Labour and Partition:
The Belfast Working Class 1905–23

Pluto Irish Library
Series editor Mike Milotte

Already published

James Larkin
Irish Labour Leader 1876–1947
EMMET LARKIN

The Politics of James Connolly
KIERAN ALLEN

Forthcoming

Labour and Nationalism in Ireland
J.D. CLARKSON

Communism in Modern Ireland
MIKE MILOTTE

Labour and Partition:
The Belfast Working Class 1905–23

Austen Morgan

PLUTO PRESS
London • Concord, Mass

First published in 1991 by Pluto Press
345 Archway Road, London N6 5AA
and 141 Old Bedford Road,
Concord, MA 01742, USA

British Library Cataloguing-in-Publication Data
Morgan, Austen
   Labour and Partition: the Belfast working class 1905–
   1923.
   1. Belfast. Politics, history
   I. Title
   320.94167

   ISBN 0–7453–0326–9

Library of Congress Cataloging-in-Publication Data
Morgan, Austen, 1949–
   Labour and partition: the Belfast working class, 1905–1923/
   Austen Morgan
      p.   cm.
   Includes bibliographical references and index.
   ISBN 0–7453–0326–9
   1. Working class–Northern Ireland–Belfast–Political activity-
   -History. 2. Labor movement–Northern Ireland–Belfast–History.
   3. Belfast (Northern Ireland)–Politics and government. I. Title.
   HD8397.B45M67   1991
   322'.2'094167–dc20   90–45333
                                                            CIP

Typeset in 9.25 on 10.5 pt Stone by Stanford DTP, Milton Keynes
Printed and bound in the UK by Billing and Sons Ltd, Worcester

to
the 'rotten Prods' of Belfast,
victims of unionist violence and nationalist myopia

GLASGOW

LONDONDERRY

BELFAST

NORTH CHANNEL

IRISH SEA

LIVERPOOL

DUBLIN

CORK

A.Ioannou-Nicolaou

Contents

Acknowledgements

The research for this book was carried out in Belfast in 1972–5, and such is the passage of time that I may have forgotten some of those who helped me over the years. I tried to thank a number in 1987, in my biography of James Connolly, which was a spin-off from my work on the Belfast working class. This was funded, for two years, by the Northern Ireland Department of Education, and also by teaching work at Queen's University, Belfast. The research was written up in 1977–8 in the comfortable Warwickshire town of Kenilworth, famous only for its castle, but I must again mention Judith Watt, who taught me a lot, and Bob Purdie, whose love of books exceeds my own. My supervisor in Belfast, John Whyte, plus Owen Dudley Edwards, encouraged me to write this book, after I received my doctorate, but I hesitated for related personal and political reasons, though John Gray had a copy of the thesis made for the Linenhall Library in Belfast. John Whyte knew this book was coming along eventually in 1989, and even coming out, but his recent sudden death means I can only posthumously acknowledge the way he influenced my work by quiet diplomacy. He was one of Ireland's most eminent scholars. The usual disclaimer applies about this book being my sole responsibility. I should also mention Peter Gibbon, whose work inspired me in a different way, and Henry Patterson, who was researching similar problems at the same time; I hope we have reached proximate ends even if the means have been different. I am, again, greatly indebted to many historical actors and scholars. I interviewed Marie Johnson, Peadar O'Donnell, Denis Rebbeck, George Gilmore, Douglas Gageby, Nora Connolly O'Brien and Roddy Connolly in 1973–4, and learned the value of this research method. Scholars are referred to the original thesis at Queen's University, as the select bibliography here is simply a guide to further reading, while only direct quotations are referenced in the notes. I have tried in the preface to acknowledge my dependence on the Irish labour historians of the 1970s and 1980s, and socialist writers, both anti-imperialist and post-nationalist.

I owe my association with the reincarnated Pluto Press to Mike Milotte and Roger van Zwanenberg. As series editor of the Pluto Irish library, Mike resurrected the idea of a book on the Belfast working class. I am grateful for this, and all the editorial attention he gave me, not least because of our formal political differences on the Irish question. Roger kept telling me he knew what it was like to write books, and then got on with being a publisher. Anne Beech always found nice things to say. The rank and file are not always mentioned in despatches, but I must commend Mari Roberts and Joe Garver for considerable editorial care. Adam Wilcox and Anny Ioannou got their electronic friend to produce a map to my specifications. Seán ('don't forget the fada') Hutton acted as consultant on the first national language. I also want to mention Manuela Narjes, who was there when I was writing, and Leo Morgan, who should be able to read his name along with his brothers.

Capitalization is always a problem in historical works, and I have tried to follow the Irish convention of as little as possible; generally organizations with abbreviated titles are capitalized. There is a glossary of Irish terms, but Irishisms – other people's if not mine – remain in the text as flavouring.

Crouch End, September 1990

Abbreviations

AEU	Amalgamated Engineering Union
AOH	Ancient Order of Hibernians
ASCJ	Amalgamated Society of Carpenters and Joiners
ASE	Amalgamated Society of Engineers
ASRS	Amalgamated Society of Railway Servants
ASW	Amalgamated Society of Woodworkers
BCPC	Belfast Catholic Protection Committee
BET	*Belfast Evening Telegraph*
BSS	Belfast Socialist Society
BEU	British Empire Union
BNL	*Belfast Newsletter*
BLPES	British Library of Political and Economic Science
BPA	Belfast Protestant Association
BSP	British Socialist Party
CRA	Catholic Representation Association
CSO	Chief Secretary's Office
DORA	Defence of the Realm Act
ETU	Electrical Trades Union
EWC	Expelled Workers' Committee
EWRC	Expelled Workers' Relief Committee
FEST	Federation of Engineering and Ship-building Trades
GAA	Gaelic Athletic Association
GFTU	General Federation of Trades Unions
GOC	General Officer Commanding
IAOS	Irish Agricultural Organisation Society
ICA	Irish Citizen Army
ILP	Independent Labour Party
ILP(I)	Independent Labour Party of Ireland
ILP & TUC	Irish Labour Party and Trade Union Congress
IN	*Irish News*
INF	Irish National Federation
INL	Irish National League
IOO	Independent Orange Order
IRA	Irish Republican Army
IRB	Irish Republican Brotherhood
ISDL	Irish Self-Determination League
ISF	Irish Socialist Federation
ISRP	Irish Socialist Republican Party

ITUC	Irish Trade Union Congress
ITUC & LP	Irish Trade Union Congress and Labour Party
ITGWU	Irish Transport and General Workers' Union
ITWU	Irish Textile Workers' Union
IUA	Irish Unionist Alliance
IWC	Irish White Cross
IWW	Industrial Workers of the World
LEA	Labour Electoral Association
LRC	Labour Representation Committee
MEA	Municipal Employees' Association
NAUL	National Amalgamated Union of Labour
NILP	Northern Ireland Labour Party
NLI	National Library of Ireland
NSFU	National Sailors' and Firemen's Union
NTWF	National Transport Workers' Federation
NUDL	National Union of Dock Labourers
NUR	National Union of Railwaymen
NW	*Northern Whig*
PRO(L)	Public Record Office (London)
PRONI	Public Record Office of Northern Ireland
RIC	Royal Irish Constabulary
RUC	Royal Ulster Constabulary
SDF	Social Democratic Federation
SLP	Socialist Labor Party/Socialist Labour Party
SPA	Socialist Party of America
SPI	Socialist Party of Ireland
SPO	State Paper Office
TUC	Trades Union Congress
UESA	Ulster Ex-Servicemen's Association
UIL	United Irish League
ULA	Ulster Liberal Association
UPA	Ulster Protestant Association
UUC	Ulster Unionist Council
UULA	Ulster Unionist Labour Association
UVF	Ulster Volunteer Force
UWC	Ulster Workers' Council
WEA	Workers' Education Association

Glossary

Clan na Gael	Family of Gaels
Cumann na mBan	League of Women
Cumann na nGaedheal	League of Gaels
Dáil Éireann	Assembly of Ireland
Éire	Ireland
Fianna Éireann	Soldiers of Ireland
Fianna Fáil	Soldiers of Destiny
Fine Gael	Tribe of Gaels
Óglaigh na hÉireann	Warriors of Ireland
Sinn Féin	Ourselves
árd fheis	conference
sluagh	branch
taoiseach	prime minister
big yard	Harland and Wolff
wee yard (shipyards)	Workman, Clark

Preface

The time: spring 1921. The place: Belfast. Ireland had just been partitioned under an act of the Westminster parliament; divided into two home rule states within the United Kingdom. The British government led by Lloyd George decreed that elections be held in the divided country; on 19 May in Southern Ireland, five days later in Northern Ireland. The prohibited republican government of Eamon de Valera, formed after the 1918 election with the object of secession from the United Kingdom, announced that successful candidates, in the 26 and the six counties, would become members of the second Dáil Éireann in Dublin.

The labour movement in the south subordinated itself to revolutionary nationalism, supporting the goal of Irish self-determination while muting the social demands of an increasingly organized working class. Workers in Ireland had already divided on the national question, those in the more industrialized north, especially protestant Belfast, having a stronger interest in the constitutional status quo of the union with Britain. Irish nationalism was seen as espousing catholic domination and social backwardness, and republicanism as violent decolonization to the point of mass expulsion. The labour movement in Ulster did advance class demands, albeit in a reformist manner, and eschewed identification with unionist reaction. At the foundation of the northern state, non-sectarian labour in Belfast was considered a threat to unionist solidarity.

The 132 seats in the Southern Ireland election went uncontested, republicans virtually sweeping the board. Shortly afterwards the Irish Republican Army (IRA) agreed to a truce with the British forces. At the end of 1921 Sinn Féin signed a treaty with the coalition government in London, agreeing to the setting up of the Irish Free State. This was dominion self-government, but the country had already been partitioned. In Northern Ireland, the unionist party, led by Sir James Craig, had won 40 of the 52 seats on 24 May. He was already prime minister of the devolved regime within the United Kingdom, having served in a junior capacity in the British government. The new provincial parliament was formally opened by George V on 22 June. Belfast accounted for 20 of the seats, in the new regime established subsequently at Stormont on the outskirts of Belfast. Northern Ireland was little more than a city-state across the channel from Britain, sharing a land frontier with a new, stunted nation-state.

The cause of socialism in the country was at a low ebb in 1921, less than four years after the Russian revolution. Ireland as the western outpost of Europe had suffered from uneven development and colonial rule. The growth of democracy under the British state saw the popularization of nationalist desires for independence. The Marxist James Connolly argued from the 1890s that this objective had to be inscribed on the banner of working-class politics. He went on, to the consternation of many contemporary socialists, to identify with republicanism in the Dublin insurrection of 1916. This was in spite of the problem of a divided Ulster, where catholics constituted a minority ethnic community, especially in Belfast. The predominant protestant community had undergone a contradictory political development, some elements supporting progressive British politics while others sought to maintain their privileges. The majority working class in Belfast had been long embroiled in sectarianism, but was slowly embracing secular politics in the home rule era from the 1880s. Democracy and socialism were on offer throughout Britain and Ireland from the heartlands of political progress. British labourism did not embody all the answers, but this growing working-class force addressed the central question of social inequality under capitalism. It was part of the movement towards democracy, where lay the resolution of the Irish and all other national and minority questions. The nationalist demand for self-government met with unionist opposition in Ulster, where working-class politics happened to be most advanced. The Irish question was complex from the beginning, and was more than simply the desire of a people to rule itself.

The first labour candidate in Ireland, William Walker, had stood in 1905 for North Belfast. Walker believed in the continuing union of Ireland and Britain. This was before the 1907 transport strike in the city led by James Larkin, who went on to fight other trade-union struggles in Ireland. The advances of the Edwardian years were not strong enough to avert the unionist mobilizations against home rule before the European war, though James Connolly was active in Ulster until 1914. Belfast emerged from the war to a period of unsurpassed class struggle, the heroes of the prewar years giving way to local figures less celebrated in Irish history. The Belfast labour party put up four candidates in the 1918 election, securing over a fifth of the vote. British labour took 59 seats at Westminster in the khaki contest, not a great improvement on its prewar performance. There followed the 1919 Belfast engineering strike, the greatest industrial struggle in Irish history. Labour improved its position in the municipal elections in January 1920, taking 12 of the 60 seats in the City Hall. That July the war of independence being fought in the rest of the country finally intruded upon Belfast with a vengeance. Loyalist militants in the shipyards and other workplaces expelled labour activists and catholics. The protestant trade unionists were known to their coreligionists as 'rotten Prods'. The working class was at its most divided at the height of the Anglo-Irish struggle, catholics and some protestants being the victims of the process of state formation in Ireland. Revolutionary nationalism exacerbated sectarian divisions, and undermined working-class politics.

The Belfast labour party was in no position to put up candidates the following May, when Britain had apparently settled the Irish question. But four independents, the Revd J. Bruce Wallace, James Baird, Harry Midgley and John Hanna stood in the labour interest in Belfast's four constituencies. They were all protestants. Midgley was a trade-union official; Baird and Hanna leaders of the expelled workers. Wallace, an old Christian Socialist, accepted the government of Ireland act. The other three opposed partition, but on socialist rather than nationalist grounds. They feared working-class division and, in Northern Ireland, a tory regime. They would have accepted rule from Dublin, if this had been agreed to by elected representatives in negotiations with the British government. They were not Irish separatists, though the expelled workers were dependent upon Dáil Éireann. Baird, Midgley and Hanna decided upon a joint campaign, to begin with a 'great labour meeting' in the Ulster Hall on 17 May.

This is where Lord Randolph Churchill had spoken in 1886, following his decision to play 'the Orange card'[1] to strengthen the conservative cause in British politics. In 1912 Winston Churchill, then a member of the liberal government, was prevented from speaking in the Ulster Hall, as a result of his support for home rule. 'The Unionists were quick to point out that his departure [from Belfast] was uncomfortably like that of the "thief in the night" about whom his father had so eloquently warned them.'[2]

On the morning of 17 May 1921 notices were posted asking shipyard workers to assemble later 'for the purpose of taking possession of the Ulster Hall and driving out the Sinn Feiners'. The organizations responsible were the Ulster Ex-Servicemen's Association (UESA) and the British Empire Union (BEU). After the industrial expulsions, there was to be political suppression. The police did not seek to prevent the shipyard workers, some of whom were carrying revolvers, from entering the Ulster Hall. The crowd surged in, and the three labour candidates were found hiding in a dressing room. They quickly fled. The loyalist workers then held their own meeting, in the course of which an English journalist and a local catholic were removed. Speakers identified socialists with Sinn Féin, both being seen as opposed to the empire. A telegram was sent to Sir James Craig, asking him to address the meeting. He pleaded previous engagements, but congratulated the shipyard workers: 'Well done, big and wee yards.'[3] Sir Edward Carson, the outgoing Irish unionist leader, replied later: 'The issue is peace or anarchy, security or murder. Keep the flag of liberty flying.'[4]

The labour candidates effectively withdrew from the campaign the following day. 'Owing to Official Hooliganism', they announced, 'we have been compelled to cancel all our meetings.'[5] On 24 May, Baird, Midgley and Hanna lost their deposits, polling a total of 1,887 votes. The *Northern Whig* had hailed the Ulster Hall rout as 'a magnificent, impressive success'. 'The men who converted what was no doubt intended to be an anti-Unionist meeting into one in support of the party which alone can give Ulster workers the sound administration and good laws they desire did not exceed their legitimate rights as citizens in any way.'[6] The nationalist *Irish News*, in an editorial on free speech, included labour in the green camp as an anti-partitionist party. In blaming the rout on 'the violent and unreasoning elements of the population *under Ascendancy inspiration and guidance*',[7] it paradoxically denied the autonomy of the loyalist masses. Elite manipulation was the nationalist view of the predominant unionist community.

Labour in Belfast, at the point of partition, was a victim of unionist violence and nationalist myopia. The city's working class appeared to be broken on the anvil of the Irish national question. With the IRA active in nationalist Ireland, the unionists were determined to make Ulster a bastion. There was no room for dissension within protestant ranks, the politics of social reform being tantamount to national treachery. This was conjunctural, the unionist mobilizations of the early 1910s against home rule having, in the context of the war against Germany, ignited nationalist rebellion in 1916. The failure of constitutional politics was revolution and counter-revolution. Ireland was partitioned because the people of the country were divided on the question of British rule. The consequence from a working-class point of view was evident in Belfast on 17 May 1921. Other possibilities had been inscribed on the social formation of north-east Ulster, as this study of popular politics in Belfast before partition demonstrates. Protestant workers were less reactionary *colons*, and more the people Irish nationalism needed to win over in order to avert partition. But Belfast could no more ignore its location in Ireland than the country could have avoided being a strategic, military threat to its larger, aggressive neighbour.

For the last two decades and more, the left in Britain and abroad has viewed Ireland through republican spectacles. The military campaign of the provisional IRA, based in the minority catholic community of Northern Ireland, has been portrayed by the revolutionary socialists of 1968 and after as another modern anti-imperialist struggle. Ireland is seen as another Vietnam. Imperialism, for Lenin, was the latest stage of capitalism, while, for de Valera under the Free State, it became the explanation for the non-appearance of the Irish nation. Socialists have subscribed to this nationalist conception of imperialism, thereby confusing the transcendence of capitalism with national separation. The traditional republican version of Irish history thrives outside the country, the majority protestant community in the north being dismissed by far too many socialists and radicals as a reactionary mass. As for most of the Irish people, who live in what is now the Republic of Ireland, a sovereign, independent, bourgeois–democratic state, and have no interest in contemporary republicanism, they are generally ignored as an inconvenient fact. Britain has many enemies in the world, and 'the Irish people' of political rhetoric is too desirable as an avenging angel to allow for the intellectual intrusion of political reality.

This is the politics of left nationalism, or, as it is known in Ireland, socialist republicanism. This is identified with James Connolly, whose posthumous reputation has greatly shaped the theory, if not the practice, of the working-class movement there. In the 1970s Irish and

British socialist apologists for the IRA took to quoting Connolly's 1914 warning that partition would lead to 'a carnival of reaction both North and South, would set back the wheels of progress, would destroy the oncoming unity of the Irish Labour movement and paralyse all advanced movements while it endured'.[8] Connolly did not live to see Ireland divided into two sectarian states, but contemporary socialists continue to talk about 'a carnival of reaction', oblivious of the fact that their anti-partitionism, along with loyalism, is part of the reactionary political culture of Ireland. To repeat a polemic of the early twentieth century towards its end is to deny the changes in the north since 1968, and the south from 1958, and attempt to reverse historical time. The division of Ireland will be undone only by the consent of people on both sides of the border. The so-called war in the north has achieved nothing in two decades, except postpone the possibility of political advance. Britain has little responsibility, having long since lost the will to dominate. The Republic of Ireland is an enthusiastic member of the European community, separatism having been long abandoned by the Irish bourgeoisie. But 'the re-integration of the national territory', espoused by the 1937 constitution, partly legitimizes the gun in Irish politics. It is more credible that the catholic minority in the north will be reconciled to continuing British rule, especially with devolution, than that the protestant majority could be coerced to recognize a Dublin parliament. If socialists are to play a role in the future of the country, it will be on a European terrain. A new Irish left asserted itself in the 1970s, though it is little recognized outside the country. Based on the politics of post-nationalism, it argues that, whatever progressive role nationalism might have played in the past, the demand for a unitary state is now part of the problem. Irish nationalism is increasingly recognized as irredentist, an ugly word for a state or people claiming adjacent territory regardless of the wishes of its inhabitants. Irredentism has nothing to do with democracy, and should not be associated with socialism.

Politics and ideology have shaped the writing of working-class history in Ireland. Academics have correctly advocated objectivity, but neutrality has often been a cover for unarticulated liberal values. Scholarship is not incompatible with clear socialist commitment. The ideologues of the so-called Irish cultural renaissance of the 1890s and after, with their emphasis upon the concept of nationality, became the traditional intellectuals of the Irish state from the 1920s. The time bombs left ticking in the republican version of history, particularly the idea of unfinished business in the north, have led to considerable intellectual revision by scholars and other writers in the 1970s and 1980s. Irish culture is now riven between tradition and modernization, with the latter very much in the ascendant. Labour history could have contained a critique of the provincial bourgeois world-view in Ireland, but for working-class politics having been given a strong nationalist identity by James Connolly in 1916. Fortunately, the theory and practice of republicanism has been repeatedly challenged by socialist intellectuals in the last two decades.

Cathal O'Shannon codified the first historiography of the Irish working class in the pamphlet *Ireland at Berne* (1919), when he accompanied Thomas Johnson to the first postwar meeting of the international on behalf of the Irish labour movement. This document was made available to European socialists in Irish, French, German and English. O'Shannon had worked with Connolly in Belfast before the war, but he saw things through republican eyes. Ulster was not a minority problem for Ireland, he argued in 1919, merely a case 'where a systematic policy of denationalisation ha[d] distorted the development of an oppressed nation'.[9] His history of the Irish labour movement from 1894 stressed Larkin and Connolly at the expense of other individuals, organizations and events. Emphasis was placed on the Irish Transport and General Workers' Union (ITGWU), and Irish socialism was dated from 1896 when Connolly came to Ireland. Labour's championing of self-determination from 1918 was proclaimed, despite its history of avoiding the national question. Support for Sinn Féin was assumed to be the inevitable destiny of rural and urban workers, despite their repeated commitment to nationalist and unionist politics. Belfast, and its working-class tradition of (British) labourism, was effectively written out of Irish history. As it began, so it continued.

The two classic scholarly works of Irish labour history are by Americans. J. Dunsmore Clarkson's *Labour and Nationalism in Ireland* was published in New York in 1926. Clarkson came to Ireland in late 1921, as a Columbia University postgraduate student, and certainly visited Belfast in 1922. He was much concerned with the 'fusion of the forces of Labour and Nationalism' in the modern world, and sought 'to correlate ... the successive stages through which the working class has passed in modern Ireland ... [in] its development with the well-known story of Ireland's struggle for nationhood'.[10] He had difficulty fitting Ulster into the story, and gave Belfast a separate chapter outside his narrative flow. But Clarkson, using much original material, constructed institutional accounts, which have passed, as unexamined and unacknowledged arguments, into academic and political literature. Arthur Mitchell was a research student in Ireland in 1963–7, working under David Thornley at Trinity College, his *Labour in Irish Politics, 1890–1930* being published in Dublin in 1974. Mitchell was concerned with how 'a workers' party, committed to social and economic transformation, achieve[d] political power in a period of nationalist revolution'.[11] He worked in Dublin at an exciting cultural time, when Irish politics seemed to be opening up. While Mitchell integrates Belfast into his national chronology, this is a work conceived before the revealing current troubles. Desmond Greaves's seminal biography of Connolly had appeared in 1961 from a political publisher in Britain, and it was followed by Emmet Larkin's academic biography of James Larkin, published in London in 1965. Mention should also be made of Erhard Rumpf's published German thesis of 1959, which has been rewritten by Anthony Hepburn, under the title *Nationalism and Socialism in Twentieth-Century Ireland* (1977).[12] This is a work of social geography, which stresses rural land at the expense of urban people in its analysis of post-1918 nationalism. The rewrite fills out the story, with a chapter on Northern Ireland, without challenging the book's confusion of sociology and socialism.

The formation of the Irish labour history society in 1973, with a professional journal, *Saothar*, has done much to promote the writing about Ireland as experienced by working men and women. It probably owes most to the inspiration of John W. Boyle, whose well-known doctoral thesis of 1961 has been only recently published in the United States, as *The Irish Labor Movement in the Nineteenth Century* (1988)[13]. Politics and scholarship have interacted in the work of the Irish labour history society, as is the case with the books written by Irish socialists on Northern Ireland since 1968 and published in Britain. Eamonn McCann's *War and an Irish Town* (1974) is largely about Derry, but it included a catholic socialist historical search for the labour tradition in the north. This section was removed from the second edition in 1980,[14] the book becoming largely a paean to the provisional IRA for the benefit of British socialists. Michael Farrell's *Northern Ireland: The Orange State* (1976)[15] has become the definitive statement of Irish socialist anti-imperialism, and its author has shown little interest in more recent political developments in Ireland. Four years after the fall of Stormont in 1972, the book amounted to a historical indictment. It remains a useful narrative history of Northern Ireland, but Farrell's lack of sympathy for the majority community is evident. Geoffrey Bell's *The Protestants of Ulster*, also published in London in 1976, echoed this position with a vengeance. With all the enthusiasm of a convert, he addressed the long-ignored problem of nationalist consciousness, only to strengthen minority sectarian feeling. 'Working-class Protestants are not innocent',[16] Bell concluded. The first serious attempt to explain the protestant working class was Henry Patterson's *Class Conflict and Sectarianism*, published in Belfast in 1980. It engaged theoretically with other Marxist works, but, in avoiding an urban history approach, may have paradoxically underestimated the strength of labourism in Belfast before partition. It has not made much of an impression on the British left.

Mention should also be made of J. Anthony Gaughan's biography of Thomas Johnson (1980),[17] and Graham Walker's academic study of Harry Midgley (1985),[18] as well as monographs on the early ITGWU by Desmond Greaves (1982),[19] Irish communism by Mike Milotte (1984),[20] the 1907 strike in Belfast by John Gray (1985),[21] and Emmet O'Connor's work on Irish syndicalism (1988).[22]

This study of the Belfast working class originated as postgraduate research at Queen's University, Belfast in 1972–5, though I did not submit it as a doctoral thesis until 1978.[23] I carried out the work in a dramatic period from just after the fall of Stormont, through the power-sharing executive of 1974, to the Northern Ireland convention. The year 1972 saw 474 people killed in the province. Examining the origins of that contemporary crisis revealed the violence of unionism and the myopia of nationalism leading up to the division of Ireland. I had reached the conclusion by 1978 that socialists had consciously to dissociate themselves from both political traditions. This remained a painful position to occupy, given the cultural success of Irish anti-imperialism with the advanced left in Britain, and, after the hunger strikes of 1980–1, even within the labour party. Many British socialists became more Irish than the Irish, unable to appreciate the politics of post-nationalism then developing in the Republic. My book on James Connolly,[24] written in London during the political affair between Sinn Féin and the labour left led by Tony Benn, was published belatedly in 1988. This work was written in 1989, memorable for the transformations in eastern Europe which may yet cast a new light on Northern Ireland. 1989 was also the year the Irish left (the labour party, workers' party and three individuals) secured a historic 25 seats out of 166 in Dáil Éireann. The workers' party, with 5 per cent of the vote, won seven seats (equivalent to 33 socialists to the left of the labour party at Westminster); Sinn Féin, with a derisory 1.2 per cent, took no seats.

This political advance greatly eased the writing of Irish working-class history, but some of the key concepts of McCann, Farrell and Bell, in a socialist theoretical framework heavily dependent on republicanism, have pre-empted scholarly debate. Theory can become dogma, as happened with Irish Marxism. Some categories in left-wing Irish historical writing require reworking, while less abstraction in history often makes for better description and analysis.

The most problematic of the concepts deployed is that of *imperialism*, wielded to explain variously why Ireland is not free and under a workers' republic. It is useless as such, the terms British power, British state, British ruling class, British government, etc. being more precise. The second-most difficult concept is that of the *Irish nation*. This is simply the imagined community of nineteenth-century Irish nationalism, which challenged British sovereignty but did not hegemonize all popular classes in Ireland. The goal of an Irish state was progressive on the whole, but this does not deny the catholic, rural, bourgeois interests behind it, nor the possibility of political advance under the United Kingdom. The Irish nation became less obtainable by constitutional means, and the revolutionary version less desirable from a working-class point of view. Irish separatism as an end in itself was a product of the Enlightenment ideas of the 1790s being overwhelmed by the romanticism of 1848. A third necessary concept is that of *democracy*, whereby increasing numbers of people determine the direction of their society. Formal democracy in Ireland strengthened nationalism and unionism, but the spirit of accommodation within both traditions was too weak to resolve the national question. The fourth category is *unionism*, in which left nationalists invariably fail to distinguish acceptance of the constitutional status quo from the active defence of the link between the two countries. To accuse all non-nationalists of unionism is simply to impose a malignant polarization, which avoids addressing the question of sectarian division.

Sectarianism is perhaps the principal concept, and is defined here as the advocacy of one community's interests, largely in the north, at the expense of the other's. The phenomenon originated in the religious identities under colonialism, when forms of Christianity fought for mastery. By the time of the home rule era, Ireland's two major political traditions could be described as sectarian; nationalist in so far as the movement mobilized the Irish catholic people, and proffered the notion of a return to a pre-conquest Ireland, and unionist to the extent that the movement identified with protestantism, and embodied a superior attitude towards the rest of Ireland. A growing contemporary usage of the term *sectarian* to refer only to loyalism is itself sectarian. The sixth category is *labourism*, which subsumes the movement towards independent labour representation from the 1880s, recognizing that its progressive content came up against the political limit of parliamentarism, while being socially circumscribed by trade-union exclusivity. *Socialism* is deployed here as a seventh concept, less as a dogmatic benchmark by which to judge historical actors, and more in a pluralist fashion to situate the aspiration to replace capitalism with popular ownership and control of society's resources. An eighth notion is that of *revolution*, the overthrow of a ruling power. Here it is necessary to distinguish Fenianism and the national revolution in Ireland, from what Marxists in Europe understood by the revolutionary road to socialism. The concept of permanent revolution associated with Trotsky has led the Irish left to support republicans in the mistaken belief that separatism is tantamount to socialism.

Labour and Partition begins with a socio-political characterization of the Belfast working class (Chapter 1). Its contradictory course between 1905 and 1923 is charted in the four main parts of the book – Edwardian politics, mobilizations, war, and national revolution – the popular politics of each period being examined in terms of the dominant traditions of nationalism and unionism, and the non-sectarian alternatives of trade unionism and socialism. Part II on Edwardian politics looks at constitutional nationalism (Chapter 2) and independent orangeism (Chapter 3), before examining the career of the labour leader William Walker (Chapter 4), and James Larkin's alternative class-struggle approach (Chapter 5). Part III deals with the unionist mobilizations against home rule in 1910–14, Chapter 6 showing how the industrial expulsions of 1912 grew out of the constitutional crisis. This sets the context for James Connolly's advocacy of socialism and national independence in Belfast (Chapter 7). Part IV covers the European war, the changes produced in Belfast (Chapter 8), and the limited opportunities for republicanism in the city (Chapter 9). Part V covers the period from the end of the war to the stabilization of a divided Ireland in 1923. Chapter 10 looks at unionism's unsuccessful attempt to incorporate the labour movement, before and after the engineering strike of 1919 (Chapter 11). The fate of the Belfast labour party is considered in Chapter 12, and the more extensive expulsions of 1920 in Chapter 13. Chapter 14 looks at the formation of the northern state and the breaking of the working class, while the conclusion (Chapter 15) charts the course of labour in both parts of Ireland after 1923 in comparison with its development in Britain.

Part I

Introduction

1

The Development of the Belfast Working Class

The Belfast working class was a product of rural migration in Ulster. Colonial relations between catholics and protestants were subverted by urbanization, industrialization requiring free labour. The working class developed as technology and capital were deployed, Belfast becoming the fastest growing city in the United Kingdom in the second half of the nineteenth century. By 1905 it exuded self-confidence when other Irish towns and cities seemed demoralized. But sectarianism was not eradicated from the society. In the world of the working class, the labour market was characterized by the operation of a protestant political economy, while the pattern of residential segregation showed a catholic ghetto community. Structural inequality between the two communities persisted in the absence of an integrating liberal bourgeoisie, and because of the weakness of the organized labour movement. Belfast had a history of strikes against employers, but this was marred by ethnic rivalry in the workplace at times of political tension. When Irish nationalists demanded home rule in the 1880s, the Ulster bourgeoisie set out to defend the union. Its eventual political success, in the form of partition, owed most to the industrial strength of Ulster. By the early twentieth century the protestant working class of Belfast was the most important social force in Ireland, a fact which has been little recognized. If it was unable to remake the world according to a socialist vision, it succeeded in frustrating an Irish nation-state. The explanation for partition is to be sought in the limited appeal of nationalism, not in pseudo-Marxist theory about protestant privilege.

The story begins with the plantation of Ulster in the early seventeenth century. The most Gaelic province of Ireland, it was thoroughly settled with English and Scots by 1690. Six counties were seized by the crown in 1607, but Antrim and Down underwent informal colonization. They were only a short sea journey from the lowlands of Scotland and the north of England. The Gaelic aristocracy was undermined in Ulster, native catholics being displaced from the land. Subsistence farming on the worst land and labouring became their means of livelihood. The new tenants became part of the protestant ascendancy of 1691, following William of Orange's defeat of King James II, though differences between protestants and dissenters existed within the new community.

3

The position of the settlers deteriorated in the eighteenth century. Small-scale farming was a stable commercial industry, but their numbers meant a wide distribution of capital. Some were forced to migrate to North America, many Scotch-Irish participating in the revolution of the 1770s. Ulster Scots came to rely on domestic linen production; skills and capital were imported. Arthur Young considered this economic heresy in 1776: 'The cause of all [the agricultural] evils, which are absolute exceptions to everything else on the face of the globe, is easily found – a most prosperous manufacture so contrived as to be the destruction of agriculture'.[1] Differentiation took place within the linen industry. The emergence of drapers, who bought brown linen from the farmer-weavers, and, later, bleachers, who came to control marketing, saw a rural capitalist class come into being in the Lagan Valley. The White Linen Hall was opened in Belfast in 1784, the port town becoming a distribution centre for eastern Ulster.

Capitalization meant a free market in labour, and catholics secured entry to the linen industry. The origins of the sectarian orange order in Co. Armagh in the 1790s have been attributed to proletarian weavers trying to maintain a protestant preserve. The order came to be supported by landlords and the state, as a counter-revolutionary force against the United Irishmen, founded in Belfast in 1791. This French-inspired, and later French-supported, organization sought to make a bourgeois revolution in Ireland, which would involve, in Wolfe Tone's words, the breaking of 'the connection with England, the never-failing source of all our political evils'.[2] While Irish republicanism aspired to unite protestant, catholic and dissenter, it was a settler nationalism, based on economic opposition to the aristocracy, and presbyterian hostility to the established church. A rising in 1798 was easily suppressed, catholic peasants in Wexford engaging in simple sectarian slaughter.

The attempted decolonization of Ireland met with internal resistance, to say nothing of British power. There were of course a great many settlers in Ulster, and they had already been there a long time. The 1790s show how the political trajectory of the protestant community was contradictory, as between revolution and counter-revolution. Orangeism and republicanism were contemporaneous. It was already evident that political advance in Ulster could not imply the mass expulsion of settlers' descendants, history being irreversible in this sort of case. Few argued in the nineteenth century for the ejection of European peoples from the Americas and Australasia, in order to grant the native inhabitants justice. The successors of the Ulster Scots were as Irish as preceding waves of invaders. It was their home, and they had no other.

The legacy of colonialism was subverted, in the north of Ireland, by the development of capitalism.

Belfast became a cotton town in the 1780s. Local capital, protection and a recession in linen production saw the import of British technology and industrial organization. Steam power made possible the development of cotton-spinning mills along the tributaries to the west of Belfast. The yarn produced was woven by independent weavers in the town and nearby. Cotton manufacturing saw the entry of many catholics into wage labour, given their underemployment in rural Ulster. Many of the early factory proletariat were women, as in Britain. The first cotton spinners were children from the poorhouse. Rapid capital accumulation during the Napoleonic wars was followed by a decline, owing to the restricted home market, and Scottish competition. The removal of protection in 1823 was a consequence, rather than the cause, of cotton's demise. It saw the emigration of many spinners, but especially proletarian weavers.

The industrial technology and organization of cotton provided the base for the mechanization of linen. The invention of wet spinning in 1825 was followed by the first linen mill in 1829. The 1830s and 1840s saw the mechanization of spinning in Ulster, which was most concentrated in Belfast. Weaving was mechanized in the 1850s and 1860s. Rising demand, and a shortage of hand weavers, led to the first weaving factory, using a power loom, in 1852. The cotton famine, consequent upon the American Civil War in the 1860s, did much to develop Ulster linen. This 'period of exceptional prosperity' was followed by 'a cataclysmic reversal of fortune'.[3] Linen stagnated in the last quarter of the century, with a few occasional good years. The industry had two main social effects. Firstly, it produced an urban bourgeoisie, which was the basis of conservative hegemony in Ulster. The linen lords played a prominent role in Belfast and provincial affairs. Secondly, the low productive capacity of linen capital meant it was labour intensive – the number of workers fluctuated, with the business cycle, from 55,000 to 65,000, between 1868 and 1904. Linen employed men but mainly women, protestants but also catholics. By 1912 there were 17 spinning companies in Belfast, 32 in the rest of Ulster, and only 1 in the south. There were over a hundred companies concerned mainly with weaving, with 2,000 power looms in the south, 13,000 in the rest of Ulster, and 21,000 in Belfast.

The natural growth of the Ulster economy had come to an end in the 1860s. 'Of itself linen could not have made Belfast prosperous, and if the city had remained dependent on linen its expansion would have ceased by the end of the century … Belfast would probably have fared much the same as Londonderry.'[4] Linen manufacturing in Belfast represented the concentration of United Kingdom production of a luxury commodity with a shrinking foreign market. But the town's incorporation into the British international economy meant that 'a large-scale general industrial development drawing capital and labour from other parts of the United Kingdom could be anticipated'.[5]

This took the form of shipbuilding and engineering. Harland and Wolff started to build metal ships in 1858, and were joined by Workman, Clark in 1879. These were the so-called big and wee yards. There were two preconditions for heavy industry in Belfast in the second half of the nineteenth century. The first was the decline of shipbuilding in Liverpool, as the port authorities turned more and more of the waterfront into docks. The second had been the development of Belfast port, especially the construction of Queen's Island, by the progressive mercantile section of the town's bourgeoisie. Harland chaired the harbour commission between 1875 and 1887. The patron of Belfast shipbuilding was G.C. Schwabe of Liverpool. Owner of the Bibby Line in the Mediterranean, he set Harland up, in return for taking his nephew, Wolff, into partnership. He also ensured that the Atlantic White Star Line got its ships from Belfast. The last was the *Titanic*, sunk on its first voyage in 1912. William James Pirrie became a partner in 1874, and ran the big yard until his death in 1924. Harland and Wolff's workforce rose from 3,700 in 1884, to 10,000 by 1900, and 16,000 in 1913. But Workman, Clark's annual tonnage was occasionally larger than the big yard's before the First World War.

By the turn of the century Harland and Wolff was opening yards elsewhere in the United Kingdom, and expanding into ship repairing and even ownership. Pirrie bought a Surrey mansion in 1909, having been made a peer three years earlier by the liberal prime minister Campbell-Bannerman. It was Lord Pirrie who brought Winston Churchill to Belfast in 1912 to defend the government's Irish policy. He has been described as 'not merely the greatest Irish industrialist of his day, but the greatest shipbuilder in the world'.[6] He became a thorn in the side of Ulster unionism.

Belfast was a unique city. It grew from 19,000 people in 1800 to 349,000 in 1901. It overtook the Irish capital, Dublin, in the 1880s, becoming a city in 1888. Cork was the only other Irish city with more than 50,000 inhabitants in 1901. Between 1841 and 1911 Ireland's population fell from 8 to 4.5 million. Rural depopulation affected all four provinces, there being more emigrants from Ulster than Leinster or Connaught. Belfast grew as Ulster declined from nearly 2.5 to 1.5 million people. Most Belfast people came from nearby. In 1901, 76.7 per cent of the population had been born in Antrim and Down (including the city itself), and only 12.6 per cent came from the other seven counties in Ulster. The remaining 10 per cent came equally from England and Wales, Scotland and the rest of Ireland. There were very few foreign born. The new immigrants were catholic and protestant. Minority migration was not quite the flood that protestant ideologues feared. Between 1780 and 1800 the catholic population of Belfast rose from 8 to 16 per cent, doubling proportionately again between 1808 and 1834. This was the period of catholic influx. It only grew slightly, relative to the protestant population, in the next 27 years, which included the famine of the late 1840s. The number of catholics increased from 41,000 in 1861 to 96,000 in 1926, but this represented a proportionate decline from 33.9 per cent to 23 per cent; that is from a third to a quarter. Belfast, at the turn of the century, was the eighth-largest city in the United Kingdom. It was surpassed only by Glasgow, in Scotland, and, in England, by London, Liverpool, Manchester, Birmingham, Leeds and Sheffield. Urbanization in Britain took place in a context of significant demographic growth, from 19 million in 1841 to over 40 in 1911. Belfast grew faster and later than the other seven cities, in a context of population decline. In the first half of the nineteenth century its growth rate was comparable to Glasgow's and Manchester's, being exceeded only by Liverpool's; in the second half, Belfast was way ahead.

It was conscious of its pre-eminence. A local directory for 1905 described Belfast as 'a maritime city ... the capital of Ulster, the chief manufacturing and commercial city of Ireland ... It is essentially a modern city, and its history is simply one of industrial progress, extending back no further than to the last century. During this short space of time, however, the city has advanced from a position of comparative insignificance to be justly considered the Commercial Metropolis of Ireland.'[7] The previous year, the Very Revd Canon Doyle had welcomed the Irish Trade Union Congress (ITUC) to Kilkenny: 'This city of ours in former days, as you are aware, occupied a rather remarkable position among the cities of Ireland – it was at one time the seat of the industrial movement in this country ... I think that it is very important that the people of Kilkenny should drink in some of that enthusiastic spirit for the revival of Irish industries which animates this body today (Applause).'[8]

The first view is modern, and forward-looking; the second, looking back, and not a little romantic. The Kilkenny cleric was articulating a popular economic historiography, later codified by George O'Brien. An industrial development association had just been set up, to revive industries in accord with the spirit of Irish Ireland, as the exponents of nationality saw it. This was the concept of self-sufficiency, advanced during the Irish cultural renaissance of the 1890s and after. Contemporary revisionist social historians argue that industrialization would have required more than enthusiasm. Or home rule. The spirit of enterprise is often advanced, in popular and intellectual discourse, to explain Belfast's development. This is invariably associated with the benefits of the union of 1801. Against this tendency towards self-congratulation, the point can be made that a regional economy, based only on the twin pillars of linen and shipbuilding, two export-orientated industries, was far from being sound. Belfast's uniqueness, which became evident in the 1860s, was virtually spent by the 1920s and 1930s. But this period crucially embraces the years of the home-rule era. The ideological difference between Belfast and Kilkenny, expressed during the Edwardian years, points to what has been called 'a comprehensive *dualism* in Irish society'[9] at the time of this political climacteric.

Ireland experienced considerable uneven development. But this was in the context of the United Kingdom state, during the modernization of Europe. Unevenness was universal in the developing world. The age of progress affected people differently, between, and within, societies. This was no less the case in Belfast. It was with considerable pride that the hoardings were removed in 1905 from a building site in Donegall Square to reveal the new City Hall, boasting a dome, corner domelets, and a *porte-cochère*. It had cost £360,000. The protestant middle class was no doubt delighted, signifying its self-confidence in municipal architecture. But most of the people in this industrial city were working class. Their experience, for good or ill, had been shaped at work and in the home. Progress was about the interrelated processes of industrialization, which created a mass proletariat, and urbanization, which saw dense residential settlement. Employment and housing should be the main themes of a social history of Belfast. The key concepts are those of the labour market, by which workers were hired and fired, and residential segregation, the spatial patterning of communities. Belfast was characterized by the operation of a protestant political economy,[10] in a context of laissez-faire, and the formation of a catholic ghetto community. Both have received inadequate scholarly attention.

The labour market, in so far as it existed in rural Ulster, from the late seventeenth century, was a product of politics. In demographically mixed areas, the protestant ascendancy took on a social meaning associated with 'the maintenance of forms of structured social inequality ... represented by definite "limits" or barriers to Catholic social mobility ... enforced by landlords and their bands of private retainers'.[11] Peter Gibbon's idea of a social barrier is the most fruitful approach to the discussion of discrimination. In the domestic linen industry, catholics were excluded by protestants. The barrier was maintained. With a change in the relations of production from the 1770s, catholics became spinners and weavers, working on equipment, flax, and yarn provided by protestant employers. Economics was becoming more important than politics. There was an attempt by lower-order protestants to preserve the barrier between natives and settlers, less because of job scarcity than fear of generalized social disintegration. Catholics only wanted work. Protestants saw it as tantamount to genocidal dispossession. 'Orangeism [from the late eighteenth century in Co. Armagh] became an ever more readily available and appealing set of symbols, rhetoric and institutions for opponents of both free labour markets and substantial farmers throughout the north.'[12]

With the arrival of a free labour market in the cotton industry, catholics swept through the barrier of structural inequality. There were opportunities in the new mills of Belfast, this being the period of significant catholic influx. Capitalism, in generating social and geographical mobility, tended to be blind to ethnic and gender differences. Work required workers. There were other segments in the labour market of the port town. The artisanate, being descended from the protestant guilds, was undoubtedly exclusive. Many of the later migrants from the other three provinces, being principally from towns, may have been protestant artisans. Belfast was also probably included in the system of tramping by British craftsmen. Freemasonry was prevalent in the eighteenth century, and persisted, largely unrecognized, through much of the nineteenth. Despite the political liberality of the late eighteenth century, equality of opportunity was lacking in Belfast. Catholics predominated in the transport industry, though protestants would also have been employed in carrying and carting. When cotton gave way to linen, catholics seem to have lost their industrial advantage. There was very little continuity between these textile industries. But some catholics did get work in the mills and factories of Belfast. The male trades probably remained heavily protestant. As for the more numerous female workforce, mills seem to have drawn on local homogeneous populations. In larger mills, there could be segregated spinning rooms, with catholics in one, protestants in another. Mechanized weaving was less geographically based. Workers were drawn from a wider area, and protestants seem to have resisted catholic advance to some extent.

Orangeism certainly developed in Belfast, in the first half of the nineteenth century. The town, after all, was growing. There were, in 1851, following reorganization of the order, 35 lodges, with 1,335 members. The first orange hall opened two years later. As the artisanate gave way to crafts, collective organization on the part of skilled protestant workers became sectarian in part. An association developed between some orange lodges and particular trades, but not, it is important to note, all. By 1889 there were six such lodges, with a total membership of 259 – out of 5,316 in Belfast. In the case of labourers' lodges in the orange order, they tended to be led by foremen, the hirers and firers of labour. Bernard Hughes, the catholic baker, was to testify in 1864: 'There are few Catholic employers in the town, the others will not take Catholic apprentices, for the workers will not work with them either as apprentices or journeymen. Every trade has an Orange lodge; and these people knew each other, for they have signs and passwords so that the Catholic population has no chance at all.'[13] Despite Hughes's anti-Freemasonry overtones, this can be accepted as a tendency, but not a universal rule. It does not necessarily conflict with the evidence of a former president of the trades association, Peter Hoey. He informed the same riot commission that, 'being acquainted with every trade in Belfast', he believed there was 'no Orangeism in the societies, except so far as the individual members were concerned, of which the society does not take cognizance'.[14] This witness was pointing to trade unionism, a secular institution which sought to restrict access to employment, using different, and superior, principles. Protestant craft workers, mainly through apprenticeships, kept out catholics and protestants indiscriminately. This was a universal process during industrialization. Orangeism in Belfast served to express earlier practices of working-class exclusion, and catholics failed to see that protestants were also victims.

Trade unionism became increasingly important in the second half of the nineteenth century, as Belfast became the site of capital-intensive industry. It was initially the preserve of skilled male workers. But trade unionism spread to the unskilled from 1889, following the pattern in Britain. A trades council had been formed in Belfast earlier in the decade, in 1881. This predominantly male institution sponsored organization in the higher-status linen occupations in the 1890s. But it was not until the First World War that unskilled women organized themselves in any significant numbers. This again was part of a general process throughout the United Kingdom.

The resistance of workers everywhere was always spasmodic, the power of capital being greater. While orangeism may have declined in time, its legacy persisted. Trade unionism certainly became more important, but, as a defensive institution, it was not up to challenging structural inequality. Protestants came to be overrepresented in higher-status occupations, and catholics in lower-status occupations. Occupational census data is always problematic, and, in the case of Belfast, is only available from 1871 to 1911. An analysis of the 20 largest industrial occupations, across those 40 years, for men and women separately, shows there was structural inequality between catholics and protestants, and that this got worse over time. In 1911 catholic men were overrepresented, in descending order, in general labour, flax spinning, factory labour, and boot and shoe manufacturing. They were underrepresented, in descending order, among shipwrights and carpenters, shipbuilders, boilermakers, engine and machine makers, house carpenters, plumbers, fitters and turners, drapers/mercers, and printers. Catholic women were similarly disadvantaged. Forty-four per cent of linen weavers were catholics, in 1871, but, by 1911, this had dropped to 29 per cent. Catholic women comprised just under a half of all spinners in 1911. While catholics may have become identified with lower-status jobs, this does not mean that protestants had only higher-status ones. Ethnicity is not simply an expression of class fractions. There was an unskilled protestant working class, which played an important role.

Orangeism and trade unionism were polar opposite orientations for protestant workers. An out-and-out sectarian was more attracted to the order, and, later, to forms of popular loyalism. A protestant trade unionist might not do much to build a united working class, but he – or she – cannot be blamed for sectarianism. The concept of 'sectarian trade unionism'[15] is a sectarian ideal-type, which conflates a relationship in Belfast requiring analysis.

Structural inequality in Belfast was acknowledged, but treated as natural in a free-enterprise society. A minority report on the 1886 riots noted, defensively, that catholics 'took their full share in all the occupations ... to which their number and education entitled them'.[16] It took someone outside the sectarian political culture of Ulster to draw attention to the fact of inequality between the communities, albeit among the middle class. In 1893 Gladstone met a delegation from the Belfast chamber of commerce, which was expressing opposition to home rule. The prime minister lectured them on the low proportion of catholic members. 'It had never occurred to them', wrote a sympathetic observer, 'to consider [their activities] from a sectarian point of view!'[17]

Nor did catholics complain inordinately about discrimination under the union, given their objective disadvantage in Ulster society. They saw themselves as part of an Irish nation, with support throughout catholic Ireland. Whatever the problem under British rule, it would be solved by home rule. The concept of discrimination was to enter the political vocabulary of Northern Ireland only much later. There were a number of necessary conditions. First, the transcendence of northern catholic visions of Dublin rule by the realization of their minority status in the new northern state. Second, the existence of protestant state power with control over social resources. Third, increased state intervention in the economy after the Second World War. And fourth, the perception, through the electronic media, of an analogous case in the United States, during the civil rights movement of the 1960s. Discrimination in Northern Ireland was a profoundly political phenomenon, on the part of its apologists as well as victims. It entered local ideologies, already well formed, to assume a contested sectarian meaning.

Structural inequality was inscribed on Ulster society, catholics being buffeted in the labour market by advantaged and disadvantaged protestants. The mechanisms and justifications were to be found throughout Britain and Ireland. There was nothing unusual, anywhere, in a skilled craftsman's securing the entry of his son to the trade. But it was only in Ulster, with its sectarian political culture, that it became a grievance related to the national question, after 1921. Before partition, catholics were underrepresented in local government in Belfast, and overrepresented in national government activity in the city. There was a warning here about a possible northern state, if the post–First World War British government had cared to note it. Catholics were discriminated against by the unionist administration, while they had no difficulty in securing employment in 'imperial' services. In the absence of countervailing policies from the British or northern governments, overrepresentation and underrepresentation were reproduced by economic development, in the private and public sectors. The ending of discrimination never implied the transcendence of structural inequality. In the absence of a serious strategy for tackling the latter, which must involve considerable economic growth, it is possible for republican ideologues to allege discrimination in order to challenge the legitimacy of British rule. States may be responsible for everything in their jurisdiction, but it does not mean all social phenomena are the result of conscious political action. Different political choices, such as affirmative action, and even positive discrimination, can alter social reality. But that is another argument, deliberately eschewed by republican ideologues.

Fairness was perceived, by unionists in Ulster, as simply dispossession. Justice for catholics was injustice for protestants. The idea of the 'raffle' or 'lottery' appears to have been invented by militant landlords in 1886, presumably with memories of the land league several years earlier. This was on the occasion of the first home rule bill. Preposterous though the detail is, there is every evidence of its being believed. Protestants feared their property was to be raffled by catholics. National self-government meant the expulsion of unionists. The myth even had an urban context. 'I have good reason for believing', a unionist was to recall of Belfast in 1886, that there were

> several 'raffles' for desirable properties at that time held by Unionists. There was no intention on the part of the Nationalists to rush things, but they thought it as well to be prepared for the great change they believed to be impending ... and their 'turn' should come. Thus it was that lots were drawn for certain houses, with the grounds, timber, and live-stock. Several gentlemen were surprised to come suddenly upon strangers measuring their lawns and examining their fences.[18]

There was a great deal of such talk then and later.

Commenting on an 1892 nationalist claim that 'the slaves have become the masters', a unionist writer noted later: 'History tells us what use slaves [make] of their newly-found freedom, especially when they [find] their former masters left in their power'.[19] Political freedom meant economic loss. It is easy to see unionist fears about home rule as a case of the colonizer projecting his own consciousness on to the colonized. There was not a little guilt involved. In the sectarian context of Ulster, fears were occasionally confirmed as real. Some nationalists saw their political advance in terms of protestant expulsion. This was usually implicit, but not always. Much later, about 1960, an official of the Dublin government urged *rapprochement* upon northern nationalists. 'There was one man', the emissary recalls,

> a local chieftain in a remote village in a desolate hilly part of South Armagh who made no reply at all to my message. He was sitting in front of his little shop and looking out across the glen in the stillness of the summer evening. Uneasily, to break the silence, I asked him whether there were many Protestants in the district. Then he spoke, quietly: 'There's only one Protestant in this townland. And with the help of God, we'll have him out of it by Christmas.'[20]

This sounds like Crossmaglen country.

Residential segregation is again universal, but in Belfast the spatial patterning of communities resulted in considerable civil strife. The first Northern Ireland census, in 1926, was blind to ethnic differences, ignoring the existence of a then considerably embattled catholic ghetto. The authorities described the families of skilled workers as better housed than unskilled, there being a progressive decline, in terms of standards, from shipbuilding, through other engineering occupations, to linen. Housing was a form of consumption, dependent upon the wage earner's place in the system of production. But the dynamics of community formation had a cutting edge in periodic inter-ethnic rivalry. Sectarian street rioting did a great deal to maintain a divided working class. The home and local community in Belfast had an impact on the world of the proletariat at critical times.

The nucleus of the catholic community in Belfast is as old as the town itself – 1613. 'It is tempting to read into the first map of Belfast [1685] a parallel to those bastide towns where the quarters of the native population were in fact a mere appendage to the invaders' walled town.'[21] Catholics lived on the southwest periphery. Their first church, St Mary's, was built in Mill Street in 1783. The community developed along the arterial Falls Road, as is clear from the pattern of church building; St Peter's (1866); St Paul's (1887); St Teresa's (1911) on the Glen Road, a natural extension of the Falls Road; and St John's (1928) to the south. (There was also a church in Ballymacarrett, in east Belfast. And, in the twentieth century, one in north Belfast, and another in Derryvolgie Avenue in south Belfast.) The siting of cotton and linen mills along the line of the Farset river determined the geography of the minority community. It was relatively compact. There was only one church until the 1860s, serving the lower Falls or Pound area. Urbanization did not extend much beyond the Springfield Road/ Grosvenor Road intersection, even by the end of the century. When local government was reformed in 1898, giving Belfast 15 municipal wards, two – Smithfield and Falls – were predominantly catholic. This is not surprising, since community leaders had been arguing for eight safe nationalist seats in the town hall where municipal government had been centred from 1871.

A social geographical analysis of the 1951 census, which plotted Belfast's residential segregation using enumerators' returns, describes the catholic areas of Belfast in detail: the first one, along the Falls Road from the city centre, with a northern boundary along a line of factories on the Farset, and with a southern one constituted by 'the low-lying floodable meadows of the Blackstaff river';[22] the second, the 'markets' area of Cromac; the third, both sides of York Street; the fourth, Ballymacarrett; and the fifth, lower Crumlin Road. The last four areas made their contribution to the history of Belfast's catholics, but the Falls Road was, throughout, the centre of the community. It justifies the term *ghetto*. More usually associated with European Jews, a ghetto has been defined as

> a form of accommodation through which a minority has effectually been subordinated to a dominant group. The ghetto exhibits at least one historical form of dealing with a dissenting minority within a larger population, and as such has served as an instrument of control. At the same time the ghetto represents a form of toleration through which a *modus vivendi* is established between groups that are in conflict with each other on fundamental issues.[23]

Survival and containment are opposite faces of the same phenomenon. The dynamic of ghetto formation was the series of sectarian riots in the nineteenth century. Territory was an important principle of their social organization, but it took some time for the protestant subordination of catholics to be achieved.

Between 1813 and 1852 there were six recorded riots in Belfast. None warranted an inquiry by Dublin Castle, the seat of the colonial Irish government in the capital. By 1835 the adversaries were being identified territorially as the catholic Pound (around Durham Street) and the protestant Sandy Row. These two districts were to be described, by the commission on the 1857 riots, as lying 'at some distance from the mercantile and improved parts of the town'. The two areas were seen as socially similar, 'inhabited by the poorer and least educated classes, with feelings not disciplined or kept in check by the influences which education and social intercourse exercise upon the higher classes'. The relationship between catholics and protestants was one of domination. The riot that year was due to 'a feeling of dominancy and insult on the [protestant] side ... [involving] the celebration of the triumph of one class over another, and the establishment of Protestant Ascendancy', and 'opposition to its display' on the part of catholics.[24]

The relatively faster growth of the minority community had probably ceased by 1857. In the second half of the nineteenth century, protestant Belfast spread over an extensive area, including that east of the Lagan. The Shankill Road developed as a protestant preserve in west Belfast.

After 1857 there were seven recorded sectarian riots in Belfast. They were more frequent, and also on a larger scale. Periodic rioting and residential expulsion served to maintain segregation between the two communities. Catholics were variously cleared out of protestant, mixed and even isolated minority areas. Some protestants suffered if they got too close to the catholic ghetto. The need for such segregation suggests countervailing integration in working-class areas in years of relative peace. These were much more numerous, if less historically dramatic. Rioting was mutual, but unbalanced as between a minority and majority. Extensive residential expulsions may have been a later phenomenon of the twentieth century, associated with the effect on Belfast in 1920 of the war of independence. The city's sectarian riots are usually discussed in terms of a breakdown in public order. This was certainly the view of the riot commissioners, in 1857, in 1864 and again in 1886. By then Dublin Castle had got the message. The Irish government felt it knew enough about the more political manifestations of opposition to home rule. In a seminal study of Belfast riots, Peter Gibbon has pointed to the growing importance of the Shankill Road as the site of the later confrontations. He sees riots as 'integrated into the local social order, and represent[ing] an articulation of it'.[25] His ideal-types of Sandy Row and the Shankill Road are sociologically interesting, though historically imprecise. His analysis neglects the fact that riots occurred between catholics and protestants. More importantly, he is wrong to attribute such behaviour, initially seen as characteristic of a lumpenproletariat, to the labour aristocracy of the city. It was more the disadvantaged among the protestant community who took direct action against their catholic neighbours throughout the city's development.

Ghetto formation was also the result of internal factors. The catholic community was predominantly unskilled working class, but with a petty bourgeoisie constituting the minority's leadership. Its patterns of work and housing were located within a sectarian universe.

The catholic middle class was not numerically large. In 1911 there were only 17 catholic merchants out of 132 enumerated, and just over 1,000 male and female catholic clerks out of well over 7,000 in the city. In the professions catholics were underrepresented in law, medicine, civil engineering and teaching – except music teaching! They were fairly represented in government service. The catholic petty bourgeoisie was otherwise dependent upon the minority, not being a fraction of the city's dominant groups. The key group was the clergy, which had no relationship with other ministers of religion. The role of catholic priests was the prototype for lawyers, doctors and teachers. The only catholic presence on the chamber of commerce was through the affiliated Licensed Vintners' Association. Arthur Savage, who owned two pubs in the 'markets', and was elected a Sinn Féin councillor in 1920, battled alone for home rule. In 1912 at a general meeting of the council of the chamber of commerce he had two supporters, and 146 opponents, when he tried procedurally to prevent the commercial interests of the city from coming out in favour of the maintenance of the union. The drink trade was the principal catholic one in protestant areas, publicans and spirit-grocers (who sold alcohol in food shops) being expelled from east Belfast in 1920. Another was butchery, which had been identified as a catholic trade from an early period.

The catholic middle class did not disperse in the main to mixed sub-urban areas. It formed its own suburb within the ghetto. The upper Falls Road and Andersonstown were, at the turn of the century, a considerable distance from the catholic masses. The Springfield Road/Grosvenor Road intersection was also a social divide. Whereas 'kitchen' houses had been typical in the lower Falls, the twentieth century saw 'parlour' houses constructed further from the city centre for 'social types who regarded themselves as one step above the mill workers'.[26] A social geographer found in the early 1950s that a small number of streets, bounded by the lower Springfield Road, Falls Road and Cavendish Street, contained 'a large number of schoolteachers, civil servants and skilled tradesmen'[27] – and no workers from the nearby Springfield Road mill. Social exclusiveness was also characteristic of the minority community.

The catholic working class had squeezed into the extramural area of the town. In the cotton years new arrivals occupied the 'tiny streets and courts ... [with] closely packed houses'[28] along the line of the Farset. By 1830 there were about 8,700 of these houses, 2,000 of which were still standing in 1850. The market in housing was private, being almost entirely for rent. In 1831 10 per cent of houses had become uninhabited. This suggests that high rent, rather than protestant landlords, kept catholics from spilling out of their area. They may have first occupied old property, and land in any case was restricted. The mechanization of linen spinning saw the housing stock increase by 50 per cent in the 1830s, when the Pound and Sandy Row were laid out. Even more houses were uninhabited in 1841, suggesting a high degree of speculative building. The break-up of the Donegall estate freed considerable land, and the rate of house building continued, in the 1850s and 1860s, to the west of the Lagan. At this point catholics settled outside the ghetto, in the classic 'zone of transition and decay', such as the 'markets' and lower Crumlin Road. The absence of multi-tenancies suggests working-class catholics were occupying protestant family houses vacated for better properties. Catholics had little to do with subsequent developments, especially in east Belfast, which was laid out in the 1880s. The housing stock there doubled again in the 1890s. By the end of the century half of Belfast's houses postdated 1878, when the second, and more important, set of municipal regulations had been imposed. Only a tiny proportion of working-class housing was tied to specific employment. Public housing was not envisaged until 1919, when an act of parliament required the corporation to prepare its own housing scheme.

Belfast had a unique pattern of industrial action, that of working-class cooperation being marred by ethnic conflict. Virtually all strikes were against employers, there being little sign of this weapon being used by one group of workers against another. Demarcation disputes were a complicated variant, the employer being the object of criticism for his managerial policies. Trade unionism was predominant, there being much less evidence of sectarian organization at the point of production. But there was a pattern of ethnic rivalry, when politics and residential rioting spilt over into the workplace. This took the form of some workers expelling others, almost always protestants attacking catholics. This became more extensive over time, and was largely a product of political division in Ireland having an impact on Belfast. Such industrial expulsion was characteristic of shipbuilding and engineering, there being little evidence after 1864 of its occurring in the linen industry. The reason has to do with greater managerial control in the spinning mills and weaving factories. The first extensive expulsions occurred in Harland and Wolff in 1886, the year of the first home rule bill. In a workforce of over 3,000, there were only, according to Harland, 225 catholics. 190 of these were expelled, most being unskilled. The perpetrators were not the labour aristocrats. Protestant rivet-heaters, unskilled workers who assisted riveters, were largely responsible for industrial expulsions.

Such intra-working-class violence disturbed the employers, though, as members of the protestant bourgeoisie, they had an interest in popular unionist mobilizations from 1886. These demonstrations had to be disciplined, and not interfere with the working day. The employers were mainly concerned to keep the state's repressive forces off their property. Hunter, of Ewart's mill, refused to let the police interview his workers in 1886, as did Combe, of Combe, Barbour and Combe. Harland, though mayor of Belfast at the time, argued that the employers could control their works. This did not prevent the army from occupying Combe, Barbour and Combe, though Combe may have segregated his workers. 'We consider that our control', he told the riot commissioners, 'has ceased as soon as they have done their day's work'.[29] The vulnerable points were the beginning and end of the working day, as well as meal times. Hunter, at Ewart's mill, stationed 'leading men' during meal breaks to prevent conflict. When some catholics were intimidated, he promised them protection if they stayed at work. If they chose to go, he kept their jobs for them. A great many returned when the riots outside stopped. Harland was much more indulgent of loyalist autonomy in his yard. He had threatened to close his yard in 1864, when an elderly catholic worker was attacked. By 1886 he was protesting his relative powerlessness. 'You cannot knock them off and take them on again, and feeling that [they] have lost nothing but the wages'.[30] But he had closed the yard twice in the previous two years, in order to enforce wage reductions. He also denied that the taking of 'Belfast confetti', rivets, bolts, etc. for use in street rioting, was theft. The riot commissioners concluded that the employers could have controlled their workplaces better. This was to ignore the fact that the protestant bourgeoisie, as the political leadership of unionism, had to be more tolerant of such undisciplined mass action. Workers worked for money. They rallied to the unionist cause out of fear and conviction.

Inter-class conflict in the mills, factories, yards and works has a much greater social weight in Belfast's history. Strikes are only the visible tip of industrial relations, but the profile of the city's workplace stoppages allows for comparisons. Between 1888 and 1913 the government's labour correspondent recorded 'principal' strikes in the board of trade's annual reports. There were 174 such strikes in Belfast in this 26-year period. The city's profile is normal, with a sustained peak in the 1890s, followed by a trough in 1899–1907, and the prewar strike wave of 1910–14. The significant years were 1897, 1900, 1907, 1911 and 1913. There were local and national strikes in shipbuilding and engineering, and local disputes in linen – 57 in shipbuilding and engineering, 50 in linen, and 66 others as well as 1 unique strike.

Forty of the shipbuilding and engineering strikes involved skilled workers. Union density among craft workers may have averaged 50 per cent in 1888, the close relationship between the Belfast yards and their customers meaning less variation in the trade cycle. Belfast workers had greater security and, with stronger organizations, were able more actively to pursue wage demands. The national consequences of this local characteristic were evident in the Amalgamated Society of Engineers (ASE). In October 1895 there began an engineering strike in Belfast, which lasted until the following January. This led the national employers to impose a lock-out in 1897, which ran from July until the following January. A severe defeat was inflicted upon the ASE, and it was forced to restrain its more advanced branches. These were the two major industrial struggles of the period under analysis. Fourteen of the 40 skilled strikes were demarcation disputes. Carpenters were prominent encroachers, and shipwrights, who had built wooden ships, were invariably engaged in defensive actions. Half of these demarcation struggles were against deskilling, that is, the breakdown of apprenticeships and the introduction of machinery to be used by semiskilled workers.

The 17 strikes of unskilled workers were very different, all but one occurring in the 1890s – the decade of new unionism. They were on a smaller scale. Plater's helpers and rivet-heaters were to the fore, attempting to free themselves from the craftsmen, who were often their direct employers. In a series of eight strikes, the plater's helpers won wage increases, breached the system of subcontracting, achieved direct payment from the firm and forced out non-union men, only to concede partially to the platers in the end. More bitter struggles by rivet-heaters were less successful, probably because they were more easily replaceable by unskilled labour.

The economic fortunes of linen were much less certain, and, after the 1860s, the industry was in a permanent slump. There was an upturn in the late 1880s, again in the late 1890s, and a recession in the early 1900s. The number of strikes declined after 1900, a greater proportion being among lower-status workers. These were women spinners, who were on time rates. The upper-status workers, on piece rates, were men as well as women wareroom workers (stitchers) and weavers. Trade unionism was confined to the upper-status workers in this period. Thirty-five strikes were conducted by this group, 15 being in male occupations. The men were able to fight long struggles against wage cuts, but they were invariably defeated. The preparing trades in linen were being undermined by new technology, and often simply by lay-offs. Hemmers and weavers were the most strike-prone women workers.

A characteristic of the industry was the infrequent, large-scale strike. It was usually provoked by a lock-out, and it was only on such occasions that the mass of spinners became involved. In the period 1888–1913 there were major struggles in 1897 and 1906. The first was a general stoppage in one of the larger works against the system of fines which had been restricted by the 1896 truck act. The 1906 dispute, which occurred with returning prosperity, was the greatest in the industry. It was largely a spontaneous reaction and, given weak organization, it soon turned into a lockout by the employers.

The one unique strike in the period 1888–1913 took place in the linen industry. It was explicitly sectarian, and occurred in 1893 – the year of the second home rule bill. According to the local press, 264 weavers 'refused to work with [a] member of another religious denomination during a political demonstration'.[31] It may have been only a workplace disturbance. There is no similar action recorded for shipbuilding and engineering. One has to go as far back as 1864 to find a sectarian strike in Harland and Wolff. This was the year the foundation stone of the statue of Daniel O'Connell was laid in Dublin, in memory of his achievement of catholic emancipation. The riot report records ship carpenters, presumably shipwrights, striking against informers and a catholic apprentice. The informers were catholics, and their leaders were named in a protestant ballad as Harkin and Macnaughten. They were accused of identifying protestant rioters to the authorities. In 1912 the *Irish News* revealed that the former catholic apprentice, William F. George, of 126 Cavendish Street, was an executive member of the shipwrights' association. He claimed that the firm got the protestant shipwrights back to work by promising he would be the last catholic taken on in the trade. He clearly survived until the third home rule bill, in what was a dying craft.

Contemporary Ireland is constitutionally the outcome of the home rule era in modern British political history. This was the product of political modernization, in particular the extension of the franchise in the United Kingdom. An act of 1884, known when introduced as the third reform bill, trebled the electorate in Ireland. The Irish question, as it came to be called in Victorian political parlance, created division within, rather than simply between, both islands.

The majority of the British ruling class considered that the maintenance of the union strengthened the heart of the empire. A minority came to believe that the same objective could be achieved, if Irish grievances were silenced with self-government within the United Kingdom. In the election of 1885 the Irish party of Charles Stewart Parnell captured 85 of the 103 seats, the unionists winning Trinity College (Dublin) and eastern Ulster. With the nationalists holding the balance of power at Westminster, Gladstone, once he had formed a government, introduced a home rule bill in 1886. It was defeated in the Commons, when a section of his party, henceforth the liberal unionists, came out in opposition. There was a second bill in 1893, the nationalists supporting another Gladstone government against unionists and liberal unionists. More of the battle was fought in Ireland. The

Irish party, after Parnell's removal from the leadership in 1890, was weaker. Ulster unionists, following their convention of 1892, and the formation of the Ulster unionist clubs, were stronger. Home rule passed in the Commons, only to be defeated in the Lords.

Gladstone soon retired, and the unionists held office from 1895 to 1905. The Irish party continued to decline, only to recover partially. It reunited, under John Redmond, in 1900. With the constitutional hiatus produced by conservative rule, other forms of nationalism developed. This was also the period of 'constructive unionism' in Ireland, when social reform within the United Kingdom was posed as the solution. But killing home rule with kindness included the devolution crisis of 1904–5, when changes in the Irish administration were mooted.

This saw the formation of the Ulster Unionist Council (UUC). The liberals returned to office in 1905, securing an electoral landslide the following year. The government did not need the votes of the Irish party, though the nationalists were offered an Irish council in 1907. Redmond had to support Campbell-Bannerman, and, from 1908, his successor as prime minister, Asquith, in the hope of home rule in the future. But it was the Lords' opposition to Lloyd George's budget of 1909, leading to the 1911 Parliament Act, which cleared the legislative way. In the first general election of the previous year, with the liberals and unionists evenly matched, the Irish party once again became important. This saw Sir Edward Carson, one of the two unionist MPs for Trinity College, and a former solicitor general, take over the Irish unionist party in February. He was a Dublin lawyer who had moved from the Irish to the English bar. Carson became the effective leader of Ulster unionism. The second general election in 1910 did not alter the balance at Westminster. This parliament saw the unionist mobilizations, mainly in Ulster but also in Britain, against the third home rule bill, introduced by Asquith in April 1912. After unprecedented parliamentary scenes, it was enacted in September 1914, having passed through the Commons three times. This Government of Ireland Act provided for a Dublin parliament, and Irish administration, within the United Kingdom. But the First World War had broken out the previous month, and the act was suspended for the duration. More importantly, special consideration was promised for Ulster when the war was over. Partition was born.

It first emerged as a solution in constitutional politics in 1913–14, but Ireland then became preoccupied by the war. There followed the Dublin rising of 1916, when revolutionary nationalists, including James Connolly, tried to seize independence with German help. Nationalist Ireland reorientated from the Irish party to Sinn Féin, and de Valera's party swept almost all of catholic Ireland in the 1918 election. An alternative, separate state was set up, but its power was more symbolic than real. There ensued a war of independence (1919–21), colloquially known as the 'tan war' after the colour of a British uniform. The Anglo-Irish treaty of December 1921 did not undermine partition, and the northern government survived. The new regime in the south, the Irish Free State, fought a bloody civil war, the republicans refusing to accept dominion status. Under this status Ireland was a member of what became the British Commonwealth. Northern Ireland remained in the United Kingdom. By 1923 the country was well and truly divided, the governments on either side of the border having created new political stabilities based on the traditions of nationalism and unionism.

The home rule era in Irish politics runs from the 1880s to the 1920s. In 1905 there began the decisive series of events which led to the outcome of 1923. It was the return of a liberal government to office, later becoming dependent upon the Irish party, which led to the third, and last, home rule bill. This period from 1905 includes what there was of an Irish revolution. It is invariably dated from 1916, when revolutionary nationalism took the stage. But the gun had returned to Irish politics courtesy of the unionists, with the formation of the Ulster Volunteer Force (UVF) in 1913. In Ireland the counter-revolution came first.

The home rule era was above all the clash of nationalism and unionism, over Ireland's partial secession from the United Kingdom. There can be no doubt about the democratic validity of home rule, given the elections from 1885 on, nor about the fact that the unionists chose to resist it using reactionary arguments. But the Irish, especially Ulster, unionists constituted a significant regional minority. It was centred on Belfast, where the protestant bourgeoisie and working class were concentrated. This was also borne out by general election results. For all the British conservative attempts to play the orange card, the Irish minority was a problem for nationalism. Minority problems are not uncommon in national questions, and Irish nationalism was not unusual in denying the problem of unionism. The winning, neutralizing or defeating of the minority, was something the nationalist majority in Ireland had to consider. It chose either to place responsibility firmly with Britain, or simply to ignore the problem. This was the undoing of the Irish nationalist goal of a unitary state in Ireland. In terms of the notion of self-determination, popularized towards the end of the European war, the Irish undoubtedly had a claim, but not to the whole of the island. The Ulster unionists never made any such claim, being content with the constitutional status quo. In so far as Irish nationalism claimed Ulster, it was irredentist. The constitutional nationalists, in accepting the temporary exclusion of the province from home rule in 1914, showed they could be forced to be conciliatory.

The revolutionary alternative, having been re-created by the romantic cultural nationalism of the 1890s and the Edwardian decade, was intellectually more dogmatic about the territorial home of the Irish people. 'There are ... three pictures ... in the history of the Irish nation', wrote James Connolly in 1915. 'The first is a picture of ... a system evolved through centuries of development out of the genius of the Irish race ... The second picture is ... of the destruction by force of the native system ... The third picture must be drawn by each, as it suits his or her fancy, who wishes to visualise to the mind's eye the complete reversal of all that was embodied in the second.'[32] The following year Connolly set out completely to reverse British rule, his distinct picture of a free

Ireland being lost in the vision of the revolutionary nationalists. Arthur Griffith and Michael Collins were also caught up in the 1916 rising, albeit in different ways. Five years later they led the Irish delegation in talks with the British. On 14 October 1921 Griffith told Lloyd George:

> We do not feel ourselves to be a colony but a nation. It is much more than a question of administration and economics. There is an intense national feeling. The people of Tyrone think of their poets and warriors as living people not as you do of King Alfred as dead. You may think it foolish but you must take account of that sentiment in making a settlement.[33]

Two weeks later Collins told C.P. Scott of the *Manchester Guardian*: 'Ireland *was* a nation. Every Irishman felt it in himself. It was not a theory. "It was there."'[34]

In the first half of the home rule era, 1886 to 1905, the political traditions of nationalism and unionism confronted each other. Between 1905 and 1923, they fought the struggle through, achieving a partitioned Ireland. Neither side had expected, much less desired, this outcome. Could Irish catholics or Ulster protestants have modified the struggle, in such a way as to alter the outcome? Were there any bourgeois or proletarian social movements, liberal or socialist forces, which could have constructively crossed the sectarian divide, reconciling the majority yearning for self-government with the minority's desire to remain British? A number of so-called third forces put in a historical appearance between the traditions of nationalism and unionism.

First, the south. This is where the greatest challenge was made to the polarization of catholics and protestants. The social upheavals of rural Ireland, in particular the land war of 1879–82, raised the question of the modernization of agriculture. Sir Horace Plunkett's Irish Agricultural Organisation Society (IAOS), and, later, the department of agriculture and technical instruction, did much to stimulate producers' cooperatives and improve farming techniques. But it was the land conference, chaired by the reforming landlord, Lord Dunraven, which led to the establishment of peasant proprietary in the early twentieth century. Wyndham's land act of 1903, as amended in 1909, provided state loans for tenants to buy out their landlords. Dunraven went on to found the Irish Reform Association, a progressive unionist body, to solve other Irish problems. When Sinn Féin set up the new state after the war, Arthur Griffith was most concerned to win the defeated, but unreconstructed, representatives of southern unionism. Also in the Edwardian decade William O'Brien, the nationalist leader, formed the All-for-Ireland League, which had a handful of MPs. An agrarian and political radical, he came to advocate conciliation between the two political traditions in Ireland. Such bourgeois currents overshadowed proletarian ones. In the towns of Ireland, craft trade unionism was long established. The nascent Irish labour movement, associated with James Larkin, and, to a lesser extent, James Connolly, was only founded late in this decade. The Irish Transport and General Workers' Union was involved in the Dublin lockout of 1913–14, but only took off in 1917–18 during an agricultural boom in wartime. The Irish Trade Union Congress had been established in 1894, as a regional trade-union centre in the United Kingdom. It agreed only in 1912 to put up labour candidates, and, given deference to Sinn Féin, an Irish labour party did not appear on the political field until the Free State had been set up. Connolly's involvement in 1916 did much to incorporate the working-class movement politically in revolutionary nationalism.

Second, the north. There were fewer alternatives here to sectarian polarization in the province which needed liberalism and socialism the most. But there were progressive bourgeois currents in rural and urban Ulster. The land struggle, particularly in Co. Antrim, saw the involvement of T.W. Russell, MP. He took over Plunkett's agriculture department in Dublin in 1907. This movement also saw Lindsay Crawford's involvement in the Independent Orange Order (IOO). There was a possibility of the revival of Ulster liberalism, on the occasion of the party's electoral landslide in 1906. It even had a presence in Belfast. But it had no significant social basis, despite the leadership of Lord Pirrie, Ulster's leading industrialist, who was singular among his peers in lacking a provincial view. Proletarian movements were relatively more important in Belfast, as might be expected in Ireland's leading industrial city. But they had difficulty surviving under the conservative hegemony which had been constructed as a result of home rule agitation, and they were troubled by the presence of minority nationalism within Belfast. Trade unionism was strongest here, and labour municipal and parliamentary activity developed first in this city. There was even a variety of socialisms on offer in the 1890s, 1900s and early 1910s. None were quite up to dealing with structural inequality between catholics and protestants, and the political divide in the city between nationalism and unionism. No labour leaders developed the politics of democratic accommodation, much less the idea of socialism as the answer to the Irish national question. Partition never became a working-class solution.

The position of a nationalist majority in Ireland was reversed in Belfast, where unionism was in the ascendant. Without the city, and its two great social classes, Ulster unionism would not have been the force it was. The historic goal of a unitary state in Ireland was frustrated by the Ulster bourgeoisie's ability to secure a mass protestant following in Belfast and the surrounding counties. Its success was the weakness of Irish nationalism. The working class of Belfast was the most important social force in Ireland during the home rule era. The failure of Irish nationalism to win over more than the city's catholic minority, combined with the success of Ulster unionism in securing the protestant majority, is the tragedy of Ireland exaggerated in geographical concentration. This is all the more so, when it is appreciated that, in the second half of the home rule era, a labour movement developed in the city, a movement which refused unionist hegemony, while it rejected nationalist blandishments. This book is about how labour fared in those choppy social and political seas, before being overwhelmed in the early 1920s. Such a historical outcome represents no moral condemnation of the men and women who rallied to the cause of labour in

Belfast from 1905 on. The suffering of the catholic masses, before and after partition, is not in doubt, but this work is dedicated to the 'rotten Prods' of 1920 and after, in the hope that they may yet be allowed to contribute to the political future of Ireland.

Part II

Edwardian Politics

2

Joe Devlin and Constitutional Nationalism, 1906–10

The Belfast catholic community was a distinct section of the Irish people, and had a chequered political history from the onset of mass male democracy. It became a case of what the city's minority could do for Ireland, rather than what nationalists could do for their besieged brethren in this industrial capital. The working class fared worst. Thomas Sexton, the Parnellites' financial expert from Dublin, represented West Belfast at Westminster from 1886 to 1892. The catholic bishop, Dr Henry of Down and Connor, then gained political control of the ghetto, seeking to advance communal interests in Belfast. It was not until 1906 that Joe Devlin, a Belfast political journalist, recaptured this marginal seat from the unionists for constitutional nationalism. He was a consummate organizer, and became one of the leaders of the Irish party. Devlin was no parochial political boss, though he ran West Belfast as a populist. He believed in a national movement for self-government, and always put Ireland before his constituency. The sectarianism of Irish nationalism was indigenous to the south, and not simply a product of Belfast intrusion in the form of the Ancient Order of Hibernians (AOH). An anti-labour organization in the south, Hibernianism was a communal movement in rural Ulster which Devlin used to underpin constitutional nationalism. He presented himself in Belfast as on the side of the working man and woman, and even as an advocate of catholic–protestant reconciliation, but this was for Irish and British political consumption. He was no socialist nor even a thorough democrat. Home rule was the only solution Devlin offered to the problems of Belfast catholics, republicanism being given short shrift. Minority politics is inextricably connected with his name from the Edwardian years on.

Politically christened 'Wee Joe' on account of his stature, Devlin was born at 10 Hamill Street in 1871 to catholic parents. His father was a jarvey (driver) at St Malachy's Church, his paternal grandfather an evicted Bannside tenant. His mother came from a Dundalk farming family. He attended a Christian Brothers school, and left at the age of eleven. Young Joe was refused a job as a clerk in a mill, and became a potboy in a public house. He was clearly ambitious, but able as well. The nationalist political organization, the Irish National League (INL), was belatedly established in Belfast in January 1885. That November

Sexton fought West Belfast, losing narrowly. He had been returned as an agrarian radical for Co. Sligo in 1880, and had won South Sligo in 1885. By then the 14-year-old Joe Devlin had founded the Thomas Sexton Debating Society, to attract young men into national political activity.

The Irish party had held only 3 of the 29 Ulster seats, Tim Healy beginning the 'invasion' when he won a by-election in Monaghan in 1883. Following the third reform bill, and the redistribution in 1885, Parnell aimed for a significant national majority of the 103 Irish seats. Thirty-three of these were in Ulster. The nationalists won 17 in 1885 to the unionists' 16, the liberals being wiped out. (They had not won the support of Belfast catholics, though Bernard Hughes became a member. Ulster liberalism went unionist the following April.) The political combatants saw the split in the province as, antagonistically, victory and defeat. When Willie Redmond, brother of John, took North Fermanagh, a local conservative blamed the nationalist victory on 'the abstention of many *rotten* renegade Protestants'.[1] The unionists had failed to organize a considerably enlarged electorate, divided between conservatism, liberalism and orangeism. 'Ulster is Ireland's at last', proclaimed the *Nation* from Dublin. 'Nevermore will a West-Britain faction or a bitter Orange clique be able to rise in the House of Commons and deny that a united Ireland demands the restoration of a native parliament.'[2]

The nationalists had formally won Ulster in 1885, only to lose Belfast. The majority of parliamentary seats went uncontested in the home rule era, being safe nationalist or unionist. The faultline of marginals ran through Ulster, where the most keenly fought contests took place. West Belfast was the most crucial of all. When Sexton won it in 1886, the unionists claimed electoral malpractice. The judges concluded there had been no generalized personation, and, of 13 cases proved, only 5 were counted against the nationalists. The Belfast unionists had been divided between orangemen and conservatives, but the union had 17 Ulster supporters. This overshadowed Sexton's gain, and he went on to become high sheriff in Dublin in 1887, and lord mayor in 1888–89. But he helped secure the extension of the municipal franchise for Belfast, all householders gaining the vote in 1887, twelve years before the rest of Ireland. He lost the west division in 1892, having deserted Parnell the previous year in the interests of home rule, but double indemnity saw him safely returned for North Kerry.

Thomas Sexton was Joe Devlin's political model. From the age of 15 he expanded the activities of the debating society, of which he became chairman. By 1890 Devlin had joined the committee of the Belfast INL. He was quick to turn against Parnell, following the split in the Irish party that December. The nationalist leader had been having an affair with Catherine O'Shea, the wife of an Irish MP, and he was cited in a divorce suit. British nonconformists wanted nothing more to do with Parnell, and Irish catholics found their political rejection of a weakened leader religiously virtuous. Devlin became local secretary of the anti-Parnellite Irish National Federation (INF) in April 1891. The following year he represented Belfast at the Dublin convention. He also organized

Sexton's unsuccessful campaign in 1892. Devlin had got a job as an assistant on the *Irish News*, Belfast's catholic newspaper, and, in 1893, moved to the local office of the *Freeman's Journal*, a national paper now under the control of Sexton in Dublin. Devlin combined journalism with being assistant manager of a public house in Bank Street. He was already the local representative of anti-Parnellite nationalism, whose national leader was Justin McCarthy, and, later, John Dillon. John Redmond had succeeded Parnell, upon his death, in October 1891, and this ensured factionalism in nationalist politics. There was a third national leader, Tim Healy, who advocated local autonomy in the movement. This meant a greater role for the catholic church, which Bishop Henry was seeking in West Belfast.

Priests had been involved in the INL, but, following the O'Shea divorce case, Henry became sympathetic to the emerging Healyite wing of nationalism. The defeat of the second home rule bill was followed, after a short interregnum, by the return of a conservative government in June 1895. That October Henry set up the Catholic Representation Association (CRA) in Belfast, which came to embrace 'the clerical party and more respectable Nationalists'.[3] The CRA was the bishop's personal political vehicle. A later copy of the association's rules, obtained discreetly by the Royal Irish Constabulary (RIC) in Belfast and forwarded to Dublin Castle, showed it was under his strict control. Henry was president, and he appointed the officers and later selected the political candidates. The literature contained pledges of personal loyalty to the bishop. 'Catholic householders' elected the committee, 'to do all that may be required when called upon by the President'. The CRA's objective was 'the Protection and Advancement of Catholic Interests, Congregational and General'. It was created for 'the religious, moral, social and educational benefit of the District'.[4] This was a clear statement of local interests, but was not necessarily sectarian. Parnell, and Devlin, had sought politically to overwhelm the city's majority. Henry was looking for the minority's just deserts.

The precipitating event for the CRA was municipal reform, the bishop wanting safe catholic wards carved out on the electoral map. The city boundary was extended in 1896, and the wards reorganized, under a special act of parliament. Since there had been only three catholic councillors in the history of the corporation, the CRA argued that wards should be based on the parliamentary divisions of north, south, east and west. Henry hoped to win some of the local seats in West Belfast. He had the active support of the Healyite MP, Vesey Knox, who ensured that Falls and Smithfield were two of the 15 new wards. With 4 seats per ward, catholics could be sure of 8 of the 60 in the corporation. William Johnston, the orange MP for South Belfast, claimed that 'these two wards were pencilled out by a Roman Catholic priest',[5] and the *Irish News* admitted they had a 'permanent Catholic majority'.[6] A general municipal election was due in November 1897, the first for 10 years. Henry swept the board, the CRA having 2 aldermen and 6 councillors on the new corporation. The bishop's men looked after catholic interests for the next few years, until Henry was forced to dissolve the CRA.

Devlin was eclipsed in West Belfast until 1905 as the advocate of a strong, united Irish party at Westminster. He had not totally opposed Henry's political project from 1895, serving on the catholic committee, as it was called, and probably writing the brief for Vesey Knox. In September 1896 he sent a friend to Glasgow to study the catholic bishop's scheme for municipal representation. But the Belfast INF censured Knox, for refusing to have Dillon on his select committee, supporters of the latter having left the CRA in March. Devlin told Dillon he would stay and fight: 'Healyism won't gather strength here by using our position and our claims here for the purpose of gaining a foothold in this city.'[7] That October Henry pushed the CRA into municipal politics. Devlin tried to stop the new constitution at a public meeting and stormed out when he failed. By July 1897 he had linked the Dillonite INF and Parnellite INL in order to stop Henry that November. He argued that the aim of the joint committee was 'the upholding of the flag of a broadminded nationality and the safeguarding and promotion of Catholic interests',[8] there being no apparent contradiction. The committee secured only 4,953 votes to the CRA's 9,414, and the association went unchallenged for seven years. Henry had taken control of the daily *Irish News* in 1895, and Devlin was forced to bring out the weekly *Northern Star* in 1897. It was named after a publication of the United Irishmen, but sought to promote Dillonite nationalism through the medium of catholic piety. Catholic successes across the globe were reported, and the evangelization of England envisaged. There were also tales of orange outrages. Devlin had been secretary of the Young Ireland Society in Belfast, and he became president in 1898 of the Belfast and Ulster United Centenary Association – to celebrate the United Irishmen. Henry ignored it, and shortly after the centenary celebrations in Dublin, Devlin was described as being demoralized about Belfast and looking for a pub to run in the capital.

Belfast catholics had never found it easy to march in their city, usually rallying at Hannahstown in Co. Antrim. This is where Wolfe Tone was commemorated in 1898, the commemoration meeting with opposition from the Belfast Protestant Association (BPA), led by the fundamentalist lay preacher, Arthur Trew. He was back the following year. Henry organized 'Belfast's first Catholic religious procession for fifty years'[9] in 1901, to a Corpus Christi service in St Malachy's Church. 'The Pope's Brigade', BPA posters announced, was 'preparing for an illegal procession through the streets of this Protestant city.'[10] Dublin Castle was forced to intervene against Trew.

The Wolfe Tone commemoration had seen the INF in Belfast and the '98 clubs dissolve in 1899 into the new national organization, the United Irish League (UIL), founded by William O'Brien, MP. The national club was opened in Berry Street in Belfast. The following year Redmond became leader of the reunited parliamentarians, and Devlin was recognized as their representative in Belfast. He accompanied Willie Redmond on a fund-raising tour of the United States in 1902, being elected unopposed in a by-election in North Kilkenny while crossing the Atlantic. Irish MPs were then paid by the party, and duties kept him away from Belfast. Devlin never married. He was appointed secretary of the United Irish League of Great Britain in 1903, and, in September 1904, of the parent body in Dublin. He took a great deal of the administrative burden off Redmond's shoulders, and intervened repeatedly in local UIL affairs. Devlin became the key organizational figure behind the Irish party, this being the basis of his elevation into the leadership of constitutional nationalism.

Dr Henry had been trying to break into national politics, CRA branches being reported in Sligo, Derry and Boyle. Dublin Castle was told it was 'a Catholic Political Party ... to look after the interests of the members of that persuasion in all walks of life, particularly with regard to employment in Railways, Banks and other Industrial concerns where Catholic capital is invested'.[11] A vacancy had arisen in West Belfast in October 1903, and the unionists were confident of retaining the seat, given nationalist division. Devlin invited Henry to chair the selection committee, but the bishop refused. Patrick Dempsey, proprietor of the Linen Hall Hotel in Donegall Square East, was then run by the UIL. Henry refused to hand over the CRA's electoral register, and the nationalists were unsuccessful. This led the UIL to retaliate in the January 1904 local elections, the Devlinite slogan being 'Avenge West Belfast'. Two supporters of Redmond were defeated in Smithfield. Samuel Young, a distiller who lived at Derryvolgie Avenue, and was one of the oldest nationalist MPs, wrote to Henry: 'Devlin wants reverence and due respect for his superiors, and I really fear, owing to the hero worship now paid to that uncultivated young man, that he may become totally spoiled for any good to his party.'[12] It was the beginning of the end for Henry.

Archbishop Walsh condemned him from Dublin, and Redmond refused a financial donation. The Licensed Vintners' Association then ousted its CRA chairman in early 1905. Twenty-two priests revolted in March, claiming their bishop had done 'incalculable injury both to religion and nationality'.[13] The CRA was dissolved in May, though Henryism survived as a political irritant for a number of years. A catholic defence society came into being in 1906, 'approved'[14] by the bishop. His men were cleared out of the corporation between 1907 and 1909, though one, P.J. Magee, first elected in 1897, fought Devlin in West Belfast in the first 1910 general election. 'Catholics of West Belfast', read a Magee tract about the recently deceased bishop,

> a voice from a lonely and unadorned grave in Milltown Cemetery, deserted, except by the prayers of the Faithful and True, calls upon you to remember the falsehoods and calumnies of the past twelve years, to revere the bishop's memory and thus free the sacred soil of West Belfast from all connection with this puerile and vulgar little leader of an ecclesiastical rebellion.[15]

West Belfast, embracing the Falls and Shankill areas, was a microcosm of division in Ireland. In 1911 there were 36,605 catholics to 30,523 protestants. Among males over nine years old, there were only 12,966 catholics to 11,234 protestants. Demographically, the parliamentary division was catholic, while, electorally, it was protestant.

Catholics were socially underrepresented on the electoral register, and the protestants won the organizational battle to get names listed. Catholic and protestant newspapers were able to state, in 1906, that there were 4,168 catholic voters and 4,704 protestant. It was a marginal seat, which the unionists, polling well in their community, might be expected to hold. Third candidates, or nationalists able to appeal to some protestant workers, could upset this certainty. So also could rivalry among unionists. Sexton had lost by 35 votes in 1885, and won the following year by 103, owing to orange–unionist differences. This was also a year of economic depression. West Belfast was undoubtedly the most organized, and contested, electoral division in Ireland. In 1906 Devlin won the seat with a majority of 16 votes. A third, unionist candidate gave him the victory. The third, nationalist candidate in January 1910 did not deprive him of West Belfast, and he had a majority of 587 votes. In December 1910 there was a straight fight between orange and green, Devlin securing a healthy majority of 463 votes. These three electoral victories, which saw Devlin speak for Belfast, and even northern, catholics throughout 1918, were a product of UIL organization and the candidate's astute handling of electoral strategy and tactics. Ideology, and respective political programmes, were of little moment. Electoral politics were about communal assertion, and the constitutional status of the country.

Devlin's opponents in 1906 were Capt. J.R. Smiley, of the North of Ireland Imperial Yeomanry, a liberal unionist in politics, and a so-called independent liberal unionist, Alexander Carlisle, managing director of Harland and Wolff, and Pirrie's brother-in-law. The two last-named had been moving back towards liberalism, Campbell-Bannerman having just become prime minister. Pirrie was at increasing odds with the Belfast bourgeoisie. He had wanted to become unionist candidate, in South Belfast in 1902, and then in West Belfast for the general election. Carlisle's intervention in 1906 was seen as a vengeful move. He obtained only 153 votes, but, with Smiley's 4,122 votes, this would have defeated Devlin with his 4,138 votes. The UIL was keen to see the protestant vote split. As for the rest of Devlin's election strategy, this comprised organization within the ghetto, and rhetorical appeals to working-class protestants. The unionist press made the usual fair allegations about electoral malpractices, but the *Northern Whig* concluded that Devlin must have attracted some protestant support in one polling district – Model School. Since he obtained a vote which was only 30 short of the number of all the catholics on the register, a combination of personation and some protestant dissent must have made all the difference.

Devlin was also running in his Co. Kilkenny seat, and was elected there. At his adoption meeting in Belfast, the chairman 'appealed to all Catholics and Nationalists to lay aside their differences'. Devlin's claim in his speech that 'he did not seek the suffrage of any man on the ground of religion' was pretty thin.[16] The *Northern Star* showed the depth of his catholicism, but there was very little reference to nationalism. Devlin did not mention home rule in his election address. He admitted he was 'leav[ing] old shibboleths and old war cries'[17] to Smiley, the Falls being firm in its nationalist conviction. A supporter had suggested he campaign in the Shankill, but Devlin joked in reply that Smiley 'could [not] say anything'[18] if he came to 'the Pound'. He was able to state, at one meeting, that no protestants were present. Devlin's social politics was petty bourgeois. A nationalist councillor argued, at one meeting, for the taxation of land values, so 'the rich capitalists' would take the burden off 'the working classes, the shop-keeper, the traders'.[19] J.P. Nannetti, who represented College Green in Dublin, and was active in keeping trade unionists in the nationalist camp, also spoke at this meeting. The catholic clergy were not seen during the campaign, but, according to the *Irish News*, 'the priests turned out and showed their delight ... by the vigorous waving of their birettas'[20] at the victory celebrations.

Devlin had been concerned mainly with the protestant working class, and playing the trade-union card. 'I hold the cause of Ireland and the cause of Labour to be identical',[21] he said in his address (anticipating by ten years a similar claim from James Connolly!). If protestants were 'true to the principles of Labour and Trade Unionism',[22] argued the *Irish News*, they would rally to Devlin. He boasted that he had supported labour as an MP, but showed himself reluctant to make specific commitments to particular trade unions. The nationalist demand for better financial relations between the two countries was pressed, along with those transposed from rural Ireland – railway nationalization, taxation of land values, better housing, and security of tenure. The only working-class demands were old-age pensions, which the liberals were to grant, and reform of the poor law. The trades council sent an 18-point questionnaire to each parliamentary candidate. Though Devlin's address corresponded on only three issues, he gave 'full replies to all questions' with an enthusiasm uncharacteristic of a parliamentarian. He begged to differ on only two: he favoured manhood rather than adult suffrage, though he later supported votes for women; as for the temperance question, he argued that the solution was 'proper housing'.[23] Given that Smiley did not reply to the trades council, and Carlisle referred to his record as an employer, Devlin should have easily secured the endorsement of Belfast's trade unionists. The trades council voted for Devlin against Carlisle, by the narrow margin of ten votes to nine, when many delegates were busy campaigning in the election. Devlin did not receive much active trade-union support, though he was presented as the 'Irish Nationalist and Labour candidate'.[24] Labourism, for him, never meant trade-union organization, much less working-class self-activity. It was a force to be incorporated, before it became an alternative to nationalism. Nannetti recalled having first met Devlin at a meeting of the Trades Union Congress (TUC), in Belfast, in 1893, without explaining that the latter was probably there as a journalist.

On 14 January 1906 Nannetti supported Devlin at a meeting in the national club. Also present was the elderly Hugh McManus, a printer and leading trade unionist, who opposed an independent labour party. The nationalist press conjured up a protestant audience. The *Irish News* referred to 'a large number of Protestants present ... [who] took no small part in the applause',[25] and Devlin's own *Northern Star* detected an audience of 200 orangemen! Devlin meeting the protestant working class is most unlikely. On polling day (18 January) the *Irish News* carried a letter from a 'North Belfast Unionist Voter', J.M. McVeigh of 43 Elmfield Street, urging support for Devlin on labour grounds. 'No matter what his religion is, vote for Devlin, as we Unionist workmen of all creeds are going to vote for Walker'. By no means all unionist working men were supporting the labour candidate in North Belfast. A quick look in a local street directory would have revealed no such person at that address. Five days later the *Irish News* carried a disclaimer from the only McVeigh in Elmfield Street. The letter must have come from a section of the UIL, if not from within the *Irish News*.

Apart from Devlin and William Walker, the unionist party was opposed, in South Belfast, by Tom Sloan, an independent orange candidate. He had won the seat in 1902 in a by-election. The three candidates had in common opposition to the unionist bourgeoisie, but there similarity ended. They had no electoral agreement, much less an understanding about acting in concert if victorious. But Devlin sought to create the myth of a popular anti-ascendancy alliance. Hugh McManus had referred to a 'triumvirate of democrats' at the national club meeting, and Devlin waxed lyrical about 'Belfast workmen ... trampl[ing] down the things that had divided them in the past, and stand[ing] together for labour, progress, democracy and Ireland (Applause).'[26] This amounted to the *Irish News* calling, on election day, for catholics in North and South Belfast to vote for Walker and Sloan, in return for labour and independent protestants supporting Devlin in West Belfast. It was an exercise in tactical voting, but it is not clear why a Walker-, much less a Sloan-, supporter would have voted for Devlin against a choice of two unionists.

The announcement of Devlin's victory saw 'the industrial population ... in a state of ferment'. 'Rule, Britannia' and 'The Protestant Boys' competed with 'God Save Ireland' and 'The Boys of Wexford'. The old land war cry, 'The West Awake!', was the theme of the victory.[27] It created a 'sensation ... in the business portions of the city'. There 'was a regular irruption of the Shankill residents into the centre of the city, some thousands of men, girls and boys ... the leading parties carrying aloft an effigy ... bearing the legend "The Man Who Sold the West".' This was a reference to Alexander Carlisle. The leader, accompanied by 'youths and roughs', was the ubiquitous Arthur Trew.[28] He addressed the crowd from atop the railings surrounding the new City Hall. At the end of his victory parade Devlin praised 'the whole of the electors ... irrespective of class or creed'.[29] A supporter who then asked for cheers for the victorious Sloan was quickly rebuffed. This was a nationalist victory, and nothing else.

Devlin was no stranger to the House of Commons, when he was returned, in his mid-30s, as the member for West Belfast. 'A tiny, little man' is how he is remembered. 'The head is large and striking', a fellow Irish party member wrote later; 'the face – clean-shaven, boyish –

suggests strength of mind and of temperament; but at a distance you might well have thought you were about to listen to an inspired school-boy who had never grown up. Nor, though the voice is powerful, is the accent such as to win the ear; for it has all the hardness of the accent of Belfast.' And this from T.P. O'Connor, the nationalist member for the Scotland division in Liverpool! He went on to describe Devlin as 'gentle, shy, almost morbidly sensitive' in private. 'Unconscious of his powers, he shivers before a speech; cannot sleep, cannot eat; if he could, he would run away; has almost to be forced to his feet by friends who realise his gifts more than he does himself. Even then, he begins with trembling voice and trembling hands.'[30]

Devlin was the source of his own political reputation. Towards the end of 1906 Redmond stated, 'It would have been impossible for Mr Devlin to have headed the poll were it not that hundreds of so-called Orange Protestant working men of Belfast voted for him.'[31] O'Connor reproduced the myth of Devlin the unifier of catholics and protestants several years later:

> If Belfast ... were ever embodied in a man, it is Joe Devlin. He has the fierce energy of that pushful town; he has its sternness of principle; he has intense pride in it; and in him is strongly developed that intense democratic spirit which, by a curious paradox, runs through all its working masses. Joe Devlin has intense sympathy with the poor; he loves them; he goes to all their homes; he knows nearly every man, woman and child in his constituency by sight and by name; he addresses them, as they address him, by their Christian names. His own view is that the real work for which he was intended was the creation of a Labour Party in Belfast which would obliterate all the old and stupid feuds in a general crusade for righting the wrongs of the sweated workers of that city.[32]

In 1911 a sketch writer described Devlin as probably as well known as the new king, George V, on the basis of their respective travels in Britain. He had already been to the United States four times since 1902. Devlin also visited Australia and New Zealand in 1906, raising money from the Irish abroad for the nationalist cause. His speeches about his journeys to the countries where the Irish emigrated undoubtedly con-tributed to the political fantasy of Belfast catholics. In the autumn of 1910 he spent ten weeks in America. The *Irish News*'s report of his first election meeting, that December, was headed 'The Irish People's Success in Other Countries'. Devlin was quoted as saying he saw 'wide-spread prosperity, splendid freedom, progress unexampled, and com-mercial greatness unrivalled ... [This was due to the] Celtic genius ... I saw Irishmen the mayors of great cities, Senators and Congressmen in Washington, leading merchants, powerful advocates, prominent lawyers, leaders and captains of public opinion.'[33] Devlin was, above all, a political organizer, certainly in West Belfast, but mainly in nation-alist Ireland. 'The Government of Ireland', Redmond had just claimed in the United States, 'is carried on in 39, Parnell St., Dublin [headquar-ters of the UIL] and Mr Joseph Devlin is the Real Chief-Secretary.'[34] 'He is an organiser of the most efficient type', commented an observer, pos-sibly William O'Brien, a useful quality which he is bound to misuse because of his limitations ... It is a bitter thing to have to say that so much cannot be said of him in his public life. He is the most dangerous, because the most unthinking force in Irish politics. Perhaps the best way to sum him up is to call him the triumph of the American quality of 'getting there'. Mr. Devlin set out to get there, and he has got. It does not matter to him where. He has never thought of it.[35]

There was a number of important changes during the 1906 parliament, which altered the character of the two contests in West Belfast in 1910. The first was the movement in national politics, in particular the struggle between the liberal government and the House of Lords. Redmond extracted an electoral commitment from Asquith in late 1909 to legislate for home rule. A second was Joe Devlin's growing pre-eminence in the Irish party. To his responsibility for the UIL, he had added, in 1905, the presidency of the Ancient Order of Hibernians (Board of Erin). The AOH, or Hibernianism, a catholic movement, was used by Redmond further to organize the nationalist bloc. It became notorious in 1909 when Devlin allegedly used members as stewards, at the UIL meeting on the new land bill. The principal dissident, William O'Brien, who quit the Irish party, subsequently referred to it as the 'baton convention'. A third change was the fact that catholics in West Belfast were now a majority on the electoral register. Much work had clearly been done since 1906. But the *Northern Whig* predicted a unionist victory in January 1910; some nationalist rioters were in jail, and other catholics had left the city to find work. The catholic majority on the register meant there was little need for Devlin to win a minority of protestant voters.

His opponent, in January 1910, in the absence of an ill Smiley, was Boyd-Carpenter. The *Irish News* described the latter as 'the possessor of an undoubted English "Haw haw" accent, and the accompanying lisp which one has come to naturally associate with those pseudo-military men who divide their time between an army connection and "society".'[36] He was a tariff reformer, the sort of conservative Pirrie disliked the most. Boyd-Carpenter secured 4,064 votes to Devlin's 4,651, giving the latter a safe majority. This was barely threatened by P.J. Magee's 75 votes, though the unionist press gave the independent nationalist considerable coverage. The unionist vote was slightly down, and Devlin gained over 500 votes.

John Redmond chaired the West Belfast selection convention, described as 'represent[ative of] every element of its population ... merchants and wage-earners, professional men and employers of labour'. Devlin was nominated by the vicar-general of Down and Connor, the church now embracing this former ecclesiastical rebel. 'I am here tonight one of the people', Devlin said, 'moved with the people's compassion, guided by the people's will, controlled by the people's influence, a labourer for the people in whatever vineyard they ask me to toil in their interest.'[37] The House of Lords was the principal issue, though it was clear that home rule would follow. Redmond repeated the old claim that the Irish party was 'the oldest and original Labour Party'. Devlin harped on social reform, citing old-age pensions and workmen's compensation. He also opportunistically came out as a free trader, to embarrass the unionists. Devlin argued that tariffs would damage Belfast's two main industries, but also defended the right of an Irish government to impose them.

A new characteristic of Devlin's electioneering was a series of enthusiastic rallies. He had the help throughout of Willie Redmond, who now occupied the safe seat of East Clare. A parade was held on 11 January despite snowstorms. At Clonard Gardens enthusiasm became 'so intense' that 'several attempts were made to take the horses from Mr Devlin's brake [carriage] and draw the vehicle among the streets.'[38] A rally of 20,000 was reported three days later. 'With the toilers and the shopkeepers of the West Division', reported the *Irish News*, 'it is not "weather permitting" but enthusiasm inspiring and gratitude urging to deeds of self-sacrifice.' The headline on this report read: 'Vast Multitudes of His Constituents Give a Series of Royal Greetings to the Past – and Future – M.P. for West Belfast'.[39] So much for opposition to the House of Lords! Men, women and children were the participants in these events.

Devlin had begun to appeal to women. Though he went along with the Irish party strategy of deferring to the liberal government on the question of female suffrage, he may not have accepted Redmond's argument that Irishwomen would follow the priests. The women of West Belfast were predominantly working class. Given the structure of the family among the unskilled, they probably had influence over the political behaviour of the men. Many of these women were mill and factory workers. The inadequacy of relief during a recession in 1908–9 had seen Devlin force the government to increase its grant to the distress committee in Belfast. He had also argued unsuccessfully for linen to be included in the industries brought under public scrutiny, when a member of the committee considering the trades boards bill. This was Devlin the tribune of the people, trying to act as broker on behalf of his clients in West Belfast. Little patronage was forthcoming from a British government, though he continued to receive popular loyalty. In 1911 Devlin secured from the government a committee of inquiry into the linen industry. During the first 1910 election a meeting was arranged for female workers at St Mary's Hall. The 3,000 were considered representative of the '35,000 of their toiling sisterhood of the city', though protestants were hardly present. 'Every girl in the hall wore Mr. Devlin's colours, and the majority, in addition, displayed the card surrounded by Orange and Green flags, he had issued the electors [bearing the slogan] ... "Vote for Devlin and Labour".' 'There was no class in the community', said Devlin, 'in whose welfare he took a greater interest [than the women workers], and none for whom he was determined to do more in the future as time and opportunity offered (applause).' But the purpose of the meeting was simply to get the men out to vote. It ended with 'God Save Ireland' and 'A Nation Once Again'.[40]

The third contest, in December 1910, occasioned by the continuing battle over the Lords, saw Devlin in a straight fight with Capt. Smiley once again. He beat him by 4,523 votes to 4,080. The unionist vote held remarkably constant, but Devlin's was slightly down on that of January. He concentrated on the House of Lords in his address, arguing that landlordism drove 'thousands of men and women into Belfast to provide cheap labour for the grasping and heartless capitalists who monopolise the linen trade of the world'.[41] The unionists had block-booked the Ulster Hall, to prevent Devlin from holding a meeting there. On the question of home rule, he stated there was no fear of a 'Unionist Revolution'. Michael McKeown, a UIL councillor, and dockers' trade-union official, claimed that only a small number of prot-estants would withhold taxes from a Dublin parliament. 'He thought the RIC would be able to cope with them (Laughter and applause).'[42] There was a greater degree of inter-communal hostility. Alleged members of the AOH were reported to have attacked Smiley's car. For the declaration, 'formidable cohorts of baton men and plain clothes constables' had to deal with the catholics, according to the *Northern Whig*. The *Irish News* saw none of this, reporting that unionists 'irritat-ingly paraded the Crumlin Rd, waving Union Jacks with a fanaticism that would disgrace a Dervish'.[43]

It was during this campaign that Devlin was reported to have held a meeting of protestants in St Mary's Hall. This is improbable. The venue was identifiably catholic, as Devlin admitted in his reported speech. The *Irish News* carried the report on 6 December, under the heading 'Mr Devlin's Protestant Constituents', with a related editorial, 'To an Audience of Protestants'. The paper claimed that five-sixths of the audi-ence were 'Protestant artisans and labourers'. The fact that such precise ethnic data could be given is an indication of the problem of division. (The *Irish News* also played up the Ulster Liberal Association's mani-festo, signed by Pirrie and other protestants, as 'A Great Employer's Words'.[44]) If Devlin had been able to fill a hall with such working-class supporters, he would have been well on his way to finding a solution to sectarianism. The fairest assessment is that he still received a small anti-tory protestant vote. He still retained the support of the trades council, as the more desirable of the two candidates. The function of such a claim about protestant supporters was to minimize, for nationalists, unionist opposition. Thomas Sexton described Devlin as 'link[ing] his native city with the movement of the nation'.[45] The member for the west division had claimed to be 'the first Catholic in twenty-five years, the second Catholic in one hundred years, sent to represent the great Protestant industrial capital of the North of Ireland'.[46] As is often the case, such a claim performed an opposite function in unionist ideology. The existence of putative protestant nationalists served to alert union-ists to the need for renewed endeavour. Smiley noted that their ranks 'unfortunately comprised men of many different moods', including 'a portion holding Socialist views'.[47]

Elections in West Belfast were, above all, about registration, and getting the vote out. In December 1910, given that Redmond was hoping to continue holding the balance of power at Westminster, organization was at a premium. The catholic majority on the register riled the unionists. Devlin was accused of packing the division with his coreligionists: 'dirt and double tenancies and the beautiful provision of "revision by party"' were seen as responsible. Smiley wept crocodile tears about its being 'a disgrace to civilisation that people should be asked to live in such surroundings'.[48]

Personation had long been alleged by unionists, only to be denied by nationalists. In 1906 the *Northern Whig* accused the UIL of being 'prepared to poll every man on the register, dead or alive, absent or present'.[49] Devlin was credited with harnessing the workhouse vote, precisely the same charge levelled by the *Irish News* at the unionists. Similar accusations were made in January 1910. 'It was suggested prior to the polling', the *Northern Whig* noted in an uncharacteristically humorous vein, 'that a special force of police would be required around the cemetery to keep the dead men from coming out to poll'.[50] A future leader of Ulster unionism retained, in his papers, a postcard, possibly from 1910. It shows a picture of Devlin, labelled 'Joe Gabriel', blowing a trumpet over the cemetery, with the captions 'Rise to Vote' and 'West Belfast – Devlin's Reserve Voters Depot – Joe's last call'.[51] At a nationalist meeting in the Ulster Hall the chairman said: 'By right the West Division of Belfast belonged to the Nationalists ... It was theirs by justice and fair play, and they meant to have it and to hold it.'[52] Foul means might well be justified by such an end. The *Northern Whig* reported 50 arrests for personation on polling day: 'A large section of hangers-on and the cheers which greeted each prisoner as he was driven off by the police showed how this form of electioneering is regarded.'[53] The *Irish News* had a not dissimilar figure, and an implicit denial: 'At least forty respectable Nationalists were subjected to the indignity of arrest on criminal charges ... grossly and illegally outraged.'[54]

It is often assumed that Devlin's formidable electoral machine was the Ancient Order of Hibernians. He had long used catholicism for nationalist ends in West Belfast, but the order was designed to advance the same cause in rural Ireland. Hibernianism was relatively unimportant in the northern capital, and the order and its national president are not mutually reducible. Nationalism in Ulster was sectarian, but this ugly feature was also indigenous to the movement in the other three provinces. It was not some contagion, carried out of the catholic ghetto in Belfast by Wee Joe Devlin.

Though it has been traced back in Irish history, the AOH started in the nineteenth century as a community organization for Irish immigrants in the United States. It became a battleground for constitutional and advanced nationalists, and was established in Ireland at the turn of the century. It was a powerful organization, whose resources attracted various types of nationalists. The Board of Erin eventually came under Irish party control, the AOH having become a constituent of the UIL. When Devlin took over in July 1905, he set about weeding out erstwhile Fenians or revolutionary nationalists. The Board of America became a rival centre for republican influence. It recognized a Scottish section only in 1909, where there had been some moves to found a friendly society. The AOH there had been banned by the catholic church, as a front for a secret society, and elements of the Irish hierarchy continued to oppose Devlin's communal organization. It was 1910 before Redmondism was accepted on both sides of the Atlantic as the political expression of Hibernianism.

The AOH was a catholic organization, it being decided, in 1907, that converts had to wait five years before being accepted into membership. It was William O'Brien, from 1909, who advanced a nationalist critique of this sectarian organization. He pointed out that Parnell, as a protestant, would have been excluded from membership. But it is not clear that it was Belfast hibernians who wielded the batons at the UIL convention on the land bill of that year. There were contradictions in southern nationalism. From 10,000 members in 1905, the AOH grew to 60,000 in 1909, reaching a high point of over 90,000 in 1913. It was under Devlin's presidency, during the 1906 parliament, that the order grew most rapidly. Under a quarter of the members in 1913 were in Britain, mainly Scotland. In Ireland, Ulster accounted for 23,767, Leinster 15,051, Munster 13,200, and Connaught 5,993. Though Ulster had 35 per cent of the Irish membership, there is no direct relationship between membership and ethnic balance. The AOH was not simply a rival to the orange order. Hibernianism was not its mirror image in time and space. The growth of the AOH occurred at a time when orangeism appeared to be weakening. Hibernianism's development has to do with the social structure and ideology of catholic communities. The membership in Ulster was strongest in Donegal (5,210) and weakest in Fermanagh (1,167). It was a response to important changes, democratic local government in 1898, and land reform in 1903 and 1909. Between the citizen and the state stood the order and the Irish party, sowing the seeds of Irish clientelism in local and, it was hoped, central government. 'There was most demand for AOH divisions in areas where the UIL had atrophied as a result of the settlement of the land question, or in towns, where it lacked the appeal to oppose Sinn Féin ... Between 1910 and 1916 the Board of Erin spread its organization substantially through the whole of Ireland, to such an extent that the police of many southern and midland counties regarded it as the leading nationalist society.'[55] The AOH was a freemasonic body. Its role was social, in the creation of a community espousing certain values in which inter-class relations were constructed, and economic, in allowing a petty bourgeoisie to transact business with the urban, but mainly rural, working class. Its culture was traditional and making for security, lacking the revolutionary promise of cultural nationalism. The Irish party used it to help hegemonize nationalist Ireland, and keep down other potential forces.

The AOH seems to have provided very few benefits initially, Devlin leaving it to the Irish National Foresters, the main Irish-based friendly society, to compete with English and Scottish organizations. He appears to have opposed registration under the friendly societies act in 1904. The national insurance act of 1911 established limited compulsory schemes for health and unemployment, using existing societies and trade unions. Approved societies were to be publicly funded for non-profit-making activity. The AOH opened a special insurance section, as did the orange order and Sinn Féin. From that date it functioned increasingly as a friendly society, accounting for possibly one in every four insured catholics in Ireland. In 1913 the separate insurance section had 168,926 members. More than a quarter were in Britain, the Irish in England and especially Wales showing a new-found interest in Hibernianism because of national insurance. In Ireland, Leinster had 64,455 such members, Ulster 31,250, Munster 21,265, and Connaught 6,956. Leinster accounted for over half of the Irish insurance section, new interest in Ulster being only slightly greater than in Connaught.

Belfast had 2,005 ordinary members in 1913, just over 8 per cent of the provincial membership. There had been 950 Hibernians in the city in 1901, though there was also a smaller, but more active, Board of America branch. The growth of the AOH in Belfast was slight in the years before the war, compared with the rest of Ireland. Bishop Henry had not endorsed it at the turn of the century, it being seen initially as a challenge to Healyism. Devlin was already busy, from 1899, building the UIL in the ghetto. He had already seen off Henry by 1905, when he added the presidency of the AOH to his work as secretary of the UIL in Dublin. There is little evidence of the AOH, or the Molly Maguires, as its members were known, being involved in Devlin's three electoral contests in West Belfast. The insurance section was 5,779 strong in the city in 1913, 18 per cent of the provincial membership. There had been 13 branches of the Foresters in 1905, all with good nationalist names. The Foresters' Hall in Divis Street had opened in 1884, and most of the branches dated from that decade. It had 1,300 members. There were also 9 small local organizations, and 104 branches of the leading United Kingdom friendly societies, catering mainly for protestants. When insurance became compulsory, the AOH was able to attract more than four times the Foresters' voluntary membership.

The AOH, as a sectarian organization, contributed to the division in the working class, in Belfast and Ireland as a whole. While the nationalist leadership sought to incorporate the labour movement, it is not clear that Redmond and Devlin deliberately fomented strike-breaking. But the order became involved in anti–trade-union activity, particularly in Dublin, as a consequence of the mobilization of catholic Ireland. The true colour of the clerical elements so encouraged was yellow, as James Larkin and James Connolly testified in the early 1910s.

The AOH certainly came out in opposition to the Irish Transport and General Workers' Union, formed in Dublin by Larkin in 1909. *Socialism: A Warning to the Workers* and *'Larkinism': What it is and What it stands for* were pamphlets published by the order. It also became involved in promoting clerical 'company' unionism to frustrate the growth of Larkinism. There is mention of an unsuccessful AOH attempt to oppose the (British) Amalgamated Society of Railway Servants (ASRS) in 1913, and of efforts among the tram workers of Dublin, shortly before the lock-out of that year. It was certainly the AOH which prevented two socialist feminists from England providing temporary homes for workers' children outside Dublin. James Connolly first confronted the AOH in Co. Cork in 1911, where it was fighting O'Brien's All-for-

Ireland League. Local hibernians believed Connolly was simply an anti-clerical socialist, and drove him out of Queenstown (Cóbh). Two years later he described 'the rank and file of the A.O.H. as generally honest, hardworking Irishmen, Labour in all their sympathies'.[56] While he criticized the *Irish News* for its false labourism, Connolly hinted that Devlin, though president of the AOH, might not know about the yellow union activity.

> Mr. Joseph Devlin, M.P., used it for Nationalist purposes; it now seeks to use, if not already using him, for quite other purposes. As soon as Home Rule is passed into activity, and the inevitable reconstituting of parties takes place, should 'Wee Joe' elect to follow the democratic path, I should not be surprised to see the A.O.H. break him and brush him contemptuously aside.[57]

Maybe this was Connolly's sarcasm, but he perceived correctly Devlin's instrumental attitude to Hibernianism. In 1911, during a strike of Irish railway workers, Devlin lectured both sides on the need to cooperate. He had nothing to lose in attacking the unpopular railway magnates. He made no statement in 1913, despite the gravity of the Dublin lock-out. This was because he was as opposed to the employers' leader, William Martin Murphy, a former nationalist MP and associate of T.M. Healy, as he was to Larkin. Both were a threat to national unity at a time of great dependence on the liberal government.

Joe Devlin was the greatest obstacle facing the labour movement in Belfast if it hoped to appeal to the catholic working class. He did not bother unduly with the sectarian communalism of the AOH, preferring the rhetoric of labourism, given the electoral exigencies of West Belfast. He was happiest deploying a populist appeal, which is characteristic of nationalist movements. But Devlin must have appreciated the working-class base of the catholic ghetto, and he observed the new labour party at Westminster. Class and nation were incompatible in Belfast under the liberals, their fusion by Devlin strengthening Redmondism. Irish nationalists in Britain moved easily into the labour party after partition, and Devlin preferred to remain at Westminster, and even to become a labour MP, to coming to terms with the Sinn Féin brand of nationalism in Ireland. Thomas Sexton had taught him the politics of Parnell and after, and he served Redmond as a functionary. The existence of Devlin also ideologically obscured the problem of Ulster unionism in the Edwardian years of 1906–10. His organizational and political achievement in West Belfast was considerable, but at the expense of the most exploited sections of the city's working class. He helped originate the clientelism which later disfigured Irish politics. By linking his native city with the movement of the nation, as Sexton put it, Devlin showed himself to be objectively sectarian. Nationalism was bent on totally routing unionism with the help of the British government. The majority community in Belfast was not convinced by Devlin non-sectarian rhetoric about fairness for all, nor did many in the ghetto believe Dublin rule would herald catholic–protestant equality.

3

Independent Orangeism, 1902–10

Belfast was predominantly unionist in the home rule era. In 1885, when its parliamentary representation increased from two to four seats, opponents of Irish nationalism swept the board. West Belfast was the chink in the armour, as Sexton showed, but Devlin did not take the seat until two decades later. Throughout, candidates in favour of the union contested all four Belfast seats. Conservatism in Ulster was troubled by opponents to left and right, in its attempt to form a provincial party, within the orbit of parliamentary unionism. This is to say nothing of socialism and the labour movement. Most local liberals followed Joseph Chamberlain in 1886, becoming liberal unionists, but the tradition revived in rural Ulster in the early 1900s at a time of conservative rule. The tradition of popular independence, or orangeism, whereby various elites were considered insufficiently protestant by the masses, was more important. The Edwardian years saw the Independent Orange Order (IOO) challenge the unionist leadership, to the delight of nationalists. This breakaway body from the orange order has been seen inaccurately as weakening dominant politics in Ulster, and even as a boon to a non-sectarian labour movement. It owed most to the reactionary sectarian populism of Thomas Sloan in Belfast. The IOO also contained an emerging liberalism, until Lindsay Crawford was driven out of the new order. The role of Alex Boyd shows that trade-union militancy, within the universe of orangeism, fell short of a labourist commitment. The IOO, and later loyalist movements, served to recompose the unionist alliance in a more active form, to mobilize against home rule in the early 1910s, and even to form a state after the European war. The leaders of Ulster unionism might try to manipulate their followers, but the rank and file strengthened the movement through manifestations such as independent orangeism.

A leading orangeman, William Johnston of Ballykilbeg, had captured a Belfast seat, in 1868, in protest at Dublin Castle's suppression of the order's marches. He was seen as a representative of the protestant working man. A liberal took the second seat. Johnston sold out to the government in 1878, but returned to politics in 1885, becoming the orange MP for South Belfast. There was also an orange victory in East Belfast. Though the order revived under the threat of home rule, there was little room for independence within organized unionism. Conservatives were able to dominate more populist elements, who largely wanted to share in political representation. Johnston was easily

43

integrated. In 1895 the unionists returned to power at Westminster. Irish policy came to involve concessions to nationalism, as an alternative to self-government, and the apparent build-up of catholic Ireland. The Ulster Unionist Council (UUC), embracing the orange order, emerged in 1905, in response to alleged conservative talk of devolution. Johnston had died three years earlier, creating a vacancy in South Belfast.

His mantle of militant protestantism was taken up, in 1902, by the shipyard worker Thomas Sloan, a member of the orange order. He did not achieve political longevity. Sloan won the seat against conservative opposition, and went on to found the breakaway Independent Loyal Orange Institution of Ireland (as it became) in 1903. It is better known as the Independent Orange Order (IOO). This new institution soon attracted the protestant journalist Lindsay Crawford, who became an advocate of liberalism. As if this was not confusing enough, the IOO had, in the trade-union official, Alex Boyd, a third potential leader, who seemed more in the developing stream of secular labourism. The IOO expressed a populist, if not popular, hostility to the class ascendancy within protestantism, on the part of sections of the masses. In Sandy Row this was about government policy eroding protestant interests across the kingdom. The land question was more important in rural north-east Ulster, though protestant tenant farmers were also keen to mobilize within their community on general political questions. The orange order's participation in the UUC confirmed that it had sold out to the unionist bourgeoisie, but the IOO developed alongside mainstream orangeism. Independence embodied a notion of the class enemy, but the issues were more religious than social. It was sectarianism of a particularly virulent kind. The solution was for the unionist leadership to become more protestant, simply by including its critics within the organizations of the movement. Protestant independence was provisional in this first decade, breakdown or transformation being its alternative destinies. Though the Independent Orange Order continued to exist, it came to an end as a movement in 1910. Alex Boyd had become caught up in the 1907 strike of dockers and carters, though he did not go on to slough off his protestantism. Crawford was expelled in 1908, for becoming a non-sectarian reformer outside the universe of unionism. Sloan lost his seat in the first 1910 election, and failed to regain it in the second.

Thomas Sloan had been born in Belfast in 1870, and he became an unskilled worker in Harland and Wolff. Starting as a red lead-er, painting iron ships, he was upgraded eventually to a cementer. He seems not to have been reconciled to this station in life, and later described himself as an 'artisan'.[1] As a member of parliament, his wearing of an overcoat with a fur collar offended erstwhile associates. He may have been a member of the unskilled union, the National Amalgamated Union of Labour (NAUL), but was certainly not active. He dissociated himself later from 'any Trade Union'.[2] Sloan was above all a protestant, of a strong evangelical bent, and held dinner-time meetings in the platers' shed at Harland and Wolff. This was in his capacity as a member of the Belfast Protestant Association, in which Arthur Trew held sway. Ritualism in the once-established Church of Ireland was their current obsession. Romanism was the eternal enemy. On the occasion of the Corpus Christi procession in June 1901, Trew was sentenced to a year in prison, and Richard Braithwaite, secretary of the BPA, to six months, for disrupting Dr Henry's catholic manifestation. With Trew out of the way, Sloan emerged as the BPA's 'lecturer' in 1901–2. His first parliamentary intervention was a defence of 'disorderliness and rowdyism',[3] when the BPA, according to Joe Devlin, secured the expulsion of a protestant clergyman from Belfast, for being reputedly soft on catholics. Thomas Sloan was, in the year of his election to parliament, master of St Michael's total abstinence LOL (Loyal Orange Lodge) 1890.

On 12 July (the Twelfth, as the anniversary of the Battle of the Boyne is known) 1902 Sloan led a group of BPA hecklers at the annual celebration in Belfast. The object of attack was Col. Saunderson, a Co. Cavan landowner, who was grandmaster of the grand lodge of Belfast, and leader of the Irish unionists at Westminster. In this position he had supported the conservative government of Lord Salisbury, who was now being replaced by Arthur Balfour. Saunderson, Sloan believed, had voted against a clause in a bill, providing for the inspection of convent laundries. Working conditions were of little concern to Saunderson, but Sloan's obsession was state control of catholic nuns. Protestant evangelicals had long been fascinated by their imagined sexual exploitation by priests and bishops. For challenging Saunderson, Sloan was later expelled from the orange order, much to his distress. Five days after the Twelfth, the now legendary William Johnston died. His orange heroics of 1867 overshadowed not only his government employment but also his parliamentary accommodation with conservatism. South Belfast, which included Sandy Row, had been independent, in the opinion of protestant electors, from 1885. The orange order believed the seat should be contested by local conservatives in the name of the union, showing how feeble the order's leaders had become. The BPA considered the Association was the legitimate heir to the seat. The day after Johnson's death, 18 July, Arthur Trew emerged from prison. Having served a year, when Johnston's martyrdom lasted a month, he no doubt felt the candidacy should be his. This was to reckon without Thomas Sloan, who had been causing trouble in Belfast for a far shorter time.

Sloan became an independent candidate in South Belfast, nominated by the BPA, the conservative association putting up C.W. Dunbar-Buller, a fellow of All Souls, Oxford. Dunbar-Buller had become a landlord in Co. Down, and master of an orange lodge, though his wife's family had business interests in Belfast. Since this is how the unionist bourgeoisie, under orange influence, treated the protestant electorate, it is not surprising it had populist difficulties that August. The fact that Dunbar-Buller was also a liberal unionist may not have helped. This is the candidacy William James Pirrie failed to be offered, as a result of which he seems to have financially supported Sloan. This relationship may well have endured. Saunderson remained the object of attack, the leaders of unionism being considered not sufficiently anti-catholic, or temperance inclined. Sloan had the support of some temperance lodges in the orange order, as well as temperance organizations and some friendly societies. The trades council had finally sent a letter of condolence to Johnston's widow, and Sloan, on the basis of replies to an election questionnaire, might have expected the council's endorsement. Some delegates considered him on the side of labour, but his overt protestantism was considered sectarian. He lost by 19 votes to 11. Sloan secured the active support of Alex Boyd, organizer of the Municipal Employees' Association (MEA), which recruited workers from the corporation. This was a protestant preserve in Belfast, there being, among the officer caste, only 23 catholics out of 274 employees. Boyd had resigned from the conservative association when it declined to nominate Pirrie as candidate. Some trade unionists found it easy to support such employers. Boyd was also an orangeman, master of the Donegall Road temperance lodge. Sloan characterized his opponent as fighting 'protestantism, Orangeism, total abstinence, trade unionism, and in a word ... protestant Belfast'.[4] Local protestants gave him 3,795 votes to 2,969 on 18 August, a majority over Dunbar-Buller of 826. South Belfast was safely independent.

Arthur Trew had supported Sloan during the campaign, but, sometime after the election, their followers clashed. Trew was expelled later from the BPA, and Dublin Castle noted considerable rivalry between the two men. Sloan's South Belfast victory seems to have increased his political ambition. Whatever had been Saunderson's support for Balfour, once in Westminster, Sloan was easily reconciled with the leader of Irish unionism. He now blamed a clique in Belfast orangeism. The BPA took the fight against the conservative association into municipal politics. Braithwaite, as secretary of the BPA, stood unsuccessfully in the Ormeau ward in 1903. Sloan, though the member of parliament, was equally unsuccessful the following year, when he stood for alderman in the St George's ward. Braithwaite fought the BPA's last electoral struggle in 1905. While the organization was still active in Belfast, Sloan began to distance himself, flying new political colours in 1906.

The orange order, in the form of Saunderson and the Belfast grand lodge, had come out against Sloan in 1902. Members were asked not to vote for him. The new MP later apologized verbally to the grand lodge, but stuck at giving a written apology. He was suspended for two years, along with some supporters. An appeal to the imperial grand lodge of Ireland failed in June 1903, and the warrants of three supporting lodges were withdrawn. One of these was the Donegall Road temperance lodge, whose master, Alex Boyd, then suggested a new order. The IOO was formally established on 11 June, those assembled agreeing that Sloan should not submit a written apology. He was standing on his dignity as a public figure. This was a halting series of events, and Sloan proved to be a reluctant rebel. A future officer of the IOO said later that they were 'trying to bring the Orange Society back to the standard set up for it when it was started by workingmen in 1795'.[5] The only thing wrong with the order was its leadership; it had to return to the path of protestantism. The idea of an independent order was less a hope for the future, and more an admission of failure. Sloan had wanted to stay in the orange order, but was unable to temper his independence. He was setting out to capture the protestant community with a breakaway organization, something which proved beyond his abilities.

The IOO organized its first Twelfth, at Dundonald outside Belfast, in 1903. Five hundred people attended, and 8 lodges marched. By 1905 there were 27, the peak of 38 lodges being reached 2 years later. The number then dropped off, there being only 12 lodges in 1912 at the IOO's Twelfth. The official order in Belfast grew from 188 lodges in 1903, through a peak of 200 in 1906, rising again to 219 lodges in 1914. Most of the growth occurred in 2 of the city's 10 districts. Before the IOO could win a section of the official order's membership, both were caught up in the growth associated with the devolution crisis, the formation of the UUC, and the return of a liberal government. The independent order declined from 1907, while the official order, as part of the emerging regional unionist party, grew in the years before the war. The IOO must be considered, in its own terms, an unsuccessful revolt.

While it obtained adherents throughout the world of orangeism, the IOO was significant in only two areas, Belfast and Co. Antrim. In the city, there were three districts – Sandy Row, Shankill and Ballymacarrett. Sandy Row was the heart of the IOO, being part of Sloan's South Belfast constituency. Its headquarters was in Great Victoria Street. Sandy Row district had the fastest growth rate, peaking in 1907 with 16 lodges. Boyd's was the only LOL in Belfast to defect to the new order, Sloan being unable to bring his own over. There were two others in Co. Antrim. These were Magheramorne LOL 26 and Ballycarry LOL 64. (The old names and numbers were retained, suggesting a certain provisional quality about the IOO's leadership.) The Co. Antrim lodges came under a separate district, Maralin, which accounted for 9 of the 38 lodges in 1907. The IOO was really two movements in one. Its urban and rural bases were described, as late as the 1914 Twelfth, by the chairman that year: there were 'two classes represented there that day – those who, whilst staunchly Protestant had never been able to agree with Orangeism of the type they had been accustomed to, and those of Liberal stock who took exception to the old Institution becoming the tool of landlord and capitalist'.[6]

This combination was the work of Robert Lindsay Crawford. He had been born in Lisburn in 1868 of planter stock, his early years being spent in business and journalism in Dublin. Between 1901 and 1922 he was involved in religious, and then political, journalism. At the turn of the century, he was an active evangelical protestant in the Irish capital. Crawford was a member of the general synod of the Church of Ireland, and also on the orange order's imperial grand lodge of Ireland. Here he suggested an independent protestant parliamentary party, which would not be linked through unionism to the government. Crawford founded the monthly, later weekly, *Irish Protestant* in 1901, to propagate his brand of reformation protestantism. He was editor until 1906, fighting an intra-episcopalian battle on behalf of evangelicalism against ritualism. He did not change his religion, only his politics. From a sectarian, public conception of protestantism, he shifted to a liberal, private one. Crawford addressed his coreligionists throughout Ireland, while Sloan, presumably a presbyterian, was concerned in Belfast about the catholic enemy at the gates. When Sloan appealed to the imperial grand lodge of Ireland, Crawford saw in the new MP a democrat railing against the orange elite. Sloan referred to those who 'had attempted to place the iron heel on the face of the democracy of Belfast'.[7] The Dublin propagandist of protestantism saw a Belfast leader of protestant people. Though still a member of the old order, Crawford came north to chair the IOO's first Twelfth the following month. While identifying with Sloan, he articulated his political project in terms of 'Liberty of Thought' and 'the genius of progress'.[8] Later he set up a lodge in Dublin, the only one in the rest of Ireland. By early 1904 Crawford was imperial grandmaster of the IOO, formally its leader. Also on the governing body, as grand chaplain, was the Revd D.D. Boyle, a presbyterian minister of St James's Church in Ballymoney, and a friend of Crawford. Sloan became deputy grand chaplain, an interesting appointment for a lay preacher, and Braithwaite grand secretary. From the first then, the IOO represented an alliance of evangelical protestants, whose varying base in Co. Antrim and Belfast undermined the revolt against orangeism.

For the 1904 Twelfth Crawford wrote a pamphlet, *Orangeism, its History and Progress: A Plea for First Principles*. 'The unholy alliance between Orangeism and toryism', he wrote, 'has been marked by the betrayal of protestantism, and the promotion on every possible occasion of the power and influence of the Church of Rome.' He hoped the 'Orange democracy' would become 'a powerful factor in our national life – softening the acerbity of religious and political strife'.[9] Crawford made his first appearance as grandmaster at Ballymoney in Co. Antrim. While 300 turned out to hear Sloan and Boyd at the Giant's Ring near Belfast, there was 'a very large gathering'[10] in Ballymoney. The Revd Mr Boyle later congratulated Crawford about the politic way in which he avoided reference to the expulsions from the old order. This less aggressive approach, characteristic of middle-class politics, was at variance with the angry revolt of the protestant dispossessed in Belfast who rallied to Sloan.

The IOO's rural base had been stimulated by the 1903 land act. The unionist MP for North Antrim, William Moore, had opposed this, thereby antagonizing many of the protestant tenant farmers in his constituency. The first meeting of the IOO's imperial grand lodge, in February, had come out in favour of 'proper independent parliamentary representation'[11] in North Antrim. This was reaffirmed at Ballymoney. Crawford was siding with T.W. Russell, liberal unionist MP for South Tyrone, who had advocated land purchase within what was a party of landlords since 1892. Russell inspired the North Antrim Land Association in 1900, which had the support of the *Northern Whig* in Belfast. He even joined the three nationalist leaders, as representatives of the tenants, at the 1902–3 land conference, speaking on behalf of Ulster unionist tenant farmers. This conference had been called by Capt. Shawe-Taylor, who later supported Lord Dunraven's Irish reform association. In September 1904 the association came out with the solution of devolution, a solution which had originated with Sir Antony MacDonnell, the catholic undersecretary at Dublin Castle. This was less a constitutional undoing of the union, and more a development of local government at the centre in Ireland. It created a furore within unionist ranks, and led eventually to the resignation of the chief secretary, George Wyndham. The legacy of the scheme was the UUC, Ulster unionists feeling the need for a regional party, given the weakness of British tories in the face of political progressives. The UUC was launched in March 1905, having been formed at a conference in Belfast the previous December. Crawford, no doubt to further the political education of the orange democracy, had Shawe-Taylor invited to speak in Belfast on 16 December in the YMCA hall in Wellington Place. Crawford was strongly critical of the UUC, seeing it as a new attempt by unionist parliamentarians to woo the protestant masses. Sloan and William Walker were also asked to contribute to the debate, as new figures in Belfast politics. Shawe-Taylor argued the politics of conciliation, but Sloan attacked the unionist party. Walker came out against home rule, and Crawford advocated bourgeois reforms in Ireland in the spirit of democracy. Something of a political shift can be detected from his July pamphlet, but he criticized Shawe-Taylor for calling for a non-denominational solution to the university question. Irish catholics were pressing the government for their own university, Trinity College, Dublin being considered exclusively protestant. Crawford apologized for the status quo, arguing that protestant domination was due solely to catholic educational policy.

In 1905 he considered turning the IOO into a political party, this being agreed to by the grand lodge on 3 June. Protestantism was still dominant in Crawford's mind. Sloan now seemed uninvolved in the BPA, at least when it came to political activity. This was probably because of the new UUC, which provided something of an opportunity for unionist regroupment. The IOO had been refused official representation, but two members, 'in their capacity as Protestants',[12] had served on the council for a matter of months. Sloan announced this at the 1905 Twelfth in Belfast, where Crawford was the main speaker. The latter waited until the following day, 13 July, before revealing his would-be party programme at an IOO meeting at Magheramorne, near Larne. The order had the use of a demesne of a member, James Lowry, for the celebration. Sloan was beside Crawford on the platform, to hear him read what came to be known as the Magheramorne manifesto.

Crawford's document was a development of the ideas first expounded in the debate with Shawe-Taylor the previous December. There was British misgovernment in Ireland, Crawford asserted. Current political alignments, nationalism and unionism, had to be transcended. There was a need for new progressive politics taking Ireland as their starting point. He opposed nationality to sectarianism, condemning the two major traditions. '[A] false conception of nationality ... prevails both among rulers and people ... our own country has been governed not on national but on sectarian lines.' He rejected both the British unionist government and catholic nationalism, and called upon protestants and catholics to 'reconsider their positions and in their common trials unite on a basis of nationality ... There is room in Ireland for a patriotic party with a sound constructive policy that will devote itself to the task of freeing the country from the domination of impractical creeds and organised tyrannies and to securing the urgent and legitimate redress of her many grievances.' Crawford specifically itemized a redistribution of parliamentary seats (which would have helped unionists), a revision of Irish finances, the ending of clerical control of education, the ending of protestant control of Trinity College instead of an alternative catholic university, compulsory land purchase, and for rural labourers 'ultimate ownership' of a house and plot of land.[13] There was nothing in the programme for urban workers, the reference to town tenants meaning shopkeepers in leased premises. Its 'land and labour' section showed Crawford to be a champion of tenant farmers. He differed from nationalist, and unionist, advocates of peasant proprietary, in his essential liberalism. Crawford wanted considerable political reform, albeit within the union. Protestantism as private belief was the foundation of his politics, and this allowed him to argue for the first time, on the university question, for the secularization of Trinity College. But his deliberate anti-sectarianism appeared, in the context of Irish catholic advance, as a new form of protestant resistance to nationalist demands for a university. The IOO after all was to be the independent protestant party he had long considered necessary.

The Magheramorne manifesto was a statement of Irish, or Ulster, liberalism, despite its subsuming of liberalism in Britain in the general critique of colonial rule. The principal officers of the IOO, including Sloan, put their names to the document, despite its radical tone. The *Irish News* had originally detected the 'cloven foot of militant Orangeism',[14] but, when it saw the hostile unionist reaction, it warmed to the manifesto. The member for South Belfast had been hesitant at Magheramorne, and, under unionist pressure, he reaffirmed his protestantism. But he tactically accepted the document, and Crawford's leadership, in so far as they were part of a popular challenge to the unionist leadership. He had not yet grown to dislike the former more than the latter. Other members of the orange democracy were more decisive. John Keown, a trades council delegate who had supported Sloan in 1902, and was a BPA activist, resigned almost immediately from the independent order. Days after the manifesto was issued to the press as a pamphlet, Crawford told a Dublin newspaper that, as an Ulsterman, he regretted to say that 'the evil influences of feudalism and clericalism prevail north of the Boyne just as strongly as they do south.'[15] The leadership of the new order was breaking up. The imperial grand lodge officially accepted the manifesto on 29 July, and Belfast followed two days later. But it had more of an appeal in rural Ulster than in the back streets of Belfast. The manifesto caused a furore among IOO members there, and a meeting had to be called in Belfast in August to consider it. Twelve hundred are said to have attended. A few days later Sloan told a BPA meeting that 'Romanism, devolution had not caught him ...

Lindsay Crawford with all his ability and all his pluck had not thrown the mantle of mesmerism over him.'[16] He had, but not for long.

Crawford's patriotic party was stillborn. It was the BPA which put up Braithwaite in the September 1905 municipal by-election, against Lord Shaftesbury, for the aldermanship of a Belfast ward. At Magheramorne, Sloan had claimed to be a member of the unionist party in parliament, contrasting this with the hostile attitude towards him of the orange order. But the UUC seemed not to want to take the orange democracy in the form of the Sloanites on board. With the change of government in December 1905, Sloan became fearful for his seat in South Belfast. The local conservative association, now involved in the UUC, was keen to see off the independents. On 1 January 1906 Sloan dissociated himself from the Magheramorne manifesto, in so far as it conflicted with unionist policy. He was a member of the platform party at the UUC's rally in the Ulster Hall the following evening. 'I may say I have always dreaded the surrender of Mr. Sloan',[17] Crawford told a Dublin journalist. He suggested the IOO might put up a candidate against Sloan in the election. The unionists were not prepared to take Sloan back into the fold, and Lord Arthur Hill was put up against him. Hill was a scion of the aristocratic family which had once owned land in Donegal and Down. The sitting MP christened his organization the South Belfast Parliamentary Association. This was probably the BPA, elements of the IOO, and local followers dubbed Sloanites by the unionist press. The *Belfast Evening Telegraph*, something of a protestant paper, was later to carry a cartoon of Sloan with a discarded 'no pope'[18] hat on the floor. A number of the 'peak and muffler' brigade, 'led by a few officials of a local organisation posing as friendly to the protestant interests of the community',[19] had used forged tickets to gain entrance to the UUC meeting. With this motley crew, he retained the seat, securing 4,450 votes to Hill's 3,634, a slightly reduced majority – 816 – in a somewhat increased poll.

The general election saw the last successful independent protestant mobilization in Belfast before partition. 'In 1906', as the *Northern Whig* reported four years later, 'the great majority of the windows in those streets [around Sandy Row and Donegall Road] displayed portraits of Mr Sloan often associated with some enthusiastic tribute to his virtues.'[20] He certainly appealed to one of the oldest, and least skilled, sections of the Belfast working class, but also to the petty bourgeois shopkeepers of the area. At a meeting of businessmen he denied all knowledge of those who had set out to disrupt the election gathering in the Ulster Hall. The Sloanites harried the conservative candidate throughout the campaign. 'In view of a possible incursion in force of the opposition partisans there was a big army of stewards, and every applicant for admission was closely questioned before being permitted to pass', the *Northern Whig* reported of a Hill meeting in a hall on Botanic Avenue. 'Upon each side of the long corridor ... a row of "deacons" armed with their formidable half-pikes was stationed ... Outside the hall a crowd ... congregated and amused themselves by cheering and booing for this and that public man whose name was mentioned from time to time amongst them. A strong force of police was on duty.'[21] Hill came under criticism for complicity in the proclamation of an orange march. Shades of William Johnston! This Hill refuted with a letter from George Wyndham, the former chief secretary. The Sloanites also criticized Hill for having maltreated a widow tenant – in 1889!

Sloan variously presented himself as a populist and as an upholder of protestant principle. 'He would make his enemies tremble with the desire to do the will of the people', he said during the campaign. '[He was] the tool of no political party ... [and] had been elected by the people, for the people, independently and irrespective of political parties.' But earlier he had said it was not 'a struggle between class and mass, between wealth and humble means, between a lord and democracy, but it was a struggle for principle, for justice, for independence, for civil and religious liberty and their common rights (Applause).'[22] This contradiction indicated his ambivalence about the orange leadership. He opposed it because of its weak protestantism, but did not develop a full social critique of the aristocracy, much less the bourgeoisie. Sloan felt ultimately that ordinary people were undervalued in unionism. One of his favourite images was that of 'the penny in the slot',[23] the party manipulating its electoral support. He had received the endorsement of the trades council this time, having, unlike Hill, replied to its questionnaire. Sloan claimed to support all its demands, in addition declaring himself in favour of home ownership, outdoor relief and temperance. On the question of the vote, he had an open mind on adult suffrage.

Lindsay Crawford did not actively support Sloan in South Belfast in the 1906 election. He had intended standing as an independent in South County Dublin, one of the few territorial seats outside Ulster within the unionists' grasp. Crawford wanted to challenge Walter Long, the recent chief secretary, who had held a succession of English seats. Long later became leader of the Irish unionists. But there was an error in Crawford's nomination papers, and he was not a candidate. As editor of the *Irish Protestant*, he supported T.W. Russell in South Tyrone, who was returned as an independent unionist, and R.G. Glendinning, who defeated William Moore in North Antrim. Sloan spoke for Glendinning. Another six so-called Russellites, unionists who opposed the conservatives, were unsuccessful in other rural constituencies in Ulster. Pirrie was behind this challenge to the conservatives. He was also the backer of Carlisle in West Belfast, and possibly still funding Sloan. A liberal actually won North Tyrone from a unionist.

The liberal landslide throughout the United Kingdom encouraged the revival of the movement in Ulster, and allowed Crawford to come out in his true political colours. In April 1906 the Ulster Liberal Association (ULA) was set up. The newly ennobled Pirrie was behind it, but the momentum was provided by Russellism. The following year the MP for South Tyrone became a junior member of the government, when he succeeded Plunkett as vice-president of the agriculture department in Dublin. He held this position until 1919, becoming in time a liberal home ruler. Other liberals had not yet conceded to nationalism, it being late 1909 before Asquith made his home rule commitment. In Dublin Crawford's involvement in the IOO had caused difficulties for him with the *Irish Protestant*'s new owners, who were conservatives in the main. Shareholders challenged his editorship in August 1905, when he was acquiring a national reputation as the author of the Magheramorne manifesto. Crawford was finally ousted in the early summer of 1906, but his role in Co. Antrim politics saw him offered, in September, the editorship of the *Ulster Guardian*, the ULA's new weekly paper. His first number appeared in January 1907. Crawford moved north in November 1906, settling, appropriately, at Magheramorne. Local IOO lodges gave him a tremendous welcome, but a mob, possibly from Belfast, attacked him at the railway station. This was because of the North Armagh by-election. Following the death of Saunderson, Crawford had stood as an independent against William Moore. He was accused of being sent to Armagh by 'the little Russellite-Pirrie gang in Belfast'.[24] Moore returned to parliament, winning the seat on 16 November by 4,228 votes to 1,433. It was Crawford's only electoral outing on behalf of liberalism, or, as it appeared, a progressive reworking of unionism which did not to lead to nationalism.

He was still grandmaster of the IOO, and had resumed political relations with Thomas Sloan. The member for South Belfast even spoke for him in Portadown during the by-election. The Belfast members of the IOO almost certainly distrusted the Ulster liberals as upper class, considering them soft on catholics and home rule. While the ULA hoped to use the orange democracy in Belfast, it probably saw Sloan and his independent orangemen as unreliable. From 1906 Lindsay Crawford tried to link the order and the association, as he had balanced urban and rural interests in the IOO for three years. When he took over the *Ulster Guardian* in 1907, he was a liberal democrat. Crawford was concerned to develop a non-sectarian and social concept of nationality, in which the protestant tenant farmers of the north would become the cornerstone of progress. In February Lloyd George was the first liberal minister in over 20 years to speak in Belfast, at the Ulster Hall. During the 1907 strike of carters and dockers in the city, led by James Larkin, Crawford discovered the working class. This was not the orange democracy, in which he had lost faith. Crawford embraced the politics of social reform across capitalist society. The abandonment of protestantism as politics, as opposed to personal belief, saw him ousted from the IOO by May 1908. Taking up social questions had not pleased the liberal bourgeoisie, and he also lost the editorship of the *Ulster Guardian*. Both sides rejected him as a home ruler, the harshest condemnation in protestant Ulster.

At the 1907 Twelfth in Belfast Crawford described his audience as the 'vanguard of the Protestant democracy'. He was coming to see Irish protestant politics as reactionary, describing Ulster as 'the blacklegger of the land strike'.[25] The strike of transport workers was then taking place. It was Boyd's involvement in the struggle which strengthened Crawford's faith in the IOO. Sloan's refusal to become involved, plus Boyd's growing divergence from independent orangeism, weakened this. Crawford's active involvement in the strike, at the behest of Boyd, dates from 17 July, when he became a regular speaker on strike platforms. Crawford favoured trade unionism as a liberal democratic right, the passing of the trades disputes bill in 1906 being a landmark in labour history. Crawford saw class polarization, and struggle, as being transcended by an industrial compact or citizenship. This had nothing to do with socialism. He 'was not a socialist, nor did he believe in the accepted theory of socialism ... But the socialistic theory was preferable to the economic heresy of the linen trusts and monopolists.'[26] This was not written until February 1908, when he had been running a column, 'Labour World', in the *Ulster Guardian* for some time. Crawford took up the question of sweating in the linen industry, describing the linen merchants as 'the last buttress of toryism and Castle ascendancy in Ireland'.[27] 'To denounce landlord rights as tenants' wrongs', he was to argue, '[was] a cheap passport to political fame for some liberal employers of labour, who own no land, but these men, if linen merchants and manufacturers, have a different code of ethics in their relations with flax growers and workers.'[28]

This was too much for the Ulster liberals, and the board of the paper gave him an ultimatum. Crawford was eventually forced to resign, writing to the chairman in May 1908:

> More than once I alluded in leading articles to the necessity of grounding the liberal revival in Ulster on something more patriotic and statesmanlike than the transference of social power and influences from the tory to the liberal side by the wholesale creation of magistrates and the shuffling of offices ... It will scarcely be denied that to the Independent Orange Order, the labour party and the nationalists, the Ulster Liberal Association owes the fact that, after wandering in the wilderness for twenty years, it has been able once more to speak with its enemies within the gate. But for the fact that Ulster Liberalism was regarded as a progressive and democratic force, and that Lord Pirrie's powerful influence was behind it, the working men of Belfast would never have rallied to its support as they did.[29]

The excuse for Crawford's sacking was his advocacy of home rule or devolution, this also being the attitude of the IOO. He was initially suspended by the Belfast grand lodge for his writings on 19 May. Crawford attended the meeting, and 'disorderly conduct and insulting language'[30] provided the excuse for his suspension. Of the 14 out of 15 present, 6 voted for the suspension, 3 opposed and the rest abstained. When his 3 supporters walked out, the rest agreed to the suspension. He appealed to the grand lodge of Ireland, at a meeting presided over by Sloan. The grand lodge seems to have condemned the suspension, and Crawford claimed that his appeal was upheld by 20 votes to 13. But Sloan was in the chair, and it was the end of Crawford's time in the Independent Orange Order.

Crawford was expelled for having advocated home rule, though he had not done this. His critique of unionism drew on other political traditions, admittedly thin on the ground in Ireland. The contradiction between unionism and nationalism saw, as Edward Dowden put it in

1904, 'two ideas, essentially antagonistic, ... confront[ing] each other – now as in 1886 – until one or the other has obtained the mastery'.[31] It was winner take all. Crawford had begun to embrace elements of the nationalist world-view, but his political ambivalence on self-government was no different from that of British liberalism. Home rule was acknowledged as inevitable, but it could come only gradually. This was then the position of the British government, Asquith, who succeeded to the premiership in April 1908, not having become a Gladstonian yet.

Crawford had opposed Irish hostility to Britain. He also believed self-government had to be earned, and that this could be demonstrated only by the construction of a progressive Ireland. He did allow for the possibility of home rule, as long as it was not sectarian and divisive of the people of Ireland. All this had been implicit in the Magheramorne manifesto. He had returned in the manifesto to the thinking of the late eighteenth century, to Grattan's parliament and even the United Irishmen. His concept of nationality was profoundly realistic, referring to the social and political conditions of the people in Ireland. This was very different from the nationality of romantic nationalism, with its emphasis upon the Irish language and Irish literature. In 1906 Crawford embraced the crucial characteristic of nationalism, belief in the uniqueness of one's own nation. 'Ireland has an individuality all her own', he said at the Twelfth that year. 'Her true destiny lay in its natural growth and development. Ireland could only develop along her individual lines.'[32] This was more the thinking of Young Ireland in the nineteenth century. Crawford went on to say that Irish protestants did not believe the preconditions for real self-government existed yet in the country. That November, in a lecture to Sandy Row members of the IOO on 'Democracy and Nationality', Crawford argued that protestantism, which stood for 'private judgement ... [and] individuality ... [against] the old feudal system', also implied 'individuality' in the development of a 'country or community'.[33] This concept of protestantism was a long way from the anti-catholic evangelicalism of the orange democracy.

Crawford had lasted five years in the Independent Orange Order, and he lingered in Ireland from the summer of 1908, eventually emigrating to Canada in 1910. He lived and worked there for twelve years, becoming a member of the editorial staff of the Toronto *Globe*. He remained with this liberal paper until 1918. In 1914 the *Globe* sent him back to Ireland, and, between April and July, he wrote 60 despatches which were published. These show he was still very much a liberal democrat, interested in social progress. He accepted the British liberal commitment to home rule, expecting that the government would vanquish unionist opposition. With the unreconstructed nationalists likely to assume power, he, for the first time, bestowed the accolade of democracy on Irish catholics. Crawford and the *Globe* supported the war, and he saw the rising in 1916 as signalling the end of British rule. He insisted catholics and protestants 'must learn to live together in the same social order and in one national unity'.[34]

After the war Crawford was a leading member of the liberal party, with his own journal, the *Statesman*. He founded the protestant friends of Irish freedom, as an auxiliary to the North American organization supporting the republican struggle. He later joined, and became president of, the Self-determination for Ireland League of Canada and Newfoundland. Irish self-determination, he argued, was part of 'the great struggle between privilege and the right of the people to equality of opportunity'.[35] He accepted the treaty solution, and considered the civil war disastrous, though the Irish Free State had 'neither freedom nor statehood'.[36] Partition, especially the creation of Northern Ireland, he considered a victory for sectarianism.

In late 1922 Lindsay Crawford quit the world of political journalism, and became the new Irish government's trade representative in New York. An Irish-American judge, helping the family settle, recommended schools for the Crawford children – catholic ones! He has 'been able to reconcile adherence to the cause of Irish Nationalism', noted a biographical entry, 'with the most ardent attachment to Reformation principles ... He fought stubbornly to justify the Unionist position only to find that his position was becoming intellectually untenable.'[37] Crawford died in New York in 1945.

Alex Boyd, who probably exercised an influence over Crawford in 1907–8, seems not to have been a member of the BPA in 1902. As a trade-union official he had the organizational capacity to realize, in 1903, the IOO. He moved from conservatism to independence for reasons of democratic assertion, albeit within the dominant protestant community. He remained a unionist, but failed to become a critic of sectarianism. None of this was incompatible with his trade unionism. By 1905 he was vice-president of the trades council. At the IOO's Twelfth that year, he said that the UUC 'should stand determinedly on Protestant principles ... As working people they could not support the policy of the Craigs and Moores who, although returned by the working class had never cast a vote in their interests.'[38] Boyd was unmoved by the manifesto for a new popular party read at Magheramorne the following day. The all-Ireland and bourgeois social reform perspectives probably meant little to this Belfast would-be labourist. Robert McElborough, a conductor on the municipal trams, who joined Boyd's union in November 1907, became a member of the Ulster Liberal Association after reading Crawford's paper. In 1906 Boyd was talking of 'the democracy of labour', and of Sloan's electoral victory as the first in 'a series of successes for the workers (Cheers)'.[39] He may have included Devlin in this. The 1907 strike largely involved members of the protestant community, and took on something of the nature of a social uprising by the unskilled. The strike reached to the heart of Boyd's politics. He proved himself a militant industrial leader, and an advocate of intensified struggle. While he opposed the introduction of politics, he openly embraced catholics as part of the working class. This was much further than the IOO or Sloan was prepared to go. The order did take up a collection on the Twelfth, though it referred to the strike as 'deplorable' and the cause of 'suffering'.[40] Boyd appears to have quit the IOO as early as 1907, on the grounds that protestant independence had nothing to offer the working class. His stand on the strike also saw him lose his seat on Belfast corporation, where he represented the St George's ward. The defeat of Larkin that summer probably arrested Boyd's political development. He was a member of the trades council executive in 1908, but seems to have become unpopular when he tried to oppose the recruiting of corporation employees by the workers' union. He disappeared from active participation in 1909, but not before opposing the formation of the Irish Transport and General Workers' Union in Belfast on the grounds that it was a Sinn Féin organization.

He was active again by 1916, there being an A. Boyd on the executive of the trades council in that year. The Municipal Employees' Association, which had been excluded from the TUC and labour party on account of its restricted membership, was soon discussing amalgamation with the workers' union and NAUL. Boyd ceased being an organizer, but he became an independent labour member of the corporation in 1920, being elected alderman for the St George's ward. Protestantism remained dominant in his politics, and Alex Boyd seems to have died shortly afterwards while undergoing an operation. He had influenced Crawford on the social question, but stuck with Sloan, more accurately the UUC, on the national question. Liberalism was not to his liking as a trade unionist.

Thomas Sloan had become grandmaster of the IOO in 1908, replacing Crawford. Only one lodge dissolved in protest, but many members seem to have drifted way. The order had passed its peak, and it was now declining. This was immediately evident at the Twelfth celebrations, the IOO attracting progressively fewer people from 1908 on.

Sloan was a member of the historic 1906 parliament. While he had claimed to be a member of the unionist party, in touch presumably with the UUC, he insisted later that he voted 'on the Radical side'[41] with Campbell-Bannerman and then Asquith. Sloan favoured old-age pensions, and reform of the poor law, but he showed himself to be a tory working man in his support for tariff reform. He supported Lloyd George's budget of 1909, but, the following year, he favoured the retention of the House of Lords as 'a safeguard against rash or ill-considered legislation'.[42] Sloan was no doubt thinking of home rule. When his unionism was called into doubt, because he had voted alongside Irish nationalists, Sloan expressed himself in favour of 'every Social Measure for the Good of the People'.[43] His parliamentary questions had been of two principal sorts. The number of catholics in, for example, the police in Newry and Belfast was his very first question. These questions ranged as far as Malta. Secondly, he posed questions about specific groups. He was mainly interested in teachers, post office employees and members of the armed forces. Sloan's favourite question was about nuns begging in Dublin. His concern with social issues was invariably located within a perspective of protestantism. He had very little time for the labour movement, though he had expressed himself in 1906 in favour of a trades disputes bill. Two years later he voted against a bill on unemployment, because it was 'an incentive to loafing'.[44] After he ceased to be an MP, his achievements were listed in a letter from 'An Independent True Orange Blue',[45] published in the *Belfast Evening Telegraph*: expelled over convent laundries issue; introduced temperance bill twice but failed; got public houses closed earlier; helped handloom weavers' bill; raised surgeon Anderson case; exposed plot to stop Warrenpoint orange march; got roman catholic demonstration in London stopped; helped ex-nun Moult to escape; opposed home rule; supported old-age pensions; opposed changing the king's oath; lectured on protestantism in England and Scotland; chairman of the Protestant Alliance; befriended teachers and postmen.

In the January 1910 election Sloan was described as 'strutting about like a very small gallus gallinaceus and crowing as assertively ... carrying with him the unmistakeable atmosphere of the Custom House Steps, which no amount of Westminster perfume can dispel'.[46] He was defending South Belfast, again as an independent, but with the backing of his parliamentary association. Local conservatives, at the behest of the UUC, were determined to get him out, and James Chambers, a Dublin lawyer, was put up against Sloan. The *Northern Whig* reported a great change from 1906: 'There have not been witnessed scenes of greater enthusiasm than greeted Mr Chambers in Sandy Row and on the Donegall Road ... It is in the smaller streets where one notices a significant change.'[47] Perhaps because of his loss of support in Sandy Row, Sloan returned to Harland and Wolff to canvass. He played the trade-union card, uncharacteristically, only to find himself accused, by the unionist press, of socialism. He received the backing of the trades council, along with Devlin and a labour man in North Belfast, on the grounds apparently that a delegate reported having heard Sloan denounce the anti-trade union Osborne judgement of 1909. Sloan was on the run in this campaign. Conservative hecklers turned up at his meetings, and the dwindling band of Sloanites had difficulty defending him. He kept up his personal attacks on the leaders of unionism. When he accused Chambers of being an atheist, the latter brought his clergyman from Dublin to refute the charge. Chambers was safely returned, securing 5,772 votes to Sloan's 3,553. The two men refought the seat in December 1910. This time Sloan's vote dropped to 2,722, while Chambers held fairly steady at 5,585 votes. Pirrie must have been behind his campaign still. Sloan had the backing of the Protestant Alliance, a London-based evangelical organization. He opened what was to be his last campaign with a lecture, 'Are the Principles of the Reformation being Maintained?' Sloan showed slides of himself 'escorting countesses and hob-nobbing with "the quality", which were pointed out with special pride by [him and] aroused good-humoured badinage'![48]

The end of the Sloanite version of independent protestantism was messy. He still had the IOO, which continued to decline. In 1911 Sloan and Devlin were burned in effigy on the Twelfth by unionist militants, when the orange order marched. At the IOO's Twelfth in 1912 one speaker said that, for a year, 'open violence [had been] threatened ... [and] tactics had been resorted to and a madness had been taken to crush them that were simply disgraceful.'[49] Blame was laid on members of the old order. The IOO's protestantism took the form of an absolute commitment to the union, being more concerned about Ireland than Ulster. The independent order opposed the idea of a provisional government for the province only. Sloan does not seem to have returned to work in Harland and Wolff after losing his seat, and he became a justice of the peace. He was ill in 1912, at the time of the industrial expulsions. When these spilt over into residential areas, he became a victim of loyalist harassment. At the 1913 Twelfth, Sloan's last, he opposed the abandonment of southern protestants to Rome rule. He may have died in the following year. On the eve of the Great War, the IOO condemned exclusion as a 'Jesuitical proposal'.[50] The order staggered on through the war, holding its last parade in 1920. It was later revived, and exists today.

If organized conservatism and the UUC, including the orange order, were the political enemy of the labour movement in Belfast, the IOO was no friend to those interested in working-class politics. Alex Boyd was the best candidate in the order's leadership to turn it in a left-wing direction, but he failed. His exclusive trade unionism in the municipality probably undermined his militancy, as much as his protestantism and unionism. Lindsay Crawford was responsible for giving the IOO a progressive historical reputation, despite his protestantism, which initially endorsed a populist revolt within orangeism. Crawford became an exponent of Ulster liberalism within, and then in alliance with, the IOO, before being driven out of both organizations as a democratic exponent, interested in social and political reform. He never became a nationalist, despite the fact that his opposition to protestant sectarianism led him eventually into the arms of the wing of Sinn Féin which created the Irish Free State. The IOO was most authentically Thomas Sloan's movement, its historical uncertainty reflecting his hesitant revolt within orangeism and unionism. It was only after his time as an MP (1902–10) that Sloan's fundamentalist protestantism was manifested in an Irish unionist opposition to the growing regionalism of the movement in Ulster. In the Edwardian years he had represented dispossessed protestants, including sections of the petty bourgeoisie, with a strong independent suspicion of dominant social groups. Protestant spirituality rather than class consciousness was Sloan's destiny. Independent orangeism only thrived in Edwardian Belfast at the time of the foundation of the UUC, when the protestant bourgeoisie was harnessing the orange order in its political interest. The IOO marked a transition from a less reputable orange order of the nineteenth century to new – loyalist – forms of independent activity by elements of the protestant masses in the twentieth century.

4

William Walker, Socialism and Unionism, 1905–12

Although beset by ethnic political rivalry, Belfast also experienced a normal political development to a not inconsiderable extent. The home rule era in Ireland was coterminous with the growth of trade unions and the development of labour and socialist parties, in the United Kingdom and across Europe. Belfast shared in this historical experience. Independent working-class politics, in a city divided on sectarian grounds, were represented by William Walker. A protestant joiner at Harland and Wolff, he was very much in the tradition of a British leader of the labour movement. As a member of a skilled workers' union, he promoted the organization of unskilled men and women, through the Belfast trades council in the 1890s. He was active in the Irish Trade Union Congress (ITUC) in the early 1900s, while also attending the British Trades Union Congress (TUC). As a supporter of the constitutional status quo, Walker tended to see the Irish regional trade-union centre as nationalist inspired. In 1901 he became a full-time trade-union official in Belfast. He had already joined the local branch of Keir Hardie's independent labour party (ILP) in 1892, only to find that socialists on the streets were unacceptable to Arthur Trew's BPA. The trades council successfully put up labour candidates for Belfast corporation from 1897. Walker became a member in 1904, and attempted to lead the labour group of three. Two years earlier, the trades council had affiliated to the Labour Representation Committee (LRC), later the labour party. It was with broad working-class support that Walker fought a by-election in North Belfast in 1905. As the first labour parliamentary candidate in Ireland, independent of all other parties, he was building on a trade unionist's fight for the seat 20 years earlier. Walker admitted he was an opponent of home rule, while dissociating himself from the unionists in parliament. Tragically, he became entangled with the BPA, endorsing some sectarian positions. But for this by-election, he might have won the seat in the 1906 general election, joining Devlin and Sloan in parliament. Walker stood a third time, in a 1907 by-election in North Belfast, but it was clear the conservative association was determined to see off the labour threat. The ILP, owing partly to his earlier efforts, was at its most influential in Belfast from this time. Walker became involved, through his trade union, in the labour party nationally. He was elected to the executive on four occasions, and served as vice-chairman in 1911. In the first general election of the previous year, he had stood, unsuccessfully, as a labour candidate in Leith near Edinburgh. Walker tried, in 1910–11, to prevent the ITUC from becoming an Irish labour party, in expectation of home rule. In doing so, he came up against James Connolly, recently returned from the United States. At the 1912 labour conference Walker was one of seven candidates for the party secretaryship, in succession to Ramsay MacDonald. He quit politics shortly afterwards to become an official under the national insurance act.

William Walker was born in Belfast, like his grandfather, in 1871, the son of a worker at Harland and Wolff, who later became a trade-union official. He attended St George's national school, and became founding secretary of the mariners' young men's debating society. He became apprenticed as a joiner in 1885 to Harland and Wolff. This was the year Alex Bowman, secretary of the non-political trades council, stood against a linen lord in North Belfast. Bowman represented flax-dressers, and had helped found the united trades council of Belfast in 1881, to advance 'the moral and social elevation of the operative class, as well as the consideration of such questions as affect the political and social interests of labour'.[1] He stood in the labour interest, and, though known as a working-class liberal, tried to hide his home rule sympathies. These led to his resigning as secretary of the trades council the following year, though a number of prominent conservative working men continued to be active in unionist politics. Walker joined the local branch of a Scottish carpenters' union, and became a delegate to the trades council in 1892. He must have soon joined the larger Amalgamated Society of Carpenters and Joiners (ASCJ), becoming a member of the Belfast 9th branch. He had assisted in organizing the plater's helpers in 1891 into what became the National Amalgamated Union of Labour (NAUL), at a time when new unionism, the organization of the unskilled, saw the number of delegates to the trades council double. In 1892 it represented about three-quarters of Belfast's 16,000 trade unionists.

Walker was one of the first Irish socialists. The Revd J. Bruce Wallace, the congregational minister and Christian Socialist, was active in the 1880s. He brought Henry George, the American agrarian socialist, to Belfast in 1884, and debated in the Ulster Hall with the Revd Hugh Hanna, the presbyterian fundamentalist. The Fabian Society also had a presence, advocating the municipalization of trams in 1891. Its local secretary, William Knox, had founded the Belfast Co-operative Society in 1889. A trade-union member of the Fabians, Alexander Stewart, failed to establish a branch of the labour church. He was more successful with the ILP, a branch being listed in the 1894 and 1895 reports. Walker was a member from the beginning, the ILP preaching socialism at the Custom House steps close to Donegall Quay, where crowds assembled each Sunday afternoon to listen to religious preachers. Arthur Trew, who had been educated at the military school in Victoria Barracks as the son of a staff sergeant, first appeared in Belfast as an industrial agitator. He may have been involved in an unsuccessful strike in the York Street mill in 1891–2. 'He was not thought much of here by his employers', the Belfast RIC reported to Dublin Castle in 1901, 'as he seemed to be trying to get up agitation for more pay among the linen-lappers'.[2] Their union was run by Alexander Taylor, a prominent member of the trades council. A labour demonstration in their support on 5 March 1892 was hailed as the 'blending of orange and green',[3] given the presence of communal bands. Trew then went to the United States, but returned to join the Salvation Army, which he soon abandoned. He then, according to the police, started 'advocating ... with a man called Walker a sort of socialism or rather he attempted to reconcile the principles of Socialism with Christianity'.[4] This is extremely interesting if correct, since Trew appears to have been some sort of socialist, and Walker, by implication, associated with him as a protestant. Trew became a regular speaker for the BPA at the steps in 1894, and soon afterwards an active rival of William Walker.

The Belfast ILP had been encouraged by the decision of the TUC to meet in Belfast in September 1893, when the second home rule bill would have received its third reading. A trades council demonstration on Saturday, 9 September showed a degree of working-class division. Will Thorne of the gasworkers angered a section of the crowd in Ormeau Park by wearing a union sash containing the colour green. John Burns, MP, who had voted for home rule, was forced to flee. But Alex Stewart chaired a successful ILP Sunday meeting at the Custom House steps, addressed by Edward Aveling, Ben Tillett and Keir Hardie, MP, who had also voted for the bill. The following week an 'attempt to introduce a Socialistic and Secularist platform' at the steps led to a 'Socialistic Disturbance'.[5] Several years later Arthur Trew claimed 'the overthrowal of the local society of Socialists'[6] as one of his achievements. In 1894–5 Walker had to be 'almost continuously under police protection, because of his advocacy of the principles of Socialism'.[7] Years later he recalled they 'preached the Gospel of Socialism ... faced [with] the batons of the police; the deacon poles of the Orangemen; the assaults of the hooligans; the execration of the rabble.'[8] 'We think it advisable', read a report in Robert Blatchford's *Clarion* of 1 June 1895,

> to discontinue the Custom House meetings until the spirit of the pious and immortal William cools down a bit ... On Saturday evening, however, we went to the Queen's Bridge. As usual bigotry and brutality were well represented in the audience, but amidst cries of 'Throw him in the dock' 'You're a Home Ruler!' 'Drown him!' Walker held his ground, and said all that he went there to say. A large crowd followed through the streets, but we divided. Walker jumped on a tram-car, and they dispersed. We sold fifty *Merrie Englands* [a socialist classic by Blatchford] at the meeting. We advertised it as an exposure of Socialism: that sells it and minimises the risk of getting hit with something.[9]

Walker was more successful on the trades council, where he became secretary of its organizing committee. Its predominantly male members had been worried about the largely unorganized women workers for a number of years. An attempt in 1890 to found three societies, with the help of national women's organizers, was unsuccessful. A second effort was made in 1893, Walker organizing a demonstration in the Ulster Hall, at the time of the TUC, addressed by Lady Dilke. Walker became temporary secretary of the textile operatives' society in 1894–5, which was handed over to Mary Galway in 1897. The trades council was certainly paternalistic, but Walker believed in trade unionism for all workers. Women hardly threatened the aristocrats of labour, and the institutions of collective bargaining locally and nationally. Unskilled men did, with the growth in mechanization of industry. Walker had helped the beetling enginemen's union, and also the National Union of Dock Labourers (NUDL). He was honorary president in 1896 of the short-lived National Sailors' and Firemen's Union (NSFU) local branch, and helped Alexander Bowman, who became involved with the Municipal Employees' Association (MEA) in 1897. Walker was elected secretary of the trades council the following year, still only in his late 20s.

'Some of us', he wrote, a little sanctimoniously, a few years later, 'have been *doing* something to improve conditions ... [through] the Trade Union branch. Amongst the textile workers, the sweated and oppressed, the dockers and carters, we have gone to help to lift them to a better condition of life.'[10] This is not quite how he put it at the 1900 ITUC, when he urged Irish trade unionists to meet the following year in Newry because 'the men of Belfast and other Northern towns were handicapped by the constant migration of non-unionists from Newry.'[11]

Walker worked as a joiner through the 1890s, his rise in the ASCJ strengthening his position on the trades council. His union was involved in 7 of the 14 demarcation disputes in shipbuilding and engineering during the period 1888 to 1913, the last taking place in 1900. He was probably one of the 4,500 Belfast workers indirectly caught up in the strike of 1,100 ASE members in 1895–6, when the directors of Harland and Wolff were in alliance with employers on the Clyde to resist a wage claim. Walker urged the trades council to help unorganized workers affected, while the ILP used the strike to promote trade unionism and raise political consciousness. Sir Edward Harland, like Wolff, a conservative MP, died on 24 December 1895. 'To the credit of those shipwrights', it was observed later, 'be it recorded that, despite the inclemency of a December rain, many hundreds of the Island men marched abreast in the funeral procession.'[12] Walker criticized two prominent trade unionists, Alex Taylor and Hugh McManus, for attending the funeral, and, in January 1896, suggested that the trades council should put up Pete Curran, an ILPer, in the North Belfast by-election. A socialist, and suspected home ruler, was too much for the conservative trade unionists in control of the council. Walker may have been affected by the retaliatory lock-out against the ASE in 1897–8, as he went to work for Thomas Gallaher, the tobacco king, in his York Street factory. He was probably involved in the 'expensive and long drawn-out struggle'[13] of 650 joiners in seven town shops, who came out on 1 May 1900 and remained on strike for nearly a year. By 1901 Walker was blacklisted, and in receipt, exceptionally, of victimization money from the trades council. He was soon appointed district delegate, or full-time official, of his union, 2,300 of the 4,900 Belfast joiners being in the ASCJ. Fewer than 700 were catholics, namely 54 ship joiners and 614 house joiners. He gave up the secretaryship of the trades council, but was elected president in early 1902 – a position he held for five years.

Walker earned a reputation for 'ruthlessness'[14] in his conduct of interunion disputes, even though there were no principal strikes involving joiners during his time as an official. But he had to resign temporarily as president of the trades council in 1905, when it attempted to mediate in a dispute between woodworkers at the new City Hall. 'It was a gloomy outlook for trade unionism', said John Murphy, the council secretary, 'if the spirit of co-operation was to be dropped and the strong unions were to crush out the small ones.'[15] There were further difficulties in 1906, when Harland and Wolff sacked an engineer after a letter from Walker to Carlisle. Murphy maintained it 'could have been settled between the two district executives',[16] and Walker survived a motion of disapproval.

Belfast's trade unionists were localized within the amalgamated unions of the United Kingdom. Close economic ties with Glasgow and Liverpool mitigated this to some extent, but they joined with other Irish workers' leaders in complaining that the TUC was insufficiently attentive to their particular interests. Dublin Castle was a colonial administration, despite direct rule from London. Belfast was integrated into the imperial economy, but its citizens were viewed as part of the Irish people. The TUC had met in Dublin in 1880, and Belfast in 1893, but Ireland failed to secure a special seat on the parliamentary committee in 1894. Irish attendance at British congresses was low, this being dependent upon the executives of British unions including Irish members in their contingents. There were about three Belfast delegates at each TUC from 1900, until the joiners dropped out in 1906, and the boilermakers a year later. George Greig of the NAUL was the major, often sole, attender until 1918. He and his Belfast colleagues had long nursed the grievance that the Irish party was considered by the TUC to speak for the whole country. When Ireland was occasionally referred to at annual congresses, it was invariably in a nationalist context – though Belfast was mentioned in 1907.

The trades council had welcomed an Irish attempt in 1889 to set up a trade-union centre, until its Dublin advocates held a sports day on the sabbath. The national leaders did not respond to a letter of protest from Belfast. The ITUC was established in 1894, Belfast accounting for 15 of the 119 delegates at the founding congress in Dublin. The first chairman of the parliamentary committee, Hugh McManus, a printers' official and also leader of the Belfast trades council, argued in 1895 that the 'mining and manufacturing' bias of the TUC meant that 'a community largely agricultural, assisting in reviving the languishing manufactures of Ireland,'[17] was overlooked. Though there was unevenness in Ireland, it was that within the United Kingdom which concerned trade unionists throughout Ireland. The revival of Irish industry, whatever its Irish-Ireland connotations for cultural nationalists, had an appeal to trade unionists still located in an artisanal universe. A Scottish TUC was set up in 1897, and Wales followed suit. The TUC bemoaned 'the unfortunate existence of these sectional congresses', a leading member writing that such regionalism 'divides the forces of Labour, weakens their influence and makes them an easy prey to the capitalistic classes'.[18] The ITUC responded that its existence strengthened trade-union organization in both countries. Alex Bowman, who presided at the 1901 congress in Sligo, justified the Irish organization in terms of

> the disparity between the industrial development of England and Wales and indeed, of Scotland also, as compared with Ireland ... The duty of Trade Unionists in the one set of circumstances is utterly unlike their duty in the other ... Our people are so sharply divided by race, by religion and by politics, that they have never been able ... to make a really effective, hearty and unanimous effort for the well-being of our common country.[19]

It was the best address since the foundation of the ITUC, though Bowman, who was bowing out of the movement, allowed his national frame of political reference to portray Belfast trade unionists as first Irish and then British.

The city, nevertheless, played an important role in the ITUC. The 1898 congress was held in Belfast, as was the one in 1908. It also met in Londonderry in 1899, and in Newry four years later. The lord mayor, James Henderson, had addressed the 1898 congress:

> Trade union workmen were the best class of workmen that any employer could possibly find ... [Belfast] provided abundance of employment for the working classes and made Belfast ... an elysium for the working men ... He thought instead of resorting to strikes, which affected not the employer in the first place, but was felt most keenly by the wives and families and the workers, some system could be evolved by which strikes might be rendered unnecessary.[20]

Ten years later, after a struggle on the trades council, it was decided not to ask for a civic reception on the occasion of the second Belfast congress. Between 11 and 23 Belfast delegates attended each annual meeting, the figure being consistently over 15 in the 1900s. There were 34 local delegates out of 108 in 1908. The trades council was represented every year, except 1913, Belfast having usually 2 or 3 seats on the 9-person parliamentary committee until 1912.

William Walker was one of the four men and two women from the Belfast trades council at the first ITUC, and replied at the congress banquet to the toast, 'the labour cause'. He was not included in subsequent delegations in the 1890s, nor could he get to the British TUC. There was a prohibition on trades council delegates to the latter, and the ASCJ in Belfast was not prepared to send a delegate to either meeting. He attended the Londonderry congress in 1899 as trades council secretary, and was a delegate to each subsequent ITUC until 1906. He also represented the Belfast joiners at the TUC from 1901 to 1905, being their full-time official. Walker made little impact at British meetings, being overshadowed by the Yorkshire-born William Hudson, who represented the Amalgated Society of Railway Servants (ASRS) in Dublin, and became a labour MP in Newcastle upon Tyne in 1906. Walker succeeded in becoming a member of the parliamentary committee of the ITUC in 1902 at Cork, when he was finally successful in getting delegates to hold their next congress in Newry. As one of three northerners elected to the executive that year, he was made chairman of the ITUC. Thus he presided at the 1904 congress in Kilkenny, where the Very Revd Canon Doyle delivered his homily on industrial revival. Walker was 'received with loud and prolonged applause' when he rose to give his address. He showed his world-view to be an imperial one, though this was a form of Belfast particularism which refused to make any concessions to nationalist Ireland. He discoursed on British politics, declaring himself a free trader on the tariff reform question, and criticized the 'hordes of German Jews' in South Africa who had imported indentured Chinese labour. The working classes had believed 'rightly or wrongly', he argued, that the war against the Boers had been 'to establish freedom and the paramountcy of English opinion'. As for Ireland, Walker supported 'a just and equitable land tenure', and railway and canal nationalization, measures acceptable to reform-minded unionists.

His theme was the need for 'a strong and vigorous Labour Party',[21] and he called upon Irish trade unionists to affiliate to the LRC. This had been established four years earlier as a result of a TUC initiative, though the socialist Ramsay MacDonald became its first secretary. Independent labour representation was an important advance for trade unionists, and Walker argued that fighting elections was cheaper than strikes and more likely to be successful. Working-class unionists, who had broken from conservatism, were interested in labour representation, but their fellow nationalists still had some faith in the Irish party for social and political reasons, and were disinclined to support a new British party. The parliamentary committee of the ITUC had interviewed Redmond and colleagues at the Mansion House in Dublin on 30 January on the question of trade-union funds, the Irish leader boasting that his party was 'really the Labour Party in the House of Commons'. J.P. Nannetti had wished Walker and Hudson well in North Belfast and Newcastle, neither, of course, being a nationalist seat. Walker acknowledged then that the Irish party had supported the cause of labour, and said that 'if the Unionist Party in Ireland were energetic in their support the position would be very different'. He articulated a non-political definition of labour interests, though this was a diplomatic refrainment on the part of the LRC to avert conservative and liberal reaction: 'The questions which affected them as working men were entirely separate or apart from party politics, and were concerned solely with the solution of economic and industrial problems.'[22] This British argument for labour representation carried even less weight in Ireland.

Walker was the first congress president to argue for labour representation in an address. Nationalists and, to a lesser extent, unionists had united to oppose all such motions at the ITUC since 1900. That was the year Walker moved unsuccessfully on behalf of the Belfast trades council that trade unionists should not support candidates unless endorsed by their local councils. It was carried the following year, and, in 1902, Walker tactically supported a motion from P.T. Daly, a member of Sinn Féin, calling for an Irish labour party. It was carried in the confusion, but the parliamentary committee did nothing, 'viewing generally the political opinion of the industrial workers of Ireland'.[23] MacDonald and Hardie addressed the 1903 congress, their presence in Newry helping delegates vote, for the first time, to affiliate to the LRC. This was endorsed on eight subsequent occasions, the LRC becoming the labour party in 1906. The Belfast trades council was the only Irish body to affiliate, though Irish members of British unions attended as delegates. Supporters of the Irish party continued to exploit the difference between affiliating to the LRC and pushing the ITUC into politics, arguing all the time that the Irish party was a labour party. From a socialist point of view, Walker had been absolutely correct to argue for labour representation, and affiliation to the LRC was the only practical option from 1903. Supporters of the Irish party may have considered him to be simply anti-nationalist, but he was not arguing for some sort of working-class unionist position. When the issue became one of turning the ITUC into an Irish labour party, Walker was more of a unionist in seeing such a party as a secessionary challenge to the British party. He had begun to play down the ITUC after 1904, when his political career in Belfast began to take off. (He may not have attended the 1905 TUC, and he was not sent to any more British congresses.) He failed to attend the 1905 ITUC, perhaps because trade-union duties kept him in Belfast. He was the only trades council delegate due to attend the 1906 congress in Athlone, but Walker chose instead to lead a deputation of linen workers on strike to the lord lieutenant in Dublin.

The *Belfast Labour Chronicle* had appeared in October 1904, as a joint publication of the trades council and the local LRC. It lasted a little over a year. The editor was John Murphy, and Walker the major contributor. His differences in 1906 with the former, who represented the typographical association, may well have been connected with the paper, because he told the trades council on 7 June that 'he would never write a line for the "Labour Chronicle" nor read it either while it was printed by Mr Adams, who had betrayed them over the "Chronicle".'[24] Walker may or may not have been involved in the July 1905 number in which, in an editorial on 'Labour and Nationalism', interest in the ITUC was described as becoming 'beautifully less' each year. Declining 'local interest in ... its deliberations' was justified in terms of a concept of internationalism. 'Capital is not national, but international. So also must Labour be. That is the truth which the Irish trade unionists outside Belfast do not seem to recognise ... Failure to recognise this truth may mean the complete failure of the ITUC.' The paper also criticized the industrial revival speech of the mayor of Wexford to the congress. He 'gave much offence to the Belfast men ... we northern men are just as much convinced that a Government composed of the gentlemen who follow Mr. J. Redmond would be somewhat "alien" to the people of the North ... things Belfastian seem to find no more favour in the sight of the average Dubliner than do men and things English.' William Walker is not the most likely person to have penned these efforts in the early summer of 1905. Hugh McManus, Irish organizer of the typographical association, lost his seat on the parliamentary committee to P.T. Daly, also a printer, but representing a Dublin society. This was seen as an attack on a British union. Walker was correct from a working-class point of view to criticize aspects of Irish nationalism, but his defence of British trade-union interests in Ireland could at times seem like an apology for imperialism.

His political career had begun when the trades council became involved in local politics in the 1890s. It had been renamed the trades and labour council in 1894, signifying the unity of skilled and unskilled workers. It occasionally endorsed a sympathetic candidate for a seat on Belfast corporation, until the municipal reforms of 1887 and 1896 stimulated the desire for local labour representation. It was claimed later that Pirrie, conservative lord mayor in 1896–7, wanted four labour, and four nationalist, members. The extension of the franchise encouraged the trades council to put up candidates in the early 1890s, but only a sympathetic lawyer won a seat. In the local general election of 1897 for the new 15 wards, the six labour candidates supported by the trades council were successful. Each elector had to choose four candidates for the ward, so it was possible to vote labour as well as unionist or nationalist. The six – elected in different protestant wards – were Alex Taylor, then editor of the trades council's *Belfast Citizen*; Alex Bowman; Robert Gageby, secretary of the flax dressers; Murray Davis, of the bakers' union; William Liddell, of the house painters; and Edward McInnes, organizer of the NAUL. This was the first group of labour councillors in Ireland, though the ILP in Britain only noticed the successes elsewhere in the country in 1899. All were stalwarts of the trades council, tending to be conservative in industrial and political matters. Bowman was more radical, and McInnes represented unskilled workers. The conservative association in Shankill left a seat free for Gageby, who was disqualified in 1899 for not being on the electoral register. They stood for trade-union interests, including fair wages for corporation employees, direct labour, fair-wages clauses in contracts, and municipalization of the trams. Such labour representation was seen as complementing municipal trade unionism, this being particularly the case with Bowman.

The year 1897 was the high point of a period descending to 1920. The number of labour councillors dropped to three in 1901, returned to six in 1905 and 1906, and then dropped off again. The trades council planned to put up 13 candidates in 1907, but eventually backed seven ILPers. Labour candidates had been envisaged, for the first time as deliberate policy, in the catholic wards of Falls and Smithfield. As things turned out, McKeown, a delegate to the council, was allowed to win in Falls for the UIL. The LRC had unsuccessfully put up Danny McDevitt there, in 1905, at the point when the catholic association was disappearing. There was a net loss of three labour seats in 1907, no more were won after 1908, and, by 1911, there were no labour councillors. Robert Gageby was the longest serving. He joined the trades council only shortly before 1897, and left soon afterwards, though he attended the ITUC from 1899 for a number of years. Gageby may have left when Walker became secretary in 1898. The latter was soon elected to the poor law board, serving for four and a half years. The unionist press perceived a difference, at the turn of the century, between the old-school trade unionists and the ILP socialists like Walker. Gageby was described as 'true to the interests of [his] class ... [but] he never forgets that his duty is towards the whole community.'[25] Walker, in contrast, was 'always seeking to set class against class and to jump into place on the shoulders of the great majority of the working men, who are antagonistic to socialism'.[26]

A safe labour man was supported in 1899, while John Murphy, the first ILPer to run, was condemned. Bowman stood down in 1901 in Duncairn, probably to become superintendent of the Falls Road baths. Walker was asked to take his place, but he felt unable to accept, possibly because of the ASCJ job. He and Murphy were both unsuccessful the following year, though Walker won Duncairn in 1904. In his election literature he appealed to householders to 'cast aside every consideration but those which will tend to improve our City life'.[27] He joined two other labour councillors, though they did not act as a coherent group. The major issue was probably tram municipalization. Walker supported a proposal to give free passes to councillors, and McManus proposed unsuccessfully a sarcastic motion of opposition at the trades council in January 1905. It was not until June 1907 that the trades council was asked to form a municipal labour party. In 1905 two ILPers joined Walker, and three other labour men. The year 1907 was the big ILP challenge, and rout, the unionist press claiming that tram municipalization was unpopular. The seven unsuccessful candidates included Joseph Mitchell, assistant secretary of the trades council; D.R. Campbell; Alex Boyd and William Walker. This slate had to do with the return of the ILP to the city, after the 1906 general election. Walker, after his two parliamentary contests, quit Duncairn. He stood for alderman in Victoria, losing by 562 votes to 1,657. His conservative opponent was the shipyard owner, Frank Workman, the former liberal. The labour defeats were due to a conservative association's fight to regain its position. Walker had entered the parliamentary arena, in defiance of the unionists, and he and his comrades had to be politically destroyed even at local level. It was the end of Walker's time on the corporation, though he fought the Dock ward in 1908, and Duncairn again in 1911. This was something of an attempt to return to Belfast politics. By 1911 the possibilities for his brand of local labourism were being undermined by the national question. It was claimed his conservative opponent had 150 vehicles and 900 election workers.

The real terrain of the fight between Belfast conservatism and Walkerism was parliamentary politics from 1905 to 1907.

The first outings of the trades council in municipal politics had coincided with its affiliation to the Labour Electoral Association (LEA) in 1891. This was a lib-lab body in national politics promoted by the TUC, but it collapsed in 1895. Belfast had played no role in the organization, and a local branch was not established in the city. This was not the case with the Labour Representation Committee in 1900. It was more independent of the major political parties, but its future was not guaranteed. The Belfast trades council affiliated in 1902. McManus and Thomas Hughes represented the council at the 1903 LRC conference in Newcastle upon Tyne, and Edward McInnes was one of the 18-strong NAUL delegation. Walker joined McManus the following year at Bradford, and William Hudson was present from Dublin. Following the 1903 ITUC at Newry, Ramsay MacDonald and Keir Hardie had come to Belfast. They addressed a conference, called by the trades council, on labour representation. At a second conference that November, Walker was selected to fight North Belfast. The Belfast LRC dates from 1903. Walker and Murphy, having got so far with Belfast's trade unionists, were keen not to have the ILP involved. North Belfast was the obvious choice. In East Belfast, Wolff remained the MP, not having fought a contest since 1892. As for the candidates, Walker and Robert Gageby started with the same number of nominations, but the latter was much less active in the labour movement. In January 1904 Walker secured his seat on the corporation, Duncairn being in North Belfast.

By 1905 the ASCJ had selected Walker and two others as parliamentary candidates, agreeing to finance them if elected. This was crucial. He was on the LRC's approved list, by the time of the 1905 conference at Liverpool, when he attended as one of seven ASCJ members. Murphy and Boyd represented the trades council, and Murphy was also listed as secretary of the Belfast LRC. This was the year Walker was first made a member of the standing orders committee. Belfast was also chosen as the venue for the next conference, though this had to be put back a year because of the general election. Walker and his trade-union supporters were behind the Belfast LRC. McInnes was its first president, and the vice-presidents included Alex Boyd and Thomas Hughes. It had an office in the Engineers' Hall in College Street, and there was a close relationship with the trades council. They shared secretaries and treasurers. Five of the LRC's 8 officers were also council officers, but only 5 of its 17-strong executive were on the council's executive. Some trade unionists were more interested in labour representation than in the trades council, though the *Belfast Labour Chronicle* was a joint publication.

The LRC, from the time of its foundation, made North Belfast its priority, setting up labour clubs in the constituency. It was a predominantly protestant, and working-class, constituency. But there was a sizeable middle-class population, and the conservative association managed to hold it. Bowman had secured 1,330 votes in 1885 to the conservative's 3,915. The following year a nationalist secured only 732 votes to Sir William Ewart's 4,522. Thomas Harrison, former secretary of the Ulster liberal unionist association, and the trades council's lawyer, ran unsuccessfully in 1900 against Sir James Haslett. He had joined the conservatives, but stood as a working-men's candidate. The major issue in Irish politics in 1904 was devolution, and Walker referred, in the *Labour Chronicle* of January 1905, to the 'revival of the landlord's ascendancy under the guise of the Irish Reform Association'. Shortly afterwards the UUC came into being, linking constituency associations and orange lodges. The *Labour Chronicle* had excluded Sloan from general criticisms of Belfast MPs, but, in June 1905, it supported the trades council's decision not to endorse him immediately . 'A Body which represents men of all shades of religious and political opinion should not support one man because he is a Unionist, and refuse to support another who happens to be a Home Ruler ... It is the only policy applicable to a city like ours where Trade Unionists are so sharply divided on questions of party politics.' Walker had been intending to fight on labour issues, on the basis of his municipal campaigning. The lord mayor, Sir Daniel Dixon, then in his seventh term, had started as a timber merchant, but was now one of the two largest builders in Belfast. Walker accused him of selling land to the corporation at an inflated price, and he successfully sued the *Labour Chronicle* for libel. Dixon was also chairman of the harbour board, which had taken four local labour candidates to court for speaking at Queen's Island. 'It allows men like Mr Wolff and Sir James Haslett', read the *Labour Chronicle*, 'to hold meetings on the quays or about the docks without let or hindrance.'[28] Haslett suddenly died in August 1905, and a by-election was called for 14 September. The electoral tide was running the liberals' way, and labour had picked up four seats during the 1900 parliament. William Walker was the LRC's first Irish hope. As if to confirm this, the conservative association in North Belfast selected Dixon. The liberal unionists had initially opposed him, and the independent protestants did not like him.

Sir Daniel Dixon, despite his position as first citizen of Belfast, was the proverbial political ass. He was described as 'a man of action rather than words'.[29] He 'would refrain as far as possible from making political speeches'.[30] Unionist propaganda stressed his position as a business-man. 'Vote for Dixon and local employment'[31] was a widely used slogan. 'Rainbow chasing may be all very well for Kerry peasants', electors were lectured, 'but the Belfast workman prefers ... good trade, good wages, and regular employment ... [to] the Socialist millennium ... [They] will do well to stick to the plain practical principles and men who have built up our industries and made the city what it [is].'[32] His campaign met with opposition. There was 'a rowdy element' at Dixon's first meeting, 'consisting chiefly of tatterdemalion youths ... their shouts and yells being kept up persistently throughout the meeting, rendering the utterance of the speakers inaudible except to a small proportion of the audience.'[33] 'More Walkerite Rowdyism'[34] was the head-line of a later press report. Popular entertainment was an important part of the unionists' campaign. A magic lantern was used to project slides on to gable walls or a screen mounted on a horse-drawn van. One programme showed 'the King, Sir Daniel Dixon, Indian cowboys, the running match, the cycle parade, cycle racing, football celebrities, the great sea serpent and funeral of Japanese standard-bearers'.[35] Dixon, apart from his unionism, presented himself as a social reformer. 'I will support', he said in his address, 'any feasible efforts to solve such difficult and pressing problems as the reform of the Poor-Law system, the case of the Unemployed, the Housing of the Working Classes, the provision of Old-Age Pensions, and the peaceful settlement of Trade Disputes. The Workmen's Compensation Act should be improved and extended.'[36] There was no commitment here. The conservatives concentrated upon discrediting Walker and his associates. A labour leader was described as 'a typical English Radical'.[37] The *Northern Whig*, the paper of liberal unionism, did everything it could to damage Walker's campaign. It published letters from those who considered the labour candidate insufficiently protestant.

Walker had been endorsed by the trades council at a special meeting on 22 August, four days after Haslett's death. This was shortly after his resignation as president, but trade-union rivalry was now forgotten. On 7 September the council agreed to a trades demonstration in support of Walker. The LRC sent Ramsay MacDonald to be his election agent. He also had the support, for four days, of Arthur Henderson, the treasurer, who had become an MP in 1903. The degree of trade-union support for Walker, during an economic recession, occasionally breached the virtual press embargo on the labour campaign. He, too, was subjected to disturbances at his meetings. Alex Boyd described hecklers, on one occasion, as 'a few beardless boys who could be bought for a penny each'.[38] Walker cited land taxation, railway reform, and improved conditions for seamen as 'significant omissions'[39] in Dixon's programme. These were areas in which Sir Daniel had personal financial interests. Walker's programme was not published in any of the Belfast newspapers, but a later 'final address' shows his theme to have probably been democracy. The 'Non-Party Section of the community' was unrepresented in parliament, while 'the interest of the Land Owners, the Lawyers, the Brewers and Distillers, the Railway Magnates, the Shipping Combines, and the Textile Manufacturers'[40] were well looked after. He left out shipbuilding, but North Belfast was not where most shipyard workers lived. Walker's programme, on this occasion, amounted to 'Land Reform, Railway Reform, the Re-adjustment of Taxation, Temperance Reform, Old Age Pensions, Amendments to our Poor Law, Amendments of the Workmen's Compensation Act, etc. etc.'[41] He addressed himself, in 1905, to the broad interests of the citizenry:

> He appealed to them on the platform of citizenship, did they not think that the system of party government which had been tried for the past 73 years [since 1832] ought to be displaced by some other system whereby the people would have the power and not the few. He appealed to them to try and alter the government of his country that the voice of the working classes would become effective in the Legislative Chamber of the Nation.[42]

Walker's position on the national question was central, in what was his first parliamentary outing.

He had been associated with Arthur Trew, a short time before the second home rule bill. There is no evidence of Walker's supporting home rule, even when he backed Pete Curran's candidacy in 1896. His tactical support for P.T. Daly at the 1902 ITUC was unknown in Belfast, and it has to be set in the context of his British view of politics. 'Imperialism is the transition stage to international union of the proletariat all the world over', the *Labour Chronicle* argued later. 'The base of true Unionism is that equal rights and privileges shall be accorded to Ireland as to all other parts of the United Kingdom.' There was here the making of a theory of international relations. 'Nationalism', the paper argued, 'is dead or dying.'[43] But it was little more than the anti-nationalism of northern protestants. Walker's argument was, not that Ulster protestants were opposed to an Irish state, but that nationalism was bad for the catholic Irish, who aspired to self-government, on the grounds that the existing union underpinned their economy. As such, this argument was not too far removed from protestant views of the priest-ridden south and west. The *Labour Chronicle* had carried an obituary, in April, of 'Frank' Ballantine, a member of the ASCJ killed at Harland and Wolff. He had been a noted evangelical preacher at the Custom House steps. Walker had espoused independent labour representation with some success, during a quiescent period of the home rule era. The more conservative versions of labourism, offered to trade unionists, insisted that the new movement was non-party political. It was more a special interest group, not a solution to all political problems. But the labourism of the ILP, as Belfast conservatives pointed out, was rooted in a form of socialism, located on the progressive wing of British politics. On a question like Ireland, nationalism and home rule were already existing answers.

Walker seems to have entered the by-election campaign playing down the national question. There were catholic votes to be garnered in North Belfast, and the national LRC figures helping him were sympathetic to home rule. MacDonald was not yet an MP, but Henderson was rumoured to have had support, in Barnard Castle, from the UIL of Great Britain. Sir William Ewart, who had held North Belfast from 1885 to 1889, accused Walker of being 'a veiled supporter of Home Rule',[44] because of the constitutional silence of his first address. The *Newsletter*, in its first editorial on the by-election, had cleared Walker as a sound unionist. Five days later the *Northern Whig* carried a letter from 'A Protestant': 'the man who associates with bad company lays his character open to suspicion, and the Parliamentary candidate who is being strenuously supported by a tool of the Irish Ultra-Montanes [Arthur Henderson] may well arouse the suspicions of all real, friends of Protestantism'.[45] Walker was forced to argue that the labour party supported the Irish party only on the grounds of anti-toryism. MacDonald portrayed himself as a good imperialist, and implied that Walker was not bound to home rule. The labour candidate was a unionist, but the secretary of the LRC did not want this fact to become an issue. On the other hand, Walker emphasized the historic significance of a labour victory: 'If they returned to the House of Commons a man who was a Unionist, plus a Labour representative, they would be striking the greatest blow that could be struck against the maintenance of Home Rule opinions in England (Cheers).'[46]

It was not Walker's unionism, whether passive or active, that was his undoing. It was protestantism. He had not been a prominent protestant, and suffered at the hands of the BPA. The association offered its hall for a Walker committee meeting, only to withdraw the facility. It may be that the BPA saw him initially as a good anti-conservative, only to suspect his British labour friends. As for the LRC in North Belfast, it was simply being practical. But Walker tried to play loyalist politics when he asked, rhetorically, of the BPA about-turn, 'was that civil or religious liberty?'[47] This seventeenth-century protestant slogan, 'civil and religious liberty', whatever its juridical meaning, was simply sectarian.

The key figure in 1905 was Richard Braithwaite, secretary of both the BPA and the IOO, who was fighting his own municipal by-election that September. The BPA was affiliated to the imperial protestant federation in London. Braithwaite secured an electoral questionnaire, and set out to raise the profile of protestantism in the parliamentary by-election. It is not clear how he felt about Walker, the enemy of Dixon, but no friend of Sloan. It is probably the case that the BPA was simply out to do down the conservative association. If so, the intervention produced the opposite result. Braithwaite was unable to get to Dixon, who later crowed about how he did not make promises to deputations at election time. It is true that Walker sought to respond to all entreaties, and the BPA may just have been another one. But the content of his reply was crucial. In answering the questions with affirmatives, negatives and some fateful elaborations, Walker, *inter alia*, 'committed himself to the retention of the sovereign's declaration against transubstantiation, to the inspection of convents and monasteries, to the exclusion of Catholics from the office of lord lieutenant of Ireland, and to the statement that, "Protestantism means protesting against superstition, hence true Protestantism is synonymous with labour."'[48] This last was a way of harnessing protestantism to labour, but Walker should have perceived the corollary as sectarian. Cornered, he responded within a protestant view of the world, at a time when labour, to say nothing of socialism, had tentatively alluded to the divided working class in Belfast. 'The independence of labour must be maintained at all costs', the *Labour Chronicle* editorial had argued in June. 'So long as that man [Sloan] stands as the nominee of an association that puts questions on which trade unionists cannot see eye to eye on in the forefront of his programme, we must decline to officially recognise him.'

Walker's electoral opportunism soon backfired. It was not simply a case of conciliating the BPA within the majority community, and guaranteeing the populist vote. Lindsay Crawford in Dublin published Walker's replies in the *Irish Protestant* on 9 September. He was not yet sympathetic to labour, but he probably thought he was helping Walker. Crawford could not have been more wrong. The *Northern Whig* picked up the material, and published it on 11 September, three days before polling. Someone seemingly with Dixon's interests at heart produced a leaflet, addressed 'to the Catholic Voters of North Belfast', and printed on green paper, which accused Walker of being a 'sham, narrow-minded bigot'.[49] This was distributed outside catholic churches in the constituency. The leaflet has been attributed to the conservative association, but there is some evidence of its being printed by a catholic,

Hugh Quinn of Church Street, a supporter of the bishop. Walker admitted he had erred, but did not acknowledge the seriousness of what he had done. MacDonald, it is said, had to be dissuaded from resigning. He certainly had had enough of Belfast politics. 'My own feelings always have been that the business was muddled from beginning to end', he wrote later to a Belfast socialist. 'I was never more sick of an election than that at North Belfast and then the religious replies coming at the end of it knocked everything out of me. I am afraid that those answers of his will make it impossible for Walker to win the constituency.'[50]

There were about 1,000 catholics in North Belfast out of an electorate of over 10,000. Walker had started the campaign as the opponent of the conservative association, and therefore likely to attract catholic votes. His unionism would not have been an overwhelming deterrent, and his labourism was attractive to many catholics. The *Irish News* took little interest in the campaign, as it was a by-election in protestant Belfast. Local nationalist leaders had an interest in seeing off Dixon, thereby weakening opposition to the Irish party. When the *Northern Whig* published Walker's replies, it became more difficult for them to endorse the bigot Walker. The UIL met on the evening of 11 September, but issued no statement. The unionist press talked of a split, but this may have been wishful thinking about Walker not picking up the catholic vote. The green leaflets represented the view that defeating Dixon was not necessarily the most important objective. Catholics had to be warned about Walker. They had not been mobilized to support labour, but Walker's replies may have led a few more to abstain (it is unlikely that catholics voted for Dixon). Walker subsequently distinguished between 'Nationalist Labour electors' and 'Nationalists of all shades',[51] suggesting he got a share of the catholic vote. Dixon's tally-room figures, showing how the vote was divided in North Belfast between the 13 polling stations, suggest that Walker secured a majority in four. Three of these, Old Lodge Road, Crumlin Road and Baden-Powell Street and Avoca Street, were the most catholic areas in the constituency. Here, protestants and catholics were voting labour. But the catholic vote was clearly split. Given the narrowness of the result, the best that can be said is that Walker's replies to the BPA probably encouraged more catholic abstentions, in a context where the UIL had not called for votes for Walker. It cannot be asserted that Walker's replies lost him the by-election. They may, after all, have increased his protestant vote. But the whole episode tainted Belfast labourism in its first major struggle.

The electoral outcome was determined mainly within the protestant community, Walker's challenge to Dixon being a class one. Polling figures show that Dixon did best in middle-class areas, and Walker in working-class ones. Dixon was reported to have done well in Antrim Road, Courthouse, Berlin Street, and Ligoniel, and his success was later attributed to 'the solidity of the Antrim Road'.[52] Old Lodge Road was described as 'a stronghold for the Walker Party', and Avoca Street considered 'exceptionally favourable' to him.[53] But Dixon won because he attracted sufficient working-class support. The unionist press suggested that the shipyards being closed would help the conservative candidate. But the *Northern Whig*, fearing, on 15 September, a Walker victory, bemoaned the fact that Pirrie had not stood. He would have better attracted the skilled working-class vote. But this is where Walker drew his support from, labourism being his appeal. The parliamentary franchise still fell short of full adult male suffrage, and registration was a lengthy procedure. Only 12.5 per cent of North Belfast's population had the vote in 1911, the figure being 13.1 per cent for Irish cities and boroughs, and 16.0 per cent in England and Wales. Walker claimed that 'a large number'[54] of his supporters had been disqualified from voting, and the *Northern Whig* confirmed that only 'the very lowest order of society ... the chronic unemployed'[55] was hostile to Dixon. If so, Walker's protestantism, or simply his opposition to the conservative association, may have attracted some independent support – but not necessarily votes. The *Irish Protestant* thought he would have won as an independent. This result was historic, not simply because 'it was a fight between capital and labour',[56] as MacDonald put it, but because the protestant working class in Belfast challenged the leadership of unionism, on a more or less principled basis. Walker secured 3,966 votes, on an 82 per cent poll in a by-election, to Dixon's 4,440. The conservative majority of 474 votes must have come as a shock to the city's bourgeoisie.

Electoral politics is always a matter of organization, and, in Belfast, this was often aided by corrupt practices. 'Perhaps there has never been in a non-party bye-election in Belfast', the *Northern Whig* reported on 15 September, 'so large a band of workers employed on either side'. Walker had claimed, two days earlier, that the conservatives had 'equipment sufficient to deport not only all the voters of the division, but all the inhabitants of the city'.[57] He later reported to his union that Dixon had over 1,000 paid canvassers, 725 vehicles, and funds to pay first-class fares and expenses to those returning to vote in North Belfast. The official history of the joiners' union notes that the by-election was 'memorable for the wholesale use of corrupt practices', and went on to quote possibly Walker: 'so patent was the corruption to even the man in the street that eight days before the election [that is, on Wednesday, 6 September] Mr ... .MacDonald ... advised doing no more fighting but to permit matters to run their course and then claim the seat on petition.'[58] This is partly borne out by MacDonald's subsequent comments on North Belfast. Walker may have been partly making an excuse to his union, shifting the blame on to conservative corruption and away from the BPA questionnaire. The ASCJ was levying members a shilling (5p) a year to provide election expenses and pay salaries for up to three MPs.

The 1905 North Belfast by-election made an impact on the LRC nationally. Shortly afterwards, Pete Curran, now a member of the executive, representing the gasworkers, publicly criticized Walker for calling himself a unionist, in a letter to the liberal *Daily News*. Curran alleged Walker was in breach of the constitution, which prevented candidates from identifying with another party. Clause II specifically dissociated labour from the liberal and conservative parties. The unionists were, then, the majority in parliament, and the party of government. Curran admitted to supporting home rule, and was thought to be concerned about Irish voters in Britain not coming over to labour. J.R. Clynes, a fellow organizer in the gasworkers, sent out a circular, on behalf of Oldham trades council, supporting Walker on 'the Political question'.[59] Lancashire unionism was a minority current in the labour movement. At its meeting on 4 October the LRC executive exonerated Walker. He had been a labour candidate, and his unionism was no more a party label than Curran's nationalism, it might have been argued, was a breach of the constitution. Walker had been summoned to the meeting, and his election literature inspected. A series of leaflets included the injunction: 'Vote for Walker and show the English workmen that besides being unionists you are also in favour of social reforms.'[60] The labour leaders were not inclined to have a debate on Ireland, with a general election in the offing. They wanted independent labour representation advanced in Belfast, but not Walker's unionism conflicting with the predominant home rule sympathies. The chairman told Walker privately that the LRC thought it improper to accentuate religious strife during the contest. The Belfast trades council also followed the LRC executive's public line, though Murphy suggested framing a resolution for the next conference.

The question of Walker's protestantism was being swept under the carpet. Hugh McManus raised the BPA questionnaire at the next trades council meeting on 2 November. 'The LRC had not the whole of the facts before them when they arrived at their decision. In his opinion Mr Walker should not have answered the questions of the Belfast Protestant Association. These questions had no connection with Labour.'[61] Others considered Walker's replies as, at best, an unfortunate slip, and, at worst, an occasion for sowing discord among trade unionists. The chairman effectively ruled McManus out of order.

At the next meeting on 18 November the council's executive suggested adding the nationalist and unionist parties to clause II of the LRC's constitution. Such a proposal was anathema to supporters of the Irish party in the ITUC. It was to associate Ireland with the work of the LRC, while allowing unionism to be propagated from labour platforms just like nationalism. The Belfast trades council's resolution came up at the 1906 party conference, held in London because of the intervening general election. James Sexton, the Liverpudlian leader of the dockers' union, made a spirited defence of the Irish party, arguing that MPs had travelled from Ireland to vote for the trades disputes bill. Walker, an ASCJ delegate, retorted that many liberals voted for their government's bill. 'They must remember that the bulk of the men from whom they must draw their recruits in Ulster and in Lancashire were Tories, and how were they going to do that if it could be said that the labour movement was open to an alliance with the Nationalist Party.' The constitution was amended with a 'few dissentients' opposing the dissociation from the Irish party.[62] Sexton came back the following day, trying to maintain the alliance between labour and nationalism.

Before Sir Daniel Dixon could take his seat as member of parliament for North Belfast, the Balfour government resigned on 4 December 1905. The liberals immediately took office, while a general election was called for 12 January to 7 February 1906. Belfast was to poll on Thursday, 18 January. Walker was endorsed by the trades council on 12 December 1905, by 36 votes to 2. A delegate from the ASCJ asked if he would vote with the labour party on Irish questions. 'Mr. Walker replied that on Irish questions he would vote as the majority of his constituents desired.'[63]

Dixon was once again the nominee of the conservative association, its campaign being revamped as social toryism. He was standing down as lord mayor, and was committed to 'every measure calculated to improve the position of the working classes'.[64] More importantly, working-men were found to grace unionist platforms. They were hardly typical trade unionists, and, according to conservatist ideology, could be capitalists. One, David Flack, was a spinning master. They went down best in Ligoniel, where paternalism still persisted. A leading orangeman praised Ewart, who had recently died, as 'the best friend of the workmen in North Belfast'. 'What would be the result of all this so called labour agitation?' he asked. 'It could only have the result of widening the breach between capitalists and workmen.'[65] Another 'did not believe in class legislation for class legislation never built up their Constitution or Empire (Hear, hear)'.[66]

Walker's campaign was again largely ignored by the Belfast press. The trades council demonstration in favour of his candidature, on Saturday, 13 January, was reported, though the *Northern Whig*, now predictably, described it as 'not as large as on previous occasions'.[67] The paper had claimed he refused to mention unionism in his election address, for fear of the LRC. He was untrammelled by national concerns, and certainly expressed himself on the national question in his 'final address'. He admitted that home rule 'must have a deciding part with the electors'. Walker then contrasted two types of unionists. The first opposed all 'social legislation', and belonged to the 'Ulster Landlord Party'. The second sought 'every advantage' for Ireland from the union, along with efficient and economic Irish government.[68] Walker was clearly rejecting the unionists as tories, but advancing a socialist justification for the union. In espousing, for the first time, a sort of labour unionism, Walker was seeking to build the labour party, among protestants, rather than pull the unionist party to the left. In this, he differed from the majority of trade unionists in Ireland, who still had some faith in the Irish party.

There were, in this general election, contests in three Belfast seats, Wolff holding East Belfast uncontested. The trades council did not draw up its questionnaire for all candidates until 11 January. Replies were considered on 13 January, the Saturday before polling day. This was the day of the trades demonstration, and many delegates were busy in North Belfast. Devlin received endorsement, by the narrowest of margins, Murphy writing to him the following Monday. Sloan received unanimous support. On the grounds of replies received, the trades council also endorsed opposition candidates in East and North Down, and East Antrim. This might have pushed catholics and protestants in North Belfast to support Walker, who was closely identified with the trades council. More likely, it was the *Irish News*'s reporting of Devlin's campaigning, in which much was made of labourism, which led catholics in North Belfast to see Walker as the opposition candidate. Quinn, the catholic printer, was again active with anti-Walker leaflets. He was standing by the bishop, and not Devlin's national politics. The BPA was not active during the general election, but Walker had done nothing since the by-election to damage whatever support he had from independent protestants.

Walker gained 650 votes in 1906, giving him 4,616, while Dixon, with 4,907 votes, obtained another 467. Dixon retained the seat, but his majority had shrunk to 291 votes. When the trades council congratulated Walker on 'his vigorous and energetic fight', by acclamation, on Saturday, 20 January, the 'splendid poll ... [was considered] indicative of a glorious victory on the next occasion'.[69] This must have been seen as several years hence. It would seem that Walker fared better with catholics in North Belfast in the general election. The *Northern Whig* claimed that 700 to 800 nationalists, who had been 'a neutral quantity'[70] in 1905, supported Walker at the instruction of Devlin. If this is the case, Dixon improved his position relatively among protestants. But this should not detract from the significance of Walker's achievement, in a general election. He did not have the active backing of the national LRC, while the local unionist machine was fully mobilized. Death, or rather two deaths, soon scuppered the trades council's hopes for William Walker as Ireland's first labour MP. Sir Daniel Dixon lasted little more than a year, dying in early 1907. Walker also lost his wife about this time, the trades council passing a vote of sympathy on 7 March. He was reluctant to fight what became his third contest in 20 months, and the second by-election in North Belfast.

In August 1906 the Belfast LRC amalgamated with the trades council, but delegates only accepted the merger by 17 votes to 11. The two bodies had overlapped, sharing the same leaderships, but drawing on slightly different sections of the trade-union movement. The LRC claimed about 30 branches had been affiliated. But so also were the ILP and clarion fellowship, which caused some anxiety on the part of conservative trade unionists. It was also revealed that nine or ten branches of the ASCJ had affiliated to the LRC, presumably because of the union's commitment nationally to labour representation, while only one was on the trades council, undoubtedly because of the joiners' aggressive approach to demarcation. Money was also an issue, it being thought that the LRC was in poor financial straits. There is some evidence for this, given the difficulty the LRC had in getting affiliations. Walker's candidature in the general election had cost nearly £1,000. He and Dixon had each to find £430 for the returning officer's expenses. Walker spent £500, while Dixon claimed £733. Most, or all, of Walker's election expenses must have come from the ASCJ. But the commitment to labour representation might prove costly for the trades council, particularly at local level.

The London conference of the labour party had agreed to meet, the following year, in Belfast, between Thursday, 24 and Saturday, 26 January. This was just after the 1907 municipal elections, which proved disastrous for labour. Walker had just stood down as president of the trades council, and lost a seat on the corporation. He did not represent the council at the labour conference, but attended as one of seven ASCJ delegates, as on two previous occasions. This was a chance for big unions to send local delegates, and some 26 Belfast trade unionists attended the conference in the Wellington Hall. William Hudson was active as a member of parliament, and had been selected as a member of a party delegation to tour the empire the previous autumn. Hudson was vice-chairman of the party executive, and, in Belfast, became chairman for the coming year. William Walker also stood for the executive, being elected fifth. Hudson had represented the labour party at the funeral of Michael Davitt in 1906 'in recognition of his great services to [their] cause', the former nationalist MP having been a champion of social reform. Davitt was also mentioned in the presidential address to the conference by J.J. Stephenson. George Greig, as president of the trades council, welcomed delegates, though he was 'sorry to say' the cause of labour had 'received a considerable setback'. He went on to say that 'if any of the delegates during their stay ... wished to study Belfast politics, they would find the study a most interesting one. If however, they wanted to master them thoroughly their stay in Belfast would have to be longer than a weekend (Laughter).' George Greig, like most of the delegates, was not Irish. Walker was one of the speakers, at the meeting in the Ulster Hall, on the Thursday evening, and presumably attended the trades council's reception, the following evening, in the Exhibition Hall. He made no major contribution during the conference, save a comment on election agents, in the discussion of the executive report. They could not get one 'suitable for every constituency', said Walker, perhaps thinking of his relationship with MacDonald.[71]

When Dixon died in March 1907, the conservative association looked for a better candidate. It drafted Sir George Clark, who had been born in Scotland. An orangeman, he became an active leader of unionism. In 1907 it was his role as partner in Workman, Clark which was considered important, the wee yard being partly located in the constituency. During the by-election, he stated that he had founded the Scottish unionist club, which had a membership of 2,000 workers. The liberal unionists endorsed him as a supporter of 'remedial legislation' for Ireland, and 'conversant and in sympathy' with working-class needs.[72] Clark had his working-men supporters, and the distinction was drawn yet again between the good type and the Walker type. He even claimed he would have hesitated to stand, if a 'bona-fide Unionist workman' had been put up by the conservative association. As for Walker, he was condemned as less than an 'out and out Unionis[t]', while socialism was the putting of 'self-interests before ... patriotism ... [and] Imperialism'.[73] Clark was an unashamed apologist for capitalist endeavour. 'It is by the energy and enterprise of the capitalist that the admitted prosperity of this city has been built up', he said, and that the working classes have been enabled to attain the measure of comfort which they enjoy. Its mills and shipyards are monuments of the capacity and courage of the men who, through good times and through bad, held faithfully to their posts, and make Belfast the city we know – a city of which, in spite of all its shortcomings, every man who lives in it has reason to be proud.[74]

He was able to answer in the affirmative a question about whether he paid trade-union wages. On the issue of workmen's compensation, he had more difficulty. Workman, Clark workers seeking compensation were sued by the insurance company supposedly looking after their interests.

Walker was endorsed as the candidate by a special meeting of the trades council on 21 March. The ASCJ was supporting him once again, and 40 delegates enrolled as election workers. There is some evidence that the labour leadership had been thinking of sending over another trade unionist, which would have been difficult with Walker now a member of the executive. His view that North Belfast could only be fought by a local man prevailed. His election agent was Joseph Mitchell, of the bookbinders, and assistant secretary of the trades council. MacDonald's offer of trained agents was rebuffed, as was a large supply of party leaflets. On 22 March Keir Hardie spoke in favour of Walker at the Ulster Hall, the trades council being 'mustered in force on the platform'. Hardie played down the number of socialists in the labour party. Recalling the 1893 TUC in Belfast, he talked seriously about sectarianism in the working class. 'If the landlord party could succeed in keeping them divided [the unionists] were secure.' Walker had joked that the *Belfast Newsletter* would describe it as a meeting of nationalists, 'but they were all up the Falls Road that evening listening to Joe Devlin'. He was moved to talk about the 'emancipation of their entire class', and another English speaker described Walker as in the 'van to change the present abnormal social system'.[75] A 'troupe of imported speakers'[76] was reported at Walker's nightly meetings, and even Ramsay MacDonald put in an appearance. John Hill of the boilermakers, who had been mooted as the candidate, supported Walker at a lunchtime meeting outside Workman, Clark's. A member of Hill's union accused him of coming to Belfast 'at the bidding of a pack of Home Rulers'.[77] The heckler was invited to address the meeting, which the *Northern Whig* described as a disaster for Walker. Hill denied he was a home ruler.

Walker's third campaign in North Belfast was fought after the liberals had won a general election. The labour party was supporting the Campbell-Bannerman government, voting, as Hardie explained to the 1907 conference, for 'progressive policy both at home and abroad'.[78] Labour might have argued, hitherto, that it had no policy on home rule. After the 1906 landslide, it was difficult to dissociate itself from the liberals. They were not going for home rule, but Augustine Birrell, the new Irish chief secretary, had got Sir Antony MacDonnell in Dublin Castle to revise his plans for devolution. There was much talk of the Irish council bill during the by-election, though it was rejected, in May, by a national convention in Dublin, and subsequently dropped by the government. Walker's British supporters took various positions on the rumoured Irish council bill. At least one supported it. Henderson argued that Ireland would still be within the empire, and he was opposed to separation. 'He did not care whether the Nationalists were pleased or not', Walker said at one meeting, 'he was opposed to Home Rule. He thought the fewer parliaments they had the better. They wanted the Irish railways nationalised but that could not be done if they had a parliament in Dublin because where was the money to come from.'[79] In his election address Walker had declared: 'I feel that as we are on the eve of legislation affecting the future of Ireland, I must again declare that *I am, as I always have been, a supporter of the legislative union.*'[80] He even considered trying to challenge Clark's unionism. Walker believed that his opponent's father, as a Glasgow MP in 1886, might have voted for Gladstone's first bill.

The by-election was held on 17 April. It represented the apogee of organization in North Belfast, on the part of the new labour party nationally, but especially of Clark's aggressive brand of unionism. There was a poll of 10,215, greater than at the general election (the electorate grew from 10,752 in 1905 to 12,726 in 1911). Walker's vote of 4,194 represented a drop of 422 on the general election, while Clark gained 1,114 votes to give him 6,021. There was a unionist majority of 1,827, Walker badly losing the election. He seems not to have bothered too much about the 1,000 or more catholics, who were not instructed by the UIL. There was again some catholic anti-socialist leafletting against the labour candidate. But Clark, one of the city's leading capitalists, won the election. Social dependence, and even deference, on the part of protestant workers partly accounted for this. The liberal government, and the Irish nationalists, did the rest. 'At the time of the contest', the labour party executive reported to its next conference, 'there was much unsettlement in the North of Ireland caused by rumours that the Government intended introducing a Home Rule Bill and this seriously influenced the polling of a straight Labour vote, and drew out maximum support for the Unionist contest.'[81]

Walker had done his best to state he was a unionist, while not a supporter of the UUC or the unionist party in parliament. But the weakness of his case was the labour party. As a trade-union pressure group, it was seen as advocating a number of legislative reforms, and avoiding party politics. On the other hand, it was seen as inspired by socialism, which, presumably, covered the full range of political issues. The trade-union leaders, and members of the ILP, were variously dependent upon liberalism, where Gladstonian home rule still survived. William Walker was less caught up with the two main parties, at least on the question of Ireland, than were many of his supporters from Britain. But he was a local figure from Belfast, representing only a section of the city's working class. His acceptance of the union, and attempted socialist justification, was only relevant in a period of political quietude in Ireland. When the national question became active, many other Irish trade unionists favoured home rule, a different socialist justification being advanced.

The ILP had reappeared in Belfast in the 1900s. By 1903 a branch existed, covering the west, south and east divisions, though no affiliation fee was paid in 1904–5. North Belfast was considered Walker territory, and he was operating through the LRC. He had not been actively involved in the ILP since 1897. Local socialists had the Belfast Socialist Society (BSS), which may not have been established until October 1905. Thomas Johnson, an English commercial traveller, who had settled in Belfast, and joined the shop assistants' union in 1903, was a leading figure. He joined the executive of the trades council in 1907, a year after D.R. Campbell, who represented insurance agents. The BSS may have continued to exist through 1911. Johnson was appreciative of Walker's unionism, to the extent that he asked Ramsay MacDonald, in late 1905, to send to Belfast only ILP speakers who could be circumspect about home rule. 'We want to influence the Labour Party here in the direction of socialism and won't interfere in the Home Rule question until we are compelled – and then the majority of our members would favour that policy I think.'[82] This did not make them nationalists. The members of the BSS were predominantly democrats, in a context of British politics, probably seeing Irish self-government as progressive. Popular unionism might have caused them to hesitate, but it was seen as a conservative cause.

The arrival of James Larkin in Belfast, in January 1907, had less to do with the foundation of an Irish trade-union movement than with the propagation of British socialism. He had joined the ILP in Liverpool in 1893, and attended the annual conference in 1908 (Huddersfield) and 1909 (Edinburgh). During the Belfast strike of dockers and carters, W. Stewart, the Scottish member of the executive, spent 14 days in the city. He organized five ILP branches, one for each of the four divisions, plus a central branch, which attracted most of those in the BSS. This was after the North Belfast by-election. It was an impressive beginning, but the ILP seems to have been down to three active branches within a year. Keir Hardie laid the stone for an ILP hall in Langley Street, by the Crumlin Road, and this became a centre of socialist activity.

William Walker represented Belfast at the 1908 conference, the first time this had happened. He was elected to the standing orders committee. Walker had run for the ILP in the Dock ward, in the municipal election, earlier in the year. Also in 1908, the North ILP, as it was coming to be called, published *The Irish Question*, the text of a lecture by Walker. This, his only publication, expressed an opposition to Irish self-government worthy of the name Walkerism. His account of Irish history, drawn in the main from Lecky, was critical of British rule. Walker condemned nationalists and unionists for being concerned about the location of government, rather than the defects of government in Ireland. 'I am convinced', he said, 'that not merely can the British Parliament do good work for Ireland if it cares to, but that if the representatives of Ireland set themselves to the task of dealing with the Irish problem as business men would in their private concerns, that we would get benefit from our legislative connection, and not wasteful extravagance.'[83] His universal solution was local autonomy, not more parliaments.

Ten Belfast ILP members were listed in the directory of speakers: Richard Elliot, Joseph Harris, the Revd T. Harrison, James Hutchinson, Thomas Johnson, J. Moreland, W.J. Murray, Alex Stewart, H.R. Stockman and William Walker. Stewart was the ASE official in the city, who had come on the trades council executive in 1907. Harrison, now a minister of religion, was its former lawyer. He and Stockman were the only two who were not delegates to the trades council. Five Belfast branches, plus one in Lisburn, were listed in 1909. Belfast Central and Belfast North each sent a delegate to the conference, and Stockman was elected to the executive for a new division dominated by Ireland. He lasted only a year. Two groupings within the Belfast ILP had already emerged. The first, based on the Central branch, was not hostile to home rule. It drifted in an Irish socialist direction from 1910. The second was anti–home rule, became centred on Walker and North Belfast, and spawned many of the postwar labour leaders.

The five Belfast branches were listed in 1910 and 1911. The executive of the ILP had recommended, in March 1910, that 'Irish branches [were] to become a separate federation [attached to the Scottish division] for organizing purposes'.[84] There were no further delegates in 1912 and 1913. ILP MPs had supported home rule (and Welsh disestablishment), to clear the way for social reform, 'on the ground that it is a democratic reform to which we all have been pledged for many years'.[85] Then in April 1914, Hugh Campbell and Sam Kyle turned up at Bradford, as delegates from North Belfast. It was the last conference before the war.

The significance of the ILP in Belfast, from 1907 to 1910, is considerable. It was drawing on the national party, with cross-channel speakers, and an essentially British view of politics. This was the period of social liberalism under Asquith, associated most closely with Lloyd George, at the treasury, and Winston Churchill, at the board of trade. More socialists emerged in Edwardian Belfast, and were formed for life in the labour movement, than in the preceding two decades. The three electoral struggles in North Belfast, in 1905–7, had a great deal to do with this. They owed much to William Walker, and his trade-union and political work from the late 1880s. In 1907 he was only 36, but a widower. He took his first holiday in 15 years that summer, after the third electoral defeat. While he undoubtedly exercised a profound influence on Belfast socialism over the next few years, he was not to the practical forefront of the ILP. Nor did he play much of a role in the party nationally, beyond attending one conference. He was still the joiners' official in the city. Though he served on the general council of the ASCJ in 1910, he did not go to the TUC after 1905. His work was in the political field. Walker returned to the trades council executive immediately after the 1907 by-election, to be re-elected each year. He never again held office. Others, particularly some members of the ILP, were becoming leaders.

Walker was preoccupied with his work in the labour party. As a member of the executive in 1907, elected as a trade unionist, he attended ten of the eleven meetings in London. These were more concerned with organization than policy. He got the trades council to send him to the 1908 conference, at Hull, so he might become a candidate for the trades council seat on the executive. Another member of the ASCJ was being put forward. Walker got only 8 votes, to Clynes's 37, there being 3 other candidates. He was back for the union in 1909, at Portsmouth, and elected seventh on to the trade-union section of the executive. He attended 16 of the 17 meetings that year. Walker unsuccessfully moved a resolution, on behalf of his union, that the exchequer should fund national insurance. 'A nation which could provide an Army and Navy to protect its industry should also be able to provide for the insurance of its workpeople.'[86] Walker must have been on the labour party visit to Germany that Whitsun, 'one of the happiest and most auspicious events in the whole of [its] history'.[87] Members of the executive visited the Reichstag, and were addressed by, amongst others, Bethmann-Hollweg, soon to be imperial chancellor.

The 1906 parliament came to an end in January 1910. William Walker had remained on the labour party's list of approved candidates. The ASCJ was willing to fund him, but probably not in North Belfast. As a tried candidate, and a member of the executive, he probably had little difficulty in finding another seat. In the general election of January/February, William Walker was labour candidate for Leith Burgh. This was essentially a working-class Edinburgh seat, and he was fighting a liberal candidate. His political past followed him to Scotland. 'Irish Socialists',[88] though it is not clear who they were, issued a manifesto against him. Walker was unsuccessful. It was his fourth, and last, defeat in a parliamentary election. He seems to have given up any idea of another contest, since he withdrew his name from the list of ASCJ candidates. His replacement on the panel was unable to find a seat in time for the second 1910 general election in December.

Without Walker, the trades council was forced to put up Robert Gageby in North Belfast, in the first 1910 election. He was unanimously selected at a 'well-attended'[89] labour representation conference, of about 170 delegates, held in the Ulster Hall. The trades council had 14 shillings (70p) in its political fund, and £90 in liabilities. Gageby was the sort of working man driven to break from conservatism, because it was insufficiently attentive to particular social and political interests. 'As a workman representing workers', he said later, 'he had tried to show in the fight what was best in the worker, and he thought he had succeeded in that though he had failed in the election.'[90] 'He held strong religious and political convictions', he said during the campaign. 'He was not a Home Ruler, and had stated so over and over again.'[91] Gageby seems to have been a liberal unionist, but this current was subordinate to conservatism in Ulster. He certainly stressed that he was a free trader, his conservative opponent being a tariff reformer. But he had shown no interest in the liberal revival promoted by Pirrie. Labourism in Britain was predominantly concerned with seceding from liberalism, where the question of the state was not in question. Ireland therefore differed in two respects. Gageby had eschewed socialism, and even the trades council after 1898. He was the sort of labour representative the conservative association repeatedly recommended to Belfast workers. In municipal affairs, he had been more a social worker than political agitator. He fought the campaign on the basis of his personal reputation, and did not import any outsiders. Trade unionists and Belfast ILPers supported him, but the likes of Keir Hardie were kept out of the city. Home rule was much more of an issue. Asquith had made a commitment, and it was likely the liberals, if returned as the government, would be more dependent upon the Irish party.

Even so, Gageby was able to tap the working-class vote first mobilized by Walker. He obtained 3,951 votes, 15 fewer than Walker in 1905. The electorate had of course grown, but the poll was only 11 more than in 1907. The conservative obtained 6,275 votes, which was 254 more than Clark's in 1907. The majority in 1910 was 2,324, whereas it had been 1,827 in Walker's last contest. Gageby may have been less attractive to catholics than Walker, but he remained the anti-unionist candidate. Given the increased political tension, as a result of the battle with the House of Lords, it might have been expected that the conservative would do better. But Walker and Gageby both affirmed their unionism. A more modest labour man does not seem to have appreciably slowed the return of protestant working-class support to the conservatives, as one might expect from an affinity between anti-socialism and unionism. Walker, it may be surmised, might have done worse than Gageby in January 1910, because he was seen as a socialist, but he could quite easily have done better. There was a class vote in North Belfast seeking expression.

This contest is significant for giving the lie to the idea that the conservative association, and the UUC in general, were interested in constructing a democratic all-class movement to defend the union. It remained socially conservative, and politically exclusive. The job of the masses was to vote, and not to cause too much bother. Col. Wallace, leader of the orange order in Belfast, claimed that the socialists had been 'cute' in getting 'an honest man to fight their battles'. He would vote, if elected, with 'the Keir Hardie Little Englander brigade and with the Rosemary St. brigade [possibly a reference to the liberals, based at the Central Hall]'.[92] Praise was heaped upon Gageby: 'One could not help feeling that a man so full of the milk of human kindness and of old world chivalry, figuring among the blatant leaders of the I.L.P ... is as much out of place as a wood-dove among a flock of jackdaws.'[93] When he was asked if he would try to convert the labour party from home rule, Gageby could only joke: 'Some people seemed to think he would be able to exercise enormous influence if returned to Parliament and yet they were doing their utmost to prevent his going there (Laughter and cheers).'[94] At his last meeting, he boasted that the conservatives had failed to prove that he was 'against the Union or that he was a Socialist'.[95] Robert Gageby fought and lost.

William Walker was also near the end of his political career in the labour party. He attended the Newport conference, just after the first 1910 election, and was elected, for the third time, to the executive. He attended all twelve meetings during the year. He again secured a seat on the trade-union section, at the 1911 conference in Leicester, the year he became vice-chairman of the labour party. He welcomed the setting up of labour exchanges. During a recent campaign against sweating in Belfast, trade unionists had had difficulty in acquiring knowledge about wage rates. Walker missed only 2 of the 17 meetings of the executive. He represented the labour party at the seventh annual conference of the peace association in Edinburgh in June, but had to leave for Belfast on urgent business on the second day. This presumably was a union matter. Later that month, the trades council held a special meeting on Lloyd George's national insurance bill, covering ill health and unemployment. It adjourned to 4 July, when Walker successfully moved deputations to the chancellor, to have small unions included, and to the Irish party, to have health insurance extended to Ireland. He joined a deputation from the parliamentary committee of the ITUC to London on 17 July. The chairman of the ITUC had learned that many members of the Irish party were opposed to the bill entirely, while the supporters of both sections being included were apathetic. Devlin secured an interview with Lloyd George, and Redmond, with some colleagues, accompanied the deputation. On medical benefits, the chancellor told them: 'You had better settle it amongst yourselves.'[96] They saw the labour party the following day.

On 20 January 1912 the annual report of the Belfast trades council mentioned that Walker had become a lecturer with the northern district to administer the national insurance act. This was a public appointment, requiring him to sever all contact with the labour movement. He turned up at the trades council on 1 February, with two colleagues, to lecture on the act. Owing to the Irish party's supporting the doctors, health insurance had not been extended to Ireland. The labour party, much to the distress of socialists in Ireland, had been unable to exercise much influence at Westminster. Walker, as a lecturer, met with opposition from some Irish local authorities, his former colleagues on the trades council considering this a form of political discrimination. He later became inspector for north-east Ireland under the act. He had been renominated for the labour party executive, at the 1912 party conference in Birmingham, between 24 and 26 January, but was not a delegate. If successful, he would have become chairman of the labour party, and presided at the 1913 conference. Before leaving the labour movement, he had put his name forward for the position of party secretary. Ramsay MacDonald had stood down to become chairman of the parliamentary party. Arthur Henderson was envisaged as his successor, and was indeed elected at the 1912 conference. Walker, and six others, had withdrawn, leaving only one aspirant to run against Henderson. If Walker had stayed in the labour party, he would not have become secretary. But he would have heard MPs report, to the 1913 conference in London, on home rule and Welsh disestablishment: 'The Party generally had made most definite promises to the constituencies and it did its best to get the measures carried and put out of the way.'[97]

He was in a sense vindicated by this admission. But Walker, as a unionist in Ireland, had sought to integrate with a labour party in Britain which clearly supported home rule for Ireland. Walker got out of politics weeks before the third home rule bill was introduced. One can only speculate about how he would have behaved from 1912, if he had not opted out. He had attempted, within the labour movement, to preserve the union; in 1910–11, he had done this by opposing the ITUC becoming an Irish labour party. From a man who had done so much for labour representation in Ireland, this was decidedly a case of putting his nation before his class.

Walker, as a member of the labour party executive in 1910, was in agreement with his British colleagues. This was after Asquith's legislative promise of December 1909. He was not an active supporter of the ITUC, and they, at least this side of home rule, did not want the British party's organizational interests in Ireland jeopardized. The political funds of the big unions included Irish contributions. Walker had not attended an Irish congress since 1904, and tried to prevent the civic reception's being held, on the occasion of the 1908 congress in Belfast, while hoping for a labour representation motion. This may have been motivated, in part, by a desire not to boost the reputation of the ITUC. Belfast corporation, after the 1907 strike, was probably not inclined to honour trade unionists of any sort, and John Murphy, as president of congress, gave a Walkerite exposition on the need for the British labour party. Walker was determined to go to the 1910 congress in Dundalk in May. He was elected a delegate from the trades council, along with D.R. Campbell, on 7 April. The two successfully opposed an attempt by James Larkin, once he was admitted to the congress, to instruct the parliamentary committee to set up 'an Independent Labour Party in Ireland'.[98]

James Connolly returned to Ireland from the United States that July. He came quickly to believe that home rule was inevitable, and wanted labour represented in the first Irish parliament. He was working as a socialist organizer from Dublin, and spending some time in Belfast. He settled there in late May 1911, and became an official in Larkin's union in July. He was hardly in a position to attend the ITUC, arranged for 5 to 7 June in Galway. Walker had again been selected by the trades council, and he was the only delegate this time. When Connolly sat down to write an article for the 27 May number of *Forward*, a socialist paper published in Glasgow, he can have had little idea that he was about to cross ideological swords with Walker. The resultant exchange, running through June, became an important socialist debate. The editor of *Forward* closed it down on 8 July, on the grounds that it fell short of being a discussion of principles.

William Walker was, it is important to recall, the more eminent figure in 1911. He read Connolly's plea of 27 May for unity between socialists in Dublin and Belfast. The latter espoused the principle of Ireland as a nation, but he used a pragmatic argument about the likelihood of home rule. Unionism, he insisted, no longer represented the interests of any economic class. The ITUC had quickly to become a labour party, rather than continue to advocate affiliation to the British party. Connolly accused the ILP of imperialism, and retrospectively welcomed Walker's defeats in North Belfast, on the grounds that a socialist unionist would have put nationalists off socialism. 'Why sacrifice all Ireland for the sake of a part of Belfast?' he asked. Walker's reply, covering three points, was published on 3 June. 'You are obsessed', he told Connolly, 'with an antipathy to Belfast and the black North, and under your obsession you advocate reactionary doctrines alien to any brand of Socialism I have ever heard of.' Walker attributed the lack of sectarianism in Belfast to the municipal socialism of the ILP. Secondly, he responded to a point Connolly made about the protestant democracy's not inspiring the rest of Ireland, by ironically listing famous Ulster protestant nationalists. On the question of an Irish labour party, Walker cited the example of Scotland, where labour was orientating to the United Kingdom, and accused Connolly of 'viewing the class war as a national question instead of, as it is, a world-wide question'. He cited the 1909 labour party visit to Germany as an example of internationalism.

Connolly came back with a characterization of Belfast parochialism, in an article written before the Galway congress, but published on 10 June. He offered an assurance that he was not against British unions in Ireland, Walker having been concerned about the severing of relations. Connolly referred to his sectarian statement in the 1905 by-election, and asked if Walker was in step with his labour executive colleagues on the question of an Irish party. Tom Johnson, about to attend his first Irish congress on behalf of his union, wrote to Connolly, asking for information on the Scottish labour party – in case Walker mentioned it. Johnson favoured an Irish party, but wanted it 'federated as closely as possible with the English Labour Party'.[99] On the third, and final, day at Galway, Walker again defeated Larkin, after a considerable row. He had the votes of those who still believed in the Irish party. But he was losing the support of some Belfast delegates. He had a majority of only three. John Murphy, who voted with his old comrade, said: 'If they started an Irish Labour Party it would be regarded as a hostile act. When they got Home Rule they could form an Irish Labour Party'.[100] This was a considerable concession, and one that Walker did not make. Connolly was being equally absolutist, since he was taking a stand in nationalist Ireland. It was a victorious Walker who penned the second reply, published on 17 June. He was not inclined to endorse Marx, whom Connolly had introduced, and wrote off the BPA incident as a closed chapter. In a somewhat heated article, he defended the Belfast ILP's parochialism, and the British labour party, suggesting that Connolly was trying to get him expelled. He alluded to the latter's recent arrival in Belfast. The protagonists went a third round, before being finally separated. Connolly showed himself to be intellectually superior, but he did not succeed entirely in politically trouncing William Walker.

The controversy in *Forward* occurred after Walker had made his contribution to Irish, and British, history. He was soon to leave politics, at the beginning of 1912. Walker, as a public official in Belfast, could not have been involved in the unionist mobilizations against the third home rule bill. There is no reason to believe he would have wanted to be active. In 1911 he made much of good Anglo-German relations as being the epitome of internationalism. He may have supported the war effort from 1914, though it is possible he was more of an ILP pacifist. William Walker died on 23 November 1918, after a long illness, in the Royal Victoria hospital. The war had ended twelve days earlier. He was only 47.

He warrants a place in Irish history for challenging conservatism in Belfast. Walker was the champion of independent working-class politics, and he deserves the respect of socialists for his attempt to build a labour party (despite his error with the BPA in 1905). He of course belonged to the predominant community, and, despite his support for trade-union organization, was blind to the position of the catholic working class. His anti-nationalism is not in doubt, but his labourism saw him leave politics rather than collapse into militant unionism. He shared the limited political and industrial vision of his British colleagues, but that is to apply a general criticism to a particular context. Walker, and much of Belfast, has been written out of Irish labour history, but this invariably has been because of his opposition to nationalism. His weaknesses were also those of most leaders of the Irish labour movement. If he was unrealistic about the rest of Ireland, socialist supporters of nationalism can be criticized for failing to appreciate the protestant working class. Walker's contribution in the form of the Belfast labour movement is significant, though his leadership was premised on there being a rank and file to make history in the first place. He took a stronger line than some of his contemporaries on the national question, but labour figures who came after Walker were not dependent upon an active and conservative unionism. They were not Walkerites in the sense of labour unionists, the independence of Belfast labourism owing a great deal to him. It is to his credit that he never established a tradition of left unionism. Walker was a victim of division in Ireland. He certainly was a parliamentarist, he would have opposed syndicalism, and his internationalism was hollow. He deserves praise for refusing to align with his own sectarian bloc in prewar Ireland.

5

James Larkin and the 1907 Strike

Following Walker's 1907 by-election challenge, there was a transport strike in Belfast that summer, during an economic boom. A change in the law governing trade unions was an important precondition. In terms of numbers of workers involved, and the duration of stoppages, this industrial action by fewer than 3,000 dockers and carters was not significant. It was easily overshadowed by the engineering disputes of 1895–6 and 1897–8, and even the 1897 and 1906 linen strikes. An iron-moulders' strike in June/July 1907 warranted listing as a great labour dispute in the board of trade's annual report. The transport strike, which began on the cross-channel docks, spread through picketing, causing considerable economic and social dislocation in central Belfast. The RIC and Dublin Castle took a great deal of interest. Thomas Gallaher, chairman of the Belfast Steamship Company, refused to recognize trade unionism in the industry, anticipating William Martin Murphy, in Dublin, six years later. The strike occurred after the appearance of new unionism, in 1889–92, in which Belfast shared, and anticipated the syndicalist strike wave in the United Kingdom, in 1910–14. It became a veritable social uprising of the unskilled, owing to the tactics espoused by James Larkin – particularly the sympathetic strike, marches and nightly meetings. He acquired a charismatic reputation, not always borne out by his qualities as a leader.

But the struggle did reveal much about society and politics in Edwardian Belfast. Larkin was working for an English union, led by James Sexton, the Irish Transport and General Workers' Union not being yet in mind. This union became the basis of new Irish unionism before the war, and significant subsequent developments. Larkin was a socialist, and a supporter of home rule, but above all a man in revolt. He had some committed supporters on the trades council, but there was no general strike in Belfast in 1907. Intervention by national trade-union leaders undermined the workers' resistance, and there was also mediation by the state. Action on the waterfront, and in the streets, was met by repression, elements of the police expressing discontent, while the use of troops became a major national issue. The strike took place within the protestant community, contrary to historical mythology. When action spread to the catholic ghetto, it ignited more traditional ethnic rioting. Nationalist leaders were simply opportunist. This was Larkin's undoing, and Walker was among those who helped defuse the crisis. The limits of trade-union consciousness were breached in Belfast in the summer of 1907, but not by the development of revolutionary politics.

William Walker was largely instrumental in attracting the labour party conference to Belfast between 24 and 26 January 1907. A printers' delegate referred later to 'a cargo of revolution [being carried by steamer] across the Irish channel'.[1] Few delegates warranted the description more than James Larkin. He had arrived from Liverpool, according to police intelligence, on Monday, 20 January, a day before his 31st birthday. Larkin was a delegate from the National Union of Dock Labourers (NUDL), and he was intent upon combining trade union with political work in this major Irish port.

James Larkin was born in 1876 in Liverpool. His father, a fitter in an engineering firm, hailed from Co. Armagh, but died relatively young in 1887. His mother was also Irish, and catholic, and reared James and his four siblings on her own. His brother Peter and sister Delia were later active in Ireland. James and an older brother were apprenticed in 1887 in their late father's firm, but James resisted the discipline of industry. He eventually became a docker, and, at the age of 17, a seaman. By 1903 he was the youngest foreman on the Liverpool docks, working for the firm of T. & J. Harrison, and nicknamed 'the Rusher'. At 27 he married Elizabeth Brown, the daughter of a Baptist lay preacher, in a civil ceremony. He remained a catholic, and had engaged in social work among the poor. Larkin was soon father to two sons, James and Denis, a third, Fintan Lawlor, being born later. As a working-class militant, Larkin had first been interested in politics, not trade unionism. He had become a socialist at the age of 16, joining the Liverpool ILP in 1892. He helped found the Toxteth branch in Liverpool two years later, and described trade unionism in 1895 as a 'played-out economic fallacy'.[2] This was in accord with the views of the Social Democratic Federation (SDF), the major Marxist organization in Britain. When Tom Mann, secretary of the ILP, established the Workers' Union in 1898, to recruit the great mass of unorganized workers, Larkin helped with the Liverpool branch. It failed to secure the support of Mann's fellow socialists, because existing unions saw it simply as a rival. Larkin did not join, the ILP remaining the focus of his attention.

He became active in the labour party in Liverpool, and acted as agent in 1906 to James Sexton in West Toxteth. Sexton was general secretary of the NUDL, one of the new unions catering for unskilled labourers. He was, at 50, the leading trade unionist in Liverpool, and a member of the parliamentary committee of the TUC. 'Larkin displayed an energy that was almost superhuman', Sexton recalled.

> The division was one of the storm centres of religious strife, and the stronghold of the Orange Order ... My being a Roman Catholic naturally made the situation still more lively. But nothing could frighten Jim. He plunged recklessly into the fray where the fighting was most furious ... and ... competed with our opponents in the risky game of impersonation they played at almost every election in Liverpool.[3]

The NUDL had been founded in Glasgow in 1889, by two protestant followers of Henry George from the north of Ireland – Edward McHugh and Richard McGhee. The latter became a nationalist MP in 1896. Sexton, a Liverpool catholic, took the union over in 1893. A strike on Merseyside in 1890 had seen the NUDL greatly weakened at the north end of the docks, where the steamship companies were located, but not at the south end, where there were fewer permanent berths. Sexton was then a strong supporter of the not yet reunited Irish party, as well as a member of the ILP. Larkin became a member of the union in 1901, but was hardly active, as a foreman. Union membership may have been a requirement where he worked, under an existing agreement. T. & J. Harrison had a permanent berth, on the south side of the docks. Then in the summer of 1905, during a period of economic decline, Larkin led an unsuccessful strike against fellow foremen in his firm, who refused to rejoin the NUDL. He had his first experience of blacklegs, as they were called, supplied by the employers' organization, the shipping federation. It was a fight for the survival of the union in Liverpool, the NUDL being broken in Harrison's company. In 1905 the city accounted for about half the union's national membership of about 12,000. Larkin left the docks to become an organizer for Sexton, working in Liverpool, Preston and particularly Scotland. He became general organizer of the union in 1906, and it was in this capacity that he sailed for Belfast the following January. There was already rivalry between Larkin and his general secretary.

The Irish ports were closely related to those on the west coast of Britain. Sexton had of course tangled with William Walker over his unionism, at the 1906 labour party conference in London, but this was no block on industrial organization. The NUDL had established branches in Ireland after 1889, and these were in serious need of revival. Larkin was following in the footsteps of Michael McKeown in Belfast. A catholic and nationalist from Co. Armagh, he had worked in Birkenhead, before becoming secretary of the NUDL there in 1889. It was as an organizer that McKeown came to Ireland in 1891, arriving in Belfast in July. A Dublin branch was involved in a two months' strike that year, but it had disappeared by 1900. Though 14 Irish branches were established by the end of 1891, only Derry and Drogheda were listed in 1905. The NUDL congress met in Belfast in 1891, and a local branch of 367 members was affiliated to the trades council in 1892. McKeown was recorded as its secretary, with an address at 112 Corporation Street. Four hundred dockers were involved in a strike that summer, but the use of 'free labour' brought it to an end. Some NUDL members lost their jobs, and the branch appears to have split during the strike, after McKeown spoke with Michael Davitt in public in Glasgow. Protestant dockers working the cross-channel steamers quit the NUDL. The branch may have continued formally to exist, but McKeown cannot have been around to keep it running. He was living in Belfast in 1907, but does not seem to have been active in the labour movement. He was elected to the corporation that January, standing as a UIL candidate in Smithfield. Daniel McDevitt, representing the tailors on the trades council, and reporting that a labour candidate had stood down in the ward, told his colleagues McKeown 'was a very good labour man'.[4] Dockers worked closely with carters. A carters' association with 500 members had affiliated to the trades council in 1892 and continued to exist, perhaps organizing tram and vehicle workers from 1900. R.J. Moore represented the tramway men's association at the ITUC in 1905 and 1906, but it was probably eclipsed by Alex Boyd's Municipal Employees' Association. By 1907 it was said of the carters' association, 'only a few men belonged to it; and it had practically fallen into desuetude, and was of no real value to the members.'[5]

Larkin quickly found his way to Michael McKeown, and persuaded him to resume his position as dockers' secretary. But the people he contacted upon arrival were Tom Johnson and his wife Marie. Johnson, the socialist commercial traveller, had joined the ILP in Liverpool in 1893, and apparently met Larkin the following year. But the latter came bearing an introduction, and stayed for a few days with the Johnsons, at 2 Frederick Terrace, off the Malone Road. By mid-February Larkin had organized 400 dockers. The NUDL branch was formally re-established by late March, and affiliated to the trades council. There were 3,100 dock and quay labourers in Belfast, and 1,500 carters working the docks; 4,600 in all, a smaller number than in some of Belfast's major industrial concerns. Two-thirds of the dockers were 'spell-men', hourly paid casual workers. The other third, about 1,000, were 'constant men', paid by the week. One-third of the carters were employed by ship owners, the majority by carting employers. Carting provided more regular employment. The police considered that Larkin organized most of the 4,600 dockers and carters in three months, and *Forward* even claimed there were 6,000 NUDL members. The figure of 2,000 was reported in April. His organizing ability is not in doubt, and there was spontaneous recruitment into the NUDL, but observers, most likely, were equating forms of mass action on the streets with the enrollment of workers into an industrial organization. Casual workers were notoriously difficult, if not impossible, to recruit into trade unions on any permanent basis. James Larkin did not totally organize the port of Belfast, though he came to command a considerable following among its workers. There was some industrial skirmishing in the first few weeks. He won an increase for spell-men, working for Burns at Dufferin dock, on 28 April. When Kelly's coal merchants locked out 400 of the fillers, Larkin got them back within a few days. Industrial relations were becoming unstable. '[A] delegate ... [would see] something or some person that was not satisfactory', an employers' representative recalled later, '[and] he would order the men off'.[6]

Docking in Belfast was integrated with shipping, and private firms made use of the harbour commission's public facilities. There were 17 shipping firms on the Co. Antrim, or west, side of the Lagan. They coexisted with 10 coal firms, and there were 12 more of these on the Co. Down, or east, side of the river. Belfast ran on coal like all cities. The Belfast Steamship Company employed the most dockers and carters, but there were three groups of employers – ship owners, carriers and, within the latter, coal merchants. The labour market on the waterfront, as in transport generally, was extremely casual. Economic insecurity for workers produced geographical stability. An excessive supply of workers was always on call, and coteries formed around individual foremen. This resulted in a highly segmented labour market. The port employers in Belfast generally subcontracted to stevedores, 'gangers' or 'labour masters', who were often from the ranks of labour, and 'sometimes [had] no capital'.[7] They contracted to do a job, employed the workers, and kept much of the piece-work bonus for themselves. This was investigated by a board of trade committee later in the year, a gang's wages being often paid in a regular pub. Such workers were unable to control the overall labour market, but cooperation, in residential areas and the workplace, could lead to spontaneous action.

Sexton attributed the weakness of trade unionism to 'the prevalence of what I can only describe as the caste system throughout the dockers' fraternity, which [leads] to the creation of almost innumerably small clubs and societies all hostile to each other ... Quite frequently religious and political differences kept these bodies apart, and, indeed, alive.'[8] This was Liverpool, and Belfast must have been similar. Catholics were increasingly overrepresented in docking, and carting was contemporaneously perceived as protestant work. But the ethnic barrier ran within, rather than simply between, both branches. There were protestant and catholic dockers and carters, and they occasionally worked side by side. Permanent and casual dockers worked, respectively, on the cross-channel or 'high' docks and the deep-sea or 'low' docks. The former was regular traffic; the latter less predictable foreign trade. In 1912 an employers' representative described this as a difference between protestant and catholic workers, this perception of separation showing the strength of sectarian consciousness in Belfast. Catholic dockers lived close to their work, in the area between York Street and Corporation Street known familiarly as Sailortown. Protestants also lived here, but were more dispersed through the city. As for carting, the large number of small firms with permanent workforces meant that these were probably integrated into both communities. There were protestant and catholic carting firms. This did not make for a pattern of simple segregation on the waterfront, more a social complex built up over time with a theme of ethnic differentiation, which ideologues often simplified.

The employers were more united. Most of those in the port seem to have belonged to the shipping federation. It had been founded in 1890, for the purpose of 'maintaining liberty and resisting the new union methods of coercion'. The federation set out to destroy the seamen's union, and it attracted most of the large ship owners, except the Atlantic passenger lines, to its ranks. These were the companies for which Harland and Wolff built ships. The shipping federation was 'founded ... from the first', as its official historian admitted, 'as a fighting machine to counter the strike weapon and it made no secret of the fact'.[9] The federation's telegraphic address was 'Nemesis'! Its Belfast branch dwarfed the local master carriers' association, which represented about 60 firms with small workforces. The coal merchants were also organized, seemingly alongside the master carriers. In 1907, once the labour troubles began, the chamber of commerce called a meeting for 26 June. An employers' protection association was formed, embracing the port employers, and 'a substantial amount of financial support was forthcoming'.[10]

The general labour superintendent of the shipping federation was invited to visit Belfast on 6 May, in anticipation of a 'local dispute'.[11] Larkin's activities had yet to attract widespread attention, and the trades council was more concerned about a problem George Greig's NAUL was having at the Sirocco engineering works of Samuel Davidson. The coordinates of industrial action can be summarized, though the 1907 strike came to be experienced as a wider confrontation of classes. There were six phases in all, the first beginning on 6 May, and the second on 26 June. The first saw the lock-out of 160 dockers, the second a strike by 300 dockers and 200 carters, followed by further lock-outs in July of 1,680 carters. The struggle continued through four further phases into August and early September.

On Monday, 6 May, 70 spell-men at the Belfast Steamship Company's York dock, working the SS *Optic*, struck against two non-unionized workers. This was the beginning of the strike, though attempts were made to get the men back. Apparently at the behest of the shipping federation, the company, undoubtedly at the instigation of its chairman, Thomas Gallaher, virtually dismissed the 70, plus 90 permanent men. Larkin was faced technically with a lock-out, that is, an employer's denying his workers employment until they agreed to accept his conditions. It is a phenomenon in labour history difficult to distinguish from a strike initiated by workers. The following day black-legs took over. On 16 May, 350 young women at Gallaher's tobacco works came out. They had been organized by Larkin, and the sacking of seven leaders provoked the strike. The young women rejected Larkin's advice to return, but the strike had collapsed by the following day. The 160 dockers remained locked out, and industrial guerrilla warfare was breaking out. 'At the quay during the past few weeks', the *Northern Whig* noted on 20 June, 'various grades of workers have been busy sending in ultimatums to their employers, mainly on the question of wages, and in some instances they have been successful in obtaining their demands.' This was the day Larkin demanded an increase from all cross-channel companies, the NUDL following this up with the threat of a complete standstill.

It was on 26 June that 300 dockers on the Barrow, Heysham and Fleetwood steamers came out on strike, because they had not been granted the increase. The lines were owned by three English railway companies, the London and North-West, the Lancashire and Yorkshire (Fleetwood), and the Midland (Barrow and Heysham). The shipping federation may have responded again with its so-called 'free labour', as it did in the case of the Belfast Steamship Company's Liverpool line. Seventy of the dockers were employed by the London and North-West Railway Company, which arranged for their immediate replacement by

15 of its workers from Dublin, and 5 from Greenore. Some, it was alleged, were members of the Amalgamated Society of Railway Servants (ASRS). Other Dublin employees may have blacklegged in Belfast. The strike began on the day the employers' protection association was formed in the chamber of commerce. The following day, 27 June, 80 carters at Cowan's, and 120 from Wordie's, came out in sympathy, but also with their own demands. These carters had been working the three lines. It was one thing to replace dockers on the quays, quite another, carters who moved about the city. Blacklegs were started at Cowan's, and Larkin threatened to bring out all carters, if blacklegs were used to cart from the Barrow, Heysham and Fleetwood, or Liverpool boats. On 4 July the master carriers locked out 800 workers, and 880 coal carters followed on 15 July.

At the height of the struggle, then, 2,340 dockers and carters were involved. Only 370 dockers and 200 carters had come out on strike, the rest being locked out. The number of strikers approximates to that for the NUDL branch, and locates the membership at four points on the waterfront – the Liverpool, Barrow, Heysham and Fleetwood boats. Just over half the total workforce of 4,600 in the port was involved at the height of the disturbances. Others may have been laid off subsequently, as the docks became crowded with goods that could not be moved, and there was less and less work for casual labourers. The shipping federation was responsible for locking out only 160 dockers, from the larger group of workers in the port, on 6 May. It was the locking out, on 4 and 15 July, by, respectively, the master carriers and coal merchants, of 1,680 workers which created the greatest impact. While the lock-out of dockers was followed by a strike, on 26 June, it was the strike of carters, on 27 June, which led to the subsequent lock-outs. Thomas Gallaher brought in the shipping federation, but local employers were determined to resist trade unionism in the port of Belfast.

Larkin was slow to affect the working of the port. Up to 1 July the tonnage figures recorded in Belfast exceeded those for the comparable period in the previous year. The shipping federation's dockers were obviously coping. The locked-out carters made more of an impact, tonnage in the 'high' docks declining in the period up to 3 August. The contrary was the case in the 'low' docks, where catholic dockers tended to work. Some activity had been reported there on 5 July, the day after the carters' lock-out, but nothing subsequently. Larkin did not manage to organize the 'low' docks, with the higher propensity for casual work. Alexander McDowell, the solicitor working for the Belfast Steamship Company, testified, in 1912, to an official inquiry, that they did not strike. There was only some picketing done by casual dockers, though workers there may have been laid off later as trade was affected. When Larkin found himself with a struggle on his hands, it was at the head of largely protestant workers. There were only 70 spell-men involved, those who had struck at York dock on 6 May, most affected workers being permanent employees. Joseph Mitchell, assistant secretary of the trades council, told delegates, on 12 September, that there were 190 dockers at the Liverpool sheds. He had charge of the records during most of the strike, and stated that 170 involved from the beginning were protestants. (Estimates are as low as 140, for Belfast Steamship Company workers affected, but the figure of 160 seems to have been used at the time by the men's leaders.) On 22 August, in Derry, Larkin claimed that seven out of ten of his members were orangemen, and they were 'the best men we had'.[12] He must have been referring to the Liverpool, Barrow, Heysham and Fleetwood boats, Larkin probably using the term *orangeman*, as a catholic, to mean simply protestant.

The first phase of the strike began with the lock-out of 160 dockers on 6 May, and ran up to the strike of 300 on 26 June. The use of black-legs became the immediate focus of attention. The 70-strong harbour police, plus the RIC, were detailed to protect the Liverpool sheds on Donegall Quay. On Saturday, 11 May, 'scores of young fellows' stormed the boat, the SS *Caloric*, where the blacklegs were accommodated. She was then moved to York Dock. A demonstration, behind the banner, 'Down With Blacklegs', was stopped in Corporation Square, and crowds cheered as fire engines rushed to put out fires started at the sheds. 'It is not so much the dockers', Sir Antony MacDonnell in Dublin Castle observed, 'as the rabble which the excitement had called out [who have] caused the damage.'[13] Armed troops were brought in on 16 May, to assist the 300 police being used round the clock. On 31 May, Richard Bamber, a blackleg, became separated from his companions, in a public house on the corner of North Street and Rosemary Street, when attacked by dockers. Bamber drew a knife outside, and proceeded down Waring Street, towards Victoria Street. Larkin, who had been sum-moned from the nearby strike headquarters, lobbed a paving stone at him. Three dockers were stabbed, and Larkin arrested and charged with assault. Bamber was also arrested. Larkin appeared in court a number of times, before being acquitted at a trial in Dublin the following January.

Larkin's leadership made an immediate impact. He held nightly meetings in Corporation Square, as well as demonstrations, parades and street collections. These often took on the character of more traditional protestant manifestations. involving more than the locked-out dockers, and the membership of the NUDL. Between 6,000 and 8,000 were reported present on 16 May, the day the army appeared. When 'rivet boys and youthful roughs'[14] attacked the police, there were two baton charges. After the meeting, the crowd split into two. One group, carry-ing two Union Jacks, marched through Great George Street, York Street, Royal Avenue, and back to Corporation Square. Larkin meanwhile led another crowd along the quays to the Custom House steps, past the offices of the Belfast Steamship Company, asserting the right of the workers to march in defiance of the police. This suggests he ignited activity, over which he did not have control. Two days later, two Union Jacks were carried at the head of a march, along with the placards 'Support Labour' and 'Smoke Murray's Tobacco'[15] – the latter was a Belfast-manufactured alternative to Gallaher's. A flute band and a man with a 'blackened' face marched, after Larkin's court appearance, behind the banner 'Support Larkin and No Surrender'.[16] Arthur Trew was losing his following to this Liverpudlian. He had initially opposed the strike. On Sunday, 12 May, he was surrounded by police, after he attacked 'the Larkinites',[17] and had to be led to safety. Larkin was described as 'a corner boy of the worst type',[18] on 2 June, but the usurper Sloan was now being described as a blackleg. Trew never rallied to Larkin, but he subsequently 'confined himself to criticizing the police'.[19]

In the first seven weeks Larkin concentrated his rhetoric upon Gallaher. He demanded the company negotiate with the NUDL; in other words he demanded union recognition. Larkin described his opponent on 14 May, as one of the snakes St Patrick forgot to drive out of Ireland, and, five days later, as a man who could not be hanged, 'for no honest rope would do it, and no respectable hangman would put his hand to the job'.[20] It was a personal style he perfected, such attacks resonating well with his followers. Larkin's strategy seemed to be to force Gallaher to climb down. The Belfast Steamship Company claimed it was willing to talk to its men; it just did not want a union involved. On 14 May Gallaher declined an offer of mediation from the lord mayor, Lord Shaftesbury, who was also president of the chamber of commerce. Larkin replied that he would have Gallaher's tobacco boycotted at the Dublin exhibition; in reply, Gallaher said he would halt plans for new premises in Belfast, shut down his existing plant, and move it to England, where he already had three factories. Larkin had few troops at his disposal, and generally acted cautiously about bringing workers out – in spite of what he said.

In this he was following trade-union practice. Alex Boyd had offered the Municipal Employees' Association's offices, at 11 Victoria Street, as strike headquarters. The NUDL also seems to have opened an office at 41 Bridge End. Boyd, Mary Galway of the textile workers, and Joseph Mitchell were the first trade unionists to join Larkin on his nightly platform on 16 May. William Walker appeared two evenings later. His wife had recently died, and he was in the depressing wake of his third North Belfast defeat. He seemed intent upon Larkin running a proper industrial dispute, of the sort the ASCJ would have conducted. Walker described the strike as 'an error of judgement', though it is not clear he was entirely blaming Larkin. He thought Gallaher could get on with dockers, when he managed 'harmoniously with joiners and members of skilled workers' unions'.[21] This was an argument for union recognition. William Walker was not much in evidence subsequently, partly because he was out of the city on holiday, but mainly because he had, as a parliamentary candidate, left industrial fighting, like socialist politics, behind. Two days later Larkin was in Dublin for the ITUC, as a delegate from the NUDL (with an address in College Street, Belfast). It was his first such appearance, during which delegates dined at the Gresham Hotel with prominent citizens, and rode free, courtesy of the Dublin Tramway Company. Larkin got delegates, including 15 from Belfast, to express 'heartiest sympathy' with the dockers, and condemn 'the tyrannical action of Mr. T. Gallaher, the tobacco king, organiser of the new tobacco trust, in denying to his employees the right of combination, and his despicable conduct in importing foreign blacklegs'.[22] It was the strongest-worded resolution to be carried by a trade union congress in Ireland. The Belfast trades council passed the same resolution on 6 June. It recommended the dockers' case to all trade unionists, and circularized the trades councils of the United Kingdom.

Larkin had already introduced politics into the industrial dispute. He objected to the *Belfast Evening Telegraph*'s coverage, and hoped there would soon be a 'democratic evening paper'[23] in the city. Charles Darcus, a printers' representative, had taken exception, at the ITUC, to an attack upon a paper which employed trade unionists only. Larkin also seems to have antagonized Belfast's catholics, since he had to deny he was going to challenge Devlin. 'Mr Devlin was a working-class member, and they were determined to maintain his hold upon that constituency.'[24] The unionist press seemed unaware of his association with Sexton, but it would have been difficult to portray the action on the quays as nationalist-inspired. The *Irish News* had declined to offer an opinion on 'this particular disagreement', describing Gallaher's line as 'a popular local steamship company'.[25] He was a unionist in politics, though he seems to have been a catholic. The paper became interested only in the blacklegs, referring to 'The English Importations'.[26] Larkin was not above a similar chauvinist response, as his ITUC resolution suggests. On 25 June police in – of all places – Bangor, Co. Down, tore down a large blue poster addressed to 'Irishmen!': 'Remember what the English blacklegs suffered – And don't betray your fellow countrymen.'[27] Larkin's name appeared at the bottom. Anti-English sentiment was not the monopoly of nationalists. Protestant workers would not have minded being addressed as 'Irishmen!', but Larkin seems to have been insensitive, at this stage, to the problem of national identity in the Belfast working class. The RIC in the city suspected that Larkin had some of his propaganda material printed by the *Irish News*, but lacking proof, they took no action. Police chiefs did not want to upset nationalist susceptibilities.

The strike of dockers on 26 June, followed by the exit of 200 carters the next day, opened a second phase of the struggle. Action shifted from the quays, the preserve of the harbour commission, to the streets of central Belfast. When the first van worked by blacklegs appeared in High Street, on 27 June, it was attacked by a crowd of 2,000 to 3,000. 'Illegal picketing increased rapidly', the police noted.

> Bands of pickets wandered all over the City interfering with whatever they thought a fit object for their violence. Gross and open intimidation was used and there was really no attempt to try the effect of peaceful picketing ... The strikers used as much violence as would achieve their object and openly said they would allow no carting of any description.[28]

Picketing, and its control by the police, was crucial in this as in many industrial disputes. Unskilled workers, lacking industrial power, were dependent for success upon a liberal interpretation of law and order. The government had carried the trades disputes act the previous year, undoing the effects of the House of Lords' Taff Vale decision of 1901.

Legal immunity was restored to trade unions, and the right peacefully to picket re-established.

Larkin had telegraphed Ramsay MacDonald, presumably as secretary to the group of labour MPs, on 26 June, saying that pickets were being harassed by the police. This was passed to Augustine Birrell, the chief secretary. Larkin presented himself, two days later, at the military cordon on the docks, bearing a copy of the 1906 act. He informed the officer in charge that all workers wearing union badges were entitled to be on the docks, though not the property of the harbour commission. This was a liberal concept of picketing. The lord mayor had started to use cavalry to protect vans travelling through the streets, this being entirely his prerogative as chief magistrate. Larkin led a twelve-man deputation to a meeting of the corporation on 1 July, it being introduced by McKeown, NUDL secretary, but also a nationalist member. 'The Lord Mayor is no use', shouted a voice from the gallery. 'I'd shoot the Lord Mayor.'[29] Members of the corporation voted not to withdraw the troops. There was a tendency on the part of respectable citizens to associate the industrial with agrarian disturbances. 'Tipperary in Belfast' was the subtitle of an article, in the *Northern Whig*, by 'A Puzzled Citizen', on 'A Study in Peaceful Picketing'.[30]

The strike of 200 carters on 27 June, following the 300 dockers, was a major escalation. It was an accession of strength to the workers' cause, but also a provocation to the employers. There was a considerable risk. Larkin met the master carriers on 29 June, following his threat of a general transport strike. He gave them until the following Tuesday (2 July) to start negotiations. They appeared willing to increase wages, but not to recognize the NUDL. The master carriers thereupon wrote to R.J. Moore, secretary of the carters' association, the barely surviving respectable union branch, since Alex Boyd was looking after corporation carters. Moore was in favour of the carters continuing to work the Barrow, Heysham, Fleetwood and Liverpool boats, but he was unable to influence the course of the struggle. A meeting of 960 carters on 1 July decided to black the Belfast Steamship Company, plus the three railway concerns.

The following day, something surprising happened. Larkin announced he was handing over the leadership of the strike to Boyd and McKeown. The employers had called his bluff, and he hoped they would negotiate with new leaders. Larkin was not able to deliver a general strike of carters, and his politics and religion were also involved. That morning, the *Ulster Echo*, in describing Larkin and McKeown as catholics and nationalists, stated they were using Boyd. Larkin admitted to being 'a Socialist all his life', but noted that it was not a requirement for NUDL membership. 'Political and religious motivations' on the part of critics made it desirable for him to hand over to 'a Protestant in the person of Mr Alex Boyd'.[31] Boyd was, if anything, even more militant than Larkin, having talked of pulling out MEA members in the corporation's gas and electricity departments. It is also unclear how McKeown, who was more catholic and nationalist than Larkin, would be more acceptable. (The latter had denied twice in May that he was related to one of the nineteenth-century Manchester Martyrs, also called Larkin.) Possibly Larkin came under criticism for being an outsider, and maybe he thought Boyd and McKeown would appeal, respectively, to Belfast protestants and catholics. Larkin decided to stand down only as negotiator. 'Loud cheering' greeted his return to the Custom House steps, on 3 July, and Boyd warned against attempts to divide dockers and carters by 'work[ing] up party feeling'.[32]

Larkin now threatened a general strike in the port by the weekend, and a 'dockers' manifesto' was issued on Wednesday, 3 July, promising the stoppage of 'general cargo, coal quay, and cross-channel traffic, together with the Carters' Union'. The strike committee, Larkin said, had been sworn to secrecy about the plan of campaign, and a headquarters staff appointed, with Boyd 'general adviser' on communications.[33] He may have known the master carriers were going to lock out 800 workers the next day, and on 4 July wagons and vans began to be attacked in the streets. Boyd again hinted at the MEA joining the strike, but he may have been unable to bring his members out. The lord mayor appealed, in vain, for the employers to meet the men's leaders. Twelve of the smallest firms settled with Larkin, as did Harland and Wolff. It employed 27 carters, and had participated in the lock-out, but Larkin visited A.M. Carlisle, and persuaded him to take the workers back.

The trades council held a regular meeting on 4 July. It had passed a motion a month earlier, but done little for the dockers. With 1,000 carters now involved, the dispute had become much more serious. Boyd and Joe Harris of the upholsterers, who soon became organizer for the Workers' Union, moved a resolution condemning the railway trade unionists who were blacklegging. A minority of delegates had been actively supporting Larkin, and the council as a whole now became more sympathetic. But a minority of reactionaries, such as Keown of the plasterers, were none too enthusiastic. He disliked a motion condemning the use of troops in industrial disputes. The trades council appointed a committee 'to act with the Dockers',[34] and promised a contribution of £100. Lock-out pay for a single man was 10 shillings (50p). By 14 July, 1,000 men required paying, at a cost of about £400 a week. There was then only £600 available, and the strike committee had repeatedly to borrow from local gentlemen – whose identities are unknown. The strike committee came to require about £1,500 a week, when all 2,340 workers were involved. The lock-out of the 880 coal carters, from Monday, 15 July, by 18 of the 20 coal firms, had effectively taken place the previous Thursday – on the eve of the Twelfth.

On 1 July Commissioner Hill, of the Belfast RIC, had telephoned Dublin Castle. 'The question of religion', he reported on the strike, 'does not enter into it at all – a fortunate circumstance, in view of the approaching Orange celebrations. I understand that there was never less party spirit in Belfast than at present. The strike is being conducted purely as a Labour dispute.'[35] Larkin's short-lived resignation, with hints about local politics intruding, came the following day. By 5 July, with the carters still locked out, the strike committee had decided not to hold a regular meeting at the Custom House steps on the Twelfth. On Sunday, 7 July, Joe Harris, speaking for the Belfast Socialist Society, said 'they would differ on one day of the year, but their interests were the same for the other 364.'[36] Trade unionists and socialists were well aware of the ethnic division in the working class. While the workers directly involved were predominantly protestants, catholics coexisted in Sailortown. Larkin took the opportunity to leave Belfast, his mother being ill in Liverpool. It is unlikely he sailed courtesy of the Belfast Steamship Company, and he may have crossed from Dublin. On the morning of Friday, the Twelfth, the *Northern Whig* wondered 'whether the rank and file [would] comply with the wishes of their leaders, and show that the movement [was] a purely trades one'. They did and it was. 'We got over yesterday very well', Commissioner Hill told Sir Neville Chamberlain, the inspector general of the RIC, on 13 July. 'No friction whatever.'[37]

While orangeism did not become an issue of the strike, some of Larkin's followers were members of the Independent Orange Order (IOO). Alex Boyd was still a leader of Sloan's order, with Lindsay Crawford grandmaster. The latter had claimed that nine-tenths of Gallaher's male employees were members of the orange order living on the Shankill and Crumlin roads.

The strikers were overwhelmingly protestant, but the independent order had originated in the area of Sandy Row. This was not a scene of conflict during the strike. Some members of the IOO were undoubtedly involved, but the dockers and carters would not have been marching, *en masse*, to Shaw's Bridge, to listen to Boyd, Sloan and Crawford on the Twelfth. More would have been members of the orange order proper, in lodges spread across protestant Belfast. The order refused to allow a collection for the strikers at its Twelfth celebration, it being reluctant to take sides in industrial disputes, especially when they challenged law and order to such an extent. The IOO, in contrast, allowed a collection along the route, and £59 was raised. This does not mean that the Sloanites were on the side of the workers, and in favour of direct action against blacklegs. This is in spite of the new order's tradition of independence, and the often militant expression of protestantism. The attitude of the members of the two orders cannot be derived from the respective existence, and non-existence, of strike collections. The rank and file of the orange order was variously described as sympathetic and hostile to Larkinism. The leadership's ban on a collection was enough to persuade the independents to do the opposite, and Boyd probably made sure the correct decision was taken. He espoused the cause of the strikers, and envisaged working-class unity, 'in one solid organization for their own interests ... [where they did not have to] sacrifice one iota of their Protestantism or Catholicism'. This apparent challenge to sectarianism was compatible with polarization on the national question. Sloan supported the demand for arbitration, but did not come down on the side of the workers. Crawford supported the strikers, but his attack on the employers was still populist. A resolution condemned those who did not recognize trade unions, 'to which is due the deplorable strike that at present paralyses trade and inflicts such suffering upon the poor'.[38] Independent orangeism was hardly running in the same direction as the dockers and carters on the streets of Belfast.

The third phase of the strike began on 15 July, ten weeks after Gallaher locked out his dockers. All 2,340 workers were out together until 25 July, though the number requiring assistance towards the latter date may have been closer to 3,500. The Belfast police were worried, because the lock-out of coal carters coincided with the annual closure of the shipyards for a week. There would be more people about, not just employees of Harland and Wolff, and Workman, Clark. Meetings had hitherto been confined to the docks, but, with the Twelfth over, the strike committee took to holding them in working-class residential areas, presumably with the intention of building popular support. There was to be a meeting at noon each day, at the Custom House steps, and one each evening at 7.30 p.m., at a different venue. Larkin, Boyd and Crawford, making his second appearance on a strike platform, spoke at Clonard Gardens in the Falls on 17 July. Crawford appeared only after the Twelfth, and this was his first venture into a catholic area. He talked of Davitt, and 'the dawn of a great day for Ireland ... because the working classes were sinking their political differences and uniting together for the cause of labour'.[39] The following night they were in Sandy Row, 'the attendance being large'. 'If he had done nothing else', Larkin said, 'since he came to Belfast than to draw Protestant and Catholic together he had done a great work.'[40]

The theme of catholic and protestant working-class unity was being distilled out of the strike. Crawford may have begun the process, but Larkin was a political activist, before a trade-union organizer, and Boyd favoured a united industrial fight. All were well aware of sectarian division. Larkin had stayed behind at Clonard Gardens to meet 'female textile workers',[41] and he also wanted to arrange for house-to-house collections, presumably only locally in the catholic ghetto. A women's strike committee was formed, though no women were directly involved. Supplies to linen mills may have been affected, but the 'low' docks were still working. Ewart's mill closed on 25 July, and the power-loom manufacturers' association announced closure later, owing to shortages of yarn and coal, and the difficulty of carting. Women of course were also consumers. Hughes's bakery, a catholic firm, had started using blackleg carters on 9 July, attracting conflict from the docks to the area of his works. On 18 July, the day after meeting Larkin, some women overturned one of Hughes's carts, scattering the bread. Challenges to public order in catholic areas had usually been nationalist-inspired.

The leaders of the trade-union movement in Belfast were sensitive to such public violence, and they would in any industrial city have sought to circumscribe a strike of dockers and carters within the realm of an industrial struggle, and certainly prevent its becoming political. In Belfast, politics was particularly divisive. Socialists in the city were keen on secular escalation, and Larkin needed the support of the rest of the trade-union movement. The shipyard holidays were due to end on

Monday, 22 July, but not all the workers returned, seemingly because of a meeting at the Custom House steps. 'The Island men to a very great extent no doubt sympathise with the strikers', the *Northern Whig* reported,

> but they mixed with them yesterday more with the object of satisfying their curiosity than of taking an active part in any demonstration which might be organised. They chaffed the police from a safe distance, and directed shafts of wit and irony at the drivers of vehicles passing along the quay, but all was said and done in the best of humour and no attempt was made to cause trouble.[42]

On 14 July it had been suggested, from a Belfast Socialist Society platform, that the Belfast Co-operative Society (the Co-op) should look after those strikers who were being refused further credit in their local shops. The following day the coal carters were locked out. The Co-op was an institution primarily of the respectable working class, having been established on the Shankill Road in 1889, though it was to have fewer than 1,000 members in 1901. There were 3,540 in 1907, and there would be over 6,000 by the end of the decade – when the share capital was £45,504. The society was then to run twelve grocery shops, five drapery shops, and one boot and shoe shop, plus a bakery and stables. It would also have a choir, orchestra, and ambulance classes, as well as the usual educational activities. Tom and Marie Johnson were active in these. James Larkin was almost certainly not, and few of his members could have afforded to pay when they shopped at the Co-op. The society did not extend indefinite credit, as suggested, after 14 July, and it moved into the coal business. W.M. Knox argued that, by opposing the coal dealers, the society was helping the dockers and carters. It was not so simple. The Co-op ordered several shiploads of coal, which were distributed by the normal 'bell-men' in residential areas. A healthy profit was presumably made, as the society donated £50 to an unemployed fund. The 'famine in coals'[43] was countered, and the regular merchants commercially threatened. In order to preserve their businesses, they relented, and allowed the 880 coal carters back to work on 26 July.

This certainly weakened the employers' offensive. But it did not strengthen the resistance of the remaining 1,460 workers, it being a considerable de-escalation. As a result of the Co-op becoming commercially involved, the end of the struggle began to be envisaged. It was not clear that the calling off of the lock-out would see all workers reinstated, much less the NUDL recognized for the purposes of collective bargaining.

Larkin was responsible to the executive of his union in Liverpool. He needed money from the NUDL and the trade-union movement generally. Britain, rather than Ireland, was the source. The Dublin trades council had sent three guineas and sympathy. By the end of the struggle, just over £70 would have been raised in the Irish capital. In contrast, the *Northern Whig* reported on 22 July that £48,000 had been sent, or at least promised, by British unions. Larkin had sent deputations to

England and Scotland. James Sexton turned up in Belfast on 19 July, promising all of the union's £20,000 reserve, though he brought only £200 with him. The NUDL would contribute a little under £5,000 to the strike fund, a mere £1,692 coming collectively from other unions, though there must have been individual contributions from unions and branches. Total income did not exceed £9,000. Larkin returned to Liverpool, his mother having died. He was about to lose control of the strike.

Sexton was accompanied by Isaac Mitchell and Allen Gee, officers of the General Federation of Trades Unions (GFTU). The federation was able to fund strikes after eight weeks, but its main function was to '*promote* Industrial Peace ... by all amicable means'.[44] The three British leaders visited the lord mayor and the coal merchants, reporting back to the GFTU executive on Monday, 22 July. They succeeded in getting the coal carters back, on the understanding that there would be no objection to the employment of non–trade unionists. This was in the context of the Belfast Co-operative Society's moving into the coal business. They also settled the ironmoulders' strike, the 350 men returning on 27 July after eight weeks. One thousand other workers had been indirectly affected. Richard Elliot on the strike committee considered that Mitchell, Gee and Sexton had thrown away the men's best card when they settled the coal dispute. The power-loom manufacturers' association's closure was announced for 27 July. With a coal famine, the union might have expected employers and the municipal authorities to lean on Gallaher and his collaborators. The return of the coal carters on 26 July was greeted with hints in the press about the end of the strike.

This was the very day on which the dockers and carters began to get trade-union support. The trades council had arranged a march for Friday, 26 July, this marking the beginning of a fourth phase in the struggle. 'Practically all the trade societies in the city took part ... [in] a very extensive demonstration.' A 'large red banner' was carried in front, bearing the exhortation, 'Support the dockers and carters in their fight for trade unionism.'[45] The route of the march was designed to embrace working-class Belfast. It began at the new City Hall, and headed for Ballymacarrett, returning to west Belfast across Albert Bridge. It wound its way up May Street, Howard Street and Durham Street, to the Falls Road. Then across to the Shankill Road, down Crumlin Road, to Queen's Square – where four platforms had been set up. Larkin, Boyd and McKeown were joined in the leading brake by Crawford. For the first time, certainly since 1892, the unity of the working class was symbolized. This time, skilled marched with unskilled; men with women. 'The older established societies', noted the *Northern Whig*, 'preceded by banners ... marched two by two with almost military preciseness, whilst the members of the more recently organised unions were collected in an irregular formed but solid body, sometimes twenty abreast, rendering a computation of the total number ... practically out of the question.' The *Irish News* reported: 'The procession also attracted a kind of vanguard, composed of young mill-girls, who wore strips of coloured cloth, and manifested their feelings by singing, cheering or groaning, as the fancy took them.'[46]

The police had been involved in attempting to control strikers and their supporters since early May. On 24 July the authorities were confronted with trouble from within the ranks of the Belfast RIC, which was not solved until 3 August. Instead of being a new front in the workers' struggle, the so-called police mutiny, given the opportunism of nationalists in the city, led to the end of the strike.

The history of policing in Belfast was related to that of sectarian rioting. Originally under the municipality, Dublin took charge with the formation of the RIC as a national police force, to the chagrin of the local bourgeoisie. After the 1886 riots it was decided not to use catholic police officers, the majority of the force, in protestant areas of Belfast. Officers were especially selected to serve in the city, and, at the time of the strike, just under a half of the Belfast RIC were catholic. They served mainly in minority areas. By the 1900s there was considerable dissatisfaction in the ranks, over pay and conditions. Dublin Castle treated it as a matter of discipline, rather than industrial relations. A Belfast police commission, in 1906, acknowledged 'a deep and widespread feeling of discontent'[47] about promotions, but the report was 'kept by the State as a secret document'.[48] Given the need to concentrate protestant officers in Belfast, their promotion chances within the force were restricted. Recently arrived officers in Belfast were often younger than those already there, and it is hardly surprising that the 1907 strike should have provoked a 'police *emeute*'[49] – as the authorities dubbed it. The employers, through the lord mayor, had been demanding that the police restrain the pickets, while Larkin was insisting that the letter and spirit of the 1906 act be respected.

On 28 June the *Irish News* carried a letter from 'Justitia', complaining about the long hours the police were being forced to work. This was at the critical point when dockers and carters struck. It was 10 July before 'Willing to Strike', again in the *Irish News*, said that the police needed a Larkin of their own. Further letters appeared on 16 and 23 July. The author, judging by subsequent open epistolary efforts, was William Barrett, a detective constable in B division, stationed at Roden Street in west Belfast. It was on 19 July, four days after the lock-out of coal carters, that Barrett revolted. Wearing civilian clothes, he was assigned to ride with a blackleg driver in a motor-van, this being less susceptible to attack. Barrett refused and was suspended. Three days later the *Irish News*, which was proving indispensable, published a circular from Barrett, calling for a meeting of police officers at the Musgrave Street RIC barracks. It was planned to petition the government, with the permission of the inspector general of the RIC. Between 200 and 300 men turned up on 24 July, and Barrett, and four others, signed the application to the head of their force. A full account appeared in the following day's *Irish News*, side by side with a story about a police strike in 1882, headed 'Belfast Police Mutiny'. Barrett was dismissed. That Saturday, 27 July, the day after the trades-council march, at least 500 men, out of a force of over 1,000, assembled at the barracks in central Belfast. A crowd got into the yard, and Barrett was carried to the Custom House steps, where he urged restraint on both strikers and police. At Musgrave Street, Barrett had urged his colleagues to give their senior officers eight days to respond to their demand for more pay and better pensions. 'Belfast Police Make History', proclaimed the *Irish News* the following Monday. It subsequently published telegrams of support from RIC stations throughout Ireland.

On Tuesday, 30 July, 1,200 troops were brought into Belfast. Some had been used, at an early stage, in the docks, but the police then took control. 'The troops were brought to Belfast', Dublin Castle subsequently claimed, 'solely for the purpose of dealing with the situation created by the threatened police strike and for policing the city if the strike became an actual fact.'[50] But it was the presence of troops which brought the strike of dockers and carters to an end. Sir Antony MacDonnell had told Birrell, the previous day, that 500 to 600 police might strike, from 4 August. This was roughly the number which had assembled at Musgrave Street on 27 July. His source was Assistant Inspector General Gambell. The RIC's senior officers felt that non-striking policemen could not be used, and that those striking would ally with the dockers and carters. This seems a considerable overreaction, but it justifies the number of troops. There was no police strike, and it is by no means clear that there would have been when Barrett's eight days expired.

On Friday, 2 August, Dublin Castle struck, transferring 273 men, about a quarter of the force. The idea had been MacDonnell's, but the RIC executed the transfer. Discontent, judging by transfers, was not spread evenly through the Belfast police. 'The trouble had clearly been organised in 'B' District, which is the Nationalist or West Division of the city', noted Dublin Castle, 'and the men in that district were more deeply implicated.'[51] Over 100 out of the 184 officers in 'B' district were transferred out of the city. They would have been mainly catholics, but protestants were included in those transferred out of the other four divisions. While they may have been motivated by sympathy for the dockers and carters, who were not, after all, from the minority ghetto, it is more likely that the discontented police officers were responding to their increased duties. Dublin Castle set out to replace the 100 or more men in 'B' division, with those serving elsewhere in Belfast, only letting 37 new officers go there. West Belfast required above all experienced officers. Drastic action solved the authorities' problem, though discontent was to simmer. The day after, Saturday, 3 August, Barrett, as a former policeman, spoke at a meeting of dockers and carters at the Custom House steps. As a result of the police strike that never was, there was now a full complement of officers in the city, and there may have been as many as 6,000 troops.

The *Irish News* covered the threatened police strike in great detail, in contrast with its lack of interest in the dockers and carters. It was not pay and conditions which concerned the paper. 'The English Government has used the "Irish Police"', an early editorial noted, 'to keep hold of their mastery over Ireland: perhaps we may soon see the "police" figuring as acknowledged masters of the English government. Anything is possible in a country like ours.'[52] The paper had been interested in a by-election in Jarrow to be held on 4 July. Tyneside was a long way from catholic Belfast, but there was a nationalist candidate, Alderman O'Hanlon, who had a trade-union background. He was opposed by Pete Curran, the socialist trade unionist, who had declared his commitment to home rule. The latter had supported Larkin during the strike, and the Belfast ILP came out in favour of Curran quite naturally. The catholic paper had to walk an ideological tightrope, refusing to back Larkin and the ILP in Belfast, while supporting Devlin's playing up of O'Hanlon's labourism in order to get working-class votes in England. It finally settled on O'Hanlon's distinction between himself as a labour man, and Curran the unacceptable socialist. The ILPer won. Devlin had been espousing the cause of labour everywhere but Belfast, and with the defeat in Jarrow behind him, he sought the support of Sloan and Wolff in an appeal to Birrell. The chief secretary was willing to intervene, but the member for West Belfast could not get his three unionist colleagues to agree to approach both sides in the strike.

The would-be police mutiny also aroused the interest of the Dungannon Club, an advanced nationalist, or republican, group. It allowed the strike to proceed without comment until 1 August, when it leafletted a meeting in Corporation Square. It had also posted bills throughout the city. In contrast to the nationalists' opportunism, the Dungannon Club proffered an explanation of the strike as national oppression. It was a struggle 'on Irish soil' waged by 'Irishmen', against 'great English carrying companies … [and] Irishmen who are relying on English capital'. Capitalism was British domination! This reinterpretation of reality was not much use to the strikers, fighting Thomas Gallaher for their jobs and union recognition. It made even less impact on a protestant leader like Alex Boyd. He later condemned the 'Sinn Fein' leaflet from the strike platform, and threatened that the club members would be removed 'by physical force, if necessary' from the square, if they tried the same thing again.[53] This attempt to raise the national question resulted only in Arthur Trew's becoming politically rehabilitated at the Custom House steps the following Sunday.

A fifth phase of the struggle began on Saturday, 3 August. The transfer of police disrupted the RIC's relations with the catholic community, and also saw Belfast flooded with troops. The former event meant the traditional leaders lost their power over the police, while the latter led the protestant bourgeoisie to think of the use of soldiers against strikers. The employers had been demanding this for some time, but the British government hesitated to override the right to picket so recently restored. On 6 August the *Northern Whig* came out in favour of the use of troops in an industrial dispute. This was the day the government approved a scheme, supported by the lord mayor, 'for the protection of carters by the combined efforts of military and police'. It had been drawn up by the Belfast RIC, not the lord mayor as chief magistrate. The plan involved 43 military pickets, of 25 men each (some had 50), 'practically in sight of each other, so that in the event of any disturbance, a large force could be collected at a moment's notice'. The police were interspersed, and 'the experiment turned out a complete success'. The troops were deployed, from 7 August, only from 9 a.m. to 5 p.m., as it was 'not deemed judicious to have [them] on the streets ... owing to the thousands of workmen and women leaving off work at about that hour [when] friction might have been caused'.[54]

Larkin must have been furious. William Walker had reappeared on 31 July, after his summer holiday, in fighting mood. With troops saturating Belfast, they rushed to London on 7 August. They were accompanied by Victor Grayson, the recently elected MP for Colne Valley. Larkin and Walker failed to see the chief secretary, but drafted a letter to Birrell on 8 August, complaining about the denial of the right to picket. A protest meeting had been called in Belfast for Saturday, 10 August, in Custom House Square. The strike committee decided to invite the city's four MPs, and it was to be the last great gathering of the strike. Larkin, in London, secured undertakings from Devlin and Sloan that they would attend. Walker was keen to leave the question of troops in Belfast to the labour party in parliament. Sloan pulled out at the last moment, leaving Devlin as the sole parliamentary representative. Larkin, Boyd, McKeown, and Crawford, were joined by Murray, of the boilermakers, and Morley, president of the Workers' Union. Murray threatened a general strike, but Larkin was clearly on the defensive. He promised £100 to charity, if it could be proved that the NUDL had unfairly allocated strike funds. Sectarianism was clearly emerging in working-class communities. Devlin was reported as having 'dealt fully' with the strike, without prejudicing hopes of a peaceful settlement. 'The Member for West Belfast on the Situation', was the *Irish News's* subheading. 'He Speaks on the Invitation of the Strike Committee'.[55] Devlin dissociated himself later from the strike, claiming he had only spoken to Larkin for two minutes. The *Northern Whig* was equally keen to report Devlin's addressing the strikers, in order to frighten the protestant community with nationalism.

It had no need. About noon on Saturday, 10 August, before the meeting at the Custom House, a group of women in Divis Street attacked three seed wagons, belonging to Hughes, and manned by blacklegs. 'Get back to your own country', they shouted at the military escort. 'We want no English here.' This was to be expected, following the strike committee's decision to spread the struggle. Larkin left Belfast after speaking, to address a meeting in Dublin that night. When he mentioned the troops, a member of the audience called out 'kill them'. 'That day had not yet arrived', Larkin was reported as saying. 'The day will come when these men will come to our side, and then there will be some killing done ... Things had come to a desperate pass in Belfast. The only danger was that the men might lose their heads and attack the military. That must be stopped by any and every means. Their men could not fight against bullets and bayonets.'[56] This was an orthodox socialist position, and Larkin clearly did not see British troops as an Irish nationalist. He may have seen anarchy threatening, but national struggle in west Belfast led only to sectarian confrontation. The next day, Sunday, 11 August, two men were arrested in Leeson Street for engaging in a drunken fight. When attempts were made to free them in Grosvenor Road, the police baton-charged. The army was called out, and, later that night, dragoons charged four or five times in Cullingtree Road.

This was a manifestation of catholic attitudes towards the authorities, rather than an aspect of the struggle between protestant workers and the central and local state. At 5.15 p.m. the following day, Monday, 12 August, Gambell reported to Dublin Castle that 'the critical time is when the factory hands leave off work'. Troops were brought into the catholic ghetto again, and stationed in the grounds of the Royal Victoria Hospital. 'Their appearance set in a blaze the fire that had been simmering all day.' Trouble started at the Cullingtree Road barracks, and spread to the Falls Road. 'It became a question of retreating in the face of this mob or firing. Major Thackery [the resident magistrate] elected to fire, read the Riot Act' – and the soldiers, with seven rounds, killed two, and wounded five. One of the fatalities was a young woman out looking for a younger brother. This effectively ended the Falls riots. The troops had marched down the Shankill Road, and, later that night, a crowd in (predominantly protestant) Northumberland Street threw stones into (predominantly catholic) Albert Street. Intercommunal rioting threatened, troops and police being withdrawn for the funerals on 14 August. The RIC considered, five days after the deaths, that 'at any moment some trifling circumstance [might] lead to a renewal of the rioting'.[57]

'Had he been in the city on Sunday', Larkin told a meeting the following night at the Custom House, 'he would have done all in his power to avoid any disturbance, because he realised that the people who would suffer were the workers.' At the time of the shooting, he was trying to prevent the rioting. 'Drink was at the bottom of all that occurred', he said later, 'and he urged the strikers and those friendly to them to abstain from all excess during the present crisis and to show that they were anxious to maintain the law.'[58] Whatever control Larkin and the strike committee had exercised over the catholic masses, they were about to lose to the traditional leaders. 'This is not a fight between Protestant and Catholic', the strike committee said in a leaflet, 'but between the employers, backed by the authorities, and the workers ... Not as Catholics and Protestants, as Nationalist or Unionist, but Belfast men and workers stand together and don't be misled by the employers' game of dividing Catholic and Protestant.'[59] Larkin was cheered when he appeared on the Falls Road, at 5 p.m. on 13 August, only to be asked by priests to leave. A deputation of 'influential citizens, clerical and lay', comprising five justices of the peace, three priests, and nationalist councillors, had asked for the withdrawal of troops. By the evening of 13 August 'practically all well-known inhabitants' had enrolled as 'volunteer guardians'. They included 'the veteran and respected Hugh McManus', the old trade unionist. Devlin appeared, and promised everything that could be done 'by constitutional means'.[60] Walker later claimed that he had organized 350 shipyard workers to patrol the other side of the sectarian divide, the only trouble being from 'a few irresponsibles'[61] in Northumberland Street.

The Falls riots of 10–12 August marked a decisive turning point in the strike. They 'had a sobering effect on all parties',[62] and a sixth, and final, phase opened on 13 August. The cessation of picketing the previous week, as a result of the troops, had led the government to intervene. Late on Saturday, 10 August, before the troops were deployed against catholics, Sir Antony MacDonnell and Sir Neville Chamberlain, of the RIC, arrived in Belfast. They met the lord mayor and prominent citizens. The local bourgeoisie, which had lost control of the police and army to Dublin, was willing to accept a solution from the liberal government. So also was the strike committee, for the different reason that intervention might force Gallaher, the shipping federation and the master carriers to move.

MacDonnell saw Carlisle, of Harland and Wolff, on the Sunday, Sabbatarianism being no obstacle for either man. Carlisle told him that 8,000 workers would have to be laid off within the week. It is difficult to believe that Larkin was disrupting the work of the big yard, and Carlisle was probably trying to encourage the Irish government. MacDonnell telegraphed Birrell in London, on Monday, 12 August, advising the chief secretary to have a word with sympathetic labour MPs. This was with the purpose of persuading Gee and Mitchell of the GFTU to return to Belfast, though Mitchell had quit the trade-union movement to become a government official in the board of trade. Interventionism was a new way of handling industrial disputes, consequent upon the accession of the liberals to power, and the emergence of a labour party based on the trades unions. Larkin telegraphed Birrell on Tuesday, 13 August, after the deaths on the Falls Road, saying he was willing to settle with MacDonnell or Carlisle, 'who had fought and worked with Tradesmen for so long'. He admitted that it had been made 'a political or religious dispute' by the press, and this had 'carr [ied] away the outside public from the real issue namely Trade Unionism'.[63] Larkin was declaring a willingness to talk, and the liberal government had a new card ready to play.

This was George Askwith, who arrived in Belfast from London on the morning of Tuesday, 13 August, having been summoned by MacDonnell. At the board of trade Lloyd George, under Campbell-Bannerman, had just appointed him assistant secretary of the railway department in anticipation of industrial disputes. Three railway companies were involved in the Belfast strike, but the appointment was not made with this in mind. Askwith became the government's industrial trouble-shooter, between 1907 and 1919, presiding over significant developments in state intervention in industrial relations. His first assignment was Belfast where 1,000 carters and 460 dockers were still in dispute with the master carriers' association and four shipping companies. Askwith first formulated the carters' demands with Larkin, during which the latter 'gave [the carters] lectures which no employer would have dared to utter ... [because of their] differences of opinion and changing proposals'.[64] He then met McDowell, the solicitor, and some of the employers. An agreement was thrashed out, providing for wage increases, shorter hours and no victimization. The employers were to retain the right to employ whomsoever they wanted. The agreement seems only to have applied to the 800 carters locked out on 4 July, not the 200 who had struck on 27 June against Cowan's and Wordie's. Sir Antony MacDonnell, representing the full might of the Irish government, put this to a meeting of the master carriers' association.

Askwith handled the strikers, at a meeting in St Mary's Hall on 15 August, an interesting combination of venue and date for largely protestant workers. The carters were in the body of the hall, while dockers observed the proceedings from the gallery. Larkin was present, as was Sexton, secretly carrying a firearm for protection! This suggests that the NUDL was representing the carters working the four shipping lines. Both sides accepted the agreement, and work resumed on 16 August. The carters were delighted with Askwith. The *Northern Whig* crowed that it was 'a complete victory for the employers', the new wages being 'practically the employers' list'.[65] The concession of no victimization, extracted from the master carriers, was a considerable gain for workers in this sort of dispute. It allowed members of the NUDL to resume work, and Murray, of the boilermakers, maintained that this allowed for a closed shop within a year. This was overoptimistic. Larkin, according to Askwith, had thrown himself into the negotiations, relieved, not only at the prospect of a return, but at the fact that the NUDL was not destroyed.

Though the 880 coal carters had been working since 26 July, Askwith became involved in handling their relations with the local coal merchants. It is possible that the carters' association of old may have continued to represent these men, and Askwith was certainly approached by both sides. He was involved in this until 24 August. In 1911 R.J. Moore, the carters' secretary, told the trades council that he could not engage in sympathetic strike action, having signed a three-year agreement, presumably no earlier than 1908.

As work resumed on the docks, Larkin was left, on 16 August, with 460 dockers still locked out, plus the 200 carters from Cowan's and Wordie's. He had hoped Askwith would be able to intercede with Gallaher, and the three English railway companies. But the shipping federation held to its position of no negotiations, not even with a government mediator. Sir James Dougherty, assistant undersecretary in Dublin Castle, told Birrell on 22 August that the three companies were refusing to make any concessions in Belfast, in case it prejudiced their handling of labour relations elsewhere. Dougherty had urged 'grace and concession' in view of the 'danger of leaving unsettled any part of the late dispute'. He asked Birrell to see the managers of two of the companies, and 'move them to order reinstatement'.[66] Larkin may, or may not, have been aware that the head of the Irish government and a member of the cabinet were being advised to lean on two managers, because a minor industrial dispute in Belfast had become a major issue of public order.

MacDonnell reported, on 26 August, that Gallaher had agreed to take back his 160 dockers, 'with very few exceptions'. Over the next seven days the undersecretary was involved in chasing Belfast employers of, mainly, carters. But Gallaher was again being difficult. On 31 August he saw a two-man deputation from the dockers. He was obviously not talking to Larkin or the NUDL. McDowell described the two dockers, who had been without work since 6 May, as 'exceedingly hostile and bitter',[67] an attitude he attributed to Larkin. Gallaher arranged to see them again on 2 September, and a deputation of dockers came. According to the *Northern Whig*, they 'expressed their sorrow for what had happened, their intention if reinstated in their employment of working harmoniously with any fellow employees'.[68] They had been forced to abandon the NUDL, and Gallaher took most of them back on 6 September. The troops had been withdrawn, finally, from the quays, two days before. By the end of the month the last few dockers had rejected Larkin. The 160 at the Belfast Steamship Company had stood by him for four months, on whatever strike pay was advanced.

The fate of the 300 dockers who had struck on 26 June, and of the 200 carters who had struck the following day, is not clear. Presumably Birrell made some impact on at least two of the three railway companies, there being reports of individual arrangements in the case of the Barrow, Heysham and Fleetwood boats. Maybe Cowan's and Wordie's came under pressure from other employers in Belfast. Some carters and dockers never returned to work as a result of the 1907 strike.

Things were not entirely over, and there was considerable discontent on the waterfront after Larkin quit the city. Stevedores reported that 'the men [were] less amenable to discipline, and [were] more independent, knowing that they have the Union at their back. They [were] inclined to do less work, and [were] more addicted to drink than formerly.'[69] In the autumn there was a resumption of industrial confrontation. On 1 November, 500 dockers struck for a day. Unlike the carters, they had not been offered wage increases in August/September. The dockers' demand for an increase was granted immediately. On 14 November 500 coal heavers came out. They were refusing to work with members of another union, an anti-Larkin organization for carters only. It was thought to be employer-inspired and not a little sectarian. Local blacklegs were employed. The coal heavers, members of the NUDL, were forced back twelve days later, without making any gains. Some of the coal heavers were replaced. The return to work was arranged by Sexton, on a flying visit from Liverpool.

The strike during the summer, if only because of the intervention of the troops, and the Falls riots, had attracted national attention. On 5 September the trades council executive recommended a full public inquiry into the use of the military. A motion was carried 'deploring' the deaths, and claiming that the army had been used 'against the wish of the great majority of citizens'. The latter part led to a 'lively debate', but Keown and Whitley, of the printers, secured only one supporter for an amendment to delete.[70] At a special meeting a week later, delegates demanded an 'exhaustive inquiry'[71] into who had been responsible for the use of troops. Murray and Boyd accused the lord mayor of siding with the employers. Keown, and Spence, of the ASE, defended their use on the docks and in the Falls. A number of British trades councils – at least five – protested to the government about the use of troops in an industrial dispute. At the TUC, in Bath, on 5 September, standing orders had been suspended, to allow Boyd and Greig to move a motion, demanding an inquiry into the two deaths. This was carried unanimously.

The parliamentary committee was not so certain. It was 5 February 1908 before the TUC wrote to the prime minister, Campbell-Bannerman, who rejected their demand six days later. In May a committee of nine MPs, including Devlin and Curran, was appointed to consider the power of chief magistrates over troops in trade disputes. It was to recommend increased powers for the police. Walker and Larkin both attended the 1908 ILP conference, in Huddersfield, that April. They joined in pursuing MacDonald, on the question of compensation for riot victims, when the conference considered the parliamentary report. MacDonald replied that the matter was being dealt with. Larkin also ran up against Philip Snowden, also an MP, who, in attempting to argue that the government should control the use of troops, seemed to be endorsing what happened in Belfast.

On 10 August 1907, at the last great meeting of the strike, Larkin had revealed that – presumably – some protestants thought the strike committee was favouring catholics in the disbursement of strike pay. The *Belfast Evening Telegraph*, if it did not originate the rumour, did a great deal to circulate the accusation of sectarianism against Larkin. The paper was virulently opposed to the strike, and its vans were attacked by pickets and their friends in retaliation. Whether or not Larkin had favoured catholics, there was no gainsaying that some protestants would be ready to believe it, but only in conditions of extreme demoralization, such as set in during the summer. It was also alleged that catholics were allowed to work, while protestants had to strike. Catholic coal merchants were not being disrupted.

The executive of the trades council recommended, on 5 September, an investigation into 'certain charges of sectarian favouritism in the administration of the Dockers' and Carters' Strike Fund'.[72] This fund was distinct from the NUDL's financial resources. Larkin denied the story, and claimed that the press had refused to publish his rebuttals. He claimed to possess a signed retraction, from one of those who had first made the charge. Larkin was willing to accept an inquiry by three protestants. A week later the trades council decided to approach Robert Gageby, and the editor of the *Belfast Evening Telegraph*. This was trusting a great deal to Gageby. The allegations now included not only the strike fund charge, but also that Larkin had attempted to make the docks a 'close borough' for catholics.[73] Boyd and Mitchell came to Larkin's defence. Gageby pleaded he was too busy, and the editor of the *Telegraph* stated he wanted a royal commission! His refusal to participate seems to have finally convinced the trades council that 'the charges ... [were] utterly incapable of proof'.[74]

Larkin's entry into Irish labour history, with the 1907 Belfast strike, was a grand one. Despite the role he played in the rest of the country until 1914, and from 1923, when he returned from the United States, he never again had much to do with the city.

He still had a family in Liverpool, and was employed by the NUDL as an organizer. After Belfast, Larkin moved on to other Irish ports, particularly Dublin. He left a small NUDL branch in Belfast, which survived among the carters who had benefited from the 15 August agreement, and possibly among the dockers of the four shipping lines, not all of whom may have been taken back. In November 1907, to refute charges of catholic favouritism, the Belfast NUDL stated that nine of its ten-strong committee were protestants. Seven out of twelve on the dockers' committee were protestant, all on the cross-channel committee, and five out of seven on the carters' committee. Union rivalry and ethnic hostility were part of the legacy of Larkin in Belfast in 1907. Still a peripatetic official of Sexton's organization, Larkin turned up at the 1908 ITUC in the Ulster Hall in June. He was listed as a delegate from the Belfast NUDL, the others being P. Cummins and J. Flanagan – all with an address at 146 Corporation Street. Larkin even managed to get himself elected to the parliamentary committee with 32 votes. So also did George Greig, who had first been elected in 1906. They were the first two representatives of unskilled workers on the executive. The following month, Larkin was presented with an illuminated address by the members of the Belfast NUDL.

The coming year saw Larkin break away from the NUDL, and establish the ITGWU in Dublin. After a series of differences, Sexton suspended him as general organizer on 7 December 1908. A meeting of the non-existent Irish executive of the NUDL was called for Dublin on 26 December. Michael McKeown, Belfast secretary, attended the hurriedly rescheduled meeting on 28 December, when Irish members of the NUDL decided to break away and form the ITGWU, with Larkin as general secretary. The new union formally came into being on 4 January 1909.

McKeown had the books of the Belfast branch, but he must have found it uncomfortable at 146 Corporation Street. Alex Boyd, still organizing the MEA, called a meeting of the NUDL for 6 January. He argued that the ITGWU was 'a Sinn Fein organisation that not even a decent Nationalist in Belfast would have anything to do with'.[75] The Larkinites met on 8 January. Though James Flanagan, a protestant, took the chair, most of the 400 ITGWU members were catholics from the 'low' docks. Larkin attended, and seemed to be arguing for his reinstatement in the NUDL. The union was to record, 50 years later, that 'a personal attempt [by Larkin] ... to unite conflicting elements and extend the membership failed after a stormy meeting which turned into an angry inquest on the 1907 strike and the loss of employment resulting from its termination'.[76] The trades council took the view that there should be reconciliation among the dockers.

There wasn't. Boyd brought Sexton to Belfast for a meeting on 12 January, only to be confronted by the new ITGWU members. By 15 January Sexton, with the support of Boyd, had begun legal action against McKeown. The NUDL regained its office and records, but the employers were ready to exploit division among the dockers. Inspired by the shipping federation, they had recently set up a free labour bureau. Workers had to be members to be hired on the docks. Larkin quickly accused the NUDL of being in the pocket of the employers, and the ITGWU was then taken on by the employers in the 'low' docks. In February Michael McKeown wrote to the parliamentary committee, from 11 Victoria Street, asking the ITUC to inquire into the NUDL branch, 'at present blacklegging on the members of the union'.[77] Boyd must have moved the headquarters of the MEA from this building. With Larkin dissenting, the matter was referred to the Belfast trades council. The parliamentary committee also decided not to invite the new union to the 1909 congress. There the matter rested, but only for a time.

James Larkin left no significant legacy in the city, though 'Belfast 1907' exposed political and social relations to the light of history. Their character was quickly forgotten when he became the founding hero of Irish labour history, the Belfast strike being interpreted as an example of working-class unity created through industrial struggle. Larkin had mobilized mainly protestants, who may or may not have been orangemen, but who were certainly excluded from Walker's labourist universe of respectability. If they had a history of sectarianism, they exhibited a class consciousness in action very different from the populism of Sloan and the IOO, which sought to make communal leaders more protestant. Unskilled catholic workers were not, in the main, caught up in the transport strike, though the spreading of the strike involved the minority ghetto. Social struggle saw constitutional nationalists seek to embarrass the government over the police, and republicans on the margin to see the strike as a contradiction between the Irish people and British rule. James Larkin appeared as very much a British socialist, anticipating the syndicalism of a few years later. If fighting trade unionism was not to the liking of the organized movement, Larkin showed no inclination to stir up sectarian conflict. He moved swiftly to help defuse the crisis, after the introduction of troops, and de-escalate the industrial struggle, with the help of an interventionist government. It is ironic that the myth of Larkinism owes its origins to a section of the protestant working class invariably condemned by Irish socialists as privileged reactionaries.

Part III

Mobilizations

6

Unionist Reaction in Belfast, 1910–14

Working-class assertion in Belfast rapidly gave way, with the loss of the liberals' majority in 1910, to the unionist mobilizations against home rule. Social liberalism under Asquith had been a response to labour movement secession, but Lloyd George's 1909 budget led to the constitutional crisis over the House of Lords. The politics of class gave way to those of nation. The third home rule bill of 1912, and unionist opposition to any devolution in Ireland, extended this crisis to the outbreak of war. Unionist reaction swept the United Kingdom, but, following Sir Edward Carson's elevation to the leadership of Irish unionism in 1910, it was in Ulster that most of the resistance took place. The Ulster Unionist Council (UUC) was to the fore, the key organization being the revived unionist clubs. These saw the industrial expulsions of 1912, when loyalist militants drove catholics and protestant labour activists out of the shipyards. This spontaneous outbreak was a problem for the unionist leadership, who were trying to orchestrate a disciplined rebellion. The labour movement failed to prevent the intrusion of political controversy into the workplace, and Irish nationalists saw the split in the Belfast working class as simply the persecution of catholics which required a strong stand by the British government. Sectarianism was more a part of the politics of the working class than was socialism. An Ulster Volunteer Force (UVF) was set up in 1913 to defend a planned provisional government, but the British government had from the first considered a line of retreat – the exclusion of several northern counties. The unionist mobilizations had an effect on the governing class in the second half of 1913. The Irish party accepted the idea of partition in March 1914, but negotiations broke down in the summer. The high politics of the third home rule bill was related to events on the streets of Belfast, the industrial expulsions representing a climax in sectarianism little appreciated in accounts of the Ulster crisis.

It was on 30 November 1909 that the House of Lords rejected by 350 votes to 75 the so-called people's budget, designed to pay for the old-age pensions enacted the previous year, but also for the building up of the Royal Navy. Most attention focused on the provisions for the redistribution of wealth – supertaxes, death duties and especially land taxes. The Irish party was not enamoured of Lloyd George, given that his budget penalized brewers, distillers and publicans, and that he envisaged a welfare state. Redmond did not want a future Irish government encumbered with extensive financial commitments, and the drink trade was influential in the party. But he was committed to the liberal alliance, as Irish support for the government was described. This had delivered the supposedly secular National University of Ireland in 1908, based on existing colleges in Dublin, Cork and Galway, but also the Queen's University of Belfast. Educational partition anticipated the constitutional solution reached later. When Asquith called an election on the Lords' veto, he needed Redmond's support. The Irish leader saw the upper house as a block on home rule, and extracted a price for encouraging the Irish in Britain to vote liberal. It was on 10 December 1909 in the Albert Hall that the prime minister promised to 'set up in Ireland a system of full self-government in regard to purely Irish affairs'.[1]

Asquith lost his overall majority at the beginning of 1910, and needed Irish and labour support to prevail over the conservative opposition. Redmond and William O'Brien, who had openly opposed the budget, secured 81 of the Irish seats, leaving 22 to the unionists mainly in Ulster. Conservatives saw off the labour and independent candidates in Belfast, Devlin alone standing for the national cause in the new parliament against three unionist MPs. If the country as a whole was behind the nationalists, Belfast and the surrounding counties favoured the maintenance of the union. Redmond and Asquith renewed the liberal alliance, each ironically going back on his earlier position. The former had argued in 1894–5 that the nationalists had to win support in Britain by conciliating unionists, while the latter warned in 1901 about a liberal government's becoming dependent upon the Irish party. The threat of the loss of office effectively concentrated the prime minister's mind, and the liberals set about tackling the House of Lords, having reaffirmed Gladstonian home rule.

Irish and labour support was forthcoming for Asquith, and the budget passed both houses in late April 1910. Redmond had threatened to vote against the budget, unless the government promised to pack the upper house with new peers to vote down the power of the Lords. The parliament bill, introduced on 14 April, provided for the abolition of their veto on money bills, and, in the case of other measures passed by the Commons, their delay for two years only. A controversial bill could be enacted after passage in three successive sessions, though parliaments were shortened from seven to five years. An elected second chamber was envisaged, but the conservatives denied that the government had a mandate for constitutional reform. The death of Edward VII in early May was followed by a constitutional conference on 17 June, but the new king, George V, was politically inexperienced. Lloyd George privately suggested in August a coalition government of statesmen, to solve this problem and other major questions without party warfare. The constitutional conference broke down in the autumn, largely on the question of Ireland, and Asquith called a second election. The king secretly promised him on 16 November that, if the liberals were returned, he would create enough pro-government peers to overwhelm the Lords. The conservatives came to consider this an underhand manoeuvre. In the second general election of 1910, in December, the government was returned with the same number of supporters as the opposition. The 42 labour, and 83 Irish nationalists (10 led by William O'Brien), continued to hold the balance of power. The number of Irish unionists dropped to 20, but there were 17 in Ulster to 16 nationalists. Belfast again had 1 nationalist to 3 unionists. (The provincial balance was reversed in a 1913 by-election in Londonderry, when a local protestant liberal was elected without declaring for home rule.)

The regional minority in Ireland opposed to home rule was firmly integrated, in 1911, into the parliamentary defence of the House of Lords. The parliament bill passed the Commons on 15 May, and was sent to the Lords. George V was well received in Ireland in early July, before visiting Wales and Scotland. Asquith privately advised him to create new peers, but the king refused at this stage. Most conservative peers followed their leader, Lord Lansdowne, in wanting to give up resistance, but a minority, led by Lords Halsbury, Selborne and Milner, declared itself ready 'to die in the last ditch'.[2] They had the support in the Commons of Lord Hugh Cecil, George Wyndham, Sir Edward Carson and F.E. Smith. It was only when the king made clear his intention to create new peers that the Lords voted, by a majority of 17, on 10 August, to accept the parliament bill. The way was now clear for home rule.

The government introduced its bill on 11 April 1912 (this being associated, for tactical reasons, with a Welsh disestablishment bill). It was greeted in Ireland with nationalist jubilation and unionist wailing, the division in Belfast being clearly reflected in the city's newspapers. The *Irish News* hailed the dawn of a new era, while the protestant papers carried casualty reports of passengers, crew and workers from the *Titanic*. Stormy parliamentary sessions were promised for 1912 and 1913, in both houses, the home rule bill being expected to pass the Commons finally in 1914. The conservatives, under a new leader, Andrew Bonar Law, whose father had come from Ulster, had until then to force the government to back down.

The key figure was Sir Edward Carson, who had been born in Dublin in 1854, and called to the Irish bar in 1877, when he was a liberal in politics. He became a liberal unionist in 1886, and prosecuted for the crown during the land agitation of 1889–91. The chief secretary, A.J. Balfour, secured him the Irish solicitor generalship in 1892, when he became one of the two unionist MPs for Trinity College. He continued to hold this university seat until after the European war, and was called to the bar in London. Carson was a member of the protestant ascendancy in Ireland, and a strong defender of the union. British liberals became his enemy, but, when the conservatives returned to office in 1895, he was not invited to join the government, being opposed to land reform in Ireland. He became estranged temporarily from Balfour, but was made solicitor general, and knighted, following the general election of 1900. Carson remained a law officer until 1905, serving Balfour when the latter was prime minister. He was then forced on to the opposition front bench to observe the doings of the liberal government.

Irish unionists were prominent, under Carson from 1910, in the parliamentary defence of the House of Lords. They and their British colleagues wanted to maintain this bulwark against home rule, believing that any weakening of the union was tantamount to undermining the constitution. They accepted the authority of the House of Commons, given the doctrine of the electoral mandate, but they also affirmed the role of the sovereign, and believed that the Lords was a restraining force on an ambitious government. They saw the Lords as forcing a general election on a controversial issue. Unionists differed in their interest in Ireland. British conservatives were concerned about the union, seeing this as integral to the constitution, and any reform a threat to the empire. They were imperialists, believing in Britain ruling the waves. Their Irish allies also wanted to keep Ireland within the union, but they held seats mainly in Ulster. Carson, a southern unionist, who had been resident in London since 1892, and led mainly Ulster unionists, embodied the differences. All unionists loathed the liberals, but there were three strands to their reaction to the government: those, initially northerners, concerned to defend Ulster against the threat of Irish nationalism; others, mainly the Anglo-Irish, seeking to use Ulster to maintain the protestant ascendancy throughout Ireland; and, finally, those in Britain, who sought to use Ulster and Ireland as a whole to maintain the empire, and see off the liberal government. Unionism as a whole was reactionary in British politics, though protestant Ulster had a democratic right to be suspicious of a Dublin parliament. In so far as Ulster accepted the leadership of Carson, the alliance with southern and British unionists contributed to sectarian irresolution in Ireland. Ulster unionists denied the democratic right of Irish nationalists to have a home rule parliament. But the support of the latter for the budget, and their opposition to the Lords, had more to do with the exigencies of parliamentary politics than with a commitment to radicalism.

Carson spoke on Saturday, 23 September 1911, at Craigavon outside Belfast, the home of the unionist MP for East Down, Capt. James Craig. The powers of the Lords had been curtailed, and this was the first in a series of semi-regal visits by Carson to the province. A crowd of 50,000 assembled to hear him speak (the police estimating that 18,000 marched from the City Hall, while 300,000 lined the route). Carson assumed a commanding position on the UUC, its president being the Duke of Abercorn, who was to be succeeded in 1913 by Lord Londonderry. 'I now enter into a compact with you', Carson said at Craigavon, 'and every one of you, and with the help of God, you and I joined together ... will yet defeat the most nefarious conspiracy that has ever been hatched against a free people.' This 'conspiracy' was the liberals' plan to introduce home rule, as a result of Redmond's powerful parliamentary position. In the next three years Carson divided Ireland, and threatened civil war in Britain, retaining the support of the parliamentary opposition. He came increasingly to be the leader of Ulster regionalism, while speaking in the name of Ireland, but the movement across the United Kingdom remained remarkably coherent. 'We must be prepared', he announced at Craigavon, 'the morning Home Rule passes, ourselves to become responsible for the government of the Protestant Province of Ulster.'[3] A commission of five, headed by James Craig, was appointed the following Monday to frame a constitution for rebellion. There was a gesture towards the loyalists of the other three provinces, but nothing more.

Unionist clubs had been formed in 1893 by Lord Templetown, but the provincial organization was suspended two years later. The intention was to have one club in each polling district, recruiting active unionists on a local basis. Towards the end of 1910 the UUC asked Templetown to revive his organization. The UUC then comprised representatives of conservative associations, electoral bodies, and the orange order, still a mass organization. The order had taken the initiative in 1910 of compiling a register of members with military skills, and the Craigavon demonstration was organized jointly with the new unionist clubs. Templetown's organization became more important. It had 55,596 members in 297 clubs by November 1912, Belfast accounting for 15,665 in 26 clubs (at a time when the orange order in the city numbered at least 18,000). The following May there were 16,628 members in 25 Belfast clubs, and 61,454 Ulster members in 315 clubs. They had taken an early interest in military drilling, and there were even sporadic attempts to arm members. The police noted that 'in nearly every household in Ulster there was a firearm of some description, either shot-gun or converted rifle, while in Belfast and the large towns revolvers were in the possession of the working classes to a very considerable extent'.[4] But these were not the weapons of a military force, and the leaders of the unionist clubs were faced with the problem of controlling popular enthusiasm.

Even while the home rule bill was being drafted, government ministers were attentive to Ulster. Churchill, as first lord of the admirality, and Lloyd George became early advocates of excluding the northern counties. They wanted to get on with other political business, though both were ready to use force in Ulster. Whatever the liberal commitment to the memory of Gladstone, the crucial role was played by John Redmond. When 'special treatment ... for the Ulster counties' was envisaged in the cabinet as early as 6 February 1912, the Irish leader was duly informed. It was agreed to proceed with the home rule bill, while 'careful and confidential inquiry [was] to be made as to the real extent and character of the Ulster resistance'.[5] Two days later Churchill spoke in favour of the government's proposals in Belfast. He had probably overestimated the strength of the Ulster Liberal Association, but advised discretion on the question of the Ulster Hall booking. The first lord retreated, with Redmond, Devlin and Pirrie, the chairman, to a marquee specially erected in Celtic Park near the Falls Road. Also present on the platform were the Revd James Armour, a presbyterian minister from Ballymoney, and Capt. Jack White from Ballymena, son of Gen. Sir George White of Ladysmith fame. Churchill was quickly spirited back to Britain, police and troops having to deal with a major threat to public order in Belfast. His feelings for Ulster unionists were not strengthened by this episode. On Easter Tuesday, 9 April, they held a huge demonstration at Balmoral, on the outskirts of Belfast. One hundred thousand Ulstermen marched past platforms adorned by 70 conservative MPs from Britain, the marchers having been mobilized by the orange order, but mainly the unionist clubs. 'Once again you hold the pass', said Bonar Law, 'the pass for the empire ... The Government have erected by their Parliament Act a boom against you to shut you off from the help of the British people. You will burst that boom.'[6]

The home rule bill was introduced in the Commons two days later. 'It was impossible', Asquith told Carson, 'to concede the demand of a small minority to veto the verdict of the Irish Nation.'[7] In June, Agar-Robartes, a Cornish Liberal MP, suggested in committee stage the exclusion of four counties – Antrim, Down, Armagh and Londonderry. The government, and Redmond, opposed any division of Ireland. Carson also wanted Fermanagh and Tyrone excluded, but the unionists were forced to support the amendment for fear of being seen to be opposed to any solution. Asquith reaffirmed the government's policy on 20 July at a nationalist meeting in Dublin, only to have the unionists show the strength of their opposition a week later at Blenheim Palace. 'I can imagine', Bonar Law told a crowd of 15,000, 'no length of resistance to which Ulster will go, which I shall not be ready to support and in which they will not be supported by an overwhelming majority of the British people.'[8]

Carson signed the Ulster covenant, pledging 'to refuse to recognise [the] authority ... [of] a Home Rule Parliament in Ireland',[9] at the City Hall on Saturday, 28 September. This piece of political theatre had to be restaged to be properly recorded by cameras for the early cinema! As many as 218,206 Ulstermen signed the covenant, and 228,991 Ulsterwomen signed a declaration of association, a phenomenal demonstration of Carson's following. But it was still a minority in Ireland, whatever its support in Britain. Unionist ideologues placed considerable weight on the parliament act, arguing that, with the change and, indeed, suspension of the constitution, the royal prerogative now included the right to refuse assent to home rule on the grounds that it was bad for the country. Bonar Law had suggested to George V that he should dismiss the liberal government, and ask the opposition to form an administration which would hold a general election. The conservative leader told the king he would antagonize half his people, whether he supported Asquith or vetoed home rule. He hoped the king would lean on the prime minister at an early stage, to avoid having to confront such a dilemma. But Bonar Law also suggested, through Churchill, secret talks with the prime minister.

It was during the first passage of the home rule bill through the Commons that Belfast was subjected to industrial expulsions in July 1912. They were an indication of the strength of popular protestant power, but an unintended consequence of the unionist mobilizations.

On Saturday, 29 June, 500 children from the Whitehouse presbyterian Sunday school left Belfast by train, under the supervision of adults including the Revd Mr Barron. The party enjoyed a day out, in a field lent by the local bleachworks, at Castledawson, in Co. Londonderry. That evening the group marched back through the village, to the local railway station. Headed by a flute band, the children carried 'a large number of texts mounted on poles, one Union Jack and the school banner'. Coming in the opposite direction were four divisions of the catholic Ancient Order of Hibernians (AOH), about 200 men, 'all fully grown ... apparently of the labouring type'. They were returning from a rally in the nearby town of Maghera. 'A Welshman' from Belfast later reported seeing an AOH banner bearing 'the likeness of the Pope', and claimed that some of the AOH marchers 'were under the influence of drink ... more like wild beasts than men'. As the two parties passed, one of the Hibernians grabbed the Union Jack. This – according to unionist accounts – was the signal for an attack on the children and their guardians. Women were stabbed 'promiscuously with the [Hibernians'] pikes', a banner holder got a pike through his hand, 'many of the children's faces were cut', and flags and banners were torn. While the six local RIC rushed for their weapons, some protestant youths came to the defence of the Belfast children. After the firing of some shots, 'the cowardly [AOH] ruffians fled precipitately'. The next morning in Whitehouse the presbyterian minister told his congregation that he had 'never seen anything of so savage a character right through the [Boer War] campaign – it was a miracle no one was killed'. But he went on to ask the children's parents, and an attentive reporter from the *Northern Whig*, not to discuss the matter further. He feared 'local ill-feeling' between catholics and protestants.[10]

The incident was already public property, and was variously treated in the Belfast newspapers of Monday, 1 July. The *Irish News*, not surprisingly, made no reference to Castledawson, but it covered AOH rallies in Maghera and Clones. Two days before the Castledawson incident, on 27 June, the paper had carried a report on 'A Lisburn Outrage', when children from the local Sacred Heart convent had been attacked while on their way to Ardglass. It was the first such disturbance since the December 1910 election. 'Nationalist Outrage – Women and Children Stabbed' was the *Northern Whig*'s headline that Monday, with a full, emotive account of the attack, and the protestant children's ordeal. The *Belfast Newsletter* carried a shorter report on a 'Belfast Excursion', giving more prominence to an 'Outrage at Innisrush', where a local outing of Sunday school children had been fired upon. It had been a normal weekend in rural Ulster at a time of heightened political tension, the attacking of communal excursions being integral to the struggle for control of territory. The orange order and, to a much lesser extent, the AOH symbolized defensive and aggressive intentions by marching, both communities being alert to any movement of groups of people. There were more such incidents in the summer of 1912. The *Irish News* reported, on 9 July, that a group going to an Irish *feis* (or festival) had been fired upon in Co. Armagh. The *Northern Whig* found 'Another Nationalist Outrage' at Kilrea, for 15 July, and, on 26 August, the *Irish News* retaliated with a story of a protestant plot to prevent Hibernians from marching in Co. Antrim.

Yet *Castledawson*, despite the best efforts of the Revd Mr Barron, entered the lexicon of sectarian outrages identified by place-names. In this generally quiet Ulster village, protestant workers at the bleachgreen (where brown linen was turned white in the open) came out on strike, on 1 July, against a catholic, alleging he had been involved in the attack the previous Saturday. Whitehouse was a small community north of Belfast, and the *Northern Whig* was largely responsible for making Castledawson an issue in the city. It was a case of the messenger energetically broadcasting the message, and there was little direct connection between Whitehouse and what ensued in Belfast as a result of this coverage. Charles Craig, brother of James, and unionist MP for South Antrim, claimed later that one of the boys attacked at Castledawson worked at Workman, Clark, though he was unable to name him. A manager there stated that one of their riveters, by the name of Larmour, had two sisters on the outing. The city had seen the Balmoral demonstration on Easter Tuesday, and the unionist clubs and orange lodges were recruiting in protestant districts. There had been 'a general feeling of unrest at the beginning of the year', District Inspector Keaveney of the local RIC testified later, when 'they had to put police at the mills and factories to protect workers.'[11] John Flanagan, a protestant supporter of home rule, who was a plater's helper at Workman, Clark, claimed subsequently that the warning 'All Fenians Clear Out'[12] had been painted up before the Castledawson incident. Peter Ward, a catholic cabinet-maker, made a similar allegation about anti-catholic slogans in Harland and Wolff. But D.R. Campbell, as president of the trades council, stated that there had been 'nothing ... out of the ordinary'[13] happening in workplaces, except for one incident in a mill. Belfast was booming in 1912, and industry carried on despite the political crisis. The unionist leaders were preparing for Ulster Day on 28 September, when the covenant would be displayed to be signed.

They were taken by surprise on Tuesday, 2 July, when the industrial expulsions began. Trouble started at Workman, Clark's north yard (on the Co. Antrim side), spreading quickly to the nearby Milewater Wharf. And, in the afternoon, it spread to the firm's south yard, across the Lagan (on the Co. Down side). The following day, 3 July, a group from the north yard arrived at Harland and Wolff, and expulsions started there. This was the first wave. There was a second wave, in the fourth week of July, when the expelled attempted to return after the shipyard holidays, on the 23rd and 26th. By then the catholic community, and its representatives, were thoroughly convinced they were the victims of a unionist plot, hatched by the political leadership and carried out by the clubs. In fact the expulsions were a response to Castledawson, carried out by workers who judged that their employer, Sir George Clark of the wee yard, would not interfere in this spontaneous action. Having given up being the MP for North Belfast, Clark was one of the most militant leaders of the unionist mobilizations. He later chaired the committee responsible for gun-running, and even landed arms at his yard. The expulsions had little or nothing to do directly with the unionist clubs, but the intrusion of unionist politics awakened sectarianism in the workplace. It was no accident that the expelling began where it did.

The trouble started with 'a party of young men' in the north yard, who attacked catholics, possibly Hibernians, in the plumbers' and joiners' shops. The offenders were described by the *Irish News* as 'drillers' and 'heater-boys – many of the latter being men of mature years'.[14] The *Belfast Evening Telegraph* referred to 'a large number of young fellows',[15] youth and low status being conflated in the idea of boy. Catholic leaders initially sought to play down the first wave of expulsions, attributing them to a minority in the shipyards. They did not want the home rule case jeopardized, the unionists claiming a Dublin parliament would lead to such trouble. 'The great body of the higher grade workmen on the [Queen's] island', the *Irish News* noted on 5 July, 'are quite out of sympathy with this class of ruffianism [and] leading hands ... were inclined in the interests of peace to get their Catholic workers out of the place as quietly as possible.' By 9 July the paper was more ready to condemn the protestant masses, their 'religious and political passions [having been] aroused [by the] recently established ... Unionist Clubs'. The unionist press was also involved in constructing interpretations. The *Northern Whig* attributed the second wave of expulsions to 'Disorderly Rivet Boys',[16] and 200 to 300 'irresponsible youths'.[17] 'The vast majority of artisans have no sympathy with the continuance of the present state of affairs', claimed the *Belfast Evening Telegraph* on 29 July. 'It is for them to try and put a stop to it.' The expulsions were as much an embarrassment to protestants, damaging the unionist cause. The prepetrators in both shipyards were mainly young, unskilled labourers and assistants, consistent with a historical pattern of shipyard behaviour.

The expulsions from the shipyards on 2 and 3 July inspired action elsewhere. Thirty to 40 workers were driven out of the Sirocco engineering works on 5 July. Threatening letters with 'the skull and crossbones'[18] were sent to some spinners in the Linfield mill, and boiling tea was thrown at workers considered undesirable on 4 and 6 July. Some workers left the shipyards when they saw trouble, many stayed at home, and yet others left the city for work elsewhere. In the first week of July about 2,000 were expelled. A further 1,000 may have been involved in the second phase in the fourth week of July. Altogether – 3,000. Just over 600 came from Workman, Clark, over 2,000 from Harland and Wolff, and the rest from Sirocco and a number of other works. Vacancy figures held by the head timekeeper at Harland and Wolff rose from 496 on 9 July, to a peak of 1,787 on 2 August, falling back to 1,213 a week later. Workers claiming relief reached a peak on 9 August with 1,544, falling back to 727 on 30 August, and 200 on 25 December. Seemingly, some expelled workers were never taken back at Workman, Clark's. A proportion found other work in Belfast, and across the channel, but the majority seem to have slowly drifted back, as and when circumstances allowed. 'The bitter feeling', it was observed early the following year, 'still existed in Workman, Clark's, in the linen mills, in Davidson's [Sirocco] works, and in many other places.'[19]

Catholics, in the main, were victims of the industrial expulsions. Peter Ward, the cabinet-maker at Harland and Wolff, claimed that all

70 in his trade were expelled. At the Sirocco works, according to Davidson, only half the catholics were intimidated out. It is clear that the expellers identified catholics as Fenians, and associated them with the home rule threat. But they also turned on protestants, being paradoxically less sectarian than earlier generations of pogromists. It was not 'a question of religion solely',[20] said David McRandall, who became a leader of the expelled workers. All who were not actively behind the unionist mobilizations were considered suspect. These included English and Scottish workers, trade-union and labour men and all protestant dissidents of the Edwardian years, such as liberals and independent orangemen. Non-catholics may have numbered 400 in the first wave, and 200 in the second – 600 workers, or 20 per cent of the total expelled. The majority of protestant workers kept their heads down, this being a conflict between easily identifiable non-unionists and unorganized Carsonite shock troops.

The catechism of loyalism was described as being: '1st Are you a Papist? / 2nd Are you a Liberal? / 3rd Are you a Socialist? / 4th Are you an Independent Orangeman?'[21] This was quoted by W.H. Davey, a liberal supporter of home rule in Belfast, in a letter to the *Manchester Guardian*. He was one of the first to point out that the expulsions were not simply a form of sectarian polarization. 'However paradoxical it may seem', he told British liberals, 'all progressive men have no cause to be disheartened by the present position in Belfast. The line of demarcation is no longer what it was ... This, indeed, is proof of a changed Ulster.'[22] The realignment was not an active cross-community alliance pursuing a common goal, but a passive gathering of victims of loyalist direct action, who were treated as honorary catholics by Irish nationalists. Catholics denied Castledawson, as unionists came increasingly to use this provocation as a justification for the expulsions.

The *Irish News* initially attributed sectarianism in the workplace to 'the political mountebanks whose incendiary incitements to outrage and "civil war"' appeared daily, but took comfort in the fact that the 'spasmodic outbursts [were] begotten of a consciousness of defeat'.[23] When, on the evening of 4 July, the Queen's Island unionist club marched to the City Hall, the paper sarcastically headlined a story, 'Unionist Clubs begin "Civil War"'.[24] This was greatly to underestimate the opposition to home rule, and offer a false theory to the expelled workers. If the expulsions were organized by the unionist clubs, this would have been a sign of a greater determination than Irish nationalists conceded. The Queen's Island club may have been trying to control the movement in the shipyard by rushing to put itself at the head, though it was not entirely successful. Windows were broken at the *Irish News* and St Patrick's Church, and 'the Italian ice-cream saloons [were], as usual, prominent points of attack.'[25] (When the club went on a route march in Belmont and the Hollywood hills, on 19 August, there were 'special police', appointed by the club, to 'keep a watchful eye on irresponsible juveniles who follow the route-marches'.[26]) Also on 4 July, in parliament, Devlin accused Clark of having instigated the expulsions, a charge he repeated on 1 August. The member for West Belfast claimed to be in possession of a circular sent to all unionist clubs, asking them to secure the dismissal of catholics. This is not inconceivable, but it does not incriminate Clark. When the Cliftonville unionist club submitted a resolution the following February, asking 'Protestant employers' to dismiss, as occasion offers, 'their home rule employees',[27] the council of the organization succeeded in having the motion withdrawn from the agenda for the annual meeting. The expulsions were a great embarrassment to the unionist leaders in the summer of 1912. Clark denied all involvement, and was, in any case, on holiday in Switzerland.

But he had been responsible for raising the political temperature, by using – particularly – the north yard for drilling purposes. Sir George Clark and his manager, John Campbell, denied later the existence of a unionist club within the yard, though they conceded there had been drilling for the Balmoral demonstration. Whether the club was particular to the yard, or, more likely, to a residential area, Clark's son was in charge. John Flanagan claimed later that it had started in February, that schedules for each occupation were posted at the time office, and that 'many of the men used to clear out as quickly as possible because they thought it was silly-looking, although they were unionists.'[28] Not all supporters of the union were active Carsonites. Accounts of the number vary, but there is a contemporary report, from March, of 700 workers being drilled at Spencer Basin by eight instructors. The north yard employed some 2,000 to 3,000. The 700 respectable workers drilling were the least likely to engage in expelling or even intimidation. But their very presence was an incentive to other workers to defend Ulster in their own immediate way. The unionist clubs were conceived, partly, to prevent direct sectarian action, by providing an alternative focus, and some employers saw the clubs as instruments for disciplining their workers. Clark did not foment the expulsions, and the management may have tried to stop them. But he, as an employer, consciously embarked upon a dangerous political strategy of resistance to home rule. Most importantly, Workman, Clark acquiesced in the introduction of sectarian direct action. Promises seem to have been made by a manager, on 4 July, that no more catholics would be taken on. This was to accept a protestant political economy, for reasons of public order in the workplace, when catholics may, or may not, have been required to work in the shipyard. There was probably a labour shortage generally. Clark did not have to be quite so impotent, as an employer of labour and leading political figure. The drilling was not bluff, and he admitted later to a readiness to fight even the forces of the crown, if they were used to impose a Dublin parliament.

The expulsions were perceived outside the catholic ghetto as spontaneous. Some unionists were worried that the workplace movement would affect the Twelfth. The orange order quickly condemned the expulsions, as did the UUC. On Saturday, 6 July, Harland and Wolff had posted notices in the big yard, threatening closure if the expelled were not allowed to return. Workman, Clark did not do this. It was implied, by the big yard, that the majority of protestant workers would bring the expellers under control. A letter from Carson to Colonel Wallace, leader of the Belfast orangemen, dated 11 July and published that evening in the *Belfast Evening Telegraph*, urged 'self-control and discipline and the preservation of the peace'. The celebrations passed off without incident, though protestants attacked North Queen Street on 13 July. The annual closure of the shipyards for a week, it was believed, would allow anger about Castledawson to dissipate. Significance was attached to the resumption of work on Monday, 22 July, when, it was hoped, the expelled could return peacefully. Only towards the end of the month did Dublin Castle come to view the industrial expulsions as a major public-order matter.

The expelled workers, to say nothing of catholic leaders, were not so sanguine. A meeting of 'Catholic clergy and laymen' was held in St Mary's Hall on Sunday, 7 July, the bishop of Down and Connor, Dr Tohill, presiding. The meeting protested against the lack of protection given 'Catholic workmen and property', and called for the use of police and the military. This was addressed to the lord lieutenant, Birrell as chief secretary, and Devlin, the *Northern Whig* mischievously noting, 'Roman Catholics Want Troops'.[29] A vigilance committee was established by supporters of the bishop, and, later, a separate women's committee was formed to look after the unknown number of women expelled. This was catholic power such as it was. The following morning the *Irish News* asked catholic workers to 'assert their right to work and live in their own city and country'. Ireland may have been catholic but Belfast was not, and discretion proved the better part of valour. The expelled workers met that day, also in St Mary's Hall. While the *Irish News* was able to detect 400 protestants, in a gathering of 2,000, this 20 per cent had already been absorbed in a catholic consciousness.

The expelled workers' committee formed that Monday, and, representing a wide range of trades, addressed itself to 'the good sense of the right-minded public',[30] to the employers, and to the trade-union executives. This was a very different strategy from the one suggested the previous evening. The expelled workers appointed a deputation, comprising D.R. Campbell of the trades council; Daniel McRandall, the only catholic and nationalist; John Flanagan, who was a lay official in the NAUL; and a third protestant. Campbell was treasurer of the ITUC, as well as president of the trades council. The deputation went to London, where, accompanied by two MPs, they saw Redmond, and then Birrell. Both played down the gravity of the expulsions. The deputation reported back to the next meeting of expelled workers on Monday, 15 July. The committee stated that Workman, Clark had not responded to their appeal for 'fair treatment',[31] but it was agreed to attempt a collective return to work when the shipyards reopened.

Catholic attention then shifted to Asquith's visit to Dublin, between 18 and 20 July, the first by a British prime minister. The prime minister and his liberal colleagues were then attracting the attention of militant female suffragists. Redmond had also experienced demands for full adult suffrage, as the would-be leader of a future Irish parliament. On the morning of Friday, 19 July, four women attacked a carriage bearing the two men. One, Mary Leigh, threw a hatchet, missing the prime minister, but slightly injuring Redmond. The fact that one of the four came from Belfast greatly distressed the *Irish News*.

The expelled workers met for a third time on Monday, 22 July, and it was agreed to return to Harland and Wolff the following day, and to Workman, Clark on the Friday. The management of the big yard had seemingly promised to address the 'head foreman and all the principal journeymen and apprentices'[32] in each department, instructing them to keep order. The meeting also passed a vote of thanks to the vigilance committee, St Mary's Hall, the *Irish News* and Devlin. The last-named had probably been in touch with Dublin Castle. The next morning the Co. Down side of the river was 'practically "held" by a large armed force, consisting of the military, RIC and harbour police'. The last-named had been moved from the Co. Antrim side on 5 July, to Queen's Road, separating Harland and Wolff from Sir George Clark's south yard. As for the RIC, the Belfast police, according to the commissioner, were unwelcome on Queen's Island, 'even in ordinary times'.[33] This was for historical reasons, dating back to 1886, when shipyard workers perceived catholic RIC officers as defending the home rule interest at the behest of liberal ministers. The army was acceptable, on what was its first appearance during the expulsions. At breakfast time, when discipline was relaxed, 2,000 workers reportedly surged out of both yards, to attack those returning. The army was later withdrawn, and the police were attacked at dinner time. With the authorities backing off, the expelled workers abandoned the attempt to return to work. Three suspected catholics had been expelled from Workman, Clark's north yard. One man, who was chased all the way to Royal Avenue, where he jumped on a tram, was later revealed to be a member of a unionist club! Further workers were expelled later in the week, the shipyard holidays having done nothing to soothe loyalist anger. Again, young men from Workman, Clark stimulated expulsions, at meal times, in Harland and Wolff.

'Decisive Action Imperative', the *Irish News* thundered on 25 July. It called for 'instant repression', criticized the police for 'lack of courage' and rejected the idea of a fund as 'acquiescence'. The following afternoon the expelled workers, meeting in St Mary's Hall, decided to set up a campaign fund. They also called for the replacement of the police commissioner, copies of the resolution being sent to the lord lieutenant, Birrell, Devlin and Ramsay MacDonald as labour leader. This stimulated the catholic vigilance committee, as it was now being called. When it met on Sunday, 28 July, supporters of the bishop established a relief fund. This was in keeping with the spirit of the St Vincent de Paul Society, which was the basis of the committee. Two catholic priests and two justices of the peace were appointed trustees of the fund, which was administered by the committee. All nationalist papers were requested to publish an appeal from the 'public meeting of Catholics'. 'Catholics of Ireland [were asked] to come to the aid of [their] persecuted brethren.' 'Nearly 3,000 Catholic working men' had been expelled, though reference was made in the small print to some hundreds of protestants 'who dar[ed] to have aspirations in harmony with those of the majority of their fellow countrymen'.[34] There is no evidence that the expelled protestants were nationalists, but this was the same sectarian logic used by the expellers. Father McCotter of St Joseph's drafted the appeal. When asked later why he sent a non-political appeal to nationalist papers only, he replied: 'We looked upon the Nationalist papers as synonymous with Catholic papers.'[35]

The *Irish News* described the appeal as on behalf of 'the Wounded Soldiers of the Home Rule Struggle'.[36] The bishop contributed £50, and so did Devlin. The sum of £500 came from the home rule fund of the Irish party, and £400 in personal subscriptions from members. The rest came in small sums, mainly from parochial collections. Hibernians in Bruree, Co. Cork, came to the aid of 'the faithful Nationalists of Belfast in their glorious fight for God and Country'.[37] A section of the All-for-Ireland League declined to support the appeal, as it was a 'matter between two secret societies'. This and the league's policy of conciliation the *Irish News* considered to be the 'surrender [of] a winning flag and [the] substitut[ion of] a white one, so that we might have quarter'.[38] The UIL in Belfast, fearing the re-emergence of a bishop's party, requested two seats on the vigilance committee. This the chairman, Father McCashin from St Malachy's, refused. He believed Devlin's organization was mainly concerned that catholic workers should continue to pay rent, for fear of losing their registration in West Belfast. There was contact between the vigilance committee and the UIL's registration agent. (On 3 August a columnist on the *Belfast Evening Telegraph* had alleged that the vigilance committee's relief fund was not for the distressed, but to advance the home rule cause. The fund certainly became dressed up in political colours, but its purpose was genuinely economic. Three of the four trustees took out libel suits of £1,000 each against the paper. There were two indecisive trials in Dublin, one in January 1913, and the other in April/May. Fifty-five witnesses gave evidence, many a second time, the *Irish News*'s extensive coverage of both constituting an excellent source on the 1912 expulsions.)

The relief fund was established only after many of the expelled had been out for nearly four weeks. All were eligible to apply, and D.R. Campbell subsequently described it as necessary. The expelled workers' committee cooperated with the vigilance committee. Eventually £4,764 was disbursed. A payment was made for the week ending 27 July, to 428 workers. The following Saturday 1,366 claimed, and the number declined from 1,031 on 16 August, through the autumn and into the winter. Most of the 1,700 from Harland and Wolff were trade unionists, according to Patrick Flood, who chaired the expelled workers' committee. He was a joiner, and claimed that 175, out of the 600 to 800 ASCJ members, received relief. The union looked after the rest. Not all trade unionists could get benefits, since they were customarily paid only during a recession. A labour MP claimed, in parliament, that the big national unions spent a great deal on their members in Belfast. Not every skilled worker was a trade unionist, and some unskilled workers were in general unions. But most of those requiring relief were from the ranks of labourers, and probably from Workman, Clark's. 'While the trade unionists were bad enough [off]', one had said at the meeting of expelled workers on 15 July, 'he maintained that the labourers, who were the worst off of all, should have their case attended to.'[39] Most likely it was unskilled catholics from the wee yard who were dependent the longest upon the vigilance committee.

These catholics had no direct claim on the trade-union movement. But the denial of the right to work, because of the incursion of sectarian politics into the workplace, cut at the foundation of trade unionism. D.R. Campbell was an important adviser to the expelled workers' committee, but he seems to have been unable to bring it under the aegis of the trades council. A special meeting was convened on 1 August to consider the 'shipyard troubles'. 'It was a deplorable thing', Campbell told delegates, 'that many persons had allowed their political feelings to run away with their better judgement and resorted to violence. He hoped that before long a better feeling would prevail among the workers in spite of their religious or political opinions.' Few of the delegates would have attempted to justify the expulsions, but they found themselves impotent as trade unionists in the face of political division – and even violence. A report was sent to the labour party. The trades council also passed a motion regretting that an executive member, O'Connor, had fled to Southampton, 'owing to his being a marked person in the Queen's Island shipyard'.[40] The executive of the council instructed Campbell and its secretary, John Murphy, to act as they 'thought best, according to the exigencies, as they would arise'.[41] This seems to have amounted to securing police protection for returning workers, and generally calming feelings. When Murphy was preparing his annual report in April 1913, the council 'eventually ... decided that it was unexpedient to revive controversy ... by any reference in the report'.[42]

With this response in Belfast, little was to be expected from the national trade-union and labour leaders. Jim Middleton, assistant secretary of the labour party, replied to a letter, dated 9 August, from the flax-dressers. He would have met William Walker at executive meetings, and seems to have relied upon him for information about Belfast. They shared a culture of historical optimism. Middleton thought that trade unionism would have stamped out 'this deplorable sectionalism [*sic*]'. 'One was justified', he wrote, 'in believing that at this time of day sectarian bitterness had been dispelled by the progress of ordinary education.'[43] 'Very few of the unions', Campbell told the trades council on 21 September, 'had taken any action regarding the assaults on shipyard workers.'[44] This was admitted later by the Federation of Engineering and Ship-building Trades (FEST), a small but powerful bureaucracy built up to coordinate trade-union action in this leading industry.

It was the most appropriate body to intervene with the employers. The federation was particularly struck by the fact that, while some of its affiliates' members had been expelled, and others might have been doing the expelling, the great mass of members, to say nothing of non-trade unionists, were probably not too inclined to have the unions come down on the side of those identified with the home rule cause. 'Perhaps the most remarkable feature of the disturbances', read a report, 'was that the protection of "marked" workmen by their shop mates was not more general.'[45] The local district committee of FEST, comprising local activists and officials, was more concerned about this absence of trade-union solidarity. 'Every member of the District Committee repudiated the lawlessness which had recently disgraced the shipbuilding yards and the town of Belfast, and almost every trade connected with this Federation sent deputations to their employers repudiating the terrorism which was being manifested.'[46] Patrick Flood dismissed the report on the expulsions, prepared by the executive committee of FEST. Its officials had talked only to workers still in employment, ignoring the expelled workers' committee. He also make a similar point about a trade-union delegation from Newcastle, which had, apparently, queried figures for the number of workers still without employment.

A condition for trade-union action may have been managerial opposition to sectarianism. Harland and Wolff had threatened, after the first wave of expulsions, to close their yard. The *Northern Whig*, albeit for political reasons, speculated about managerial prerogative. There should be, it opined, 'some further delegation and sharing of responsibility which would make every man having an industrial stake in the shipyards a special constable, zealous and active in the maintenance of order'.[47] The *Belfast Evening Telegraph*, ever ready to apologize for loyalist violence, called for 'special constables ... [to] protect those who were in danger of violence at the hands of the younger fry'.[48] But this strategy had not worked. When there was a second wave of expulsions, in the week after the summer holidays, the management had to assert its control over hiring and firing. The power plant at Harland and Wolff had been badly affected by the loss of key men, and the management predicted a progressive shutdown. Finally, on Saturday, 27 July, the big yard issued notices of closure for the following Tuesday. That day 500 men working on the SS *Darro* – informally renamed 'the Orange boat' – were laid off. 'This caused a great furore ... Strenuous agitation was immediately started through the trade societies.'[49] Deputations from the shipwrights, boilermakers and drillers approached the management, and this may have been the occasion on which members of the FEST repudiated terrorism. The workers' representatives promised to use their influence on the younger elements. Work resumed the following day. Harland and Wolff seem to have persisted with this managerial pressure. On 3 August the plumbers decided to ask that their members be restarted, on condition that they used their 'best endeavours to protect our Roman Catholic members who were employed in Messrs. Harland and Wolff'.[50]

The big yard was also cooperating with the authorities. On Sunday, 28 July, Commissioner Smith, and Deputy Inspector-General O'Connell, of the RIC, met Kempster, a manager at Harland and Wolff. O'Connell had been sent north to take charge of the police. They told Kempster the RIC assumed 'everything reasonable ... would be done to prevent further assaults within the yard.' He reiterated the policy of using leading workers to police the others, but it would 'take time'. O'Connell reported to Dougherty, undersecretary at Dublin Castle, the following day. There was 'persistent provocation on the one side, and natural and growing exasperation on the other'. He explained the unpopularity of the police, and the inadequacy of the three military pickets in Queen's Road. On Tuesday, 30 July, the day Harland and Wolff acted, Birrell told parliament that, since 2 July, there had been 80 assaults in the shipyards, most just outside the gates. 157 workers had been prosecuted. He was sending a third battalion to Belfast. This announcement followed considerable discussion within, and between, the police, army and executive. Count Gleichen, the military commander in Belfast, seems to have been prepared to respond only to a direct request from Smith. The army would then be acting in aid of the civil power. Smith had relayed his request up the RIC. It then went to Dougherty, to the Irish command, and finally back down to Gleichen in Belfast. The lord mayor was kept in ignorance of the request, the municipal authorities being reluctant to see troops used against loyalists. Though the army had camped in Ormeau Park in 1907, the corporation's parks committee voted not to allow this in 1912. The lord mayor reversed the decision, but Gleichen snubbed the municipal authorities, accommodating his new troops at Victoria Barracks.

The use of troops brought about a change. 'The situation is growing more peaceful',[51] Gleichen wrote to Dougherty on 31 July. Trouble ceased in early August. The army remained in full force in Queen's Road, some troops being withdrawn on 14 August. This had again caused a flurry of communications about local police–army relations. An element of farce had recently entered the story, when some workers were seen to beat up a man, and throw him in the water, attracting soldiers to the incident. The victim turned out to be a dummy! The *Northern Whig* gleefully observed that English radical papers, which had been contacted by the vigilance committee, would now run stories about protestant violence. The unionists continued to refer to Castledawson as a provocation, while acquiescing in the repression of loyalist direct action. Carson, who visited Ulster as little as possible, was indulging his hypochrondria at a German spa. On 21 August he wrote to James Craig from Bad Homburg with great feeling for the expellers: 'I am very distressed about the men who are being prosecuted for the rows in the shipyards. Do you think they or their families ought to be assisted in any way? You know how much I feel about others suffering when I don't, and they received great provocation.'[52] Craig's reply is unknown. The loyalist militants in the shipyards probably never knew how their leader felt, but it is likely that he was impressed with the nature of the Ulster revolt. This spontaneous action by a section of the protestant masses probably convinced Carson of the need for a military organization, the better to control their resistance.

Smith reported to the inspector-general on 29 August:

By the use of the military with the police, the town is saved the turmoil, dislocation of business, and damage to property, not to speak of the loss of life, consequent upon a serious riot ... The history of rioting in Belfast, the experience of my predecessors, and traditions handed down by those who successfully maintained the peace in times of excitement and trouble – all point to the necessity for the prompt use of military in sufficient force at the very inception, or perhaps before rioting occurs.'[53]

The inspector-general had written, on 15 August, to Smith's predecessors, going back as far as 1885. Former Commissioner Singleton (1889–96) referred to the use of 'older and more respected employees' to police workers inside the shipyards. Leathem (1901–6) stated he had always used the harbour police on the Co. Down side. 'The unpopularity of the RIC does not appear to have extended to [Workman, Clark's north yard] to the same extent'. Hill (1906–9) reported that, in 1907, he was able to use the RIC in the docks, but not near the shipyards. District Inspector Clayton, now in Ballinasloe, stated police would have to be 'armed' to go into the shipyards, which would be 'madness', since they would be 'cockshots for the workers on the various ships, gantries etc.'.[54]

The expelled workers helped the authorities. On 12 August Devlin had written to Peter Ward, secretary of their committee, stating he would forward a map to Dougherty to guide the army. Ward replied, on 14 August, complaining about the partial withdrawal of troops, and enclosing his own map of likely flashpoints on Queen's Island. The army was finally withdrawn from the area on 16 September, and there was a momentary resurgence of sectarian violence outside the shipyards. (Two days before, at Celtic Park, Celtic had played Linfield, a protestant team. Rival fans clashed during the game, and the police drove them from the field. Order was only restored when the protestants returned to their areas.) But the expulsions, as a breakdown in public order, were over. In regaining control, the police had thought deeply about working-class action. Industrial expulsions were an extension of sectarian rioting in the streets, and totally unrelated to industrial disputes. But the class struggle had not been totally stilled by intra–working-class hostility. On 20 August, as peace was being restored, 200 red-lead-ers from, probably, Harland and Wolff, met in the Artisans' Hall. They were threatening to strike, in order to secure a closed shop. One speaker even called for a general strike in the shipyards!

The presence of the army had allowed some workers to return, probably to Harland and Wolff. The relief figures halved from 1,544 on 9 August to 727 on 30 August. Patrick Flood claimed that 200 of the expelled joiners left the city to return to 'Cork and Dublin ... to Scotland, to Derry and to Liverpool'.[55] The sum of £64 was even provided from the relief fund to help with emigration. Six hundred platers and their helpers, in Workman, Clark's north yard, had struck on 31 July, when the three workers attempted to return. In September a deputation of expelled workers was told there might be a possibility of returning after Ulster Day on the 28th. Sir George Clark was being disingenuous. He seems to have advertised for a – presumably protestant –

foremen in the *Glasgow Herald*. Clark was not inclined to go against his employees' desire to work only with protestants. When one catholic attempted to return to the north yard in April 1913, there was again a downing of tools. A fitter in the engine works, Maguire, stated that only one catholic had been allowed back there, probably in the south yard. The expelled workers did not all return to work in the remaining months leading to the outbreak of war.

It was on 1 January 1913 that Carson unsuccessfully proposed an amendment, that the nine counties of Ulster should be excluded from home rule. The bill passed in the Commons on 16 January, only to fall in the Lords two weeks later. In the debate on the address at the beginning of the new session, on 12 March, the opposition called upon the government to proceed with the promised Lords' reform and hold a general election, before introducing the bill again. 'The bitterness engendered was such that, for the first time since the Reform Bills, members of the opposing parties refused to meet each other socially.'[56] The second circuit of the bill was much shorter, being introduced in the Commons in March, and rejected in July by the Lords.

The year 1913 also saw the establishment of the Ulster Volunteer Force, a retired general, Sir George Richardson, taking command in the summer. It recruited from the unionist clubs and oranges lodges, and was therefore an inter-class paramilitary force. The UVF was limited to 100,000 men who had signed the covenant, and the force numbered about 90,000 when recruitment ceased in February 1914, with ancillary units bringing it close to the total. This was before the force was extensively armed. The cabinet was informed, by the Irish attorney general, in August 1913, that the activities of the UVF were illegal, on the grounds that they represented attempts to intimidate the king and both houses of parliament, but ministers declined to act. The UVF was intended as a serious military organization, though it was, at all times, subordinate to the political strategy being pursued under the singular leadership of Sir Edward Carson. He, and many leading members of the local bourgeoisie were concerned, above all, with disciplining the protestant masses. 'Efforts were made in Belfast to enlist the hooligans', the RIC noted, 'as the leaders were anxious to acquire a disciplinary control over that class.'[57]

Belfast had one division of the UVF. On Saturday, 27 September 1913, it was reviewed at Balmoral, by Richardson, Carson and F.E. Smith, who earned the nickname 'galloper' for the services he rendered the general that day. The police estimated a parade of 11,000 men, with a crowd of 50,000 observing. The division had four regiments, one for each of the parliamentary constituencies. North, South and East Belfast each had four battalions. West Belfast had only two, but it made up for numbers in the enthusiasm of its first commander, Maj. F.H. Crawford. He was to pull off the UVF's daring gun-running exploit. A former commander of the Somerset Light Infantry, Col. G.H.H. Couchman, was brought in to take over the Belfast division, with his own staff within the UVF organization based at the Old Town Hall. This had become unionist headquarters when the municipality moved to the City Hall.

Three other English officers were appointed as regimental commanders, one replacing Crawford. East Belfast was commanded by Col. Spencer Chichester.

Towards the end of the year Belfast accounted for about 25,000 volunteers, organized in 20 battalions. (Police reports, as of 30 September 1913, gave 10,700 members in Belfast, out of a provincial force of 56,551. The figures for 30 November were 22,061 out of 76,757, and for 31 March 1914, 24,509 out of 84,540. On the latter date, East Belfast had 9,113, North Belfast 7,596, South Belfast 6,400, and West Belfast 1,400 members. They drilled, during Easter 1914, at, respectively, a private residence at Orange Field, Lord Shaftesbury's residence, Belfast Castle, a camp near Templepatrick, Co. Antrim, and a private residence at Glencairn and Fern Hill.) Belfast accounted for about a third of the UVF, making it the most important of the ten divisions. The unionist leaders decided, in January 1914, to raise a special service force (later called a section) of 3,000 in Belfast, each battalion supplying a company. Comprising mainly former soldiers and reservists, the force was to act as a vanguard. Belfast was considered the most militarily important area, given the possibility of government pre-emptive action, such as the securing of public buildings. The special service force was also a way of regulating the mass of volunteers who flocked into the Belfast division. The section attached to the West Belfast regiment, some 300 strong, recruited mainly from the Shankill Road area, was to be commanded by Capt. F.P. Crozier, who later commanded the auxiliary division of the RIC. It was chosen to protect the Old Town Hall the night the UVF secretly imported weapons from Germany. Perhaps a measure of unionist seriousness was the suspension, in January 1914, of the football season, to allow the members of the principal clubs to drill.

In the summer of 1913 the unionist mobilizations began to make an impact on the governing class. On 24 July Birrell told the king that, while the Ulster revolt would not amount to much, the solution was for the opposition to propose temporary exclusion, say, for ten years. There would then be a referendum on coming under the Dublin parliament. The king considered that the government was drifting, and taking him towards his Scylla and Charybdis. He summoned Asquith on 11 August, to suggest a settlement between government and opposition, based possibly on the idea of devolution to Scotland, Wales, southern Ireland and northern Ireland. George V showed he was being considerably influenced by the opposition, their arguments becoming his. The prime minister warned the king against dismissing the government, and conceded there might be an election after the enactment of home rule. To appease the unionists, Asquith argued, would be to enrage the nationalists. This was to anticipate the formation, in Dublin, on 25 November, of the Irish Volunteers, a body Redmond came to control the following June. Asquith dismissed the likelihood of civil war in Ulster, believing the catholic minority there would aid the British government. While the king, on 22 September, stated his opposition to the Ulster leaders' countenancing of illegality, he stressed that Bonar Law and his colleagues would accept home rule if the liberals were returned in a general election. Asquith had already conceded to George V the possibility of exclusion on 11 August, and this he reaffirmed in a letter of 1 October, as long as it was 'not inconsistent with the fundamental principle and purpose of the Bill'.[58]

There was here, at the very highest level, the makings of a settlement, but this was surrounded by the treacherous waters of a royal dissolution of parliament, and a revolt in Ulster or, alternatively, the rest of Ireland. On 9 September Lord Loreburn, the former liberal lord chancellor, had suggested, in *The Times*, a conference behind closed doors to find a settlement. On 24 September the Ulster Unionist Council agreed to the setting up of a provisional government, if home rule should be enacted. It arranged to delegate its powers to a 77-strong administration, with Carson as chairman of its central authority. This was to be the basis of loyal resistance to a Dublin parliament. Asquith agreed, in early October, to enter into secret talks with Bonar Law, the two leaders meeting in great secrecy on 14 October, 6 November and 10 December to little effect. The exclusion of Ulster was mooted, but Asquith's idea of a local legislature and executive was strongly resisted. The prime minister also had a secret meeting with Redmond on 18 November. The latter was opposed to exclusion at this stage, but thinking of 'Home Rule within Home Rule',[59] some sort of federal Ireland. Asquith privately put a variation of this to Carson, after meeting him on 16 December. The Ulster leader rejected the idea of a veto in an Irish parliament, even before a second meeting on 2 January. Asquith also saw Redmond again on 2 February, and further explored the idea of home rule within home rule.

The home rule bill was to be introduced, for the third, and final, time, in the 1914 session, beginning on 10 February. The king sent his private secretary to Carson, asking him not to make a violent speech. He and the conservative leaders were thinking of denying the government control of the army, by holding up the annual army bill in the Lords. Birrell and Lloyd George had been working on Redmond, who eventually agreed to accept exclusion, but only on a temporary – three-year – basis. This was extracted, by the prime minister, on 2 March. The – third – second reading of the bill was held on 9 March, and Asquith, for the first time, publicly offered exclusion for six years. The news of exclusion for three years had leaked on 5 March, only for the period to be doubled the following day. This had first been suggested by Lloyd George, the previous November. Partition was now out in the open. The government's concession allowed for two general elections in that period, but Carson characterized it as 'a sentence of death with a stay of execution for six years'.[60] Bonar Law wanted it made permanent. The area of disagreement had been narrowed, but the gulf between the two sides widened.

On Thursday, 19 March, with rumours of military manoeuvres in Ulster, Carson stormed out of a parliamentary censure debate to take the boat train to Belfast. Sir Arthur Paget, the general officer commanding in Ireland, had been instructed, the previous day, to secure all military and naval installations against the UVF. A letter from the army council, dated 14 March, specifically mentioned Armagh, Omagh, Carrickfergus and Enniskillen. A special cabinet committee on the issue had been set up on 11 March, following the discovery of a plan to isolate communication with Ulster. This seems to have been discovered by the Omagh RIC, but it required an active imagination on the part of key ministers to turn a UVF contingency plan into an immediate conspiracy. Churchill hinted, in a speech at Bradford on 14 March, that there might be military action. (He subsequently made reference to 40–50,000 troops, the use of the navy to support the army, the arrest of leaders, the seizure of arms and the prevention of drilling.) Four days later Gen. French, chief of the imperial general staff, told the director of military operations at the war office, Gen. Henry Wilson, that the government proposed 'to spray troops all over Ulster as if it were a Pontypool coal strike'.[61] Wilson, a strong unionist from an Anglo-Irish background, had no time for liberal ministers, and spilt the beans to Bonar Law and Carson.

On 20 March, in Dublin, Paget told his commanders to prepare immediately for operations in Ulster. It seemed to be a way of flushing out officers sympathetic to Irish loyalists, and it had been agreed at the war office that officers with direct family connections in Ulster 'should be permitted to remain behind either on leave or with details'.[62] At the Curragh the commander of the third cavalry brigade, Gen. Gough, and 59 other officers, decided to offer their resignations. The government backed down, and stated, on 22 March, that it had never intended to flood Ulster with troops. 'Whatever may be said about provocation [of the UVF by the authorities], there can no longer be any doubt that an operation was planned for the coercion of Ulster, and that it was badly planned.'[63] There was no political preparation, since the cabinet committee, in particular Churchill and Seely, the minister for war, were acting behind the backs of their colleagues. There was also inadequate technical preparation, shown not least in the confusion over the role of Gen. Sir Nevil Macready, who was sent from the war office to Ulster. He was to take command of the Belfast garrison and also of the RIC, but this was aborted. Later, when the government tried to put him in charge of the police, it was found he could be made only a resident magistrate of the whole of Ulster excepting Belfast, where an act of 1911 required six years' legal experience. The Curragh mutineers, as they were to be dubbed, were ordered to resume their duties. Gough extracted from Col. Seely an undertaking that troops would not be used to crush political opposition to home rule, but this was repudiated by the government, Asquith taking over the war office on 30 March.

Carson escaped whatever military repression had been intended for Saturday, 21 March. He did not, as was thought possible, proclaim his provisional government, since home rule had not yet been enacted, much less imposed on Ulster. The unionist leader was not bluffing, but he was engaged in a game of deterrence. Military manoeuvring had the purpose of encouraging the government to retreat politically. Carson wielded a metaphorical sword, even if he had no intention of drawing blood. Bonar Law also declined to go the last step, and interfere with the army act. On 24 April the UVF landed at Larne (as well as at Bangor and Donaghadee) 25,000 rifles and 3 million rounds. This was the work of the unionist leadership in Ulster, the so-called business committee of the UUC having masterminded the importation. Drilling with arms, in defence of the constitution, could be made legal by two justices of the peace, but not importing them wholesale. This had been banned by the government the previous December. The cabinet, though it met the following week on four successive mornings, dithered about prosecuting Carson for treason. Redmond and Birrell were opposed to strong action.

On 1 May the king pressured the speaker of the House of Commons to offer to preside over all-party talks. George V suggested such a conference on 17 May and 19 June. Talks had been resumed with Bonar Law and Carson on 5 May, lesser members of the government handling Redmond. The Irish party, it seemed, was prepared to accept permanent exclusion, but it was not inclined to give up as many as six counties. Fermanagh and Tyrone were in dispute. The home rule bill, which received its – third – third reading on 25 May, was proceeding towards royal assent, scheduled for 25 June. But an amending bill, providing for exclusion by county option, was introduced in the Lords on 23 June. This had been promised on 12 May. It was quickly amended to provide for nine-county permanent exclusion without any vote, and returned to the Commons on 14 July. Five days earlier James Craig had released part of the constitution of the provisional government. This showed that Carson intended to hold the province 'in trust for the constitution of the United Kingdom', rebellion coming to an end only 'upon the restoration of direct Imperial Government'.[64] The amending bill now became the object of disagreement. The problem of the border was reported to the king on 17 July, Asquith being now willing to hand it over to a speaker's conference.

The Buckingham Palace conference began four days later, involving government and opposition, the Irish unionists and nationalists, the four leaders and their seconds meeting daily between 21 and 24 July. The British leaders wanted a settlement, but Carson and Redmond could not agree on the excluded area. The conference broke down, before the question of time could be considered. Asquith resolved to proceed with the amending bill, without a time limit, and Redmond and Dillon agreed to press this on their colleagues. Having 'toiled for hours around the muddy by-ways of Fermanagh and Tyrone'[65] at Buckingham Palace, as Churchill wrote of a cabinet meeting on the evening of 24 July, the liberal government was suddenly confronted with the threat of war in Europe. The Archduke Franz Ferdinand of Austria, heir to the Habsburg throne, had been assassinated, by a nationalist student, at Sarajevo in Serbia on 28 June. On 24 July Austria finally issued an ultimatum to Serbia, due to expire in four days. That Sunday, 26 July, the Irish Volunteers illegally landed 1,500 used rifles at Howth (and Kilcoole), outside Dublin. It was not on the same scale as the landing at Larne, the relative costs being £1,500 and £60,000. But guns in the hands of nationalists were a greater threat to Dublin Castle.

The amending bill was put back from 28 to 30 July, Ireland now being overshadowed by Europe. It was on 29 July that Britain began to prepare for war. The unionists proposed the postponement of the amending bill on 30 July, given the likelihood of war. Redmond concurred, since he did not want to be seen to be putting Irish above national interests. The home rule bill was to be enacted, but suspended until the Ulster position could be settled. As late as 4 August, Redmond believed this would happen in the 1915 parliamentary session, before an election expected in June. On Saturday, 1 August 1914, Carson committed the UVF to home defence, and even service overseas. Redmond was under pressure to follow suit. Sir Edward Grey, the foreign secretary, effectively committed Britain to entering the war, in a speech in the Commons on Monday, 3 August. 'The one bright spot in the very dreadful situation is Ireland', he said. 'The position in Ireland – and this I should like very clearly to be understood abroad – is not a consideration among the many things we have to take into account now.'[66] The foreign secretary was probably thinking more of Ulster than of the rest of Ireland. Redmond then offered to protect the country, perhaps in alliance with the UVF, so that troops could be sent to the front. At 11 p.m. on 4 August, Britain's ultimatum to Germany, about troops in Belgium, expired. Ireland was now of little moment. All the evidence suggests that the UVF would have risen against the imposition of home rule, whatever the brinkmanship of Carson and his British allies. The outbreak of the European war closed off this progress towards counter-revolution. If Asquith and Redmond had not been conciliatory, Carson would have been forced to make the Ulster provisional government a reality. Ireland escaped this malignant development, only to have the tragedy of a wartime insurrection in Dublin.

7

James Connolly, Socialism and Nationalism, 1910–14[1]

It was the misfortune of James Connolly – the father of Irish socialism – to be in Belfast during the unionist mobilizations, following his return from the United States in 1910. As national organizer of the Dublin-based Socialist Party of Ireland (SPI), he saw home rule as the imminent solution of the national question, and looked forward to the ITUC becoming a labour party. He successfully proposed this at the 1912 congress in Clonmel, but it was ten years before the trade-union based party fought a general election in a partitioned Ireland. The SPI had become the Independent Labour Party of Ireland (ILP[I]) in 1912, but Connolly did not attract all Belfast socialists into this first all-Ireland organization. Connolly's belief that home rule was a socialist principle contributed to the growing gulf between the two communities, despite his profound opposition to sectarianism. He took up residence in the city in 1911, and became local organizer of the Irish Transport and General Workers' Union (ITGWU). Despite his syndicalist experience in the United States, he did not see union work as the main way forward in Ireland. But Connolly came to lead a group of men and women, in a catholic area outside Devlin's control, his first, and last, personal political following in Ireland as a socialist agitator. He became a leader of the Irish Trade Union Congress and Labour Party (ITUC & LP) in 1914, shortly before moving to Dublin to succeed Larkin as acting general secretary of the ITGWU. Connolly's years in Belfast gave him an opportunity to consider the divided working class at the time of the third home rule bill. He went along with the optimism of the Irish party, believing the British government might have to coerce the Ulster unionists, until he was shocked in March 1914 by the threat of partition. From an Irish catholic background, Connolly was intolerant at times of the protestant community, and it was in Belfast that his personal political transition began. Talk of partition and the outbreak of the war strengthened his nationalism, and propelled him towards the Dublin rising in 1916. But it was the defeat of Dublin workers in the lock-out of 1913–14, followed by the collapse of working-class internationalism, which weakened his socialism. He left Belfast a revolutionary nationalist in October 1914, having written off constitutional politics.

James Connolly had become a socialist propagandist in the Edinburgh of the 1890s, the city of his birth to Irish parents in 1868. By his 20s, he was a believer in the evolutionist Marxism of the second international, founded in 1889. This theory proved a poor guide to political practice, Connolly's Marxism obscuring the agrarian backwardness of Ireland when he came to live in Dublin in 1896. His time in Ireland, which saw the Boer War, was filled, politically, with the Irish Socialist Republican Party (ISRP), and the *Workers' Republic* newspaper. He had an orthodox view of socialism, on the left of the international, and accepted the progressive British view that Ireland, one day, would again have a parliament. He sought to recruit republicans to the socialist cause, where the question of an Irish or British state was not immediately central, while propagandizing through the medium of nationalism. He failed to appreciate the political significance of regional industrialization in Ulster, areas which he probably never visited, and left for the United States in 1903.

There he joined the followers of Daniel De Leon in the Socialist Labor Party (SLP), but he soon rejected their political substitutionism, whereby the revolutionary party was emphasized at the expense of the working class. Connolly was disarmed as a critic of reformism, though he remained a member of the party. Connolly became a syndicalist, ironically under the influence of De Leon, and remained one for the rest of his socialist life, though he did not seek to advocate American industrial unionism for Europe. He worked for a time as an organizer for the Industrial Workers of the World (IWW), but he also founded the Irish Socialist Federation (ISF), with its paper, the *Harp*. Connolly had joined the Socialist Party of America (SPA) in 1908, and it employed him as a speaker touring across the United States. He belonged to the revolutionary wing, but the SPA was above all a tolerant party, which the reformist element was able to dominate.

There was no talk of socialist revolution in Ireland from 1910, when he returned to undertake a four-week propaganda tour on behalf of the SPI, before going on to Britain. One week was to be devoted to Belfast. William Orr, a supporter of Connolly, had written to William O'Brien, of the SPI in Dublin, that an Independent Labour Party (ILP) organizer in Belfast now believed 'they would never make any progress in Ireland so long as they remained a tail of an English party, that they were losing Ireland to get Belfast, and that they were not even getting Belfast.'[2] Connolly landed at 'Derry on 25 July, towards the end of the government's constitutional conference with the opposition, and he established the Belfast branch of the SPI on Sunday, 7 August. It initially comprised 24 members, and was to include William Orr and his brother James, D.R. Campbell, Danny McDevitt, Tom Johnson and Joe Mitchell, plus William McMullen, a young protestant who worked in Harland and Wolff, and even Bulmer Hobson, the nationalist. Connolly also spoke at two ILP meetings, some of the Belfast members welcoming the idea of Irish socialist unity. (It may possibly have been members of the [British] SLP in Belfast who objected most strongly to what they perceived to be Connolly's nationalism.) He returned to Belfast at the end of the month for a week, and wrote to William O'Brien in Dublin that the new SPI members wanted a national conference. He advised the

Dubliners to extend a special welcome on Sunday, 18 September, Language Day, when reduced railway fares were available. O'Brien organized only an informal meeting, out of which emerged an all-Ireland national executive, Belfast having two members out of the eight.

Connolly was reluctant to take a job with the ITGWU, founded by Larkin in Dublin in 1909, and he was dismissive of this new Irish union as late as May 1911. He finally forced the SPI, in late October 1910, to issue an appeal for funds, to allow him to stay in Ireland as the party's organizer. He was spending considerable time in Belfast, though meeting resistance from the ILP to the SPI. His family returned to Ireland in December and settled in Dublin. The second general election of the year had seen Connolly draft a manifesto for the SPI, containing an apocalyptic view of Irish politics. 'We live in times of political change, and even of political revolution', he wrote. 'More and more civic and national responsibility is destined to be thrust upon, or won by, the people of Ireland.' He argued that existing political forces would disappear with Dublin rule, and the new Ireland would see untrammelled class struggle. 'In this great awakening of Erin', he continued, 'Labour, if guided by the lamp of Socialist teaching, may set its feet firmly and triumphantly upon the path that leads to its full emancipation.'[3]

While continuing to make political tours of Ireland and Britain, Connolly moved to Belfast in March 1911, lodging with Danny McDevitt at 5 Rosemary Street. He appealed, through *Forward*, for socialists 'of any nationality ... in Londonderry, Newry, Dundalk or Drogheda'[4] to join the SPI, the three last-named towns being on the road from Belfast to Dublin. His eldest daughter, Nora, joined him, but it was a few weeks before he found a house, 1 Glenalina Terrace, on the Falls Road, opposite Belfast cemetery, which allowed him to bring the rest of the family from Dublin. He was making a serious bid for the ILP, still largely under the political influence of William Walker. '[We] were nurtured', William McMullen recalled of his time in the ILP,

> on the British brand of socialist propaganda, and all the literature we read, as well as all our speakers were imported from Great Britain ... Our school of Socialist thought had no nationalist tradition, and was not conscious of, and even if it had been would have been contemptuous of, a Socialist movement in any other part of this country ... The members of the Socialist movement in the City were Protestants, as the Catholics were in the main followers of ... Devlin.'[5]

This was the context of Connolly's *Forward* appeal in late May, where he ran up against William Walker. Connolly argued that 'only the force of religious bigotry remain[ed] as an asset to Unionism', and that the Twelfth parade would 'be as the last flicker of the dying fire which blazes up before totally expiring'. 'The Orangeman of to-day', he wrote, 'may hate the Pope, but he hates still more to lose time by rioting, when he might make money by working, and in this he shows the "good sense which pre-eminently distinguishes the city by the Lagan".'[6] Walker agreed in his reply, when he affirmed that it had 'now become *impossible* in Belfast to have a religious riot', but Connolly's snide anti-utilitarianism clearly annoyed him. He rushed to defend the ILP, against its new socialist critic, collapsing into self-righteousness. 'My place of birth was accidental', Walker concluded, 'but my duty to my class is world-wide, hence MY INTERNATIONALISM.'[7] He then went off to represent the trades council at the ITUC in Galway, leaving Connolly to draft his retort. He accused Walker of 'overwhelm[ing] us with a mass of tawdry rhetoric, cheap and irrelevant schoolboy history, and badly digested political philosophy, all permeated with an artfully instilled appeal to religious prejudice and civic sectionalism carefully calculated to make Belfast wrap itself around in a garment of self-righteousness, and to look with scorn upon its supposed weaker Irish brethren.'[8] Referring to Walker's first by-election, Connolly alluded to the fact that Richard Braithwaite, of the BPA and IOO, had now come over to the SPI. Braithwaite had indeed crossed the sectarian divide.

Having defeated Larkin at the congress, Walker, in his second reply, acknowledged Connolly's arrival in Belfast. 'I am glad to think that I am going to welcome him as a *citizen* within its borders. Democracy, my friend, has no geography.'[9] Connolly then countered, in his article published on 1 July, that, since they were 'but representatives of two opposite policies', nothing he said about Walker could be considered personal. Connolly went on to refer to Walker's 'unctuous self-glorification and holier-than-thou attitudinising'.[10] The latter, on 8 July, then described Connolly as

> sometime of Edinburgh, sometime of Dublin, then of New York, again of Dublin, now of Belfast, and several other places, all of which had the unblushing temerity to refuse the Gospel of the new Messiah, and to demand some earnest as to the qualifications of the man who, refusing to WORK either in Scotland, Ireland, or America, in any existing organisation, demands as the price of his allegiance to Socialist propaganda that the organisation must be his, and either GENERAL secretary or NATIONAL organizer must be his title.

He noted – correctly – that Connolly had taken to referring to the late ISRP as 'the Irish Socialist Party'.[11] 'The I.L.P.', Walker concluded, 'have enabled the Irish in Belfast to unite, James Connolly (Catholic) can – thanks to the spade work of the I.L.P. – come to Belfast and speak to audiences mainly Protestant, and be patiently heard.' Whatever the struggle over an Irish labour party, it is clear that Connolly's SPI overture to the ILP was perceived, by Walker, as an attempt to usurp his leading position in Belfast.

Connolly's controversy with Walker, whatever his earlier pragmatic arguments about the inevitability of home rule, 'had not the effect', according to William McMullen, 'of detaching many members of the ILP from their allegiance to it'.[12] This was in spite of his socialist diplomacy, whereby he had called for a joint convention between the two parties, giving to the delegates 'the power to debate and agree upon all questions of tactics, policy, and name for a new organisation to embrace all sections of the movement in Ireland.' (Like most such offers, Connolly's was rigged in advance, since a precondition was 'recognising Ireland's right to self-government'.)[13] This was precisely the point on which Walker did not agree. In Belfast, in the summer of 1911, it was not so evident that he was wrong about Ireland's future. The Lords' veto was coming to an end, but the unionist clubs and orange lodges were growing. With Connolly away from Dublin, the SPI there waned. The money to employ him also ran out, and he ceased being national organizer after approximately six months. In September 1911 the Belfast ILP began to talk to the SPI, 'the Walker element remaining away'.[14] Connolly considered that he was winning one of the two active branches. North Belfast remained loyal. East Belfast was 'practically unanimous in our favour'.[15] But Connolly also wrote, on 7 December, that lecturing on 'Irish subjects ... [did] not do [him] much good from the point of view of the Union in this Orange hole, but ... [he] must take the chance'.[16]

Walker retired from politics the following month, leaving the way open for Connolly. It still took some time for the ILP(I) to emerge. Four of the five formally existing ILP branches in Belfast came over, but Connolly may not have taken over a majority of the active members. William McMullen recalls the novelty of travelling by train to Dublin with Connolly, at Easter 1912, in the company of Johnson, Campbell, McDevitt and Mitchell, for the first all-Ireland socialist conference. He knew only William O'Brien and Francis Sheehy-Skeffington, among the Dublin delegates, at the foundation of the new party. The SPI was not keen to lose its name, or shift from socialism to labourism, for the purposes of winning the ILP over to an Irish political terrain. Some Dublin members, in what they may have taken to be a joke, placed a Union Jack on the doormat of the conference room, thereby driving back to Belfast some members of the British Socialist Party (BSP).

Connolly lost his job with the SPI in June 1911, just after settling in Belfast. 'The trade union world', he had written to O'Brien on 22 April, '[was] not nearly so important *at this stage* as the keeping up of the movement proper.'[17] Connolly had spoken at a meeting of the Belfast ITGWU branch, and, though there is no evidence of his joining the union in March, he was keen, in May, that it should send him to the ITUC. Larkin may have suggested that he could become the delegate, but Michael McKeown remained a champion of the Irish party. Connolly attended the meeting of seven members which decided to send McKeown to the congress. The ITGWU had been readmitted to the ITUC at the 1910 meeting, Larkin attending as a delegate from the trades council in Dublin, because the new union had been expelled after complaints from dockers' leaders. He rejoined the parliamentary committee in June 1911 in Galway, when William O'Brien, a member of a tailors' union, was also elected. The ITGWU had established a base among catholics in the 'low' docks in Belfast, in early 1909, only to engage in rivalry with the NUDL. Attempts were made by P.T. Daly, who became congress secretary in 1910, as well as a Larkin intimate, to revive it that summer. It was during this time that Connolly spoke from a union platform, but Larkin was in the dark, in October 1910, about whether there was a Belfast branch.

On 15 June 1911 there began a national strike of seamen, led by the National Sailors' and Firemen's Union (NSFU). Action was coordinated by Tom Mann's National Transport Workers' Federation (NTWF), to which the NUDL was affiliated. It was only a matter of time before dockers in various ports, those of Ireland included, became involved. The NUDL had been revived at the cross-channel docks in Belfast, but the ITGWU was not affiliated to the NTWF. Connolly was introduced to trade unionism in Belfast on 27 June, when he spoke at the Custom House steps, at the invitation of the NSFU's Irish organizer from Dublin, J.H. Bennett, in the company of McDevitt and Campbell. In mid-July Connolly became Ulster district organizer of the ITGWU, in time for the commencement of the local seamen's strike on the 19th. His base was the 'low' docks, and his office at 112 Corporation Street, several hundred catholic dockers comprising the branch.

On 19 July between 300 and 500 dockers, working seven boats in the 'low' docks, came out in sympathy with certain seamen. The latter were working the *Innishowen Head*, owned by the Belfast Steamship Company (since all but one of its boats were named after an Irish headland, it was known locally as 'the head line'). This was not to be a repetition of 1907, though the dockers demanded better pay and conditions, as well as the abolition of the free labour bureau. The cross-channel docks were picketed on 20 July, but the men did not come out. Two years later Connolly described the heroes of 1907 as having scabbed in 1911. The York dock came out on 20 July, and, by Monday, 24 July, the remaining dockers were locked out. Between 100 and 150 returned in the face of employer intransigence, and, by 25 July, work had restarted on three boats on the Co. Down side. Several hundred workers in total were involved. The separately organized carters refused to join the strike, because of their agreement with their employers. 'War Is Declared'[18] proclaimed a dockers' banner, on the day the lock-out was announced. Connolly, like Larkin, held nightly meetings at the Custom House steps. At the first, on 19 July, he had described the strike 'as the greatest crisis and the greatest opportunity in the history of labour in the city'.[19] On the day of the lock-out, he led a demonstration through the principal streets, a 'Shipping Federation'[20] coffin being tipped into the Lagan.

The trades council called a special meeting for 29 July, to consider the seamen's strike, though the NSFU was not then affiliated. Negotiations had opened with the seamen after the dockers' lock-out. The ITGWU was not yet acceptable to the trades council, and it was A.T. Cox of the NSFU who told the delegates of the dockers' involvement. He stated he had been 'very courteously received by the shipowners' in the past few days, and that Heyn, of the head line, was 'reasonable'.[21] Cox said he would intercede on behalf of the dockers, and the trades council agreed to raise funds for the seamen. The NSFU secured a local settlement, but the Belfast seamen stayed out in solidarity with the dockers. Heyn then showed himself unreasonable, falling back into line with other shipping federation employers on 2 August. This led Connolly to threaten blacking of the Belfast Steamship

Company's boats throughout the United Kingdom, an action he was hardly in a position to command. There followed, on 3 August, scenes of cart-overturning reminiscent of four years earlier, and mounted and foot police patrols were put into the docks. The next night Connolly told strikers to keep 'within the law', but to pursue the struggle with the same spirit. That Friday night, Connolly announced a settlement was imminent, and it is likely Cox was mediating with Heyn on the ITGWU's behalf. The following morning, Saturday, 5 August, talks were broken off, and a direct offer to the men posted up on the waterfront. The dockers were ready to accept. Connolly had been outmanoeuvred, and he made the best of it at the steps on Sunday. The new wage rates, though the lowest in the United Kingdom, would, he said, enable them to secure concessions in the future. The promise of 'no discrimination' was of 'the highest value', members of the ITGWU being allowed back to work. Connolly appealed to 'the public' to ensure that this 'pledge' was kept.[22] The employers, the *Northern Whig* was to note, 'were prepared to recognise the [union] so long as it did not interfere with the freedom of labour'.[23]

Connolly consolidated the small ITGWU branch in the 'low' docks after the strike, drawing on the ties of the dockers' community in the area of York Street. Dockers and carters had also taken action in Dublin in July 1911. There the seamen won the same terms as in Britain, and there was a return to work in the Irish ports in August. Transport workers remained out in Liverpool and London. The first national rail strike took place in the middle of the month, to be followed by another strike on Irish railways in September. Connolly was approached in Belfast by women workers from the York Street area on the occasion of a spontaneous spinners' strike in local linen mills.

Several hundred spinners refused to enter a mill in Henry Street on Monday, 2 October. It was owned by the York Street Flax Spinning Company, one of the largest in Belfast. They were protesting at short-time working, a practice possibly owing to a downturn in trade. Within hours, workers at three other mills had struck. The company announced a lock-out from the following day. The Henry Street and York Street mills were reported to be out, along with 100 to 200 workers at the Blackstaff Mill on Springfield Road, and several weaving factories on the Falls Road. When the mills reopened the following Monday, 9 October, about 200 older women returned, despite picketing. More returns took place in the following week, and, by Wednesday, 18 October, the strike was over. It had not been general to the linen industry, involving, at the very most, between 1,100 and 1,300 workers.

In 1911 fewer than 3,000 women linen workers were members of Mary Galway's textile operatives' society. There were more than 11,000 female spinners, and most were unorganized. Mary Galway had first been elected to the executive of the trades council in 1899, and, in 1907, she joined the parliamentary committee of the ITUC, becoming the most prominent woman trade unionist in Ireland. A Belfast protestant, she had worked in the better end of the industry, and this is where she recruited her members. She shared the views of her male trade-union colleagues, underestimating the domestic and social difficulties faced by many linen workers. James Connolly's sympathy for the exploited extended naturally, but his view of domestic labour as oppressive coexisted with idealized notions of patriarchal care. And he, too, underestimated women's social labour, either ignoring it altogether, or assuming that working women were too difficult to organize. Connolly had no recruiting ambitions in the linen industry, and he would have recognized Galway's claim. Larkin established the Irish Women Workers' Union (IWWU) in September 1911, with his sister, Delia, as secretary, alongside the – male – ITGWU. But Connolly did not share this British conception of general unionism, with sexual segregation, having experienced American industrial unionism, where all workers in one industry were seen as belonging to one union. Partly in response to this Dublin initiative, but mainly because of the overture from the Belfast women, Connolly set up the Irish Textile Workers' Union (ITWU) after the York Street Flax Spinning Company strike. (He saw it initially as the textile section of the ITGWU, but Larkin was to consider it part of the IWWU.)

Connolly appeared in the middle of the day, at dinner time, on 2 October, on the corner of Henry and York Street, in the company of Marie Johnson. He addressed the striking spinners, hinting that ITGWU dockers could hold up flax supplies. The raw material was most likely imported through the 'low' docks, and Connolly may have been invited along by female relatives of his dockers. '[As] a number of the women and girls', he wrote the following day, 'are relatives of the members of our union they knew me.'[24] This was to be used as a justification for his initial involvement. Connolly may have exaggerated the relationship, but he was making an impact on a section of the catholic working class. He subsequently argued that the women had approached Mary Galway, but received no help. She, with George Greig of the NAUL, had appealed to the spinners, from the other side of the street, not to strike. Connolly got them to organize a strike committee, and appoint their own treasurers. Three days later, when Galway called upon the women to return to work, and they refused, Connolly issued temporary membership cards for the ITGWU. This was on 5 October. Thereafter, he led the women. During the strike, he organized a meeting at St Mary's Hall, seemingly to establish the 'textile branch'[25] of the ITGWU. Connolly may have put in a claim for an increase, possibly as a negotiating ploy. He seems to have been more concerned with industrial discipline, an apparent grievance, which the spinners articulated in terms of the truck act of 1896, which required the display of rules. But Connolly does not seem to have been able to negotiate on their behalf. A deputation of spinners approached the York Street Company on Monday, 9 August, only to be told to await a meeting of the employers' association. It was after this meeting – on 13 October – that the drift back started.

The spinners' strike was a volatile outbreak of self-activity over which Connolly had little control. On the first day, the women – most likely young and unmarried – congregated 'in light-hearted and merry mood'.

They set off in a 'singing procession' through the streets, liberating newsagents' bill-boards on the way. 'The female contingent were in so hilarious a mood', when Connolly and Johnson addressed them, 'that they made it difficult for the speeches to be heard.'[26] When the older women returned a week later, 'boohing and cheering alternated with the lusty rendering of popular music hall ditties.'[27] Connolly referred to the strikers as 'cheering, singing, enthusiastic females, and not a hat among them',[28] the shawls of the mill girls distinguishing them from their more respectable sisters within the working class. But such defiance could only be short-lived, given the precarious nature of their families' incomes, and the absence of a strong trade-union tradition. 'They've great spirit', Connolly's oldest daughter, Nora, would recall his having said at the beginning of the strike. 'They are not in the Union; they've no funds. It's going to be difficult.'[29] And so it was.

On Sunday, 15 October, the day before the women started to drift back, the catholic church intervened. Connolly had been born a catholic in Scotland. He abandoned the practice of his faith in 1893, when he was 25, but did not broadcast his non-belief. He had already come under attack from the militant catholics of the AOH in Cork, but in Belfast protestants would have considered him a member of the minority community. At the beginning of the third week of the strike, Nora Connolly, as she recalled in a sentimentalized published account, took her father to mass in St Paul's on the Falls Road. It is unlikely he normally attended, and probable that he was expecting some sort of reaction from the autocratic priest, who acted as a 'knocker-up'[30] for workers. The priest stared from the pulpit at Connolly, his daughter recalled, and the sermon was directed entirely at him and against his labour activities. Connolly sat silently, later explaining to his indignant daughter that self-control was necessary 'in face of attack'.[31]

This would suggest that Connolly was condemned as some sort of undesirable in the catholic ghetto. The Irish church, at this time, was becoming alert to the threat of socialism, and Connolly's trade-union activity would have alarmed the local nationalist political leadership. The *Irish News* opposed the strike, proffering the Devlin-initiated official inquiry into the Ulster linen industry as the way forward, even though the spinners' grievances did not come under its terms of reference. It is certain that the church tried to break their strike, though the action of the employers, and the passage of time, may also have contributed to the return to work on the Monday. Connolly had come up against clericalism of the catholic variety, though he chose to be discreet about its impact, given the sectarianism in the city. On Tuesday, 17 October, he ordered the members of the ITWU to return to work, the better to continue the struggle within the mill.

This strike of October 1911 brought James Connolly to the attention of the trade-union movement in Belfast. The ITGWU branch had only affiliated to the trades council on 7 September, after the seamen's strike. On 3 October the *Belfast Evening Telegraph* enquired in a heading, 'Who Is Mr Connolly?', only to supply the answer, 'Repudiated by Operatives' Officials'. Mary Galway, presumably, was reported as describing

Connolly as 'a menace to trade unionism ... If he would organise the dockers of whom only one in ten are in his union, he would find plenty to do.' Connolly immediately dashed off a letter of reply, stating that he was only helping the women, and that he hoped they could work alongside the textile operatives' society. He denied there was a rival union, only to have the paper lambast him again – 'Mr Connolly's Bona-Fides / Emphatic Reputation / Union Official Disavowal'.[32]

The formal establishment of the ITWU was delayed until the end of 1911, partly because of Larkin's insistence in Dublin on giving the new women's union to his sister, but mainly because of Mary Galway's opposition. She was to allege poaching, but Connolly is unlikely to have attracted existing members of her society. Galway meant that all women workers in the linen industry were her potential members. At the trades council on 21 October, three days after the return to work, she moved that the ITGWU be disaffiliated. Connolly had written to defend his organizing the women 'with the union',[33] and to suggest a working relationship with the textile operatives' society. The executive divided on the issue. Galway described Connolly as an 'adventurer',[34] at the meeting on 2 November, but was forced to withdraw the remark. The recently affiliated NSFU came to his defence, but the issue was again referred to the executive. Connolly attended for the first time on 18 November, when John Murphy, the secretary, attempted to bring the textile society back 'under the wing of the Council'.[35] (It was denied that Greig had suggested to Joe Harris, that the Workers' Union should organize in the 'low' docks.) The executive was keen to avoid conflict, and, on 16 December, Campbell successfully suggested a conference of all interested parties to reach 'an amicable basis of working'.[36] The ITWU had now been set up, with an office at 50 York Street, Connolly's persistence being rewarded with quiet support from within the council.

This only encouraged Galway to persist with her charge, the poaching allegation being taken to the 1912 ITUC at Clonmel in May. Larkin was to become chairman of the parliamentary committee for 1912–13. Belfast hostility to Connolly was reinforced by the resistance of Irish party supporters to the ITGWU in the rest of Ireland. On the second day, the standing orders committee recommended that Delia Larkin be admitted as the IWWU delegate. John Murphy, representing the printers, then talked about 'adventurers' and 'bounders' in the trade-union movement, especially in Belfast. He wanted the congress to oppose new unions, but was ruled out of order. While some Belfast delegates supported Galway, who was still on the parliamentary committee, others were clearly for peace. Campbell, and McConnell of the bakers, stated that the Belfast trades council had discussed the issue for months, and would be holding a conference. 'There is a clique in the Belfast Trades Council', said Galway, 'who back these people up.'[37] The standing orders report was accepted. Galway came back during the discussion of the parliamentary committee report. Referring to the insurance act, she said that in Belfast they had to contend against church societies and burial societies, and, in addition, they had to meet the competition of so-called trade unionists who were making an attempt to further divide the workers (hear, hear). They had organisers only recently arrived in Ireland increasing the trouble which sectarian and political bigotry were causing to the genuine trade unionists of Belfast (hear, hear).[38]

The strikes in the summer and autumn of 1911 represented a high point in Connolly's career as Ulster district organizer of the ITGWU. In late January 1912 he was summoned to Wexford, where ITGWU iron-workers had been locked out the previous August, returning to Belfast in early March. In August 1913, Larkin summoned him to Dublin, during what became the famous lock-out, a historic struggle which kept him away from his duties in Belfast until the following March.

Marie Johnson had become honorary secretary of the ITWU following its establishment in December 1911. It did not have more than 300 members at any point. Open-air recruiting meetings were started in the Falls, in May 1912, though Johnson considered that the initiative had been lost. She refused a full-time job, possibly because of family commitments, and Connolly had difficulty in finding other women. She became honorary treasurer, and he the union's organizer. Connolly tried to attract mill workers by holding Irish dances in June. He had shown little interest in cultural nationalism, and may have thought this was a way to reach Belfast catholics. Some of his children had integrated into the ghetto in this manner. He was wrong about working-class women, and the ITWU had more success with ballroom dancing. Johnson seems to have disapproved of a Miss Savage, from Glasgow, who became secretary. Helena Maloney turned down an offer to come to Belfast, and it was 1 September before Winifred Carney, a secretary, took on the work. She had been introduced by Johnson, and Connolly seems to have antagonized Johnson by dispensing with her services as honorary secretary. Nelly Gordon (later Grimley) also became an organizer about this time, having worked as a 'doffing mistress'[39] in charge of spinning frames. Some members of the ITWU seem to have suffered in the expulsions that summer, and it was only in the autumn that the union got off the ground.

In November Connolly issued a manifesto, 'To the Linen Slaves of Belfast'. The home office inquiry into the industry, set up by Churchill in July 1911, had created considerable public discussion, and this was the background to Connolly's intervention. He described the mills as 'slaughter-houses for the women and penitentiaries for the children'. Reference was made to Irish women in the land struggle. Connolly appealed openly to spinners, whom he saw as having the power to disrupt the entire industry. 'A programme of industrial reform' was proposed, including a trade board for the industry and proper government inspection. In the interim, he argued for better pay, the abolition of fines, and the reduction of stoppages to the hourly pay rate. Connolly argued that these demands could be achieved within a year, if the women organized. He hinted at a general strike. The union was willing to establish an office, or women's club room, in each district, if there was sufficient response. 'Talk about success', he concluded, 'and you will achieve success.'[40]

In March 1913 Connolly issued an 'Ultimatum to the Linen Lords', but it does not seem to have precipitated a struggle. He claimed, in *Forward*, on 7 June, that 'ceaseless propaganda' had led to 'more active and intelligent discontent in the mills ... than at any time in the past.' Two days later, on Monday, 9 June, he held a demonstration in Smithfield, to further the demand for the extension of the trade boards act to linen. Mill workers and their supporters were addressed by a Leeds trade unionist and a councillor from Dublin. While Connolly claimed the ITWU was recruiting 'by hundreds', there is no evidence for this scale of activity. But the ITWU clearly achieved a small coherent membership. Nelly Gordon had represented the Belfast IWWU, as the branch was formally known, at the 1913 ITUC in Cork the previous month. Larkin was re-elected chairman, for 1913–14, but Connolly had yet to join the parliamentary committee. Gordon also spoke on an ITWU platform in Blackpool, a district of the city, and for the ILP(I) in Queenstown (Cóbh). Back in Belfast, she was largely responsible for the textile union through to the spring of 1914. She again represented the Belfast IWWU at the ITUC in Dublin that June. It was probably after the Dublin lock-out that Connolly showed his increasing nationalism. Constance, Countess Markievicz, the Anglo-Irish wife of a Polish count, came to Belfast to talk 'on cultural activities but these were bad days and very hard for poor girls', Gordon recalled. Constance Markievicz probably came north to address the ILP(I) on the Balkans, 'few of the small audience', according to William McMullen, '[knowing] anything whatever of the subject'.[41] Maud Gonne also spoke later on 'the duties of Irishwomen'. 'All we could do', Gordon would remember, 'was [stare] at her open-mouthed as she was so beautiful and also beautifully dressed.'[42]

As for the ITGWU, Connolly kept the branch going in the 'low' docks from 1911. (A branch had been established in Newry in July, but the Ulster district organizer was confined largely to Belfast.) Connolly later claimed that he organized a closed shop. He would have drawn on the communal ties of the local dockers' community, which had been formed in the days of a free labour market. He expressed confidence in the support of his members, in the autumn of 1912, though the association of the union with Larkin and 1907 caused problems. 'There is a strong feeling against him in the Union here', Connolly told William O'Brien on 13 September, 'and the feeling for him is summed up in the phrase that "He was a great fighter, but too reckless". So a fight by him upon me would wreck the branch again, and he is headstrong enough to make it.'[43] The following month he was complaining about the impact of the insurance act, 'the struggle – the battle in fact – that I have to hold my own against the myriad of sectarian societies with which I am surrounded'.[44]

By January 1913 these duties were squeezing out time for politics: 'I am up to the neck in trade union and Insurance and other allied work, and scarcely have a moment especially as Jim withholds all books etc. until the day after the last legal minute.'[45] He continued to look upon the cross-channel dockers as scabs, as he told *Forward* readers that May. But he also stated that some had joined the ITGWU, after being referred by unions 'across the water'.[46] Connolly claimed he had won improvements for casual labourers employed by eight companies. 'The Awakening of Ulster's Democracy' was hailed in the *Forward* of 7 June, a singularly optimistic piece. He claimed that dockers, hitherto 'under the influence of religious prejudice and political intriguing', were now joining the ITGWU in great numbers. This had probably been written on Sunday, 1 June.

On 6 June, Connolly wrote to O'Brien: 'I am in the midst of strife and tribulation here ... a rival union established on the docks to fight us – the Belfast Transport Workers' Union. This is an Orange movement fostered by the employers, and directed by a Councillor Finnigan, an Orange leader. I see ahead the fight of our life.'[47] By late July he was unfavourably contrasting his Belfast members with those in Dublin, in a 'city ... so violently Orange and anti-Irish at present that our task has been a hard one all along'.[48] He soon lost the cross-channel members, as a result of his involvement in the Dublin lock-out. According to William McMullen, men on the Liverpool boat read a newspaper report of a Connolly speech (possibly on 29 August), which led them to resign 'owing to [his] political opinions and ungodly propensities'.[49] Shortly before he left for Dublin, Connolly unburdened himself to O'Brien about Larkin. 'I confess to you *in confidence*', he wrote,

> that I don't think I can stand Larkin as a boss much longer. He is simply unbearable. He is for ever snarling at me and drawing comparisons between what he accomplished in Belfast in 1907, and what I have done, conveniently ignoring the fact that he was then the Secretary of an *English* organization, and that as soon as he started an *Irish* one his union fell to pieces, and he had to leave the members to their fate. He is consumed with jealousy and hatred of anyone who will not cringe to him and beslaver him all over.[50]

That *Forward* article of 7 June may have been inspired by a breakthrough, for the ITGWU, in, of all places, Larne, a town 'noted for its irreproachable loyalty'.[51] Connolly mentioned that the dockers 'to a man' had joined the union, but he also, more significantly, referred to 'the poor slaves' of the British Aluminium Company 'produc[ing] a revolt'. They were working an 84-hour week, 12 hours a day. He had recently recruited 300 labourers, 'the overwhelming majority of these workers [being] Protestants'.[52] On Wednesday, 4 June, the night shift came out, because the manager refused to meet union representatives. The men had wanted to request a reduction in hours, and they were joined by the day shift the following morning. A strike committee was elected at a meeting in Victoria Hall, and later that day Connolly spoke at an open-air meeting on the harbour. This is the only known occasion – Thursday, 5 June – of his being in Larne. He told O'Brien the next day that he was also handling a strike of 300 men in a brickworks, seemingly in Belfast, while the Smithfield demonstration of linen workers was arranged for the following Monday. The strike proceeded without much reference to the ITGWU's organizer, and Connolly relied eventually upon press reports. But he did appeal, through *Forward*, for any information on another aluminium works at Kinlochleven in the Scottish Highlands. Some strike pay was issued eventually on Saturday, 14 June, and more aid promised for the following week. Even so, the men went back to work on Monday, 16 June, after twelve days. The strike committee had been attempting to raise its own funds.

On Sunday, 15 June, the strikers – according to a report in the *Belfast Evening Telegraph* – had been asked to stay behind after church services. 'It was decided that the men should go to the works [on Monday at 10 a.m.] and interview the manager.'[53] The *Telegraph*'s reporter predicted an amicable settlement. Nothing else is known of the outcome, but Connolly embellished this press account, probably on Sunday, 22 June, for the following Saturday's *Forward*. 'Upon Monday', he wrote, 'the work gates were besieged by a mob of men clamorously begging for leave to return at any terms the manager chose to impose.' He claimed the strike had nearly been won, the management being about to concede. But exception had been taken to the ITGWU with headquarters in Dublin, and 'the twin forces of scabbism and Carsonism won a glorious victory'. An eight-hour day had been granted, but greater output was demanded, and there was a reduction in wages. Some strikers were also victimized, and the union branch broken up. Connolly alleged that this was 'the first strike broken in Ireland by the direct intervention of the clergy', but then went on to rebut notions of Irish catholics as priest-ridden. 'Clerical interference in industrial disputes has been common in Ireland', he wrote, 'but it is a matter of bitter comment in Labour circles here that the only occasion upon which this clerical dictation succeeded in acting the part of strike breaker should be among and with Protestants, in an Orange community, in the most Orange part of the North-East of Ulster.' He compared Larne with Wexford, where, the previous year, he had established an Irish foundry workers' union, which later became a branch of the ITGWU. There 'the men resolutely but respectfully told the clergymen to mind their own business ... The boys of Wexford fought on, and suffered on, until they won.'

It was less than two years since Connolly had been condemned from a pulpit in the catholic ghetto, a clerical intervention which certainly seems to have broken the spinners' strike. No doubt he was reacting to British views of Ireland, but Connolly was evidently at a low point. His distance from unionists, and from protestants, had been evident early in the Larne strike, when he remarked that 'a people who have been brought up on such mental pablum [as the *Belfast Evening Telegraph*'s labour column on Saturdays] ... cannot be expected to believe as a progressive people would'.[54] Afterwards he wrote of the aluminium workers 'bit[ing] the hand that fed them', namely his own. There is evidence that the Larne strike collapsed, because of inadequate strike pay, and some sort of managerial offer. Connolly was in no position this time to allege successful clerical interference, and certainly not to do it in a sectarian manner. He was thinking less of the position of protestant workers, and more of unionist political opposition to home rule. 'A great victory for the apostles of "civil and religious liberty"', he ended his account, 'in the very home of their apostolate!'[55]

After the disappointment of Larne, Connolly had to endure the much greater defeat in Dublin with the lock-out of 1913–14, when Larkin railed against wealth and power. A leading employer, William Martin Murphy, set out to destroy the ITGWU, and almost succeeded. Belfast did not play a major role during the struggle, though the trades council condemned the attack on trade unionism on 14 September 1913. Keir Hardie addressed the meeting, and the delegates called for an inquiry into the behaviour of the police. Connolly had a mixed reception, on his return to Belfast, three days later, having become identified with the workers' resistance in the capital. Opposition was expressed at Great Victoria Street railway station, but, when he reached Glenalina Terrace, a bonfire in his honour was blazing in the city cemetery. Nora Connolly claimed later that collecting for the Dublin workers 'was an uphill task. The Church, the clergy, the press, the Hibernian organisation were all against them.'[56] No doubt this was the case in the minority ghetto, given that Devlin was responsible for the AOH. It is likely that opposition increased because of the Montefiore episode in October, when two socialist feminists tried to take workers' children to England for the duration. Connolly's speech in the Albert Hall on Sunday, 1 November, at a meeting chaired by George Lansbury, editor of the *Daily Herald*, would have led catholic nationalists to be more suspicious of him. The Belfast trades council had recommended the Dublin appeal to its affiliates on 2 October, and it condemned the imprisonment of Larkin at the end of the month. Ina Connolly, another of Connolly's five daughters, suggests that most financial support came from the shipyard workers on Friday evenings. Larkin's release in Dublin, on 13 November, was celebrated, in Belfast, at a meeting in King Street, opposition being expressed by a group of militant catholics.

The question of sympathetic industrial action arose only following the closure of the port of Dublin in November. Earlier in the year, Connolly had lost 200 members from the Belfast ITGWU. They had been on strike against the Clyde Shipping Company, but Larkin, having signed an agreement in Dublin on 26 May with six shipping companies, ordered them back to work. The Belfast dockers were not prepared to have him surrender the sympathetic strike weapon for money. Connolly paid a flying visit to Belfast around 20 November, and 150 dock labourers were later reported to have come out because the Belfast Steamship Company was transporting blacklegs to Dublin. Local officials had difficulty in sustaining this strike. In Dublin, on 13 December, Connolly insisted that the NSFU should not work the company's boats. By the middle of January 1914, the ITGWU in the 'low' docks was faced with the problem of blacklegs. With the NSFU unwilling to help, Connolly was burdened with his own minor lock-out. Workers were drifting back in Dublin. On 6 March he met the executive of the Scottish dockers in Glasgow. He was optimistic that the union would put some pressure on the Belfast Steamship Company, but later reported that the NTWF – which the ITGWU never joined – had been unable to rally other transport unions.

Connolly resumed his post in Belfast in the middle of March, and was soon faced with an attack from the engineering firm of Davidson & Company at the Sirocco works. Employees there were asked to sign a declaration that they were not members of the ITGWU. This was Dublin all over again, though Davidson had done the same thing in 1906, when he objected to labourers organizing, and again in 1913. Davidson was then prominent in the unionist leadership, and Connolly made much of UVF drilling in the Sirocco works, at the 1914 ITUC & LP in June, when he asked delegates to condemn the company. An end to government contracts was demanded, but, since the state was concerned only about the wages paid by its contractors, Davidson was able to impose his anti–trade-union views. Connolly also had to deal with the continuing lock-out by the Belfast Steamship Company. The NTWF had protested in April, but Robert Williams was unable to organize industrial action to help ITGWU members. In June Connolly was refused permission to address the conference of the federation in Hull. He intended to attack the NSFU, and Scottish dockers, for working the company's boats. Things were hardly any better in Dublin, where the same company was also refusing to take back workers. When Larkin momentarily released his grip on the union, in the middle of June, Connolly showed no sign of aspiring to become general secretary.

He had remained primarily interested in politics, from the formation of the ILP(I) at Easter 1912. The party's manifesto, in keeping with Connolly's desire to reconcile Belfast socialists to home rule, contained no reference to the struggle for national independence. The branch argued, in May, for democratic reforms to be included in the home rule bill. When the expulsions occurred in July, the party called upon all progressive forces to show their opposition. An office had been acquired in Upper Donegall Street, and William McMullen became chairman of the Belfast branch. Open-air meetings were held at what was known as the lamp in Library Street. 'Being in the business centre of the town', Connolly explained later, 'the passing crowd is of a mixed or uncertain nature'.[57] When a heckler brandished a copy of the covenant, challenging Connolly's affirmation of home rule, he advised him to have it framed for his children to laugh at in the future. During the winter, members met above McDevitt's tailor shop at 5 Rosemary Street. This was known as the bounders' college, possibly because of John Murphy's attack upon Connolly at the ITUC in Clonmel over the textile operatives' society. Later, maybe in 1913, and certainly in 1914, the open-air meetings were transferred to the safety of Clonard Street, off the Falls Road. The ILP(I) survived two years in Belfast, its fortunes declining from the beginning. On 16 October 1912, Connolly asked O'Brien for a list of speakers, who might come to their indoor meetings on Sunday nights. 'We want to work up an interest here in Socialism from the Irish standpoint, and also to develop a feeling of comradeship, and believe that this would be served rather by Dublin lecturers than by imported ones.'[58]

But he did not have things all his own way. In January 1913 a majority of the members decided to hold joint propaganda meetings with the ILP. The average Walkerite, Connolly argued later, 'repeats in the Labour movement the same feelings of hatred and distrust of his Catholic brothers and sisters, as his exploiters have instilled into him for their own purposes from infancy'.[59] This was his attitude, in 1913, when he shared a platform at the lamp in Library Street. When a former ILPer argued that the protestant ethic explained the north, while the south was the product of a slovenly spirit, McMullen refused to let Connolly reply. (He had his own – inverted – explanation of catholic/ protestant differences, which was equally non-Marxist.) 'Things are in a terrible tangle here', he told O'Brien on 29 July. A member of the North ILP, by the name of Daniels, had argued – seemingly – for the exclusion of four Ulster counties from home rule. Connolly wanted to withdraw from the joint committee, but Johnson insisted that acceptance of home rule should be a condition for further cooperation. The ILP refused, and sympathisers and former members then quit the ILP(I). 'Bigotry and anti-Irish prejudice', Connolly concluded, 'dies hard.'[60] He left shortly afterwards for Dublin.

The revelation on 9 March 1914 that the government was considering partition occurred shortly before Connolly's return to Belfast. He got the ILP(I) to hold a protest meeting in St Mary's Hall, though it attracted less the organized working class and more the catholic elements loyal to Devlin. Connolly published in *Forward*, on 18 April, 'Ireland Upon the Dissecting Table', a statement of opposition to partition. This was drafted for the Belfast ILP(I), but hardly advocated in the city. The branch had declined during his absence, Connolly finding it 'nearly wiped out ... [and] almost bankrupt and broken up'. In order to dispel the notion that he did 'not regard the branch here as of any importance', Connolly told O'Brien on 4 May he intended to keep 'to the fore ... [as much] as possible'.[61] In early June he asked his faithful Dublin friend to see if Larkin would grant the ILP(I) a room in Liberty Hall, the headquarters of the ITGWU.

Weeks before the outbreak of war, Connolly was evidently still attached to the strategy he had conceived in 1910. At Library Street shortly after the beginning of the war, Connolly expressed his opposition to militarism. He was shouted down by, as he put it, 'a dozen young Orange hooligans', and an angry crowd followed him up Royal Avenue, as he was forced to retreat to the Falls. Connolly considered that things were being 'magnified into an awful danger'. On 21 August the ILP(I) decided to postpone the Library Street meetings for the duration of the war. He urged their continuation, on the basis of the ITUC's recent proclamation on the need to retain food in Ireland, but he had only three supporters, including William McMullen. Connolly attributed the opposition to 'the machinations of McDevitt'. Campbell spoke and voted against him, Johnson saying and doing nothing. 'Campbell and Johnson and McDevitt have always been of that style', Connolly wrote to O'Brien. 'Ready to cheer every stand made in Dublin, but always against any similar attempt in Belfast.' He announced he was about to resign from the ILP(I). 'I have spent myself pushing forward the movement here for the past three years, and the result of this is that my activity is labelled as a desire for "cheap notoriety". I am sick, Bill, of this part of the Globe.'[62]

The ILP(I) had been conceived in 1912 to push forward the ITUC. Connolly, as Ulster district organizer of the ITGWU, had no difficulty in becoming delegate of the Belfast branch to the Clonmel congress of, what became, the Irish Trade Union Congress and Labour Party (ITUC & LP). It was his first attendance at this parliament of labour since its foundation in 1894. To him fell the honour, in the company of R.J. Moore of the Belfast carters, of moving the first motion, on labour representation: 'That the independent representation of Labour upon all public boards be, and is hereby, included amongst the object of this Congress.' With Walker out of the way, there was no one to argue for affiliation to the (British) labour party. Connolly's motion was, if anything, less immediately political, since few Irish trade unionists were prepared to stand out against the idea of labour representation. His slightly veiled call for an Irish labour party was pressed in terms of home rule. 'The years in which they would be waiting for Home Rule', he said, 'should synchronise with the preparation of labour for Home Rule (applause).' Greig, still a member of the parliamentary committee, warned it would lead to the loss of trade-union members, an Irish labour party being a divisive issue. It 'was premature and should be left over until they knew exactly where they were (applause).'

The discussion ran into the second day, 28 May, Connolly closing the debate by arguing that 'differences of expressed opinion were the very lifeblood of discussion (hear, hear).'[63] The motion was carried by 49 votes to 18, with 20 not voting. There were 19 delegates from Belfast, many of whom probably opposed the ITUC's going into politics. Connolly must have reassured Irish party supporters that they would not be launching a challenge before the formation of an Irish parliament. It was a historic decision, though it probably did not seem like that at the time. Murphy and Galway went on to attack Connolly over his trade-union work in Belfast, though the opponents united, later that day, to support a motion from Larkin and O'Brien, calling for adult suffrage and payment of MPs in the new Irish parliament.

Connolly had realized that the parliamentary committee would have to push trade unions into political activity. His motion included the provision for an annual levy of a shilling (5p) per affiliated member, and a day at congress to discuss labour representation. Campbell as president, and Murphy as secretary, of the Belfast trades council, probably voted on opposite sides at Clonmel. On 21 September, in the aftermath of the expulsions during the summer, Campbell moved that a meeting on labour representation be held in Belfast. This was carried by 11 votes to 9, the envisaged meeting being one of a series across the country. Larkin, O'Brien, Campbell and P.T. Daly were the four office holders on the nine-strong parliamentary committee in 1912–13. On 29

June 1912 Connolly had asked O'Brien if any action had been taken on his resolution. 'The Committee has now the chance', he wrote, 'to create a great Labour movement on sound political lines, and should not hesitate to go out of the beaten track and create precedents instead of following old ones.'[64]

This was to reckon without Larkin, as chairman of the ITUC & LP. He refused to appear at a labour representation meeting, arranged for the Antient Concert Rooms in Dublin. O'Brien informed Connolly, who replied, on 13 September, that Larkin was seeking to dominate the labour movement, and would 'pull [them] all down with him in his fall'. He advised cancelling the meeting, even though he realized that this was to give in to an ultimatum. 'I am sick of all this playing to one man', Connolly wrote, 'but am prepared to advise it for the sake of the movement. In fact, the general inactivity since the Congress has made me sick and sorry I ever returned.'[65] A meeting was held later in Dublin, O'Brien presiding, and also in Wexford, Sligo and Waterford. There is no record of one in Belfast. When it was proposed at the trades council, on 15 March 1913, that two delegates should be sent to the Irish congress, Greig asked about the previous year's resolution. Delegates voted 11 to 10 to adjourn the issue. On 3 April the council decided, by 19 votes to 18, to miss that year's congress.

Connolly attended the Cork congress of the ITUC & LP, between 12 and 14 May, fearing the Irish labour party resolution might be reversed. 'As the Orangeman says "We will not have Home Rule"', he wrote in *Forward*, 'so the Belfast dissenters from the position accepted by most Socialists in Ireland say "We will not have an Irish Labour Party".'[66] Larkin, Johnson, Campbell and Daly were elected officers for the year, from the now twelve-strong parliamentary committee, which also included O'Brien as a Connolly supporter. Larkin and Daly had been to the labour party conference in London to press legislative amendments concerning Ireland – without much effect. 'The English Labour Party was their natural ally', Connolly said in reply to an Irish party supporter, 'and appealing to men of their own class across the water was more natural than appealing to their enemies of the master class in their own country.'[67] William O'Brien proposed that there should be a new constitution, with an executive of twelve, the six Dublin members meeting monthly. George Greig had an amendment for a one-day labour conference after the following year's congress. Delegates finally voted, by 63 to 4, to refer the whole matter to a small committee, comprised of Connolly; Richard O'Carroll, a Dublin member of the parliamentary committee; and P. Lynch, a Cork opponent of a labour party.

It was the parliamentary committee of the ITUC & LP which entered into negotiations with the (British) labour party. On 15 July Larkin and Campbell met MacDonald, Arthur Henderson and Keir Hardie in the House of Commons. Larkin protested against the labour party's consulting the Irish party on all matters to do with Ireland. Campbell wanted a share of the funds, collected in Ireland by the British unions, and passed on to the labour party. The British leaders talked about the need for closer relations. The question of money was discussed at a further meeting, on 6 September, in Dublin, in the early stages of the lock-out, G.H. Roberts and Arthur Henderson representing the British party. An Irish labour party was seen, on both sides, as concerning itself with local matters, the British party still looking after general United Kingdom issues. Campbell admitted that there was not much prospect, at present, of organizing in Ireland, other than Belfast. W.E. Hill, of the railway clerks, admitted it would be a trade-union party, not one federated with socialist organizations. Henderson considered that the admission of socialist groups was a precondition for the return of funds, arguing that the British model of organization was the most appropriate.

Daly, Johnson, Campbell and Hill travelled to London for a third conference on 9 May 1914 with MacDonald and colleagues. Two legislative issues were uppermost. The ITUC & LP had been pressing for better representation for urban areas in the new Irish parliament. The parliamentary committee had also, on 18 March, come out strongly against the exclusion of Ulster. Only Daly was a catholic, Campbell was the son of an Orangeman, and Hill had been in the order for seven years. Johnson and Campbell supported Connolly's view on partition, arguing that they had practical experience of Belfast. 'If Ulster were excluded', Campbell said, 'it would be against the interests of the workers in that province, and he believed that the commercial party were as much opposed to it as they were.' Daly spoke ominously of physical-force nationalists being able to express an opposite determination to that of Carson and the unionists.

The 1914 ITUC & LP was held in Dublin between 1 and 3 June, Larkin presiding. In his address he discoursed on the evil of sectarianism, and praised Connolly, who was 'fighting against forces that few realise the strength of (hear, hear)'.[68] Connolly was again a delegate, and was elected, with 69 votes, to the new 12-strong national executive. Johnson, Larkin, Campbell and Daly were the officers for the forthcoming year. The Belfast trades council had debated a motion, from J. Mercer of the linen-lappers, on 21 February, calling for an all-Ireland labour conference, including socialists and others, given the likely enactment of home rule. This was amended to a local conference, and, on 21 March, the trades council decided to send two delegates to the ITUC & LP. Murphy had not called the labour conference as secretary of the trades council, because the electricians threatened to disaffiliate. He was also cautious, on 2 April, about a meeting against exclusion, given that the liberal party had not come out against it, and the nationalists were supporting this temporary concession. But 'he thought if exclusion were adopted the workers of N-E Ulster would be more than ever in the grip of the sweating employer.'[69] In the discussion of the executive report at the ITUC & LP, the question of a federal party was raised. Connolly, warning about sectarianism in the trade unions, argued against admitting socialist organizations, for fear of antagonizing potential labour supporters. He had the backing of Johnson and Campbell, and a motion calling for a federal Irish labour party, moved by Mercer, and Dawson Gordon of the flax-roughers, was lost by 75 votes to 6. On the second day Connolly, with the support of Richard Corish of

Wexford, moved a resolution against exclusion. H.T. Whitley of the printers made a passionate speech opposing partition, the orange leadership, he argued, being out to prevent working-class unity. The motion was carried by 84 votes to 2.

Connolly became a leader of the Irish labour movement in June 1914, as an executive member of the Irish Trade Union Congress and Labour Party. It was the 21st such gathering of trade unionists in Ireland, but this was only weeks before the outbreak of war. By the time of the 1914 congress, Connolly was recognized as an important trade unionist in Belfast, who had helped lead the Dublin workers during the lock-out. But his base in Belfast was limited, as can be seen from a series of mobilizations following the dockers' and spinners' strikes in the summer and autumn of 1911. They show that the ITGWU and ITWU proved consistently more important than the ILP(I), despite Connolly's political intentions. The erstwhile syndicalist became a leader of a section of the catholic masses outside West Belfast.

The first mobilization was the ILP(I) meeting on home rule in May 1912. The party's foundation, in Dublin, on Easter Monday (9 April), occurred the day before the unionist demonstration at Balmoral addressed by Bonar Law. This was a protest against the introduction of the home rule bill on 11 April. Connolly was on the side favouring home rule, but the bill left a great deal of room for democratic reform. (Larkin became a strong critic of the constituency schedule for the new parliament, complaining that the underrepresentation of towns would see domination by farmers, 'a class which ... had neither a soul to be saved nor a body to be kicked'.[70]) The theme of the meeting called by the Belfast branch of the ILP(I) in St Mary's Hall was the need for reform of the bill. Connolly had used this catholic venue during the mill strike, but the meeting, while an affirmation of the nationalist cause, was implicitly critical of Devlin's relationship with the liberal government. The socialists' audience most likely came from the minority community rather than the labour movement, since the trades council never took a position on home rule. But there were few catholics in the city critical of Devlin. The resolution, drafted by Connolly, referred to a 'meeting of workingmen and women of Belfast'. It welcomed an Irish parliament, 'as opening the way for much needed social reform and the reunion of the Irish democracy hitherto divided upon antiquated sectarian lines'.[71] The meeting called for the payment of members of the Dublin parliament (which had been granted in 1911 for Westminster); election expenses; proportional representation; the enfranchisement of women; and the dropping of the idea of an Irish senate.

The second mobilization was during the expulsions in July 1912. As soon as the workers were driven out of the shipyards, Connolly organized his own dockers and spinners to protest. A band had been in evidence during the strikes of the previous year, and, on 2 July, the first day of the expulsions, the non-sectarian labour band – as it was now named – appeared in the York Street area. (It was equipped by the ITGWU.) A hostile crowd had assembled that evening near Workman,

Clark's north yard in expectation of a catholic manifestation. Connolly, Campbell and Savage, of the ITWU, led a demonstration of 'some thousands' of local people, though Connolly seems to have rerouted the procession to avoid trouble. It had been intended to go down Corporation Street, across Whitla Street and then up York Street, but it cut across at Henry Street, in order to avoid the Whitla Street area. A mob assembled at the end of Donegall Street, but it did not cause trouble. The demonstration was described as 'non-political and non-sectarian'. It ended with speeches at the Custom House steps, where 'strong appeals were made ... that all workers should put sectarianism aside and work in amity and harmony for the betterment of their conditions.'[72]

It was another month before Connolly was able to act further. The ILP(I) held a meeting at its office in Donegall Street, on 2 August, to discuss 'The Present Situation at the Shipyards'.[73] A resolution condemning the expulsions 'as invincible to all progress and destructive of civil and religious liberty' was passed. Connolly called for a united front of opposition. He wanted 'a mammoth demonstration of protest', involving 'all progressive bodies, Liberals, Nationalists and all the freedom-loving organisations'.[74] The Ulster Liberal Association had recently 'deeply deplore[d]'[75] the expulsions, sending £25 for relief. The nationalists were caught up in relief in Belfast, while engaged in high politics at Westminster. There were few other freedom-loving organizations in the city. Connolly secured no united front, and thus, it seems, the ITGWU, 'the only union that allows no bigotry in its ranks', called a 'Labour Demonstration'.[76] (It is just possible this predated 2 August.) It marched from the ITGWU office in Corporation Street and up Victoria Street to – the catholic – Cromac Square. The non-sectarian labour band was again present. Connolly, James Flanagan of the ITGWU, whose brother John had been expelled, and Miss Savage addressed the marchers.

The third mobilization was the Dock ward election in January 1913. Connolly described this as 'an Orange ward', though there were a little over 8,000 catholics to just under 13,000 protestants living there. The local ILP had given up Sunday night meetings, and Connolly took over their hall for his campaign. He was not the candidate of the ILP(I), and some members were hesitant about helping him. His candidacy had been endorsed by the trades council on 5 December 1912, and he was elected to its executive on 2 January 1913. He was being put up by the ITGWU, having been adopted at a meeting of union members 'very largely composed of residents of [the] ward'. They were concerned about the new insurance commission, which would include elected city councillors. He described himself as a trade-union official, standing in the cause of 'labour'. The Clonmel congress of the ITUC & LP, he informed electors, had declared in favour of labour representation. His address combined minimum and maximum programmes. He wanted 'the voice of labour' heard on the corporation, on such demands as the currently important one of covered workers' trams. While he was 'a labour candidate ... totally independent of any political party', his 'personal views' could not be ignored, and would most likely be misrepresented.[77] Thus, he admitted his support for socialism and national independence.

Connolly was fighting a unionist. Nelly Gordon recalls that 'Connolly was well supported by the Dockers and mill workers', and that the contest 'aroused a lot of bitterness between the Catholics and the Protestants'.[78] Ina Connolly remembers turning up at the ILP hall, and finding 'a large number of the Nationalist groups, including members of the Fianna and the Gaelic League – all intent in their efforts to gain a victory for the Labour candidate'.[79] Connolly did not have the support of the AOH, given his connection with the ITGWU, but the *Irish News* commented enigmatically on the morning of the election that 'it need only be mentioned that Mr James Connolly opposes ... the official Unionist nominee.'[80] Stone-throwing prevented some people from voting, and Connolly received 905 votes to the unionist's 1,523. The *Belfast Evening Telegraph* claimed he polled a straight nationalist vote, though he must have picked up some protestant trade-union support. This is the highest vote James Connolly obtained during his political career.

The fourth mobilization was on May Day in 1913. In the absence of a labour demonstration, Connolly led a joint ITWU/ITGWU procession, on 1 May, down the Falls Road, through Royal Avenue to the Custom House steps. The meeting was addressed by Connolly, Flanagan, Nelly Gordon, Shields (unknown) and Malcolm of the railwaymen.

The fifth mobilization was a union excursion in August 1913. On Monday, the eleventh, Connolly led a procession of ITWU/ITGWU members, with the band at the front, down York Street. They were heading for the Midland railway terminus, for a day out at Portrush on the Antrim coast. Their train left at 9.15 a.m., but the mill girls and dockers were 'followed by a hostile crowd of considerable dimensions'.[81] Near Whitla Street, the procession was stoned by some local mill workers. (York Street, according to H.T. Whitley, the printer, had been orange territory for a number of years. He told the 1914 ITUC & LP in Dublin that Connolly's band was the first to challenge this. When another printer, Frederick Hall, criticized Connolly for referring only to protestant bigotry, the latter replied: 'He had been told that other districts were as bad. He was quite prepared to believe that this was as true of the Falls Rd etc. but York St was a main artery of the city.'[82]) That evening, the police commissioner prepared for the return of the excursion at about 9 p.m, a large number of men being deployed at the station. The gates were closed on a crowd of about 1,000, 'mostly composed of girls and youths having the appearance of mill workers'.[83]

When the train pulled in, stones were thrown. 'A few revolver shots were discharged into the air, while feeling evidently ran high.'[84] Connolly had a discussion with the senior police officers, and agreed to cancel the return march up York Street. The party slipped out of the station in small groups, over the space of an hour. One girl was hit on the head by a stone, and had to be treated at the Mater Hospital. Connolly reproduced the *Northern Whig* report of the incident, in his

Forward article of 23 August. He argued that the excursion was 'of a purely trade union nature', and that the band 'had never been known to play any party tunes or attend any demonstration under the auspices of either of the orthodox parties in Ireland'. The counter-demonstration stemmed from opposition to the fact that the two unions were based in Dublin, plus 'a pleasant desire to kill your humble servant'. Connolly did not contradict the *Northern Whig* report that he called off the return march even before reaching Belfast, but he presented a different position in his article on the excursion. He argued that it was necessary to make a strong stand for home rule against protestant workers. 'A real Socialist movement', he wrote, 'cannot be built by temporising in front of a dying cause as that of the Orange ascendancy, even though in the paroxysms of its death struggle it assumes the appearance of health.'[85] Whatever his theory about operating in Belfast in 1913, Connolly's practice at the Midland railway terminus that evening – fortunately for the members of his two unions – was very different.

The sixth mobilization followed Connolly's return from Dublin on 17 September 1913, in the first weeks of the lock-out. He had arrived in the capital on 29 August, only to be sentenced, the following day, to three months in jail, for refusing to give a guarantee of good behaviour in court. Connolly began a hunger strike on Sunday, 7 September, a weapon then being used by women suffragists in Britain. He was released from jail on 14 September, and was able to return to Belfast three days later. Connolly telegraphed Nelly Gordon, asking her to arrange a welcoming party at the Great Victoria Street station. Shortly after 9 p.m., a procession, led seemingly by two bands, and comprising 'a large number of girls', marched up York Street and across town. They sang 'The Robert E. Lee', and the band played 'Johnny Cope', tunes the *Irish News* thought 'could not have had any political significance'. A protestant crowd had gathered in Shaftesbury Square, behind a police cordon, singing 'Dolly's Brae'. When Connolly appeared at the station, the mill girls cheered, and the protestants booed. Stones were thrown, and revolver shots heard yet again. Two of Connolly's supporters were injured by stones. Connolly quickly mounted a sidecar, and was conveyed with his family to the Custom House steps. As he passed the City Hall, more stones were thrown. Flanagan and Gordon spoke at the steps, 'deploring the introduction of sectarianism into the labour question'. Connolly was then driven to his office in Corporation Street, to allow things to quieten down. Only then was he able to travel home to Glenalina Terrace in the Falls.[86]

James Connolly gained considerable direct experience of popular politics in Belfast. He was correct to condemn his nationalist and unionist adversaries as sectarian, standing, as he did, on the shrinking middle-ground of trade unionism. But he contributed to working-class polarization when he argued that socialists had to support home rule. Some local socialists and trade unionists were going along with him, but others, even without Walker, were not so sure. Connolly admitted, on 23 August 1913, that the politics of the ILP(I) 'would arouse passions immensely more bitter than had ever been met ... by the Socialist movement in the past, but it would make [their] propaganda more fruitful and [their] organisation more enduring'.[87] Connolly made this confession in the belief that history was ultimately on the side of the Irish nation, looking forward to untrammelled class struggle under an Irish state. Many people accepted the inevitability of home rule, but not all did so – particularly in the Irish working-class movement. Some labour leaders showed they might be prepared to accept a Dublin parliament legitimized by the British government, and work in a new constitutional arrangement. Connolly's 1913 prediction was soon proved inaccurate, though Walker and socialists throughout Europe had also been historically optimistic in their own ways. The assumption that the Irish national question would soon be solved underpinned everything Connolly wrote about contemporary politics in Belfast from 1910 on. His views – at times from week to week – can be followed in his political journalism.

During his time in the United States, it was the 1907 strike which had elicited Connolly's first comment on Belfast, belatedly in September 1908. He again referred, a few weeks later, to 'the workers shot down last winter [*sic*] in Belfast ... not ... in the interests of the Legislative Union ... [but] in the interests of Irish capitalists'. This was in an article on Sinn Féin, the advanced nationalist organization set up after he left Dublin, published on 23 January 1909 in the *Irish Nation* by W.P. Ryan. Connolly advanced a simple socialist critique of Arthur Griffith's national capitalism. He accepted that the ILP was attractive in Belfast, while making no concessions to its putative internationalism. 'The workers in the towns of North-East Ulster', he wrote,

> have been weaned by Socialist ideas and industrial disputes from the leadership of the Tory and Orange landlords and capitalists; but as they are offered practical measures of relief from capitalist oppression by the English Independent Labour Party, and offered nothing but a green flag by Irish Nationalism, they naturally go where they imagine relief will come from. Thus their social discontent is lost to the Irish cause.

He was already thinking in terms of socialist unity between Belfast and Dublin. 'This union, or rapprochement', he argued, 'cannot be arrived at by discussing our differences. Let us rather find out and unite upon the things upon which we agree.' By September 1909, writing in the *Harp* in the United States, he was much more critical of protestant socialists, and sympathetic towards the catholic masses in Ireland. He contended that the latter's religious culture propelled them towards 'the Revolutionary Social-Democracy of the Continent of Europe', while protestant workers had an affinity with 'Fabian opportunism'. This was a sectarian theorization, albeit a reversal of British superiority with a socialist gloss, which Connolly would have found difficult to substantiate historically. Irish catholicism was about to put up strong resistance to socialism, and he had already conceded that the protestant working class was showing a degree of political independence. Connolly even referred to William Walker, endorsing his criticism of home rule politicians.

Connolly first admitted that Belfast had a history of sectarianism, when he lectured in Glasgow in October 1910. 'It was simply a part of the policy of the governing class to keep the people at loggerheads in order that they might more effectively pick their pockets (applause).' But he went on to argue that 1907 had finally united the working class. 'Along came the Labour Movement and the propaganda of socialist ideas, and ere long religious influence had a negligible quantity.'[88] The following year, he condemned the two main Irish parties in *Forward*, on 11 and 18 March. The unionists had suppressed the 'essentially democratic ... instincts' of the protestant masses, while the home rulers were 'purblind bigots'. Ireland was locked in a reactionary contradiction: 'The question of Home Government, the professional advocacy of it, and the professional opposition to it, is the greatest asset in the hands of reaction in Ireland, the never-failing decoy to lure the workers into the bogs of religious hatreds and social stagnation.' Connolly went on to insist that socialists had to support national freedom. While the home rulers were vanquishing the unionists, working-class independence had to be maintained. 'They represent', he wrote, 'the same principle in different stages of social development. The Tories are the conservatives of Irish feudalism, the United Irish Leaguers are the conservatives of a belated Irish capitalism. It is our business to help the latter against the former only when we can do so without prejudice to our own integrity as a movement.' It was one thing to say this, quite another to maintain working-class unity while supporting home rule, and, much later, fighting for an Irish republic. There was also a suggestion in March 1911 that the catholics were more progressive than the protestants:

> When his mind is not obsessed with the fear of compromising the national demand, the Irish Catholic labourer seems to be enough of a democrat to insist upon his social rights as against his Catholic employer or representative; but his Protestant fellow-worker in the North seemingly allows a blatant parade of loyalty to 'our Protestant institutions' to compensate for all manner of treachery to the cause of labour.

On the eve of moving to Belfast in 1911, then, Connolly had a contradictory view of popular politics. His socialist belief in the working class as the force of the future clashed with his view of the Irish nation as the subject of history. He argued that the protestant masses were progressive, having hinted that they were reactionary. It was their unionism which accounted for the latter, the former stemming from their labourism. The resolution of this contradiction lay in Connolly's view that, after a period of constitutional restructuring, would come an age of internal political development in Ireland. This was an untenable political position, not least in Belfast in 1911. The inevitability of self-government was assumed simply on the grounds of desirability. 'The development of democracy in Ireland has been smothered by the Union. Remove that barrier', he insisted, '... and ere long that spirit of democratic progress will invade and permeate all our social and civil institutions.'[89] Connolly wanted to embrace class politics, and it was possible to make a democratic case for Dublin rule. He went some distance along this route, but the major political problem for Irish socialists was the protestant working class.

Connolly's controversy with William Walker occupied his first weeks in Belfast, from 27 May to 8 July. His claim that no class had an economic interest in the union – thinking of the end of landlordism – was a myopic observation for a Marxist. It was in the 1900s that the uneven development of Ireland was at its most extreme. The economy of Belfast and its environs was clearly integrated into the imperial structure. That of the rest of Ireland was equally dependent, but proponents of self-government did not envisage economic separation. National questions were about statehood, and Irish nationalists assumed a thriving society with national sovereignty. Connolly's argument flowed quite simply from his nationalism, which had long occupied a space in his Marxist theory. When he went on to characterize unionism as reaction in its death throes, this – paradoxically – was derived from his socialism. It was a voluntaristic theory, premised on the belief that all reactionary ideologies could be historically overcome. Just as the protestant bourgeoisie had divided the working class, so socialists, Connolly argued, could unite all workers. Proletarian propaganda could be counterposed to that of the bourgeoisie. The moral stature of this assertion was only slightly dented by its empirical improbability in Belfast in the early 1910s. But it was heavily contested when Connolly, as the prophet of proletarian action, was prepared to accept increasing working-class division, in the short term. And it was finally obliterated with the view that the nationalist–unionist contradiction should be transcended by the physical power of the British state.

Things would get worse, Connolly believed in 1911, before getting better! They got considerably worse with the denouement of Churchill in Belfast on 8 February 1912. When the first lord of the admiralty spoke in Celtic Park, with Pirrie, Redmond and Devlin on the platform, he did so a very short distance from Connolly's home. Connolly may, that wet Saturday afternoon, even have been a member of the audience, which comfortably occupied the alternative tented venue! It was well over two years before Connolly wrote about Churchill's rout in Belfast, in an article on the liberal government's handling of the Ulster crisis. He recognized that the rank and file were probably willing to fight, but suggested that the protestant bourgeoisie, by virtue of its ownership of property, would not rebel against a capitalist government. Connolly went on, in a sarcastic vein, to say that it was widely expected that the police would be used to enforce law and order. In so doing, the government could present itself as upholding free speech. 'The occasion called, and called loudly, for a firm application of force to establish, once and for all, the right of public meeting in Ulster.' He accused Churchill of running away, and the government of using more troops and police in the Falls than would have been necessary to regain control of Belfast from the unionists. This retreat, Connolly argued, did a great deal to encourage unionist reaction. Even before the introduction of the home rule bill, Connolly – by the evidence of later writings – was banking upon the British repression of Ulster.

His first lectures from the ILP(I)'s platform in Library Street were published in the May/June 1912 issues of the *Irish Worker* (a weekly which James Larkin had founded in Dublin the previous May). After the Clonmel congress of trade unionists, Larkin suggested that these pieces could be published as a pamphlet by the new Irish labour party. Nothing came of this suggestion, and Connolly seems to have written little in 1912–13 for the *Irish Worker*. Some articles from *Forward* were to be added to the text at the end of 1913, and other bits later reworked. But it was 1915 before Connolly himself published *The Re-Conquest of Ireland*, a pamphlet of 9 chapters (plus appendices) and 64 pages. It is ironic that the political conditions in which it was written had been left behind by the time it was published.

The Re-Conquest was a political text, embracing history and sociology. The compilation was very different from *Labour in Irish History*, his book published in 1910 in Dublin shortly after his return from the United States, which said very little about Ulster. This intellectual omission must have become apparent to Connolly, in Belfast in 1912–13, when he was drafting what became the first two chapters of his historical pamphlet. His concern at the time was building the Belfast branch of the ILP(I), and winning over the socialists hitherto attached to the ILP. The basic historiography employed was nationalist, but with socialist overtones. Thus, the foreword referred to the 'plebeian Conquerors' and the 'Conquered plebeians' of seventeenth-century Ulster. There soon emerged a 'commonality', argued Connolly in the first chapter, 'the Catholic dispossessed by force, the Protestant dispossessed by fraud', while the aristocracy exploited old fears. Ulster protestants, he continued in the second chapter, were now 'an integral part of the Irish nation', 'the historical development of Ireland [having] brought the same social slavery to the whole of the workers'. The sectarian character of Ulster, in other words, lacked a social basis.

Connolly, then, had a liberal historical view of a divided Ulster, which was derived from his socialist culture. But it was difficult to sustain, given the actual behaviour of protestants in Belfast. Connolly came close in this text to admitting there would be no simple political transformation.[90] The fifth chapter, on 'Belfast and its Problems', followed two chapters on Dublin, all three being drafted when he was preoccupied with the foundation of an Irish labour party. While some of the analysis was forced and unconvincing, it was the writing of a passionate socialist. 'Its industrial conditions', he argued of the city, 'are the product of modern industrial slavery and can be paralleled wherever capitalism flourishes. The things in which Belfast is peculiar are the skilful use by the master class of religious rallying cries which, long since forgotten elsewhere, are still potent to limit and weaken Labour here.'[91]

Connolly commenced what was intended to be a regular series of articles in *Forward* in May 1913. He had the responsibility, as Belfast correspondent, of interpreting Irish, especially Ulster, events for a British socialist audience. Connolly returned to his religious theory of politics in order to explain the peculiarity of Ulster. Irish protestantism, he argued, was 'almost a convertible term with Toryism, lickspittle loyalty, servile worship of aristocracy and hatred of all that savours of genuine political independence on the part of the "lower classes"'. Catholicism in Ireland, against the European norm, was 'almost synonymous with rebellious tendencies, zeal for democracy, and intense feelings of solidarity with all strivings upward of those who toil'.[92] A year after the formation of the ILP(I), he explicitly identified himself with the Irish catholic tradition. There was a passing reference to protestant privileges, but Connolly still explained unionism in terms of false consciousness. There was a second identification with Irish catholicism, in an article published on 12 July, and, on 2 August, he pointedly refuted the – crude – Marxist argument that advanced industrial conditions made for progressive politics:

> The Irish Catholic worker is a good democrat and a revolutionist, though he knows nothing of the finespun theories of democracy or revolution ... the doctrine that because the workers of Belfast live under the same industrial conditions as do those of Great Britain, they are therefore subject to the same passions and to be influenced by the same methods of propaganda, is a doctrine almost screamingly funny in its absurdity.

Connolly had begun the *Forward* series 'believing that the tale these Notes from Ireland [would] have to tell [would] be a hopeful one, even if the hope was nurtured amid storm and stress'.[93] Part of the storm and stress had been the formation of the UVF in January 1913. He wrote of this somewhat later: 'Having allowed the Unionists to drill and arm, the Government made the fact of their military preparations an excuse for proposing the dismemberment of Ireland as a sop to those whom it had allowed to arm against it.'[94] But he remained hopeful. 'The Awakening of Ulster's Democracy', his one unconditionally optimistic piece for *Forward*, was written after the 1913 meeting of the ITUC & LP, when Connolly was probably relieved that there was no attempt on the part of Belfast delegates to reverse his Clonmel motion. He had anticipated 'many-headed opposition'[95] at the Cork congress. The Larne strike of protestant workers saw Connolly culturally react against the dominant community, as he had when he crossed literary swords with William Walker.

For the 12 July number of the paper, Connolly chose, as his subject, the Twelfth celebration. 'Some parts of it are beautiful', he wrote, 'some of it ludicrous, and some of it exceedingly disheartening.' He described watching a procession, presumably in Belfast, in 1911 and/or 1912. This article and another published on 9 August were attempts at a socialist reinterpretation of Ulster protestant history. He described them, on the latter occasion, as contributions to a 'literature that would be suitable for the conversion to Socialism of Orangemen'. (They formed the basis of the second chapter of *The Re-Conquest*.) 'The Socialists of this district', he wrote, 'seem to have been possessed with the idea that it was good tactics to talk about every place under the sun except the North of Ireland, to read every history except Irish history, and to profess unlimited faith in the democracy of every country except Ireland.'[96] This was the hopeful side of Connolly's politics expressing itself, but some Belfast socialists may have considered him disingenuous, given his adhesion to a stormy political scenario.

Connolly had initially been critical of the Irish party from a class perspective, though he later did a great deal to defend the politics of Ulster catholics. It may have been out of a desire to correct this bias, in the context of the overture to Ulster protestants in the summer of 1913, that he wrote a critical article published on 30 August. This was the point at which he went to Dublin to help Larkin, but the piece had been composed shortly after the union outing to Portrush. It was an attack upon the *Irish News*, and its argument, which Connolly had made from the beginning, was that a progressive commitment to political independence, such as that expressed by the Redmondites, was perfectly compatible with positions which were socially reactionary. 'In all Ireland', he wrote, 'there is no journal more ready to proclaim from the housetops its readiness, and the readiness of the party whose mouthpiece it is, to do something for the working class, and in all Ireland there is no journal more ready with poniard to stab to the heart every person or party that dares to organise the workers to do anything for themselves.' The Belfast catholic newspaper, he argued, had 'brought to bear against the Labour movement the most refined and insidious arts of character assassination'.

He attributed the labour pretensions of the *Irish News* to Devlin's need to hold on to a crucial minority of labour votes in West Belfast. Connolly predicted that Devlin might lose, in the election expected by 1915. He himself had come under challenge from the AOH in 1910, and he referred to the order's campaign against trade unions, including the ITGWU. There is no doubting Connolly's opposition to Hibernianism, and his desire to turn members against the leadership, but he hesitated about politically condemning Devlin. He was, after all, politically dependent upon the MP for West Belfast's denying the unionists' political hegemony in the city and province.

The lock-out of 1913–14 began the transition in Connolly's politics, by raising his proletarian political expectations, only to dash them. The defeat of the Dublin workers challenged his socialism. Almost simultaneously, his nationalism was threatened by partition, this undermining the political vision he had held since 1910. From 9 March 1914, Connolly's political journalism became focused on the division of Ireland.

He had less support from nationalists in Belfast, and more from socialists and labourists. It was in the *Irish Worker* of 14 March, that Connolly wrote, in Dublin, about the dangers of a carnival of reaction both north and south. He immediately criticized the Irish party:

The trusted guardians of the people, the vaunted saviours of the Irish race, agree in front of the enemy and in face of the world to sacrifice to the bigoted enemy the unity of the nation and along with it the lives, liberties and hopes of that portion of the nation which in the midst of the most hostile surroundings have fought to keep the faith in things national and progressive.

This was a reference to the Belfast ghetto, where his family lived, and his trade-union members worked. Partition saw Connolly write about 'the national democracy of industrial Ulster' for the first time. He wanted 'Labour in Ulster [to] fight even to the death, if necessary, as our fathers fought before us'. The historical subject was being confused with the political present in Belfast. He returned to the possibility of 'armed force if necessary', against 'the proposal to leave the Home Rule minority at the mercy of an ignorant majority with the evil record of the Orange party', in *Forward* on 21 March. 'Such a scheme', Connolly argued,

> would destroy the Labour movement by disrupting it. It would perpetuate in a form aggravated in evil the discords now prevalent, and help the Home Rule and Orange capitalists and clerics to keep their rallying cries before the public as the political watchwords of the day. In short, it would make division more intense and confusion of ideas and parties more confounded.

Connolly returned to Belfast after writing this article. Saturday, 21 March, was the day of the aborted Seely/Churchill military raid on Ulster. Sunday's papers were full of stories about the government plot and Curragh mutiny, when he sat down to write his next *Forward* piece. Connolly poured scorn on the idea of a crisis, insisting that it was a conspiracy by the political leaders to enforce partition. Few of his observations were apposite, and he revealed a romantic disdain for the protestant community in his description of the city:

> Belfast itself seems bent upon its usual lines of strict attention to the business of profitmaking, and when I look around for the 'grim, determined faces', so celebrated in the song and story of the Tory Press, I fail to see them, and see instead in all the shop windows the usual alluring advertisements of next week's sales; in the columns of the Tory Press the usual invitation to buy and sell and leave all sorts of property; and in the faces of the people in the streets the same unimaginative smugness, tempered by the effects of a Calvinistic theology in some cases, and by drink in many more.[97]

This appeared on 28 March.

That Tuesday (24 March) had seen the ILP(I) meeting to protest against partition, in St Mary's Hall. William McMullen chaired, and was joined on the platform by, in addition to Connolly, Johnson, Campbell, Braithwaite and Capt. Jack White. Five of the six were protestants. 'This was the first big political demonstration I had addressed indoors', McMullen recalled, 'and the hall was packed to capacity, mainly by a Falls Road (Nationalist) audience.'[98] It probably comprised members of the ITGWU and ITWU, plus individual catholics worried about developments. White had been involved in the lock-out in Dublin, and his head was still bandaged following a clash with the police. He was cheered by the Belfast audience as a unionist turncoat.

Connolly 'was received with tepid lukewarmness and had to shout above the subdued hum of conversation of the audience to make himself heard and understood by those who desired to hear him'.[99] The reason was his reputation, among local nationalists, of being less than a loyal follower of Devlin. His speech did not help, Connolly coming out against the stand of the Irish party in the negotiations. Despite this, the ILP(I) secured support for its resolutions of opposition to exclusion. While Connolly was more honest than the Irish party about partition's becoming permanent, he was not a major political threat to Devlin's position in West Belfast.

Connolly followed the meeting up with 'an appeal to the working class', which appeared in *Forward* and the *Irish Worker* on 4 April. He attacked the position of the Irish party, stressing that two general elections would be held during the six-year exclusion period. While he called for 'an Ireland broad based upon the union of Labour and Nationality', he was still attempting to maintain a socialist perspective. But he was appealing only to Belfast catholics, and in language he had criticized Devlin for using. His *Forward* article of 11 April beseeched British labour to oppose exclusion. Only by settling the national question would the Irish vote in Britain be released. Connolly claimed that 'the organised Labour movement in Ireland ... would much rather see the Home Rule Bill defeated than see it carried with Ulster or any part of Ulster left out.' This was hardly a considered retreat from sectarian confrontation, though some of his socialist colleagues began to hesitate about pushing on to solve the national question. 'Ireland Upon the Dissecting Table' appeared the following week, as a statement of the Belfast ILP(I)'s position. Connolly again appealed to the catholic minority, warning them that four counties, plus Belfast and Derry, would be left outside home rule. There would be no social reforms in the excluded area, he argued, the corollary of his assumption that a home rule Ireland would have a strong labour party.

Connolly's strategy for home rule in 1912/13 had allowed for British repression, the nationalists holding firm and the unionists collapsing. On 22 March 1914, he had begun to query the determination of the government, insisting that a home rule parliament could control all its territory. 'Nationalists, Socialists, Liberals, to put them in the order of their numerical importance, feel quite confident that were the forces of the Crown withdrawn entirely, the Unionists could or would put no force into the field that the Home Rulers of all sections combined could not protect themselves against with a moderate amount of ease.'[100] He had been aware of nationalist concessions since 9 March, but could not easily revise his belief that the unionists were bluffing. On, probably, 24 May, he reviewed the major events of the Ulster crisis. Connolly acknowledged there had been unionist defiance, accused the nationalists of timidity, and argued that there had been government treachery. This assessment was made on the eve of the bill's final passage through the Commons. But the amending bill had been promised on 12 May, though it was not introduced in the Lords until 23 June. The absence of any political prescription in Connolly's *Forward* article of 30 May suggests the eclipse of his apocalyptic view of political transformation in Ireland.

This was two days before the 1914 meeting of the ITUC & LP in Dublin. Its parliamentary committee, the formal leadership of the Irish labour movement, had considered home rule inevitable until 9 March. No position had been taken on the bill, out of a desire not to divide the movement. Nine days later, under Larkin's chairmanship, the parliamentary committee condemned exclusion, arguing that 14 of the 34 urban seats would be lost from an Irish parliament. The labour party in parliament, according to the *Irish Worker* of 28 March, was asked to go as far as opposing the home rule bill in its entirety. (This was the source of Connolly's claim on 11 April.) In early April, a national labour demonstration against exclusion was held in Dublin. Congress officers, not including Larkin, travelled to London a month later, and made further representations to labour MPs. They also met the Irish party and Birrell. In his presidential address to the congress on 1 June, Larkin claimed – erroneously – that home rule had now been enacted. 'That question was settled once and for all (cheers).' Discussing the parliamentary committee's report immediately afterwards, Connolly stated that 'he was not so sanguine as the chairman'.[101] But he did go on to talk about the payment of members being crucial. It was the following day that his resolution of opposition to exclusion was overwhelmingly carried, delegates endorsing the parliamentary committee's stand. Connolly had inspired this, through Johnson and Campbell from Belfast, and, to a lesser extent, William O'Brien in Dublin.

He became a member of the new national executive in Dublin that June, but it was the beginning of the end for Connolly, Larkin and the Irish labour movement, or, at least, of the prospect of a labour party in the first home rule parliament.

In the middle of June, after the physical and mental strain of the lock-out, Larkin suddenly resigned as general secretary of the ITGWU. Connolly was keen to see him go, but a meeting of Dublin ITGWU members persuaded Larkin to resume his post. In an article written for *Forward* on 4 July, Connolly queried the future of the Irish labour party. He argued that labour representation was by no means inevitable, but still did not doubt the emergence of an Irish parliament. His concern was the lack of finance for labour candidates in the first Irish election. 'The dice are heavily loaded against us in Ireland', he wrote. 'They are loaded by the evil traditions of the past, by the cowardice of many working class elements in the north especially, by the awful poverty of the country, by the ignorant obstinacy of the capitalist class, by sectarian animosities, by the unscrupulous politicians, by a lying press.' The subtext of the article was the Ulster difficulty. Connolly ended by appealing to 'all those workers everywhere who desire to see an effective force carrying the green flag of an Irish regiment whilst unconditionally under the red flag of the proletarian army'. A month later the ITUC & LP executive, including Connolly, decided to put up candidates in 'the forthcoming elections for the first Home Rule Parliament'. This was reported in the *Irish Worker* of 8 August, four days after Britain had gone to war! Electoral funds were still the big problem, and a six-month speaking tour of the United States was mooted. Campbell was selected on 29 August as a 'Belfast man',[102] but Larkin refused to go. Samuel Gompers of the American Federation of Labor, which Connolly had opposed when in the United States, agreed to an Irish tour. The war prevented the departure of the delegation.

It also altered a great deal else, completing Connolly's political transition which had begun when he went to Dublin on 29 August 1913. The perceived collapse of international socialism subverted 25 years of political certainty, his socialism being severely shaken. But the war also energized Connolly's nationalism, since it promised medium-term revolutionary nationalist possibilities after the deadlock of the preceding five months, if not four years. National patriotism swept Europe in August 1914, and, while Connolly witnessed in a revolutionary way for a secessionist state in Ireland, it had been demonstrated politically that an Irish nation did not have sufficient popular consent. Connolly was no socialist apostate who intellectually dismissed a tradition that had failed him. But a seed of nationalism was nurtured in a historic crisis, until it dominated his politics. By 30 August 1914, when he first alluded to England's difficulty being Ireland's opportunity, in a speech in Dublin, socialism had ceased to be his guiding ideology. The moment of socialist internationalism on the question of European militarism had passed.

But Connolly was still a trade-union official in Belfast, trying to knock at the door of the revolutionary underground. He had to move to Dublin. Larkin continually returned to the idea of going to the United States, thereby vacating the general secretaryship. Connolly certainly knew by 5 September that Larkin was planning to go in three weeks' time. The executive committee of the union then resigned over Larkin's indulgence of his sister Delia, and this reconciled the members to Larkin's departure. He told Connolly in Belfast on 5 October that he could have the insurance section of the ITGWU plus the *Irish Worker*. P.T. Daly would take temporary charge of the union. Connolly thereupon wrote to O'Brien, arguing that Daly would make it impossible 'to maintain an understanding with the Nationalists'.[103] Connolly evidently wanted to use the union in some way, but his relations with the republicans were weak at this point. Two days later he wrote that he would refuse to serve under Daly even if he lost his job as an organizer. He put these points in a letter to Larkin on 9 October, but the latter proposed Daly at an executive meeting on 13 October. O'Brien had been lobbying Thomas Foran, the general president, on Connolly's behalf, and a majority voted for him to become acting general secretary. The ITGWU bid formal farewell to Larkin on Sunday, 18 October, and Connolly took over Liberty Hall the following day. He left his family in Belfast. It was from Liberty Hall that he would march to the GPO in O'Connell Street on Easter Monday, 1916, becoming an Irish historical hero. He sloughed off a lifetime of socialist politics in his 18 months in Dublin, turning his back on the Belfast he had known in the years before the war.

Part IV

War

8

The Great War in Belfast, 1914–18

The war in Europe, which began in August 1914 and ended in November 1918, was a watershed in world history. The Irish question was set aside in British politics, only to re-emerge as the Dublin rising of 1916. The Irish party vied with the unionists to be responsible at a time of national emergency, but only the rebels of Ulster joined the coalition governments of Asquith and then Lloyd George. Redmond did not survive the war, and his successor, John Dillon, went down, in the 1918 general election, to Eamon de Valera, as leader of Sinn Féin. Opposition to conscription was a major issue that year, but the Redmondite national volunteers had been as ready to enlist as the UVF. The Ulster division was decimated at the Somme in 1916, and Irishmen from the other three provinces were also sacrificed by the war machine. This consumed a gigantic amount of armaments, the state coming to command industry. Belfast played a leading part in Ireland's contribution to wartime production, with its linen and shipbuilding industries. The wartime political truce saw peace return to the city. Though prices rose, the war provided an unprecedented opportunity for the Belfast working class to earn a living, this applying especially to the catholic minority. The gap between skilled and unskilled narrowed. The prewar unionist mobilizations in Ulster gave way, after four years of carnage, to revolutionary nationalism in the rest of Ireland.

The first day of the war was 5 August 1914. Carson wanted the status quo in Ireland maintained, but Redmond, in calling for the prorogation of parliament, was concerned to have home rule enacted without any amendment. It was not until 15 September that Asquith announced that the bill would receive the royal assent, while being suspended for the duration of the war. An amending bill was to follow in the next parliamentary session dealing with Ulster. The conservatives stormed out of the house, and home rule became law three days later. Redmond had got everything, and nothing.

The unionist mobilizations had seen the formation of the UVF in 1913, but also of the Irish volunteers in nationalist Ireland. Redmond hoped that the latter, now under the control of constitutional nationalists, would be recognized as the Irish volunteer force within the British army. Redmond did not want it committed overseas, but Lord Kitchener at the war office simply wanted recruits for the three divisions of the British army from Ireland. He refused to recognize Irish regiments as those of another nation, and initially dispersed Irish recruits throughout the army. It was on 20 September 1914, at Woodenbridge in Co. Wicklow, that Redmond, returning from London after the enactment of home rule, told a parade of Irish volunteers that they should be ready to fight 'not only in Ireland itself, but wherever the firing line extends, in defence of right, of freedom and religion in this war'.[1] This was a sudden and decided change of policy, from an Irish nationalist leader dependent upon the British government. The 10th and 16th divisions of Kitchener's new army were recruited in nationalist Ireland, though men were quickly sent to England. Five days later Asquith spoke at a home rule celebration in Dublin, 500 armed volunteers marshalling the huge crowd. Carson and Craig had demanded that the UVF be absorbed into the army, Kitchener finally agreeing that the 36th division should be dignified with the name of Ulster. Craig opened a recruiting office at 60 Victoria Street in Belfast, the UVF equipping those who signed up. The original leadership of the Irish volunteers repudiated Redmond on 24 September, and he went on to form his own national volunteers. As Irish leader, he took nearly 170,000 members, leaving a mere 11,000 to guarantee Ireland's freedom. Nora Connolly wrote to her father in Dublin on 25 October, complaining about the Union Jack and Belgian flags on the Catholic Boys' Hall on the Falls Road in Belfast, in honour of Redmond's visit to review the national volunteers in Celtic Park.

The pattern of military recruiting in Ireland was complex, and related to the existence of opposing paramilitary forces. The number of – nationalist – volunteers in Belfast in September 1914, according to police estimates, was 3,250, out of 59,892 in Ulster, and 181,732 in Ireland. There had been 22,431 members of the UVF in the city in May, out of a total of 84,865, a figure that declined to 61,982 by February 1915, when there were 13,420 in the 4 Belfast regiments. In the first months of the war, some 20,000 protestants from Ireland joined up, the figure for catholics being fewer than 14,000. The first recruits came from the UVF, but only a minority of this force enlisted. Some of the protestants also came from the other three provinces. Ulster was not quite as loyalist at it liked to boast. Fifty-seven per cent of the first catholic recruits came from the Redmondite national volunteers, but only a minority of this force joined up. Redmond lost his instructors at an early stage, since most were British army reservists. (Of the 17,804 reservists at the outbreak of war, 12,115 were catholics, and 4,074 were from Ulster.) Many of the catholic recruits also came from Ulster, particularly urban areas, and they were predominantly working class. Catholic West Belfast was particularly involved in the war effort.

In the next 12 months, to 15 December 1915, 31,000 Irish catholics came forward, as compared to nearly 20,000 protestants. By April 1916, 150,000 Irishmen were in active service, one-third of whom had been in the army at the start of the war. There were 14,013 voluntary recruits from Ireland in 1917, and, as late as 1918, more than 11,000 came forward in 11 weeks as a result of a campaign in the final months of the war. Over 200,000 enlisted in the British forces during hostilities. When the wives, sweethearts, parents, siblings, and children of some quarter of a million Irishmen are taken into account, this was a sizeable proportion of the people of Ireland. Of the 22,494 recruits from the 6 counties of Ulster in 1915, 30 per cent were catholic. In Belfast, 3,956 catholics, of whom 928 were members of the Redmondite organization, volunteered in 1915. The comparable figures for protestants were 10,507, of whom 4,017 came from the UVF. Twenty-seven per cent of the Belfast recruits that year were catholics, slightly greater than the proportion of the minority in the city.

The 36th (Ulster) division was trained in the province, leaving for England only in July 1915. On 8 May the former UVF members, now in British uniforms, had paraded in Belfast. It was October before the division crossed to France. On 1 and 2 July 1916 it lost well over 5,000 men at the beginning of the battle of the Somme, the Ulster division winning 4 Victoria Crosses. This entered the folk culture of the province, the humble village of Thiepval and its wood being forever commemorated. Only 70 of the 700 men from the West Belfast battalion of the UVF survived the first day unscathed. The 10th and 16th divisions had seen action in France and elsewhere much earlier, and, in the first 13 months of the war, catholic Irishmen won 17 Victoria Crosses. This became less and less a source of pride as the war continued, and it is possible that catholic recruitment began to slow down in early 1915. The war weakened the national volunteers, though the Irish volunteers did not immediately benefit. The UVF also continued to exist, but it was better able to safeguard Ulster's future while wholeheartedly supporting the war effort. Recruitment of protestants may have ceased in the early autumn of 1915, the myth of a possible nationalist invasion being used to justify this.

The military and naval disasters in the spring of 1915 had forced Asquith to form a coalition government, in May, with the conservative and labour parties. The Irish party refused to join. Carson became attorney general, and, when he resigned in November, F.E. Smith took his place. Redmond had failed to get the chief secretaryship, but he was able to prevent J.H. Campbell, the second unionist MP at Trinity College, from becoming lord chancellor of Ireland. Campbell became Irish attorney general on 9 April 1916.

Belfast, and the rest of the country, lost the most enthusiastic supporters of Redmond and Carson. On Easter Sunday, 1915, 27,000 national volunteers, some of them from Belfast, attended a review in Dublin's Phoenix Park. Many later left for the front. The orange order marched in 1915 on the Twelfth without emblems or banners, and observed the wartime political truce. The 1916 Twelfth in Belfast, and throughout Ulster, was cancelled. The lord mayor requested five minutes' suspension of all business at noon, in memory of those lost at the Somme, the annual holidays also being put back to 7–8 August. The RIC commissioner reported to Dublin Castle that 'there [was] much party feeling between the Catholics and Protestants in mills and factories.'[2] He predicted that the latter would not work on the Twelfth. The Independent Orange Order, or what was left of it, had intended to march, but the military authorities successfully maintained their ban in the wake of the Easter rising in Dublin, when a republic had been proclaimed – and defended between 24 and 29 April.

The Irish volunteers, or Óglaigh na hÉireann, had been formed, at the instigation of Eoin MacNeill, a professor at University College, Dublin, during the lock-out in 1913. This also saw the creation of a workers' militia, called the Irish Citizen Army (ICA) by Capt. Jack White. Followers of Larkin attempted to disrupt the foundation of the volunteers, at the Rotunda Rink, though they were contained by the Irish Republican Brotherhood (IRB) under Bulmer Hobson. This secret separatist organization, which many considered to be moribund, was controlling the nationalist response to the establishment of the UVF earlier in the year. The constitutionalists were initially scathing, but MacNeill believed it was necessary to counter the militancy of the unionists. The threat of physical force from nationalist Ireland came too late to influence members of the liberal government. (When P.T. Daly, who had been drummed out of the IRB in 1910 for embezzling funds, made veiled threats to the [British] labour party in May 1914 about exclusion, this led Tom Johnson to make the same point to Redmond and Devlin. When he also put it to Birrell, the Irish secretary demurred: '[he] was haunted by the spectre called up in Ulster', but did not believe the ITUC & LP 'would plunge their country into Civil War for the sake of the few years covered by the proposals'.[3]) MacNeill believed that drilling by nationalists strengthened the cause of home rule, and created the army of a future Irish government. The Larne gun-running by the UVF meant that the Irish volunteers had to engage in a counter-escalation.

MacNeill decided it was necessary to arm, and Sir Roger Casement, a former commercial diplomat, arranged the illegal importation. Bulmer Hobson took charge of the landing at Howth in late July. There had been 75,000 volunteers in May, and after the arms landing the organization grew to 180,000 in September. A second, and perhaps more important reason, was the constitutionalists' takeover of the organization early that summer. MacNeill and Hobson acceded to Redmond, for tactical reasons, though the decision enraged Tom Clarke and Sean MacDermott, the effective controllers of the IRB. Hobson ran the organization behind the backs of the Redmondites. All factions were willing to have the Volunteers recognized as a defence force, from 3 August, but, after 20 September, MacNeill, Hobson, and the now pro-German IRB leadership were not willing to fight for Britain at Redmond's request. MacNeill's Irish volunteers held their first convention in Dublin on 25 October 1914.

Capt. White's ICA had not survived the defeat of the Dublin workers in March 1914, but Sean O'Casey, a former IRB man and supporter of the ITGWU, suggested its revival. Larkin presided at a foundation meeting in Liberty Hall on 22 March. This second ICA was a working-class alternative to the Irish volunteers, socialism being relatively unimportant, and, under Larkin, it came to cooperate with the more militant section of the volunteers. When Connolly took over at Liberty Hall in October, he – for the first time – became actively involved with the organization. It was not just for ITGWU members, nor was it exclusively working class, but he failed in his effort to affiliate the ICA to the volunteers at their first convention. Connolly's goal was national insurrection. This he pressed upon the Irish volunteers, oblivious of the efforts of the IRB, and against the MacNeill/Hobson position of resisting disarming and conscription. Connolly, as acting general secretary of the ITGWU, met later with opposition from within the union. He had a serious confrontation with his executive on the eve of the 1916 rising, threatening to resign if it did not let him hoist a national flag on Liberty Hall.

By the end of August 1914, the IRB had decided to rise during the war, regardless of German military help. It was Casement, though not a member of the IRB, who secured a German declaration of support for Ireland, and permission to raise an Irish brigade from prisoners of war. The IRB meanwhile was gaining control of the volunteers, a secret military committee, later council, being established in May 1915 to prepare for an insurrection. This – augmented – military council asked the Germans, towards the end of the year, for arms, despite Casement's failures to interest Berlin. The IRB also knew how little enthusiasm there was for advanced nationalism, there being continuing support in Ireland for the war throughout 1915, when the membership of the volunteers remained at 13,500. They were ordered not to fire on civilians hostile to their opposition to the British war effort, after a nasty incident in May when a crowd attacked Irish volunteers in Limerick. The authorities repressed anti-war agitation, using the Defence of the Realm Act (DORA), but the army was not allowed to ban the volunteers, the Irish government fearing this would only provoke MacNeill.

Ireland's benign colonial rulers had no fear of pro-German separatism in 1915, given what they knew about Casement, the state of the country, according to police and military intelligence, and Redmond's claim still to command the political leadership of the Irish people. Armed volunteers and ICA men were tolerated by Dublin Castle. Some of Connolly's men were army reservists, and others volunteered for the British army. (In March 1917, P.T. Daly told Arthur Henderson that 5,000 ITGWU members had volunteered for the army. 'Close on'[4] 2,000 were killed in British uniform!) Connolly fashioned a small military organization of about 100 men, with the help of former British soldiers, hardly a working-class militia in wartime Dublin. On the eve of the volunteers' second convention, in October 1915, Connolly publicly threatened to act, if MacNeill did not decide to rise. Conscription of single men was enacted in January 1916, and Redmond successfully pressured Birrell to have Ireland excluded from this. The Irish volunteers were worried about Connolly, but Patrick Pearse finally reported that he would be no problem. MacNeill did not know that Pearse was a member of the IRB's military council, and that Connolly had been incorporated into the Fenian conspiracy between 19 and 22 January. The military council had fixed the rising for Easter Sunday, 23 April, though the IRB was not formally told of the plans. A rising had initially been envisaged to take place if there was a German landing, conscription was imposed, or the war was likely to end. Connolly and his five, later six, colleagues intended to use the IRB to call out the Irish volunteers, before, as they believed, the British authorities moved against them. A German military intervention was requested.

Arms and ammunition on the *Aud* were intercepted by the British navy on 21 April. Casement had landed from a German submarine, to advise against a rising, only to fall into the hands of the police. This lulled Dublin Castle into thinking it had pre-empted any action, but the military council decided, on Easter Sunday, to come out the following day. Without German arms, the insurrection was confined largely to Dublin. The plan to provoke the volunteers had also failed, MacNeill doing his best to prevent any action. Well under 1,000 volunteers, plus 152 members of the ICA, rose at noon the following day. It was Pearse who proclaimed the Irish republic, becoming president of its provisional government. He was also commander in chief of the army of the Irish republic, its Dublin division being commanded by James Connolly. The revolutionary junta of seven had launched an insurrectionary attempt at national revolution, in political conditions its members had failed to grasp, and with military forces they could hardly claim to command. By the time the provisional government surrendered unconditionally, on Saturday, 29 April, there were no more than 1,600 insurgents. They had to be protected from the wrath of Dublin's inhabitants, when they were being taken away by British soldiers. A total of 3,430 men and 79 women were arrested; 170 men and 1 woman (Countess Markievicz) were court-martialled, all but 1 man being convicted. Of the 90 sentenced to death, 15 – including Pearse and Connolly – were executed by military firing squad between 3 and 12 May. A total of 1,836 men and 5 women were interned in England, but most were discharged after further inquiry, and nearly all released by Christmas. The last of the sentenced prisoners was home by June 1917.

Lt.-Gen. Sir John Maxwell, who had been relieved of his command in Egypt, arrived in Dublin on Friday, 28 April, to tell Birrell, and the viceroy, Lord Wimborne, that he was taking charge. Martial law had been proclaimed for Dublin on the Tuesday, and for the rest of the country on the following day. The insurgents were seen simply as pro-German by the martial law authorities. The seven signatories of the republican proclamation expected to die, and the political establishment accepted that the leaders would be executed under the Defence of the Realm Act. But the administration of military justice was left to Maxwell, his courts martial handing down the 90 death sentences. He was out to get an unspecified number of the organizers and commanders of the insurrection, believing he could suppress Irish revolutionary nationalism by eliminating its leadership. Seven leaders were executed on 3 and 4 May, after which Asquith requested no further deaths. Some commutations began to be announced, but a further eight died over the following week. 'The policy of dribbling executions'[5] had an effect on public opinion, and the government believed all further executions were halted on 9 May. Eamon de Valera and Thomas Ashe, as commandants, received commutations two days later. John Dillon vented his anger in the House of Commons on 11 May: 'It is not mur-derers who are being executed, it is insurgents who have fought a clean fight, a brave fight, however misguided.'[6] But this did not stop the exe-cution of Connolly and Sean MacDermott the following morning. They were the last to die, Maxwell being determined to execute the two sur-viving signatories of the proclamation. Asquith arrived in Ireland later that morning for a two-week tour of the country, having accepted the resignations of Birrell, and his under-secretary, Sir Matthew Nathan.

With government completely broken down in Ireland, the prime minister recommended a general settlement, there being no other way of disarming the volunteer organizations. The inspector general of the RIC had reported that Ulster unionists welcomed the suppression of the rebellion, 'and think this will show the English people the dangers likely to result from Home Rule'.[7] Asquith was thinking of 'the total exclusion (for the time at any rate) of Ulster'[8] from home rule, the task of settling the Irish question being left to Lloyd George, the minister of munitions. The deaths of the insurgents were already making an impact at home but especially abroad. On 19 May the British ambassador in Washington had written that, while the rebellion was a failure, 'the mil-itary executions which have been its consequence have raised the victims to the status of martyrs'.[9] Unionists, by and large, including some in the government, considered any settlement a concession to Sinn Féin, as the insurgents were erroneously dubbed. This view was fiercely argued by Lord Lansdowne, minister without portfolio, and a landowner from Co. Kerry, and Walter Long, a former leader of Irish unionism, who was now at the local government board.

Lloyd George proposed an Irish parliament, made up of existing MPs, who were also to remain at Westminster. The six counties of Ulster would be excluded from Dublin rule, certainly until a year after the end of the war, but with provision for extension by order in council. What the unionists saw as permanent exclusion, Lloyd George hoped the nationalists would consider to be temporary. As minister of munitions he used the argument that the United States needed to be conciliated for the sake of continuing supplies. He had told Carson on 29 May that exclusion would be permanent, and the latter succeeded in having Lloyd George's proposal quietly accepted by the UUC on 12 June. The Irish party saw it as temporary, and, on 18 June, a convention of Belfast nationalists voted to accept his – as yet unpublished – plan. Redmond had to threaten to resign, to get an Ulster convention, also in Belfast, on 23 June, to back him by 475 votes to 265. This was to reckon without the southern unionists, who were influential in the coalition government. They saw partition as desertion of the south by Ulster. Asquith suggested in cabinet on 27 June a committee to consider further an Irish settlement, it being assumed that Redmond and Carson were in agreement. It was not until 17 July that Lloyd George circulated his proposals to cabinet colleagues, having taken over the war office eleven days earlier, following the death of Kitchener. The government decided, on 21 July, to end Irish representation in the House of

Commons, thereby excluding the nationalists from reconsiderations after the war. The following day, Lloyd George admitted to Redmond that exclusion would be permanent. The settlement was unravelling. Peace had been restored in Ireland, and it was with some relief that Asquith and his new war minister returned to the conduct of the war in which so many Ulster unionists had recently made the supreme sacrifice at the Somme.

Lloyd George finally unseated the prime minister, and formed his own coalition government on 6 December, establishing a small inner directorate for the war effort. The new government was less liberal than Asquith's, many of the senior positions going to conservatives. Lloyd George, and Arthur Henderson, the labour leader, sat in a war cabinet with four tories. Carson returned to the government, as first lord of the admiralty, and James Craig was given a junior position – treasurer of the royal household! No offers were made to the Irish party, and the unionist, H.E. Duke, continued as chief secretary, though Lloyd George ended martial law, and allowed internees in England to return to Ireland by Christmas. He had begun to talk about the need for conscription there. Carson joined the war cabinet in July 1917, only to resign, again, the following January, when Jellicoe, the first sea lord, was sacked, his withdrawal being bound up with Lloyd George's putative policy towards Ulster.

The labour movement in Ireland was caught up in the aftermath of the rising. Connolly of course had been a member of the national executive of the ITUC & LP, and he attended his last meeting on 4 March 1916. One other member, Richard O'Carroll, who had joined the Irish volunteers, was killed in the fighting. The 1915 meeting of the ITUC & LP, arranged for Sligo, had been postponed, 'the minds of the people for the most part [being] engrossed in the progress of the European war'.[10] The ITGWU was not involved in the rising, though the ICA's association with Liberty Hall meant it was shelled, and subsequently ransacked by troops. Maxwell included trade-union activists in his sweep for insurgents. P.T. Daly, the congress secretary, and William O'Brien were arrested, though neither had borne arms. The leadership of the movement, such as it was, temporarily fell to Johnson and Campbell in Belfast, both black-coated workers. The papers of the ITUC & LP had been seized, and they sought their return. Johnson and Campbell set about securing the release of trade-union leaders, and pressured Asquith on compensation for death and damages. Johnson, and Thomas Farren of the Dublin trades council, met leaders of British labour, and attempted to defend the ITGWU from the Sinn Féin smear. The national executive of the congress/party demanded on 10 June that Irish labour be consulted, and again came out against partition. Johnson and Campbell, and three Dublin trade unionists, met Lloyd George on 7 July – his first day at the war office – to express opposition to the division of Ireland. Johnson acknowledged he did not speak 'for the large number of Ulster Trade Unionists who were opposed to any form of Home Rule', and Thomas McPartlin admitted, in reply to Lloyd George, they would rather 'continue as heretofore'.[11]

The Irish Trade Union Congress and Labour Party met in Sligo between 7 and 9 August, having been postponed from Whitsun. Johnson, in his presidential address, paid tribute to Connolly, O'Carroll and Peadar Macken, another trade-union member of the volunteers who had died in the rising. But he also mentioned Irish trade unionists killed in the European war. Johnson admitted to being a supporter of British war aims, though he had become a critic of militarism after the rising. 'The moral of the whole story – not yet closed – for the workers is to be very vigilant against any encroachment by the military on the civil powers of the State.' He claimed that labour leaders from Belfast were prepared to wait 50 years, rather than have exclusion. 'An intelligent advocacy of ... a programme ... of social reconstruction ... and its application by public bodies wherever possible [would] be the surest way of rallying the workers of Ulster to the banner of a United Ireland.'[12] It was the first of many articulations of the possible relationship between socialism and nationalism in Ireland. The national executive had sought to dissociate the ITGWU from the ICA. W.E. Hill, the London-based delegate of the railway clerks, wanted this part of the report referred back, until Thomas Foran stated that his union was proud of the association, though the citizen army was an independent body. The congress voted to oppose partition, but Campbell got no support for the idea of leaving a settlement until after the war.

The first congress of the war did not reflect the economic changes taking place in Belfast, nor was this evident in the local trades council. The prewar mobilizations had produced a – partial – dislocation of Belfast's economic life in the summer of 1914. The prospect of civil strife, so Asquith told the cabinet after the 1916 rising, frightened English and Scottish banks and insurance companies. The outbreak of war saw a return of economic confidence, with a resumption of financial commitment.

The air was open to the combatants, and a new technology of war – aeroplanes – created a demand for Ulster linen. The cloth was used in the shells of these light aircraft. German airships had appeared over the British coast at the end of 1914, but primitive, though no less fearful, bombing of England was carried out by aeroplanes. These new machines were used by British forces in France to observe the enemy, and also engage in tactical bombing. Air combat brought the front line to the skies. The aeroplane was also envisaged by Britain, from late 1917, as a machine for mass bombing of the enemy, this being seen as a reprisal for German air attacks. It was also believed victory could be achieved by air power alone. An air ministry was set up under Lord Rothermere, then director of the army clothing department, and the Royal Air Force (RAF) formally established.

The Irish linen industry had been engaged in full production from early 1909, half the flax coming from Russia, and over a quarter from Belgium. The latter ceased with the outbreak of war, and Russian supplies became more important, until gravely affected by the revolution in 1917. Irish-grown flax accounted for over 60 per cent in 1918, the acreage having almost trebled since 1914. The flax crops in 1917 and

1918 were commandeered, at fixed prices, by the government, the industry effectively coming under state control. Flax was distributed to linen mills, licensed to spin. Before the war, spinners had earned an average of 12s. (60p) a week, on time rate, for 55 hours. This increased annually, reaching 19s. (95p) in 1917, and 26s. (130p) the following year – a wartime increase of 117 per cent. Prices did rise during the war, but these wages represented a shortage of labour, at a time of high government demand for yarn. 'Never before in the history of the Irish linen industry, nor indeed of any other industry, [had] changes so drastic and so remarkable been brought about in such a comparatively short time.'[13] There was plenty of work for women, particularly in the unskilled end of the industry, and catholics may have disproportionately benefited in Belfast from the war. Wage increases for weavers were lower; 95 per cent for plain weavers, and much lower, 62 per cent, for damask weavers, in the luxury end of the industry. Plain weavers earned an average piece-rate of 12s. 8d.(63p) at the start of the war, this rising to 24s. 8d. (123p), while damask weavers saw their wages rise from 19s. 3d. (96p) to 31s.3d. (156p). Weaving factories were also under great pressure to turn yarn into cloth, Trenchard having the impossible goal of an RAF of 100 squadrons.

The linen industry obtained its spinning and preparing machinery from local firms, which had also exported textile machinery before the war. It was this engineering industry nationally which became central to the war economy, Lloyd George's new ministry of munitions bringing it under state control in 1915. 'From first to last a businessman organization',[14] it allowed considerable profiteering, despite the treasury agreements negotiated with the unions. He organized the production of shells and other ammunition, for the guns of the western and other fronts. Engineering workers were subjected to dilution, skilled men being joined by unskilled men and women as workplaces were reorganized. The manufacture of munitions saw the development of a shop stewards' movement, in Scotland and England, which industrially confronted the government, and even constituted a serious political challenge to the wartime state. This pattern was not reflected in Belfast, where only a few textile plants were converted to munitions manufacture. Women workers were required in the linen industry, and local engineering firms made their contribution to the war by continuing their patterns of production. There was less dilution, and therefore little ambiguous resistance by organized workers in the town shops. The engineering industry was also related to Belfast's second industrial pillar, shipbuilding, though the connection may not have been as strong as elsewhere.

Workman, Clark and, especially, Harland and Wolff overshadowed Belfast, being dominant firms in the United Kingdom shipbuilding industry. They supplied the merchant and royal navies during the war, the freedom of the seas having long been a British strategic interest. A ministry of shipping was established in December 1916, when Lloyd George became prime minister, a liberal Glasgow shipowner taking charge. Carson, at the admiralty, found himself a customer of the

Belfast yards, and his ministry took over responsibility for all shipbuilding in May 1917. The state controlled the yards. The comptroller of
shipbuilding and repairs, Sir Eric Geddes, replaced the Ulster leader as
first lord in mid-1917. In March 1918, Pirrie became comptroller of
merchant shipbuilding. Lloyd George liked businessmen in government. The idea of standard ships had been drawn up in 1916, but it was
Pirrie who allocated the different sizes to the yards of the United
Kingdom. He also synchronized hull and engine manufacture. Pirrie got
his own yard to build six different merchant ships; on five of these,
Harland and Wolff had the shortest manufacturing time. In the
tonnage league for 1918, it came first in the United Kingdom, with
Workman, Clark third. The demand for labour, skilled and unskilled,
increased, and wage differentials decreased. In the first two years of the
war, prices rose faster than wages, workers maintaining their standard
of living by working over and above 54 hours a week. Shipyards had
become controlled establishments in the second half of 1916, collective
bargaining being suspended. Wage rates thereafter were set by bureau-
cratic fiat, flat-rate increases helping to narrow differences. Extra hours
were still worked. The standardization of design did not require a major
reorganization of the shipyards, and reconstitution of the workforce.
From 20,000 in 1914, it expanded to 29,000 in 1919. Craft controls still
persisted, but more employment probably improved the position of
catholic workers relative to protestants.

There was little ethnic hostility in Belfast in the course of the war,
catholics finding it a more congenial city in which to live and work.
The rising passed peacefully, due largely, so some unionists thought, to
the control the UVF exercised over more unruly protestant elements.
The government was told in May 1916 that 'a large number of [UVF
members were] now being sworn in as special constables.'[15] Martial law,
and the cancellation of the Twelfth that year, caused more protestant
anger. On 6 July, according to the inspector-general of the RIC, 14
catholics left work at Grove Mill, 'in consequence of annoyance from
Protestant fellow-workers'.[16] There were no generalized expulsions, and
catholics and protestants continued to work side by side during the rest
of the war.

The authorities, if anything, became more anxious about secular
industrial agitation. The military intelligence report for September 1916
made reference to a strike of engineers at the docks on the 14th, the
unrest being attributed to 'Socialistic propaganda and meetings'.[17] In
March 1917 there was reference to a short strike at Workman, Clark.
Some dockers were also expected to cause trouble, but 'the presence of
so many loyal men ... probably keeps them quiet.'[18] An ILP meeting in
Victoria Street on 25 August, to be addressed by a woman speaker from
Liverpool, was proclaimed by the military authorities, given it was
about peace. Reference was made to a strike of tinsmiths in Harland and
Wolff, that October, and also of tenters in the linen industry. Towards
the end of the year members of the ASE in the two shipyards struck,
their industry having been excluded from a special bonus awarded by
the government to skilled workers. When engineering officials warned

the men that strikes were illegal during wartime, they were 'hustled off the platform and the meeting was taken charge of by the rank and file'.[19] Military intelligence kept an eye on workers who had come to Belfast to avoid conscription. In early 1918 there were some strikes in the docks, which were attributed to men from Glasgow. 'They are all socialists of an advanced type and members of the ILP.'[20] It was reported that these men were predominantly Jewish, and that, by taking good jobs, they were causing resentment. In March 1918 there was a two-week strike of 2,000 carpenters. All this suggests a considerable undercurrent of discontent in the workplace.

More trouble was brewing in nationalist Ireland in the wake of the rising. In July 1916 Maxwell wrote that the Irish volunteers were 'at present sheep without a shepherd'.[21] Redmond, the leading Irish shepherd, had been elected back in 1910, and he and his colleagues were failing to get home rule from Lloyd George. His support for the war probably caused less distress among his followers, though this would change after his death in early 1918. John Dillon argued that the Irish nationalists should be more of an opposition at Westminster. The insurrection was – semi-officially – called the Sinn Féin rebellion, and the name stuck from April 1916. Sinn Féin had been founded as an advanced nationalist party, after the return of the liberals to power, by the political journalist Arthur Griffith, to propagate national self-reliance. Initially backed by the IRB, Griffith argued, against the Irish party, for parliamentary abstentionism (the so-called Hungary policy) and economic nationalism (after Friedrich List) as a basis of Irish industrialization. Sinn Féin became the expression of post-rising nationalism, though its rise was not inevitable.

Griffith had long moved away from Irish republicanism, and, as a rank-and-file member of the Irish volunteers, helped MacNeill try and prevent the rising. Sinn Féin in 1916 was a weak separatist organization, though Griffith's latest paper, *Nationality*, had the second-largest circulation – 4,539 in February – of some nine seditious weeklies. Fortunately for his future reputation, he was arrested after the rising, and interned in Britain, to be released towards the end of the year. Meanwhile a so-called Sinn Féin candidate, who declared his opposition to physical force, had come a poor third to two constitutional nationalists, in a by-election in West Cork in November – the first electoral contest in Ireland after the rising. Back in Dublin, Griffith began to look to the postwar peace conference for a solution to the Irish question, in keeping with his concept of a political strategy. But the IRB had been reactivated after the rising, and funds were raised for the families of dead and imprisoned republican volunteers.

In February 1917 Count Plunkett, the father of one of the signatories to the republican proclamation of 1916, ran successfully as an independent in the North Roscommon by-election. He declined to take his seat. Sinn Féin was revived in April, though it was not until 25 October that de Valera, as the senior surviving leader in the rising, became president. Sinn Féin clubs had been growing in number, totalling 1,240 by the end of the year. Abstentionists had taken three more seats from the

Irish party; South Longford in May, East Clare in July (where de Valera succeeded Maj. Willie Redmond, killed in France on 7 June), and Kilkenny in August. This – second – Sinn Féin was committed to securing an Irish republic, after which the Irish people would be free to choose their own form of government. This compromise was proof positive of the separatist, rather than democratic, character of the new nationalism. Eoin MacNeill, despite his role in trying to prevent the rising, was the most popular member of the new executive committee. De Valera was also elected president of the Irish volunteers, which had been reorganized in 1917. The IRB again penetrated its executive and headquarters staff, in order to further the cause of republicanism. The chief of staff, Cathal Brugha, was opposed to Fenianism, but Michael Collins, director of organization in the volunteers, was becoming dominant in this secret society. He had given the uncharacteristically brief oration in September, at the funeral of Thomas Ashe, who died in prison while on hunger strike.

The United States entered the war in April 1917, and Ireland became a consideration in Anglo-American relations. From May 1916, President Wilson had talked of the right of small nations to self-determination, providing Irish separatists with a vocabulary of international democracy. Lloyd George again offered immediate home rule, with exclusion, to Redmond, who refused on the grounds that partition would now be unacceptable to nationalists. But the Irish leader, perhaps thinking of Sinn Féin's goal of a constituent assembly, suggested an Irish convention to decide the country's future within the United Kingdom. This idea may have originated in Lloyd George's circle, and the war cabinet released all sentenced Irish prisoners on 18 June as a gesture of good will.

The Irish convention met in July, at Trinity College, under the chairmanship of Sir Horace Plunkett, and sat until the following spring. That winter the Irish party retained three seats, two in Ulster and one in Waterford, suggesting a residue of faith in the constitutional road. Sinn Féin refused to participate in the convention. Given that labour was a member of the coalition government in Britain, and, in the hope of denting the nationalist and unionist blocs, Duke, a member of the British cabinet as the chief secretary for Ireland, extended an invitation to Irish labour. This was political recognition. The Dublin and Cork trades councils refused to participate, though two supporters of Redmond – a Dublin railwayman and James McCarron from Derry, a former president of the ITUC – accepted. The Belfast trades council sent H.T. Whitley, its president. The secretary of the insurance commission also selected Charles McKay, a FEST official, and Robert Waugh, the ASCJ organizer (who attended the trades council). No invitation seems to have been extended to the ITUC & LP, though Johnson's idea of asking for admission was defeated on the executive, by the narrowest margin of O'Brien's casting vote. The five labour men were only a tiny minority of the 95 Irish delegates. Plunkett's strategy was to extract concessions from the nationalists, get the southern unionists and labour to ally in a new bloc with the Redmondites and other nationalists, and then confront the Ulster unionists.

The southern unionists were terrified of partition, and Redmond set out to win them over by diluting his nationalism. He was prepared to surrender customs duties, though this caused problems within the Irish party. He was no longer interested in negotiating with the Ulster unionists about exclusion, there being still a strong desire to maintain the unity of the country. The 1917 ITUC & LP had come out unanimously against partition. (Whitley was a delegate to the congress, and William O'Brien described him on that occasion as the antithesis of Connolly in all other respects.) A majority report finally emerged from the convention, recommending dominion home rule. This was carried by 44 votes to 29. It was envisaged that Ireland would leave the United Kingdom, but there were considerable concessions to the Ulster unionists. It was still hoped they could be attracted into a parliament in Dublin, though this was to refuse to hear what they consistently said. The five labour men signed the majority report. 'If Ulster working men could hear the debates', Whitley was reported as saying by Plunkett, 'they would see that the danger to their interests from an Irish Parliament was wholly imaginary.'[22] Whitley described himself as an imperialist on the question of customs, and supported conscription. The labour group argued, in its own convention report, that self-government was 'in the best interest of the country'.[23] For this reason, it suspended its objections to the less than democratic provisions in the majority report, principally the composition of an Irish senate. (The labour men succeeded in getting the convention to vote unanimously for a housing programme, to be partly financed by the British government, and supervised by the first Irish parliament.) Whitley and McKay voted in all 52 divisions, including the crucial second one, when they opposed exclusion. Waugh had attended only 34 of the 51 sessions, and seems to have decided to vote only on the final report.

The convention only reinforced the political division of Ireland when it reported in April 1918. It was the last British attempt to find a solution, certainly during the war. For southern unionists it was the end of their brief independent foray on the political stage. Redmond did not survive the convention, dying on 6 March, and the leaderless Irish party was shown up as having failed for the last time (his son, Capt. William Redmond, inherited his Waterford seat). Labour, or at least those elements not being attracted to Sinn Féin, had made an impressive political debut, though the three Belfast men were remembered for their disloyalty by Ulster unionists. The latter had once again stood firmly in opposition to Dublin rule, and the idea of a united Ireland was buried definitively at Trinity College in 1917–18. This was not so obvious at the time, Sinn Féin being the main beneficiary of the failure of the Irish convention. By standing outside, it was in a position to grab the nationalist mantle from the Irish party. That it did so in 1918 was due largely to the British government.

With the German offensive in March, Lloyd George looked to Ireland for recruits. The prime minister believed they would be forthcoming, once the Irish question was settled, and he may have seen the enactment of conscription in Ireland, but not its enforcement, as a precondition for the further conscription of British men and boys. Conscription had been avoided in Ireland, though Sinn Féin grew strong among those social groups, the rural and urban petty bourgeoisie, who feared it most. The end of emigration had kept the sons of farmers and small-town shopkeepers at home, and considerable discontent had built up in rural Ireland. When the convention failed, the prime minister promised home rule, including exclusion. With his credibility in Ireland waning, he introduced, on 10 April, a military service bill. The convention had reported the previous day. The bill allowed for conscription in Ireland, but only when implemented by order in council. This was to test the legitimacy of British rule to breaking point.

The Irish party withdrew from parliament on 16 April when the bill was passed. This might have strengthened its following in nationalist Ireland, but it was about to concede its hegemonic position. It allowed Sinn Féin to take Tullamore on 19 April. Patrick McCartan was also returned – unopposed – for North King's County on the same day. On Sunday, 14 April, Johnson and Campbell had addressed an anti-conscription meeting at the Custom House steps in Belfast. There was a basis for resistance, as the presence of the crowd suggests, but not if it was simply identified with nationalism. Arthur Trew was present, and, when Johnson and others spoke outside the City Hall three days later, the meeting was broken up by loyalists. The next day, Thursday, 18 April, the lord mayor of Dublin held a conference at the Mansion House, to organize a campaign of resistance throughout Ireland. Dillon and Devlin represented the Irish party, William O'Brien and T.M. Healy dissident nationalists. De Valera and Griffith spoke for Sinn Féin, and the ITUC & LP – being politically recognized for the first time – sent Johnson; William O'Brien, chairman for 1917–18; and Michael Egan from Cork. The conference agreed upon a pledge to be taken at – catholic – church doors the following Sunday, 21 April. The lord mayor then led a delegation to Maynooth, where the bishops where meeting. The catholic church came out against conscription, a considerable boon but also a constraint. The Mansion House conference also decided to appeal to the president and congress of the United States. Johnson, who had been discreet about his involvement with the labour movement, was sacked from his job in Belfast following his appearance at the anti-conscription meeting. Subsequently he became secretary of the Mansion House conference in Dublin, which remained in being to lead an anti-conscription campaign.

A special labour convention was held in Dublin on the Saturday, at which the congress/party affirmed the right to national self-determination for the first time. A one-day general strike against conscription was called for 23 April. This, the first in Irish history, was a national, or communal, strike and not a class action. 'The whole Nation – outside Belfast – ceased work on Tuesday', British workers were told in a circular from the national executive. 'If conscription be enforced we warn you, comrades and friends of liberty, that massacre and rapine will follow.'[24] Rhetoric was becoming infectious. The British TUC and labour party appealed to Lloyd George not to proceed with conscription in Ireland. Irish labour, in taking a democratic stand, had identified with the national cause, and two members of the national executive declined to sign the circular summoning delegates to the Dublin convention. D.R. Campbell, treasurer since 1911, considered it of 'an unduly alarmist character', and he did not stand again for the executive. J.H. Bennett – the seamen's organizer in Dublin – 'thought the Executive were allowing themselves to be used for political purposes and there should not be any politics in the Trade Union movement'.[25] He was not re-elected at the 1918 congress. The two dissidents were not in general political agreement, because, at a special conference later in the year, Campbell voted for the expulsion of Bennett and other delegates. The NSFU had encouraged merchant seamen to take industrial action, to prevent socialists from meeting after the Russian revolution to discuss international peace.

Anticipating considerable resistance to conscription, Lloyd George made Lord French viceroy, the field marshal being despatched to Dublin on 11 May. A new chief secretary, the liberal Edward Shortt, had also been put in place. On the night of 17 May, the leaderships of Sinn Féin and the Irish volunteers, with the exception of Brugha and Collins, were arrested. The republicans had decided to allow this to happen, the better to strengthen the anti-government cause. According to a proclamation issued the next morning, there had been a German plot. This was nonsense, the authorities were two years late. There had been a pro-German insurrection, but the volunteers were now interested in mass political and military resistance. One of Casement's men had been landed recently from a German submarine, but this was a case of Berlin's trying to stir up Irish discontent. Despite such weak evidence, French's document outlining a German plot had been approved by the cabinet three days earlier. It was clear that collaboration with Germany was being used in order to justify repression of nationalists fighting conscription.

Opposition was authentically a Sinn Féin position, given that the argument was about Irish sovereignty. The constitutional nationalists found themselves defending another parliamentary seat, while the Mansion House conference was organizing the campaign against conscription. Sinn Féin may have decided not to resist the arrests, in order to help it in the by-election. On 20 June no less a person than Arthur Griffith, arrested during his campaign, won East Cavan on an abstentionist platform. 'Put him in to get him out'[26] was the political message. On 3 July all public meetings were banned. Summer turned to autumn without conscription, as Britain gained the upper hand in the war. Volunteers were still coming from Ireland. Sinn Féin was driven underground, only to strengthen itself and grow, this owing much to the leadership of the IRB, in particular Harry Boland, a close associate of Michael Collins. This would not have been possible without the continuing threat of conscription in Ireland, Sinn Féin building a pan-nationalist following from the cardinal, the head of the catholic church, by way of constitutional and revolutionary nationalists, to the socialist leaders of the labour movement.

The armistice was signed on 11 November, and parliament dissolved ten days later. An election was called for 14 December, with all men over 21 and women over 30 entitled to vote. On 13 November hostile crowds in Dublin, including many Irish soldiers, attacked and wrecked Sinn Féin's head office in Harcourt Street. This not inconsiderable section of the Irish people – those who had been involved in the British war effort – was about to disappear from history. The Irish party, still out of parliament, was influenced by the events of 1918, to come out in favour of dominion home rule. Sinn Féin, in contrast, was for appealing to the peace conference, and establishing a constituent assembly. This implied a continuation of the struggle against Britain. Irish labour – now calling itself the Irish Labour Party and Trade Union Congress (ILP & TUC) – had decided to fight the 1918 general election, only to withdraw to give Sinn Féin a clear run. This it did at a special conference on 1–2 November. 'Was it', D.R. Campbell asked, 'to be left to the Nationalists and Sinn Feiners in the South and to give a walkover to the Conservative crowd in the North?'[27] He saw the carnival of reaction assembling. Belfast had been left behind in the course of the anti-conscription struggle, though the working-class movement there was showing its opposition to the idea of tory rule by Ulster unionists. At dissolution Dillon had held 68 seats, William O'Brien and other nationalists 10, de Valera 7, and Carson 18.

When the results were declared on 28 December, the unionists had 26 of the 105 Irish seats. Sinn Féin, many of whose candidates were still in prison, came back with a staggering 73 seats. De Valera ousted Dillon in East Mayo. The Irish party was reduced to 6 seats, including Devlin and Redmond's son, the other four in Ulster having been agreed with Sinn Féin. The landslide was not quite so dramatic, in terms of contests and votes. Twenty-five of Sinn Féin's successes were uncontested, the battle having been won – by whatever means – in those constituencies before polling. But uncontested seats in nationalist Ireland were not unusual. The turnout in 1918 was about average, though many soldiers, absent at the front, were not able to vote in time. De Valera attracted under half a million votes, while the Irish party had over a quarter of a million, and the unionists many more. Sinn Féin, in fact, secured only 47.7 per cent of those polling. It would not have been the outright winner under a system of proportional representation. Even taking uncontested seats into account, de Valera had the support of only a minority of Ireland's nearly 2 million electors. 'Probably what most Sinn Fein voters were voting for was simply the greatest measure of independence, without partition of the country, which Ireland could get ... The one thing they were certainly not voting for was an attempt to win sovereign independence by force of arms or a campaign of terrorism.'[28] What they got was the war of independence.

9

Belfast Republicanism, 1905-18

Advanced nationalism did not appeal to the minority in Belfast in the early twentieth century for three principal reasons. First, Irish republicanism was inimical to industrialization. Second, it was unrealistic about the protestants of Ulster. Third, it could not challenge catholic nationalism with a labour slant. In the formation of a national revolutionary leadership, catholic and protestant individuals from the city played important roles in the separatist movement. But the Irish Republican Brotherhood (IRB) was not the underground force in Belfast it became elsewhere in Ireland during the war. The topic of Belfast republicanism remains microhistorical – big individuals in small organizations who leave for Dublin. Despite the sea change in Irish politics after 1916, Joe Devlin fought off the challenge from de Valera in the general election. Sinn Féin was rejected in 1918 by the majority of the city's catholics.

Organized republicanism in Belfast dates from 1858, when the IRB was founded in Dublin on St Patrick's Day. The American wing of the movement was known as the Fenian Brotherhood, after the Fianna, the warriors of the mythical Finn McCool. Frank Roney, whose father recruited carpenters into a union, was a catholic artisan in Belfast – a moulder. In 1862 he became Ulster 'centre', or head, of the IRB, and later deputy director for the province. Roney recruited from among the artisanate and petty bourgeoisie, 'intelligent young men ... few of [whom] had ever been the victims of landlord oppression or felt the lash of the evictor. Almost all of them were in comparatively easy circumstances.'[1] He described the catholic members as simply anti-orange, and claimed that protestants were forthcoming from rural areas where the tradition of 1798 survived. There is little evidence that the catholic labourers involved in the 1864 riots in Belfast were Fenians. This was becoming a pejorative term used by protestants. The town does not seem to have been implicated, to any significant extent, in the abortive rising of 1867.

This put revolutionary nationalism on the map of Irish history. After the insurrection, American Fenians formed the more secret Clan na Gael, which John Devoy led after his release from prison in 1871. Knowledge of the Fenian movement subsequently in Ireland is largely dependent upon surviving police reports. In 1879, with the new departure, revolutionary and constitutional nationalists united in the land league struggle. In October 1882 the commissioner of the Belfast RIC reported the existence of sympathisers only. 'I do not think any Secret Society exists and as far as can be learned no active steps are being taken to further Fenianism.'[2] Reports the following year mention a society comprising four publicans, three dealers, two drapers, a pawn-broker, a linen merchant, and two special constables dismissed from the RIC. The employment of informers towards the end of the decade suggests that the police remained suspicious of the Parnellite move-ment in Belfast, though Thomas Sexton, MP, had been considered 'to be moderate in his views'.[3] By 1901 the police were reporting 600 IRB members of good standing in 11 circles. This was undoubtedly a guess, local officers finding it irksome to fill in monthly forms for Dublin Castle.

Fenianism, by the 1900s, was becoming an endangered revolutionary species, under the leadership of three Dubliners, P.T. Daly, Fred Allen and John O'Hanlon. With the rivalry in Belfast between the bishop's men and Devlin, there was less room for advanced nationalism. The UIL's candidate in the 1903 by-election, Patrick Dempsey, was consid-ered by the police to be a Fenian. It is unlikely that the proprietor of the Linen Hall Hotel, in Donegall Square East, was keeping an open revolu-tionary house, but the RIC continued to report on him as a leading member. The 400 alleged members or supporters of the IRB were described as having divided on the advisability of electoral politics. Devlin was certainly capable of disorganizing the republican move-ment, by winning a section of it to the UIL on the occasion of a West Belfast by-election. P.T. Daly had spent two weeks in Ulster in March reorganizing the movement, and it seems that quarterly meetings of the three-member IRB executive of Great Britain and Ireland were held in Belfast for reasons of geographical convenience. By August 1905 the brotherhood in Belfast was reported to be in a 'disorganised state',[4] shortly before Devlin won the west division. According to a younger member, it 'consisted for the most part of elderly men who were quite inactive politically. There were some very good men among them, but there were also some who drank too much and who, had they been engaged in any serious enterprise, would have been a danger to all con-cerned.'[5]

This was the opinion of Bulmer Hobson. Born in Hollywood, Co. Down, in 1883, the son of a Quaker tea traveller, he did a great deal to revive the IRB. Hobson attended the Friends' school in Lisburn. His parents introduced him, at an early age, to a small circle of protestant nationalist intellectuals, as isolated from the catholic masses as they were removed from the dominant community. The central figure was F.J. Bigger, a protestant solicitor, who lived at *Ardrigh*, a house on the Antrim Road. He was unmarried, and may have been a homosexual. Bigger was also a Freemason. In 1906 he was Carlisle's election agent in West Belfast. Bigger edited the *Ulster Journal of Archaeology*, but he was mainly a cultural nationalist, active in the Gaelic League from 1895. Each year from 1904 he organized a *feis*, or festival, in the glens of Antrim, where some Irish was still spoken. Bigger first met Roger Casement on this occasion, and *Ardrigh* was the latter's base on subsequent visits to Belfast. Casement was an active homosexual, and also unmarried. The police believed Bigger was printing anti-recruiting literature in 1905, but 'it [was] difficult to probe the matter to the bottom owing to Mr Bigger's position'.[6]

The young Hobson became a subscriber to the *Shan Van Vocht*, a national monthly magazine published in Belfast between 1896 and 1899, by Alice Milligan and Ethna Carbery. It was a separatist publication, though Milligan was generous enough to allow James Connolly to advocate socialism in it. Milligan and Hobson's mother were joint secretaries of the Irishwomen's Association, and a home reading circle met in young Hobson's house. The cultural nationalists tried to appropriate Wolfe Tone in 1898 for the cause of Irish Ireland, only to find Devlin fighting separatism with parliamentary nationalism. In 1900 Hobson started the Ulster Debating Society, for protestant boys, and later, with William McDonald, the Protestant National Society. This evolved in 1904 into the Ulster Literary Theatre, when he and David Parkhill set out to provide 'a commentary on the political and social conditions of the North of Ireland'.[7] According to their short-lived magazine, *Uladh*, this regional theatre would tap the 'strong undercurrent of culture' and 'turn [it] into native channels'.[8] Hobson also joined the Gaelic League, in 1901, and the Gaelic Athletic Association (GAA), establishing the first hurling team in Ulster. The following year he organized junior members of the GAA into the Fianna Éireann, meeting in the Catholic Boys' Hall on the Falls Road. Hobson hoped to interest working-class youths in the culture and politics of Irish Ireland. Between 1901 and 1903 he worked for a printer, thereafter becoming a professional revolutionary. He was recruited into the IRB in 1904, at the age of 21.

Hobson was spotted by Denis McCullough, the son of a catholic publican, also 21, who had joined the republican organization in 1901. The young McCullough was sworn in by a tailor, at the side door of a pub on the Falls Road. McCullough then set out to rejuvenate the Belfast Fenians. He was described as a piano tuner, and would become a manufacturer of musical instruments. By 1903 he had formed two new circles. He became head of his father's circle, expelling his father and his drinking companions. A third important member of the IRB was Sean MacDermott. The son of a Leitrim farmer, he went to Glasgow for a time. MacDermott then came to Belfast, where he worked in a bar, before becoming a conductor on the trams. He was initially involved in the AOH, and it was not until 1906 that McCullough swore him into the IRB.

Hobson, McCullough and MacDermott were to the fore in Belfast in the 1900s. In 1901 the former also joined Griffith's Cumann na nGaedheal, later serving on the executive. This was a precursor of the Sinn Féin party, though the term became an articulation of self-reliance from 1905. Griffith was then a member of the IRB, though developing a third course, between physical force and constitutional nationalism, in his *United Irishman* paper. He looked back to Grattan's parliament, or the constitution of 1782, and, having started as a republican, became an advocate of a dual monarchy for Britain and Ireland. Griffith believed this could become a popular demand. His Hungarian policy was presented in 1904. The following year Hobson established the Dungannon club in Belfast, 'to push the Hungarian Policy in Ulster'.[9] Dungannon, in Co. Tyrone, was where the original Irish volunteers had met, in convention, in 1782.

Three or four Dungannon clubs were established in Belfast, comprising 30 to 40 'young men at a white heat of enthusiasm', with 'an unbreakable psychological strength', and an 'intense conviction and ... passionate faith'.[10] Some 14 clubs in Ireland and Britain existed in 1905–7. One was founded in Carrickmore, Co. Tyrone, by Patrick McCartan, a mature medical student in Dublin who had become a Fenian in Philadelphia. It was short-lived. A manifesto of 1905 referred to building Ireland up intellectually, materially and physically, and achieving political independence by passive resistance. Copies were sent to many in Ulster. William Walker denounced the idea of nationalizing the trade-union movement in the *Labour Chronicle*, and Hobson was the main speaker in a debate on socialism on 19 November 1905. The following March, O'Donovan Rossa lectured to the club. In July 1906 Hobson was accused of being a rent collector, the meeting breaking up in confusion. The Dungannon clubs' main intervention was during the 1907 strike. Hobson had brought out a newspaper, the *Republic*, from late 1906, which was supported by the IRB. It merged after six months with W.P. Ryan's *Irish Peasant*, and Hobson worked later on this in Dublin. *The Creed of the Republic* was the title of Hobson's pamphlet published in 1907. Denis McCullough was also active in Hobson's organization, but kept more in the background. Sean MacDermott recruited some tram workers, before becoming travelling organizer for the clubs, in Belfast, Dublin, Glasgow, London and throughout Ulster.

Hobson was still a follower of Arthur Griffith, both having joined the National Council in 1903. This was formed to protest against a visit to Ireland by Edward VII. Griffith announced his Sinn Féin policy at its first convention in 1905, and changed the name of his paper to *Sinn Féin* the following May. In April 1907 the Dungannon clubs and Cumann na nGaedheal merged to form the Sinn Féin League. When the National Council joined in September 1908, the party became simply Sinn Féin. MacDermott had moved to Dublin earlier in the year to become organizer, and Hobson was also in Dublin in 1908–9 working on Ryan's paper. He returned north, and was active in the West Belfast branch of Sinn Féin. This was the high point of Sinn Féin activity, though events were soon to swing in the direction of the parliamentarians. At its peak Sinn Féin had 106 clubs in 1909. But there were only 581 paid-up members that August, few outside Dublin, when *Sinn Féin* became a daily paper. Griffith then became interested in the All-for-Ireland League of William O'Brien, of Co. Cork, and the paper reverted to being a weekly in January 1910.

Denis McCullough had been coopted on to the supreme council of the IRB in 1908, and the following year he became Ulster representative. The police came to regard him 'as one of the most dangerous suspects in Ireland'.[11] He helped secure MacDermott's appointment, at the end of 1908, as IRB national organizer. MacDermott later joined the supreme council. He formed a close relationship with Tom Clarke, who had returned to Ireland in 1907. Clarke had served 15 years in prison for dynamiting, followed by a spell in New York working for John Devoy's *Gaelic American*. Clarke was coopted on to the supreme council in 1909, and behaved very much like a traditional Fenian. In August that year Hobson, with the assistance of only Constance Markievicz, reformed his Fianna Éireann in Dublin. Many members graduated into a special circle of the IRB in 1912. Hobson – at this stage – was close to Clarke.

It was in 1910 that Griffith was thrown over by P.T. Daly, and the young guard, including the 53-year-old Clarke. Daly, who had become editor of the Dublin trades council's paper in 1909, was shortly after expelled from the brotherhood. He had earlier been unseated as one of the handful of Sinn Féin councillors on Dublin corporation. From 1910 Daly was exclusively active in the labour movement. The Belfast police, reporting on his visits to the city, first exonerated him of Fenian activity in March. That November the IRB brought out a monthly, *Irish Freedom*. The Irish freedom clubs later challenged Sinn Féin. Patrick McCartan, who had filled Daly's seat on the corporation, became nominal editor, working as a hospital doctor in Dublin. The monthly paper was the brainchild of Hobson, who now moved to Dublin as editor. He was coopted on to the supreme council in 1911, where Allen and O'Hanlon, the two remaining members of the executive, were peeved at their loss of control. After an internecine struggle of unrecorded complexity, they both resigned from the IRB in 1912. The previous year Clarke had become treasurer and MacDermott secretary of the organization. This was the basis of the 1916 conspiracy. By the time of the third home rule bill, the 2,000-strong IRB, in Ireland and Britain, was under the new revolutionary management of 'the old chap' Clarke, and his young acolytes – several with experience of Belfast.

Irish Freedom, which Hobson edited from November 1910 until 1914, was the most sophisticated republican paper published in Dublin. In commenting on contemporary events, it showed a grave misunderstanding of Ulster opposition to home rule. Many contributors had a positive view of the unionist mobilizations, either because they were seen as simply anti-British, or because government action might drive the Ulstermen into the arms of radical nationalists. The IRB welcomed volunteering and arming in Ulster, largely because the political ante was being raised, and partly because it would force the nationalists to follow suit. Patrick McCartan, who had returned to Co. Tyrone in 1913, to work as a dispensary doctor, let the UVF have his motorcar in April 1914, in order to distribute arms run into Larne.

Back in Belfast, Denis McCullough continued to run the IRB, and its various front activities. The Belfast freedom club was founded in June 1912, in the Fianna hall in Victoria Street. This venue was directly across from unionist headquarters in the Old Town Hall! It later met in the national club in Berry Street. Leading members included Ernest

Blythe and Cathal O'Shannon. Blythe, a protestant from near Lisburn, had joined the Gaelic League in Dublin, when working there as a civil servant. He ran an IRB circle in Belfast from 1909, while working as a journalist on the *North Down Herald* in Bangor. He remained an active republican, joining the national leadership after the rising. Cathal O'Shannon, from Co. Derry, had been educated at St Columb's College in Derry. He was a member of the IRB. Employed as a shipping clerk in Belfast, he came to work for James Connolly in the ITGWU. O'Shannon was an advocate of left republicanism in *Irish Freedom* in 1913, losing the argument before the Dublin lock-out. (He became the principal interpreter of James Connolly. At the ILP & TUC's special conference in 1918, O'Shannon, protesting at the exploitation of Connolly's name, stated his preparedness to follow in the latter's footsteps. He meant – metaphorically – back into the GPO, the headquarters of the Dublin insurgents in 1916. O'Shannon went on to argue for labour's participation in the election, so the party, through the socialist international, could aid the cause of self-determination.)

Cathal O'Shannon provided a link with younger republicans, including the Connolly family. He founded the Betsy Gray *sluagh*, or branch, of Markievicz's Fianna, which met in former army huts on the Falls Road. Nora Connolly was a leading member, and her sister Ina became secretary. On the occasion of the 1913 Twelfth, it posted a Connolly leaflet along the route, chiding the marchers with the – erroneous – fact that the pope had supported William of Orange. In October 1913 O'Shannon founded the young republican party, a junior version of the freedom club. On 21 June 1914 Ernest Blythe gave the oration at MacArt's Fort, overlooking west Belfast, on the occasion of Wolfe Tone's birthday, to a gathering comprising the young republican party, the Fianna and the ILP(I). The presence of the latter heralded the imminent collapse of Connolly's socialism, though Blythe claimed he was then 'a bit of a Socialist'.[12] The following month Connolly's two daughters attended the *árd fheis*, or conference, of the Fianna, camping at Contance Markievicz's cottage in the Dublin mountains, and helping with the distribution of arms landed at Howth. At the beginning of the war the Belfast Fianna paraded the Falls Road singing 'The Watch on the Rhine'.

Bulmer Hobson and the IRB had been – to a considerable extent – behind the formation of the Irish volunteers in November 1913. It was Hobson who, that December, swore Patrick Pearse into the IRB, and thus into Irish history. Until June 1914 the Belfast volunteers were little more than the IRB on parade. Denis McCullough was the leader, and the police thought there were at most 150 members. The 100 who drilled on the Falls Road in March 1914 were probably members of the Fianna. National membership estimates for April show 7,881 volunteers in Ulster, out of a total of 19,206, Donegal alone accounting for 3,648 members. Jack White became an organizer for the volunteers in May, and found catholics in the hinterland of Derry fearful of exclusion. It was the Larne gun-running which stimulated recruitment in Belfast, the police estimating 1,800 members in May.

The Redmondite takeover of the volunteers saw George Fitz Hardinge Berkeley, a former army captain, take command in Belfast on 6 July. He was approached by Roger Casement. Of southern, landed stock, though then a member of the Warwickshire gentry, Berkeley was a supporter of the Asquith government, and in indirect contact with Churchill. Berkeley had put up much of the £1,500 to arm the volunteers, having been involved with MacNeill, The Rahilly (as he called himself), Casement and Hobson in planning the Howth gun-running. The landing helped recruiting in Belfast, McCullough claiming 4,100 members in September. Joe Devlin had become one of the keenest members of the volunteers' executive in June, and he worked hard to keep the guns under his control. Only 25 of the Howth rifles reached Berkeley, and Devlin arranged his own importation of 800 rifles, less ammunition, sometime in August–September. Berkeley appointed former British soldiers, plus McCullough, to lead 5 battalions, each with 8 companies. He claimed they reached their establishment of 120 by September. There was also a cycle corps, a signal section and a Red Cross corps of 60 nurses. The military committee of the Belfast volunteers 'considered that it would be more to the credit of the movement if the officers came from the richer classes'. Col. Cotter, formerly of the royal engineers, was second in command. To drill they had to march seven miles out of the city, to find a sympathetic farmer willing to lend his land. Berkeley left Belfast on 18 September upon the enactment of home rule, 'full of keenness to work for the Empire'[13] in the war.

Seven hundred volunteers, including the two instructors, Joseph Burns and Sgt.-Maj. Cussick, who had initially helped McCullough, joined up in the first ten days of war. They were undoubtedly reservists in the British army, and the first to be called up. The general committee of the Belfast volunteers came out against enlisting, but Berkeley and Devlin got Col. Moore, their inspector-general, to impose Redmondite discipline. The enactment of home rule saw another 700 leave to join the British army. Though the split began on 24 September, Devlin and McCullough were sharing a platform in St. Mary's Hall on 4 October, when the audience turned against the latter. To effect his escape, McCullough had to pull a gun on the MP for West Belfast, persuading him to calm his followers. There was even less enthusiasm in Belfast than in the rest of the country for nationalist opposition to the parliamentary leadership. Between 100 and 200 members of the Irish volunteers remained loyal to the MacNeill/Hobson leadership, all the rest going off into Redmond and Moore's national volunteers. This was the wing scheduled to appear in Celtic Park on 25 October, armed by Devlin, until rain caused the cancellation of the parade. By November over 1,000 former volunteers from Belfast were reported to be under training, before being sent to the front.

MacNeill was not a member of the IRB, and was looking forward to the Irish volunteers sitting out the war. Hobson, for acquiescing in the Redmondite takeover in June, had quickly lost the editorship of *Irish Freedom*, and was forced to resign from the supreme council of the IRB as Leinster representative. He greatly angered Clarke. McCullough remained a leader, and accepted the decision of a wartime rising, which had been initiated by the American Fenians. McCullough, like his revolutionary colleagues throughout Ireland, probably placed less emphasis on a German landing, and more on a British suppression of the Irish volunteers, or conscription. These were the necessary conditions for MacNeill to order the volunteers to fight. Few members of the supreme council can have been attached to the idea of a rising, simply because the end of the war might be imminent. But this was clearly most important to Clarke and MacDermott, the two key members of the executive.

In late September 1914 McCullough spoke to Blythe, now a member of the Belfast volunteers, about 'the raising of privates to the rank of sergeants and of sergeants made lieutenants, in an effort to keep influential individuals from resigning'.[14] He claimed that only 142 remained loyal to the MacNeill leadership, the organization being once again the IRB on parade. McCullough kept his small band of volunteers in a high degree of readiness. A variety of arms was available, some of which must have been stolen from the national volunteers. The following March, his 200 volunteers were reported to have 117 rifles. In the summer of 1915 the authorities moved to suppress anti-recruiting activity. On 10 July expulsion orders were served on McCullough, Blythe, Liam Mellows, a member of the volunteers' general council, and Herbert Moore Pim, a recent convert from unionism to Sinn Féin. They were all volunteers' organizers. Mellows went on the run, but the other three were imprisoned in Belfast for refusing to leave the city. McCullough got four months, his companions three. Though a member of the supreme council, McCullough had been kept in ignorance of the formation of the military committee in May, and he would not have heard of Clarke and MacDermott joining the renamed council in September. At the December meeting of the supreme council, the two latter proposed McCullough successfully as president of the IRB. Pearse was coopted to the supreme council at this time, but Clarke and MacDermott had other plans for him. Total power remained with them in Dublin, McCullough being in Belfast. They fixed the date of the rising towards the end of the year, but the supreme council was not informed of this on 16 January 1916 at Clontarf Town Hall. Most of its members still believed the IRB and the Irish volunteers would only act if conditions were correct. Patrick McCartan, who had been coopted to the supreme council in late 1914, actually opposed the decision at Clontarf to rise, believing there was no clear evidence of a German plan to invade Ireland.

In March 1916 in Dublin McCullough received specific instructions from Pearse and Connolly, 'to be implemented should a Rising take place'. Ulster was to be abandoned. McCullough would bring his Belfast volunteers to Coalisland, link up with McCartan's Co. Tyrone force (which would be in touch with Joe O'Doherty's Derry group), and converge on Belcoo, Co. Fermanagh. No shots were to be fired in Ulster, and the combined body was to march on to Connaught. They were to link up with Liam Mellows behind the line of the Shannon.

McCullough thought the plan for Ulster absurd, and said so to Pearse and Connolly. 'From Dungannon to Galway', he wrote much later,

> is a distance of well over two hundred miles and the most direct way is through Enniskillen ... [which] had a strong British garrison and the chances of taking it with our assorted supply of arms and a few home-made gelignite bombs was remote indeed. Besides, two hundred miles would tax the marching ability of the most seasoned soldiers. Apart from all that, we were forbidden to fire a shot in the north ... When I questioned the possibility of carrying out this plan the answer I got from Pearse and Connolly was: 'That is an order, obey it strictly!'[15]

McCullough was again in Dublin the weekend before Easter. Though president of the IRB, he had to pursue Sean MacDermott into his office to hear about the military council's overall plan. This was on Monday, 17 April, six days before the intended rising. He still remained ignorant of the date of the rising, though he had his suspicions about the mobilizations scheduled for Easter Sunday.

On Easter Saturday, 22 April, 132 insurgents, including women members of Cumann na mBan, and the Fianna, left Belfast by train for Dungannon. It was ostensibly an outing of cultural nationalists. Only single tickets were purchased, a fact to alert suspicious persons. They marched to a hall in Coalisland, to await mobilization at 7 p.m. the following evening. Patrick McCartan wrote later of the preparations in Co. Tyrone: 'Long before Easter I had not heart in it as it came, and could not inspire others with courage when I had none myself.'[16] He had first heard of the intended rising on the Friday in Dublin. When McCullough later told him of the plan in Tyrone, he 'refused point blank to take the orders'.[17] The two men then motored to Dublin that Saturday, to be told by Clarke of the plan to come out the following evening. Sunday was the day the rising was put back to Easter Monday. Given that the Tyrone volunteers refused to leave their area, McCullough had no option but to order his men and women back to Belfast on Easter Sunday. Archie Heron bought the tickets at Cookstown for the journey back. MacNeill's countermand had appeared in the press that morning, and Belfast was to play no part in the rising. No shots were fired in Ulster, but for reasons very different from those intended.

Nora Connolly and several companions had left Tyrone for Dublin on the Saturday. Her father sent her back, to try to get the volunteers out on the Monday. This had been rendered impossible, and she spent the week trying to get back to Dublin, not arriving until it was all over. Connolly had moved his wife and younger children to Markievicz's cottage before the rising. In its aftermath Danny McDevitt, according to Marie Johnson, had to board up the house in Glenalina Terrace, when it was attacked by irate dockers and their wives. McCullough and some others in Belfast were arrested, but only 83 of the 1,600 held came from Ulster. Sean MacEntee, who hailed from Belfast, and had been out in Dublin, was the only man from the province court-martialled. (He, too, claimed later he had been interested in Connolly's socialism, and even a member of the SPI.) MacEntee had applied for a commission in the

British army, when working in Dundalk, only to throw in his lot with the volunteers.

Devlin did not have things all his own way in the immediate wake of the rising. Lloyd George's attempt to find an Irish settlement caused anxiety among northern catholics. On 5 June Devlin wrote to Dillon that only Belfast had accepted exclusion so far, but he was confident the Irish party could swing catholic Ulster. Belfast nationalists came into line 13 days later, but, on 20 June, UIL delegates from Derry, Tyrone and Fermanagh, meeting in Derry city, came out against exclusion. It was believed they had the support of the bishops. Three days later they constituted many of the 265 delegates, at the Ulster convention in Belfast, who voted against Redmond. The AOH, according to the police, helped Devlin get his majority, and his opponents alleged the payment of bribes and help from civil servants. When the UIL's national directory met in Dublin, on 3 July, Fermanagh and Tyrone, according to Tom Kettle, were the only counties opposed to a settlement. On 20 July the inspector general of the RIC reported that 'the feeling against [Redmond was] increasing ... and some of the Belfast Nationalists [were] now siding with the anti-exclusionists.'[18] Lawrence Ginnell, a dissident MP, had addressed a meeting on 17 July. 'There [was] little doubt', the RIC reported, 'that the Sinn Fein movement [was] gaining strength in Belfast, and Mr Devlin's [was] waning'.[19] By the time this was written, on 27 July, the Lloyd George scheme had collapsed.

Sinn Féin, so called, was reported to be growing in Ulster in the summer of 1916. On 18 September, in St Mary's Hall, Arthur Savage, the publican, and Bernard Campbell formed a branch of the Irish nation league. This was opposed to the Irish party, but not for abstention. It expressed the fears of Ulster catholics who thought they might be left out of home rule. Archie Heron, who had led the Belfast volunteers back from Co. Tyrone, shouted out during Savage's speech: 'To hell with the Empire.'[20] Supporters of the league were not prepared to go that far. As a regional anti-partitionist organization, it grew in the autumn, only to decline in the winter. But the formal organization became involved in the all-Ireland developments in 1917. It supported Plunkett in North Roscommon in February. In April, at his convention in Dublin, Plunkett formed his Mansion House committee, as it was to be called, linking Sinn Féin and the Irish nation league. It eventually dissolved into the second Sinn Féin in October, though de Valera's new party contained no particular faction of Ulster catholics.

It was Herbert Moore Pim, the volunteer organizer before the rising, who did much to raise the separatist standard in Belfast, following his release from prison in August 1916. He had not participated in the rising, though the police had described him as 'a very clever, well-educated man, and capable journalist ... one of the most advanced and dangerous pro-Germans in Ireland'.[21] Pim was an admirer of Griffith, particularly his ideas of social reconstruction. In January 1916 he had started a monthly, the *Irishman* in Belfast, a non-political journal. He adopted the pseudonym A. Newman. The *Irishman* reappeared in

September, and he also helped with *Young Ireland*, an advanced nationalist paper for boys. Pim set about re-establishing Sinn Féin, against the
wishes of some leading IRBers. He was also active in the West Cork by-
election in November. Sinn Féin, Pim argued, was 'a system whereby a
people may, by the daily actions of each individual, and by the associated action of the community, set up immediately a state of intellectual independence, and, by degrees, of social and economic
independence'.[22] It was January 1917 before the Pearse club was set up
in Belfast. There followed the Irish-Ireland club, in Divis Street, a Sean
MacDermott club, and a fourth club in Ardoyne. By June there were
150 members of Sinn Féin in the city. The political rise of de Valera was
too much for Pim. He considered that Griffith sold out to the physical
force men in October, and he left Sinn Féin in June 1918. Pim rapidly
returned to the unionist fold, and got Carson to write the foreword to
one of his books. He no longer believed Irish catholics could embrace
the protestant ethic:

> There seemed to be growing among the people a business instinct, and a respect
> for the sterling qualities of the Ulster people ... Then de Valera came forth from
> prison endowed with what Le Bon calls 'accidental popularity' ... Sinn Fein
> became a glorified Donnybrook Fair. Industrial revival was forgotten in the joy
> of preparing to 'wipe out the British Empire' and in the raiding of decent homes
> by parties of armed men.[23]

After June 1918 Sinn Féin in Belfast lacked a leader of the literary and
organizational capacity of Pim. Soon the city was caught up in the new
party's plans to hegemonize Ireland at the general election. This was
announced in August, Lloyd George seeking a mandate, in December,
so it was thought, to finish the war. The country still had 101 territorial
seats, but also 4 university ones, following the redrawing of boundaries
in 1917. Sinn Féin planned to contest all 105, but its desire to turn the
election into a referendum on self-determination came up against the
reality of sectarian division in Ulster. Cardinal Logue, worried about a
split catholic vote helping the unionists, distributed 8 seats equally
between the Irish party and Sinn Féin. Eoin MacNeill's acceptance of
this plan greatly sullied the party's electoral strategy. Catholic Belfast
was not considered. The city's allocation had been increased from 4
seats to 10, including 1 for Queen's University – as it were. Each of the
1910 seats was essentially divided into two. The new Falls division was
a very safe catholic seat, though there were nationalist minorities in
other seats. The Belfast nationalist registration and election committee
opposed the redistribution, solely on the grounds that catholic representation would decline from 1 in 4 to 1 in 10 seats. The size of the
electorate had also been greatly increased, the presence for the first time
of female and many more male electors causing some anxiety for the
established parties.

Sinn Féin stood in all 10 Belfast seats, de Valera, in Lincoln jail, being
nominated for Falls (as well as East Clare and East Mayo). Joe Devlin
was determined to hold on to the catholic ghetto. The UIL did not put

up candidates in any of the other 9 seats, but the liberal, Maj. W.H. Davey, who had written to the *Manchester Guardian* in 1912, advocated home rule in Duncairn, where Sir Edward Carson, having quit Trinity College, was standing in the Ulster unionist cause. The 1918 election saw 9 unionists returned for Belfast, and an important nationalist side-show. The 10 Sinn Féin candidates picked up 8,882 votes, to the 11,937 for Devlin and Davey. In Falls, de Valera, the leader of the nation, secured only 3,245 votes to Devlin's 8,488, when the Irish party was otherwise obliterated. It was a freak result, but it also represented Sinn Féin's inability to do better than the Irish party on partition, given the Ulster unionists.

The coalition government's manifesto, signed by Lloyd George and Bonar Law, and issued on 22 November, offered little to Ireland. It promised 'to explore all practical paths towards the settlement of this grave and difficult question on the basis of self-government'. Two options were excluded: 'a complete severance of Ireland from the British Empire', and 'the forcible submission of the six counties of Ulster to a Home Rule Parliament against their will'.[24] This was a particularly unionist statement. It excluded Sinn Féin's desire for an Irish republic, but de Valera was interested only in the peace conference, and the party was prepared to use 'any and every means available'[25] against British rule. Devlin was a House of Commons man, with all the tradition of the Irish party behind him. While his dominion home rule, what he called 'complete Self-Determination for Ireland',[26] was not ruled out, Lloyd George, having just won the war, had signalled that Ireland would be partitioned.

The contest between de Valera and Devlin in Falls was a clash of political cultures, Sinn Féin's romantic nationalism meaning little, given the social and political reality of Belfast catholics.

'What did these visitors to West Belfast know of the conditions under which the West Belfast people had to work?' Councillor Jamison asked on 8 December. 'Yet, knowing nothing of the actual conditions they asked the people to wait for fifty years until an Irish Republic was established – (Laughter) – until the young men of Kerry and Cork had strangled the military power of England (Laughter and applause). Belfast however was going to lead Ireland back to sanity.'[27] There were only 50 or so Sinn Féin election workers in Falls, but the party sent so-called 'peace patrols' to west Belfast, from – allegedly – Co. Clare and other distant places. Great fun was made of these young idealists. The trade unionist, Michael McKeown, still with the UIL, hoped they would report the rejecting 'manner of the people'[28] when they returned home. Devlin's prewar rivalry with Bishop Henry was tapped to express an anti-clerical opposition to Fr O'Flanagan, vice-president, with Arthur Griffith, of Sinn Féin. It was believed he had made a sacreligious reference about Dubliners wanting to throw Redmond's coffin in the Liffey. The Sinn Féin manifesto, which invoked 'the dead generations'[29] of republican mythology, in the uncensored version, was accused, by the *Irish News*, of referring to 'the damned souls' who had died in the war. 'Horrifying Insult to every Catholic With Soldier Relative', was one typical political advertisement.[30] The paper was also chauvinist and sectarian. Bulmer Hobson was described as one of a number of Englishmen in Sinn Féin, while Herbert Pim was reported to be 'somewhere in the unplumbed depths of Carsonism'.[31] The UIL practised what it preached, and Sinn Féin's first meeting was disrupted. 'A large number of mill girls sang and cheered lustily, and also blew shrill whistles.' According to the *Irish News*, Sinn Féiners 'armed with bludgeons, rushed at the mill-workers'.[32] One woman received a violent blow on the head, while others had salt thrown in their faces. It was de Valera's supporters who retreated, and the UIL seems to have harassed Sinn Féin throughout the campaign. Even Michael Davitt's daughter, a visiting speaker for de Valera, was not safe from Devlin's mill girls.

Sinn Féin made it extremely easy for Devlin, by concentrating upon the national question. Its manifesto emphasized 'march[ing] out into the full sunlight of freedom', in the censored version, after which it would 'develop Ireland's social, political and industrial life'.[33] Its candidates in Belfast betrayed their ignorance of social issues. Three of them peppered their joint election address with quotations from Patrick Pearse. 'As Irish Catholics', they wrote, 'we will, by all and every effective means in our power, urge the Church and the Nation to oppose ... a demoralising and Godless educational system which a Foreign Parliament would impose upon a partitioned North-East corner.' And this in protestant St Anne's, Woodvale and Ormeau! On modern urban industrial life in general, Pearse was cited on 'Godless Cities'. 'We know', they admitted plaintively, 'that on the great ideals of Nationality and Religion we are fundamentally at variance with the majority of you.'[34] At the 1917 Sinn Féin *árd fheis*, de Valera had said that when labour helped free the country, it could 'look for its own share of its patrimony'.[35] It was Tom Johnson, in *Irish Opinion* of 1 December, who described Sinn Féin as asking that 'Labour should wait until freedom is achieved.'[36] Johnson was acceding to de Valera in late 1918, but he had formulated the 'labour must wait' position ascribed critically to Sinn Féin. (Virtually all the famous quotations attributed to Irish political figures originate with their opponents.) By the time of the general election, the Sinn Féin candidates in St Anne's, Woodvale and Ormeau were telling labour to wait until 'an Independent Ireland [was] an established fact'.[37]

The statement, 'Labour must wait', Devlin ascribed to de Valera on 8 December, 'and wait for fifty years if necessary', a period of time long bandied about in the labour movement as regards home rule. 'Never', his audience replied. 'He can wait.' 'I decline', Devlin went on, 'to tell the shipwrights and mill workers, the street sweepers, or any section of the working people that they must wait fifty years on a Republic before their grievances are redressed ... we are out for one thing, to improve and elevate the people.'[38] This sort of populism had been characteristic, designed to unite rhetorically the working class in West Belfast. There was no need for this in the Falls, but Devlin's nationalism was now in greater sympathy with British labour. The labour party came out in favour of 'the right of self-determination within the British

Commonwealth of Free Nations'[39] for Ireland and India, that is, dominion home rule. Labour had recently become socialist, but Devlin continued to believe in 'the right of individual liberty and ... the inviolable
sanctity of the home'.[40] He would, as a House of Commons man, move
towards the parliamentary labour party, but had begun, in 1918, to
accept aspects of a programme of social reform. He favoured minimum
wages, equal pay for women and state arbitration – all providing 'at
least frugal comfort'.[41]

Organization was, once again, crucial in the election campaign.
Given the sectarian balance in West Belfast, registration had long been
a precondition for success. With the extension of the franchise, the UIL
was well placed to encourage male and female catholics to register. Sinn
Féin had little experience of this, and it was now the enemy. (Orange
and green had been Devlin's electoral colours before the war, but the
Irish tricolour of 1916 now belonged to Sinn Féin. The UIL stuck with
the old national colours, which slid towards the green and gold (or
yellow) of the Vatican. Irish nationalists always had difficulty in distinguishing orange and yellow!) Devlin symbolically got a 'brewer' to
nominate him for Falls, and the administrator of St Mary's to second
his candidacy. But he then did something which must have been
unique in electoral politics in the British Isles. The UIL went round the
houses of the division getting electors to sign Devlin's nomination
papers. Eight hundred papers, with 10 signatures each, were handed in
on nomination day. This made 8,000 electors. Since Devlin secured
only 8,488 votes, most of them were in the bag from an early stage. The
Irish News then published the names and addresses, street by street,
devoting whole pages, on 5, 7 and 11 December. It was easy to locate
those who had not affirmed for Devlin when approached by his election workers. If this amounted to political finger-pointing, serious
efforts were made to persuade the remainder against de Valera. Devlin
spent much of his time visiting electors, presumably the 4,000 or so
who had not yet been signed up.

Devlin had long sought to mobilize women. He did so again in 1918,
even though many of them must have been under the voting age of 30.
The war had brought work, if not prosperity, to the ghetto, and the
member for West Belfast must have been credited with the linen boom.
Devlin set up a 'Belfast Workers' Fund'[42] for women workers only. The
Irish News claimed it had been initiated by the women themselves, and
it published the names of those who donated. Most were unmarried
workers. Joe Devlin remained single, and, in his nomination papers,
had variously described himself as a gentleman or a secretary. A deep
bond of affection seems to have been built up, judging by the evidence
of gift-giving in Falls during the election campaign. Women workers
clubbed together to buy the nationalist candidate presents, the *Irish
News* again documenting the source of the gifts. On Wednesday, 11
December, a Devlin parade was held in the division, which 'established
a new precedent in manifestations of popular enthusiasm'. His brake
was surrounded by 'a stalwart bodyguard of young men carrying
camans [hurling sticks]'. Young men and women made up the

procession. 'Rockets flared into the air and exploded in cascades of coloured lights.' '[It was] a picture reminiscent of Carlylean descriptions', reported the *Irish News*, 'of great popular outbursts in the French revolutionary period ... The fiery enthusiasm which [the crowd] displayed could not have been excelled by the most emotional populace in Ireland.' Devlin's brake pulled alongside another in Clonard Street, occupied by women. McKeown asked for silence. The women then presented Devlin with their gifts – a gold signet ring, a gold pin, a box of handkerchiefs and a silken scarf, a cigar case and silver box with initials, a dressing case, a pair of gloves, and more handkerchiefs. Referring to political desertions elsewhere in the country, Devlin said that 'the women of West Belfast [did] not know the meaning of the word'.[43]

There was more of this at his victory parade on 29 December. The range of gifts was even more extensive, and the workers in the various spinning rooms acknowledged in the *Irish News*. Devlin had been abstaining from the House of Commons since April, when he had nearly 70 parliamentary colleagues. After the declaration on 28 December, he had the support of Redmond's son, plus four fellow Ulster nationalists (as well as T.P. O'Connor in Liverpool). Devlin was the most senior, but the rump Irish party does not seem to have met to elect a new leader. Devlin, in what was undoubtedly a personal decision, hinted he would not take his seat in the new parliament, in solidarity, presumably, with the rest of nationalist Ireland. But he was too attached to the Palace of Westminster, and was quickly to find an excuse for returning, in order to speak for his constituents. He had once been a leader of the Irish nation. Now he was just a ghetto boss, and one who was not prepared to link his city to the march of the nation under the new regime beginning to emerge in Dublin.

Part V

National Revolution

10

The Ulster Unionist Labour Association, 1918–22

The 1918 election saw the Ulster Unionist Labour Association (UULA) secure three of the nine unionist seats in Belfast. It was a creature of the Ulster Unionist Council (UUC), Sir Edward Carson believing that an inter-class movement, such as Ulster unionism, had to appeal directly to protestant workers. This was especially the case after the sacrifices of the war. Labour unionism was social toryism, in the form of a regional movement of opposition to Irish nationalism. It did not frighten middle-class voters, who supported the UULA as unionist. Nor did its putative labourism impress the working class, and undermine support for the Belfast labour party. This was seen most clearly in the 1920 municipal elections, held under proportional representation, when the unionists had difficulty in hegemonizing the protestant vote. The UULA was designed to counter working-class independence of a secular kind, the greatly strengthened trade-union and labour movement, since this threatened unionist solidarity. The Irish labour movement was seen as having identified itself with Sinn Féin, though Belfast remained very much a part of the British movement. The UULA did nothing to impress the British labour movement with the democratic pretensions of unionism, nor did it alter the balance between the classes in Ulster. The three UULA MPs at Westminster in the 1918 parliament were conservative on social issues, and loyalist on the constitutional question. They were deferential in the main and highly sectarian. The UULA was kept in being for the 1921 elections to the northern parliament, under the leadership of Sir James Craig. But the labour unionists were redundant, following the establishment of the state. The UULA was a failure, though it lingered on as a member of the unionist family.

The origins of the UULA lie in the prewar unionist mobilizations. In early 1912 Churchill had been told that if he tried to speak in the Ulster Hall, he would find it occupied by unionist militants. The first lord of the admiralty was confronted by loyalist demonstrators, when he and his wife were driven from the Midland station to a hotel in Royal Avenue in central Belfast. After lunch with prominent Ulster liberals, they left by car for the meeting in Celtic Park. Shipyard workers had now joined the throng, and – according to protestant folklore – were intent upon overturning Churchill's car until they noticed his wife. 'Mind the wumman'[1] was reportedly shouted. One of the shipyard men was William Grant, from Harland and Wolff, then in his mid-30s. He was president of the shipwrights' society, and an active member of a conservative association. 'They had every intention of killing Churchill', it was later said of Grant and his fellow workers, 'till suddenly they saw his wife beside him and that cooled them down.'[2] Shipwrights belonged to one of the more traditional crafts in Belfast, having their own orange lodge. Their society had three branches in 1912 and 812 members. When a former district secretary, James Baird, was killed in an accident at Workman, Clark in September, his funeral attracted a 'cortege ... of an imposing character'.[3] William Grant was a working-class orangeman of some influence in 1912, but it is questionable whether he can be considered a leader of the shipyard workers.

Within organized unionism working men, as they were still called, played a subordinate, but often important, role. So-called labour unionist contingents, probably unionist clubs from predominantly working-class areas, were present at the various mobilizations, from the Craigavon meeting in September 1911 onwards. An organizing secretary for the Balmoral parade, in April 1912, was Thompson Donald, also a shipwright. He had been one of two Belfast delegates, at the Ipswich TUC in 1909, and the only one at Newcastle two years later. The shipwrights did not customarily attend, and Donald had no opportunity to speak about Ireland. His working-class conservatism would not have impressed British trade unionists, who were, in the main, liberal going on labour. The Belfast shipwrights had given up on the trades council some years earlier, probably because of Walker's ventures into politics, though two branches reaffiliated just as the war began.

On the occasion of the third home rule bill, the Ulster unionists fought an extensive propaganda battle in Britain, in conjunction with the southern unionists. They intervened in by-elections, arguing the case against home rule. It was hoped that, by influencing public opinion, they could force the government to call a general election. In putting over the unionist case, they had to counter liberal and Irish nationalist propaganda about Carsonism being an aristocratic and bourgeois movement. In seats previously held by labour, Ulster was portrayed as the progressive part of Ireland. Unionists sought to present it as a place of inter-class harmony. The UUC could not manipulate the labour movement in Belfast, and Dawson Bates, its secretary, formerly a solicitor, was to show himself ignorant about its workings. He had to find working-class unionists, from within the party, to send to Britain. 'A body of Belfast working men' was included among unionist canvassers, during a by-election in north-east Derbyshire in May 1914, 'seeking quietly to convince their fellow trade unionists of the justice of Ulster's opposition to home rule'.[4] The same individuals were also put on display, when working-class delegations, inspired no doubt by local conservatives, visited Ulster in 1914. There were 102 such deputations, firstly to the south, to see how bad a home rule Ireland would be, and then to the north, to appreciate the virtues of its industrious inhabitants. These groups of a dozen or so liberal and unionist working men were personally received in Belfast by the lord mayor.

On 7 April, what purported to be 'the overwhelming body of trade unionists in Ulster', appealed, through the unionist press, to British workers, to support their cause on trade-union grounds. A home rule Ireland, it was argued, would jeopardize British unions. The appeal was signed by only 20 officials, mainly from the shipyards. The shipwrights accounted for one-third, including Grant and Donald. They were hardly representative of the protestant working class. This labour unionist manifestation was against the trades council and the ITUC, the opposition of the Irish labour movement to partition being considered essentially nationalist. The ITUC had held a public meeting in Dublin on 5 April, but the Belfast trades council executive announced, on 16 April, 'that in the present state of divided public opinion no meeting should be held'[5] in the north.

Grant and Donald, no doubt with the help of the Old Town Hall, then called a meeting of trade unionists, to be held in the Ulster Hall on 29 April. It was filled to overflowing by the unionist democracy, the men being addressed by conservative trade unionists. John Murphy, the secretary of the trades council, wrote later to the press disavowing the views expressed. No. 10 branch of the ASCJ protested against the misrepresentations at the Ulster Hall, and other trades council delegates concurred on 4 June. The Ulster Hall meeting represented the apogee of labour unionism before the war, and there was no organizational outcome, though it was remembered, by Grant, as the foundation of the UULA. It went down in unionist history as a unique event. Much later, after the war, the UUC referred to the meeting, in a 1921 pamphlet, by way of rebuttal to a critical labour party report on Ireland. It had been 'the most remarkable Labour demonstration ever seen in Ireland', its author – erroneously – claimed. '[The meeting] consisted of officials and members of every great trade organisation in the city and district. It was a purely spontaneous demonstration originating with the workers and conducted solely by them. It issued an appeal to the trade unionists of Great Britain pointing out that [home rule] ... would be disastrous for the solidarity of labour.'[6]

The next labour initiative of the Ulster unionists was during the war, when 95 delegates were appointed to the Irish convention in 1917. Given the presence of three independent labour men from Belfast, and two pro-Redmond trade unionists, the Irish and unionist parties each included one labour man in their delegations. John Hanna, who had spoken at the April 1914 meeting, was selected by the UUC. He was later a member of the UULA. Hanna was not a leading trade unionist, and his claim to represent the shipyards was hollow. He attended all 51 sessions, and was the only one of the seven so-called labour delegates not to make a presentation. This was a good precedent for the role of the UULA within organized unionism. Hanna seems to have spoken only once, in support of the amendment favouring exclusion. He also lined up with the Ulster unionists in the final vote, the only bloc not to support the majority report. Hanna signed their minority report, blaming the failure of the convention on the nationalists. He broke once from the Ulster unionists, and to the right, on an offer from Sir

Horace Plunkett. The chairman's compromise sought to attract the
unionists into a home rule parliament, by reserving 40 per cent of the
seats in the Irish senate for commercial, industrial and agricultural
interests. The Ulster unionists rejected it, ironically, as undemocratic,
but Hanna liked the idea of such discrimination. This was hardly out of
a desire to compromise with nationalism. A deputation of loyalist
workers was sent to Lloyd George, undoubtedly by the Old Town Hall,
when it was feared the prime minister might be listening to Plunkett, to
reinforce Ulster's opposition to the report of the convention.

Later in 1918, in May, a working men's unionist association appeared
on the UUC, with twelve representatives. The council had been reorganized, in anticipation of a general election. The UUC's working-men's
association seems to have been the party's way of appealing to the
working class. But the term 'working-man' was dated, and evocative of
conservatism. 'Labour' had already taken root, and was an acceptable
social category. The party's organization quickly became the Ulster
Unionist Labour Association (UULA), which formally dates from June
1918. It may have come into being, to counter, in the United States, the
Mansion House conference, through which the Irish labour movement
was opposing conscription. A labour representative from Belfast had
been included among the Ulster unionists who signed a statement to
President Wilson, arguing that there was support for the war. An organization of *'workers* formed to support and maintain the Legislative
Union', membership of the UULA was open to 'Unionist worker[s] ...
deemed to be eligible'.[7] There was also provision for honorary members
and women workers. 'Though many politicians are said to have sought
to avail themselves of the provision' of honorary membership, it was
observed later, 'they have been rigorously excluded.'[8]

Sir Edward Carson became president, and J.M. Andrews chairman.
The latter, a businessman, was an honorary secretary of the UUC, and
would be, much later, prime minister of Northern Ireland. Carson and
Andrews were still liberal unionists, not frightened of the organized
working class. The UULA was undoubtedly a creation of the Old Town
Hall, and the party bureaucracy under Bates. 'Sir Edward Carson', it was
recalled later, 'was increasingly conscious of the need to have card-
carrying Trade Union Members associated with the Unionist Movement
to disarm the obvious criticism that it was a movement largely dominated by Conservative Landowners.'[9] A membership of 30,000 was
claimed, but this seems fanciful. The UULA was never a rank-and-file
organization, like a trade union. Its constitution provided for branches,
as in a political party, and an annual meeting to elect officers, the executive and delegates to the UUC. Organizational activity was considerably lower than the voter support the UULA attracted in the 1918
general election, for reasons which had little to do with labour unionism as such. Its secretary was Wilson Hungerford, formerly a political
secretary of the UVF, who took over from Bates as secretary to the UUC
in 1921. The most important worker was William Grant, soon to be district chairman of the shipwrights, who later became vice-chairman of
the UULA. The first vice-chairman was J.A. Turkington. The honorary

secretaries were J.F. Gordon, who claimed to be a member of the ASE, and H. Fleming, a boilermaker. Gordon was a company secretary about this time, and was considered for employment as a party official. The honorary treasurer was R. Williamson, a plater. The executive committee, comprising 15 trade unionists, included some who had been outspoken conservatives on the trades council. William Grant seems to have been dependent upon a limited number of fellow trade unionists to constitute the leadership of the UULA. Of the 20 honorary vice-presidents in 1919, no fewer than 14 were on the executive. Between 1919 and 1923 the seven officers remained the same, except for James Turkington, who moved beyond the patronage of the party. Eleven of the original executive were still in place in 1923.

In the final months of the war, Carson, on his visits to Belfast from London, showed himself to be a politically changed man. During the unionist mobilizations, he had become the leader of protestant Ulster. It was the means to the defence of the empire, but Ulster was also the issue which might lead to a compromise on home rule. Leader and followers had been locked in determination. During the war, Carson played less than successful roles in the Asquith and Lloyd George coalition governments. Just as Sinn Féin had looked to Wilson in the United States from 1917 on, so revolution in Russia came to alarm the ruling powers in Europe. Bolshevism became the great fear for the bourgeoisie in 1918. Carson had long dreaded mass desertions to socialism, even in Ulster. But the global threat of bolshevism was the central issue of international relations. Carson was more of a British politician by the end of the war, and looked on Ireland principally as a place where nationalist revolt might fan dangerous bolshevik embers. The protestant working class might even rise in anger against the Ulster unionist leadership. He saw the south of Ireland being abandoned to a struggle between Sinn Féin and the British government, and Ulster integrated more into the United Kingdom. Home rule was dead, partition almost a reality, and unionism concentrated even more in Ulster.

This regional movement, Carson believed, had to be recomposed on more modern political lines. The model was the way the British state had been transformed during the war by coalition government. The working class had been harnessed, to fight abroad and work at home, in a spirit of national unity. Carson announced his 'new policy', as he called it, to the UUC in November. Sinn Féin was not acceptable to the British government, so there would be no negotiations with Irish nationalism. The days of the Ulster provisional government were therefore over, and loyalists had to become good British citizens within the United Kingdom. 'In the course of the war', Carson told the UUC, 'men's minds [had] been occupied with all the problems that [were] necessary for the greater advancement of civilisation and the betterment of what all called the working classes.'[10] The franchise had been recently extended, under an act of parliament, to cover virtually all men over 21, and all women over 30. Carson was symbolically re-elected president of the UUC on a motion, proposed by Lady Londonderry, leader of the Ulster Women's Unionist Council, and seconded by Samuel McGuffin, a conservative working-man. Without Carson, there would have been no UULA.

With the increase in parliamentary seats in Belfast from four to ten, there was considerable jockeying, on the part of aspiring unionists, for the eight safe territorial ones. Carson wanted a number of working-class MPs returned from the city, seemingly as many as 3 out of 9. In the summer of 1918 the UUC set up a labour sub-committee to implement this policy. Though the UULA was represented on the UUC, it was not directly involved in the sub-committee. This was chaired by H.T. Barrie, MP, who had led the Ulster unionist delegation at the convention, and it included Belfast worthies. Andrews was a member, and Bates the secretary. Falls was ignored, the rest of the old West Belfast seat being Woodvale. North Belfast had been divided into Shankill and Duncairn, and South Belfast into St Anne's and Cromac. East Belfast, the largest seat, was split into Victoria, Pottinger and Ormeau. The sub-committee, meeting first on 2 August, selected Shankill, Victoria and Pottinger, only to alter its plans to Shankill, Victoria and St Anne's, in the three existing unionist seats. The new unionist associations were reluctant to have labour candidates foisted upon them by the Old Town Hall. Hungerford did the rounds, only to meet with a negative response. Clark, a member of the sub-committee, had a word with Ewart, president of the Shankill organization. As for the other two, a consultative central council had to be set up. This included the UULA, but it did not play a major role. Donald was selected for Victoria by a committee chaired by Frank Workman.

Three candidates eventually emerged at Carson's insistence. Samuel McGuffin for Shankill, Thompson Donald for Victoria and Thomas Burn in St Anne's. McGuffin had been born in 1863. Starting as a postboy, he became a hackle-maker. He was a foreman in the Irish Flax Spinning Company for 16 years, but by 1918 he had his own drapery business on the Shankill Road. He had been the first president of No. 12 ASE branch, but gave up trade unionism when he became a foreman. He was a methodist, but not an orangeman. Thompson Donald was a member of the order, and a Freemason. Born in 1875, he had been a shipwright at Workman, Clark. He became chief assistant foreman in 1912. Donald had been, for three years, district secretary of the shipwrights' society, but gave up trade unionism when promoted. He was the most active of the three labour unionists, having been involved in the Belfast FEST, a member of arbitration boards and the advisory committee on Irish labour exchanges. Less is known about Thomas Burn, also born in 1875. He was a lithographic printer. All three had been active members of conservative associations, and at least two were upwardly mobile. Their trade-union reputations lay in the past, where they had undoubtedly been opposed to the tradition represented by William Walker.

The three UULA candidates were, first and foremost, protestant loyalists. McGuffin mentioned that he had written to the *Northern Whig* in 1886, at the age of 22, arguing that home rule was essentially a 'religious' question.[11] Thompson Donald accused Robert Waugh, his labour opponent in Victoria, who had signed the majority report at the convention, of having sold 'his birthright for a mess of pottage'. He claimed Waugh was an orangeman, and 'was speaking that night in the midst of a Roman Catholic district'.[12] Thomas Burn distinguished 'two classes of Labour', those 'selected by Unionist workers of the city' and those 'without a proper prefix'.[13] Labour unionism had little to say about social questions. The UULA was committed to class collaboration, and opposed to the industrial and political independence of labour. J.M. Andrews, supporting McGuffin, 'claimed he was proud to know that an employer could still attend a meeting such as that one and be still looked upon as a friend'.[14] At a meeting at Ewart's mill, chaired by the owner, McGuffin warned workers not to be led away 'by illusory doctrines that young men preached and did not understand'.[15] He later claimed that he could get a testimonial from his old union branch, but that 'there was a certain amount of Bolshevism in the ranks of the ASE.'[16] Carson was described, by J.F. Gordon, as having shifted from a unionism of 'negation' to one of 'advance'.[17] The leader of Ulster unionism was standing in a working-class constituency – Duncairn. He came to Belfast supporting the coalition government, and seeking to relegitimize the union, in the eyes of protestant workers, with social reconstruction. Carson specifically mentioned education, housing and temperance reform, only to have Maj. Davey, his opponent, issue a document outlining his conservative opposition to progressive measures in the past. The UULA candidates variously repeated Carson. Donald was for municipal control of education (which the catholic church opposed), better housing, a local option on temperance, shorter hours if output was kept up, and a peace based on revenge. Burn and McGuffin stressed their support for ex-servicemen.

Carson had difficulty in coordinating the unionist electoral campaign. 'When is a Unionist not a Unionist?' he asked on one occasion, giving the answer, 'When he creates disunion.'[18] There was even talk of an independent unionist opposing him in Duncairn. His candidate for Woodvale, R.J. Lynn, editor of the *Northern Whig*, secured the nomination by only 80 votes to 58. By the close of nominations there were only two independent unionists running in the city. W.J. Stewart opposed Thomas Moles, of the *Belfast Evening Telegraph*, in Ormeau, while, in St Anne's, W.H. Alexander opposed the UULA candidate. Both stood for local independence. The fact that Stewart did so much better than Alexander suggests that the imposition of an outsider – Moles – caused more offence than a labour unionist candidate. The latter did not frighten the middle class. The three UULA candidates won their seats. McGuffin, in Shankill, with 11,840 votes, got the second-highest unionist poll in the city. The other two were well up – Donald in Victoria with 9,309 votes, and Burn in St Anne's with 9,155. Though McGuffin and Donald were opposed by labour candidates, labour unionism did not weaken the independent labour vote. The Belfast labour party got 23 per cent of the vote in Shankill, and 26 per cent in Victoria, its two best results in the general election.

Elected members of the 1918 parliament, McGuffin, Donald and

Burn went off to Westminster. They made no impact. The three were submerged in the Ulster unionist party, doing nothing to give it a democratic reputation. They were entertained by the likes of the duke of Abercorn and the marquis of Dufferin and Ava, and the experience – according to Hungerford – 'went to their heads'.[19] The UULA men were unable to live on their salaries as MPs, and had to be further assisted by the UUC. They made few contributions on the floor of the house.

The three mainly asked questions, and even these dropped off after 1921. Donald was the most active, then McGuffin, and Burn a very poor third. 'I do not usually take up very much of the time of this House',[20] he said in March 1922. The three were strong supporters of the government, in its campaign against Sinn Féin and the IRA in Ireland. McGuffin was worried, on one occasion, about the number of catholics in the RIC in Belfast. Donald complained about loyalists receiving harsher treatment from the courts than republicans. The three were unhappy with the treaty settlement towards the end of 1921, which led to the setting up of the Irish Free State. Donald thought Ulster was entitled to nine counties, and threatened that if the boundary commission took territory from the north, protestant trade unionists 'would begin differentiating against Roman Catholics'.[21] Hostility to Irish nationalism extended to the people of the south, including trade unionists. The arrest of William O'Brien, then secretary of the ILP & TUC, in early 1920, was welcomed. When it came to protestant workers, the UULA MPs adopted sectional stances, often against other trade unionists. McGuffin, for example, complained about an iron-moulders' strike affecting other workers. Most of their questions concerned government intervention in disputes, strike-breaking by official action being welcomed. No criticism was made of those responsible for the expulsions of 1920. When Devlin attempted to raise the issue, he was accused of helping Sinn Féin.

Carson was appointed a lord of appeal in 1921, having resigned the leadership of the Ulster unionist party, and then his seat in the Commons. Retirement from politics did not deprive him of a platform in the Lords. For the 1922 Westminster election, Belfast was reduced, once again, to four territorial seats. Northern Ireland had 13, including a university seat. The UULA experiment was discontinued by the UUC. Thompson Donald wanted to stand in East Belfast, but Herbert Dixon secured the candidacy and seat.

The UULA had continued to exist as an organization, principally in Belfast. The monthly meeting for February 1919 was cancelled, because of the engineering strike. It had not even been mentioned at the annual meeting held on 18 January. That June, Bates, in a letter to Carson, articulated the unionist leadership's view of the UULA. 'The working people in Belfast', he wrote, 'have felt for a very considerable time past that means should be placed at their disposal whereby domestic matters could be discussed by them under Unionist auspices.' Political discussion was prevented in trade unions, except labour questions, and, in any case, their officials often held home rule views. 'The result has been frequently that opinions of the working classes in Belfast on the question of the Union are misrepresented in Belfast and elsewhere.'[22] Bates was particularly concerned that young workers were joining labour and socialist organizations. He admitted that the UULA's monthly meetings were inadequate, but the only solution to come from the association was four working-men's clubs in Belfast. A programme of winter lectures had also been suggested. The UULA passed these requests to Andrews, who forwarded them to Bates, who was now consulting Carson. Andrews, as an honorary secretary of the UUC, appreciated that he was considered pro-labour, so he wanted Carson's approval for any development of the UULA. Later that year, the association sent a deputation to the chief secretary, on the all-important question of housing. It 'received a most sympathetic hearing'.[23] It was also reported to the 1920 annual meeting that the UUC was sympathetic to the idea of working-men's clubs. A building was being purchased in east Belfast.

It was 1921 before it was open. A second club, in north Belfast, did not appear until 1924. The association was now largely concerned with adult education and social facilities. 'It is part of the duty of the [UULA]', the UUC's annual report for 1926 noted, 'to expose the real aims and objects of Socialism and other anti-British movements.'[24] That year, the UULA executive had congratulated Carson on a speech he made in the Lords. Following the general strike, reference was made to the 'great and effective work [he did to] lessen the hardships associated with unemployment'.[25] And so it continued. In 1931 Hungerford, now secretary of the UUC, asked Carson for 'a line' to read at the UULA's annual meeting.[26] Carson died eventually – at a relatively old age – in 1935. A statue was erected to him at the new parliament buildings at Stormont. It was the UULA which appropriated the right to lay a wreath each year on the anniversary of his death.

The 1918 general election had not been the electoral end of the UULA. The unionist leadership considered that it had a role to play in the 1920 municipal elections in Belfast, and in the first northern parliament general election in 1921. Both of these were held under proportional representation.

In the wake of the 1919 engineering strike (discussed in the next chapter), the Old Town Hall decided to use the UULA in the municipal general election the following January. It was the first such election for over 30 years. All 60 seats were to be contested, the wards being those of the parliamentary elections. Most of the 9 wards had 6 or 7 seats. Eight UULA candidates were selected. Two of these were in Shankill, the only ward with 8 seats. There was 1 in each of the other wards, with the exception of Falls and Ormeau. The UULA backed an independent, William Lorimer, in Ormeau, who claimed to be a defector from the ILP. The UULA candidates worked in the older crafts, and included a coach builder, a machine man, a merchant tailor and a linen lapper. They were drawn from the small circle of conservative working-men associated with organized unionism. Six of the eight were honorary vice-presidents of the UULA, three being members of the executive, including the vice-chairman and an honorary secretary. There was little contact with the labour movement. Gordon seems to have still been an ASE branch secretary, and another candidate was involved in a friendly society. A third, Turkington, the vice-chairman, was secretary of the Ulster workers' trade union, a sectarian rival to existing unions, such as the (British) Workers' Union and the ITGWU. The 8 UULA candidates were included in the unionist contingents in each ward, there being 47 official candidates (plus 5 independent unionists).

If the association's labour image was designed to reinforce the unionist appeal, or even to stop protestants from supporting independent labour, it had little to offer. The UULA had not supported the 1919 strike, and Lorimer admitted that he welcomed the use of troops. Gordon opposed 'Bolshevism Syndicalism and Socialism because he felt that the interests of the ratepayers could best be served by intelligent labour'.[27] The UULA favoured class collaboration, Lorimer considering Andrews 'the idol of the Association'.[28] Lennox, a UULA candidate, was 'under a deep debt of gratitude to his employer'.[29] He would be allowed off work, if elected, to attend to council business. The UULA was integrated into the unionists' campaign, Gordon, in Pottinger, joining other unionists in offering 'sound and progressive business ability ... a practical knowledge of Labour conditions ... [and] mature experience in Civic affairs'.[30] When the party stood on its municipal record, it effectively negated any role for the UULA. Bates admitted to Carson after the contest that 'many of the old Corporation were rather unpopular.'[31] The members of the association seemed more keen on the national question than on municipal reform. Robert Weir stated during the campaign that conscription in Ireland would have saved the lives of 'brave Ulster boys'.[32] Six of the UULA candidates, plus Lorimer, were returned, along with 29 official unionists (and 2 other independents). The 2 UULA defeats were in Shankill, where independent labour did best, securing 2 seats. In the other wards, the labour unionists had fewer first preferences than did their party colleagues. Thirty-eight seats were a majority on the corporation, but not an overwhelming one at this critical time in the history of unionism. The UUC did not harness the entire protestant working class, the labour party attracting trade unionists and the smaller number of socialists. 'It will be necessary', Bates reported to Carson after the election, 'for all Unionists to work as one Party in the Corporation, and the result will be closer cooperation between all shades of Unionist opinion.'[33]

The UULA had been eclipsed by labour in the 1920 municipal election, the latter taking 12 seats. But the industrial expulsions that summer, when the national struggle intruded upon Belfast, totally reversed things within the protestant working class. By the time of the first northern parliament election – May 1921 – the UULA was better placed to claim that it was representative.

There were 52 seats in the new Northern Ireland house of commons, Belfast being allocated as many as 20. These were divided between the pre-1918 divisions of North, East, South and West Belfast, each having 4 seats (plus 4 for the 2,528 eligible graduates of Queen's University). McGuffin, Donald and Burn were still UULA MPs at Westminster. They were now put up, respectively, for North, East and West Belfast, their existing constituencies being within these areas. William Grant, the UULA's leading activist, and district chairman of the shipwrights' society, joined McGuffin in North Belfast, the South, presumably, being considered too middle class. Andrews, the chairman, ran in Down, as a straight unionist, alongside R. McBride, a farmer and textile worker, who called himself a labour unionist, as did Gordon in Antrim. But it was only the four from Belfast, plus McBride, who affirmed their labour identity. William Grant was somewhat alone in having a recent involvement in industry.

While McGuffin, Donald and Burn had been attending at Westminster, labour unionism was overshadowed in Belfast by loyalist direct action. The Ulster Ex-Servicemen's Association (UESA) and the British Empire Union (BEU) were more popular, in 1921, than the UULA. As loyalist organizations of ex-servicemen, they did much to focus the unionist cause through their Saturday afternoon paramilitary parades during the election. The UESA, as its name suggests, was a regional, and not a British, organization. The BEU, in contrast, whose president was Carson, argued for counter-revolutionary vigilance. Bolshevism was blamed for all industrial conflict and socialist activity, Sinn Féin in Ireland, because of the stands of the ILP & TUC, being subsumed in this world conspiracy. The UESA and BEU were loyalist rather than orange, their cultural motifs being the empire, the Union Jack, and law and order. The commemoration of the recent dead was a major objective, followed by the care of servicemen's dependants. In Ulster this took on a sectarian coloration, it being believed that protestants had done all the fighting. But unemployed ex-servicemen were the major problem, given the shortage of work. Sir James Craig became parliamentary secretary at the ministry of pensions, after the 1918 election, moving, in April 1920, to the admiralty. He quit the British government in March 1921, shortly after becoming Ulster unionist leader. At pensions, and possibly the admiralty, Craig had been helped by Thomas Burn, MP, probably as a parliamentary private secretary. Burn certainly had a reputation, in Belfast, for being a friend of ex-servicemen. Catholics undoubtedly received their entitlement, but payments, in the eyes of the dominant community, were related to the existence of the union. The first Northern Ireland general election was scheduled for 24 May – Empire Day. The Belfast Union Jack Committee, on which the UESA was probably the leading body, arranged a march and service. The marchers were undoubtedly ex-servicemen, but they were joined by a small UULA contingent, led by Andrews, which had assembled at the Old Town Hall.

An 'effective working majority' was the goal in 1921, according to Craig on 25 April, soon to be installed as prime minister. Though the country had been partitioned by the 1920 government of Ireland act, he warned that Ulster might be 'submerge[d] in a Dublin Parliament'. It was therefore necessary, he argued, to 'lay aside minor issues [and] sacrifice personal interests'.[34] This caused no problem for the UULA. The unionist regime took office on 3 May, with the election due three weeks later. Though Craig referred to the need for a 'democratic Parliament ... for the benefit of the people'[35] during the campaign, he did not spell out any programme of social reform. This was the general election in which he endorsed the driving out of the labour candidates from the Ulster Hall. The UULA, if anything, was more intent upon seeing the northern parliament elections as the consolidation of a protestant political bulwark. 'The real struggle', according to Thomas Burn, MP, on 3 May, 'was between Protestantism and Catholicism. Let them make no mistake about that.'[36] As for Carson, he was still Westminster MP for Duncairn, but had given up the leadership in February. His role was confined to sending messages from London. They show a continuing commitment to social toryism, a commitment that was not articulated by Ulster unionists. The union, Carson wrote, would 'bring about such reforms as [would] ensure contentment, happiness and civil and religious liberties to all creeds and classes'.[37]

The four UULA candidates in Belfast fought alongside fellow unionists. In North Belfast McGuffin and Grant combined with two businessmen, to run a 'peace and prosperity' campaign. McGuffin promised to 'deal with all the interests concerned [in the postwar depression] in a broad and generous spirit, and to strengthen more than ever the bond between employer and employed'.[38] Westminster was making a diplomatic impact. Grant, in contrast, was more of a local populist. An Ulster parliament, he believed, would be able to tackle economic recession. British labour leaders were 'of a Bolshevik or Red flag tendency'. 'He just obeyed these people so far as it suited him, and used his own judgement on trade union affairs.' Grant wanted 'a system as would cement that friendly feeling and render impossible these disastrous disputes'.[39] Donald did not want to make any pledges, until the foundation stones of the state had been laid. He refused to help the town tenants' association, an organization of shopkeepers. 'He could not be bothered by people coming at the time of the election and harassing the candidates.'[40] Burn pledged himself, along with the other two unionists in West Belfast, to 'any reform which is for the betterment of the people'.[41] All four UULA candidates were returned. Burn was the only one to come top of the poll, possibly because of his involvement with ex-servicemen. He got 3,000 more votes than W.J. Twaddell, a unionist, who was killed by the IRA the following year. McGuffin, probably because he was already an MP, did significantly better than Grant in North Belfast. As for Donald in East Belfast, he came third, over 3,000 votes behind Bates.

Andrews was returned for Down, in company with the labour unionist R. McBride. Gordon was successful in Antrim, coming in sixth, in a seven-seat constituency, with unionist transfers. The 1921 election, despite proportional representation, saw all 40 unionist candidates elected. The campaign of independent labour had come to a halt in the Ulster Hall. There were only twelve from the catholic minority (six followers of Devlin, and six Sinn Féin). The six UULA candidates in the first Northern Ireland parliament, which met on 7 June, were a recognizable group within the unionist party. All the catholic representatives abstained from attending. But the UULA did not become an opposition, even within a wider unionist solidarity. Craig's cabinet included Andrews as minister of labour. Gordon became parliamentary secretary in the same department. Of the three Westminster MPs, only Burn was given a job – assistant parliamentary secretary in the ministry of finance. McGuffin and Grant joined Andrews on the ten-strong delegation, elected to represent the northern parliament on the council of Ireland under the 1920 act.

In the first northern parliament, which lasted until 1925, McGuffin, Donald and Grant, as backbenchers, showed that their working-class unionism was a mixture of social deference and political sectarianism.

McGuffin seconded the motion which elected the speaker in the new house of commons. Later, he had cause to complain about the labour members, so called, being passed over, when it came to the appointment of backbench MPs to committees. Andrews, for the government, replied that he thought McGuffin and Donald would be occupied at Westminster. He claimed that his department always tried to include labour men on committees. Speaking later in a debate on unemployment, the minister of labour said: 'I am told very frequently that I am bound to fall between two stools – Labour on the one hand and Capital on the other' – only to have McGuffin interject, 'Not a bit of you.' 'I ... will never have any suspicion' with regard to the ministry so long as Andrews was in charge, McGuffin said later in the debate. 'I know how the working people feel with respect to him – they feel that in him they have a friend. We are not asking him to act partially with respect to us, or to adopt the position of a partisan in regard to our claims.'[42] It was Andrews who came under attack from the unionist dissidents in the first parliament, a group of right-wingers around W. Coote, a Tyrone farmer and woollen manufacturer. He thought the government was interfering too much in industry. All unionists rallied, on the occasion of the 1922 engineering lock-out in the United Kingdom, to insulate Ulster. Andrews advised the British employers not to include Belfast, only to support them when they decided to go ahead. The UULA initially backed the government, and then advised the unions not to resist the lock-out. McGuffin pleaded for a committee of inquiry, which he hoped might allow local employers and unions to back off, but the government refused. The labour unionists were, above all, suspicious of the catholic minority, rarely missing a chance to dismiss them as republicans. Officials in labour exchanges were described as Sinn Féiners, and those on the dole as members of the IRA. The UULA reluctantly accepted attempts, in early 1922, to establish good relations with the new Irish Free State.

Labour unionism, after Carson quit Ulster in 1921, amounted to very little. McGuffin, Donald and Burn, having been removed from Westminster, remained in the Belfast parliament, with Grant, in the early, formative years of the new state. McGuffin did not stand again for North Belfast in 1925, his seat going to an independent unionist, T.G. Henderson, a more reform-minded figure. In 1929, the third general election, McGuffin tried to take Shankill from the independent, only to lose narrowly. Donald and Burn defended their seats in the 1925 elections, still under proportional representation, only to lose to two independent labour men. William Grant was the only labour unionist from Belfast to sit in the second Northern Ireland parliament, coming in third in North Belfast behind another labour man. He became a more vociferous critic of the second unionist government, following the lead of the labour party on social issues. (Gordon still called himself a labour unionist, in Antrim, and R. MacBride was also returned in Down, where there was no contest.) This was effectively the end of the UULA as a parliamentary force. In 1929, when the Ulster government reverted to the British electoral system, Grant was returned unopposed for Duncairn as a straight unionist. Ahead lay a career as one of the only two protestant working-men to serve in a unionist cabinet.

11

The Engineering Strike of 1919

Carson's fear of working-class action had been confirmed in January and February 1919, in the strike of engineering and shipyard workers for a 44-hour week. The cause was the sacrifices made in the workplace during the war, and the occasion, the short postwar boom. The Belfast strike coincided with one in Glasgow, but the movement of working-class militancy was not synchronized in the United Kingdom. There was an absence of sectarianism in Belfast at the end of the war, but the city was also unreceptive to Clydeside revolutionary socialists. Revolution had a particular national identity in Ireland, this being the major political restraint on protestant working-class behaviour. A serious challenge to legitimate authority in Belfast merely played into the hands of the IRA. Republicanism had nothing to offer Ulster except nationality and religion, neither of which appealed to protestant workers who considered themselves British. The 1919 strike was the greatest in Irish history, being – almost – general throughout Belfast. It showed the formidable unity of the trade-union movement, following its strengthening during the war. But it had limited industrial goals, and the strike's leaders were circumscribed by the institutions of collective bargaining. The resoluteness of the Belfast working class was related less to the construction of proletarian hegemony within capitalism than to claiming a legitimate share of its industrial birthright. When the army was brought in to restore municipal services, the strike committee declined to confront state repression. The Belfast trade-union movement eschewed politics in 1919, whether of ethnic rivalry or industrial militancy. But the strike did strengthen socialist leadership in the city, the May Day march that year being one of the greatest in the history of the city.

During the war workers in the engineering industry, throughout the United Kingdom, had reluctantly accepted dilution, the suspension of collective bargaining and the illegality of strikes. This was purely for the duration. Male workers in Belfast, largely in the two shipyards, but also in town engineering shops, as they were known, were relatively quiescent. They benefited more from the full employment of war work, but were no less determined that their sacrifice should be rewarded after the armistice. The war effort had required workers to put in a considerable number of hours, and attention, in the closing months of hostilities, became focused on the idea of a shorter working week. The treasury agreements had provided for a return to traditional practices, and the end of dilution, in the engineering industry, when peace returned. Similar expectations existed in shipbuilding, even though it was less affected by the entry of women into temporary employment. The engineers' union, the ASE, which was dominant in its own industry, had been involved until January 1918, through the federation (FEST), in shipbuilding, where multi-unionism prevailed. While the shop stewards' movement had seized the initiative in the British engineering industry, at crucial points during the war, it was the official leadership of the ASE which led the negotiations for a reduction in hours, from the prewar norm of 54 or 53. The engineering employers offered 47 hours, as from the beginning of 1919. This had been demanded in 1897, provoking the lock-out which lasted into 1898. Forty-seven hours was accepted, by 337,029 votes to 159,887, in a United Kingdom ballot held by the FEST at the end of 1918. Rejection by nearly a third of those voting, admittedly on a low national turnout of 25 per cent, showed there was a widespread desire for fewer than 47 hours. Some unions – the plumbers, boilermakers, shipwrights and NAUL – voted against the employers' offer, but opposition was concentrated in Belfast and Glasgow.

The movement for shorter hours had begun, in Belfast, on 21 August, as Germany was retreating in Europe. A meeting of engineering and shipyard workers, held in the Ulster Hall, formulated a demand for 44 hours. Belfast had been working a 54 hour week, with a 6 a.m. start, from the early 1870s. Putting this back to 8.15 a.m. meant a 44-hour week, with workers having breakfast at home. Forty-four hours meant an 8-hour day, with Saturday morning work continuing. The organizers of this meeting were James Baird, James Freeland and Robert Weir. Baird, a boilermakers' branch secretary from Ballymacarrett, chaired the meeting. Freeland was Irish organizer of the ASE, based in Belfast. Weir was a machine hand from Harland and Wolff. He had taken part in anti-home rule campaigns in Britain before the war, and was an executive member of the UULA. He was the odd man out, though H. Fleming, the boilermaker and one of the UULA's honorary secretaries, may have been involved initially. Baird and Freeland's unions generally ignored the trades council and ILP & TUC, and Belfast delegates rarely made it to the TUC. But Baird was a member of the ILP, and may have been active before the war. Freeland was one of the labour parliamentary candidates in the city in December. This was a rank-and-file meeting, called by activists, and involving lay officers, and full-time trade-union officials. The workers looked to the Belfast district committee of the FEST for leadership.

Forty-four hours became an issue in the general election campaign. Nominations closed on Tuesday, 3 December, and all parliamentary candidates were invited to a meeting in the Ulster Hall the following evening. The district committee of the FEST seems to have been responsible. Forty-seven hours had been agreed to in negotiations on 19 November, but the federation had yet to ballot. The two shipyards and the local engineering employers' organization were not automatically committed to this offer, and the Belfast FEST was keen on local negotiations. The district committee of, largely, full-time officials stood in much the same relationship to the national unions and federation, as did the shop stewards' movement in Britain. Glasgow and other centres had experienced unofficial or unconstitutional trade unionism. It was a case of localism in Belfast, based on Ireland's less than complete integration into the United Kingdom. The Ulster Hall meeting opened with the singing of the national anthem. The ten Sinn Féin candidates were nowhere to be seen, either because those at liberty were not invited, or because they refused to attend. James Baird was again in the chair. There were only three other absentees; one of the four labour candidates and one of the three UULA sent apologies, as did Joe Devlin. He expressed full support for the demand, and offered to do what he could. But this was undermined by his excuse of a 'slight cold'.[1] The presence of Carson and his unionist colleagues, at the invitation of local trade unionists, is a measure of the state of relations between the classes in Belfast at the end of the war.

James Baird stated that the object of the meeting was 'to assist the workers apart altogether from politics, in obtaining shorter hours of labour'. The workers' leaders were adamant about 44 hours, without any reduction in pay, or any other condition being imposed by the employers. But the labour candidates present were standing against unionists. The latter sought to impose a capitalist rationality on the issue. An independent unionist wanted increased capital investment. Lynn was 'in hearty sympathy' with the workers, but opposed to those who said 'hang the output'. The high point of the meeting was Carson's speech, in which he equivocated. He argued that the workers had secured the end of the early morning start, hinted that he would support 44 hours if Belfast workers could get this accepted in Britain, but suggested they should accept the employers' offer. It was less than total support for the Belfast workers, but not a criticism of trade unionism. He left after speaking, supposedly for another meeting, the *Northern Whig* claiming he was 'received with loud cheers'. The *Irish News* detected 'a strong under-current of groaning in the cheers which greeted him'. His speech had been punctuated, it was claimed, with interjections such as 'What about excess profits?', and 'What about your voting on the 8-Hour Day?'[2]

The Belfast workers were also looking ahead that December to the possibility of a downturn in trade, and the return of ex-servicemen seeking work. The armistice had signalled the end of wartime production. Engineering employers, and, to a lesser extent, shipyards, throughout the United Kingdom, began to dismiss workers. Unemployment in shipbuilding rose from 0.31 to 2.43 per cent between November and December. It was over 6 per cent by March 1919. There was then re-employment, to finish prewar contracts, this helping fuel a postwar boom. It did not last beyond May 1920. National figures obscure local differences. Belfast did well in 1919. The shipyards had record orders, and there were 'many new slips'.[3] It is not clear how the two Belfast yards were affected in late 1918, but the first meeting of the trades council in the new year heard that all dilutee shipwrights had been laid off at Christmas. There were 4,000 unemployed in the city. Linen may have fared better, with the ending of wartime control. There was an immediate postwar boom, then a downturn, and another downturn in late 1919. Male workers, during the first Christmas of peace, saw shorter hours as a way of coping with the threat of unemployment. Members of the ASE in Belfast, according to Freeland in his monthly report, were 'much dissatisfied' at the re-election of the Lloyd George coalition. 'The political tricksters', he wrote, 'will now tell you that you misunderstood them, and they cannot find the money for the reforms you expect, but it was ever thus.'[4]

The Belfast employers decided to introduce 47 hours as from Wednesday, 1 January 1919. When the national FEST ballot on the offer showed acceptance by over 2 to 1, the Belfast district committee refused to go along with the decision. This had been expected. The local FEST met on 27 December 1918, having become 'the most powerful combination of organized labour ever formed in Northern Ireland'.[5] Five days later workers who had hitherto gone to the engineering shops and shipyards *en masse* at an early hour in working clothes, now rubbed shoulders, on the municipal trams, with the first waves of middle-class clerks, other black-coated workers, and female secretaries, on their way to offices. The ASE led the call, on 2 January 1919, for a one-day strike, but the federation district committee decided upon a local ballot. Though the engineers had left the FEST, the Belfast ASE and several other non-affiliated unions worked with the district committee. Delegates at a FEST meeting on 4 January voted for 14 days' strike notice, but this was overturned, five days after that, when the district and branch committees of all the affiliated unions were summoned to a conference. It was agreed to hold a strike ballot on Tuesday, 14 January.

At noon that day, work stopped in much of Belfast, 'one of the indications to the employers how seriously the men looked on the question'. Dinner was normally from 12.45 p.m. to 1.30 p.m. Workers left Harland and Wolff, and were joined by those from Workman, Clark's south yard. They crossed the river, and headed down Victoria Street, towards the north yard. The procession – now estimated at 30,000 – came back up York Street and Royal Avenue, to the City Hall. Among the slogans on the placards and banners carried were '44 Hours means no unemployment'; '44 or damn all'; '47 be hanged, we want 44'; 'We are forced to this by a partial press'; and '44 means work for demobilised soldiers'. After a short meeting, the workers split into different trade groups, to go off and vote at union and other halls. The corporation's ballot boxes were used. Two questions were asked, and the result seemingly leaked that evening to the *Northern Whig*. Only 1,184 voted for 47 hours, and 13,508 against; 20,225 workers favoured 'drastic action in the way of an unofficial strike' for 44 hours, with only 558 against.[6] It was an overwhelming result in favour of industrial action. The figures were publicly announced the following day, at a mass meeting in the Assembly Hall. It was decided to strike from Saturday, 25 January, if no concession was forthcoming. Other workers – municipal employees, and men and women in the linen industry – expressed a willingness also to demand 44 hours.

The strike began as planned ten days later. The two shipyards and the town engineering shops stopped at the end of the working week. But it was not just private industry which was halted. Electricity, gas and water were essential to production, and under the control of the municipality. The electricity power station shut down, stopping the trams at 4 p.m. It started up again on Sunday evening to supply hospitals, other consumers being under an obligation not to use electricity. The gasworks also shut down by midnight on Saturday, 25 January. A skeleton workforce was allowed to remain, since it would have taken three weeks to resume supplies from a complete shutdown. All newspapers were initially affected, but a three-page *Strike Bulletin* – cost 1*d*. (0.42p) – was available. Bread rationing had begun. Shipbuilding and engineering accounted for the largest concentration of male workers in Belfast. Twenty-one thousand votes had been cast in the ballot, but many more men were now on strike. Maybe as many as 40,000 were directly affected, and another 20,000 indirectly involved – a total of 60,000. The FEST unions, which included tram drivers and conductors in the NAUL, were joined by the engineers' union, the municipal employees' union, and the Workers' Union. The 1919 strike was close to being a general strike, though there seems to have been no serious attempt to include the linen industry, which was affected by power cuts, particularly in the making-up trades, though mills had steam power, and some factories their own electricity generators.

Strike headquarters was in the Artisans' Hall. At 3 p.m. that Saturday, the district committee met delegates from affiliated unions, plus the ASE, MEA, and the Workers' Union. This body – some 150 strong – seems to have become the general strike committee. It was responsible for 'larger questions of policy',[7] and there were sub-committees for finance, organization, picketing, press, amusement and general activities. It probably elected a small executive, known as the strike committee, which was, most likely, the district committee, augmented by the leaders of the other three unions. It was about 15 strong. The chairman of the local FEST, McKay, of the pattern-makers, became the leader of the strike. The other leaders were Waugh, Freeland, Milan, Howard, Corbett, Geddes, Clark, Weir, Donaldson, McKeag, Lockett, Attwood, Baird, and William Grant. At least seven were full-time trade-union officials, the others being, in the main, lay officers of their unions. Few, if any, were shop stewards. Charles McKay may have been a catholic, as Stephen Gwynn first claimed in 1924, but the strike committee was heavily protestant. So also were the strikers, but there were catholics taking part in this mass working-class action. They were integrated into the movement, and did not seek to identify trade unionism with republicanism. McKay and Robert Waugh, of the ASCJ, had, of course, attended the Irish convention, lining up against the Ulster unionists. Waugh and James Freeland had stood as labour candidates in the general election. McKeag, of the Workers' Union, and Abe Lockett, of the NAUL, were probably members of the ILP, as may also have been

Milan, from London, who represented the electricians. Corbett was also an English electrician. Geddes represented the ironmoulders; Donaldson, the plumbers. James Baird was the most militant member of the strike committee. Others who can be identified were more conservative, and unionist. Attwood of the blacksmiths, and Harry Howard of the boilermakers, had been labour councillors of the old school before the war. Clark, a brass-founder, was identified with the unionist party, and Grant and Weir, of course, were executive members of the UULA. Grant claimed much later that he voted against unofficial action, and worked on the strike committee for a settlement. Labour unionism and conservative trade unionism were minority forces on the strike committee, the majority of the leadership being in a labourist tradition, with some involved in politics and others not.

The strike committee held a mass meeting of 'several thousand' the following day at the Custom House steps, Sabbatarian sensibilities in Belfast being ignored. The withdrawal of labour had seen the workers' leaders assume responsibility for electricity, gas and water. Seven members of the strike committee met the corporation on Monday, 27 January, to consider the use of electricity. Strikers surrounded the City Hall. A sub-committee made up of the mayor John White, a former lord mayor, and several councillors, agreed that its use should be banned, so that the hospitals and other exempted consumers might continue functioning. The strike committee was to issue permits. Electricity was used largely by industry and commerce, and only domestically by the middle class. Pickets were appointed to patrol the city, to make sure no lights burned, or machines ran. 'Holliganism [*sic*] at once became prevalent'; the RIC reported window-smashing in central Belfast, 'and for a short time the residents were in a bad state of panic.' The commissioner immediately had 300 strikers enrolled as special constables. They 'actively assisted in the protection of property in the central district of the City'.[8]

A march was held on Tuesday, 28 January, from Carlisle Square, where orange parades began, to the City Hall. It attracted 4,000 strikers. Trade-union banners and Union Jacks were carried. 'Nobody', the *Northern Whig* reported, '... could fail to be impressed by it and by the character and type of the men who marched in its serried ranks.' This paper alone had resumed publication, possibly because of independent power supplies. The *Belfast Evening Telegraph* and the *Belfast Newsletter* did not publish until 4 February; the *Irish News*, until 14 February. The *Strike Bulletin* of 25 January had described the Belfast press as 'hostile to Labour', and the strike committee ensured that an almost daily *Workers' Bulletin*, as it was renamed, appeared during the strike. There were 18 issues. The march was an exemplary display of workers' power, their resoluteness having momentarily stilled the unionist bourgeoisie and the local state. The strike committee seemed to be dictating to the lord mayor and the police. 'The fight would be bitter', McKay told the strikers at the City Hall, 'and some of them had got to suffer ... It was better to make it fast and furious, short and sharp.'[9] Short and sharp was the strike committee's intention.

The spectre of bolshevism had already been raised. 'There never was a movement in Belfast', the first *Strike Bulletin* claimed on 25 January, '... [that has] aroused such intense feeling that no compromise is now possible.' It was clear the men and their leaders were determined to be compensated for the 'four long years ... [when they] endured the grind of inhuman hours under the spur of necessity'.[10] The *Northern Whig* noted, on the same day, that 'as far as Belfast is concerned Bolshevism does not exist', while the *Belfast Newsletter*, detecting a conspiracy between red and green, thought 'the future of the whole world [was] in the melting pot.' At the first strike meeting on Sunday, 26 January, a man called O'Hagan addressed the marchers from the platform. He was described as having a cockney accent, and the *Northern Whig* reported that even members of the strike committee 'spoke with accents not generally associated with the North of Ireland'.[11] O'Hagan wore a red badge, and was heckled for his anti-employer remarks. This happened again, the following day, outside the City Hall, when he was accompanied by two companions, identified as Meehan and O'Mahon. On Thursday, 30 January, at another meeting outside the City Hall, called, apparently, by these militants, 'O'Hagan and his pals' were repudiated by a member of the strike committee for 'doing far more harm than good'. O'Hagan was summoned to a meeting of the strike committee later that day, and, when four members addressed workers outside their headquarters, he was denounced. The *Northern Whig* ran a hostile editorial on O'Hagan the following day, and, on 1 February, published a statement from the strike leaders saying 'they knew nothing of Mr O'Hagan and repudiate any claims on his part to act or speak for them.'

O'Hagan, Meehan and O'Mahon were, respectively, John F. Hedley, Charles O'Meaghar and Simon W. Greenspon. Hedley – who was English – claimed to be a member of the Workers' Union on strike. This was the sixth dispute in which he had been involved, and the sixteenth he had helped 'in all parts of the world'.[12] He had deserted from the navy, in Glasgow, in October 1918, having been a stoker, first class, on HMS *Vindictive*. He continued to be known by the name of O'Hagan. O'Meaghar had been born in Dublin, and had fled military service, in London, in 1917. He was sent to prison, but secured his release after a hunger strike. Greenspon had also been born in Dublin. He was Jewish, probably from the Polish part of Russia, and had taken part in the 1913 lock-out. He promised the Belfast workers support from 'Dublin, Cork and the South',[13] and admitted to being a member of the ILP. These three outsiders were rejected in Belfast. 'The Black North can take care of itself anyway', a heckler had shouted at the City Hall on 30 January, 'without either Larkins or O'Hagans or Russian Jews'.[14] 'Resentment is being shown', Bates wrote to Carson the following day, 'at men like the Russian Jew being brought from Dublin to teach the Belfast men their business.'[15] This was the end of their involvement in the strike, though the three remained in the city preaching revolutionary socialism. At some point subversive literature was thrown over the walls of a military barracks.

In May, after the strike, Hedley helped launch the Irish revolutionary socialist party in Belfast. This was an early supporter of the recently formed Third International in Moscow, the Comintern. The following month, he, O'Meaghar, Greenspon and Chris Ferguson, an Englishman later active in Dublin, were charged with unlawful assembly. Greenspon had spoken at an ILP meeting on 23 February and, with Walter Carpenter from Dublin, on 20 April. 'They were not afraid to hold meetings anywhere in Belfast', Hedley said at one point, 'and had men in their organisation who were not afraid to deliver their message.'[16] Hedley, O'Meaghar and Greenspon were removed from the scene, being sentenced to six months' hard labour. Hedley went on hunger strike twice, in jail in Belfast, demanding political-prisoner status. Released, he was again sentenced to six months in 1920, this time in Britain. Back in Ireland, he was one of a small cadre of trade-union officials employed by the ITGWU who attempted to foment social struggle during what there was of a national revolution. He appears to have been settled in Liverpool by 1923, and active as a member of the communist party.

James Baird was the most prominent socialist on the strike committee. Early in the third week of the strike, the *Northern Whig* published a letter from him. It was an attempt to distinguish his ILP view of socialism from what he called a 'class' one. Workers, he argued, were faced with a choice between 'slavery ... or some system of collectivism'. The latter would grant 'the citizen the right to engage in the production and share in the consumption of wealth'. This was not Marxism, but Baird showed an interest in syndicalism. He contrasted strikes of the past, 'a mob without a plan of campaign', with the engineers' current struggle, an 'assault ... made on the most vulnerable point ... as a matter of tactics'. He advanced, without attribution, some of Connolly's ideas on industrial unionism, and portrayed the strike committee, somewhat romantically, as being engaged in a historic struggle for socialism. But he then appealed to the Belfast public to take an interest in the 'welfare of the whole people and use every effort to secure the best possible conditions for all workers'. The *Northern Whig* described this as 'The "Hold-Up" Theory' in an editorial, and accused Baird of advocating 'class war and terrorism'.[17] He replied, quite consistently, that he was not advocating 'class prejudice', and a narrow conception of 'labour'.[18] Baird was some sort of parliamentary socialist, a supporter, most likely, of the (British) labour party's new constitution. He claimed, in his second letter, that he was not a member of the strike committee, and that his views were his own. Baird had been described, by the *Northern Whig*, as a member, a few days before. He may have been pushed aside at an early stage, by the trade-union officials leading the strike, but it is more likely that his advocacy of socialism was the cause, or consequence, of his ousting.

Meanwhile in Glasgow, events were unfolding in a most dramatic way. The demand for shorter hours had been formulated there in 1918. In early 1919 a conference of shop stewards called for a 30-hour week. Between 5 and 18 January, the – unofficial – Clyde workers' committee was joined by sections of the trade-union movement. A joint commit-tee, representing both currents, was formed, and Manny Shinwell, a councillor, took the chair. When the strike was called for Monday, 27 January, it was for 40 hours. This was two days later than Belfast and four hours shorter. Two representatives of the joint committee had gone to Belfast, as part of the attempt to bring about a general strike. While they addressed workers on Sunday, 26 January, the Belfast strike com-mittee seemed interested in official trade unionism only. The local lead-ership saw the Glasgow strike as helping to justify shorter hours, but there was little coordination between the two cities. The strike commit-tee diverged from the joint committee, as is clear from what happened on 31 January in Glasgow. The lord provost was due to report, that Friday, on Lloyd George's response to the demand for 40 hours. A depu-tation of strike leaders, at the head of a crowd of, reportedly, 30,000 workers, arrived in St George's Square. A battle ensued. The police arrested the strike leaders, and the military was brought in that night. There was a lesson here, which was quickly noted in Belfast. What was left of the joint committee tried to defend the Glasgow strikers by extending the struggle, the Belfast strike being portrayed as a response to this call. The strike on Clydeside dragged on until 10 February, a return to work being recommended two days later. 'The Clyde strike went down to defeat alone ... [It had involved] the dissipation of revolu-tionary capital accumulated during four years of war, on an inade-quately prepared, isolated, unplanned and ill-considered venture.'[19]

Willie Gallacher, one of the leaders arrested during the battle of St George's Square, had come to Belfast as chairman of the Clyde workers' committee in February 1918. This was shortly after the movement on Clydeside had come close to taking a stand against the war itself. Gallacher's arrival in Belfast was anticipated by the unionist press. 'I want to ask Mr Gallacher', a worker shouted out at his first meeting, 'is he loyal to his King?' 'That's a stupid question', he replied. 'You know I am a revolutionary and that the only loyalty is to the working class.'[20] The engineers refused Gallacher the use of their hall. While he subse-quently expressed himself pleased with his reception in Belfast, it is clear that Clydeside industrial militancy was not to be emulated in the course of the war.

Gallacher also wrote later about the 40 hours' strike in Glasgow: 'A rising was expected. A rising should have taken place. The workers were ready and able to effect it.'[21] But there was no revolutionary leadership. The lord provost of Glasgow had panicked, at his first meeting with the joint committee on 29 January, on the hoisting of a red flag on the municipal buildings. He and others in London were all too ready to see this as a revolutionary threat. Henry Wilson, as chief of the imperial general staff, had walked out of a cabinet meeting in December 1918, when it 'refused to consider either that a state of war existed, or that a Bolshevik rising was likely'. Sir Basil Thomson of Scotland Yard later considered February 1919 'the high water mark of revolutionary danger'.[22] Willie Gallacher – certainly when writing in 1936 – con-curred in one respect. The hoisting of the red flag had not for us [the workers' leaders] the significant meaning it had for our enemies. They saw it as the symbol of an actual rising; we saw it as an incident in the prosecution of a strike. We were all agreed on the importance of the strike for the 40-hour week, but we had never discussed a general line against capitalism, and never could have agreed to it, even if we had discussed it.[23]

There was no revolutionary situation in Glasgow after the war. The Belfast strike leaders had supported the Glasgow workers until 31 January, the *Workers' Bulletin* being critical of the joint committee thereafter. 'The events in Glasgow', according to Charles McKay,

> were a warning to their men of the folly of unconsidered action. They in Belfast were determined they would be an object lesson to the world as to how a strike should be conducted ... they appealed to the authorities and to the public in general to see that nothing provocative was done to try the temper of the men to breaking point.[24]

A meeting of strikers in Belfast did call for the release of those arrested in St George's Square.

Revolution, of a sort, was stirring in nationalist Ireland. Dáil Éireann, Sinn Féin's attempt after the 1918 election to create an Irish assembly, had met on 21 January 1919 in Dublin's Mansion House. The British government allowed it to gather. On the same day volunteers in Co. Tipperary, acting autonomously as the army of the Irish republic, killed two policemen at Soloheadbeg. Irish labour was not represented in the Dáil, but Tom Johnson, with the help of William O'Brien and Cathal O'Shannon, had produced the first draft of its democratic programme. Though members of the national executive of the ILP & TUC, they acted on their own initiative. On the eve of the Belfast strike, the *Belfast Newsletter* warned that it would 'rejoice the heart of Sinn Fein ... for it [would] be a provocation to disorder bordering upon anarchy'.[25] When Hedley was repudiated on 30 January, one heckler shouted, 'We want no Sinn Feiners or Bol-shee-viks.'[26] But this was the day an ILP & TUC executive circular summoned a conference in Dublin, on Saturday, 8 February, to advance a 'national wages and hours movement'. Labour wanted the 44-hour demand of the Belfast workers taken up throughout Ireland. 'Moral and financial' support was offered by the conference, a collection being taken up for the Belfast workers.[27] This was a token gesture, the Irish labour movement failing to appreciate the importance of the Belfast struggle. But the strike committee declined to approach the national executive of the ILP & TUC, the Irish labour movement being viewed from Belfast as implicated in nationalism. 'The forces which control Sinn Fein and Irish Labour', the Irish Unionist Alliance (IUA) claimed later in 1919, 'are marching hand in hand on the lines of approved Bolshevism ... [and are] fast undermining the very foundation of social order.'[28]

Anti-bolshevism also had an appeal in Belfast. Carson, in London, sought to guide the Ulster unionists' response to the strike, through Bates in the Old Town Hall. The policy in the first few days was to keep quiet. On 31 January and again on 1 February, Bates wrote to Craig, reappointed a junior member of the coalition government, that he was keeping in touch with Hacket Pain, the military commander in Belfast (formerly of the UVF!). This soldier was currently acting as police commissioner. They were refusing to do anything that might 'make the workers think they were being intimidated'. Bates hoped the workers would realize that it was a national issue, a local struggle being unnecessary. He was glad the army refused to be deployed 'for the alleged protection of property'. 'Once one of the workers got injured in a mêlée with the troops', he went on, 'nothing would save Belfast from becoming a scene of disorder and tumult, the consequences of which would be far-reaching.'[29] The Belfast unionists did not want Carson to intervene, in case industrial dissatisfaction, after any return to work, might become political disenchantment. Bates could not see the employers shifting from 47 hours. He sketched out a political line for the party, the basis of an ideological intervention. Fewer than a quarter of the strikers, he told Craig, were 'out and out socialists and "extremists"'. Another quarter were satisfied with 47 hours, and half the workers went along with constitutional trade unionism. If this was sanguine, his view of the strike committee as 'practically Sinn Feiners' was hysterical.[30] Writing to Carson also on 1 February, Bates enclosed an anti–Sinn Féin leaflet, the source being unidentified. Belfast, it argued, was part of a Sinn Féin plot to bring about an all-Ireland strike. All would be revealed at the ILP & TUC conference on 8 February. If Bates and the Old Town Hall were not writing such black propaganda, the unionists seem to have been putting it into circulation.

It was the orange order, ostensibly in response to working-class members who wanted the strike ended, which sought to regain control of the protestant community. On Monday, 3 February, Col. Wallace, the Belfast grandmaster, issued a manifesto. Bates had sent it to Carson two days earlier, with his own comments. It was designed, according to the former, to get 'the decent men to secede from the Sinn Fein Bolshevik element'.[31] The orange order hinted that the strike was 'engineered by parties' out to discredit the 'fair name' of Belfast. Wallace claimed that unionist MPs favoured better conditions and shorter hours, if they were obtained by parliamentary means. He offered to arrange a conference with the employers, 'with a view to returning to work'. The grandmaster, in saying nothing practical, inadvertently committed Carson to supporting shorter hours.

The engineering strike, certainly by the end of the first week, was a case of many workers doing nothing together. Trade-union organization was proving itself in the solidarity of the strikers. 'The workers were as full of grit and determination', said Howard of the strike committee, 'as the boys who went over the top [at the Somme] on 1st July 1916'.[32] Presumably, a member of the strike committee, writing 'About Ourselves', in the *Workers' Bulletin*, announced the existence of a 'Labour Parliament in Belfast'. 'The E. and S. Federation', he continued,

is that Parliament, and the work of this body is going to be an education to the workers of Belfast. Belfast this week has found itself. The workers have discovered their friends. They are not in the City Hall, nor yet in the Elected Legislature. They, like themselves, were always to be found on the Queen's Road and on their way to the engine shops all over the city at 5-30 each morning. Labour in Belfast has discovered that when it must fight, it must fight alone. No helping hand is stretched out to help on the way. Labour will fight, and labour will be right. LABOUR CAN STAND ALONE![33]

The transmogrification of Randolph Churchill's slogan of 1886 is indicative, at least in the case of one member of the strike committee, of an absence of subordination to the unionist leadership.

The idea of a labour parliament shows the existence of a proletarian consciousness, a commitment to working-class self-reliance. But it was one still circumscribed by survivals of craft exclusiveness, and a strong conception of respectability. It was also highly parochial, Belfast trade unionists having ignored the rest of Ireland, while also cut off from the British movement. The small branch of the ITGWU was offering to join the struggle, but the strike committee was more interested in the NTWF. This made more industrial sense, but there may have been a fear of a repetition of Larkinism. Trade unionists in the linen industry were keen to join the movement for shorter hours, but the engineering and shipbuilding workers did not have faith in the women's ability to endure privation. 'Custom has decreed that amelioration of onerous conditions is generally secured by the craftsmen first, though we do not think there is any inherent reason this should be so.'[34] Belfast had already turned its back on Glasgow, and industrial militancy with, or without, revolutionary socialist leadership.

While descriptions of the metaphorical 'labour parliament' anticipate those of the Italian, Antonio Gramsci, a few months later, it is equally clear that Belfast was no Turin. It was going to take more than a display of workers' solidarity to force the employers to make a local offer, while the local and central state continued to abdicate responsibility. The strike committee was no factory council, the war of industrial position it was waging allowing only for retreat.

The strike committee cooperated, from the first, with the RIC. There was also a sort of joint control, with the municipal authorities, over gas and electricity. On 3 February the strike leaders approached the City Hall, requesting a joint committee to handle the distribution of coal and food. Much of industry had been stopped, but the strike committee had no desire totally to dislocate civic society. The strikers, with their families, were a part of the community, and they sought only to impose fairness on the employers. The lord mayor did not reply. Unbeknown to the strike committee, the first citizen of Belfast was in discussion with the employers and the central government about bringing the strikers' hold on the city to an end.

On Tuesday, 28 January, the strike committee had written to the lord mayor, asking him to arrange a conference with the employers. This they immediately rejected, the reply being received by the workers' leaders the following day. The employers were standing by the 47 hours, an offer which had been accepted by the national trade-union leaders. The district committee of the FEST was an official body, but the strike committee was engaging in unconstitutional behaviour. The *Workers' Bulletin* referred to 'the obscure working of executive machinery in England', while a leader like Weir, of the UULA, could stress that 'every member of the present Strike Committee was an accredited Official or Delegate of his Union.'[35] Meeting rejection in Belfast, the strikers' leaders turned to central government. London should lean on the employers, they believed, to avert 'the forces of Capital and Labour fight[ing] to a finish'.[36] Members of the strike committee may well have expected a hearing from Pirrie. The workers had, after all, done his bidding during the war, and he urged them to work now for industrial prosperity. But it seems to have been Clark, the local shipbuilder, and not Pirrie, the member of the metropolitan ruling class, who considered conceding 44 hours.

When the lord mayor learned there would be no local bargaining, he set out to regain control of his municipal services. He asked the chief secretary, the newly appointed liberal, Iain Macpherson, a Scot, for 100 naval stokers. This was on 31 January. They would restore the gas and electricity supplies. The lord mayor stated he could find 100 free labourers in Belfast to help. These had been offered three days earlier by a group of engineering employers. Macpherson declined the request on 4 February, the acting commissioner of police, Hacket Pain, wanting to move only if there was 'serious disorder'.[37] The following day electricians in London threatened to black out the capital, on 6 February, in solidarity with the workers in Belfast and Glasgow. Using an order in council, under DORA, the government prevented the electricians' trade union from taking any action. Also on 5 February the ASE suspended its district committees in Glasgow, London and Belfast. This made local actions unconstitutional, even in Belfast. That Friday, 7 February, a rumour spread that the strike committee was to be arrested. At the steps on Sunday, 9 February, Clark, the brass-founder, joked that the strike leaders 'were to be imprisoned and put with the "boys" [republican prisoners] who were providing the music on the Crumlin Road [jail] (Renewed laughter)'.[38].

While the government hesitated about Belfast, but not Glasgow, the workers had entered their second week on strike stronger than ever. A meeting was held at the Custom House steps on Sunday, 2 February. The *Workers' Bulletin* claimed an attendance of 10,000, the *Northern Whig* grudgingly acknowledging 3–4,000. Speakers emphasized the need for order, less emphasis being placed on the need for continued picketing. Another 'monster demonstration' was held on Tuesday, 4 February, again from Carlisle Circus to the City Hall. It was bigger than the previous week's. A.A. Purcell, vice-chairman of the TUC, addressed the strikers. Six years later he recalled 'an event I have always regarded as unique in Working Class history'. He had by then seen workers' demonstrations in London, Berlin, Vienna, Leningrad and Moscow. Belfast he remembered as exhibiting 'higher discipline'.[39] The previous Saturday George Cuming, managing director of Harland and Wolff, had died after a short illness. This was a cause for widespread grieving in the protestant community. Bates wrote to Carson on 1 February that Clark and Cuming 'could always hit it off between them', and that Cuming had been the 'only responsible representative of Harland and Wolff in Belfast'.[40] Cuming had been close to the unionist leadership, and his demise meant the Old Town Hall was no longer in touch with the big yard. The general strike committee, meeting that day, agreed to convey its sympathies to his relatives. 'Various delegates paid a tribute to the unfailing courtesy extended to them by the late Mr Cuming in negotiations on behalf of their members.'[41] McKay paid a 'generous tribute' at the steps the next day, while the strikers removed their hats (they were, presumably, dressed in Sunday best). On the Tuesday, while the strikers were assembled outside the City Hall, Cuming's funeral passed. Some workers spontaneously joined the procession, there being no evidence that this dramatic moment was planned in any way.

Cuming's funeral brought Pirrie to Belfast. He was still controller general of merchant shipping, though he was more than willing to act on behalf of Harland and Wolff. The Old Town Hall and the local bourgeoisie were momentarily out of the picture. Representatives of the strike committee met Pirrie on Wednesday, 5 February, and he asked for the restoration of gas and electricity. This was to be in return for a resumption of the 54-hour week, overtime being paid after 47 hours. Pirrie was offering the resumption of national negotiations, though he was in no position to do this. The strike leaders requested him to meet them as a representative of Harland and Wolff; in other words, to engage in local bargaining. A 16-strong negotiating committee was appointed, which was 1 more than the strike committee.

On the opposite side of the table, on Thursday, 6 February, were five representatives from each of the two shipyards. Their leaders were Pirrie and Clark. The town employers were not included. Negotiations continued on the Friday and Saturday and were resumed on Monday, 10 February. This was the beginning of the third week of the strike. A possible settlement was announced. The rumour about arresting the strike committee had circulated during the talks, but it was unlikely that the government would have intervened when there was the possibility of a settlement. The threat of repression may have encouraged the strikers' leaders to accept the best they could get. Shipyard, and engineering, workers were to return to the 47-hour week. This would be on the understanding that Harland and Wolff, and Workman, Clark called a national conference within 30 days, recommending fewer than 47 hours. If national negotiations were not resumed, there would be a local settlement within a further 21 days. The workers were guaranteed fewer than 47 hours. The employers had the chance of making this national, and therefore of no relative economic cost to the Belfast yards. '[They] had extracted from these men', McKay claimed, 'the very last ounce they were willing to give ... [and hoped] to have the 44 hours or perhaps a little less for every worker in the city.'[42] If the former was true, the latter was most unlikely.

This settlement was to go to ballot on Wednesday, 12 February. The Glasgow strike was called off by the joint committee that Monday.

Electricity was restored in Belfast on the Tuesday for a time, and some workers drifted back. The shipyard workers on the strike committee were dragging the engineering workers in the town shops with them. The latter had been offered nothing. The ASE, angry at the suspension of the Belfast district committee, revolted against the domination of the FEST unions. A mass meeting of ASE members rejected the strike committee's interpretation that 44 hours had been offered. The ballot was put back until Friday, 14 February, in order to allow the strike committee to reach a similar agreement with the town employers. They refused to shift from their statement of 1 February, signed, ironically, by 44 members of their local federation. The ASE then backed off, and decided to participate in the ballot. (A reporter from the *Belfast Evening Telegraph* tried to insinuate himself into this private meeting on 13 February. His paper had been arguing for the use of troops, as in Glasgow. He was 'shown the door'[43] in no uncertain terms, and regaled his readers that evening with a long diatribe against the strikers.)

The strikers voted, by 11,963 to 8,774, to reject the 10 February offer. The turnout on 14 February – 20,737 – was only 46 down on the 14 January ballot. This is yet another demonstration of the remarkable solidarity of the workers. Both turnouts were reportedly about 60 per cent, giving the FEST and other unions a Belfast membership of about 33,000. Things had changed after almost three weeks' industrial action. On 14 January the vote had been 20,225 to 558 for drastic action in the form of an unofficial strike. The workers' union – according to a banner carried later on a march – voted by 4,027 to 60, suggesting that unskilled workers were slightly more militant. A breakdown of the voting, by union, is available for the second ballot. On 14 February the skilled unions voted 2 to 1 against acceptance. Their members were clearly not demoralized. Joiners voted 5 to 1 against, moulders 4 to 1, and machinists, and painters, 3 to 1. The unskilled unions split more evenly, as might be expected from workers with less in the way of savings, and perhaps more in the way of commitments. Strike pay was available, but in no consistent way. Even the TUC, in the form of A.A. Purcell, recognized the strike. The ASE had been the only union not to do so, but the different head offices in England would have managed their Belfast branches in an uncoordinated manner. Local district committees most probably had their own resources. The ASE, interestingly, was only 2 to 1 against the offer, perhaps because the national leadership had supplanted the local militants. By 14 February, then, the two shipyards' offer had been rejected by 58 per cent of those voting. The town engineering employers reiterated that they had not made an offer.

The Glasgow strike was over, that in Belfast about to enter a fourth week. Ulster unionists, and Carson in particular, had probably lobbied what was, after all, still a coalition government in London, urging caution. At stake was their political following in the protestant community. Both strikes had been considered at length by the cabinet, in what were the first weeks of peace. McKay and his colleagues, while they might still be on strike, had not posed the revolutionary threat, after the struggles of wartime, of Shinwell and his comrades. Macpherson, in

Dublin Castle, and the Irish office in London, should have been preoccupied with the activities of the new alternative Dáil regime, such as it was. The Belfast strike, it seems, was the major issue in Ireland in early 1919. The lord lieutenant, Lord French, a soldier, reported that it was occupying everyone's attention within the Irish government. Bonar Law had refused him the use of troops, given the possibility of a settlement. On 7 February French endorsed the preposterous view of the General Officer Commanding (GOC), Northern Command, that the strike was organized by bolsheviks and Sinn Féiners. Thursday, 13 February, was the beginning of the end. With Glasgow over, the government was able to concentrate more on Belfast. The Ulster unionists probably had little direct influence on Dublin Castle.

Following the abortive meeting between the strike committee and the local engineering employers in Belfast, 17 of the 44 employers wrote to the corporation. An earlier letter of 28 January had gone unacknowledged. The lord mayor had appealed to Dublin on his own initiative, but now an important section of the local bourgeoisie attacked him for cooperating with the strike committee. The local authority, it was alleged, had done nothing about 'act[s] of violence ... committed by an irresponsible section of the community'.⁴⁴ Also on 13 February, Maj.-Gen. Shaw, GOC, Irish Command, travelled to Belfast to meet the lord mayor. The following day, that of the second ballot, the lord mayor issued a proclamation. Troops were being made available 'for the protection of the workers – whether ordinary employees or volunteers'. He appealed for volunteers to assist in ending the 'wholly unjustifiable attack on the common rights of the citizens'. The *Belfast Evening Telegraph* reproduced the proclamation on the evening of 14 February, the *Northern Whig* and the *Belfast Newsletter* simply carrying the text the following morning. It is not clear whether the lord mayor and the head of the army in Ireland waited to hear the result of the ballot. The *Belfast Evening Telegraph* did not carry it until the following day. That Saturday the troops moved into the gasworks and power station. They were 'fully armed infantry, wearing shrapnel helmets and accompanied by machine guns'.⁴⁵ (The government claimed that only the six armoured cars normally stationed in Belfast were used.) All municipal services were restored by the Monday, Belfast having been without gas or electricity for three weeks.

This was official strike breaking and belated, but hazardous, militarism, given the number of workers who had voted to end the strike. It enraged the strike committee and possibly many of the workers who had voted to continue the struggle. McKay and his colleagues responded, on Saturday, 15 February, by pulling out the two workers, described as shop stewards, left in the power station, who had been keeping up sufficient electricity for the hospitals. The lord mayor retaliated by offering a reward for information, and the government used DORA against the two workers. The strike committee appealed for calm. It met on the Sunday, and resolved to continue the strike. This information was relayed to the Custom House steps, where some 3,000 workers, according to the *Northern Whig*, were gathered. The strikers were told that their leaders were then meeting. Members of the strike committee spoke, and there was a vote at the end in favour of continuing the strike.

The town employers announced they would be open on Tuesday, 18 February; the two shipyards on the Thursday. On the fourth Monday the strike committee found it had lost control of gas and electricity. Work was resuming. The strikers' leaders were offered a meeting with Pirrie and Clark. The big and wee yards, not unexpectedly, refused to move beyond their offer of the previous Monday. The committee returned to its headquarters, and finally recommended a return to the shipyards when they opened on Thursday. A crowd of angry workers had assembled outside, demanding a continuation of the strike. There was again unevenness in the response of the different unions, when they balloted over the next two days. The Workers' Union and NAUL were reported to be 'practically unanimous' in favouring return. Municipal employees had been drifting back from the time of the proclamation. With the gasworkers back, the boilermakers voted to return by 60 to 40. At the meeting of joiners, 'the proceedings took a lively turn ... [and the discussion was] of an intensely lively character.'[46] Some picketing was evident on Tuesday when the town shops opened, but, when the shipyards started up two days later, the majority of workers went back. It was 85 per cent at Harland and Wolff; 80 per cent at Workman, Clark. All were back by Monday, 24 February. The *Northern Whig* had rhapsodized, on the Friday, about the two groups of 'dour Ulstermen', employers and workers, who had ended their struggle. The fortitude of the workers was 'the same quality which saved Ulster from Home Rule five years ago, and may be needed again to save her in the future'. The strike leaders were condemned as 'red-flaggers'. 'On reflection the great majority of the men must see that orange is a much better colour than red.'

The 10 February offer, the strike committee believed, still existed. 'Yielding now is only a matter of tactics', the last *Workers' Bulletin* argued. 'To know how and when to retreat, it is said, is the mark of a great general.'[47] The workers went back to 47 hours. Freeland took the view that the 10 February offer contained the germs of substantial progress. Writing on 28 February, he believed that it had been lost. A national ballot in March voted overwhelmingly to go for 44 hours. It was 5 June before the unions in shipbuilding and engineering put in this demand. At a conference on 24 July of the FEST and the ASE with the employers, a federation representative stated, 'We were given to understand that the 44 hours was likely to be conceded by the largest employer ... in Belfast.'[48] Pirrie, of course, had premised this on other employers granting shorter hours. The employers nationally refused even to discuss 44 hours. The workers had to make do with a joint committee to consider anomalies which had arisen with 47 hours, these mainly concerning piecework. The Belfast district committee of the FEST was equally unsuccessful in local talks. On 18 October 1920 it would receive a final rejection from Harland and Wolff. 'The Federation decided to defer this matter owing to the unsettled and uncertain position at present prevailing in Belfast.'[49]

The 1919 engineering strike was remarkable, not just for the withdrawal of labour, but also for the swift manner in which the employers and the state regained control. The strike and its undermining followed from the conception of working-class action held by the leaders. This was endorsed by Purcell's attendance at the 4 February demonstration, the TUC being associated with an important local action. Only a minority of the strikers at the City Hall chose to follow Cuming's coffin, the struggle as a whole showing a lack of deference or fear of employers. The local bourgeoisie, and the municipal and central state functionaries, were, in contrast, immobilized by the workers. There is no doubt the workers wanted a shorter working week, were not fooled by the economic and political arguments of the employers, and showed massive solidarity in organizing the strike. This solidarity was not threatened at any stage by communal tensions. The action of 1919, as an example of working-class power, was much more impressive than that of 1907. The Belfast strikers emphasized that they were fighting only a trade-union struggle, but the description of the local FEST as a labour parliament shows the strength of working-class independence, evident in support for labour candidates, among leaders, activists and a section of the protestant working class. The strikers remained unionist in politics, in the main immune to the blandishments of Joe Devlin or Eamon de Valera. If there was an affinity between their trade unionism and unionism, as socialists who argue for a notion of protestant privilege maintain, it was the theory and practice of labourism which threatened to break any relationship. The Belfast working class did not respect ruling-class economic or political interests.

Willie Gallacher had been irreverent about the king when he came as an emissary from Glasgow towards the end of the war. 'You know I am a revolutionary and that the only loyalty is to the working class.' This future British communist had been more of a working-class leader during the war, than, say, McKay or Baird, but it is debatable whether he was as good a leader in the 1919 strike in Glasgow. His republicanism was a secular kind, applicable to all monarchies and princely states, and derived from a commitment to democracy. There had been a few in Belfast in February 1918 who hated George V just as much, but these Irish republicans would not have been interested in Gallacher's meeting. Their republicanism was nothing more than separatism, some of the leaders of the rising in 1916 having no objections to – German – princes. Hostility in Belfast to the monarch had a strong sectarian coloration, being associated with the political defeat of the majority community. (Unionists were equally divisive in their celebration of imperial power.)

Willie Gallacher was not the first, or last, British socialist to be insensitive to the peculiarities of Belfast. His revolutionism did have an affinity with Irish republicanism in a shared will to revolt, and this identification undermined his socialism in Belfast in 1918. He had nothing to offer the protestant working class, a fact which is a better theory of the limits of the 1919 strike in terms of the goals of social and political revolution. Gallacher quite correctly protested his loyalty only to the working class, without fully developing the democratic implications in a divided society like Ulster. His opposition to the British ruling class saw him ignore the Belfast working class, catholic and protestant, when he went on to champion republicanism, and, following the foundation of the Irish state, work more closely with de Valera than with Irish communists. Willie Gallacher was not the only socialist to put the Irish nation before the working class, as is evident from the ILP & TUC's attempt to celebrate May Day in 1919 – while Belfast came out alone. A critique of the Irish nationalism of the labour movement is not that it should have subscribed to the constitutional status quo, for whatever reason, but that it refused to mitigate the divisions between north and south, and within Belfast, when it was clear that the labour movement there was not sectarian or anti-democratic.

Irish labour, though it never formally recognized Dáil Éireann, helped Sinn Féin in the national struggle. It called for self-determination, from the ruling British government, in Ireland and abroad. Johnson and O'Shannon attended the Berne meeting of the International, in February 1919, doing much to promote Ireland's cause in Europe. There was some overlap, between trade unionists and members of Sinn Féin and the IRA, but the small labour leadership, mainly in Dublin, was remarkably willing, at times, to do the bidding of the republican command. In April there was a general strike in Limerick, led by the trades council, against British militarism, a communal affair, rather than class action, which helped the IRA. Tom Johnson visited the city, but the national executive had difficulty in raising sufficient funds for the struggle to continue. No attempt was made to advance class demands, much less challenge the republicans' strategy. The labour leadership was engaged in a selfless political gesture, from 1919, based ultimately on limited aspirations, and a failure to lead a trade-union movement which had grown, throughout Ireland, because of the wartime economy. The ILP & TUC was already heavily dominated by the main beneficiary, the ITGWU – a general union which exploited Connolly's ambiguous reputation to give the working class a place in an independent Ireland. 'We ... know', de Valera told the 1921 ILP & TUC meeting, 'what your support has been to us and what your refusal to put forward even your own interests has meant to the cause of Ireland in the past two years.'[50]

This Irish trade-union movement had grown out of, and away from, the British movement, which was dominant in Ulster. Some 220,000 workers were associated with the ILP & TUC in 1919, out of a working class estimated to be 700,000 strong. Between 30,000 and 80,000 organized workers were not affiliated. Only a handful of Belfast delegates were to attend the annual congress, in Drogheda, in August 1919. The national executive, in reporting, praised the Belfast strike. 'The Strike Committee controlled the city.' But Irish labour conveniently blamed the failure on English and Scottish workers. Implicit was an admission that Belfast was integrated into a United Kingdom economy, an excuse which cast doubt on the viability of an Irish nation. A one-day strike had been called by Irish labour for Thursday, 1 May, 'to demonstrate

the solidarity of the workers and to reaffirm their adhesion to the principle of self-determination.' This, in the context of Ireland in 1919,
meant only separatism, as interpreted by Sinn Féin. 'The response was
magnificent', the national executive reported. 'Practically the whole
country, outside the Belfast area, kept holiday, again proving ... that
the workers when united are all-powerful.'[51] This had been, in no sense,
a proletarian manifestation against the national and imperialist bourgeoisie, but a clear assertion of Irish labour support for Sinn Féin, in a
country where the working class was seriously divided. In Ulster, a
march in Derry was banned. Four hundred took to the streets in Newry,
carrying red flags.

Belfast continued to work on 1 May, but the trades council had called
a march for the Saturday afternoon. It was the largest labour demonstration in the city's history, the ILP claiming responsibility for the
organization.

The procession assembled in Donegall Place, to march to Ormeau
Park. Virtually all the unions participated. The labour representation
committee, and the socialist Sunday school were also in evidence, as
was even a wagon of blind men and women. Women linen workers
marched behind their union banners. The route of the march suggests a
protestant demonstration, but catholics were being integrated into the
working-class movement. The small ITGWU participated in the march,
and among the bands was one dressed in Irish kilts, which may, or may
not, have been a manifestation of cultural nationalism. Tens of thousands marched, according to the *Belfast Newsletter*. It estimated that the
march took 40 minutes to pass, the *Irish News* putting it at an hour. The
Northern Whig commented on the small number of workers behind
each banner, not unusual in labour marches. And the *Belfast Newsletter*
estimated a crowd of 100,000 in Ormeau Park. The strike was still very
much in mind. The plumbers carried a banner reading 'Solid for 44'.
One of the resolutions called for shorter hours, sufficient to absorb all
unemployed and demobilized. The release of the Glasgow leaders was
demanded.

Three platforms had been set up in Ormeau Park, for speakers simultaneously to address the crowd. Thomas Cassidy, a printers' official,
from Derry, who was currently chairman of the ILP & TUC, expressed
the wish, in a letter of apology, that Belfast would participate, in future,
with the rest of Ireland, in celebrating May Day. When a labour candidate in the general election claimed that the workers of the city were
unrepresented in parliament, a member of the crowd shouted out
Devlin's name. 'That is so', was conceded from the platform. If such
catholic and nationalist gestures irritated protestant workers, they did
not lead to any perceptible working-class disharmony. The only outside
speaker was a labour candidate from Motherwell, Walton Newbold. He
accused the city's textile workers of having been 'unconscious blacklegs'
in the past, being less organized than the cotton workers of Yorkshire
and Lancashire.

There was no attempt to eschew politics in the speeches from the
platform. A resolution was even carried, supporting Woodrow Wilson's

fourteen points of January 1918. This democratic statement had been seized upon by Sinn Féin, but it also inordinately influenced Tom Johnson of the ITUC & LP. Since Lloyd George was able to subscribe to the American president's conception of international democracy, including the reference to 'absolutely impartial adjustment of all colonial claims',[52] this was not seen in Belfast as justifying Dublin rule. Dáil Éireann, which demanded recognition, on the basis of the right to national self-determination, had failed to secure a seat at the peace conference in Paris, the British retaining the support of the Americans and French. The *Belfast Newsletter* had – correctly – attributed the march to 'the little band of disgruntled Red-Socialists who opposed the Unionist Labour candidates ... and who figured prominently in the strike'. It was less sound when it described the demonstration as anti-unionist, 'Sinn Fein tricked out as Labour with its red flag'. The theory of a bolshevik conspiracy did not have a popular resonance in May 1919, and the jingoistic appeal of anti-Germanism was – on the evidence of this march – slight. Internationalism was affirmed, 'without reservation of either creed or colour ... with the workers of all lands ... in renewed hope of a new earth'. Another resolution called for 'the withdrawal of all "regulations" having for their object the curbing or repression of the fullest and freest criticism of all acts bearing on the welfare of the working classes at home and abroad'. The theme of the meeting was the need for 'undiluted, uncamouflaged [labour] representatives'.[53] It is a moment worth savouring.

12

Belfast Labourism, 1918-21

The desire for labour representation had persisted in the city through-out the war. The ILP affirmed socialism, and, in 1918, helped form the Belfast labour party based on the trade-union movement. Partly legiti-mized by the Irish convention, four candidates stood in the general election of December that year. Belfast labourism was more independent than the ILP & TUC, opposing the Ulster unionists' desire for partition, while Irish labour stood down for Sinn Féin. Belfast labour was not nationalist, though three of its candidates were prepared to accept a Dublin parliament. The Belfast labour party secured over a fifth of the protestant vote, the UULA failing to impress the working class. This was a good result for Lloyd George's khaki election, jingoism having little appeal in Belfast. The ILP and the Belfast labour party thrived as a result of the engineering strike shortly afterwards. The municipal general election in January 1920 saw the party and individual trade unions put up 35 candidates, labour taking 12 of the 60 seats. Again a fifth! ILPers were included among the labour councillors, and Belfast enjoyed another successful May Day celebration.

Two developments halted working-class assertion. The end of the postwar boom, combined with the continuing unemployment of ex-servicemen, saw sectarian hostility within the working class in the form of the July 1920 expulsions. But the Belfast working class would not have divided in such a fundamental way, without the impact of the national revolution on Ulster. One IRA operation came too close to Belfast. What Sinn Féin sowed in the south, catholics reaped in the north. The new administration there was constructed by the forces of unionism and loyalism, as a result of enactment by the Westminster parliament. The undemocratic nature of Northern Ireland was seen most sharply, not in partition, or even the suppression of northern nationalists, but in the way the four labour candidates suffered at the hands of loyalist direct action in the first northern parliament election in 1921.

The key to the Belfast labour party of 1918 and after was the ILP. Socialists drew more on Walker than Connolly, but, with the prewar unionist mobilizations in mind, members of the ILP were strongly opposed to partition. This did not make them nationalists, but it cer-tainly made them anti-unionist.

The ILP(I) had not long survived Connolly's departure from the city, in late 1914, to take charge of the ITGWU. But his concept of a future for Irish labour was carried by his erstwhile socialist comrades, even if they took varying positions on the national question. William O'Brien, in Dublin, remained a sort of political confidant, but he did not become a republican, of any ilk, until 1917. While supporting Sinn Féin, he became secretary of the ITUC & LP at the 1918 congress. He became general treasurer of the ITGWU in January 1919, and – with Larkin's continuing absence in the United States – acting general secretary. Tom Johnson, who helped lead the anti-conscription campaign in 1918, became treasurer of the ITUC & LP and, in 1920, secretary. D.R. Campbell stayed in Belfast, after quitting the executive at the 1918 congress. He remained active on the trades council, continuing to serve as secretary of the life assurance workers. He led the labour councillors elected in 1920. Danny McDevitt also remained in Belfast, collecting £20 of the £34 the city sent to the Limerick workers in 1919. William McMullen seems to have continued to work at Harland and Wolff, becoming secretary of the Belfast ITGWU in 1920. Cathal O'Shannon had quit Belfast after the rising, becoming editor of the ITGWU's paper, *The Voice of Labour*, in late 1918, after a spell in Cork. He was elected that year to the congress/party executive. James Grimley – who married Nelly Gordon – had been a member of the socialist party of Ireland (SPI), and a devoted follower of Connolly. Opposed to conscription during the war, he was active in the Belfast labour party from 1918.

Most Belfast socialists remained orientated to the (British) labour party, the north ILP, as it continued to be called, maintaining continuity during the war. Its secretary, from 1910 all the way through to 1925, was Sam Kyle. Born in 1884, Kyle had joined the ILP in 1907. He attended his first party conference in 1914, and the north ILP continued to send a delegate during the war. Walker's old branch must have been a reservoir of pacifism in Belfast, though it was possibly overshadowed for a time by the central branch – until the early 1920s. (A leading ILP pacifist in the central branch was Margaret McCoubrey, a prominent suffragist and cooperator.) Kyle worked for the textile operatives from 1916, until becoming an official of the Workers' Union at the beginning of 1919. He was the leading socialist in Belfast, and an active speaker during the strike. His wife Mary had been Ramsay MacDonald's secretary. Kyle had also been secretary of the Workers' Education Association (WEA) from 1910, 'maintain[ing] that the W.E.A. ideal of the broad highway of education [was] the proper one'.[1] The figure of about 70 students fell by half during the war, though it rose to a record 187 in 1923–4. But there was 'a steady drift from social and economic questions to the more innocuous subjects so dear to the ears of the idle person who yearns "to be educated"'.[2]

Other individuals identified with the north ILP were: Alex Stewart, a founding member, who, in retirement, was the senior figure in the 1920s; Robert (Bob) Dorman, an early secretary of the Dublin ILP, who returned to Belfast in 1912, becoming superintendent of the socialist Sunday school in 1916; Robert (Bob) McClung, a socialist from 1905, who was an official of the Workers' Union in 1919; Dawson Gordon, who joined the ILP in 1907, worked for the flax roughers, had been elected to the congress/party executive in 1910, 1916 and 1919, and was Kyle's predecessor as secretary of the branch; George Donaldson, who took an interest in labour politics from 1906, and became the plumbers' official in 1918, in time to be a member of the strike committee; Harry Midgley, who may have joined as early as 1906, and helped Walker in North Belfast the following year; and William McMullen, who had certainly joined the ILP by 1910, though he left to support Connolly. He did not, apparently, return to the fold.

The principal socialist intellectual in Belfast, by the 1920s, was Hugh Gemmell. His father had been born in Conlig, Co. Down, but moved to Scotland. Gemmell came to Belfast during the war, to avoid conscription. A member of the ILP from 1907, he had been active among the shop assistants in Glasgow. He seems to have continued in this occupation in Belfast. Gemmell was founder and tutor of the Belfast Labour College, at 41 Albertbridge Road, conducting classes in economics, general industrial history, Irish industrial history and public speaking, from towards the end of the war. (Part of the national council of labour colleges, it became an alternative to the WEA.) In the mid-1920s Gemmell was described as having 'trained all the young men and women who have recently become speakers for Socialism'.[3] He wrote for left-wing papers under the *nom de plume* of Hotspur. In 1925–6 he would edit *Labour Opposition*, a monthly publication of the north branch ILP. It had an address at 48 York Street (next door to where Connolly had found an office for the Irish textile workers' union), this being the ILP hall. The north branch contributed a staggering £108 to a special party fund in 1923, the central branch managing £5 (and the whole of Scotland only £133). This may have seemed unlikely, from the perspective of 1920, but it shows the existence of a strong socialist cadre. By the mid-1920s, meetings, with a speaker, were being held in the ILP hall, each bleak Sunday evening. Fellowship night proper, with singing and dancing, was Friday. 'Great names that are gone', Gemmell was to write, of the launch of *Labour Opposition*, 'rise up before us and inspire us with their steadfast courage and noble manhood. Had it not been for the pioneers who blazed the trail in the dark days of Ulster Labour we could not have launched this venture now.'[4] He was thinking, no doubt, of William Walker, though the concept of Ulster labour was a recent creation.

The Belfast labour party was certainly being mooted by 1917, but it seems to have been formed in April 1918. Its base was the trades council, which attracted sections of the trade-union movement in the city. Many of the big amalgamated unions, which dominated in shipbuilding and engineering, were no longer affiliated to this local centre. April 1918 saw the Irish convention report in Dublin, the three labour men from Belfast – H.T. Whitley, Charles McKay and Robert Waugh – supporting the majority view in favour of dominion home rule. Whitley and Waugh were active on the trades council, and McKay, of course, led the 1919 strike. Like the British parent of old, the Belfast labour party was a federal body – membership was through an ILP or trade-union branch. The year 1918 saw (British) labour adopt a new constitution, allowing for individual members, and a programme which represented the party's new commitment to socialism. The Belfast labour party was denied affiliation by the British party, a decision that would be cheered at the 1919 meeting of the ILP & TUC. A properly constituted labour party in Ireland, combined with the imminence of some sort of self-government, it was argued in London, meant that all labour representation should be orientated to Dublin. (Irish labour reciprocated, advising Irish workers in Scotland and England to affiliate to the British party.) The Belfast labour party, whatever its commitment to the union, would be localized. It was to be 'representative of practically all Trade Unions in the city'.[5] Figures of 150,000 to 200,000 affiliated members were being bandied about; these must have been estimates of the whole Belfast working class.

As the war neared its end, labour activists in the city were determined to participate in the expected general election. This was initially the position of Irish labour, the executive in Dublin deciding to stand, on 10 September, in what was expected to be a war election. The 1918 congress had decided, the previous month, to adopt a new constitution, allowing for political action, this to be presented to a special conference in November. A manifesto was even drawn up by the four officers, providing for abstention from Westminster, though attendance was to be allowed if a party conference so decided. There was no intention of attending Sinn Féin's alternative Irish assembly. The response to this from trades councils was not enthusiastic. Belfast lay beyond the writ of the congress/party, and the executive had considered electoral possibilities only in Dublin, Cork, Limerick, Waterford, Sligo and Derry – at the very most 15, most likely 6 candidacies. Belfast was against self-determination being interpreted as separatism, its democratic solution being closer to British labour's dominion home rule. Others in the Irish labour movement were prepared to leave the national question to Sinn Féin. The national executive of the ITUC & LP reckoned in 1918 without P.T. Daly. O'Brien had just unseated him as secretary of the congress/party, and was on his way to driving him out of the ITGWU. Daly was still very much a republican, but sought to embarrass his former colleagues by reporting on secret talks between labour and Sinn Féin.

Sinn Féin would have stood down for labour, in certain seats, if its candidates had signed a pledge refusing, if they were elected, to attend at Westminster, regardless of the wishes of a labour conference. This became public at the Sinn Féin *árd fheis*, held in Dublin on 30–31 October. The Sinn Féin pledge would have amounted to a takeover of labour, so, faced with the possibility of a fight, the national executive backed off. Johnson, O'Brien and their colleagues, changed their minds on 1 November, recommending non-participation to the special conference later that day. The war would be over by 14 December, the date of the election. O'Shannon, and Thomas Farren, also of the ITGWU, voted against. It was D.R. Campbell, still representing the Belfast trades council, who said at the special conference, of his old friend Johnson's argument, that 'he had not been able to understand the subtle distinction between a War Election and a Peace Election.'[6] Irish labour did this by way of support for self-determination, though the attempts of several leaders to dissociate the movement from Sinn Féin were hardly credible. Johnson, closing the debate, then admitted that Irish labour would have contested the election if Belfast had subscribed to the manifesto. He went on to suggest that the national executive was trying to avoid a disaster in the south, given the determination of Sinn Féin to contest all seats. Withdrawal represented a failure of political will, the policy being carried by 96 votes to 23.

The Belfast labour party went ahead without the ILP & TUC, deciding to put up candidates in four of the nine territorial seats. James Freeland, the ASE organizer, who was to be prominent in the strike, stood in Cromac (formerly part of South Belfast). Robert Waugh, who was also to be a member of the strike committee, as ASCJ organizer, stood in Victoria (East Belfast). The two trade unionists were joined by two members of the ILP. Sam Kyle, also a trade-union official, stood in Shankill (North Belfast). In Pottinger (also East Belfast), the ILP put up S.C. Porter, a barrister, who had sought a liberal nomination in East Belfast in 1910. All were protestants, standing in protestant seats. But the four labour men were opposing unionists. In the case of Waugh and Kyle, they were fighting UULA candidates. Sinn Féin put up the third candidate in all four seats. Porter, in Pottinger, was also faced by an independent labour candidate, J.H. Bennett.

As Irish organizer of the NSFU, Bennett followed Havelock Wilson, his general secretary, in deriving his politics from anger at the 17,000 merchant seamen who had reportedly died in the war. The NSFU was violently anti-German, and sought to put up six candidates in 1918 against the (British) labour party, which was calling for a peace of reconciliation. The 1916 rising had been a pro-German affair, and Irish labour, welcoming revolution in Russia the following year, sought to advance national interests through international socialist means. Bennett was elected to the ITUC & LP executive in 1917, but not before he and others, including Whitley, had objected to the executive's having accepted invitations to a socialist conference in Stockholm. Frederick Hall, of the printers, stated that he would 'take a note of all belonging to Belfast' who voted in favour. When the delegates backed the executive by 68 votes to 24, Bennett shouted out: 'I am glad there are 24 Britishers in the room anyway.'[7] He refused to sign the anti-conscription circular in April 1918, claiming that he opposed trade unions being involved in politics, and later lost his seat on the executive. The expulsion of the NSFU from the congress/party, given the action of seamen in preventing socialists from meeting in Europe, was carried, that November, at the special conference, by 99 to 10.

Bennett retreated to Belfast, hoping to exploit unionist sentiment for chauvinist ends. He was to fail. He joined the ILP, in order to be considered as a candidate by the Belfast labour party, only to be rejected on 23 November on grounds of his politics. He went ahead as an independent in Pottinger, opposing the unionist candidate. Bennett was an empire man, and, in reply to a question, admitted that he favoured the exclusion of Ulster. He believed in class collaboration, and was able to cite a commitment to trade unionism going back 40 years. Porter was attacked for being a middle-class socialist, out of touch with ordinary working people. Bennett's anti-Germanism was a minority current in the Belfast labour movement in 1918, and he received only 659 votes in Pottinger – 5 per cent of a poll of 12,139.

Sinn Féin, of course, was making a bid in all ten Belfast seats, but the unionists were unable to stampede the protestant working class on the national question. The Belfast labour party was, most certainly, not Carsonite, few identifying it as unionist. At a rally in the Ulster Hall, James Freeland was interrupted:

> You will excuse me, Sir, but what about the Union? (Laughter) / Chairman – Order / A Voice from the platform – It's on the Lisburn Rd (Laughter) / Freeland – He did hope that in this new era that they heard so much about that the Union at all events would disappear – (applause) – and that no longer would the people of this country be fed on shadows. Their interest lay in their bread and butter. Only by workers' hands will workers' wrongs be righted (Applause).[8]

Bread and butter socialism was the predominant position of the Belfast labour party, a not ignoble tradition where the question of the state was settled. Irish labour was effectively supporting Sinn Féin in 1918, in the name of self-determination, while British labour advocated self-determination within the empire, for Ireland and India. This was close to the dominion home rule of the Irish party.

The Belfast labour party affirmed a commitment to Wilsonian international democracy, including the League of Nations, but was vague on its application to Ireland. Most leading members probably interpreted self-determination, as British labour did, to mean dominion home rule rather than separation. The party's manifesto came out against the politics of 'Celt against Saxon, or Catholic against Protestant' (first used by Connolly for the ILP(I) in 1912), a decided statement of opposition to sectarianism. Three of the four labour candidates clearly supported self-government. Freeland made no reference to it in his address, but, in reply to a question, stated that he would vote with labour on all issues, except home rule for Ireland. This minority position was Walkerism. Waugh, of course, had already declared himself at the Irish convention, and sought to argue that the Irish working class would remain close to Britain even with a Dublin parliament. The ASCJ would survive. He avoided the issue in his address, and was on the defensive during the campaign. Kyle in Shankill made no secret of his support for the ILP's programme, which included home rule. Porter was the only labour candidate to argue for the 'fullest measure of Self-Government in accordance with the principles of self-determination'.[9] He had the support of John Flanagan, who had helped Connolly before the war, only to recruit in Ireland as a lieutenant in the Connaught Rangers, a regiment of the British Army.

The Belfast labour party was concerned principally with social questions, the election taking place on the eve of the 44 hours strike.

The party opened its campaign with an Ulster Hall rally on 30 November, appealing for the first time to both protestants and catholics. The advertisement for the rally in the *Northern Whig* read: 'Come and hear the unanswerable case for the creation of a strong *Independent Working Class* parliamentary party in Ulster.'[10] That in the *Irish News* of the same date exhorted 'women [to] come and hear the case for the Working People's Own Parliamentary Party'.[11] This Devlinesque populism situated the female proletariat, voting for the first time, in the ghetto, while a class appeal was addressed to protestant workers. The *Irish News* advertisement stressed the organ recital before the rally, though it is not clear how many catholics were in the Ulster Hall to hear 'England, Arise' as the closing rendition. The minority would have been receptive to Freeland's discussion of labour's economic demands, and the majority not at all offended by his attack upon the UULA as the enemy who had captured their programme. Three of the four labour candidates were back in the Ulster Hall four days later, in the company of Carson and his colleagues, for the FEST meeting on shorter hours. It was Freeland who moved the main motion, after the speeches, calling for 44 hours, and pledging 'to take whatever steps may be necessary to secure the same'.[12]

The Belfast labour party's manifesto was more radical than the national one. 'Too long', it argued, 'has Labour been content to be governed and dealt with as a subject class, exploited for the benefit of a few who utilised every possible appeal to racial sentiment, patriotic devotion and religious bigotry causing dissension in the ranks of the workers to cloak their ever present desire for wealth and power.' It stood for the socialization of wealth under 'democratic control', a national minimum wage, and better housing. Specific Irish demands were the nationalization of railways, and the development of agriculture, mines, and canals and other waterways. It called for such things as free education, under 'democratic control', and local option on temperance.[13]

None of the four labour candidates was elected, but they all did surprisingly well. In the four seats, labour secured a total of 12,164 votes, to 41,176 for the unionists and a derisory 2,319 for Sinn Féin. This was an average of 22 per cent of the poll for labour. Waugh did best in Victoria, with 26 per cent (3,469 votes), despite his association with the Irish convention. He lost to Thompson Donald of the UULA. Kyle, who fought Samuel McGuffin in Shankill, did second best, with 23 per cent (3,674 votes). Both results suggest that labour unionism did not undermine a working-class consciousness. S.C. Porter had 22 per cent (2,513 votes) in Pottinger, despite the opposition of Bennett and Porter's affirmation of home rule. It was Freeland who did worst, with 17 per cent (2,508) in Cromac. He, of course, was the only Walkerite, and Cromac contained the catholic 'markets' area. Sinn Féin did best here, Arthur Savage, the local publican, receiving 997 votes. It got fewer than 400 votes in Pottinger and Victoria, and just over 500 in Shankill, suggesting that the Belfast labour party, in the 1918 general election, had begun to appeal to the catholic working class.

The engineering strike dominated 1919, as the Belfast working class enjoyed the postwar boom. At Westminster it was November before the government turned again to the Irish question. Though Dáil Éireann was in existence, the IRA made little impact on Belfast. With municipal urban and rural elections due, respectively, in January and June 1920, London imposed proportional representation to lessen Sinn Féin's expected majorities. (It had first been used in Sligo in January 1919.) This system of voting had been advocated by the proportional representation society of Ireland, in 1911, there also being an Ulster extension committee. The society and committee re-formed for the 1920 elections, and D.R. Campbell was one of seven lecturers in Belfast working for the committee from October 1919, explaining proportional representation. Belfast was included among the trades councils, at a special ILP & TUC conference on 24–25 October, when Irish labour decided to contest the 206 town and city elections throughout the country. Of 650 labour candidates, 341 were to be elected – there being 1,470 seats. A total of 116 trade unionists was elected for parties other than labour. Sinn Féin, with 422 seats, and the nationalists, with 213, were to have majorities on 172 of the local authorities. In the province of Ulster, nationalists controlled 23, the unionists 22. Derry went nationalist. Belfast, of 12 cities and boroughs in Ireland, was the only one to remain unionist. There were 52 unionists out of 60 on the outgoing council, but only 37 on the new one. The minority had 10 seats, divided equally between nationalists and Sinn Féin. The success of the corporation elections in Belfast was labour, which secured 12 seats.

The 1920 election was held with a considerably expanded franchise, and altered boundaries. The electorate nearly doubled, from the prewar figure, to 135,538 – 32 per cent of the population. The 9 territorial constituencies used in the 1918 Westminster election were used for wards, each having between 6 and 8 seats. The Ulster extension committee, which studied the elections in Belfast, Derry, Lisburn and Bangor, considered the allocation of seats 'fair',[14] though there were still geographical anomalies. Proportional representation saw a better translation of votes into seats for the city's minority. But catholic opinion, seeing that Falls was given only 6 seats, was slightly critical. Though the minority was to win only 4 of these, it picked up six, among small catholic minorities, in the rest of the city. One unionist was returned for Falls, simply because catholics did not vote against him, this also applying to protestant electors, who allowed a Sinn Féiner to succeed in Victoria. The Ulster extension committee's advice – 'If you can't get a *Good Man In*, why not try to keep a *Bad Man Out*?'[15] – was generally disregarded. A total of 143 candidates stood, including 20 independents. There were 47 official unionists, plus 8 UULA and 5 independent unionists. Nationalists had 16 candidates, to 12 for Sinn Féin. One of the independents was Alex Boyd in St Anne's, formerly of the Independent Orange Order (though Dawson Bates considered him a labour man).

Labour put up, in all, 35 candidates, across the 9 wards. Only 22 of these were recognized by the Belfast labour party, the rest being the candidates of individual unions. The NAUL accounted for 3 of these 13. The prominent activists of the trade-union movement stood for the

Belfast labour party. At least 7 of the 22 were members of the ILP. Half of these were trade-union officials, the rest predominantly skilled workers. Only 2 of the 13 independent labour candidates were officials, and the unskilled workers tended to be in this group. The reason for the lack of unity probably had little to do with the Belfast labour party's setting a limit. Most likely, the novelty of proportional representation, against the background of wartime trade-union growth, and the continuing short boom, allowed localized unions and branches to seek political representation. A product of strength, it was also a sign of sectionalism.

William McMullen stood for the ITGWU in Victoria, which contained the old Dock ward. The 3 NAUL candidates stood in Pottinger, Victoria and Woodvale, areas where unskilled shipyard workers lived. Half the remaining 10 independent labour candidates competed in Cromac, which had 7 seats. Presumably as a result, the Belfast labour party put only 1 of its candidates into the ward, suggesting a degree of cooperation. All 3 NAUL, and 8 of the 10 other independent labour candidates, were unsuccessful, indicating the limited appeal of particular unions. One was successful in Cromac. Of the Belfast labour party's 22 candidates, 10 were returned. D.R. Campbell was probably responsible for party strategy, and he was elected labour leader on the corporation. Sam Kyle greatly assisted him. The labour party contested all 9 wards. While it was a movement of the protestant community, it had 4 candidates in Falls, the highest number of any ward, suggesting an orientation to the catholic minority. It is not clear whether this was an attempt to appropriate Devlinism or pre-empt Sinn Féin, but the party had one success.

The combined labour forces picked up at least 1 seat in each of the 9 wards – the Belfast party in all except Cromac. Second seats were picked up in Ormeau, Shankill and Woodvale, the last-named by an independent labour candidate. Six of the 8 UULA candidates were successful, but only 29 of the 47 official unionists (there were also 2 independent unionists returned). The UULA probably did not weaken the labour vote. On the contrary, the actions of the unionist leadership may have legitimized labour support in the eyes of protestant workers. The Belfast party came top of the poll in Shankill (Sam Kyle), and second in St Anne's – to Alex Boyd. It secured 2 more seats on third and fourth counts, 3 on fifth, and the last 3 on sixth counts. Of the 34,285 transfers, 75 per cent followed the party – there were 8,409 transfers to labour, and 7,170 from its candidates. A total of 1,396 nationalist votes transferred to labour, but only 885 unionist ones. More of the latter came from official and independent unionists, suggesting a lack of affinity between the UULA and labour. As for transfers from labour, there were 1,259 to unionists, but only 241 to nationalists, in keeping with the protestant origins of the party. Belfast labour party voters were less inclined to transfer to the UULA than were supporters of the independent labour candidates. Of 79 Kyle votes transferred to unionists in Shankill, only 10 went to the UULA. A vote for the labour party may have been indicative of a more rounded labourist loyalty, while support

for a particular union candidate could have had an affinity with unionist populism.

The figure of 12 labour seats out of 60 is remarkably close to the 22
per cent secured by the party in the 1918 general election. It must be
considered a measure of the strength of class consciousness among
protestant workers at the end of the war when in political competition
with the unionists. Proportional representation in 1920 allowed for a
fairer expression of these politics. The catholic working class was even
coming over to labour. One of the Belfast labour party's four candidates
was successful in Falls. It has been estimated that 20 per cent of the –
predominantly catholic – electorate in the ward voted labour, but that
this was not reflected among the city's minority in other wards.

In Belfast as a whole, owing to events elsewhere in the country, Sinn
Féin was gaining on the nationalists. Catholics in predominantly protestant areas, outside Devlin's fiefdom, were being won to the alternative Dáil Éireann regime based in Dublin. In Falls, it was a case of a
confused breakdown of constitutional nationalism. Devlinism was still
dominant, but labour was an alternative to Sinn Féin. For a catholic
male or female worker, it became a case of class or nation. Transfers to
labour came more from nationalists than Sinn Féin supporters, suggesting a strong social aspect to Devlinism. But the transfers from labour in
Falls (159 to Sinn Féin and 82 to Devlinites) show a willingness to
embrace national radicalism. Catholic support for labour in a municipal
election, in a context of national rivalry, was not necessarily a challenge to sectarianism. Voting for the Belfast labour party was not seen
absolutely as a way of uniting with protestant workers. Catholic labourism was very probably legitimized by the propaganda of the nationalists: 'Vote no. 1 for / SMITH / [ran a Devlinite advertisment] CATHOLIC
AND ONLY / Nationalist candidate / WHO HAS ALWAYS BEEN / A
FRIEND OF LABOUR'.[16] Smith's labourism was more catholic than
nationalist.

Protestant labourism was also not essentially concerned with uniting
the working class across the ethnic divide. The 1920 general municipal
election shows a contradictory process at work in the combined labour
forces. The Belfast labour party, in 1918, had been predominantly anti-
partitionist. In 1920, a majority of the 22 Belfast labour party candidates was opposed to the division of the country. Some went further in
a nationalist direction. At least 5 of the 10 elected had a reputation as
home rulers, while only 3 can be clearly identified as unionists.
Wilsonism still reigned, however abstract in theory, and disappointing
in practice. Anti-unionism was to be expected from the most politically
conscious section of the protestant working class, given the weight of
the ILP in the labour movement. William Walker and his times had
long been left behind. But the unionist mobilizations and the war had
led to loyalist organization. The British Empire Union (BEU) was emerging, in Belfast, as early as January 1920. Its target, during the elections,
was the 13 independent labour candidates, that is, those not under the
central labour leadership. There were rich political pickings. The BEU
was still fighting the Hun, with a questionnaire to all candidates, asking

opinions on the awarding of municipal contracts locally, and on preferential employment of ex-servicemen. (Catholics might have had something to gain from the latter, but the former was an example of the localism characteristic of Ulster loyalism.) Nineteen of the Belfast labour party, so far as is known, refused to have anything to do with the BEU. Three did – James Duff, an executive member of the Workers' Union, and one of the few Belfast delegates to the TUC (and labour party in 1921); George Donaldson, the plumbers' official; and Clarke Scott, of the postal workers' union. The two last-named were elected for, respectively, St Anne's and Woodvale. All 3 NAUL candidates supported the BEU, as did 3 of the remaining 10 independent labour candidates. The UULA, of course, responded positively to the questionnaire. This confirms the suggestion that the trade-union candidates, as opposed to the ILPers, were not inimical to loyalism.

The 1920 municipal general election, while it may have been an extension of 1918 and 1919 and a harbinger of a future of class struggle, also contained, in the support for the BEU, the seeds of ethnic hostility. Three developments were to operate upon Belfast in 1920–1, before the next elections in the city: first, the partitioning of Ireland by the British government; second, the increasing intensity of the IRA's campaign in the south; and, third, economic recession, preventing the return of ex-servicemen to employment. These factors set the context for the first northern parliament election, which, in turn, gave the new state its loyalist political character.

The Belfast labour party and the working class as a whole were inordinately influenced by the industrial expulsions of July 1920 (Chapter 13). It was mass intimidation. Labour officially decided not to participate in the May 1921 northern election, because of the political condition of the city. The four labour candidates – the Revd J. Bruce Wallace, James Baird, Harry Midgley, and John Hanna – were formally independent, but the ILP was present behind the scenes, prominent members signing the nomination papers. Even Wallace was seconded by Sam Kyle, and supported by Robert McClung. The latter recalled several years later that '1921 [was] ... a time when it was considered dangerous to label oneself Labour or Socialist.'[17] (According to William McMullen, who would have been in the Belfast labour party, but not the ILP, Baird, Midgley and Hanna received financial support from Sinn Féin. McMullen had originally been mooted for East Belfast, but Sinn Féin, realizing that he would attract catholic rather than protestant votes, refused to help him. Thus, Midgley was substituted for him.) Proportional representation, having been used in the local elections, was prescribed, in the 1920 government of Ireland act, for the two Irish parliaments (it was abolished in Northern Ireland after the 1925 general election). The four labour candidates stood in each of the four-seat divisions, the pre-1918 constituencies of North, South, East and West having been restored for the local parliament.

The Revd J. Bruce Wallace, in North Belfast, stood apart from his three labour colleagues. He had been one of the first socialists, in the 1880s, when he came to Belfast as a congregational minister. He quit the city in 1896 for England, to become warden of Mansfield House university settlement, and minister of Letchworth garden city. In *Labour in Irish History* (1910), James Connolly described him as 'long a hard and unselfish worker for the cause of Socialism in Ireland'.[18] In 1921 Wallace retired to Limavady, in Co. Londonderry. James Baird, in South Belfast, had come to attention during the 1919 strike, and had been elected to the corporation in 1920 for the Belfast labour party. He suffered in the expulsions, and became a leader of the expelled workers. He was one of the few ILPers to look benignly upon Sinn Féin, though this may have resulted from the expelled workers having been driven into the arms of Dáil Éireann.

Harry Midgley, in East Belfast, was the most prominent of the four in later years. Born in Belfast in 1892, he became an apprentice joiner in Workman, Clark at 14 years. He quickly associated with William Walker and the ILP, helping to build the Langley Street hall. He gravitated towards James Connolly before the war, without joining the SPI, and was in the United States in 1912–14. Midgley was no republican, and served in the 36th (Ulster) division until May 1919. But he was in revolt against capitalism. He became a joiner in Harland and Wolff, and, in October, was appointed organizer of the linen lappers, which was now recruiting women. Midgley represented the north branch of the ILP at the 1920 conference in Glasgow, in April, when delegates voted to recognize the Irish republic. He had taken an interest in ex-servicemen, and, at the May Day meeting, showed his commitment to socialist internationalism. The Langley Street hall was burned down after the expulsions. John Hanna was also a boilermakers' secretary and a leader, with Baird, of the expelled workers. He was a member of the ILP, and seems to have represented the central branch at the 1920 conference.

Wallace ran his own campaign in North Belfast, 14 years after Walker, having a reputation as a Christian socialist. Samuel McGuffin, the Westminster MP for Shankill, was the UULA candidate. Wallace was a moralist, and he cited John Ruskin, 'certainly not a revolutionist'. He promised 'to promote conditions favourable to the freedom, health, and happiness of all citizens, by the ways of least resistance and of least shock to existing legitimate interests'. To avoid 'violent revolution', people needed to do something about 'the preventable injustices and inhumanities into which our industrialism has been allowed to drift'. He appealed to those whose 'social conscience is awakening and who mean to work for an honest, decent, and fraternal civilisation'. McGuffin had known Wallace as a socialist, but 'it depended on the kind of socialist he was now whether or not he would be well received in that constituency.' Wallace was taking an individual line on the national question, but one that was very far from unionism in theory or practice. He opposed a united Ireland, without the 'consent and conviction' of the north. Given the existence of a northern state, he expressed the wish that the catholic minority would 'suffer no disadvantage'. But this made little impression on unionists. '[He] ought to be putting himself', one said, 'on the side of Christianity and an open bible [rather than] trying to make a split and put the Protestant people ... under

Sinn Fein.'[19] Wallace was too benign a political creature for this time and place, but he showed considerable courage, as an elderly man, in making a stand for decency at the beginning of the new regime. It is not known how much he campaigned, but he certainly seems to have survived unscathed. Wallace came bottom of the poll, losing his deposit. He secured 926 first preference votes, just over 2 per cent. He got 18 transfers from the unionist elected first, and 28 from McGuffin.

Baird, Midgley and Hanna did worse, despite their joint campaign. All lost their deposits. Baird was now known as a labour councillor, and Hanna an unsuccessful trade-union candidate in 1920. Midgley had a reputation as an ex-serviceman who had tried to look after the interests of former comrades. The three – independent – labour candidates, as members of the ILP, had the support of active socialists. All, no doubt, saw themselves trying to build, or at least defend, the politics of class, at a time when the country was gripped in turmoil, and the city divided by sectarian polarization. The national question was uppermost, and the Ulster unionists were well on their way to finding their answer. Midgley had been a socialist since the days of Walker, and Baird and Hanna had experienced loyalist direct action. They were in the tradition of labourist anti-partitionism, first expressed by the ITUC. Thus they were opposed to the government of Ireland act. They described the settlement, in a joint manifesto, as 'an unworkable stupidity, as the inner circle of political wire-pullers well know'.[20] They had expressed the conviction that de Valera, Craig and Devlin would shortly agree, in conference, that two parliaments could not work. The interests of workers lay in 'an unpartitioned Ireland based on the goodwill of all who love their native land – North to South and East to West'.[21] This is what they said in the *Irish News*. The three candidates were acutely aware of economic changes, and tried to mount a campaign on social issues. 'It is the Poverty, Unemployment and Insecurity question that matters most to working people',[22] read one political advertisement. The 'real politics', they said later, '... the things that matter for the people',[23] were unemployment, poverty, dread, and insecurity. But to gain a hearing for social politics, they had to invoke the – orange – slogan, 'Civil and Religious Liberty'.[24]

The question of ex-servicemen was to the fore in May 1921. From early 1919 two United Kingdom organizations – the Comrades of the Great War and a second known as 'the federation' – had organized in Belfast. On 6 December Bates informed Carson that the Comrades was 'very socialistic in its management', and that the federation was likely to go the same way.[25] He may have been responding to press reports of a deputation to the City Hall on 1 December, when Sam Kyle, Dawson Gordon and Harry Midgley, all concerned with linen workers, called upon the corporation to feed necessitous school children. Midgley actually spoke for an ex-servicemen's organization, this being a case of the left seeking to provide leadership.

Shortly before, some members of the Comrades of the Great War in Belfast had broken away, to found the Ulster Ex-Servicemen's Association (UESA). 'For Ulstermen Who Enlisted for Ulster' was its motto. On 24 November the association wrote to Carson, asking him to become their president. 'Our members are all loyal Ulstermen and 95% are Orangemen.'[26] It believed loyalism was the answer to the problem of unemployed ex-servicemen. Carson asked Bates's advice. The secretary of the UUC admitted the UESA was 'run on more or less Unionist lines', but identification with Carson would not attract members of the Comrades. The UESA was small, and had, in its leadership, few people of 'standing'.[27] Carson did not touch the association, but it clearly grew throughout 1920. As labourism gave way to loyalism, the ex-servicemen became the shock troops of reaction on the streets of Belfast. For the first northern parliament election, the UESA came out in support of loyalist candidates who favoured the retention of the Union Jack, a constitutional monarchy and British 'law and order'.[28] Each Saturday during the election campaign, the association held military-style marches in the four divisions. They were the most characteristic aspect of the 1921 election.

The UESA worked closely with the British Empire Union (BEU). The latter had a more respectable pedigree, having been founded by some conservative members of the House of Lords. The BEU was an all-party organization, including former pro-war members of the labour party who refused to leave the coalition government at the end of the war. The BEU considered that the empire needed defending against the bolshevik conspiracy, a number of different fears coalescing in Britain and Ireland. *Red Terror and Green* was the title of a book, by Richard Dawson, published by the BEU in 1920. In it Sinn Féin was portrayed as a totally unacceptable expression of Irish nationalism, while the 1919 strike was seen as revolutionary. Carson's assumption of the presidency of the union, in mid-1920, no doubt cheered the members of the Belfast branch, though it is difficult to believe it had 5,000 members. The BEU had, as noted, intervened in the municipal elections, and, by the time of the May 1921 northern election, it was actively supporting the unionist candidates. On the 20th the lady mayoress presided at a BEU meeting. It was a bourgeois and petty-bourgeois movement, though the Belfast branch was ready to take to the streets when the cause of loyalty needed defending.

It was the BEU and UESA which drove Baird, Midgley and Hanna out of the election campaign. The notices posted up in Ballymacarrett on 17 May, asking shipyard workers to assemble at Hamilton Road, at 5.30 p.m., to march to the Ulster Hall, were the work of Robert Boyd, secretary of the UESA, and Leo Thomas of the BEU. The labour candidates were considered a threat, because Baird and Hanna had organized what was called the catholic expelled workers' fund. Boyd and Thomas travelled in the leading brake from Queen's Island, in the company of two organizers of the expulsions the previous July, plus Thomas McConnell, a unionist councillor (who became a Westminster MP in 1922). He was the only speaker identified with the unionist party who addressed the shipyard workers once they had taken over the hall. 'The canaries had flown', Boyd said of Baird, Midgley and Hanna's hasty departure, 'and … the Ulster Hall was once again free from the stigma of Fenianism.'

Baird, as a councillor, had, apparently, voted to allow Sinn Féin to rent this municipal venue. The chair was taken by R.H. Tregenna, a member of the UULA prominently associated with the expulsions. 'It is a terrible thing', he said, 'that you, the working men of the city, cannot be trusted by the[se labour] men.' When loyalty was offered Craig and Carson, both accepted. Neither had been responsible for the routing of the labour candidates, but endorsement of this action came strangely from a provincial premier, and a future lord of appeal. The BEU and UESA had done more than simply oppose labour because it was social-ist, during an election campaign. They had affirmed that democratic political rights were not to be extended to any catholics or protestants who were not thorough loyalists.[29]

Baird and Midgley came bottom of the poll, in South and East Belfast, while Hanna did better than the second nationalist in West Belfast. Though a leader of the expelled workers, he obtained only 367 votes (less than 1 per cent), while Burn of the UULA topped the poll with 13,298. Joe Devlin got 10,621 first preferences, and Denis McCullough, for Sinn Féin, 6,270. Midgley got 645 votes (a bit under 2 per cent), in a seat where Dawson Bates came first with 10,026, and Donald of the UULA third. Baird did best with 875 votes (2.4 per cent), in the only Belfast seat with no UULA candidate. The industrial expulsions had clearly spilled over into politics.

13

The Industrial Expulsions of 1920

In July 1920 there were industrial expulsions in Belfast on a greater scale than before the war. This was the second year of Dáil Éireann, and after the British government had delineated the six-county area of Northern Ireland. The postwar boom came to an end in May, but it was a diatribe by Carson against Sinn Féin on 12 July, and the killing in Cork by the IRA of an RIC officer from Banbridge, Co. Down, five days later, which precipitated the expulsions. They commenced on Wednesday, 21 July, in Workman, Clark's south yard, spreading quickly through the shipyards and engineering works. The 1920 expulsions rapidly sparked sectarian street rioting. A total of 7,500 catholics and labour activists, including 1,800 women, lost their jobs. Ex-servicemen were included, the 'rotten Prods' being about 1 in 4 of the expelled. The expellers were, again, young labourers and craftsmen's assistants. The Belfast Protestant Association (BPA) fomented the expulsions, and vigilance committees were established to maintain the new industrial status quo. This was in a context of workers being laid off, and the continuing unemployment of ex-servicemen. A myth of catholics taking protestant jobs during the war spread. The British state was about to begin to devolve power to the Ulster unionists, so a protestant political economy, arguably a precondition for Northern Ireland, became a characteristic of civil society. The expelled workers were overshadowed, partly because the 'rotten Prods' became dependent upon a British trade-union movement on the defensive, but mainly because Belfast catholic power was being absorbed into Sinn Féin. A second police killing, in Lisburn on 22 August, intensified sectarianism in Belfast. The self-styled 'Black and Tans of Industry' politicized the workplace with counter-revolutionary fervour, the unionist leadership seeking to harness this in a new regional political stability. There is no end to the story of the 1920 expulsions, the expelled workers of Belfast being the unknown victims of the Irish struggle.

The year 1920 was the beginning of the end for Belfast's industry, though few could have appreciated that at the time. Unemployment in shipbuilding throughout the United Kingdom started to rise in May, though it was August before engineering went into recession. In July, 27,000 men were employed in the city's two shipyards, 2,000 fewer than in the previous year. The fortunes of the two Belfast yards may have diverged. Workman, Clark experienced financial problems in 1919, and changed owners the following year. Harland and Wolff may have been more robust. Linen also benefited in the postwar boom, but, by December 1920, it was to undergo its worst depression. After a month's short-time working, 30,000 were laid off. Unemployment in the north rose in the early 1920s, reaching 18 per cent in 1923.

Carson and the Ulster unionists had supported Lloyd George's government after the 1918 election, Craig, of course, being a junior member. The suspended home rule act of 1914 forced the British government to reconsider Ireland towards the end of 1919. The restoration of order was believed to be a precondition for an Irish solution, but Sinn Féin – it was felt – had to be repressed. The idea of two parliaments was advanced, even though Ulster unionists had never demanded self-government. The aspiration of Irish unity survived, or was anticipated, in the provision for a council of Ireland. The thinking in London was that Irish nationalists would be less critical of the British government if it ceased to control the north directly. The Ulster unionists, after all, were Irish. By February 1920 it had been agreed to divide Ireland so that six counties would go to the new northern state. This was less territory than the historic province of Ulster, but more than the protestant heartland. There had been, in 1911, 820,370 protestants to 430,161 catholics, in this area. Virtue was made of necessity in a truncated Ulster, and this regional parliament came to be seen as a bulwark against Irish nationalism. A future British government, dominated by the liberal and/or labour parties, it was thought, might otherwise put the six counties out of the United Kingdom. A new government of Ireland bill was introduced, to be enacted by late December 1920. It was known, from the beginning, that it would not satisfy Sinn Féin, but the government was consoled by the thought that the Ulster question was being answered. This was to reckon without the impact of southern resistance on the north, to say nothing of the new catholic minority being legislatively created, by way of solution to the problem of a protestant minority in Ireland.

In May 1920, dockers in Dublin refused to unload what they called war material. They were inspired by workers in the London docks, who, opposing the British government's intervention in the Soviet Union, had refused to allow the *Jolly George* to sail for Poland with arms. Unlike the (British) National Union of Railwaymen (NUR), the ITGWU supported action in Ireland, when its members joined in, refusing to transport troops or munitions. The IRA intimidated train drivers who continued to work. The munitions strike, as Irish labour called it, was more a transport embargo, with widespread catholic support. The ILP & TUC appealed to 'Nationalists, Republicans or Trade Unionists'[1] to support laid-off workers. In June attempts were being made to have workers reinstated, British unions being asked to be more supportive of the Irish struggle. The NUR executive was influenced, in part, by northern railwaymen who refused to help the IRA, a position affirmed at the national conference in Belfast between 5 and 10 July. This strike had a bearing on the expulsions.

So also did events in Derry, Ulster's second city. The catholic majority had, of course, secured control of the corporation in January.

'Ireland's right to determine her own destiny', the new nationalist mayor said, 'will come about whether the protestants of Ulster like it or not.'[2] This was followed by the government's decision to go for a six-county Northern Ireland, just locking Derry into a unionist state. The IRA had been relatively inactive in Ulster, but unionists alleged the incursion of southern gunmen. Tax offices in Belfast and other northern towns were attacked, in April and May, as part of an IRA offensive against British civil administration throughout Ireland. Trouble broke out in Derry in April and May, and the first RIC man in the north was killed. Between 19 and 26 June there was rioting between catholics and protestants, the UVF having been re-formed locally by ex-servicemen as a popular defence force. The violence was brought to an end by troops and a curfew, but not before up to 20 lives had been lost. The IRA then folded its tents, while a local conciliation committee of leading citizens sought to prevent provocative sectarian displays.

The Twelfth was approaching. Though Carson had declared the days of Ulster resistance over, he was dependent upon the British government's repressing Sinn Féin. The previous year he had threatened to restore the UVF in order to protect the – political – rights of Ulster, only to meet with criticism from British unionists. In 1920, at Finaghy outside Belfast, he hinted at the same thing, as being the way to deal with Sinn Féin. This was in spite of having talked down shipyard workers during the Derry riots. 'I say that if the British Government are unable to deal with these matters they ought to ask somebody else to deal with them', Carson told the orangemen. 'We know well that the real battlefields of Ireland in relation to a republic must be Ulster (Cheers). We know well that their ambition is to penetrate Ulster ... Do not let us close our eyes to the realities of the situation.' Carson went on to articulate his conspiracy theory about the revolutionary threat.

> The most insidious method is tacking on the Sinn Fein question and the Irish Republican question to the Labour question. (A voice – 'Ireland is the most Labour centre in the United Kingdom'). I know that. What I say is this – these men who come forward posing as the friends of Labour care no more about Labour than does the man in the moon ... Beware of these insidious methods ... We in Ulster will tolerate no Sinn Fein – (cheers) – no Sinn Fein organisation, no Sinn Fein methods ...[3]

The Ulster unionist leader was clearly worried about disunity, having been affected by the assertion of labour from 1918. In the wake of the Derry riots he portrayed protestant labour men as the tool of Sinn Féin, used to undermine unionist resistance. In Carson's mind Sinn Féin and labour merged, but there is no evidence that he was exhorting loyalists to wage war on Sinn Féin by attacking the labour movement. It was irresponsible rhetoric, a measure of his failure as a political leader. Ulster was being politically guaranteed by the British government, but there was insecurity about the failure to repress Sinn Féin. Political rebellion had been abandoned with the outbreak of war, and it was now a case of the unionist state inheriting, and/or building up its own, repressive institutions. The *Irish News* of 13 July thought Carson's

speech 'a harmless and commonplace harangue ... [comprising] plati-
tudes and conditional threats'.[4] The *Northern Whig* referred to the possibility of unionists taking 'the matter into [their] own hands ... in a
disciplined organised fashion under the leader who had served us so
well in the past'.[5] The *Belfast Evening Telegraph* referred to the UVF's
being remobilized. There followed a spate of letter writing to the *Belfast
Newsletter*, on the theme of a Sinn Féin incursion into Ulster. Whoever
might have been behind this campaign, it was on 23 July that Lt.-Col.
Spender took command of the UVF, calling upon all loyalists to report
to their battalions, to be 'at the disposal of the Government if and
when they were required'.[6] If this was an attempt to control elements of
the protestant masses, as seems likely, the UUC was too late.

The Belfast expulsions had their origins in Cork, where the Sinn Féin
lord mayor, Thomas MacCurtain, had been killed in his home in
March. MacCurtain was the leader of the local IRA, and an inquest
blamed the assassination on the RIC acting at the behest of the British
government. District Inspector Swanzy, Divisional Inspector Clayton
and Acting Inspector General Smith were specifically named. The two
last-named had served in Belfast, and Swanzy was soon transferred to
Lisburn, Michael Collins having ordered that he be killed. On 19 June
the divisional commissioner of the RIC for Munster, Brig.-Gen. Smyth,
told police officers in Listowel, Co. Kerry, that they would not be
disciplined for shooting suspects. An account appeared in the *Irish
Bulletin* of 9 July. Eight days later, on Saturday, 17 July, Smyth was
killed by the IRA in the county club in Cork. This young former army
officer hailed from Banbridge in Co. Down, south of Belfast. Railway
workers in Cork refused to load his body for conveyance home for
burial. It had to be taken by road, newspapers in Ulster announcing
that it would arrive on Wednesday, 21 July.

It was nine days since Carson's Twelfth speech, and the end of the
shipyard holiday in Belfast. The Belfast Protestant Association (BPA),
which had sought to destroy William Walker, posted notices that
morning on Queen's Island. They summoned a 'mass meeting of the
Unionist and Protestant workers of the shipyards',[7] to be held outside
Workman, Clark's at 1.30 p.m. There a resolution was adopted, to the
effect that all workers had to sign a declaration of opposition to Sinn
Féin. Expulsions began spontaneously in the south yard at 3.30 p.m.
'The gates were smashed down with sledges', one worker recalled, 'the
vests and shirts of those at work were torn open to see were the men
wearing any Catholic emblems, and then woe betide the man who
was.'[8] The *Belfast Newsletter* claimed, in an editorial, that a worker had
provocatively shouted 'up the rebels', 'during the dinner hour',[9] only to
locate this, in its news report, after the BPA meeting. The following day,
Thursday, 22 July, the expulsions spread to the town engineering
shops. Unlike those in 1912, the 1920 expulsions immediately ignited
street rioting, this tending to overshadow intra–working-class hostility
in the workplace. Three catholics were killed on the Wednesday, seven
the following day, and four more on the Friday in street rioting.
Residential expulsions had begun, catholics being driven across the

river to west Belfast. The origins of the expulsions are difficult to determine, given the subsequent political exchanges at Westminster. 'There was a good deal of looting especially of spirit dealers' shops in the east district',[10] Sir Hamar Greenwood, the liberal chief secretary, told the Commons on 22 July. Devlin referred to Carson's Twelfth speech, only to admit later that the expulsions had not been deliberately planned. Carson did not push the connection with Smyth too far, and showed a concern to have 'the best men of the labouring classes'[11] enrolled in the police force.

The 1920 expulsions were extensive, spreading through the industry of Belfast. Those of 1912 had begun in Workman, Clark's north yard. This seems to have been relatively peaceful, either because the workforce had remained purged, or because economic difficulties were making an impact. This time, trouble began in the south yard on Queen's Island. It spread to the much more formidable Harland and Wolff, then to the large engineering firms, followed by the smaller ones, and finally into linen mills and factories. Nearly 7,500 workers suffered, in comparison with 3,000 in 1912. The figure of 7,410, of the very many quoted, seems to be the most accurate. Most were unionized male workers, both skilled and unskilled. But some 2,000 were not unionized, and 1,800 were specifically identified as women. (Some of these women would have been trade-union members.) The expulsions affected production, and were coterminous with growing unemployment, so the effect on the working class, in terms of loss of earnings, was even greater. Over the next two years, Harland and Wolff cut its workforce from 20,000 to 15,000, and Workman, Clark from 7,000 to 1,800. The corresponding figures for expulsions in July 1920 were 2,000 and 250 (the latter figure confirms the relative unimportance of Workman, Clark). Unemployment was a result of a global reduction in demand, while the expulsions were the product of an Irish political crisis. Queen's Island was the centre of the expulsions, and the shock waves spread in concentric circles of decreasing intensity through the working class. Of the 5,610 expelled men, 1,390 were skilled workers, comprising 400 joiners, 300 fitters and 690 in 18 other crafts. Most of the expelled men were unskilled, and nearly half of them ununionized. Of the remainder, 800 were members of the workers' union, and 500 of the NAUL. There were also 120 NSFU members, and 100 dockers and carters (probably from the cross-channel docks).

Most of the expelled were catholics, but the proportion of 'rotten Prods' – a term which was widely applied in 1920 – was greater than before the war. Vulnerable and identifiable catholics were the first to suffer, and about 5,550 were expelled. Any contact with the minority community made a worker suspect in the eyes of loyalists. 'Even the sons of a Protestant by his first wife, who was also a Protestant', an expelled worker claimed, 'had to go because their father remarried and took a Catholic woman as his wife.'[12] Approximately 1,850 protestants were expelled, 1 in 4. In 1912, it had been 1 in 5, or about 600 workers. '"Rotten Prods"', another worker told the 1920 conference of the ILP & TUC in Cork, '[were] the same as a "Mickie".'[13] John Hanna, who became the leader of the expelled workers, described the protestants as 'the backbone of Trade Unionism in the North'.[14] F. Lowe of the painters told the 1920 TUC that 'every man who took part in the Trade Union movement and in the Labour movement had been absolutely driven from the [Queen's] island.'[15] James Baird, the most politically alert leader of the expelled, explained the expulsions graphically to the following year's congress of the British trade-union movement:

> Every man who was prominently known in the Labour movement, who was known as an I.L.P.-eer was expelled from his work just the same as the rebel Sinn Feiners. To show their love of the I.L.P. they burnt our hall in North Belfast. The Chairman of our Central branch had to flee to Glasgow for his life. The secretary had to fly all the way to London. The district chairman of the Amalgamated Engineering Union [AEU, as the ASE had recently become], a very moderate and quiet Labour man, was beaten not once but two or three times because he persisted in returning to his work. A member of the executive of the Joiners' Society was also expelled. He was not a Catholic, and he was also a moderate Labour man.[16]

The 1,850 protestants must have included almost the entire cadre of working-class leaders in the industrial and political wings of the labour movement.

The perpetrators, the expellers, were, again, young labourers and craftsmen's assistants, platers' helpers being prominent. But the 1920 expulsions were less spontaneous in execution, the BPA being evident in the first few days. This evangelical organization was probably the one which had been behind the Independent Orange Order. Thomas Sloan had preached at dinner time in the platers' shed at Harland and Wolff before going into politics. This sort of activity may have continued, but the BPA seems merely to have ignited the expulsions, rather than planned and carried them out. The BPA was also described as the Ulster Protestant Association (UPA) in 1920, and an organization of this name was in evidence from the autumn, with branches in Ormeau, Shankill Road, York Street and Ballymacarrett. It was set up, according to later police intelligence, 'following on the disturbances which ... began in the City', and was an organization of 'well disposed citizens for the protection of Protestants and Loyalists against Sinn Fein aggression'.[17] The UPA may, or may not, have been in the shipyards in July. What is clear is that its membership became much less well disposed, and committed to an extremely aggressive form of defence.

The 1920 expulsions differed from those before the war in that leaders could, and can, be identified. They were predominantly plater's helpers, though craftsmen tended to chair meetings. Fourteen leaders have been identified from press reports. The most prominent was Alex McKay, a UULA member of Bangor council, employed at Workman, Clark. Another, a joiner in the north yard, was William Barclay, who was later prominent in the UULA. D. Campbell and J. McIlhagger also worked there. Eight of the 14 were from Harland and Wolff. John Holness, a riveter, was probably the second-most prominent leader, and also active in the UULA. Other first-rank leaders were James Connolly (not, of course, the republican leader) and John Crumlin, both plater's helpers. Second-rank leaders were William Blair, an ex-serviceman; William Taylor, a fitter; J. McQueen, an electrician's helper; William Wilson, a plater; and N. Gordon, again a plater's helper. H. Ford worked at Harland and Wolff, but less is known about G. Wells, a former navy man. These were mostly unknown men otherwise. Only Holness seems to have been an active trade unionist, in the boilermakers, while McKay, with a political background, was not to the fore in the UULA organization.

These leaders saw to it that there was counter-revolutionary institutionalization, in the form of vigilance committees in the workplaces. The idea was first mooted at Workman, Clark's north yard on 28 July. Two days later, at a dinner-time meeting chaired by James Connolly, at Harland and Wolff, such a committee was established. The UPA was reported on 19 August as having suggested vetting committees in each shop, the idea being to maintain loyalist integrity among the workforce. The following day, a representative body, very like the UPA, met Harland and Wolff's board of directors. By late September, vigilance committees had supplanted trade-union organization in the workplace. They represented the men who had carried out the expulsions, or acquiesced in the intimidation of catholics and disloyal protestants. This reactionary emulation of a shop stewards' movement had in common merely a certain obscurity. There is evidence of a joint vigilance committee of the shipyards emerging, but it is not clear how representative it was. Local papers were not too determined in their reporting of this underworld.

Unemployment, particularly of ex-servicemen, was an immediate preoccupation. By October there were 6,226 registered unemployed workers in Belfast. Of these 2,800 were ex-servicemen claiming unemployment benefit, and another 2,500 receiving out-of-work payments. Most had been employed before the war, and military service was seen as the epitome of loyalty. Those who had taken their jobs during the war were, almost by definition, disloyal. This was so regardless of where they had come from, what their politics was, and whether the catholics among them had actually supported Sinn Féin in the 1918 or 1920 elections. A number of catholic, and protestant, ex-servicemen had been expelled, perhaps as many as 700 – 1 in 10. (The Irish nationalist veterans' association opened a register for former Redmondites.) The expulsions were a conscious attempt to impose a protestant political economy on the postwar labour market. William Barclay, speaking outside the north yard on 28 July, justified them in terms of the need to replace disloyal workers with ex-servicemen. A resolution was passed 'respectfully suggest[ing] that the first consideration be given to loyal ex-servicemen and Protestant Unionists'.[18] He went on to complain about trade unionists getting involved in divisive political issues. There was no doubt that the disloyal workers, in Barclay's mind, posed a threat to the security of the protestant community, while the ex-servicemen, again in his opinion, deserved employment in return for being in the forces. 'If you people forget there was a war in 1914–18', read a placard displayed at a meeting of the corporation, 'we don't.'[19] William Blair, the ex-serviceman, had said on 28 July, that, 'before the war there was no Sinn Fein ... [and] if Sinn Feiners ever got back to work in their midst all the efforts of the last week would have been in vain.'[20]

The expulsions were also a reprisal against catholics and socialists in Belfast, for the behaviour of Sinn Féin and the IRA in the rest of the country. William Barclay specifically mentioned Sinn Féin outrages, and the refusal to transport Smyth's body. The resolution at that meeting also insisted upon the end of Sinn Féin's campaign, as a condition for workers being taken back. The Belfast minority was being held hostage against the behaviour of nationalist Ireland. The vigilance committees, McKay argued on 5 October, were 'the Black and Tans of Industry'.[21] It is a striking analogy, identifying the expulsions with British state policy.

The Irish government acquiesced in sectarianism, London letting the executive, police and army get on with it in Ireland. British rule amounted to a combination of differing responses to Sinn Féin and the IRA's campaign. Greenwood was appointed chief secretary in early April to strengthen the Irish executive. There was increasing repression, the RIC, under Maj.-Gen. H.H. Tudor, being augmented by the so-called Black and Tans, as well as by the auxiliaries. The former, demobilized British soldiers, dressed in black (dark-green) police trousers and khaki soldiers' jackets, had started to arrive in March. The latter, which were sent in September, were former military officers. They were commanded by Brig.-Gen. F.P. Crozier, formally of the UVF, who resigned in protest at government policy in February 1921. The army, under Maj.-Gen. Sir Nevil Macready, was not central, staying much more in the background. If the IRA was the foe of the British government, then the Ulster unionists were its friends. The devolution of state power was only slightly interrupted by the Derry riots, and the Belfast expulsions. But it was September before Sir Ernest Clark was sent from Dublin to become assistant undersecretary in Belfast, the source of the new regional administration. On 29 July the cabinet's Irish committee welcomed the remobilization of the UVF, to help counter Sinn Féin but also to control the protestant masses. It was to be an arm of the new state. Greenwood's first response to the expulsions had been an assertion of his duty to maintain peace. When the actions in the private realm of capital were rapidly overtaken by rioting on the streets, he quickly forgot them. The chief secretary refused to answer Devlin in parliament on 29 July, and, four days later, washed the government's hands of responsibility:

[I have] no power to insist upon employers employing Roman Catholics, Orangemen, or anybody else ... [or] to compel one trade unionist to work alongside another, against whom he had an antipathy, as I think, an unreasonable antipathy ... It is impossible for any Government to compel employers to employ or workmen to work.[22]

Belfast corporation was quickly involved in the issue of the expulsions. It had in 1920 five nationalist and five Sinn Féin members, and the twelve labour men plus Alex Boyd, the only independent elected. On Monday, 26 July, James Baird and D.R. Campbell, leader of the labour group, requested a special meeting of the corporation. They had the support of three Sinn Féin councillors. This was possibly to make up a quorum, which begs the question as to why the labour group did not make the request. That Friday, 30 July, at Harland and Wolff, loyalist workers expressed their opposition. James Connolly, as chairman, attacked the labour councillors as 'disloyal demagogue[s]', accusing them of wanting to 'advertis[e] the Sinn Fein policy and reviv[e] religious and political bigotry'.[23] Baird and Campbell tried to withdraw their request. They had failed to bring the labour group with them, and had become associated with Sinn Féin, this being spotted by the loyalists. The lord mayor insisted upon proceeding with a special meeting on the Saturday, when a regular meeting was scheduled for Tuesday, 3 August. When councillors assembled on 31 July, eleven were absent. This may have been Campbell's group, and certainly there were no labour contributions. The councillors elected only months before were clearly frightened of mass intimidation. 'The meeting', according to the *Irish News*, 'resolved itself into a demonstration of sympathy with the shipyard terrorists, large numbers of whom had possession of the public galleries and dominated the proceedings from beginning to end.'

'Exuberant plater's helpers' were reported to have filled the chamber with 'tobacco smoke ... [and] coarse language'. Dungaree-clad workers, presumably straight from the shipyards, were seen to be waving revolvers. William Barclay led a deputation of 15 from Workman, Clark, 'some of whom bore tiny Union Jacks in their hands'. He reiterated the position of the loyalist workers. When Denis McCullough of Sinn Féin rose to speak, he stood on a Union Jack which had fallen from the public gallery. It may not have been accidental, and the loyalists above proceeded to spit at him. The case for the expelled workers was put by Sinn Féin, in the absence of the labour men. The expulsions had been 'inspired from higher quarters', and 'responsible workmen' had not been involved. The republicans demanded that the corporation set up 'peace patrols', secure the return of the expelled, and request the local press to support its efforts. If the party showed courage in attending, its politics were naive in the extreme. One Sinn Féiner left early, and the other four received the support of only one nationalist. A unionist amendment, calling for no action, was carried by 35 votes to 5. 'There is no single cogent reason at all', councillor J.A. Duff argued, 'why we should interfere in the present situation ... The Unionist workers were strained to breaking point and were determined that the Sinn Fein poison, which was worse than any surgical operation, would be expelled from the body politic ... [Reinstatement] was beyond our wish ... There is plenty of room and plenty of work for these men outside Belfast.' Alex Boyd was reported 'professing to speak for Labour ... [He] supported the case of the pogromists, and said it was most unfair that Trade Unionism should be dragged at the tail of any political party, whether Sinn Fein or Socialist.'[24] It was a sorry position for a trade unionist to reach.

The expelled workers, as in 1912, sought to organize, but the military authorities banned a meeting called for Monday, 26 July 1920. Another was allowed to proceed two days later in St Mary's Hall, when a committee was elected to represent the case of the expelled to the employers and trade-union leaders. This was the Expelled Workers' Relief Committee (EWRC), whose leaders were to be James Baird and John Hanna. Its address was St Mary's Hall, the EWRC becoming responsible for about 90 per cent of the workers victimized. As its name implied, it was concerned primarily with providing for workers who had been deprived of their right to work. The district committee of the ASCJ also set up an organization, in the Artisans Hall. Four hundred of the 1,390 skilled workers expelled were joiners, about 1 in 10 of those working in Belfast. A third committee was set up by the engineers in the Clonard Street Hall, interestingly, a catholic area. There were 300 expelled fitters, about 1 in 17 of those in the city, though other small groups of craftsmen may have belonged to the AEU. While the 1920 expulsions were on a greater scale, they received less publicity than those of 1912. The political context was substantially transformed. The unionist leadership in 1920 was more perturbed about street rioting, and the expellers had articulated a sophisticated justification. The expulsions were a neat piece of social surgery, and the issue rapidly became the new loyalist industrial order. Devlin still looked to London, but Sinn Féin, which was growing in Belfast, was at war with the British government. Expelled catholics were thrown back on a divided nationalist movement, but with Dáil Éireann aspiring to be the Irish state. Catholics and especially 'rotten Prods' believed the labour movement of both countries might come to their aid.

Two days after Baird and Campbell called for a special meeting of the corporation, a deputation from the Belfast labour party left for London. This may have initially included Simon Greenspon, now out of jail. He must have been an engineer, since he seems to have approached the leadership of his union, the AEU. He was told to go to the labour party. The 300 and more expelled members were to be paid only lock-out, rather than victimization, pay, on the grounds that the loyalist actions were 'retaliatory'. 'That reasoning', a southern member of the AEU told the ILP & TUC, meeting in Cork at the beginning of August, 'was based on one of the officials of their Union and a member of the executive driving 40 miles in a char-a-banc and seeing a couple of police barracks burned down.'[25] James Freeland said little about the expulsions in his monthly reports, except to attribute some unemployment to subsequent dislocation. Greenspon was joined in London by Baird and Clarke Scott, also a labour councillor. They saw Greenwood the chief secretary and labour MPs, and held a public meeting. But it was difficult to raise the question of expulsions, given the political violence stimulated by Sinn Féin.

Back in Ireland, a Belfast expelled workers' fund was announced on 13 August. One of the treasurers was Father Convery, who had so acted in 1912. The other two lay treasurers happened to be the president and treasurer of the St Vincent de Paul Society. But six labour men joined in signing their appeal to 'all classes and creeds [in] ... the Industrial World for Industrial Peace'. They were Alex Stewart, now vice-president of the trades council; W.H. Carruthers, secretary of the Belfast labour party; Baird; Daniel McRandall, an office holder in the ASCJ; J.T. Clarke of the ETU; and J. Fegan, a joiner. Clarke was a member of the EWRC, and Fegan its secretary. Socialists and nationalists combined to argue that the expulsions had been planned by 'a Political and Capitalistic caucus, who sought to break up the ranks of labour'. They called for 'economic *action* ... to frustrate this manoeuvre of selfish capitalism', as well, of course, for much needed funds.[26] If the labour men were thinking of industrial action by the working class, an economic boycott of Belfast by nationalist Ireland was the outcome.

As before the money came from catholic sources. Bishop MacRory, who claimed he had waited for the labour movement to act, sent £100. He believed the employers should have closed the works, and the government used the army. A similar sum came from Hughes bakery, while Joe Devlin sent £50 for 'the soldiers in the fight for religious and economic liberty'.[27] Most of the money came from local authorities, under Sinn Féin control, and from the catholic church. J.A.M. Carlisle, now retired in London, sent two guineas. By October the EWRC had been in touch with leading figures and public bodies in France, Spain and Belgium. Another appeal, dated 19 October, stated that the workers were 'fighting for not only Religious but [also] Industrial Freedom'.[28] And, when Devlin addressed an Irish meeting in Glasgow in November, he described the expelled as 'Irish Catholics fighting for the preservation of that faith that our fathers and forefathers fought [for] along the ages – a faith that burns as brightly and shines as brilliantly today in the hearts of Irish Ulster as it does in Cork or Tipperary (Loud Cheers)'.[29] Presented with the 'rotten Prods', Devlin, the populist constitutional nationalist, could only invoke catholicism.

Sinn Féin, in the catholic ghetto, helped the nationalists in providing relief for the thousands of expelled workers. They were quickly joined by victims of more traditional rioting in Belfast. Catholics also fled from Dromore, Banbridge, Bangor, Lisburn and Ballymena to the city. On 22 August, when the IRA killed District Inspector Swanzy, at his new posting in Lisburn, the spirit of rebel Cork provoked a more violent loyalist reaction in Belfast. The remaining catholics in Lisburn sought the sanctuary of the ghetto, and there may also have been further industrial expulsions. Two Sinn Féin councillors, Dennis Barnes and Dr McNabb, opened a relief depot in Mill Street. 'Refugees, Victims of the Pogroms, are pouring into Belfast', they declared in the *Irish News*. 'They are for the most part penniless, and *All Are Homeless*.'[30] The help they were able to offer did a great deal to establish Sinn Féin, which had access to material assistance from the rest of Ireland. Devlin's political hegemony was economically challenged, though the St Vincent de Paul Society probably remained dominant. In becoming the defenders of a national minority, Sinn Féin's association with the

IRA paled in the face of growing sectarianism. By October nationalists and republicans were helping 8,140 who were registered for relief, while 23,140 were receiving it on a daily basis.

A new loyalist industrial order was created after 21 July, premised on a purging of the trade-union leadership. The Belfast labour party, said James Connolly, was 'a party of place hunters (Hear, hear) [who] cared not for King or Country, and their policy was not patriotism but pocket (Applause)'.[31] The expellers were opposed to the socialist, and allegedly nationalist, politics of labour, but not specifically to the institutions of trade unionism. These were left alone, and this helped in winning the support of the protestant workforce. But it also minimized the possibility of aggressive action by the national trade-union leaders. A TUC deputation to Belfast met with 'men of strong prejudices but claiming intense loyalty to the Empire, and bitterly opposed to the Sinn Fein movement'. The British representatives were told 'to go back and leave them to settle their own affairs'.[32] Loyalism was above all localistic, patriotic affirmations being conditional upon protestant security, if not supremacy. 'He was as strong a Labour man as any', Tregenna of the UULA said, 'but he could never find anything strong enough to put forward to Labour to override the religious question.'[33]

Nationalists and socialists, ironically, drew on the language of the Russian revolution, to condemn the loyalist leaders, who considered they were waging a crusade against bolshevism in Ireland. 'They had a workers' Soviet in Belfast',[34] Sam Kyle was reported as saying on 3 August of the new industrial order. A catholic leader later referred to 'Soviet terrorists'.[35] The *Irish News*, already anti-communist for catholic reasons, described the '"Pogrom" [as] an exhibition of Bolshevism in practice unexampled outside Russia'.[36] The vigilance committee, the paper described, on 18 September, as an 'Orange Soviet'. The critical ascription of revolutionary rhetoric, in 1920, to a reactionary workers' movement, was not the least bizarre aspect of those summer and autumn days.

The establishment of the vigilance committees was symbolized in a politicization of industry. On 25 August a large Union Jack was unfurled in the plumbers' shop at Harland and Wolff. 'Loyalists', said Crumlin, as one of the new leaders, 'would be compelled to take matters into their own hands',[37] if the British government did not stop Sinn Féin. 'Gentlemen of the Imperial guard', was the way McKay addressed another meeting on 2 September, 'we are all Imperialists, and the reason we are met today is because we believe in Imperial authority.'[38] He was calling for the arming of the UVF, and the speeding up of the recruitment of protestants as special constables. Twelve days later McKay unfurled what was reported to be the largest Union Jack in the city, in the turning shop at Workman, Clark. This self-activity of the protestant masses was legitimized, in the context of preparing for unionist rule, by the community's leaders. J.F. Gordon, then a UULA councillor, unfurled yet another Union Jack, in the valve and brass fitting department at Harland and Wolff, on 14 October. Also present was Sir James Craig, still a member of the British government. 'Do I approve of the action you boys have taken in the past?', the *Irish News* reported him as asking rhetorically, with the answer, 'I say "Yes".' Whether he was accurately quoted or not, Craig was looking forward to the new regime:

> He could not understand how it was that when any progressive movement was put forward it was always blocked by the Nationalist Party in the old days and now by Sinn Fein. All that would be changed by the new [Government of Ireland] Bill and Unionists would be able to watch them with an eagle eye. Unionists would be able to to take control of education, housing etc. – problems that could not then be blocked by disloyalists.[39]

Even Carson, belatedly, endorsed the expulsions, in the House of Commons on 25 October: 'I am prouder of my friends in the shipyards than of any other friends I have in the whole world.'[40]

This behaviour of the unionist leaders and their followers required the acquiescence of the Belfast employers. After the expulsions the joint vigilance committee in the shipyards sought to control entry to employment. Workers would be allowed back only if they signed a 'test', affirming loyalty to king and empire: 'I do not belong to or sympathise with Sinn Fein', it went on, 'and ... I deplore and abhor all murders and outrages inflicted upon humanity by this dangerous and disloyal movement.'[41] It was a statement of loyalist disavowal of republicanism. Few, if any, expelled workers signed it, presumably having no faith in the vigilance committee. They included catholic, and protestant, ex-servicemen, who had returned to work in Belfast, only to be expelled. The EWRC had put its counter-proposals to the employers. Harland and Wolff was asked to segregate the yard, allowing catholics to work under military protection. The alternative was closure, a device the firm had used in the past to enforce managerial prerogative. 'They told us', Travers, an expelled leader, reported to Irish trade unionists, 'that the hooligan element would break loose and that property would suffer.'[42] The police and army feared that street rioting would escalate. The expulsions might have helped the employers lay off workers, but their sectarian political principle was very different from managerial retrenchment. Economic dislocation rapidly became a problem. At the Sirocco engineering works, the laboratories and drawing office were badly affected. Davidson called a meeting of his workers, advanced the argument that there were some good catholics, and tried to get the vigilance committee to relent. The UPA visited the works, and secured a reaffirmation that disloyal catholics would be kept out. Davidson cannot have been amused.

On 11 September Harland and Wolff wrote to the FEST district committee. Workman, Clark followed later. Charles McKay, the chairman, had been expelled, but Speirs, the secretary, seems to have survived for a time. The district committee strongly condemned the expulsions, on 24 July, but, at a second meeting four days later, its members were forced to accept that they were unable to do anything. The big yard asked the federation to organize workers' representatives for a conference. The wee yard stated that the objective was 'to restore normal conditions of employment ... [where] all sections of the community should work together in harmony'.[43] Whatever the economic difficulties being suffered by the two yards, this initiative may have been provoked by the intended arrival of Sir Ernest Clark in Belfast five days later. The employers seemed to be alert to British considerations. The London government was to hand power to the Ulster unionists, as a party committed to parliamentary government, not to loyalist direct actionists. Conferences were held. While the FEST district committee may have been in attendance, it was the loyalist leaders who spoke for the shop floor. It was agreed to drop the written test for a verbal promise, 'an honourable understanding that any man taking advantage of a general permission to return should be regarded as having by so doing signified his loyalty to the Crown and his disapproval of attempts to subvert the Constitution by outrage and violence'.[44] The joint vigilance committee was still to control any return of expelled workers, but without a formal system of religious and political discrimination. 'We will work with any workers irrespective of religion', Harland and Wolff's employees agreed later, 'putting them on their honour that they are not associated with Sinn Fein or any other disloyal organisation.' Workman, Clark's workers were more explicit: '[we] declare we are prepared to work with any loyal man irrespective of religion.'[45]

Before these concessions could be implemented, the IRA intervened dramatically. Shortly after Clark began to prepare for devolution in Belfast, there was an attack upon the RIC in the Falls Road on 25 September. One policeman was killed, and another injured. It was the first such action in the city, but it undermined any possibility of a settlement. The joint vigilance committee reverted to its position of maintaining the post-expulsions status quo. The fate of catholic, and protestant, workers in Belfast counted for little in the war between Sinn Féin and British rule. With the employers and the state having risked their authority, the problem became one for the labour movements of both countries.

The ILP & TUC had met in Cork on Monday, 2 August, for its four-day annual conference. John Hanna led a small deputation of expelled workers, the other members being Travers and O'Donovan. The executive had earlier told the (British) labour party that it would probably ignore the government of Ireland bill. Travers recounted the events of 21 July and afterwards, on the third day, in a private session. As in times past, he mentioned that the expelled were looking to the British trade-union movement. This was not for reasons of unionist sentiment, but was merely a recognition that the Irish movement did not embrace Belfast. The unions there had been overwhelmed, and were looking to their national leaderships. Delegates in Cork condemned the expulsions, but left the national executive to decide upon action. This was to take the form of a donation of £50, and the sending of two members north to help with relief. 'We have endeavoured to assist in any way practical', the executive reported to the following year's conference, '... but regret that virulent intolerance still prevails ... We confess we can

see no light ahead and no sign of improvement.' Tom Johnson, as secretary, admitted later that there had been no contact with the British
labour movement on the question of the expulsions: 'Of course ... we
have no right to ask [the British TUC] for any information.'[46]

The British TUC met a month later, in Portsmouth, between 6 and 11
September. There were only two delegates from Belfast, a shipwright
and James Duff of the Workers' Union, but neither of them spoke about
the expulsions. A deputation of expelled workers was admitted, and
allowed to put an emergency motion. This instructed the parliamentary
committee to convene a meeting of union executives immediately, in
order 'to take a common line of action' on reinstatement. John Beard,
president of the Workers' Union, who had had 800 members expelled,
seconded, though he argued that 'both sides had prevented each other
from working', and 'the less said about the matter the better'. A
Sunderland shipwright 'made a protest', as the delegates were about to
vote in favour of the motion, '[and] amid some excitement proceeded
to invite the Congress ... to consider well about it'.[47]

The resolution was considered at the next parliamentary committee
meeting. The committee decided to send a three-man deputation to
Belfast, namely J. Hill, A.A. Purcell and A. Pugh. Hill represented the
boilermakers, and was president of the FEST. It was 4 December before
they left, for a week's visit, in order to report to the December meeting
of the parliamentary committee. The expelled had been out of work for
nearly six months. Guided by Speirs, the local FEST secretary, the three
TUC leaders met the assistant undersecretary, the lord mayor, the two
shipyard managements, the harbour commissioners and the chamber
of commerce. Of the workers, they met the FEST and ASCJ district committees, and the EWRC and committee of expelled AEU members, plus
the joint vigilance committee and an organization of joiners who
acquiesced in the expulsions.

Hill and his colleagues reported that they had met with all-round
goodwill, but were unable to come up with very much. They repeated
the loyalist justifications for the expulsions, particularly the far from
accurate claim of an influx of southern Sinn Féiners to take the jobs of
those off fighting, though the BPA was accused of being inflammatory
when it summoned the meeting for 21 July. Their report to the parliamentary committee, while condemning the expulsions, was appreciative of the new stability in industry. It was a feeble document, based on
too close an empathy with the protestants still in work, and lacking any
active commitment to trade-union principles. It was with some relief
that they turned from the irrational workers, to the responsible managers and public officials. The members of the deputation expressed the
hope that the broad-minded on both sides might be brought together,
in order to tackle the difficulty. But the TUC delegation also criticized
the ASCJ, the one union which had attempted to do something about
the expulsions.

Individual unions had been affected in different ways. A little is
known about the electricians, painters, railwaymen, engineers, plumbers and joiners – all unions for the skilled, who were only a minority

of the expelled. They constitute a mini-case study of trade-union une-venness, in the conditions of state formation, each being overwhelmed by loyalism, to a greater or less extent. This is also the case with the ASCJ, though the general secretary, and national leadership, put up something of a fight.

It is known that 83 electricians were expelled. They were supported by the central branch in Belfast, one that does not seem to have been involved in the expulsions. The painters had 26 members expelled, and Lowe, an official from Manchester, held a meeting of over 600 of the 750 members in Belfast in August. A levy of 2s.6d. (12½p) a week was voted, for the support of the expelled painters. Lowe told the 1920 TUC that, of their members who refused to sign the vigilance committee's test, over 100 were ex-servicemen, and 22 were members of the orange order. When he next visited Belfast, he found in his hotel room a note decorated with the skull and crossbones and signed 'The Ulster Division',[48] telling him to get out of the city. The railwaymen, faced with the challenge of the munitions strike, had affirmed the 'complete unity of the working classes ... [without] religious or political differ-ences'.[49] After the expulsions, protestant members of the NUR stated that they had 'no grievance against [their] Catholic fellow workmen'. They objected to Sinn Féin. It was resolved to impose a written test 'of loyalty to [the] King and Constitution',[50] though it is not known whether this occurred. Expelled engineers, as noted, organized, and got in touch with their executive. There were over a dozen branches of the AEU in Belfast. Most of the members seem to have kept their heads down, as economic dislocation and recession made it increasingly diffi-cult to earn a living. This was reflected in the contribution of a Belfast delegate, W.J. Moody, to the 1921 TUC. Claiming to 'know absolutely nothing about orange or green, or any mixture',[51] he spoke personally of the need for reconcilation between engineers, if not within the wider working class.

Some 60 plumbers, out of a craft of about 1,000 workers, were expelled (before the war, 12 per cent had been catholic). Over 800 were members of the united operative plumbers' association of Great Britain and Ireland. By April 1920 the Belfast branch had secured the establish-ment of an Irish council within the union, and attended the first meeting in Dublin. This was in anticipation of self-government. At the half-yearly meeting on 30 June, members voted, by 68 to 16, to with-draw. The seconder of this motion was R.H. Tregenna, of the UULA, one of the few vocal loyalists active within the trade-union movement. After the expulsions, the branch asked the executive for a district com-mittee for the 'Belfast branch and lodges within the radius'. By September, they wanted an Ulster district committee, on the grounds that Clark had taken up his appointment. The expelled plumbers had met in St Mary's Hall, and they appealed directly to the executive in Britain. The Belfast branch denied any responsibility for their expul-sion. But it condemned the expelled for meeting separately, while telling them to appeal directly to the executive for financial help. The 60 plumbers were, effectively, disowned. The branch took an interest only when some of the expelled allegedly prevented other members from continuing to work.

Localism saw the Belfast plumbers become increasingly hostile towards their own executive. The national leadership balloted the Belfast members, over the head of the branch committee, on the question of working again with the expelled. They voted 138 to 78 to do so, this being only a minority of the members in the branch. Disappointed, the executive then asked its Belfast members to sign a declaration by 20 December, stating a preparedness to work with catholics. The branch committee refused to hand over the names, asserting its right to 'deal with our members locally'. When expelled plumbers made threats, the branch committee had to be given police protection. The branch voted by 53 to 50 on 19 January 1921 not to help the expelled, and by 46 to 45 to withdraw from the Belfast labour party. Two executive members then visited the city, but the branch again voted, by 77 to 74, not to set up a lock-out committee. The executive members then forced the branch committee to meet the expelled, and saw to it that a seven-man committee was set up and all its proceedings minuted.

Much of this saga went unreported in Belfast. Lock-out benefit was paid by the executive in April, nine months after the expulsions. The Belfast branch also had to accept the new Irish district committee, though it grumbled about a meeting in Dublin in July. At the half-yearly meeting, Tregenna successfully moved that two members, who had been presented to the king and queen, on the occasion of the opening of the new parliament, should be congratulated. Lock-out pay continued throughout 1921 and into 1922, but the expelled received no other help from the branch. Other members were allowed to serve as special constables, while remaining in the branch, but did not get away with claiming sickness benefit. By the spring of 1922, the executive was suggesting to the expelled that they should look for work elsewhere, 'when the wages question was settled Nationally'.[52]

The largest group of skilled workers expelled was the 400 ASCJ members, about 1 in 10 of those in Belfast. A management committee linked the dozen or so branches in the city, and worked with Robert Waugh, and a second officer by the name of Kennedy. A Dublin member, E.F. McDermott, had been on the executive council since 1918, but he was replaced by one from Belfast in 1921–3. McDermott, a protestant, may have been working in Belfast, as he seems to have been expelled. Thomas McPartlin from Dublin – a leading Irish trade unionist – served on the general council from 1913, until his death in 1923. The general secretary of the ASCJ was Alexander Cameron, a Scot. A member of the ILP, he served on the executive of the labour party (and was an MP in 1929–31). Cameron was a strong supporter of Irish self-government, writing, in his union journal, in June 1920, that 'a freedom-loving people [could] not be stamped out by the iron heel'.[53] The ASCJ defended its expelled members, waging 'a tough fight for bedrock principle'.[54] It went further than the plumbers.

The executive council of the union immediately responded by paying benefit, and granting £500 to the management committee in Belfast for expenses. The ASCJ failed to get the shipyard managements to act, and a meeting of all members, called for 26 August, was banned by the military authorities. But it issued a circular on 21 September, blacking the two shipyards and five engineering firms, plus the builders, McLaughlin and Harvey. This may have been after the expulsion of McDermott, who then became the union's national organizer in Ireland. All joiners were given four days to withdraw from work. The loyalist test, Cameron had written to McRandall, secretary of the management committee, was 'an obnoxious document'. The general secretary wanted to force the employers to act, by pulling his members out. He does not seem to have doubted his own power.

On 25 September the majority of working joiners in Belfast turned their back on the union. It may have been between 2,000 and 3,000 men, but some 500 or 600 who had not been expelled obeyed their executive's instructions. (They joined the 'rotten Prods' in being workers from the majority community who refused loyalism.) The executive council of the ASCJ in Manchester then expelled the working joiners from the union. This must have been further than Cameron would have wanted to go, but, after 25 September, he had to restore his authority. He seems to have been acting on the advice of Waugh and Kennedy. Designed as a response to the industrial expulsions of 21 July and afterwards, it was the joiners' expulsion of some 2,000 to 3,000 members which became the issue for the British trade-union movement! These ex-members set up a provisional committee, showing their desire to remain in the union, while having the blacklist withdrawn. But the provisional committee widened the area of disagreement, repudiating, in October, an executive instruction, from May, forbidding members to have anything to do with munitions for Poland or Ireland.

The management committee in Belfast remained loyal to the national leadership. On 12 November Speirs, as secretary of the Belfast FEST, offered to mediate in the dispute among joiners. Nothing came of this, and the letter to McRandall seems to have been intercepted by someone sympathetic to the unionist party. (The day before, on the third reading of the government of Ireland bill, the labour party had called for a commission of inquiry. When the government refused this, the party sent its own commission to Ireland on 30 November. Cameron was one of the executive members involved, the commission reporting to a special conference on Ireland on 31 December.) When the TUC delegation separately visited Belfast, on the question of the expulsions, it tried unsuccessfully to bring the provisional and management committees together. Its report to the parliamentary committee had little to offer on the industrial expulsions. Much was made of the trade-union expulsions, though it was agreed to hold a conference of trade-union executives to consider how to prevent further intra–working-class hostility. It was held in London on 26 January 1921. The ASCJ had now become the ASW – the amalgamated society of woodworkers. The 80 delegates elected 14 of their number to help Hill, Purcell and Pugh on the sub-committee. The ASW was invited to send a representative to a meeting on 4 February, but the woodworkers refused to go along with the TUC.

Back in Belfast, the provisional committee had been fighting the executive. It even considered taking legal action. On 26 November 1920 the executive council agreed to meet the provisional committee if this was requested. On 31 December McRandall, Waugh, Kennedy and Baxter, for the management committee, met Boyce, McKinney, and Priestley of the provisional committee. It seems that the union was keen to take back its members, without conceding the correctness of its response to the industrial expulsions. But these overtures were rejected, in Belfast, by 1,000 votes to 86. Further negotiations between the two committees took place in February 1921 under the auspices of the local FEST.

The shipbuilding employers' federation, which had paid joiners an extra 12s. (60p) a week from May 1920, proposed to withdraw this increase on 4 December. Three days before, joiners in shipyards throughout the United Kingdom came out on strike. The Belfast joiners did not participate. At a meeting in the Ulster Hall, on 29 November, called by the provisional committee, joiners had voted by 900 to 299 to accept the wage cut. For this, they were berated by the ASW nationally: 'No word in the dictionary', it was argued in the monthly journal of February 1921, '... would adequately define the spirit which activates such men.' This was after the failed negotiations, in Belfast, aided by the FEST. The provisional committee had offered to join the strike, if the expelled members were readmitted to the union without prejudice. It agreed to accept 'the Trade Union card ... [as] the only credential necessary to obtain and follow employment', if this was the wish of a mass meeting called by the federation. The local FEST was not keen on being involved in this way. As for the management committee, it insisted that all records should be handed over, and the expelled members leave themselves open to discipline by the executive council. Retribution was clearly in mind. But, if the provisional committee had been readmitted, the Belfast ASW might have joined the strike, but would not have done anything about the victims of the industrial expulsions. The national ship joiners' strike continued, with support from building joiners and foreign unions. It was called off, after 39 weeks, in August, the workers accepting a gradual wage cut of 12s. (60p). Negotiations had continued on the question of the ASW's relationship to its expelled members, through the good offices of the FEST nationally and the TUC. On 23 July Cameron told the TUC that nothing had been achieved.[55]

It was a year since the industrial expulsions. And the TUC, which had been slow to intervene, and then only to concern itself with the expelled ASW members, was about to drop the issue. The ILP & TUC had done even less. The national executive reported to the August conference that the outcome would have been very different, if other British unions had followed the ASW. William O'Brien suggested that three or four large unions should have withdrawn union cards. Alex Stewart, speaking for the Belfast trades council, considered the task of securing relief of £5,000–8,000 per week to be daunting enough.

William McMullen, attending his first conference, hoped that 'the people – particularly the Protestants in the North of Ireland who proved themselves good Irishmen on previous occasions, and particularly in 1798 – will no longer allow the spirit prevailing at the moment to continue and ... be led away by shibboleths'.[56]

The TUC met the following month in Cardiff. There were only four Belfast delegates there, but Baird and Hanna, on behalf of the EWRC, were given 30 minutes to address the congress. A great deal had happened in Ireland, since the last TUC, but British labour proved it was unable and/or unwilling to do very much about the challenge to trade unionism in Belfast. This showed in the contributions of the expelled workers' leaders. Baird recounted the history of the Belfast working class, though he seemed unaware of unskilled trade unionism before the Workers' Union. He advanced a theory of the ruling class's using religion to divide the working class, the unity demonstrated in 1919 being the reason for the expulsions in 1920. He praised the ASW, but argued that Belfast should have been entirely isolated. '[If the unions had] prevented goods and raw material going to Belfast, and coal and steel, and the other things required for the industries, I fearlessly assert that one fortnight of that action would have settled entirely the trouble ... [and] might have settled what you call the Irish question.'[57]

Though the 1921 TUC carried a resolution from the assurance workers, inspired presumably by D.R. Campbell, calling upon the parliamentary committee to safeguard the interests of trade unionists, it was effectively the end. It was another year before the ASW solved its problem. On 18 September 1922 the provisional committee reached an agreement with the executive, in Carlisle, under the watchful eye of the FEST. In time the provisional committee in Belfast came, through elections, to control the management committee. The industrial expulsions were never reversed, and the status quo was rapidly reinforced by economic recession. The events of 21 July 1920 and after were never fully appreciated, given the return of sectarian rioting to the streets of Belfast.

14

State Formation and the Belfast Working Class, 1920–23

The IRA had brought its war north in 1920, igniting sectarian hostility on an unprecedented scale. The government of Ireland bill remained on course, and Britain connived with the Ulster unionists to establish repressive forces. The bestowal of legitimacy saw informal loyalist attempts at creating security, and Belfast was plunged into unprecedented inter-communal fighting. The IRA proved a poor local defence force, being part of a national guerrilla organization. The Belfast boycott, when finally authorized by Dáil Éireann, showed Sinn Féin ineffectively irredentist. Catholic political division, and disorientation, aided the creation of unionist hegemony. The opening of the northern parliament in June 1921 led to the truce between British and Irish forces, but saw protestant domination of the catholic minority in Belfast. The treaty agreed upon in December granted Ireland dominion status within the empire, and also secured partition. Irish republicans deceived themselves about reunification. The establishment of a British-supported provisional government in Dublin, in January 1922, saw its leader, Michael Collins, negotiate with Sir James Craig in an attempt to alleviate the position of northern catholics. Collins used the northern question to maintain political, but mainly military, unity, and was eventually forced to suppress the IRA dissidents. A bloody civil war, from June 1922 until May 1923, heralded the foundation of the Irish Free State. Across the Irish border, Northern Ireland also settled down, with a concept of continuing British citizenship which remained anti-nationalist and, at heart, anti-catholic.

In 1917–18 Sinn Féin had juxtaposed separatism and the nationalism of the Irish party. This refusal of British rule took the form mainly of abstentionism, but the manifesto for the 1918 general election gave 'Ireland the opportunity of vindicating her honour ... by rallying to the flag of the Irish Republic'.[1] Republicanism had been the monopoly of the IRB, and the reorganization of the Irish Volunteers, after the Easter rising, was an essential aspect of the new nationalism. When their leader, Eamon de Valera, was arrested in May 1918, one of the documents in his possession was a 'Memo on Irish Army Organisation',[2] which was published in 1921. De Valera envisaged the future IRA, in an independent Ireland, as comprising six divisions. The first division, with headquarters in Derry, would be based in western Ulster as well as

Sligo and Leitrim. Eastern Ulster was to be the territory of the second division, the Belfast headquarters of the IRA controlling the counties of Antrim, Down, Armagh, Monaghan and Cavan. The romantic notion of an Irish nation, which excluded, in thought, any internal opposition from northern unionists, was graphically demonstrated in this most practical – because military – plan. There was always a strong element of pretence in revolutionary Irish nationalism, but this amounted to gross self-deception, in the Ulster, particularly the Belfast, of 1920.

The Irish volunteers in catholic Belfast after the rising were insignificant nationally, there being about 500 members of the IRA in the city in 1920. The Belfast RIC had noted in 1918 that 'the [Sinn Féin] movement did not gain as much from [the anti-conscription] campaign here as it did by the great numbers of young men migrating into the City from rural districts, to take up remunerative employment which was plentiful here.'[3] 'The Nationalists of Belfast', it was reported in 1919, had 'not substantially thrown in their lot with Sinn Fein.'[4] The latter party was credited with less than 1,000 members the following year, Devlin's UIL having, on paper, nearly 7,000. This was the reverse of the position in the rest of Ireland. Cathal Brugha, as minister for defence in de Valera's regime, had presented an oath of loyalty in Dáil Éireann in August 1919. The Irish volunteers became the army of the Irish republic, or IRA, but, in refusing to ratify this decision, they retained organizational independence within the republican movement. There was strong local autonomy, the IRA's divisional structure being based on counties to the north, south, east and west. There were five northern divisions by the second half of 1921, but with fewer brigades than the three southern divisions. Belfast was then organized with Antrim and north Down in the 3rd northern division. Each had its own brigade. The commandant of the division was Joseph McKelvey, who became an IRA martyr. McKelvey hailed from Co. Tyrone, and he came to Belfast only when his father, who was in the RIC, was transferred to Springfield Road around the beginning of the war. They lived in Cyprus Street.

It is difficult to associate the self-styled army of the Irish republic, having on paper more than 14 brigades in the north, with what there was of a rural and urban guerrilla campaign. A figure of 4,000 members in the 6 counties, out of 72,000 nationally, was claimed – about 5 per cent. The actual strength at any time was much less. The first coordinated action was that against tax offices on Easter Sunday, 4 April 1920. Ten were attacked in the north, including one in Belfast, in following weeks. The Belfast brigade of the IRA was certainly active in the city, but volunteers from there may have been engaged more often in rural Ulster. A so-called flying column was in Co. Cavan in May 1921, at a time of great difficulty for Belfast catholics. McKelvey became a senior officer in the IRA in Dublin, but only after he lost command of his division. A few isolated police barracks in the province provided easy targets in the late spring of 1920. Derry saw the first RIC officer killed. There was another casualty, in Co. Armagh, in June. But it was Saturday, 25 September, before the Belfast brigade of the IRA claimed its first successful ambush. Smyth had been killed in Cork, and Swanzy may have been the victim, in Lisburn, of an IRA member sent north. The first IRA man killed in Ulster had died, in Co. Tyrone, in June.

Only nine republicans from Belfast were killed, between 1920 and 1923, in six major incidents. Following the killing on 25 September 1920 of the RIC man, Eamonn Trodden, Sean Gaynor and Sean McFadden – acknowledged to be members of the IRA – were victims, early the next day, of reprisals, presumably by elements of the RIC. Trodden had been a barber at 68 Falls Road, and 'was prominent in the I.R.B., Sinn Fein and I.R.A.'.[5] On 30 November Sean O'Carroll, of Gibson Street, was killed at his family home in Ardee. After the killing of two auxiliaries in Donegall Place on 23 April 1921, the brothers Daniel and Patrick Duffin died in reprisals that night at 64 Clonard Gardens. Sean McCartney of Norfolk Street was killed in action in Co. Cavan on 8 May, and Murtagh McAstocker of Ballymacarrett died on 24 September at the hands of loyalists, probably without knowledge of their victim. Finally, Joseph McKelvey himself, as a prisoner of the Dublin government, was shot in reprisal on 8 December 1922, after the death of a member of the Irish parliament. Four men killed in 1920, another four in 1921, and one in 1922 suggest that the Belfast IRA was relatively unimportant.

Sinn Féin in Belfast drew on the Edwardian cultural nationalism of the F.J. Bigger circle, a leading local intellectual after the war being William Forbes Patterson. In so far as the alternative Dáil regime gave any thought to Ulster, it was Patterson who did the thinking in Belfast. Sinn Féin's strategy was intellectually premised on, first, the theory that unionism was a British conspiracy, and, second, the practice of self-determination as totally overriding national minorities. In April 1920, that is, after the general and municipal elections, Patterson paid serious attention to the protestant community. He sent two reports to Dublin, one dealing with the military position in Ulster; another with the political. Both, for a republican, were uncharacteristically realistic. The first report acknowledged the military superiority of the Ulster protestants, and admitted that Sinn Féin would not be able to deal with an expected pogrom. The second advanced an argument about labour threatening unionism, Sinn Féin being in a position to turn the movement in a national direction to help the republic. 'The time is therefore ripe to take hold of the now fluid state of mind in Ulster and to mould it to a national outlook ... [now that] a section of the labour men led by Councillor James Baird were definitely groping their way towards an Irish national position.'[6] Patterson wanted the party to launch a paper, the *Northern Democrat*, based on the democratic programme, this to be sold by volunteers in Ulster and Irish areas in Britain. He mentioned that Eoin MacNeill, P.S. O'Hegarty and Darrell Figgis, of the leadership, supported his idea. Patterson was clearly still a nationalist, seeking to use socialism to weaken unionism. His papers were considered at two successive meetings of the Dáil ministry, as the alternative government was known. De Valera had to circulate the democratic programme among his colleagues, and Ulster policy was left to Eoin MacNeill, the minister for industry. Nothing more was done before the expulsions.

Patterson surfaced in September as the editor of *Red Hand*, a monthly literary and political magazine. This short-lived publication was uninterested in the labour movement. O'Hegarty was reviews editor, drawing on such contributors as MacNeill, Jack White and Bigger. The magazine exhibited all the Manichaeanism of Irish separatism: 'To us, in so far as it is Irish, everything is clear and sweet and good, and in so far as it is English every Irish growth is blighted. We therefore accept and endorse in 1920 the policy of Wolfe Tone in 1798.'[7] O'Hegarty predicted a settlement within a week, if Britain, including the Asquithian liberals, withdrew its support from unionism. White alone espoused a view typical of Connolly, arguing that protestants would not subscribe to an Irish nationality, but that the 'unification and ... liberation of Ireland' would result from the 'enlightenment of the Ulster workers as to their true economic interest'.[8] Such ideas made little impact on catholic Belfast, least of all on members of Sinn Féin and the IRA.

It was Britain which was still responsible for Ireland in 1920, Ulster included. Having sought to fill gaps in the RIC with the Black and Tans and auxiliaries, the repressive policy which did most to guarantee a war, the Lloyd George government considered the north separately. The prewar UVF had proved itself as a military force on the western front. On 23 July – two days after the expulsions – Winston Churchill, at the war office, proposed raising 30,000 men in Ulster, releasing troops for the south and west. The previous month the UESA had offered the king 3,000 men, seemingly to look after Belfast. Churchill's third paramilitary force, in aid of the RIC, would have been nothing more than legitimized sectarianism, even if northern protestants could have been found to serve away from their areas. The government was tempted to solve the problem of unemployed ex-servicemen, by pitching them into the battle for Ireland. Craig was present at this cabinet discussion, and must have known that the UVF was being revived that day. He was less a member of the British government than a likely leader of a future Ulster regime. Macready, in charge of the army in Ireland, expressed his opposition to the use of civilians, but remobilization of the UVF was accepted by the cabinet's Irish committee on 29 July.

The trouble in the shipyards had brought rioting to the streets of Belfast, and the unionist leaders were keen to leave it to the police and army. Such civil disturbances helped segregate the city, residential expulsions being common until the end of August – when a curfew was imposed. Catholic businesses had colonized east Belfast during the war, judging by the 82 spirit-groceries and 44 public houses in the Mountpottinger police sub-district. Many of these came under attack. Such activity damaged the Ulster cause in Britain, and opened up the possibility of property as a whole being the object of attention by the lower orders. This activity stimulated a form of vigilanteeism, ex-servicemen mainly being used to restore discipline in the protestant community. In east Belfast the Revd John Redmond gathered 60 such men at the Albert Bridge Road orange hall, sending them out to patrol the streets. This was probably the UESA. Another 100 responded to newspaper advertisements, and were put under the control of

Redmond's curate, a former army officer, at an empty catholic school. By the time Swanzy's death had stimulated further hostilities, the lord mayor, as chief magistrate, had enrolled Redmond's force as special constables under the acts of 1832 and 1914.

On 30 August 1920 the Old Town Hall announced that the unionist leaders were negotiating with the government, Craig presenting a memorandum to the cabinet on 1 September. The orange order was calling for the government to act, while the vigilance committees wanted the UVF armed. Craig suggested the latter, in the eventuality of troops being withdrawn to deal with strikes in Britain. But he wanted, above all, an Ulster undersecretary, and a special constabulary. His concern was less counter-revolutionary security than the potentially arbitrary use of power by the loyalist masses. 'Unless the Government will take immediate action', Craig argued,

> it may be advisable for [unionist leaders] to see what steps can be taken towards a system of *organised* reprisals against the rebels, mainly in order to defeat them, but partly to restrain their own followers from acts which are regrettable and in large measure ineffective ... [A special constabulary would] ensure that as large a proportion of the population as possible were brought under discipline.[9]

The purpose of a special constabulary was partly political. Craig got his part-time constabulary as part of the RIC in the north, and the UUC declared its support for the government on 3 September. But Macready was still opposed to such a force's not being under military control, and Wilson, as chief of the imperial general staff, hesitated to place security in the hands of loyalist activists. Repression was still the responsibility of London, but the idea of a special constabulary had been conceded even before Northern Ireland was set up.

The force was announced by Dublin Castle in late October, and advertisements appeared in Belfast newspapers on 1 November. It was under the command of Lt.-Col. C.G. Wickham, divisional commissioner of the RIC for Ulster. He appointed six county commandants, including Lt.-Col. W.E. Goodwin for Antrim and Belfast, and Capt. Sir Basil Brooke – a future unionist prime minister – for Fermanagh. The county selection committees harked back to the power of the protestant gentry, and Sir Ernest Clark's view that catholic constables would be recruited to look after their own areas was symptomatic of British assumptions about democracy being left behind in this part of Ireland. Three grades of special constables were planned: *As* – men who joined full-time for a minimum of six months, and were attached to the RIC; *Bs* – unpaid, part-time men who were on call about one night a week; and *Cs* – those on call only for emergencies. By December 1920, 1,500 'A specials' had been recruited for Belfast, a figure that would rise by only 100 by the following October. Most were recently demobilized soldiers, but they were not recruited from a revived UVF through the Old Town Hall. Some were attached to RIC stations, but most, outside Belfast, were organized in highly mobile platoons with their own officers. They were drawn from the protestant community, but their purpose, apart from being a bulwark against a potential IRA threat, was to discipline loyalism. The 'A specials' were the only ones used in catholic areas. The 'B (and C) specials' emerged more slowly. A total of 750 'B specials' were enrolled in Belfast, but they did not appear until February 1921. There were 16,000 in the north by October, and 19,000 by the middle of 1922. The 'B specials' were much more locally based, and given to vigilantism. The RIC considered them to be less temporary policemen than loyalists in uniform.

The setting up of a special constabulary under the RIC in November 1920, was an ill-considered British policy, even more bizarre than the Black and Tans and the auxiliaries. By September 1921 Dublin Castle was allowing the 'B specials' to be deployed in Belfast, albeit under the control of the RIC, the police, in turn, being subject to military command. In mid-1922 a British civil servant, having investigated the position in Ulster, reported critically on the whole idea of special constables. 'The case against the[ir] "usefulness"', he wrote, 'as a means of restoring and placing on a permanent basis law and order has been proved beyond a shadow of a doubt against A and B Specials ... on account of their present organisation and especially their want of discipline and want of coordination with [the police] and military.'10 Northern Ireland did not assume control of the RIC, and its 'specials', until November 1921, months after a government had been established.

Dawson Bates, secretary of the UUC from its foundation, and a party man to his core, was made minister of home affairs in the new provincial regime, and placed in charge of internal security. Without a police force, Bates, in the context of the truce between the IRA and army in the second half of 1921, and with the possibility of political negotiations, reverted to the prewar tactic of a revived UVF. A totak of 21,000 was seemingly mobilized, the target being 150,000, greater than the volunteer force before the war. The UVF was now under the command of the gun-runner Frederick Crawford, and it was the Ulster unionists' insurance against any possibility of a British sell-out to Sinn Féin. In November Wickham, in charge of the RIC in Ulster, tried to absorb the UVF into the 'C specials', on instructions from the Irish office. When the Dublin authorities protested to Lloyd George, the prime minister handed over the responsibility to the Belfast government. Thus, Bates, responsible for home affairs, came to control the RIC and the 'specials'. Craig announced a variation on the Wickham plan, a C-1 special constabulary recruited from the UVF. In April 1922 the Royal Ulster Constabulary (RUC) was formed as the new state's police force. Its basis was less the catholic and protestant RIC in Ulster than the 'A specials'.

The devolution of control over the police had not been a pressing aim of the British government in 1920. The new Northern Ireland executive took office on 3 May 1921, and obtained a democratic but sectarian electoral mandate three weeks later. The regional parliament was opened in the City Hall by George V on 22 June. His majesty was very concerned about 'my Irish people',11 as he put it, but he did more for the south than north. The king was in Belfast to bestow legitimacy on the six counties, as he described the new jurisdiction, but he went on to 'appeal to all Irishmen to pause, to stretch out the hand of forbearance and conciliation, to forgive and forget, and to join in making for the land they love a new era of peace, contentment and goodwill'.[12] This led to the truce between the IRA and the British forces, and eventually the treaty. In Northern Ireland things became worse in the summer of 1921.

The industrial expulsions of the previous July forced Dáil Éireann, and the de Valera ministry, seriously to consider the position in Belfast. In 1912 there had been some spontaneous boycotting of Belfast by catholic Ireland, and this was the policy adopted eventually in 1920 to deal with the problem of Ulster. It quickly proved counter-productive. Sinn Féin erroneously assumed that Belfast was economically dependent upon the rest of the country, and found itself, as the party of the Irish nation, attempting to coerce the citizens of the country's largest industrial city. Here were the makings of civil war.

The expulsions were first discussed in the second session of Dáil Éireann, in a private meeting on 6 August, when Sean MacEntee, who represented South Monaghan, presented a request from Sinn Féin in Belfast for a boycott, as 'the heads of the distributing trades ... [were] the chief promoters of Orange intolerance'. MacEntee, who was also a member of the IRA executive, was the only deputy born in Belfast. He had worked as an electrical engineer in the power station, before moving to Dundalk. MacEntee took an aggressively anti-unionist position, describing the expulsions as 'the first open act of rebellion against the Republic'. Military action, he argued, was not yet possible, but a boycott would be appropriate. Brugha, the minister for defence, argued that this was 'an admission that Belfast was outside Ireland', and Constance Markievicz, as minister for labour, thought it 'a good excuse for partition'. She and Ernest Blythe, who sat for North Monaghan and was notionally director of trade and commerce, suggested a selective embargo, which Brugha supported. Blythe, as a northern protestant nationalist, argued that 'the basis of every trouble in the North was sectarian', and Michael Collins, the minister for finance, interestingly, attacked those trying to 'inflame the passions of members'. The matter was referred to the ministry, and the Dáil went on to vote for the setting up of a commission to inquire into 'English Organised Opposition to [the] Republic', this to include a consideration of 'the Ulster question'. The victimization of 'nationalist' workers was mentioned in the terms of reference, but also 'local self-government' for the province, federalism and a 'liberal scheme of devolution'.[13]

On 19 August, six Sinn Féiners in Belfast, plus a representative of the bishop, wrote to Austin Stack, the minister for justice in de Valera's regime, informing him that, after a public meeting, a committee had been formed to work secretly with Dáil Éireann in running a boycott. Arthur Griffith, as minister for home affairs, thought the Dáil should recognize a boycott committee only if formed by members of the public, but, following a visit from Denis McCullough, he acceded to the Belfast request. On 8 September the ministry, with de Valera still absent in the United States, agreed to a boycott. Michael Staines, a deputy from Dublin, was appointed by Dáil Éireann to run it. This was in spite of a petition from eight eminent nationalists, including Erskine Childers, Alice Stopford Green and George Russell ('AE'), who favoured a blacklist only. They made the point that a boycott would not affect the shipyards, but would increase catholic unemployment. The commission on anti-republican activity had been reconsidered, its terms of reference now being the overcoming of opposition 'amongst certain sections of the Irish people'.[14] Collins, Griffith, Childers, Father O'Flanagan, still vice-president of Sinn Féin, and MacNeill, minister for industry, were appointed, along with five northern republicans, including McCullough, MacEntee and Blythe. Cathal O'Shannon and Thomas Johnson were also made members, though labour did not recognize the Dáil. Little was heard subsequently of this commission on Ulster, Dáil Éireann's minority problem being inadequately recognized.

It took some months for Dáil Éireann to establish its boycott, under Constance Markievicz's substitute as minister for labour, J. MacDonagh. Funds were voted in late January 1921 for eight to ten organizers for a period of four to five months. MacDonagh blamed the delay on Sinn Féin in Belfast, though MacEntee sought to apologize for northern republicans' ignorance of trade with the south. Dáil Éireann formally promoted a blacklist against selected firms, but members of Sinn Féin and the IRA invariably considered that they were engaged in an economic war against Ulster. By March, 184 boycott committees were in existence, MacDonagh having circularized all local authorities. There were 400 by May, the boycott being the ministry of labour's major preoccupation. These committees were largely controlled by the IRA, and the Irish industrial revival campaign was encouraged to provide alternative goods. The Dáil decreed in June that citizens had to inform on those using northern banks. Further funds were voted on 18 August, during the truce, with MacEntee still arguing for an all-out boycott, but action against northern goods effectively ceased in December when the treaty was signed.

It is difficult to assess the impact of the boycott. Sinn Féin in Belfast reported towards the end of 1921 that several catholic businesses had been forced to close, including, ironically, McCullough's. He employed only republicans, 'even members of the Army',[15] to make musical instruments, and cultural nationalists in the rest of Ireland were forced as a result of the boycott to purchase Irish bagpipes from England. Sinn Féin in Belfast asked for the licensing of specific catholic firms by Dáil Éireann, to 'sustain ... our colony ... in this Garrison City'. It would help 'the Irish community ... Irishise Belfast ... by getting a stronger hold upon the commercial life of the city'.[16] Belfast loyalists perceived the catholic minority as disloyal, and the West Belfast unionist club suggested a counter-boycott in September. Some unionist businesses certainly suffered a loss of trade with the south, but this was in a context of recession, where Belfast's industrial exports were affected by global conditions. In mid-1922 a British civil servant visiting Ulster observed of the boycott, still informally in being, that it could 'never ruin Ulster ... only cripple individuals'.[17] 'Belfast never regained the trade it had lost between 1920 and 1922',[18] northern banks probably suffering the most. Southern banks were keen to take over customers, and even branches. In 1921, £5 million of business may have been lost but this, whether temporary or permanent, also hurt the south. An economic historian argued in 1924 that the boycott 'revealed, in some cases, an unsuspected dependence of the South on the North', thread to repair boots in Dublin, for example, being unavailable during the war of independence.[19]

James Baird had advocated an economic boycott of Belfast by the British labour movement, when he addressed the 1921 TUC in September. It is possible he and Hanna had been involved in the original appeal to Dáil Éireann in August 1920. There can be no doubt of their growing political consciousness as socialists, but Baird and Hanna's orientation towards Dublin as leaders of the expelled workers is remarkable. It can only be explained by the absence of help from any other quarter. Sinn Féin seems to have sought to use the two men to discredit Ulster unionists in its pursuit of a separate Ireland. Baird and Hanna were active in Britain raising money, there being a Belfast expelled workers' committee at 2 Union Road in London N7. They were unsuccessful in advocating a British boycott. Dáil Éireann's representative in Britain from 1919 was Art Ó Briain, a position he combined with the presidency of the Irish Self-Determination League (ISDL). During the truce, on 31 October, a Patrick Keating, who seems to have been an Irish businessman with labour party connections, suggested Ó Briain might make indirect use of Baird and Hanna to advance the Sinn Féin cause. Keating was in touch with the expelled workers' leaders, and argued that they would 'prove that in the Nationalist districts the residents protected the property of Protestants while the Protestants in their districts ruthlessly destroyed all the Nationalist property which they could lay hands on'[20]. Keating proposed a series of meetings in 18 labour boroughs in London, but Ó Briain, concerned principally with the state of negotiations between Sinn Féin and the British government, rejected the idea on 3 November.

Baird and Hanna remained in touch with Keating, though Ó Briain was eclipsed, following the signing of the treaty, by C.B. Dutton, Collins's man in London. On 27 January 1922 Baird expressed apparent sympathy for de Valera to Keating: 'We want the English public opinion so educated that when Ireland once again proclaims a republic', he wrote, 'England will recognise it, not crush it in blood.'[21] If this was republicanism, Baird's politics were tempered by realism. He complained the following day about the lack of help they had received from the ISDL, and informed Keating that the expelled workers were winding up their mission in London. Keating pressed Dutton unsuccessfully to use the two Belfast men, but Ó Briain, now the British representative of the republicans, was keen to propagandize about the expulsions. On 23 February Baird, in Dublin, wrote to Keating that a new committee had been formed in Belfast, the Expelled Workers' Committee (EWC). He was going to recommend a resumption of propaganda work, but was distressed at the lack of support in the south, and growing demoralized after 20 months. The following month he wrote to Keating from 5 Rosemary Street in Belfast, McDevitt's address, looking forward to the defeat of the unionists in the next general election in Britain. Ulster would then be more reasonable. Baird continued to work with the new regime in the south, and even had contact with Craig's government, holding all the while to the view that the expelled workers in Belfast would find a solution only in an Irish republic.

The IRA had made little impact on Belfast after the industrial expulsions of July 1920, during what was soon known as 'the tan war'. A curfew was imposed on 30 August, and guaranteed by the RIC and army. The first two members of the RIC were shot on 25 September, after which there was no major incident until April 1921, when the two auxiliaries were killed in central Belfast. Active members of the Belfast brigade may not even have been in the city, the minority being dependent for defence on 'local Catholic defence groups mostly composed of ex-servicemen.'[22] This was the period of Craig's taking office, the first northern parliament election, and the formal appointment of the first Northern Ireland government on 7 June. It also saw the second Dáil come into being. Between 10 and 12 June two members of the RUC and a special constable were killed, five innocent catholics dying in reprisals. The king was in Belfast on 22 June for the state opening of the provincial parliament, and a train carrying troops and horses back to Dublin was attacked by the fourth northern division of the IRA (under Frank Aiken, this was drawn from Co. Armagh, parts of Down and north Louth). Between 9 and 14 July another RUC man was killed and two wounded in Belfast after a raid on Raglan Street. In reprisals, and accompanying rioting, no fewer than 16 catholics died. A police officer recalled later that 'matters remained fairly quiet throughout the whole city until July 1921',[23] because things got much worse in Belfast.

The truce between the IRA and British forces had begun on 11 July. The IRA considered Belfast an integral and ordinary part of the national territory, though the Northern Ireland government was just beginning to function with its parliament. London remained sovereign, under the 1920 act, and the Irish office still controlled the police and army. The IRA sent Eoin O'Duffy, an assistant chief of staff, to Belfast to ensure the truce. He may have been responsible for a larger area, but St Mary's Hall became the publicly recognized headquarters of the IRA's liaison officer, who dealt, presumably, with the military only. While both sides manoeuvred for advantage, the truce held generally as the politicians talked. There was very little talking in Belfast, or even between the new northern government and London. Dan Breen, a legendary guerrilla leader from Co. Tipperary, came north to help Charles Daly train the IRA in Tyrone and Derry. 'We saw a great portion of Ulster in our long walks and occasional pleasure-drives', Breen recalled. 'To make it more exciting, we paid an occasional visit to Belfast.'[24] There was an outbreak of violence in late August, following the meeting of the second Dáil in Dublin on the 16th. It still claimed to be the assembly of all Ireland, though Sean O'Mahony, who had been elected for Sinn Féin in Fermanagh, was the only Northern Ireland MP who sat in Dublin.

(De Valera, Collins, MacNeill, Griffith and Sean Milroy were the other Sinn Féiners in Northern Ireland, but they had also been elected for seats in the 26 counties.)

There was a further outbreak of violence in Belfast in September, but the IRA was a disciplined national organization, substantially under the control of Michael Collins, formally director of organisation, and director of intelligence. On 4 September Collins and O'Duffy spoke at a Sinn Féin meeting in Armagh, the latter addressing the question of whether Northern Ireland would be included in an Irish solution. If Craig refused, O'Duffy said, 'they would have to put on the screw – the boycott. They would have to tighten that screw and, if necessary, they would have to use the lead against them.'[25] He claimed later during the treaty debate that he had silenced Ulster opponents with lead. For his utterance in Armagh, O'Duffy was transferred, by Richard Mulcahy, chief of staff, to Cork. Later, when it seemed that the truce might end, because of a breakdown in the negotiations, the IRA in Dublin issued a statement on 25 September, in response to pleas from northern catholics, saying it was ready to defend the minority in Belfast. Despite a deputation to de Valera's ministers three days later, the IRA – then being reorganized into divisions – was not deployed in Belfast in a defensive capacity. This was in spite of the fact that, on 21 November, Dublin Castle gave up responsibility for the RIC in the north. From 22 November Dawson Bates controlled those members of the RIC who wished to serve the unionist government. Further violence ensued. The British policy, or practice, of reprisals gave way to a political conception of security, in which attacks upon putative Sinn Féiners were considered the best means of defence.

British policy had been based on the 1920 government of Ireland act. Following the king's speech in Belfast in June 1921, Anglo-Irish negotiations took place, resulting in the treaty of that December. Sinn Féin deceived itself about the position in Ulster, the catholic minority there bearing the consequences. This can be seen in the way de Valera and his colleagues handled the question in talks with the British.

The act had come into effect on 3 May 1921. Two days later Sir James Craig, at the behest of Sir Alfred Cope, assistant undersecretary in Dublin Castle, was brought to a secret meeting with de Valera – still a political outlaw – at a house on Howth Road in north Dublin. Craig pontificated on the binding nature of the act of union, while de Valera countered by 'harping on [the] grievances of Ireland for the past 700 years'.[26] Nothing came of the meeting. 'I do not see any hope of ending the struggle with England', de Valera wrote later, 'through a prior agreement with a Unionist minority. At bottom the question is an Irish/English one and the solution must be sought in the larger general play of English interest.'[27] Sinn Féin organized for the elections, but refused to sit in the new parliament set up by Britain, even under the threat of crown-colony government being imposed on 14 July. Craig was prepared to work the partition solution, all the time fearing a British sellout. His strong card was to do nothing, leaving Sinn Féin to continue fighting British rule.

On 25 June, following the king's speech, Lloyd George invited both Irish leaders to London. Craig declined to be involved, but de Valera negotiated, and secured the truce for 11 July. He had recognized the reality of Ulster unionism on 28 June, only to revert on 8 July to his claim to be leader of the Irish nation (after he had done a deal with the willing representatives of southern unionism). As president of the Irish republic, he met the prime minister in London on 14 July. Craig saw Lloyd George two days later, and, on 18 July, rejected five suggestions as to how Ulster could be accommodated with de Valera's unitary state. De Valera privately informed Lloyd George, on 19 July, that he was 'willing to sanction any measure of local autonomy which [Ulster] might desire'.[28] This was the county option of exclusion from prewar days. (As early as 1917, de Valera had said that 'Ulster was entitled to justice',[29] but this coexisted with his references to 'blasting Ulster like a rock from our path'.[30]) He left for Ireland after a fourth meeting on 21 July 1921, having told Lloyd George that 'unless England helped [them] to get a united Ireland, thereby undoing the greatest wrong she had been guilty of in modern times, she was not entitled to and would not get any concessions from [them].'[31] Britain was now offering Ireland dominion status. Craig had no objections as long as it involved the 26 counties only. De Valera was trying to maintain the republic, though it is not clear whether he wanted the substance or the shadow. On 22 July Thomas Jones, the cabinet's assistant secretary, informed Bonar Law of a discussion he had had with two of de Valera's colleagues: 'I found it almost impossible to make any of them admit the reality of the Ulster difficulty. They will have it that we created it and that we continue to exploit it; if we left Irishmen alone they would quickly settle their squabbles. You know the sort of stuff.'[32]

Back in Dublin, de Valera came up with the counter-offer of external association on 27 July. Ireland would be a sovereign state, but associated with the British empire as part of its external relations, the king being head of state only in this respect. The Dáil ministry rejected the British offer formally on 10 August: 'We cannot admit the right of the British Government to mutilate our country', de Valera wrote to Lloyd George, '[but] we do not contemplate the use of force'. The last eight words, 'among the most important he ever wrote concerning the north',[33] were made public later in 1921. Dominion status was debated by Dáil Éireann from 16 August, republican deputies finally endorsing the action of their government ten days later. De Valera said of the north on 22 August:

> They had not the power, and some of them had not the inclination to use force with Ulster. He did not think that policy would be successful. They would be making the same mistake with that section as England had made with Ireland. He would not be responsible for such a policy ... For his part, if the Republic were recognised, he would be in favour of giving each county power to vote itself out of the Republic if it so wished.[34]

Unfortunately for the republicans of 1921 and afterwards, this was said in a secret session, and not reported for many years, but the members of the second Dáil heard what their president said about partition. There then followed a lengthy correspondence between the Irish president and the British prime minister, it being agreed on 30 September that there should be a conference to consider how 'the association of Ireland with the community of nations known as the British Empire may best be reconciled with Irish national aspirations'.[35]

It began in London on 11 October, Griffith leading a team of five from the Dáil ministry, including Collins, with four officials, principally Erskine Childers. They were the representatives of a popular nationalist movement, whose military wing, at the time of the truce, comprised as few as 2,000 members who were not in jail. Lloyd George had five cabinet colleagues, including Churchill and Greenwood, as well as the attorney general. They represented a British empire which had won the war, only to lose the general election in Ireland, though London had been prepared to impose martial law on 14 July. Ulster had no seat at the table, and adopted a pose of studied aloofness. This greatly helped the British side, which implicitly defended the partition settlement. Lloyd George did nothing to challenge constitutional division, and successfully imposed responsibility for unity on the people of Ireland. The Irish delegates convinced, if not themselves, then their supporters, that they were discussing the future of the whole island. The Irish assumed that a separate Ireland would be united, at least in the sense of national sovereignty. (Their concept of local autonomy for Ulster, introduced on 14 October, envisaged the continued existence of a northern parliament with local government powers, so long as sovereignty was transferred from London to Dublin.) The British saw dominion status leading to the creation of an Irish state, which Ulster could join if it wished. Lloyd George and his colleagues were prepared to end the talks on the question of separation, realizing their weakness on Ulster. The Irish were even weaker on this question, but the integrity of the Irish nation was ultimately their stumbling block. It was Lloyd George's concept of a boundary commission which allowed him to prevail from 7 November, it being a more creative negotiating idea than de Valera's external association.

The conference moved forward decisively when Lloyd George, after the seventh plenary session on 24 October, succeeded in separating the Irish delegates. Political negotiating began to take place outside the formal structure of the conference. The key figure was Griffith, formally the leader of the delegation. By 27 October he had begun to believe that, if the Irish accepted less than separation, namely, retention of the crown in an Irish constitution, the British government would pull the rug from under Ulster. Griffith had long abandoned republicanism, and, as the Irish minister for foreign affairs, as he had become in the second Dáil, was hooked on a question of political honour on 5 December. A more Anglophobic Irish revolutionary might not have responded to a British appeal to personal integrity. Lloyd George rarely let this stand in his way, and he used three key external events to work on Griffith. The first was a censure motion in parliament, on 31 October, when the prime minister greatly exaggerated the weakness of his coalition government. Griffith began to see, in the British position, the possibility that a smaller and, he thought, weaker Northern Ireland might collapse in a short time. The second was Lloyd George's meeting with Craig, in the second week of November. It was after this, on the twelfth, that Griffith promised, in a private meeting with Lloyd George, that he would not reject the idea of a boundary commission over the following few days. 'I do not think that I have seen D[avid] so excited about anything before',[36] Frances Stevenson, Lloyd George's secretary and mistress, recorded in her diary. Griffith's undertaking was committed to paper by Thomas Jones on 13 November. The boundary commission pushed the problem into the future, from Britain's point of view, but Griffith saw it as the means to a united Ireland, underestimating Craig's inertial power not to give an inch. A third major event was coming up, on 17 November, namely the conservatives' conference at Liverpool, when, so Lloyd George suggested to Griffith, die-hard unionism would reassert itself. The prime minister had to struggle to keep his administration together, but the Irish question was not about to smash up the government.

The formal British offer of the boundary commission, and the recalling of Griffith's written promise of 12/13 November, ensured, on 5 December, that the Irish delegation did not reject the British draft treaty. Once Griffith had agreed to accept, the rest of the delegation followed, some more reluctantly than others. Neither Griffith nor Collins was, in principle, opposed to dominion status. The former had little faith in open war, and the latter knew how difficult it was to wage a guerrilla campaign. When Lloyd George threatened to resume hostilities, Collins could see the treaty as 'the first real step for Ireland'.[37] Both men must have known that this constitutional gradualism could not be accepted by de Valera, who had said, the day before, that 'freedom is a thing that you cannot cut in two – you are either all free or you are not free.'[38] The British government offered an Irish Free State, independence within an evolving empire. Ireland – as things turned out – would be able to join the League of Nations, but the treaty provided for continuing British control in a number of areas, particularly aspects of defence. Sinn Féin had achieved much more on paper than the constitutional nationalists, though Britain had not advanced much further than the convention report of 1918. The document, as signed by both sides on 6 December 1921, allowed for Dublin rule over the whole island. But Northern Ireland was to be given a month, from enactment at Westminster, to decide whether it wished to join the Irish Free State. If it decided against, there would, of course, be the council of Ireland, plus the boundary commission, more equitably to redraw the border. The Irish delegation too readily believed it would make significant territorial gains, given catholic majorities in Fermanagh and Tyrone, and engaged in wishful thinking when it assumed that a four-county Northern Ireland, as part of the United Kingdom, would collapse for economic reasons. The treaty also made provision for a provisional government, for up to twelve months, to be elected immediately by members of the southern parliament.

Griffith, Collins and Barton, as members of the Dáil ministry, were committed to recommending the treaty. They were joined by William Cosgrave on 8 December, leaving de Valera in a minority with Austin Stack and Cathal Brugha. The president stood by the republic, but Michael Collins, as president of the supreme council of the IRB, quickly secured its support for the treaty. The Dáil began debating its acceptance on 14 December, and continued – with a break for Christmas – until 6 January 1922. Those in favour argued that they had got much more than home rule within the United Kingdom, and that an Irish government could increase its freedom. Nothing was to be gained from a resumption of hostilities. Those against were not deterred by a continuation of the struggle. They argued that the republic, once declared, could not be abrogated. The existence of the king, as head of the Irish Free State, to whom deputies would have to swear an oath, was abhorrent. 'Ulster was not the main issue as can be seen from the negligible time spent in the Dail debate.'[39] Only 9 of the 338 pages of the official report contain any reference to partition. It was the concern of mainly three Co. Monaghan deputies, most particularly Sean MacEntee. When de Valera argued for his alternative draft treaty, to be known as document number two, it simply endorsed the Ulster clauses of the treaty. It embodied his idea of external association on the question of constitutional status. Dáil Éireann voted, on 7 January, to accept the treaty, but by the narrow margin of 64 to 57. The nation was split. Griffith was elected to succeed de Valera on 9 January, the Dáil ministry including Richard Mulcahy as minister for defence. But the pro-treatyites were also working with the British, and, at a meeting of the southern parliament on 14 January, Michael Collins was elected chairman of the provisional government. It took over Dublin Castle two days later.

All these events were watched from Belfast, the Northern Ireland government being determined not to surrender any of its powers. The city's catholics looked, from January 1922, to Collins's provisional government, which was due to work with Winston Churchill at the colonial office for up to twelve months.

On 19 July 1921 de Valera, in a letter to Lloyd George, had referred to 'six counties of Ulster, arbitrarily selected and containing a minority of one-fifth of our people, who oppose the national demand'.[40] 'North-East Ireland'[41] became the Dáil ministry's official designation, when the Irish delegation presented its proposals for Ulster on 14 October. The catholic minority in Northern Ireland was coming into political view, the terms *pogrom* and *ghetto*, taken from Russia before the war, entering the Irish political vocabulary in 1920–2. Lloyd George had said, at the cabinet meeting at Inverness on 7 September 1921, that Britain had 'a very weak case'[42] on Fermanagh and Tyrone. At the first plenary discussion of Ulster, the Irish delegates based their case on the substantial number of catholics in the six counties. Griffith described 'the Ulster question [as] a Belfast city question'[43] on 14 October. This was correct as far as unionism was concerned, but it overlooked the nationalist minority in Belfast. The latter did not come into view at the second plenary discussion three days later. When Lloyd George referred to the catholic minority, in 'non-contiguous areas'[44] of Ulster, Griffith cited the example of north-east Antrim. It was after this that Lloyd George informed Jones that the issue of Tyrone and Fermanagh was 'going to wreck settlement'.[45] The Irish delegation was arguing, implicitly, for a redrawing of the border, rather than questioning its illegitimacy, and Griffith, on 17 October, conceded that there would have to be 'a deal in exchange'.[46] They were talking about the transfer of population. Sinn Féin still found it difficult to acknowledge the existence of a catholic minority in Belfast, and this despite the economic boycott. Nothing in the Irish proposals offered Belfast catholics relief, except good relations between north and south. When the idea of the boundary commission was accepted, this implied that the catholic minority would be at the heart of a four-county protestant state collapsing economically. When the Irish leaders referred to Ulster catholics, they could not even mention Belfast. 'Most of Tyrone, Fermanagh and part of Armagh, Down, etc.',[47] is how Griffith referred to the area joining the south, on 8 November. For Collins, on 5 December, a Dublin government would be gaining catholics in 'Tyrone and Fermanagh, parts of Derry, Armagh and Down'.[48]

The treaty allowed for immediate discussions between Northern Ireland and the provisional government on a range of issues, including 'safeguards for minorities in Northern Ireland'.[49] This was only in the expectation of the Irish Free State's taking over the whole of Ireland, and it was the position of Belfast's catholics that required the intervention of Collins at the beginning of 1922. On 11 January, three days before the provisional government was elected, Craig suggested a meeting with Churchill and Collins, to ascertain the attitude of the new southern regime towards the north. The two Irish leaders met at the colonial office on 21 January, reaching agreement surprisingly quickly under British tutelage. It was decided to do away with the boundary commission, the line of the border to be fixed by the two governments. Collins offered to call off the economic boycott, and Craig promised to get the expelled workers back. This would be as conditions allowed, relief meanwhile being provided for the unemployed. James Baird saw Collins's secretary in Dublin about this time, and, on 24 January, was waiting for a message through Dutton's office in London. The EWC may have had some faith in Craig, but Baird seems to have considered that Collins had sold them out. He was summoned to Dublin on 28 January. The Dáil ministry had suspended the boycott on 24 January, the staff being released three days later. Michael Staines was later formally reappointed director by Dáil Éireann, though Griffith and Collins came under attack from MacEntee for lifting the boycott. Craig showed less willingness to act.

The two heads of government met again in Dublin on 2 February. Craig reported that the boundary commission had been intended, by Lloyd George, to defend Ulster, an intention which came as a surprise to Collins. The prime minister's duplicity was confirmed four days later, when Collins saw Churchill in London. The agreement of 21 January was unravelling. The EWC finally saw Craig on 21 March. The expelled workers' leaders heard that Craig and Collins were jointly approaching the British, but the northern prime minister was taking no responsibility for those who had been victims of loyalism. 'He ... stated that the trouble over the boundary question was responsible for failure to reinstate men in work.'[50] Craig and Collins, with their respective colleagues, signed a pact in London on 30 March, which was countersigned by Churchill and the war minister. 'Peace is today declared',[51] announced the Craig–Collins pact, a phrase inserted by Churchill. There was to be every effort to get the expelled back to work, though the British government put up £500,000 of relief money, one-third of which was for catholics. There was also to be a committee, composed equally of protestants and catholics, the chair to rotate, and with direct access to the government. It was to try to contain sectarian outbursts, and to ask newspapers to be responsible. IRA activity was to cease, and there would be joint catholic/protestant patrols of special constables. A catholic advisory committee was to be responsible for the recruitment of the minority into the police force. After the formation of the Irish Free State, there would be a further joint meeting to consider the border.

Michael Collins was probably sincere in signing, but he had been committed to the eventual collapse of Northern Ireland. More importantly, he was trying to run a provisional government in the south, with political and military opposition from the anti-treatyites. The British government, as architect of the plan, continued to betray a naive optimism about the possibility of democratic accommodation in Ulster. Sir James Craig felt the need to go along with Churchill, but he was in the business of constructing a protestant regime against internal and external threats. The pact of 30 March hardly began to be implemented. Collins and Craig again grew apart, and, by the end of April, Churchill was trying to coax them into cooperation.

Belfast had been disturbed since July 1920, and communal violence, including that by revolutionary, state, and counter-revolutionary forces, lasted until the autumn of 1922. Something under 500 people were killed in the city in that 2-year period, and over 2,000 injured (this figure is for civilians, including the IRA, the number of so-called crown forces killed, until July 1922, being 37 in Belfast and 45 in the rest of the 6 counties). All but 2 or 3 of the victims were identified by religion, a significant indication of the depth of sectarian consciousness. The estimate of 500 can be roughly allocated, between the two communities, and across time. A total of 67 civilians (35 catholics and 32 protestants) died in 1920. This total doubled in 1921, and again in 1922. But the rough numerical balance of the first year gave way to something approaching 2 catholic deaths for each protestant one. Given that catholics were about only a quarter of the city's population, this represents a considerable imbalance in communal attrition. The majority community did much more damage to the minority than the IRA did to the official and unofficial forces of unionism.

Belfast was the centre of Irish violence during the national revolution to a remarkable extent. It accounted for nearly 90 per cent of the deaths in the area of Northern Ireland, and a majority for the country as a whole – 752 people dying in Ireland between early 1919 and the truce in July 1921. This represents a stunning condensation of political hostility, in which Belfast carried the burden of the Anglo-Irish struggle. There were few deaths in the rest of the country from the truce until June 1922, but the violence in Belfast carried on, not being historically synchronized with events in the south. 'For twelve months [from July 1921] the city was in a state of turmoil. Sinn Fein was responsible for an enormous number of murders, bombings, shootings, and incendiary fires.' This was the period when Northern Ireland was established, the RIC being under Dawson Bates from November 1921 until the following April, when the RUC came into being. The IRA undoubtedly killed some catholics, but the new authorities viewed many of the deaths as legitimate repression. 'All during the spring and summer of 1922', the police officer reported, 'murder and outrage continued all over the city. It was particularly bad until June, when Sinn Fein outrages suddenly ceased with a series of incendiary fires.'[52] This was the start of the civil war. While 752 people had died, when Ireland was under direct British control in 1919–21, the erstwhile republicans – treatyites and anti-treatyites – added perhaps as many as 4,000 deaths, civilians and combatants on both sides, to the statistics of political violence in 1922–3. Belfast was spared these hostilities, the once united Sinn Féin in the south bearing responsibility for the fratricidal strife of the Irish civil war.

Figures obscure the succession of incidents of political violence in Belfast, incidents which are a better pointer to historical explanation. In 1920 there were 3 major incidents: 13 killed immediately after the expulsions; 20 killed from 24 August, after Swanzy's death; reprisals after the death of the policeman on 25 September. The year 1921 saw 6 such occurrences: the death of the auxiliaries, and reprisals against the IRA, in April; the killing of an RIC man and special constable, after the opening of the northern parliament, followed by reprisals against 5 catholic civilians; 23 killed at the beginning of the truce, as the result of an RIC raid, in which 1 policeman was killed, followed by reprisals against catholic civilians; 20 killed in late August after the meeting of the second Dáil; further activity in September, when the last IRA man in Belfast was killed; more deaths in November, when the unionists secured control of the police. There were 8 more major incidents in 1922: 14 killed during the Dáil debate on the treaty; 44 killed in February, when the IRA attacked special constables from Northern Ireland in Clones, Co. Monaghan; 61 killed in March, including 3 RIC members and 3 special constables, followed by reprisals against 5 members of the McMahon family, well-known publicans; 36 killings in April, with extensive RIC reprisals, just before the force was disbanded; 66 killed in May, including a unionist MP, followed by the outlawing of the IRA, and the introduction of internment; a continuation of violence into June, exacerbated by the IRA's occupation of the Fermanagh triangle, and the killing of Sir Henry Wilson in London; violence on the occasion of the beginning of the civil war on 28 June; a final resurgence of violence in September. This violence was political by virtue of context, whether republican- or loyalist-inspired.

Following the industrial expulsions, catholics were residentially expelled from east Belfast in the summer of 1920. The significant riot zone thereafter was west Belfast, where the catholic ghetto was surrounded by protestant areas. Catholics were also victimized in the Short Strand enclave in east Belfast, their communal solidarity allowing a degree of retaliation. The shipyard trams reminded the Short Strand of the industrial expulsions every day. In November 1921, and again the following February, bombs were indiscriminately thrown at passing workers. Belfast catholics suffered for Ireland. They did so at the hands of the RIC and RUC, though reprisals, interestingly, occurred when London had control of the police. On other occasions, the dominant protestant community, through support for the police and enlistment into the special constabulary, punished catholics. This included unofficial, or freelance, killing by loyalist activists.

They were grouped in the Ulster Protestant Association (UPA), a loyalist body first noticed in the autumn of 1920. It then had branches in Ormeau, Shankill Road, York Street and Ballymacarrett, but it soon lost its reputation for respectability. 'Before it had been long in existence this organisation', according to District Inspector R.R. Spears of the RUC, 'appears to have attracted to itself a large number of the lowest and least desirable of the Protestant hooligan element.'[53] Spears most probably had been in the RIC, and, in March 1922, was in charge of E district in east Belfast. He was most likely based at Mountpottinger Road, and concerned only with the UPA in his area. Spears acknowledges that police action in Belfast against Sinn Féin was 'greatly hampered by the fact that the rough element on the Protestant side entered thoroughly into the disturbances, met murder with murder and adopted in many respects the tactics of the rebel gunmen.'[54] He was aware of the UPA in his district, but it was not until March 1922, as the RIC was about to be disbanded, that he took action. He reported in February 1923 to Dawson Bates on the nefarious activity of the UPA.

The Ballymacarrett branch of the UPA met every Thursday evening, at 7.30 p.m. until near curfew, in the top room of Hastings's public house, at Scotch Row on the Newtownards Road. 'It was simply a terrorist organisation, having a membership of about 150.' There were about 50 active members, 'the whole aim and object of the club [being] simply the extermination of Catholics by any and every means'.[55] Names and addresses were kept in a book, and there was other documentation. A cryptic language was used to disguise murderous activity – 'dog' for revolver, 'stick' for rifle, 'a bit of work' for a shooting or bombing, 'grant' for the issue of a weapon to a member, 'deputation' for intimidation. Members swore one oath upon joining, and another 'which was practically a vow to murder'. Funds were collected in the Newtownards Road area, and even in the suburbs. There was a high degree of internal discipline, and provision for trial 'by a nominated jury of the members'. Punishment was carried out on a 'flogging horse', with a 'cat-o'-nine-tails'. The UPA had great need of its solicitor, Nathaniel Tughan, to defend its members on serious charges.

Spears referred to at least 17 members of the UPA in his report, though two informants were not identified to Dawson Bates. The district inspector believed that Robert Simpson, who lived with his mother at 124 Beersbridge Road, was chairman of the UPA, 'and its leading desperado and murderer'.[56] He was charged on 27 March 1922 with possessing ammunition, sent to jail, and interned upon his release the following January. The previous day, 26 March, Spears had failed to associate Thomas Pentland, of 14 Clonallon Street, a plumber and 'the principal bully of the club',[57] with an arms find. The flogging horse and cat-o'-nine-tails were attributed to him. Three others, two of them members of the UPA, were acquitted by a jury. (It was for such reasons that Collins agreed to a non-jury court with Craig on 30 March. Catholics might also secure justice without protestant jurors being involved.) Pentland was believed to be vice-chairman. He, and possibly three others, had been charged with killing Murtagh McAstocker, the IRA man, in September 1921. Pentland was acquitted, only to be interned, with three others, on 5 November 1922. Simpson's place had been taken by Robert Craig, of 20 Convention Street, 'a cornerboy who never did any work but who was the brain and organiser of the gang'.[58] He, too, was interned with Pentland. The treasurer was George Richards of Avondale Street. He was arrested on 20 November, and charged with possessing arms.

An informant had enabled Spears to move against the UPA in March. Between June and October, he believed, it was responsible for killing six catholics, for many attacks on catholic civilians and police, and for the attempted murder of a protestant member of the RUC. Four members of the UPA killed Mary Sherlock, the last catholic to die in Belfast, on the Newtownards Road on 5 October. They were deported to Britain, and told to stay away for two years. Another informant then began to reveal three arms dumps to the RUC, as well as the meeting place of members. Hastings's public house was raided on 25 October, Craig being found upstairs chairing a meeting of 38 members. The UPA's papers were seized, but the members were released, after identification, as none were carrying arms. William J. Morrow, of 34 Central Street, fled immediately to Liverpool, and joined the army, only to be arrested, back in Belfast in January 1923, in possession of a revolver. Spears believed he 'was the principal murderer and most active gunman in the club'.[59] Another, Archibald Pollock, of 120 Lord Street, 'the actual murderer of the gang',[60] joined the Royal Ulster Rifles on the Isle of Wight. The club no longer met, but activity continued. Spears and other officers had been sentenced to death by the UPA. There were further arrests and arms seizures, including some in the Oval football ground. This was the end of the association. Spears justified the internment of leading members, for which he required government sanction, on the grounds of the fear of witnesses, and the willingness of members to provide false alibis for those charged. He reassured the minister of home affairs that only 'a few ill-conditioned malcontents and the immediate connections of the men concerned' were opposed to the actions of the RUC. 'The general public regards it with much gratification ... especially ... the shop-keepers and publicans about the Newtownards Rd, who were simply the prey of the club.'[61]

A cause and consequence of such loyalist direct action was the breakdown of the Craig–Collins pact of 30 March 1922.

The industrial expulsions were the root of the Belfast problem. Craig immediately had a meeting with local businessmen, and informed Collins, on 3 April, that he was acting in the spirit of the pact. But the return of workers was dependent upon an economic upturn, which would not come. Collins, for his part, had not been able completely to stop the boycott. He attributed its continuation to a 'certain lawless section',[62] namely the IRA. Collins claimed that it was mainly dispossessed Belfast catholics who were waging economic war. The £500,000 was being disbursed by Andrews's ministry of labour, through a committee which included representatives of the expelled workers. A total of 469 protestants and 277 catholics were employed on 46 relief schemes, which cost £677,000 plus £232,000 in salaries. This was only a minority of the expelled, but the committee seems to have been genuinely broad-based. Collins, no doubt at the behest of Sinn Féin in Belfast, objected to the expelled workers' leaders, claiming they were not 'specifically representative of Belfast Catholicism'.[63] The Belfast Catholic Protection Committee (BCPC), with an office at 82 Smithfield, had emerged in March, 'to unite all sections of Catholic opinion in Belfast'.[64] The protestant socialists were clearly being squeezed out by more traditional community leaders, loyal to Dáil Éireann. Collins and the BCPC wanted all relief work for the minority in the hands of the Irish White Cross (IWC), set up, in late 1920, by the lord mayor of Dublin, under the presidency of Cardinal Logue. The White Cross had contributed to the expelled workers' fund until November 1921, at which point this effectively catholic body took over responsibility for relief.

The second main provision of the pact was the joint catholic–protestant committee, to avert communal hostility. Collins sent a list of six catholic nominees – Joseph Brady, George Martin, T.J. Campbell, H. McAlinden, Dr McNabb and Frank McCardle. It met six times, but Craig refused it funds, and a necessary legal basis. It was 'agreed by all concerned that it accomplished nothing'.[65]

The most immediate issues were the IRA and special constabulary. Eoin O'Duffy supported the treaty to save 'our Catholic people in Ulster',[66] but Collins was unable and/or unwilling, to halt republican activity in the north. The IRA, particularly the majority opposed to the treaty, was the major issue the provisional government had to face. Collins pressured Craig to keep his side of the bargain, but the recruitment of catholics to the 'specials' was rapidly subverted by sectarian violence. When the former demanded an inquiry into the death of some catholics, this delayed his nominations to the catholic advisory committee. The bishop of Down and Connor, plus H. McAlinden, Dr

McNabb, Frank McCardle, Alderman Harkin, D. Dempsey, Fr Murray, Fr Laverty, D. McCloskey, D. McCann, Charles Magee and F. Crummie were eventually appointed to oversee the recruitment of the minority to the RUC. Three meetings were held up until 7 June, but catholics were not inclined to join the 'specials', and two members of the committee were arrested by the RUC.

The fourth main issue was the boundary commission, which Craig had never sought. The prime minister of Northern Ireland sat tight, having momentarily hinted at quitting the United Kingdom. London found it difficult to influence Belfast, though the British government was helping construct the state, including its repressive wing. Churchill chided Craig, on 24 May, with accepting British money and weapons, while defying British policy (under the treaty, Northern Ireland was considered potentially part of the Irish Free State, then in creation). This is the closest the British coalition government came to shaping the north, under pressure from the south. 'Many thanks for your private and confidential scold', Craig began his reply to Churchill. 'The ... commission has been at the root of all evil ... I believe it would have been impossible to have found a more appropriate moment to jettison this preposterous proposal ... with ... our people ... subjected ... [to] constant unparalleled provocation.' Events in the south had made an impact on the north. In trying to avert civil war, Collins had agreed upon a political pact with de Valera the day previously. The treatyites and anti-treatyites agreed to keep the issue out of the 18 June election, the better to prevent other political forces from emerging. Craig exploited this to the full. 'If, as I am so sure, you will be yourself shrewd enough to take full advantage of this escape from an impossible position', he told Churchill, 'it will clear the air for the defence of Ulster against the Republic.'[67]

If Craig showed bad faith on the principal issue of the border, he had exhibited practical inertia on relations with the catholic minority. But Collins, in his way, had been hesitant about securing relief and even reform in the north, given that his erstwhile revolutionary colleagues throughout Ireland were intent upon resuming the national struggle. Churchill had become responsible for Northern Ireland, after the signing of the treaty, as well as for the provisional government. He tried and failed, to handle the dialectic of Irish politics in the first half of 1922. 'Your opponents in the North', he had written to Collins on 29 April, 'hope to see a Republic in the South because it will bring about *inter alia* such a civil war, in which they know they will have the whole force of the British Empire behind them.' He continued: 'Your opponents in the South hope to use antagonism against Ulster as a means of enabling them to snatch the power from the hands of the Provisional Government or else involve them in a series of events so tragic that they will break up under the strain.'[68]

Churchill was asked to report to the cabinet, particularly on the break up of the Craig–Collins pact. On 21 June, Stephen Tallents, a civil servant on loan to the home office, was sent, by the colonial secretary, to investigate the position in Belfast. He had once been private secretary to a lord lieutenant of Ireland. This secret investigation by a lone official was all that remained of an attempt, by Lloyd George, to have a judicial inquiry into the behaviour of Craig's regime, the unionists threatening to resign from his government. The British prime minister was finally taking the question of Belfast catholics seriously. Tallents, who remained in Belfast until 1 July, provided the first significant report on the Northern Ireland government, six months after the treaty. His critique of the regime touched on the particularity of Ulster, as distinct from a British form of rule. 'Ministers', wrote Tallents, 'are too close to their community and cannot treat their supporters as from a distance.' The government was failing to guarantee life and property, but 'otherwise it [had] made good progress especially since it had to establish new machinery in an anarchical country and in face of Southern obstruction.' He concluded that both Irish administrations had started with an 'honest desire' to make the pact of 30 March work, but 'they were estranged by causes which were from the start, or were soon to be found to be, outside their control.' The 'underlying causes' of the trouble in Belfast had not been tackled, being evaded with 'platitudinous sentences'.[69] Tallents described the basic issues as control of the IRA, the question of the border, and catholic refusal to recognize the northern government. This was certainly the case, from the point of view of British policy. But he could, just as easily and somewhat more liberally have added, the behaviour of the special constabulary, the partitioning of Ireland, and the existence of the unionist government. This was the republican view of the Irish question, which led to the outbreak of the civil war on 28 June, when Tallents was still in Belfast.

The civil war in the south represented the failure of Collins's project to construct an Irish state, following the apparent unanimity of de Valera's Dáil Éireann from 1919. Collins had been prepared as a revolutionary to negotiate with the British in September 1921. If de Valera, as president, had an argument for not leading the Irish delegation, Cathal Brugha and Austin Stack, his two supporters in the ministry, did not. The Irish plenipotentiaries did not refer back to their colleagues before signing the treaty on 6 December, but Brugha and Stack shared with de Valera responsibility for instructions at variance with the delegates' status. The split in the Dáil ministry was, at best, the fault equally of majority and minority. Towards the end of the debate in the Dáil, which, after all, comprised only members of Sinn Féin, Collins confided in his sister: 'I have strained every nerve to get support for the Treaty, but I'm hoping now we'll be defeated at the division.'[70] This contradiction in Collins's being was characteristic of the revolutionary statesman in the making. When de Valera opposed the treaty, in alliance with unreconstructed separatists, as being less than external association, he allowed this intellectual distinction to obscure emerging political division among the revolutionary nationalists. De Valera lost the presidency by 60 votes to 58 on 9 January, the narrowest of democratic margins, but the Irish nation, for him and others, had long been superior in their politics. Collins understood this as a leader of the IRB, but he was no less earnest in establishing the provisional government. His erstwhile adversary, the anti-bolshevik Churchill, accepted that Collins continued to love Ireland, but had stopped hating England: 'He had come in contact during the Treaty negotiations with men he liked; with men who played the game according to the agreed rules; he had plighted a new faith to act fairly by them.'[71]

Northern Ireland, in the first six months of 1922, inordinately dominated Collins's time. He relied upon the strategy of political bargaining to provide relief for the catholic minority, but, as president of the IRB, and as a member of the volunteers' general headquarters staff, he also connived at revolutionary militarism. This was always subordinate to the goal of maintaining unity, or rather preventing disunity, in what survived of the political and military wings of Dáil Éireann. Thus the pact with de Valera on 20 May, and the attempt to prevent the republican army from splitting after 7 January. Collins was building his own Irish Free State army, of which he became, in time, commander-in-chief, out of this revolutionary force. It was inevitable, given the logic of military discipline, that he would have to fight his former comrades, if they refused to abandon the republic. He did everything to avoid it for six months, and then, just as determinedly, threw himself into the fray, even to the extent of requesting British military equipment.

Dáil Éireann continued in being after 7 January, with Griffith as president. Collins had immediately proposed a joint Dáil committee, after the vote on the treaty, but he accepted the summoning of the southern parliament for 14 January, and emerged as chairman of the provisional government. This was recognized by Britain. Fearing disunity in Sinn Féin, Collins postponed a general election, which would have affirmed the treaty, and set about having a constitution drafted for the new state, to be as close as possible to the republic. A police force – the civic guards – was formed, and Mulcahy, minister for defence in Dáil Éireann, and Eoin O'Duffy, now chief of staff, sought to get the IRA on the side of the government. The new army uniforms had to be purchased in Britain. Rory O'Connor, director of engineering in the IRA, raised the banner of revolt from 11 January, soon forming an acting military council. His supporters included Liam Lynch of the first southern division. Pro- and anti-treatyite units clashed occasionally as they rushed to take over from British troops, but formal army unity was maintained until 26 March (one division seceded). Collins called his troops the republican army, and Churchill did not hold him responsible for individual IRA actions. On 11 February a party of RIC 'specials', travelling by train from Newtownards to Enniskillen, was intercepted by the local – pro-treaty – IRA at Clones in Co. Monaghan. Four 'specials' were killed, eight wounded and another four detained, their release requiring lengthy negotiations between Belfast, London and Dublin. Following the breakdown of the 21 January agreement with Craig, Collins had expressed anxiety about the IRA in the north. 'If we don't find some way of dealing with it', he wrote to his fiancée, 'all the bravos will get a great chance of distinguishing themselves once more.'[72]

Collins urged Churchill, in early March, to use British troops to maintain order, following attacks upon Belfast catholics. It was on 26 March, at an army convention summoned by O'Connor, that the IRA broke away, not only from Collins, but from Dáil Éireann. Liam Lynch became chief of staff of this new organization on 9 April. Four days later the Four Courts was seized as headquarters for this still-revolutionary IRA, O'Connor being a member of the new army council. These anti-treatyites, or irregulars, went on to occupy other buildings in Dublin, liberate funds from banks, and generally disrupt politics. It was the Four Courts headquarters which resumed the Belfast boycott, under Leo Henderson as director. The IRA saw the problem of the north as the way to resume the national struggle against Britain. Its seizure of the Four Courts coincided with the breakdown of the Craig–Collins pact, Collins's provisional government being at its weakest in late April. At a meeting of the north-eastern advisory committee, set up to keep northern nationalists in touch with Dublin, Collins argued, on 15 May, that the British government should be pressed to hold an inquiry into conditions in the north. At the time of the army split, Collins, perhaps through the IRB, had been in touch with Lynch. He tried to maintain unity in the south, while making promises about military action in the north. This was interrupted by the pact of 30 March. There is evidence that Collins sent officers and arms to the north in April, probably to Donegal, and possibly to Frank Aiken. This can only have strengthened his control. Aiken, with about 300 men in Dundalk, cooperated with Mulcahy in Dublin, as minister for defence, chairing a committee of pro-treaty IRA units. It was known as the Ulster command council. The fourth northern division was involved, at Collins's behest, in Belfast, and 72 IRA men were in the city as a paid guard from February. There were also 100 Cork IRA men in Beggars' Bush barracks in Dublin, the provisional government's military headquarters, waiting to be sent to the north. Collins preferred to keep them under his control in Dublin. In late April arms exchanges took place, British weapons being given to the first southern division, in return for their unmarked guns going north. These may have been for defensive actions, given the breakdown of the pact.

The first northern division in Donegal and the fifth in Monaghan were pro-treaty, and the fourth refused to come under the Four Courts command. This left the second and third northern divisions of the IRA, the latter now under Seamus Woods, which could operate only in predominantly catholic areas. Those most keen to fight were interested in border skirmishes. There had been some action against the RIC in March. In April plans were laid for IRA attacks on the RUC, to be carried out by pro- and anti-treaty units, all with the sanction of Beggars' Bush. Sean Lehane was sent from Cork to take charge of the first and second divisions. The attacks were due to begin on 19 May, but the IRA in Belfast failed to capture police transport two days before. There followed an incendiary campaign against unionist businesses, mainly in Belfast, but this signalled the end of military resistance. The RUC had obtained information in a raid on St Mary's Hall, and, following the killing of a unionist MP on 22 May, internment was introduced. It worked. 'The people who supported us', read an IRA memorandum, 'feel they have been abandoned by Dáil Éireann, for our position today is more unbearable than it was in June 1921 ... Today the people feel that all their suffering has been in vain and cannot see any hope for the future.'[73] 'The purpose of the campaign seems to have been not so much to try to overthrow the northern government as to reinforce Collins's attempts to pressure the British into curbing the excesses of the Northern regime.'[74] Woods was opposed to an aggressive policy in Belfast, given the vulnerability of the minority to the RUC and 'specials', but the behaviour of the anti-treaty units in the second and third divisions often caused problems for the attempt by Beggars' Bush to control IRA responses to the actions of the northern government. Dublin called off all action in the north on 3 June, no official or republican forces being allowed to travel there.

Collins had begun to regain control in the south on 4 May, when a truce was agreed, and talks were opened between government and republican forces on reuniting the army. There were already differences between Lynch and O'Connor, which the provisional government hoped to exploit. On 19 May Griffith announced an election the following month for the third Dáil, in order to strengthen the treaty. The following day the pact between Collins and de Valera was revealed, Griffith never again referring to the former by his first name. He saw the Fenian inspiration in Collins's attempt to secure the existing political leadership on the eve of an election, regardless of division over the treaty. De Valera shared the hope that a national coalition government, dominated by the old Sinn Féin, would emerge in June. Pro- and anti-treaty factions were to put forward candidates in the proportion of the 7 January vote. Sinn Féin endorsed the pact on 23 May. The coalition would build on the treaty, through Dáil Éireann, but not overturn the republic, the object being to avert civil war. This postponement of political division over the treaty did not affect the provisional government, which summoned a provisional parliament under the free state act on 27 May to meet after the election. Churchill was not amused, but continued to work with Griffith and Collins, despite their seeming concession to de Valera. The colonial secretary argued that republicans could not be members of the government under the treaty without adhering to the agreement between Irish and British leaders.

As Sinn Féin tried to rig the general election, to be held on 16 June, the spirit of the pact was absorbed by the IRA. The formation of a coalition army council, loyal to the government, was envisaged after the election. Mulcahy and O'Connor 'actually discussed co-ordinated military action against N.E. Ulster',[75] agreed upon a commander, and arranged for the further exchange of arms. This may have been before 3 June. Mulcahy was acting in accord with Collins, and the talks had the effect, unintended at the time, of lulling the Four Courts headquarters into complacency about a government attack on the republicans. Another border incident had occurred, in the Belleek/Pettigoe triangle in Co. Fermanagh, an area which might have belonged more naturally to the south. When 'specials' occupied it on 27 May, the Donegal IRA acted on its counter-claim. Craig secured the use of British troops, who quickly drove out Collins's men, the old fort at Belleek in Co. Donegal being shelled inadvertently. An earlier tripartite border commission with its own blue and-white-flag had collapsed, but Collins agreed with Craig upon a neutral zone to be patrolled by unarmed police on either side. Griffith went to London on 6 June, with the draft constitution of the Irish Free State, only to have Lloyd George reinsert the king as head of state into the document. Collins saw Churchill on 13 June, and it was not until polling day that the altered constitution was published. The Four Courts garrison split on 14 June over the terms for army reunification. Collins was due to speak that night in Cork, but, before the meeting, the IRA refused him admission to the republican plot in the city cemetery. In later 'mak[ing] a straight appeal to the citizens of Cork to vote for the candidates they think best',[76] he was considered to be repudiating the pact with de Valera. There was no way the new constitution could be accepted by the anti-treatyites, and it was on 14 June that Collins stopped trying to prevent political and military division.

The results of the 16 June election were not declared for eight days. It was then found that the pro-treatyites had secured 58 seats, to the anti-treatyites' 36. Most of the other 34 members of the provisional parliament, due to meet on 1 July, were anti-republican. The 17 labour representatives were certainly not followers of de Valera, but, like him, they would have welcomed a coalition government. The 14 June split between O'Connor and Lynch was decisive, Collins seeing the possibility of the anti-government forces becoming preoccupied with their own falling out. On 18 June O'Connor lost a vote in the Four Courts on a motion that the IRA should restart the war with Britain, but he expelled Lynch and had McKelvey made chief of staff. There was no need for a coalition government. On 22 June, two days before the results were known, Sir Henry Wilson was killed in London. Two Irishmen – later acknowledged to be members of the IRA – were quickly arrested, and later hanged. Wilson had left the war office to become an Ulster unionist MP at Westminster, and advised Craig in March on internal security. Churchill, certainly in retrospect, thought the two assassins had acted entirely on their own. One was a supporter of Collins, and the latter tried to help them after their arrest, while condemning assassination. O'Connor tried to arrange their escape, and, though he was still in charge of the British brigade of the IRA, he did not claim responsibility. Wilson had been an IRA target undoubtedly, but the date of his death exonerates Collins and probably O'Connor.

Belfast intruded once again in the play of events in the south. On Sunday, 25 June, three days after the killing of Wilson, the Four Courts, now under Kelvey, decided to send an IRA unit, under Peadar O'Donnell, to the north. This was supposedly to defend catholics, but O'Connor believed, despite the breaking of the Collins–de Valera pact, that he would be cooperating with Mulcahy on an invasion of the north. When Lloyd George had demanded, on 23 June, action against the Four Courts, a reply had been sent on Collins's behalf: 'The Government was satisfied that these forces contained within themselves elements of disruption which, given time, would accomplish their complete disintegration, and relieve the Government of the necessity of employing methods of suppression which would have perhaps evoked a certain amount of misplaced sympathy for them.'[77] On Monday, 26 June, probably as part of the republican effort to save the provisional government by provoking the British, Leo Henderson in Dublin seized 16 new cars from Belfast. The boycott was seen as part of 'the war against N.E. Ulster'.[78] Henderson was arrested in the act by Collins's men. The Four Courts was preparing for the northern invasion, but retaliated by kidnapping J.J. O'Connell, the deputy chief of staff of the government forces. Sean MacBride was one of the IRA men involved. This act on 26 June provoked the provisional government to act, Collins having been prepared to fight the IRA from 14 June. He knew the constitution of the Irish Free State would not be accepted on 1 July, when the third Dáil/provisional parliament met. Britain had been threatening to act, but General Macready, who still had troops in parts of the country pending complete evacuation, was against attacking the Four Courts. Collins believed O'Connor did not have the support of Lynch and others. Thus, he requested the loan of some pieces of artillery from the British troops, though he was denied further shells for a time. Early on Wednesday, 28 June, Mulcahy's troops began shelling the Four Courts. Unknown to them, O'Connor had, the previous evening, succeeded in reuniting the anti-government IRA, Lynch being restored as chief of staff. As pro-treatyites turned the Anglo-Irish struggle into a civil war, the catholic minority in Belfast was left to live under a protestant regime.

Conclusion

15

Conclusion

The people of Ireland have lived with the constitutional settlement imposed by Britain in 1920–2. Griffith died suddenly early in the civil war, to be followed, within days, by Collins, the victim of his erstwhile republican comrades. The Irish Free State emerged as a parliamentary democracy in 1923 under lesser men, the once-dominant Sinn Féin spawning the major parties of its political system. De Valera came to power in 1932, ironically proving Collins correct on the question of political evolution with his 1937 constitution for Éire (or Ireland). This clerically inspired document included an irredentist claim to the north in articles 2 and 3, which survive after more than half a century. Ireland proved its independence by remaining neutral in the Second World War, a republic being finally declared, by the civil war victors, in 1949. Partition now became a grievance for Irish nationalists, temporarily uniting the major parties – Fine Gael and Fianna Fáil. But 1958 saw the abandonment of economic nationalism, and the beginning of the end of the so-called Irish tradition in intellectual and political life as exemplified by de Valera. There were suggestions of political liberalization in the 1960s, and politicians discussed having merely an aspiration to Irish unity in the constitution. In 1973 the Republic of Ireland enthusiastically joined the European community, as one of the more isolated western countries of the continent.

Northern Ireland also joined, albeit reluctantly, as part of the United Kingdom.

The so-called province of Ulster had stabilized, with strong unionist government under Craig from 1923. Republicanism was an irritant, and nationalists abandoned abstentionism hesitantly. Catholics came to articulate their status as an oppressed minority, while participating in the protestant-dominated parliament at Stormont. Britain, though the sovereign power, was content to leave things to the unionists, continuing to provide a financial subvention. Ulster participated in the Second World War, and its devolved government had the benefits of the welfare state to disburse to its citizens. The IRA ran a desultory campaign in Northern Ireland in 1956–62, and few would have predicted the emergence of the provisionals in 1970. But the rhetoric of modernization in the 1960s, under O'Neill, the fourth unionist prime minister, encouraged catholics to demand civil rights. In 1968 the orange state came under an internal challenge to reform, the unionists' inability to democratize their regime leading to the introduction of British troops in 1969. Stormont

315

was closed down eventually in 1972, and Northern Ireland has been under direct rule from London ever since. Reforms had been imposed, but it has proved impossible to construct a stable inter-communal devolved administration. In the absence of structural reform, the IRA and Sinn Féin have maintained a capacity to destabilize the north.

The partition settlement of the early 1920s has been under challenge for the last two decades, but only in Northern Ireland. The problem with this constitutional outcome of the home rule era was not continued British involvement in Ireland, as nationalists would have it, but the concession to Ulster unionism of a provincial regime, with direct responsibility for a nationalist minority. This is not difficult to appreciate, with hindsight. The experience of the catholic masses over 50 years, particularly in Belfast, has inspired the provisional IRA. This guerrilla organization goes on largely because it does not want to go back to the position before 1968. The Irish question has had little to do with imperialism, as republicans claim. The minority problem of Ulster protestants in Ireland was solved, in 1920, by a partition solution which created a second minority problem of catholics in Northern Ireland. It is no answer to end the oppression of one minority by oppressing another. Contemporary republicans can trace their lineage back to 1916, still the source of political legitimacy in the Republic of Ireland (the Irish state and the IRA sharing the green, white and orange tricolour flag, while supposedly sworn enemies). 'We were probably the most conservative-minded revolutionaries that ever put through a successful revolution',[1] said one of the Irish state's first ministers. The success was the Irish Free State, later Éire and then the Republic of Ireland. The limited social goals of the Irish revolution are not in historical doubt, but he might have admitted to its political failure to unite the people of Ireland, the aim of all nationalists, whether constitutional or revolutionary. It was Sinn Féin's contribution to bequeath the idea of unfinished business to following generations. Dublin succeeded in scaring the unionists of the north, without, in any serious way, coming to the aid of the catholic minority. Both regimes came, in time, to find the border very functional to their political hegemonies – the north by stressing security, the south by harping on the grievance of partition.

This latest phase of the republicans' struggle for a united Ireland is going nowhere, and has failed to make any significant impact on the Republic. But Northern Ireland has had the status of a world trouble spot in the 1970s and 1980s, as familiar, and incomprehensible, as real proxy conflicts on the frontline of the cold war between imperialism and communism. It has contributed to the electronic media's diet of international strife, and the integrity of the quarrel in Northern Ireland, as Churchill once put it, can now be seen more clearly with peace breaking out across the globe. The historical importance of the Belfast working class, albeit in a state of sectarian polarization between catholics and protestants, is now evident. It was a communal strike in 1974, initiated by the Ulster Workers' Council (UWC), a loyalist and not a labour body, which brought down the power-sharing executive, by which catholics participated in government for a few brief months.

The anti-imperialist school of Irish socialism, inspired by the trinity of McCann, Farrell and Bell in the 1970s, has done much to propagate an apparently radical view of Irish history during the current troubles. This has drawn on a sympathy for the catholic masses, and these three writers' work has fed back into contemporary republicanism. For socialists, the varying dismissal by these writers of the protestant working class is stunning, though this is only an effect of their dependence upon nationalism. Socialist apologies for sectarianism have made the so-called struggle of the Irish people more acceptable to the left abroad in the 1980s. British radicals love to hate British reactionaries. This past decade saw Marxist conceptions of proletarian socialism, based on universalist notions, overwhelmed within the labour party. Revolutionary socialism outside the party was undermined by particularist concerns with putative, but usually unspecified, social movements. Irish republicanism is sometimes listed as one of the contemporary sites of progress under the British state, though radical metropolitan intellectuals still remain confused about Ireland. The leadership of British labour has welcomed the demise of traditional socialism as outdated, and, practising electoral politics as determined by the advertising industry, can live with any number of new social movements in suitably anodyne forms. The pro-IRA, withdrawal position among labour party members has been sanitized to unity by consent, by the leadership, this political absurdity amounting to little more than a future labour government promoting good Anglo-Irish relations.

A set of assertions has been generated by socialist republicanism in Ireland which does injury to history and makes no constructive political contribution. The first such assertion is the characterization of British interests in Ireland as imperialist, a characterization which serves to legitimize all anti-British sentiment. If this were true in the 1880s to 1920s, it is no longer so. Britain agreed to devolve power to Ireland, as home rule within the United Kingdom, and then as dominion status in the empire, remaining ties being severed later. Partition was a British compromise stemming from division in Ireland, and the establishment of Northern Ireland, paradoxically, a way of discharging responsibility. Britain has no decisive economic, social, political or strategic interests in Ulster. It stays because it cannot get out; if London shed responsibility for Northern Ireland, at an unlikely point in the future, the British state would have to return as the sovereign authority recognized by virtually all states, if only to avert further chaos. The second assertion is the teleological notion of an Irish nation, whereby the failure of this subject to appear fully in history is attributed to perfidious Albion. An Irish nation remains to be created, on the edge of the state structure of Europe, though not on a basis of national sovereignty. In so far as the notion was popularized in the nineteenth century, the identification of nationalism with catholicism meant the cultural exclusion of all protestants from an Irish nationality. The political implications were suppression or expulsion, though nationalists usually halted before reaching this intellectual point. The third assertion is a zero-sum conception of democracy, whereby the victory

of Irish nationalism is measured in terms of the vanquishing of unionism, and not by the degree of popular sovereignty resulting from cooperation between catholic and protestant rural and urban workers. A
fourth assertion is the denial of the autonomy of unionism with respect
to the British ruling class, and a conception of this inter-class alliance as
based upon elite manipulation or ideological mystification. Ulster protestants formed a community, based on shared economic and political
interests. The proof of this is catholic Ireland's failure to integrate its
claimed national minority.

A fifth, Marxist-sounding argument of the 1970s, distinct from the
above, is that sectarianism in Ulster is based on economic rivalry,
popular loyalist opposition to the blandishments of Irish nationalism
being motivated by a desire to maintain the margin of structural inequality among lower social classes. This begs the question of why the
most disadvantaged protestants were often the most vicious, while the
so-called labour aristocracy was the bearer of more progressive social
and political ideas. A sixth position is shared with revolutionary elements of the British left, namely, the dismissal of labourism as circumscribed by limited political horizons and a restricted social base. This
can be condescending in historical writing, since it underestimates the
work which went into building the labour movement, and the extent
to which the idea of working-class representation challenged the
restricted nature of British politics. A seventh proposition is universal,
namely that there existed a correct socialist theory realized in a number
of individuals or organizations who would have made things different if
only they had not been obstructed or ignored. Such Leninist certainty
collapsed historically in 1989, and this point applies especially to forms
of Trotskyism which portray the Soviet Union as a failure of Stalin the
man. An eighth argument is that revolutionary commitment is the only
viable one in advanced bourgeois democracies. This has seen Irish
socialists leave the fighting to republicans, without adequately explaining their abstention from a revolution they insist is historically necessary. Some have followed the logic of their convictions and joined the
republicans.

A theory embracing these general arguments is implicit in writing on
the Belfast working class, in so far as the topic has been addressed
directly by left nationalists.

A great deal of emphasis has been placed on Larkin and Connolly as
historical heroes, this being a measure of the weakness of the working-
class movement in Irish history. It was also highly uneven. The ITGWU
could have been excluded from this account of Belfast as marginal, but
the same cannot be argued of the rest of Ireland before 1923. Larkin's
involvement in 1907 was considered in Chapter 5; Connolly's contribution in 1910–14, in Chapter 7. Larkin ignited a social uprising of
unskilled protestants in the transport industry, which anticipated syndicalism, and retreated when it stimulated nationalist rioting against
British forces. He did not unite the working class, a claim first made by
W.P. Ryan in *The Irish Labour Movement* (1919),[2] repeated by Clarkson,
and mythologized in Larkinism. The lesson of 1907 is that protestant

workers were not immune to class struggle, and that syndicalism could threaten to spill over into sectarianism. James Connolly ventured to Belfast three years later, because of the strength of its labour movement, his goal being an Irish labour party, under informal socialist leadership, in a Dublin parliament. In very different circumstances from those of Larkin, he became perforce a syndicalist leader of a section of the catholic working class. Connolly had no more luck at uniting workers across the sectarian divide, a fact which is hardly surprising given his slippages into nationalism during a period of unionist reaction. His involvement with the ITGWU from 1911 in Belfast was exaggerated by O'Shannon in 1919, by which time his historical reputation overshadowed the transition in his politics from socialism to nationalism.

It also obscured William Walker, whose much longer career in Belfast from the 1890s was considered in Chapter 4. Walker remains a major Irish labour figure, by virtue of his parliamentary contests of 1905–7. He was a social democrat, as the term was understood after 1917, but Connolly had moved into the labourist mainstream, and Larkin's relationship with communism in the 1920s and 1930s was not unproblematic. Walker's sectarian utterance in 1905 indicated that he belonged to the Belfast protestant community, and his opposition to Irish nationalism was a product of unionism reinforced by socialism. His legacy was labourism, Walker's successors crossing the sectarian divide, and taking a democratic position on the national question. They did a great deal better than Walker, because of altered circumstances, though the left nationalist notion of labour unionism simply dismisses the progressive face of the protestant working class. Walker dropped out of politics, while Connolly became a revolutionary nationalist, and Larkin fought further struggles in the United States. The father of labourism in Belfast was easily written out of Irish history by W.P. Ryan in 1919 for having opposed Connolly, and he does not figure in O'Shannon's official historiography.

Constitutional nationalism had been dominant in Ireland in the Edwardian years, the catholic ghetto in Belfast being under the sway of Joe Devlin from 1906 on (Chapter 2). He believed in the liberal alliance, became the organization man behind the Irish party, and was on the progressive wing of British politics. His appeal to protestants in 1906 was tactical, while he strategically tapped catholicism in Belfast, and went on to promote Hibernianism throughout Ireland. Devlin recognized the role of women in the catholic working class, his labourism being paternalistic, and on a par with the liberals who tried to prevent the working class breaking away from their party.

Organized unionism also had problems with the masses in the 1900s, but Thomas Sloan's Independent Orange Order was a right-wing populist breakaway concerned about the leadership's being too soft on catholic Ireland (Chapter 3). Lindsay Crawford's temporary involvement represented a reviving Ulster liberalism in uneasy alliance with the orange democracy. Alex Boyd was associated with Larkin in 1907, but his brand of labourism did not transcend protestantism. Independent orangeism had no appeal to the mainstream labour movement, and more protestant workers remained loyal to the orange order. Nor was the predominantly protestant labour movement integral to the unionist mobilizations against home rule in the early 1910s (Chapter 6). The Irish party is open to criticism for wanting an all-Ireland parliament on the basis of a majority, but it did come to concede the principle of exclusion. Ulster unionism is open to greater criticism for resisting home rule entirely, and its acceptance of partition was more hesitant. The resistance to the government's bill was a serious reactionary challenge in British politics, Carson's political deterrence by demonstration and military organization ultimately implying a provisional government in Ulster against Dublin rule. Asquith, with Lloyd George and Churchill, had been prepared to concede to parliamentary unionism, and the outbreak of the European war suspended consideration of the Irish question.

Belfast lost unionist and nationalist volunteers to the ranks, while the city's industries provided increased employment for protestants and catholics (Chapter 8). War work had a profound impact on the social structure of Belfast, an impact which was evident in the immediate postwar years. The war, against the background of the Ulster mobilizations, increased nationalist resistance in catholic Ireland, though the involvement of southern workers in British militarism should not be underestimated. Prewar volunteering had inspired some nationalists, and the republican underground immediately saw England's difficulty to be Ireland's opportunity, with or without German military help. The constitutional nationalists, having failed to solve the national question, lost authority during the war, but it took some time for the spirit of the 1916 rising to become the source of legitimacy for mass republicanism. James Connolly's involvement came as a surprise to most socialists, despite his theorization of socialist republicanism, and socialism in Ireland was given a strong nationalist identity. He did nothing to strengthen the position of the working class in Irish politics, and acted with profound experience of division between catholics and protestants in Belfast. The city contributed a number of important leaders to the second Sinn Féin in Dublin, but separatism was a minority current in the catholic ghetto (Chapter 9). Romanticism was a petty-bourgeois alternative to working-class utilitarianism. This was evident in the 1918 election, when de Valera, despite his national reputation as a 1916 leader, failed to oust Joe Devlin, who saw his nationalist colleagues at Westminster virtually wiped out.

Unionism remained dominant in Belfast. Carson believed the British government would not deal with Sinn Féin, and certainly not over Ulster, but fear of bolshevism led him to promote social toryism in the form of the UULA (Chapter 10). Labour unionism was working-class conservatism, an equation which neither deterred the middle class, nor impressed labour sympathizers among the protestant masses. The unionist bourgeoisie could not secure social peace by raising a scare about the union, and it was in the 1918 election that the Belfast labour party secured over a fifth of the vote (easily a quarter of the protestant working class). The engineering strike of early 1919 was the greatest in

Irish history, proof of the Belfast working class's industrial assertiveness, but also of its political suspicion of revolutionary socialism (Chapter 11). The trade unions in shipbuilding and engineering were not successful, but the labour movement was not demoralized. While Dáil Éireann was fighting Britain in the south, it secured an important twelve seats on the corporation in Belfast in 1920 (Chapter 12). This labourist expression was, among voters, compatible with forms of loyalism (and nationalism in the case of catholics), but social reform was the important issue for the leadership of the labour movement and activists. Belfast labour subscribed, in the main, to Wilsonian democracy, and, while it never became nationalist or separatist, it was certainly not unionist, the idea of Carson running Ulster being rejected on social and political grounds. These predominantly protestant men (and some women) would have accepted a negotiated solution such as dominion home rule, rejecting the partition which had been inevitable since before the war.

It was the IRA war's coming north which reversed the balance in the protestant working class between labourism and loyalism. The 1920 expulsions saw elements of the workforce anticipate a unionist state by expelling catholics and 'rotten Prods' (Chapter 13). Trade-union resistance was feeble, and the expelled workers' leaders came to look to Dublin for assistance. Sinn Féin had no strategy other than the Belfast boycott, which threatened to become sectarian. But it was militant loyalism which wiped out labour in the first northern parliament election in May 1921, violence in Belfast in the following twelve months being associated with state formation (Chapter 14). The thin strand of realism in Sinn Féin's thinking about the north had been subordinate to its overall concept of the Anglo-Irish struggle. Though Collins believed Northern Ireland would collapse, he worked as chairman of the provisional government in 1922 to alleviate the position of catholics. This northern policy was integral to his attempt to avoid division in the south, and then his desire to create the Irish Free State by defeating the republicans. The civil war brought to an end the constitutional restructuring of Ireland in 1923, leaving a catholic state in the south and a protestant one in the north.

Despite Connolly's prediction in 1914 of a carnival of reaction, secular working-class politics was not totally destroyed in Ireland by the constitutional settlement of 1920–2. Labourism developed unevenly throughout the country, and its roots in Belfast and Dublin were not entirely destroyed in the violent resolution of the nationalist–unionist contradiction. It could be argued that socialism fared better in the north against unionism, than in the south, where nationalism remained a radical force. But partition saw political development in Ireland follow a different pattern from that in Britain. This is in spite of the fact that labour figures in both parts of the country looked to the Ramsay MacDonald governments of the 1920s.

The ILP & TUC finally entered politics in the south in 1922, having sat out the national struggle, winning 17 seats in the provisional parliament. Tom Johnson became parliamentary leader, and labour, in the absence of the anti-treatyites, became the official opposition in Dáil Éireann in the first years of the Free State. Irish politics in this respect seemed like those in Britain, with the pro-treatyites running a right-wing government while labour occupied the opposition benches. Labour won 22 seats out of 153 in the first 1927 election, and Johnson even came within 1 vote of the premiership, given tactical support by other parties. The entry of the anti-treatyites into the Dáil as Fianna Fáil after a second election, and then into office in 1932, saw labour drop progressively to 7 seats. This coincided with the rout of the labour party in Britain, when MacDonald formed the national government during the 1931 financial crisis. The ILP & TUC had finally split into the ITUC and the Irish labour party, but socialism meant little in the face of de Valera's strategy of nation-building. The senior survivor from 1916 had 16 unbroken years in office until 1948, during which he proved decisively that the Irish people had their own state. Labour wilted even further under catholicism, when the aim of a workers' republic was removed from the constitution in 1940. When Larkin and his son were elected to the Dáil, in neutral Éire in 1943, William O'Brien, still general secretary of the ITGWU, had five of the union's deputies break away. They formed the national labour party in 1944. Connollyism now meant anti-communism, and O'Brien went on to form the breakaway confederation of Irish unions, in opposition to British unions in Ireland. Britain helped win the war, and Attlee went on to reconstruct the country with a majority government, until labour ran out of steam by 1951.

It was 1950 before the ITGWU returned to the labour party in Ireland, and 1959 before the – united – Irish congress of trade unions emerged. Labour had participated in the Fine Gael-led coalitions of 1948–51 and 1954–7, after which Fianna Fáil had a second unbroken 16 years in government until 1973. Labour achieved an all-time high of 22 seats (out of 144) in 1965, and, four years later, 17 per cent of the vote, its maximum ever. This was the year Conor Cruise O'Brien and other intellectuals became labour deputies in Dáil Éireann, the year 1969 coming to acquire a mythical status for the Irish left. The 1960s had seen the two governments of Harold Wilson in Britain, and there were three more labour administrations in the 1970s. Coalitionism remained the Irish labour party's destiny, in the third, fourth and fifth inter-party governments of 1973–7, 1981–2 and 1982–7, which were dominated by Fine Gael, the last-named being the only one to run a full term. The 1989 election result for labour, the workers' party and three independents gave the left a historic 25 seats, but not quite labour's share of the vote in 1969. Fianna Fáil, for the first time, had to form a coalition to stay in office, this being perhaps a better harbinger of a realignment in Irish politics.

Labour in the north did worse in the same period, but it was contending with a divided society. From 1921 the unionists were the sole party of government, ministers treading a varying line between British standards of administration and popular loyalist concepts of the state. The Northern Ireland labour party (NILP), as it later became, emerged in 1923, with Harry Midgley as its first secretary. He fought West Belfast unsuccessfully, in the 1923 and 1924 Westminster elections, securing working-class supporters, but also a new catholic protest vote. The NILP's interest in the minority in Belfast seemed almost opportunist, but labour had crossed the sectarian divide after the war. With Devlinite nationalism hesitant about practising minority politics, and republicanism even more disorientated, labour became a serious political option for the catholic masses. Midgley's survival, and that of his protestant and catholic ILP comrades, was remarkable. The – largely Belfast – socialists were still anti-partitionist in the main, no one giving any credibility to the northern regime. But MacDonald's 1924 labour government in Britain, to say nothing of Johnson's opposition in Dáil Éireann, led them to articulate the idea of a labour opposition in Ulster. This flowed from their labourism rather than any residual unionism. The unionists were seen increasingly as just tories, and less in the context of Irish politics. The NILP won three seats in the 1925 northern parliament, Jack Beattie coming first in East Belfast, Sam Kyle second in North Belfast, and William McMullen fourth in West Belfast. All were protestants. Beattie had been one of the few active supporters of J.H. Bennett in 1918, and was the only NILP MP to survive the abolition of proportional representation. The 1929 northern parliament election was held under the British electoral system. Kyle and McMullen later went off to Dublin, where they held trade-union and political offices in the Irish labour movement.

Jack Beattie sat in the northern parliament until 1949, and for West Belfast at Westminster in 1943–50 and 1951–5. Given his British chauvinism in 1918, it is ironic that he became an official of an Irish teachers' union in 1934, and was expelled from the NILP, in that year, and again in 1944, for his increasingly republican views. He joined the Irish, or Éire, labour party in 1949, when it moved into the north, at the time of the anti-partition campaign by southern parties. (Harry Diamond won the Falls seat as a socialist republican in 1945, and remained at Stormont until 1969, in the latter years as a republican labour MP. He was expelled from the Irish labour party in 1951, at the behest of Beattie, having defended the claustrophobic catholicism of the south.) Harry Midgley joined Beattie at Stormont in 1933, in the new parliament building outside Belfast. Given the former's association with Connolly before the war, it is ironic that he was moving in the opposite direction to Beattie, towards unionism. Both men proved too individualistic for the small NILP. Midgley's shift owed a great deal to his support for the republicans in Spain, a touchstone of socialist commitment in the 1930s. Ireland, in the main, was enthusiastic for Franco's nationalists, who were catholic anti-communists, and this turned Midgley against Irish nationalism. Though he had been chairman of the NILP from 1933, Midgley formed the pro-war commonwealth labour party in late 1942. Patriotism and anti-fascism fused in support for the war effort. Midgley was taken into the government as minister of public security, a position he held for the rest of the war. Herbert Morrison occupied a similar post in Churchill's wartime coalition government. (William Grant had been made minister of public security in 1941, and he remained a unionist minister until he died in 1949.) Midgley joined the unionist party in 1947, replacing Grant two years later, but as minister of labour. He was in charge of education from 1950 until his death in 1957. The NILP, without Beattie and Midgley, finally committed itself to the union in 1949. This was when Attlee's labour government, in response to the declaration of a republic by the first inter-party government in Dublin, allowed Stormont the last say on its constitutional position. (This turned out to be an empty counter-gesture when London suspended the province's parliament in 1972 without consulting its members.)

If the predominantly protestant NILP was wrong to go pale orange in 1949, in the sense of supporting the majority view in Northern Ireland, it can be argued in mitigation that it stood out for three decades against unionism. The NILP had tried and failed, as an alternative, to integrate as a regional council into the (British) labour party. The Irish labour party could institutionally trace its origins to the 1894 foundation of the all-Ireland ITUC, but Irish labourism, whatever the inspiration it received from Belfast, failed to challenge its corporatist position in nationalist Ireland, remaining subservient to the Irish party, Sinn Féin, and then Fianna Fáil. It became bright green in 1949 when it joined the all-party anti-partition front in Dublin, which resulted from Sean McBride's attempt to prove he was a better republican than Eamon de Valera. It is no mitigation for the Irish labour party to justify its involvement in the north from that date, by arguing that it was invited by dissident catholic socialists in the NILP.

Harry Midgley – Ulster's own Ramsay MacDonald – was not representative of NILP members, even after the 1949 commitment to the union. They remained socialists outside the frame of Ulster's sectarian politics, though a protestant Sabbatarianism, of strong nonconformist origins, asserted itself in the 1950s. The party won four Belfast seats at Stormont in 1958, its highest number ever. The NILP even became the official opposition, catholic MPs not wishing to occupy the position. Two former shipyard workers, David Bleakley and Billy Boyd, protested about unemployment, at a time when Britain was enjoying better economic conditions. The four were re-elected in 1962, with increased majorities, the NILP getting its highest vote ever – 76,842 – at a time when the local economy was in crisis. (Gerry Fitt was also elected, as an independent Irish labour candidate in Dock, and, retaining his seat at Stormont, won West Belfast in the 1966 Westminster election for the republican labour party.) The working-class breakthrough at Stormont led to the resignation of Brookeborough as prime minister in 1963, his successor, O'Neill, being concerned principally to retain the unionist party's mass base. Thus he attempted to follow the interventionist policies of the British government, once labour had come to office under Harold Wilson promising to modernize the economy. Ten NILP candidates in the 1964 Westminster election secured a total of 103,000 votes. A snap Stormont election in 1965 saw the NILP seats reduced to two, and a reassertion of protestant populism – identified with the Revd

Ian Paisley. O'Neill raised catholic aspirations without any strategy for meeting them, given the need to reaffirm protestant loyalty as the foundation of the state. There were meetings with Sean Lemass, *taoiseach* in the Republic, in 1965, the first between the two heads of government in Ireland since the 1920s. The nationalists became the official opposition at Stormont, but O'Neill did not long survive the outbreak of the troubles in 1968. These saw the NILP pushed aside by the civil rights campaign. Paddy Devlin, elected to Stormont for the Falls seat in 1969, soon moved on politically, given a recomposition in catholic politics, leaving one labour MP to wither on the vine.

Unionism and protestantism inflicted mortal wounds on labourism in the north, the majority working class failing to integrate the catholic minority. But socialism in the south, owing largely to the weak position of the working class in a post-colonial state, was not unmolested by nationalism, catholicism and anti-communism. It is not difficult to attribute the failure of labour in Ireland to partition in 1920–2. But it requires a socialist act of political faith like that of Connolly to see a 32-county Ireland – in the counterfactual history of the Irish left – becoming a workers' republic.

If Redmond and the Irish party had held firm in 1913–14, and the British government had not been concerned primarily with maintaining constitutional politics, Ireland, in the absence of the European war, would have seen counter-revolution in Ulster. This would have been a set-back for both countries, and not least their working-class movements. If – constructing a second scenario – the 1916 insurgents in Dublin had linked up better with the Germans, it is likely that the cause of separatism would have resonated less well in catholic Ireland. The Easter rising would not have become some sort of Irish permanent revolution. James Connolly never theorized such a leap to socialism, nor did Lenin see the ICA, about which he knew little, as anything more than 'backward workers … [with] their prejudices, their reactionary fantasies, their weakness and errors'.[3] If, for a third hypothesis, de Valera, Griffith and Collins had fought and negotiated, in 1919–21, for an Ireland separate and united, it is most likely that British power would have divided Sinn Féin and the IRA, to an extent greater than the civil war, and almost certainly prevented the formation of an Irish state for a further period. The position of the catholic minority in Belfast in this eventuality would have been even worse than it became under partition.

Socialists have been forced since the 1920s to envisage alternatives to Ireland upon the dissecting table (a strong nationalist image), principally because of the difficulty of proceeding politically in both parts of the country. This has had less to do with the weakness of reformism, where socialists ultimately work in a given parliamentary arena, than with revolutionary Marxism, which, in a country like Ireland, can be both inadequately democratic, in the richest meaning of the concept, and inordinately uncritical of a zenophobic and anti-utilitarian separatism. The advance of labour and socialist politics may, or may not, have been halted by the partitioning of Ireland, but it is just as likely –

despite James Connolly's call of 1914 to the British government to press on with home rule – that the attempt to resolve the national question in Ireland through the construction of a unitary state would have created an even greater carnival of reaction.

Something of a historical perspective on the question of class and nation in Ireland can be gained from looking at Belfast in the context of the United Kingdom. It is the case that the Irish party, and then Sinn Féin, sought to secede from this state, but it is a historical indictment of Irish nationalism that, while it claimed 32 counties as its territory, leaders of the movement led only the catholic people of Ireland. Irish catholics were to be found in many nineteenth-century British cities and towns, especially Glasgow and Liverpool. These two centres of population compare with Belfast in this respect, and it is in the industrial triangle linking Scotland, England and Ireland under the United Kingdom state, where a comparative assessment of the Belfast working class, warts and all, may be constructed.

Belfast, it could be argued, was politically in advance of Glasgow and Liverpool under the union. Unionism predominated in all three cities from the 1880s, but Glasgow and Liverpool also had strong liberal traditions of bourgeois reform. The working class in Belfast had to assert itself without the help of liberalism in the home rule era. Sectarianism was common to all three cities, but working-class politics in Ireland was more developed. William Walker came extremely close to winning one of the four Belfast seats in 1906, at the time of the liberal landslide in Britain. Another Ulster protestant did not come close to being returned to parliament, in Liverpool, until the first 1910 election. It was 1918 before labour secured one of the 15 seats in Glasgow. The Belfast labour party probably did better in terms of mobilizing a working-class base against the principal bourgeois party, even though unionists, and one nationalist, captured the ten seats. Glasgow developed a reputation for Scottish Marxism and the wartime shop stewards' movement, Belfast and Liverpool being weak in such revolutionary politics. But the 1919 strike in Belfast can be compared directly with that in Glasgow, and was so compared at the time by observers on both sides of the North Channel. St George's Square certainly entered the mythology of communist politics in Britain, but the absence of a battle at the City Hall in Belfast is not necessarily a cause for regret. James Larkin, who cannot be accused of running away from fights, had been quick to sense how syndicalism could blend into sectarianism in a city like Belfast. When the twelve labour men took their seats on the corporation in January 1920, it seemed as if middle-class municipal power was about to be challenged by a resolute working class.

It took some time for the Anglo-Irish struggle of 1919–21 to make an impact on Belfast, but when it did, in July 1920, it did so in a form – industrial expulsions – which had been prefigured before the war. This was something the labour movement in Belfast had to cope with, Glasgow and Liverpool being free of a major surrounding political struggle having such an effect. It was in 1921, when political labourism was physically suppressed by loyalism, without any restraint from the

Ulster bourgeoisie, that Belfast broke from the political history of the industrial triangle. While Ireland was divided into two states, albeit one of these states still within the United Kingdom, Britain underwent an experience of muted class politics as a result of the collapse of the liberal party. Clydeside and Merseyside, as industrial areas on the mainland, benefited from this realignment in British politics. The year 1922 saw ten of the Glasgow seats fall to labour, and the Red Clydesiders take the train to Westminster. Their political contribution proved to be less than the expectations they raised at the time. It was a by-election in 1923, the year after MacDonald had been re-elected to the leadership of the labour party, before Liverpool sent a labour MP to the House of Commons.

Class politics became dominant, but sectarianism lived on in Glasgow and Liverpool after 1922. Ethnic rivalry between catholics and protestants was politically suppressed, by the pull of a – national – labour party in competition with the conservative party. Ethnic, or national, politics were the story in Belfast. The partitioning of Ireland, and the crystallization of the nationalist–unionist contradiction in catholic and protestant states, undercut the labour movement. Since the early 1920s Belfast has seemed to be a different city from Glasgow and Liverpool, given their twentieth-century political histories. It is external factors which determine the primacy of catholic and protestant identities in Belfast. The cleavage in the Belfast working class has been too great to be attributed to the communal inequality in the social structure. Disadvantaged minorities are universal under capitalism, but support in West Belfast for an armed struggle flows from an earlier, proximate, rural nationalist tradition in the rest of Ireland. When Belfast became the capital of Northern Ireland, it was cut off from the political development experienced by Glasgow and Liverpool, despite continuing membership of the United Kingdom. The British labour party refused to accept the NILP in 1949, but it is not clear that such integration would have averted the current troubles. The city's preoccupation – for both minority and majority communites – was the south, where Anglophobia was enshrined in the Irish Free State, and then the Republic. This obsession with Britain began to break down in the 1960s. Belfast catholics had variously looked to Dublin for relief from the 1920s on, despite the vested competitive interests of dominant parties there in raising, but not solving, the northern question. This became a liability only in the 1970s, when the Irish state had to start behaving like a European nation, working with Britain and taking some responsibility for the north. The predominant protestant community there, paradoxically, had the legitimacy of its fears in the home rule era confirmed from the 1920s. When Irish nationalism was realized in an irredentist state, home rule really did become Rome rule.

This book has been written in order to reinsert Belfast into Ireland's past. There was one country, with divergent forms of development at their most extreme in the late nineteenth century. Nationalism may have been the answer for the south, but the state based on Dublin could never have been a major European nation, much less the centre of Irish political development. To reinsert Belfast is to confront the limits of nationalism, whether constitutional before the First World War, or revolutionary afterwards. But it is also to highlight the conservative character of Ulster unionism, under Carson, and Craig's tolerance of loyalist violence in the formation of Northern Ireland. This book has looked at the partitioning of Ireland from the point of view of ordinary men and women in Belfast. Most followed nationalist and unionist leaders; a few did not. I have been concerned to restore the latter to their full integrity, as opposed to socialist writers who have been pro-catholic or pro-protestant, and have simply perpetuated sectarian myths about villains and heroes. The catholic working class was undoubtedly oppressed, but it was not republican. While sectarian at moments, it was resigned much of the time to a ghetto existence. The protestant working class was also exploited, whatever the structural inequality between the two communities. It exercised a democratic right not to be impressed by the possibility of Dublin rule. Protestant workers participated in the emergent labour movement, the major internal development in twentieth-century British politics.

This assertion of working-class independence came up against the problem of sectarian division in Belfast. Socialists were a sort of vanguard in the movement, and the weaknesses of the British tradition – at a time when other socialisms flourished in Europe – were all too evident in Belfast. A trade-union-based and nonconformist-inspired labourism was confronted by a minority working class, unorganized and partly female, and attached to a popular catholicism spread across Ireland. It is easy to show that Belfast socialists failed, but this also allows for the assessment of others' achievements. Irish republicans, and their socialist allies, have been battling, on their own admission, for over eight centuries! The fault of Belfast labourism was not its commitment to the British constitution, in the face of Irish revolution, but its inadequate democracy, which developed belatedly in the First World War. The Belfast socialists' anti-partitionism had little to do with nationalism, but James Connolly became committed to Irish republicanism, in deed as well as word, and entered Irish history as a hero.

The republican version of the nation's story has been in terminal cultural decline for nearly two decades, on the basis of Irish historical scholarship from the 1930s. This work has sought to assess Connolly in Belfast in objective terms, alongside the maligned Walker, but, more importantly, alongside the heroic men and women who tried, if only to fail. The year 1919 was undoubtedly the most important year, against the background of wartime social change, and with the prospect of settlement across Europe. Sinn Féin's contribution to this was slight, its inability to unite the people of Ireland, including its working class, considerable. Irish labour history has been dominated by Dublin for too long. The assertion of Belfast's importance is, paradoxically, a contribution to a growing – secular – cultural unity in Ireland. This has nothing to do with an armed struggle against partition, by a minority of a minority of a minority of the Irish people. The problem of sectarian polarization in Belfast still remains, to be addressed by contemporary and future victims of the troubles. Perhaps this record of previous socialists in the labour movement may still be an inspiration, though Irish and British socialists, long enamoured of republicanism, (and, in the case of some, of loyalism) may not be greatly moved.

Notes

Preface

1. W.S. Churchill, *Lord Randolph Churchill*, 2 vols., London, 1906, p. 59.
2. A.T.Q. Stewart, *The Ulster Crisis*, London, 1967, p. 54.
3. *Northern Whig* [NW] and *Irish News* [IN], 18 May 1921.
4. *IN*, 21 May 1921.
5. Ibid., 19 May.
6. *NW*, 18 May 1921.
7. Ibid., 18 May 1921.
8. *Irish Worker*, 14 March 1914.
9. Irish Labour Party & Trade Union Congress (ILP & TUC), *1919 Report* (page numbers not available).
10. Pp. 8 and 473.
11. P. 9.
12. Liverpool.
13. Washington, D.C.
14. London.
15. London.
16. P. 144.
17. *Thomas Johnson, 1872–1963*, Mount Merrion, County Dublin.
18. *The Politics of Frustration: Harry Midgley and the Failure of Labour in Northern Ireland*, Manchester.
19. *The Irish Transport and General Workers' Union: The Formative Years, 1909–1923*, Dublin.
20. *Communism in Modern Ireland: The Pursuit of the Workers' Republic since 1916*, Dublin.
21. *City in Revolt: James Larkin and the Belfast Dock Strike of 1907*, Belfast.
22. *Syndicalism in Ireland, 1917–1923*, Cork.
23. 'Politics, the Labour Movement and the Working Class in Belfast, 1905–1923'.
24. *James Connolly: A Political Biography*, Manchester, 1988 and 1989.

Chapter 1

1. Quoted in Conrad Gill, *The Rise of the Irish Linen Industry*, Oxford, 1925, p. 46.
2. *The Best of Tone*, Proinsias Mac Aonghusa and Liam Reagain, eds., Cork, 1972, p. 46.
3. D.L. Armstrong, 'Social and Economic Conditions in the Belfast Linen Industry, 1850–1900', *Irish Historical Studies*, vol. 7, no. 28, 1951, p. 238.
4. L.M. Cullen, *An Economic History of Ireland since 1660*, London, 1972, pp. 159–60.
5. Peter Gibbon, *The Origins of Ulster Unionism*, Manchester, 1975, pp. 16–17.
6. R.D.C. Black, 'William James Pirrie', in Conor Cruise O'Brien, ed., *The Shaping of Modern Ireland*, London, 1970, p. 184.

7. *Belfast and Province of Ulster Directory for 1905*, pp. 4 and 54.
8. Irish Trade Union Congress (ITUC), *1904 Report*.
9. Gibbon, *Unionism*, p. 9.
10. The term 'sectarian political economy' was used first by J. Dunsmore Clarkson, *Labour and Nationalism in Ireland*, New York, 1926, p. 361.
11. Gibbon, *Unionism*, p. 33.
12. Ibid., p. 42.
13. P.P., 1865, XXIII: *Report of the Commissioners of Inquiry Respecting the Magisterial and Police Jurisdiction Arrangements and Establishment of the Borough of Belfast*.
14. Ibid., p. 342.
15. Liam O'Dowd, Bill Rolston, and Mike Tomlinson, *Northern Ireland: Between Civil Rights and Civil War*, London, 1980, pp. 71–4.
16. P.P., 1887, XVIII: *Report of the Commissioners of Inquiry Respecting the Origins and Circumstances of the Riots in Belfast in June, July, August and September 1886*.
17. T. MacKnight, *Ulster as It Is*, vol. 2, London, 1896, p. 322.
18. F. Frankfurt Moore, *The Truth about Ulster*, London, 1914, p. 56; see also the Revd Mr Hanna in 1886, quoted in Gibbon, *Unionism*, p. 126.
19. MacKnight, *Ulster*, vol. 2, p. 393.
20. Conor Cruise O'Brien, *States of Ireland*, London, 1972, p. 148.
21. Emrys Jones, *A Social Geography of Belfast*, London, 1960, p. 187.
22. Ibid., p. 197.
23. L. Wirth, *On Cities and Social Life*, Chicago, 1969, pp. 84–5.
24. Riot Report, 1857. P.P., 1857–8, XXVI: *Report of the Inquiry into the Conduct of the Constabulary during the Disturbances at Belfast in July and September*.
25. *Unionism*, p. 68.
26. E. Austin Currie, 'The Growth and Development of South-West Belfast: A Regional Study in Urban Geography', BA dissertation, Dept. of Geography, Queen's University, Belfast, 1955, p. 37.
27. T.J. Hughes, 'A Study of the Working Populations of three Belfast Linen Mills', BA dissertation, Dept. of Geography, Queen's University, Belfast, 1954, p. 24.
28. Jones, *Geography*, p. 225.
29. Riot Report, 1886. P.P., 1887, XVIII: *Report of the Commissioners of Inquiry Respecting the Origins and Circumstances of the Riots in Belfast in June, July, August and September 1886*.
30. Ibid.
31. *Report on the Strikes and Lockouts of 1893 by the Labour Correspondent of the Board of Trade*.
32. In *The Re-Conquest of Ireland*, included in James Connolly, *Labour in Ireland*, Dublin, n.d. [1944], pp. 171–4.
33. Quoted in Thomas Jones, *Whitehall Diary: Vol. III, Ireland, 1918–1925*, ed. Keith Middlemass, London, 1971, p. 132.
34. Quoted in Margery Foster, *Michael Collins: The Lost Leader*, London, 1971, p. 230.

Chapter 2

1. Quoted in Patrick Buckland, *Ulster Unionism and the Origins of Northern Ireland 1886–1922*, Dublin, 1973, p. 6.
2. 12 December 1885, quoted in F.S.L. Lyons, *Charles Stewart Parnell*, London, 1978, p. 305.
3. Belfast RIC Report to Dublin Castle, 9 April 1903, CSO 29372/S, State Paper Office (SPO).
4. Ibid., CSO 29482/S, SPO.

5. Ian Budge and Cornelius O'Leary, *Belfast: Approach to Crisis – A Study of Belfast Politics, 1613–1970*, London, 1973, pp. 116–19.
6. 2 June 1896.
7. Quoted in F.J. Whitford, 'Joseph Devlin and the Catholic Representation Association in Belfast', unpublished typescript, Library of Queen's University, Belfast, n.d.
8. Ibid.
9. Sybil E. Baker, 'Orange and Green: Belfast, 1832–1912', in H.J. Dyos and W. Wolff, eds., *The Victorian City: Images and Reality*, 2 vols., London, 1973, p. 800.
10. Ibid.
11. 8 April 1903, CSO 29372/S, SPO.
12. *IN*, 19 January 1910.
13. Whitford, 'Devlin'.
14. Monthly Report RIC Special Branch for April 1906, CO 904/117, Public Record Office, London (PRO[L]).
15. *NW*, 19 January 1910.
16. *IN*, 8 January 1906.
17. *IN*, 15 January 1906.
18. *IN*, 8 January 1906.
19. *IN*, 15 January 1906.
20. *IN*, 20 January 1906.
21. *IN*, 11 January 1906.
22. *IN*, 12 January 1906.
23. *IN*, 15 January 1906.
24. *IN*, 16 January 1906.
25. *IN*, 20 January 1906.
26. *IN*, 15 January 1906.
27. *IN*, 20 January 1906.
28. *NW*, 20 January 1906.
29. *IN*, 20 January 1906.
30. Quoted in 'Character Sketch: Joe Devlin', *Review of Reviews*, March 1911, pp. 235–6.
31. *Irish People*, 12 December 1906, quoted in Paul Bew, *Conflict and Conciliation in Ireland, 1890–1910: Parnellites and Radical Agrarians*, Oxford, 1987, p. 123.
32. 'Character Sketch', pp. 235–6.
33. 1 December 1910.
34. *NW*, 29 November 1910.
35. 'Character Sketch', p. 237.
36. *IN*, 23 December 1909.
37. *IN*, 1 January 1910.
38. *IN*, 13 January 1910.
39. *IN*, 16 January 1910.
40. *IN*, 19 January 1910.
41. *IN*, 2 and 3 December 1910.
42. *IN*, 1 December 1910.
43. *NW* and *IN*, 10 December 1910.
44. *IN*, 6 and 7 December 1910.
45. Quoted in 'Character Sketch', pp. 235–7.
46. Ibid., p. 237.
47. *IN*, 10 December 1910.
48. *NW*, 7 December 1910.
49. 19 January 1906.
50. 20 and 21 January 1910.
51. D 1268/3/3a, Public Record Office of Northern Ireland (PRONI).
52. *IN*, 7 January 1910.
53. 21 January 1910.

54. Ibid.
55. A.C. Hepburn, 'The Ancient Order of Hibernians in Irish Politics, 1905–14', *Cithara*, vol. 10, no. 2, 1971, pp. 7 and 10.
56. *Forward*, 30 August 1913.
57. Ibid.

Chapter 3

1. *NW*, 15 January 1906.
2. *Hansard*, vol. 163, col. 1401, 1 November 1906.
3. Ibid., vol. 113, col. 689, 23 October 1902.
4. *NW*, 7 August 1902.
5. *Belfast Newsletter (BNL)*, 13 July 1907.
6. *BNL*, 13 July 1914.
7. *BNL*, 4 June 1903.
8. *Belfast Evening Telegraph (BET)*, 13 July 1903; *BNL*, 14 July.
9. Quoted in J.W. Boyle, 'The Belfast Protestant Association and the Independent Orange Order, 1901–10', *Irish Historical Studies*, vol. 13, 1962, p. 129.
10. *BNL*, 13 July 1904.
11. Quoted in Boyle, 'Belfast Protestant Association', p. 133.
12. *BET*, 12 July 1905; *BNL*, 13 July.
13. *IN*, 14 July 1905.
14. 14 July 1905.
15. Quoted in Boyle, 'Belfast Protestant Association', p. 136.
16. *NW*, 28 August 1905.
17. *IN*, 8 January 1906.
18. 14 July 1906.
19. *NW*, 3 January 1906.
20. *NW*, 19 January 1910.
21. *NW*, 13 January 1906.
22. *NW*, 20 January 1906.
23. *BNL*, 13 June 1906.
24. *BNL*, 12 November 1906.
25. *BNL*, 13 July 1907.
26. *Ulster Guardian*, 29 February 1908.
27. Ibid.
28. *BNL*, 2 June 1908.
29. Ibid.
30. *BNL*, 21 May 1908.
31. Quoted in F.S.L. Lyons, *Ireland since the Famine*, London, 1973, p. 223.
32. *BNL*, 13 July 1906.
33. *BNL*, 6 November 1906.
34. J.W. Boyle, 'A Fenian Protestant in Canada: Robert Lindsay Crawford, 1910–22', *Canadian Historical Review*, vol. 52, no. 2, June 1971, p. 168.
35. Ibid., p. 174.
36. Ibid., p. 175.
37. *American Biography*, vol. 35, New York, 1928, p. 262.
38. *BET*, 12 July 1905.
39. *NW*, 20 January 1906.
40. *BNL*, 13 July 1907.
41. *NW*, 19 January 1910.
42. *NW*, 13 January 1910.
43. *NW*, 13 January 1910.
44. *BNL*, 14 July 1908.
45. 3 October 1911.

46. *NW*, 17 January 1910.
47. 15 January 1910.
48. *NW*, 1 December 1910.
49. *BET*, 12 July 1912.
50. *BET*, 12 July 1914.

Chapter 4

1. An 1892 Copy of the Rules, in Col. E, Section B, XVII, Webb Papers, British Library of Political and Economic Science (BLPES).
2. CSO, 24851/S, SPO. This is contained in a file, opened in 1899, on public order at the Custom House steps, CSO RP 17289/1911, SPO.
3. *1892 Report of the United Trades Council of Belfast*, p. 6.
4. CSO, 24851/S, SPO.
5. *BET*, 18 September 1893.
6. *Belfast Protestant Record*, vol. 1, no. 1, March 1901.
7. *Labour Opposition*, vol. 1, no. 1, March 1925.
8. *Forward*, 8 July 1911.
9. Quoted in Emmet Larkin, *James Larkin: Irish Labour Leader, 1876–1947*, London, 1968, p. 286.
10. *Forward*, 17 June 1911.
11. ITUC, *1900 Report*.
12. S. Shannon Millin, *Sidelights on Belfast History*, Belfast, 1932, p. 11.
13. S. Higenbottam, *Our Society's History*, Manchester, 1939, p. 169.
14. J.W. Boyle, 'William Walker', in *Leaders and Workers*, Cork, n.d. [1967], p. 63.
15. Minutes, 3 August 1905, on microfilm, PRONI.
16. Ibid., 6 September 1906.
17. ITUC, *1895 Report*.
18. ITUC, *1901 Report*.
19. Ibid.
20. ITUC, *1898 Report*.
21. ITUC, *1904 Report*.
22. Ibid.
23. ITUC, *1903 Report*.
24. Minutes.
25. *BNL*, 7 January 1901.
26. *BNL*, 16 January 1902.
27. Leaflet dated 15 January 1904, T 2085, PRONI.
28. February 1905.
29. *NW*, 1 September 1905.
30. *NW*, 2 September 1905.
31. *NW*, 11 September 1905.
32. *NW*, 12 September 1905.
33. *NW*, 2 September 1905.
34. *NW*, 6 September 1905.
35. *NW*, 7 September 1905.
36. *NW*, 30 August 1905.
37. *NW*, 2 September 1905.
38. *NW*, 7 September 1905.
39. *NW*, 31 August 1905.
40. 1906 General Election, T 2085, PRONI.
41. Ibid.
42. *NW*, 29 August 1905.
43. 7 October 1905.
44. *NW*, 7 September 1905.

45. *NW*, 1 September 1905.
46. *NW*, 7 September 1905.
47. *BNL*, 8 September 1905.
48. Boyle, 'Belfast Protestant Association', pp. 138–9.
49. Reproduced in John Gray, *City in Revolt: James Larkin and the Belfast Dock Strike of 1907*, Belfast, 1985, p. 37.
50. MacDonald to Thomas Johnson, LRC, 28/189.
51. *Forward*, 3 June 1911.
52. *NW*, 19 January 1906.
53. *NW*, 15 September 1905.
54. *NW*, 18 December 1905.
55. *NW*, 16 September 1905.
56. *NW*, 2 September 1905.
57. *NW*, 13 September 1905.
58. Higenbottam, *History*, p. 280.
59. Belfast Trades Council Minutes, 21 October 1905.
60. Quoted in Gray, *City*, p. 221.
61. Minutes.
62. Labour Party, *1906 Report*, pp. 50–1.
63. Minutes.
64. *NW*, 17 January 1906.
65. *NW*, 10 January 1906.
66. *NW*, 12 January 1906.
67. *NW*, 15 January 1906.
68. T 2085, PRONI.
69. Minutes.
70. 20 January 1906.
71. Labour Party, *1907 Report*, pp. 16–18.
72. *NW*, 26 March 1907.
73. *NW*, 5 April 1907.
74. *NW*, 16 April 1907.
75. *NW*, 23 March 1907.
76. *NW*, 10 April 1907.
77. *NW*, 12 April 1907.
78. Labour Party, *1907 Report*, p. 20.
79. *BNL*, 9 April 1907.
80. Quoted in Gray, *City*, p. 401.
81. Labour Party, *1908 Report*, p. 3.
82. LRC, 26/235, quoted in Patterson, *Conflict*, p. 75.
83. Belfast, 1908, p. 17.
84. ILP, *1910 Report*, p. 16.
85. ILP, *1913 Report*, p. 32.
86. Labour Party, *1909 Report*.
87. Labour Party, *1910 Report*, pp. 14–15.
88. James Connolly, in *Forward*, 27 May 1911.
89. Belfast Trades Council Minutes, 2 December 1909.
90. *NW*, 21 January 1910.
91. *NW*, 8 January 1910.
92. *NW*, 14 January 1910.
93. *NW*, 17 January 1910.
94. *NW*, 20 January 1910.
95. Ibid.
96. ITUC, *1912 Report*.
97. Labour Party, *1913 Report*, p. 38.
98. ITUC, *1910 Report*.
99. ITUC, *1911 Report*.
100. Ibid.

Chapter 5

1. Robinson Bentley, in *Typographical Circular*, February 1907.
2. James Sexton, *Sir James Sexton: Agitator*, London, 1936, p. 202.
3. Ibid., pp. 203–4.
4. Minutes, 3 January 1907.
5. CSO, *Crime Branch Special: Intelligence Notes, 1907*, Official Papers, Carton No. 2, SPO. This annual publication, for government circulation, contains two relevant reports, 'Belfast Labour Strikes and Riots 1907' and 'The Police Emeute in July 1907'. The first is based on a 59-page typescript of the same name, by District Inspector Clayton of the Detective Branch of the Belfast RIC, dated 5 October 1907. It is contained in the Dublin Castle file on the 1907 strike – CSO, File No. 20333/08, SPO. I refer hereinafter to Clayton, 'Strikes'.
6. A. McDowell, P.P., 1913, XXVIII: *Industrial Council of Inquiry into Industrial Agreements. Minutes of Evidence.*
7. Larkin, *Larkin*, pp. 17–18; D.F. Wilson, *Dockers: The Impact of Industrial Change*, London, 1972, pp. 33–4.
8. *Sexton*, p. 109.
9. Wilson, *Dockers*, p. 39.
10. *NW*, 27 June 1907.
11. Larkin, *Larkin*, pp. 23–4.
12. *NW*, 23 August 1907.
13. 15 May 1907, Messages File, in CSO, File No. 20333/08, SPO.
14. *NW*, 17 May 1907.
15. *NW*, 19 May 1907.
16. *NW*, 3 June 1907.
17. *NW*, 13 May 1907.
18. *NW*, 3 June 1907.
19. *NW*, 1 July 1907.
20. *NW*, 20 May 1907.
21. Ibid.
22. ITUC, *1907 Report*.
23. *NW*, 3 June 1907.
24. Ibid.
25. *IN*, 9 May 1907.
26. *IN*, 10 May 1907.
27. A copy exists in the Dublin Castle file. See also reproduction in Gray, *City*, p. 64.
28. Clayton, 'Strikes'.
29. *NW*, 2 July 1907.
30. *NW*, 5 July 1907.
31. *NW*, 2 July 1907.
32. *NW*, 4 July 1907.
33. Ibid.
34. Minutes.
35. Messages File.
36. *NW*, 8 July 1907.
37. Messages File.
38. *NW*, 13 and 15 July 1907.
39. *NW*, 18 July 1907.
40. *NW*, 19 July 1907.
41. *NW*, 18 July 1907.
42. *NW*, 23 July 1907.
43. *Belfast Co-operative Society, 1889–1910*, Belfast, 1910, p. 13. Authorship attributed to W.M. Knox, in copy held in Linenhall Library, Belfast.

44. GFTU, *Report of Founding Conference, 1899.*
45. *NW*, 27 July 1907.
46. *IN*, 27 July 1907.
47. *Report of Belfast Police Commission, 1906*, in CSO, File No. 20333/08, SPO.
48. *Constabulary Gazette*, quoted in Gray, *City*, p. 111.
49. *Intelligence Notes, 1907.*
50. Ibid.
51. Ibid.
52. *IN*, 25 July 1907.
53. *NW*, 2 and 5 August 1907.
54. Clayton, 'Strikes'.
55. *IN*, 12 August 1907.
56. *NW*, 12 August 1907.
57. Messages File.
58. *NW*, 13 August 1907.
59. *NW*, 14 August 1907.
60. *IN*, 14 August 1907.
61. *NW*, 20 August 1907.
62. Clayton, 'Strikes'.
63. CSO, File No. 20333/08, SPO.
64. Sir George Askwith, *Industrial Problems and Disputes*, London, 1920, p. 110–13.
65. *NW*, 16 August 1907.
66. CSO, File No. 20333/08, SPO.
67. Ibid.
68. *NW*, 5 September 1907.
69. *Intelligence Notes, 1907.*
70. Minutes.
71. Ibid., 12 September 1907.
72. Ibid., 5 September.
73. Ibid., 12 September.
74. Ibid., 3 October.
75. *NW*, 9 January 1909.
76. ITGWU, *Fifty Years of Liberty Hall: The Golden Jubilee of the Irish Transport and General Workers' Union, 1909–1959*, ed. Cathal O'Shannon, Dublin n.d. [1959], p. 23.
77. ITUC, *1909 Report*

Chapter 6

1. Quoted in Robert Kee, *The Green Flag: A History of Irish Nationalism*, London, 1972, p. 463.
2. Quoted in Harold Nicolson, *King George the Fifth: His Life and Reign*, London, 1972, p. 212.
3. Quoted in A.T.Q. Stewart, *The Ulster Crisis*, London, 1967, p. 48.
4. Choille, *Intelligence Notes*, p. 21.
5. Quoted in Roy Jenkins, *Asquith*, 3rd edn, London, 1986, p. 277.
6. Quoted in Patrick Buckland, *Ulster Unionism and the Origins of Northern Ireland, 1886–1912*, Dublin and New York, 1973, p. 54.
7. Nicolson, *George*, p. 268.
8. Ibid., p. 269.
9. Ibid.
10. *NW*, 1 and 2 July 1912.
11. *IN*, 22 January 1913.
12. *IN*, 17 January 1913.
13. *IN*, 7 May 1913.
14. *IN*, 3 July 1912.

15.   *BET*, 2 July 1912.
16.   *NW*, 25 July 1912.
17.   *BET*, 26 July 1912.
18.   *IN*, 5 and 6 July 1912.
19.   *IN*, 17 January 1913.
20.   *IN*, 16 July 1912.
21.   *IN*, 10 July 1912.
22.   Ibid.
23.   *IN*, 3 July 1912.
24.   *IN*, 5 July 1912.
25.   *IN*, 5 July 1912.
26.   *BET*, 19 August 1912.
27.   Quoted in Buckland, *Ulster*, p. 58.
28.   *IN*, 17 January 1912.
29.   *NW*, 8 July 1912.
30.   *IN*, 9 July 1912.
31.   *IN*, 16 July 1912.
32.   *IN*, 23 July 1912.
33.   Report to Inspector-General, RIC, 29 August 1912, in CSO R.P. 15601/12, SPO.
34.   *IN*, 29 July 1912.
35.   *IN*, 25 April 1913.
36.   *IN*, 31 July 1912.
37.   *IN*, 15 August 1912.
38.   *IN*, 17 August 1912.
39.   *IN*, 16 July 1912.
40.   Minutes.
41.   *IN*, 21 January 1913.
42.   Minutes, 3 April 1913.
43.   *IN*, 15 August 1912.
44.   Minutes.
45.   *IN*, 1 January 1913.
46.   Ibid.
47.   *NW*, 26 July 1912.
48.   *BET*, 29 July 1912.
49.   *IN*, 31 July 1912.
50.   Minutes, Belfast branch, United Operative Plumbers' Association of Great Britain and Ireland, D. 1050/5, PRONI.
51.   CSO R.P. 16056/12, SPO.
52.   Quoted in H. Montgomery Hyde, *Carson*, London, 1953, p. 318.
53.   CSO R.P. 15601/12, SPO.
54.   Ibid.
55.   *IN*, 1 May 1913.
56.   Jenkins, *Asquith*, p. 295.
57.   Choille, *Intelligence Notes*, p. 25.
58.   Nicolson, *George*, p. 307.
59.   Jenkins, *Asquith*, p. 294.
60.   Nicolson, *George*, p. 316.
61.   Quoted in George Dangerfield, *The Damnable Question: A Study in Anglo-Irish Relations*, London, 1979, p. 87.
62.   Jenkins, *Asquith*, p. 307.
63.   Stewart, *Crisis*, p. 175.
64.   Ibid., p. 220.
65.   Nicolson, *George*, p. 325.
66.   Dangerfield, *Question*, p. 122

Chapter 7

1. This chapter is an expanded version of parts of Chapters 5 and 6 of my *James Connolly: A Political Biography*, Manchester, 1988.
2. Letter, dated 13 June 1910, in Ms 13919, NLI.
3. James Connolly, *Socialism and Nationalism*, ed. Desmond Ryan, Dublin, 1948, p. 191.
4. *Forward*, 11 March 1911.
5. Introduction to James Connolly, *The Workers' Republic*, ed. Desmond Ryan, Dublin, 1951, pp. 1–4.
6. *Forward*, 27 May 1911.
7. Ibid., 3 June 1911.
8. Ibid., 10 June 1911.
9. Ibid., 17 June 1911.
10. Ibid., 1 July 1911.
11. Ibid.
12. Introduction, p. 19.
13. *Forward*, 27 May 1911.
14. James Connolly to William O'Brien, 15 September 1911, in Ms 13908, NLI.
15. Ibid.
16. Connolly to O'Brien, 7 December 1911.
17. Ms 13908, NLI.
18. *NW* and *IN*, 22 July 1911.
19. *NW*, 20 July 1911.
20. Ibid., 25 July 1911.
21. *NW*, 31 July 1911.
22. *BET*, 7 August 1911.
23. *NW*, 8 August 1911.
24. *BET*, 4 October 1911.
25. Ina Connolly-Heron, 'James Connolly: A Biography', in 8 monthly parts, *Liberty*, March–October 1966, June, p. 15.
26. *BET*, 2 October 1911.
27. Ibid., 9 October 1911.
28. Connolly-Heron, 'Connolly', June, p. 15.
29. Nora Connolly O'Brien, *James Connolly: Portrait of a Rebel Father*, 2nd edn (first published 1935), Dublin, 1975, p. 129.
30. Interview, Roddy Connolly (son of James Connolly), 16 March 1974.
31. Connolly O'Brien, *Portrait*, pp. 134–5.
32. *BET*, 4 October 1911.
33. *BNL*, 23 October 1911.
34. Minutes.
35. Minutes.
36. Minutes, 16 December 1911; *BET*, 18 December 1911.
37. ITUC, *1912 Report*.
38. Ibid.
39. 'James Connolly in Belfast'. Recollections of Mrs Ellen Grimley (née Gordon), Ms 13906, NLI.
40. In James Connolly, *Ireland Upon the Dissecting Table*, Cork Workers' Club Historical Reprints No. 11, 2nd enlarged edn, Cork, 1975, pp. 23–5.
41. Introduction, p. 22.
42. 'Connolly'.
43. Ms 13908, NLI.
44. Ibid., 8 October 1912.
45. Ibid., 3 January 1913.
46. *Forward*, 10 May 1913.
47. Connolly to O'Brien, 6 June 1913, in Ms 13908, NLI.

48. Ibid., Connolly to O'Brien, 29 July 1913.
49. Introduction, pp. 25–6.
50. 29 July 1913, Ms 13908, NLI.
51. *Forward*, 14 June 1913.
52. *Forward*, 28 June 1913; see also *BET*, 5 June 1913.
53. *BET*, 16 June 1913.
54. *Forward*, 14 June 1913.
55. Ibid., 28 June 1913.
56. *Portrait*, p. 142.
57. *Forward*, 23 August 1913.
58. Ms 13908, NLI.
59. *Forward*, 10 May 1913.
60. Ms 13908, NLI.
61. 4 May 1914, Ms 13908, NLI.
62. Ibid., 22 August 1914.
63. ITUC, *1912 Report*.
64. Ms 13908, NLI.
65. Ibid.
66. *Forward*, 10 May 1913.
67. ITUC, *1913 Report*.
68. ITUC, *1914 Report*.
69. Minutes.
70. ITUC, *1912 Report*.
71. Connolly, *Ireland*, p. 21.
72. *IN*, 3 July 1912.
73. *BET*, 1 August 1912.
74. *IN*, 3 August 1912.
75. *IN*, 30 July 1912.
76. C. Desmond Greaves, *The Life and Times of James Connolly*, London, 1972, p. 292.
77. Connolly, *Ireland*, pp. 21–3.
78. 'Connolly'.
79. 'Connolly', June p. 17.
80. *IN*, 15 January 1913.
81. *NW*, 12 August 1913.
82. ITUC, *1914 Report*.
83. *BET*, 12 August 1913.
84. *NW*, 12 August 1913.
85. *Forward*, 23 August 1913.
86. *IN*, 18 September 1913.
87. *Forward*.
88. Ibid., 15 October 1910.
89. Ibid., 11 March 1911.
90. *Labour in Ireland*, Dublin, n.d. [1944], pp. 169, 176–7, 180.
91. Ibid., p. 210.
92. *Forward*, 3 May 1913.
93. Ibid.
94. Ibid., 30 May 1914.
95. Ibid., 7 June 1913.
96. Ibid., 9 August 1913.
97. Ibid., 28 March 1914.
98. Introduction, pp. 20–1.
99. Ibid., p. 21.
100. *Forward*, 28 March 1914.
101. ITUC, *1914 Report*.
102. Con Lehane to William O'Brien, 1 September 1914, Ms 15700(4), NLI.
103. N.d. [5 October 1914], Ms 13908, NLI.

Chapter 8

1. F.X. Martin, *The Irish Volunteers, 1913–1915: Recollections and Documents*, Dublin, 1963, p. 148.
2. CSO Rep. P., 13,805/16, SPO.
3. ITUC, *1914 Report*.
4. ITUC & LP, *1917 Report*.
5. John Dillon, quoted in Dangerfield, *Question*, p. 212.
6. Ibid., p. 213.
7. 15 May 1916, Cab 37/147/38, PRO.
8. Memorandum, 21 May 1916, Cab 37/148/18, PRO.
9. Dangerfield, *Question*, p. 224.
10. ITUC & LP, *1916 Report*.
11. Ibid.
12. Ibid.
13. William J. Larmour, 'Effects of the War on the Irish Linen Industry', Unpublished MSc thesis, Queen's University, Belfast, 1921, p. 99.
14. Taylor, *English History*, p. 65.
15. Memorandum, W.H. Long, 19 May 1916, Cab 37/148/11, PRO.
16. Report, 13 July 1916, Cab 37/151/26, PRO.
17. CO 904/157/1, PRO.
18. Ibid., 31 March 1917.
19. Quoted in Patterson, *Class Conflict*, p. 95.
20. 1 February 1918, in CO 904/157/1, PRO.
21. 21 July 1916, Cab 37/152/15, PRO.
22. R.B. McDowell, *The Irish Convention, 1917–18*, London, 1970, pp. 176–7.
23. P.P., 1918, X, *Report of the Proceedings of the Irish Convention 1918*, pp. 137–9.
24. ILP & TUC, *1918 Report*.
25. Ibid.
26. Kee, *Flag*, p. 625.
27. ILP & TUC, *1918 Report*.
28. Kee, *Flag*, p. 624.

Chapter 9

1. Frank Roney, *Irish Rebel and Californian Labor Leader*, ed. I.B. Cross, Berkeley, 1931, pp. 121–2.
2. P & C Reports, Carton No. 1, 1882–4, SPO.
3. P & C Reports, Carton No. 4, 1886–1915, SPO.
4. CO 904/117, SPO.
5. Bulmer Hobson, *Ireland Yesterday and Tomorrow*, Tralee, 1968, p. 35.
6. RIC Special Branch, Monthly Report for July 1905, CO 904/117, PRO.
7. Hobson, *Ireland*, p. 4.
8. November 1904, quoted in Brian Walker, *Faces of the Past: A Photographic and Literary Record of Ulster Life, 1880–1915*, Belfast, 1974, p. 52.
9. Minute Book, Ms 12,175, NLI.
10. Hobson, *Ireland*, pp. 8, 22.
11. Crime Branch Special Files, 1913–20, Carton No. 23, SPO.
12. *Irish Times*, 30 December 1974.
13. Manuscript, 'Experiences in Belfast 1914', George Berkeley Papers, Ms 7,880, NLI.
14. 'Ireland in 1915: National Spirit at its Lowest Ebb', *An tOglach*, Summer 1962, p. 4.
15. 'The Events in Belfast', *Capuchian Annual*, 1966, p. 383.
16. 'The McCartan Documents', *Clogher Record*, vol. 6, no. 1, 1966, pp. 41–2.
17. McCullough, 'Events', p. 383

18.   Cab 37/152/11, PRO.
19.   Cab 37/152/23, PRO.
20.   CSO R.P., 19700/16, SPO.
21.   CSO, CBS, 1913–20 Files, Carton No. 23, 1915.
22.   *Irishman*, 4 November 1916.
23.   *Sinn Fein*, London, 1920, pp. 28–9.
24.   F.W.S. Craig, *British General Election Manifestos, 1918–66*, London, 1970, p. 4.
25.   Dorothy Macardle, *The Irish Republic*, London, 1968, p. 842.
26.   *IN*, 7 December 1918.
27.   *IN*, 9 December 1918.
28.   *IN*, 10 December 1918.
29.   Macardle, *Republic*, p. 843.
30.   *IN*, 10 December 1918.
31.   *IN*, 11 December 1918.
32.   *IN*, 27 November 1918.
33.   Macardle, *Republic*, p. 842.
34.   *IN*, 10 December 1918.
35.   Quoted in Clarkson, *Labour*, p. 337.
36.   Quoted in Mitchell, *Labour*, p. 84.
37.   *IN*, 10 December 1918.
38.   *IN*, 9 December 1918.
39.   Craig, *Manifestos*, p. 5.
40.   *IN*, 7 December 1918.
41.   Ibid.
42.   *IN*, 25 November 1918.
43.   *IN*, 13 December 1918.

Chapter 10

1.   Quoted in Stewart, *Crisis*, p. 53.
2.   Terence O'Neill, *The Autobiography of Terence O'Neill: Prime Minister of Northern Ireland, 1963–1969*, London, 1972, p. 32.
3.   *BNL*, 23 September 1912.
4.   *The Times*, 13 May 1914, quoted in Buckland, *Ulster Unionism*, p. 82.
5.   Minutes.
6.   Ulster Unionist Council, *The Labour Party and Ireland: The Deputation's Report: Analysis and Criticism*, Belfast, 1921.
7.   *The Ulster Unionist Labour Association: What it is*, quoted in Clarkson, *Labour*, p. 374.
8.   Clarkson, *Labour*, p. 374.
9.   'Memo of Conversation with Sir Wilson Hungerford', PRB 987, PRONI.
10.   *NW*, 16 November 1918.
11.   *NW*, 27 November 1918.
12.   *NW*, 7 December 1918.
13.   *NW*, 12 December 1918.
14.   *NW*, 27 November 1918.
15.   *NW*, 30 November 1918.
16.   *NW*, 10 December 1918.
17.   *NW*, 2 December 1918.
18.   *NW*, 12 December 1918.
19.   'Hungerford'.
20.   *Hansard*, vol. 151, col. 741.
21.   Ibid., col. 739.
22.   30 June 1919, Carson Papers, D 1507/1/3/41, PRONI.
23.   *BNL*, 8 January 1920.
24.   Belfast, p. 60.

25. Carson Papers, D 1507/1/1926/9, PRONI.
26. Carson Papers, D 1507/1/1931/18, PRONI.
27. *NW*, 7 January 1920.
28. *NW*, 3 January 1920.
29. Ibid.
30. *BNL*, 6 January 1920.
31. 23 January 1920, Carson Papers, D 1507/1/3/47, PRONI.
32. *BNL*, 13 January 1920.
33. 23 January 1920, D 1507/1/3/47, PRONI.
34. *NW*, 26 April 1921.
35. *NW*, 11 May 1921.
36. *NW*, 4 May 1921.
37. *NW*, 3 May 1921.
38. *IN*, 12 May 1921.
39. *NW*, 12 and 13 May 1921.
40. *IN*, 6 May 1921.
41. *NW*, 11 May 1921.
42. *Northern Ireland Hansard*, vol. 1, cols. 265–6 and 276–7.

Chapter 11

1. *IN*, 6 December 1918.
2. *IN* and *NW*, 6 December 1918.
3. Intelligence Notes, 1919, SPO.
4. *ASE Monthly Report*, January 1919.
5. *NW*, 19 February 1919.
6. *NW*, 15 January 1919.
7. *Strike Bulletin*, 29 January 1919.
8. Intelligence Notes, 1919, SPO.
9. *NW*, 29 January 1919.
10. *Strike Bulletin*, 25 January 1919.
11. *NW*, 28 January 1919.
12. *NW*, 31 January 1919.
13. Ibid.
14. Ibid.
15. D 1507/1/3/34, PRONI.
16. D 1327/7/14, PRONI.
17. *NW*, 11 February 1919.
18. *NW*, 12 February 1919.
19. Walter Kendall, *The Revolutionary Movement in Britain, 1900–21*, London, 1969, p. 140.
20. *Revolt on the Clyde: An Autobiography*, London, 1936, pp. 191–3.
21. Ibid., p. 234.
22. Kendall, *Movement*, pp. 189, 194.
23. *Revolt*, p. 220.
24. *Workers' Bulletin*, 3 February 1919.
25. *BNL*, 25 January 1919.
26. *NW*, 31 January 1919.
27. ILP & TUC, *1919 Report*.
28. *Sidelights on Bolshevism, Sinn Fein, and the Irish Transport Union*, reprinted from *Notes from Ireland*.
29. D 1507/1/3/34, PRONI.
30. Ibid.
31. Ibid.
32. *NW*, 29 January 1919.
33. *Workers' Bulletin*, 1 February 1919.

34. Ibid.
35. Ibid., 3 February 1919.
36. Ibid., 1 February 1919.
37. CSO, R.P. 3663/19, SPO.
38. *NW*, 10 February 1919.
39. *Labour Opposition*, vol. 1, no. 7, September 1925.
40. D 1507/1/3/34, PRONI.
41. *Workers' Bulletin*, 3 February 1919.
42. *BET*, 13 February 1919.
43. *BET*, 13 February 1919.
44. *NW*, 14 February 1919.
45. *NW*, 17 February 1919.
46. *NW*, 19 or 20 February 1919.
47. Quoted in *NW*, 20 February 1919.
48. FEST and ASE, *Application for 44-Hour Week*, London, 1919, p. 5. Copy in British Library of Political and Economic Science (BLPES).
49. Quoted in Michael Farrell, 'The Great Belfast Strike of 1919', *Northern Star*, February–March 1971, p. 16.
50. *1921 Report*.
51. ILP & TUC, *1919 Report*.
52. Taylor, *History*, p. 163.
53. *BNL*, 2 May 1919; *IN*, *NW*, and *BNL*, 5 May.

Chapter 12

1. *Labour Opposition*, vol. 1, no. 8, October 1925.
2. Clarkson, *Labour*, p. 381, quoting secretary of Belfast WEA, 1924–5, possibly Kyle.
3. *Labour Opposition*, vol. 2, no. 11, January 1926.
4. Ibid., vol. 1, no. 1, March 1925.
5. *IN*, 3 December 1918.
6. ILP & TUC, *1918 Report*.
7. ITUC & LP, *1917 Report*.
8. *NW*, 2 December 1918.
9. Ibid.
10. *NW*, 30 November 1918.
11. Ibid.
12. *IN* and *NW*, 6 December 1918.
13. *IN*, 27 November 1918.
14. Alec Wilson, *P.R. Urban Elections in Ulster, 1920*, first published 1920, London, 1972, p. 11.
15. Ibid., p. 9.
16. *IN*, 15 January 1920.
17. *Labour Opposition*, vol. 1, no. 7, September 1925.
18. *Labour in Ireland*, Dublin, n.d. [1944], p. 113.
19. *NW*, 14 and 16 May 1921.
20. *IN*, 21 May 1921.
21. *IN*, 18 May 1921.
22. *IN*, 16 May 1921.
23. *IN*, 21 May 1921.
24. *IN*, 18 May 1921.
25. D 1507/1/3/42, PRONI.
26. Ibid.
27. Ibid.
28. *NW*, 21 May 1921.
29. *NW* and *IN*, 18 May 1921.

Chapter 13

1. Clarkson, *Labour*, p. 419.
2. Quoted in Desmond Murphy, *Derry, Donegal and Modern Ulster, 1790–1921*, Culmore, Londonderry, 1981, p. 254.
3. *NW*, 13 July 1920.
4. *IN*, 13 July 1920.
5. *NW*, 13 July 1920.
6. *BNL*, 24 July 1920.
7. *IN*, 22 July 1920.
8. Travers, at 1920 ILP & TUC, 1920 Report.
9. *BNL*, 22 July 1920.
10. *Hansard*, vol. 132, col. 616.
11. Ibid., col. 713.
12. John Hanna, at 1920 ILP & TUC, *1920 Report*.
13. Travers, ibid.
14. Ibid.
15. *1920 Report*, pp. 382–4.
16. *1921 Report*, p. 268.
17. D.I. R.R. Spears, 'The Ulster Protestant Association', Report to Sir Richard Dawson Bates, T 2258, PRONI.
18. *IN*, 29 July 1920.
19. *IN*, 2 August 1920.
20. *IN*, 29 July 1920.
21. *IN*, 6 October 1920.
22. *Hansard*, 1920, vol. 132, cols. 1974–7, 2 August.
23. *IN*, 31 July 1920.
24. *IN*, 2 August 1920.
25. *1920 Report*.
26. *IN*, 13 August 1920.
27. Ibid.
28. *IN*, 19 October 1920.
29. *IN*, 22 November 1920.
30. *IN*, 3 September 1920.
31. *BET*, 30 July 1920.
32. TUC, *1921 Report*, p. 115.
33. G.B. Kenna, *Facts and Figures of the Belfast Pogrom, 1920–22*, Dublin, 1922, p. 108.
34. *IN*, 4 August 1920.
35. *IN*, 16 August 1920.
36. *IN*, 21 August 1920.
37. *IN*, 27 August 1920.
38. *IN*, 3 September 1920.
39. *IN*, 15 October 1920.
40. Quoted in Clarkson, *Labour*, p. 371.
41. TUC, *1921 Report*, p. 113.
42. ILP & TUC, *1920 Report*.
43. TUC, *1921 Report*, p. 112.
44. C.J.C. Street [I.O.], *The Administration of Ireland, 1920*, London, 1921, pp. 348–51.
45. TUC, *1921 Report*, p. 113.
46. ILP & TUC, *1921 Report*, p. 83.
47. TUC, *1920 Report*, pp. 382–4.
48. TUC, *1921 Report*, p. 274.
49. Clarkson, *Labour*, p. 420.
50. Ibid., p. 370.

51. TUC, *1921 Report*, p. 275.
52. Minutes, Belfast branch, United Operative Plumbers' Association of Great Britain and Ireland, 10 August 1920, PRONI.
53. ASCJ, *Monthly Journal*.
54. Higenbottam, *History*, p. 226.
55. ASCJ/ASW Records, in Union of Construction, Allied Trades and Technicians (UCATT) Archives, Modern Record Centre, University of Warwick.
56. ILP & TUC, *1921 Report*.
57. TUC, *1921 Report*, p. 269.

Chapter 14

1. Macardle, *Republic*, p. 842.
2. P.P., 1921, XXIX, *Documents Relative to the Sinn Fein Movement*, p. 47.
3. C.O. 903/16, PRO.
4. Ibid.
5. National Graves Association, *The Last Post*, 2nd edn, Dublin, 1976, p. 40.
6. DE 2/89, SPO.
7. *Red Hand*, September 1920.
8. Ibid.
9. Thomas Jones, *Whitehall Diary: Volume III: Ireland, 1918–1925*, London, 1971, p. 38; Hezlet, *'B' Specials*, p.17.
10. S.G. Tallents, C.O. 906/27, PRO.
11. Nicolson, *George V*, p. 460.
12. Ibid., p. 459.
13. Dáil Éireann, *Minutes of Proceedings of the First Parliament of the Republic of Ireland, 1919–21: Official Record*, Dublin, 1921, pp. 191–4.
14. Ibid., p. 228.
15. DE 2/110, NLI.
16. Ibid.
17. Tallents, 'The Commerce of Ulster', 3 typescript pages, C.O. 906/26, PRO.
18. D.S. Johnson, 'The Belfast Boycott, 1920–1922', in Goldstrom, J.M. and L.A. Clarkson, eds., *Irish Population, Economy, and Society: Essays in Honour of the Late K.H. Connell*, Oxford, 1981, p. 306.
19. D.A. Chart, 'The Industrial History of Ulster', *Edinburgh Review*, January 1924, p. 129.
20. Keating to Ó Briain, 31 October 1921, in Ó Briain Papers, Ms 8457, NLI.
21. Ibid.
22. Michael Farrell, *Northern Ireland: The Orange State*, London, 1976, p. 34.
23. Spears, 'Association'.
24. *My Fight for Irish Freedom*, revised and enlarged edn, Cork, 1964, p. 161.
25. Quoted in Farrell, *State*, p. 43.
26. St John Ervine, *Craigavon: Ulsterman*, London,1949, p. 411.
27. To Judge O'Connor, May 1921, in Earl of Longford and T.P. O'Neill, *Eamon de Valera*, London, 1974, p. 123.
28. Macardle, *Republic*, p. 440.
29. Longford, *de Valera*, p. 63.
30. Desmond Ryan, *De Valera: Benevolent Dictator*, London, 1936, pp. 82–3.
31. Ryan, *De Valera*, p. 274.
32. Thomas Jones, *Diary*, pp. 90–1.
33. John Bowman, *De Valera and the Ulster Question, 1917–1973*, Oxford, 1989, p. 52.
34. *Irish Times*, 27 March 1975.
35. Macardle, *Republic*, p. 478.
36. Quoted in Dangerfield, *Question*, p. 335.

37. Longford and O'Neill, *De Valera*, p. 166.
38. Ibid., p. 163.
39. Frank Pakenham, *Peace by Ordeal*, London, 1935, p. 108.
40. Macardle, *Republic*, p. 440.
41. Ibid., p. 495.
42. Jones, *Diary*, p. 111.
43. Ibid., p. 128.
44. Ibid., p. 136.
45. Ibid., p. 137.
46. Ibid., p. 136.
47. Macardle, *Republic*, p. 509.
48. Pakenham, *Ordeal*, p. 274.
49. Macardle, *Republic*, p. 883.
50. James Baird to Patrick Keating, 21 March 1922, in Art Ó Briain Papers, Ms 8457, NLI.
51. Macardle, *Republic*, p. 894.
52. Spears, 'Association', pp. 1–2.
53. Ibid., p. 1.
54. Ibid.
55. Ibid., p. 4.
56. Ibid., p. 2.
57. Ibid., p. 4.
58. Ibid.
59. Ibid., p. 9.
60. Ibid.
61. Ibid., p. 11.
62. C.O. 906/29, PRO.
63. Ibid.
64. Ibid.
65. C.O. 904/30, PRO.
66. Macardle, *Republic*, p. 575.
67. Quoted in Margery Forester, *Michael Collins: The Lost Leader*, London, 1971, pp. 305–6.
68. W.S. Churchill, *The World Crisis: The Aftermath*, London, 1929, p. 327.
69. C.O. 904/30, PRO.
70. Forester, *Collins*, p. 273.
71. *Aftermath*, pp. 336–7.
72. Forester, *Collins*, p. 288.
73. Quoted in Michael Hopkinson, *Green Against Green: The Irish Civil War*, Dublin, 1988, p. 85.
74. Michael Farrell, *Irish Times*, 3 September 1982.
75. Macardle, *Republic*, p. 899.
76. Forester, *Collins*, p. 311.
77. Longford and O'Neill, *De Valera*, p. 192.
78. Macardle, *Republic*, p. 899.

Chapter 15

1. Quoted in Hopkinson, *Green*, p. 275.
2. *The Irish Labour Movement: From the 'Twenties to our own Day*, Dublin, 1919, p. 184.
3. V.I. Lenin, *British Labour and British Imperialism (a compilation of writings by Lenin on Britain)*, London, 1969, p. 167.

Select Bibliography

Geoffrey Bell, *The Protestants of Ulster*, London 1976.

John W. Boyle, *The Irish Labor Movement in the Nineteenth Century*, Washington, D.C. 1988.

J. Dunsmore Clarkson, *Labour and Nationalism in Ireland*, New York 1926.

Michael Farrell, *Northern Ireland: The Orange State*, London 1976.

J. Anthony Gaughan, *Thomas Johnson, 1872–1963*, Co. Dublin 1980.

John Gray, *City in Revolt: James Larkin and the Belfast Dock Strike of 1907*, Belfast 1985.

C. Desmond Greaves, *The Life and Times of James Connolly*, London 1961 and 1972.

——, *The Irish Transport and General Workers' Union: The Formative Years, 1909–1923*, Dublin 1982.

Mike Milotte, *Communism in Modern Ireland: The Pursuit of the Workers' Republic since 1916*, Dublin 1984.

Irish Labour Party and Trade Union Congress, *Ireland at Berne: Being the Reports and Memoranda presented to the International Labour and Socialist Conference held at Berne, February, 1919*, Dublin 1919 (reprinted as *Irish Labour and its International relations: In the Era of the Second International and Bolshevik Revolution*, Cork n.d.).

Emmet Larkin, *James Larkin: Irish Labour Leader, 1876–1947*, London 1965 and 1968.

Eamonn McCann, *War and an Irish Town*, Harmondsworth 1974 and London 1980.

Arthur Mitchell, *Labour in Irish Politics, 1890–1930*, Dublin 1974.

Austen Morgan, *James Connolly: A Political Biography*, Manchester 1988 and 1989.

Emmet O'Connor, *Syndicalism in Ireland, 1917–1923*, Cork 1988.

Henry Patterson, *Class Conflict and Sectarianism: The Protestant Working Class and the Belfast Labour Movement, 1868–1920*, Belfast 1980.

E. Rumpf & A.C. Hepburn, *Nationalism and Socialism in Twentieth-Century Ireland*, Liverpool 1977.

Saothar, Journal of the Irish Labour History Society.

Graham Walker, *The Politics of Frustration: Harry Midgley and the Failure of Labour in Northern Ireland*, Manchester 1985.

Index